OPTICAL PHYSICS

OPTICAL PHYSICS

BY

S. G. LIPSON, Ph.D.

*Senior Lecturer in Physics, Israel Institute of Technology
Haifa*

AND

H. LIPSON, F.R.S.

*Professor of Physics in the Faculty of Technology
University of Manchester*

CAMBRIDGE

AT THE UNIVERSITY PRESS

1969

Published by the Syndics of the Cambridge University Press
Bentley House, 200 Euston Road, London, N.W.1
American Branch: 32 East 57th Street, New York, N.Y. 10022

Library of Congress Catalogue Card Number: 67-15308

Standard Book Number: 521 06926 2

Typeset by J. W. Arrowsmith Ltd., Bristol, 3

Printed in Great Britain by
John Dickens & Co. Ltd., Northampton

TO MY MOTHER
—S.G.L.

TO MY WIFE
—H.L.

CONTENTS

PREFACE

There are two sorts of textbooks. On the one hand, there are works of reference to which students can turn for the clarification of some obscure point or for the intimate details of some important experiment. On the other hand, there are explanatory books which deal mainly with principles and which help in the understanding of the first type.

We have tried to produce a textbook of the second sort. It deals essentially with the principles of optics, but wherever possible we have emphasized the relevance of these principles to other branches of physics—hence the rather unusual title. We have omitted descriptions of many of the classical experiments in optics—such as Foucault's determination of the velocity of light—because they are now dealt with excellently in most school textbooks. In addition, we have tried not to duplicate approaches, and since we think that the graphical approach to Fraunhofer interference and diffraction problems is entirely covered by the complex-wave approach, we have not introduced the former.

For these reasons, it will be seen that the book will not serve as an introductory textbook, but we hope that it will be useful to university students at all levels. The earlier chapters are reasonably elementary, and it is hoped that by the time those chapters which involve a knowledge of vector calculus and complex-number theory are reached, the student will have acquired the necessary mathematics.

The use of Fourier series is emphasized; in particular, the Fourier transform—which plays such an important part in so many branches of physics—is treated in considerable detail. In addition, we have given some prominence—both theoretical and experimental—to the operation of convolution, with which we think that every physicist should be conversant.

We would like to thank the considerable number of people who have helped to put this book into shape. Professor C. A. Taylor and Professor A. B. Pippard had considerable influence upon its final shape—perhaps more than they realize. Dr I. G. Edmunds and Mr T. Ashworth have read through the complete text, and it is thanks to them that the inconsistencies are not more numerous

than they are. (We cannot believe that they are zero!) Dr G. L. Squires and Mr T. Blaney have given us some helpful advice about particular parts of the book. Mr F. Kirkman and his assistants —Mr A. Pennington and Mr R. McQuade—have shown exemplary patience in producing some of our more exacting photographic illustrations, and in providing beautifully finished prints for the press. Mr L. Spero gave us considerable help in putting the finishing touches to our manuscript.

And finally we should like to thank the three ladies who produced the final manuscript for the press—Miss M. Allen, Mrs E. Midgley and Mrs K. Beanland. They have shown extreme forbearance in tolerating our last-minute changes, and their ready help has done much to lighten our work.

S.G.L.
H.L.

CHAPTER 1

HISTORY OF IDEAS

1.1 Importance of history

Why should a textbook on physics begin with history? Why not start with what is known now and refrain from all the distractions of out-of-date material? These questions would be justifiable if physics were a complete and finished subject; only the final state would then matter and the process of arrival at this state would be irrelevant. But physics is not such a subject, and optics in particular is very much alive and constantly changing. It is important for the student to understand the past as a guide to the future. To study only the present is equivalent to trying to draw a graph with only one point.

Moreover, by studying the past we can sometimes gain some insight—however slight—into the minds and methods of the great physicists. No textbook can, of course, reconstruct completely the workings of these minds, but even to glimpse some of the difficulties that they overcame is worthwhile. What seemed great problems to them may seem trivial to us merely because we now have generations of experience to guide us; or, more likely, we have hidden them by cloaking them with words. For example, to the end of his life Newton found the idea of 'action at a distance' repugnant in spite of the great use that he made of it; we now accept it as natural, but have we come any nearer than Newton in understanding it? By being brought back occasionally to such fundamental problems the physicist is bound to have his wits sharpened; no amount of modern knowledge can produce the same effect. The way to study physics is to ask questions, as the geniuses of the past asked them. The ordinary physics student will find someone to answer them; the good physics student will answer them himself.

1.2 Historical sequence

1.2.1 Prehistory. Sight is the most important of our senses and for this reason most people take it for granted. But scientists do not take it for granted, and even two thousand years ago people

were asking the question 'How do we see?' and they tried to provide an answer in familiar terms. Since touch was the most familiar sense, they tried to provide an answer in terms of it and imagined that the eye had its own type of fingers with which it appreciated the presence of objects. These 'feelers' had to have odd properties; they could pass through transparent bodies such as crystals but not through opaque fabrics however flimsy they might be; they could operate in the presence of light, but not in its absence. The theory was quite inadequate and made no progress. But even to have thought the question worth asking was a step in the right direction.

1.2.2 Impact of experiment. Real progress was not made until the seventeenth century, when a basic obstacle was overcome—the objection to experiment. For some reason—possibly the idea that the only problems fit for gentlemen were those that could be solved by pure thought—experimental tests of theory were disdained by the ancient philosophers. There were some exceptional people such as Archimedes but their methods did not 'catch fire' and they founded no experimental schools. Mathematics shows continuous development over two thousand years; physics did not begin until about three hundred and fifty years ago.

Galileo (1564–1642) started the fire that finally caught. He tested his ideas with experiments and soon other people realized the great significance of what he was doing. In the great cities of Europe men grouped together to discuss and follow his methods, and they founded academies for the purpose; the Royal Society of London was one of the most prominent. The society employed a laboratory steward, Hooke (1635–1703), who was ordered to carry out regular experiments; the Fellows had still not quite accepted the idea that they should carry them out themselves!

Galileo's experimental work on light is not now regarded as outstanding, but his ideas were the forerunners of many more. He accepted that light is the agency by which we see: light falls upon an object and is scattered; some of the scattered light enters the eye and there produces the effect known as vision. To support this idea he tried to measure the speed with which light travels. He and a servant stationed themselves on two well-separated hills with lamps which could be covered and uncovered. The servant was asked to uncover his lamp at the instant when he saw his master

uncover his; Galileo could then measure the delay in receiving the signal. The delay tended to zero as the servant became more experienced!

That Galileo conceived the idea that light travelled with a finite speed is one indication of his genius. That he appreciated the essential points in the design of the experiment is another. That he failed is immaterial; we now know that the speed is far too great to be measured with the means available in Galileo's day. But the study of light had started.

1.2.3   Wave-corpuscle controversy. The first question we must ask is 'What is light?'. We cannot expect an immediate answer; we must find out as much as we can of its properties and we must see what sort of picture they fit into. Two schools of thought arose—the corpuscle school and the wave school.

Newton (1642–1727) threw the weight of his authority on the corpuscular theory; he was impressed by the fact that light travels in straight lines, and none of the waves that he knew possessed this property. His first law of motion gave a ready explanation of the straight-line motion, but it seems odd to us now that he should have placed so much emphasis upon this one property; the corpuscles could not be ordinary massive particles since they had to penetrate glass. Moreover, to explain simultaneous reflexion and transmission at a surface, and to account for the phenomenon now known as Newton's rings, he had to ascribe to the particles properties that made them suspiciously like waves.

Newton's authority lasted for about a hundred years, and the views of such a great physicist as Huygens (1629–95) were overlooked. Huygens showed clearly how a wave motion could account for all the then-known properties of light, and his methods of approach are still of current value. But on his contemporaries he made much less impression.

Amongst the evidence that was being amassed, and which was quite well known to Newton, was the discovery of what we now call Fresnel diffraction by Grimaldi (1618–63) in 1660 and by Hooke in 1672. It is conceivable that the discovery was made through the principle of 'taking to the limit': shadows produced by an extended source, such as the sun, are blurred; is there any limit to the sharpness if the source is made smaller and smaller? Grimaldi and Hooke found that there *is* a limit; if an object is

illuminated by light passing through a fine hole there is a residual
blurring that is independent of the size of the hole, and outside
the shadow there are fine fringes (see Fig. 6.16(*b*)).

1.2.4   Triumph of wave theory. Such evidence strongly supported
the wave theory, but the corpuscular theory was not overthrown
until the end of the eighteenth century. In 1801 Young (1773–1829)
produced his double-slit fringes (Fig. 1.1)—an experiment so
simple to carry out and so simple to interpret that the results were
incontrovertible; in 1815 Fresnel (1788–1827) worked out the
theory of the Grimaldi–Hooke fringes; and in 1821 Fraunhofer
(1787–1826) produced diffraction patterns in parallel light which
were much more amenable to theoretical treatment than were the
Grimaldi–Hooke fringes. These three men laid the foundation of
the wave theory that is still the basis of what is now called physical
optics.

Fig. 1.1. Young's fringes.

Nevertheless the corpuscularists were not quite defeated. In
1818 Poisson (1781–1840) produced an argument that seemed to
invalidate the wave theory; he used the device of *reductio ad
absurdum*. Suppose that a shadow of a perfectly round object is
cast by a point source: at the periphery all the waves will be in
phase, and therefore the waves should also be in phase at the centre
of the shadow; there should therefore be a bright spot at this point.
Absurd! Fresnel and Arago (1786–1853) carried out the experiment
and found that there really *was* a bright spot at the centre (Fig. 1.2).
Users of *reductio ad absurdum* should make sure of the absurdity
of the result they are criticizing.

The triumph of the wave theory seemed complete.

1.3   Speed of light

1.3.1   Measurement. Although Galileo's attempt to measure the
speed of light had been unsuccessful it was not long before a
successful measurement *was* made. In 1678 Romer (1644–1710) was

able to account for an apparent anomaly in the times of the eclipses of Jupiter's moons by assuming that light took a finite time to travel; since the distance from Jupiter to Earth varies, the eclipses do not seem to take place at exactly regular intervals. He found that the speed of light was very large—about 3×10^{10} cm/s.$^{-1}$—and this value was supported by another astronomical measurement by Bradley (1693–1762) in 1726. Each star appears to trace out yearly a small elliptical path in the heavens superimposed on its other apparent motions. Bradley showed that this anomaly was caused by the motion of the Earth, which adds a small component to the velocity of light; since the Earth moves round the Sun each year, so this 'aberration' also traces out a yearly path.

Fig. 1.2. The bright spot at the centre of the shadow of a disc.

The immense value of the velocity gives some idea of the difficulty facing Galileo; if his servant and he had been separated by a mile, he would have had to observe a time lapse of 11 microseconds!

It was not until 1850 that the measurement was made with self-contained apparatus. The experiments were both made by Frenchmen—Fizeau (1819–96) and Foucault (1819–68)—and both used Galileo's method, replacing the servant by a mirror. Fizeau replaced the lantern cover by a rotating toothed wheel, and Foucault replaced it by a rotating mirror; the possibility of producing rapid controlled rotation was the secret of success. Foucault's method proved the more accurate and versatile; he was able to build an apparatus compact enough for the velocity to be determined in

water as well as air. In the hands of Michelson (1852–1931) a high degree of accuracy—about 0·03 per cent—was achieved.

1.3.2   Refractive index. Was there any physical importance in making these measurements? There was indeed, for they provided another way of distinguishing between the corpuscular and wave theories, by relating the speed of light in a medium to its refractive index.

It has been known from time immemorial that light appears to bend on passing from one medium to another. Ptolemy in the second century A.D. had made measurements of the angles of incidence and refraction for water and had tried to find a mathematical relationship between them. The true relationship was not, however, found until about 1600 by Snell (1591–1626) and in 1637 by Descartes (1596–1650); they found that the ratio of the sines of these angles is constant; this ratio is called the refractive index.

Here was a piece of evidence that must fit into an acceptable theory of light. On the corpuscular theory it was claimed as a manifestation of the attraction of the corpuscles by the medium that they were entering; the tangential component of the velocity was unchanged but the normal component was increased (Fig. 1.3(a)). Snell's law fitted in beautifully. On the wave theory the law was claimed as a manifestation of the slowing down of the wave front as it entered the second medium: with oblique incidence the wave front would enter the medium progressively and the parts that entered first would be slowed down more than the later parts; the wave would thus 'slew' round to a new orientation (Fig. 1.3(b)). Snell's law fitted in beautifully.

Which theory was right? The former predicted an increase of speed of light in water; the latter predicted a decrease. Foucault's result (§ 1.3.1) was unambiguous. Light travelled more slowly in water. The wave theory again was triumphant.

1.4   Transverse or longitudinal waves?

1.4.1   Polarization. The distinction between transverse and longitudinal waves had been appreciated early in the history of physics; sound waves were found to be longitudinal and water waves were obviously transverse. For some reason—perhaps because seeing and hearing were thought to be connected—light waves were thought to be longitudinal. Huygens and Newton both seem to

have considered only this possibility, and the mistake was largely responsible for delaying adoption of the wave theory. It is easy in physics to jump to conclusions, and it is comforting to find two of the greatest physicists of all time making this mistake.

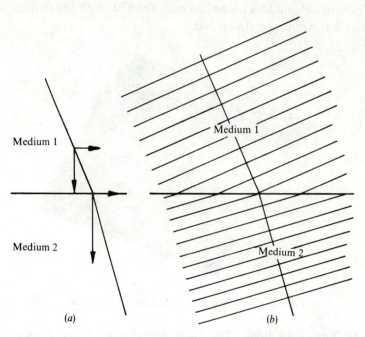

Fig. 1.3. (a) Refraction according to the corpuscular theory;
(b) Refraction according to the wave theory.

The phenomenon that enabled a decision to be made was that of double refraction, discovered by Bartholinus (1625–98) in 1669; he found that if an object were viewed through an Iceland Spar crystal—a form of calcium carbonate—two images were seen (Fig. 1.4). If these images were viewed through another crystal, four images were seen and these changed in position and intensity as the second crystal was rotated; when the two crystals were in parallel orientation two of the images disappeared. Huygens pointed out that this property must mean that the orientation of the crystal must be related somehow to some direction in the wave, and hence that the wave must have some transverse property.

To him this conclusion seemed inexplicable. But to the supporters of the corpuscular theory there was no dilemma; one had merely to endow the corpuscles with some anisotropy—for example, that

the two ends were different—and suppose that the crystal could sort them out into two streams with these properties at right angles. These could be transmitted with different velocities and so double refraction was accounted for. The corpuscles were said to be 'polarized' and this name has endured although the corpuscular theory has been long discarded.

Fig. 1.4. Double refraction in an Iceland Spar crystal.

1.4.2 Nature of light. The final overthrow of the corpuscular theory had to wait until the idea of transverse vibrations had been accepted; this came about at the beginning of the nineteenth century—the time of Young, Fresnel and Fraunhofer. The acceptance of the idea was a step forward, but it did not establish the nature of the waves. The solution to that problem came from quite a new direction—the theoretical study of electricity and magnetism.

In the first half of the nineteenth century the relationship between magnetism and electricity had been fairly thoroughly worked out, by men such as Oersted (1777–1851), Ampère (1775–1836) and Faraday (1791–1867). In 1864 Clerk Maxwell (1831–79) was inspired to put their results in mathematical form, and in manipulating the equations he found that they could assume the form of a wave equation. The velocity of the wave could be derived from the known magnetic and electric constants. Evaluation of this velocity showed that it was equal to the velocity of light, and thus

light was established as an electromagnetic disturbance. This was one of the most brilliant episodes in physics, bringing together several different branches of physics and showing their relationship to each other.

1.4.3 Implications of electromagnetic theory. If light is electromagnetic, why do water and glass slow it down? Why does Iceland Spar doubly refract? Obviously, atoms of matter must have electric and magnetic properties. Thus began the investigation of the structure of the atom, which has resulted in the vast knowledge that we now possess. Visible light is not itself of great use in studying atomic structure, but it certainly set the study on its feet. In physics we can rarely see in advance which way a subject is leading, and from which direction the answer to any specific question will come.

1.5 Instruments

1.5.1 Discovery of the lens. While all the fundamental work was going on, applications of optics were also taking place; technology does not wait for science to solve *all* its problems before stepping in. The phenomena of refraction had been known for thousands of years. Aristophanes, about the fourth century B.C., referred in one of his plays to a burning glass, and Marco Polo in the thirteenth century found that the Chinese knew something of spectacles. But without real scientific understanding no real advances on these simple applications could be made.

1.5.2 The telescope. The first step to any degree of complexity was the invention of the telescope by Lippershey (died 1619) in 1608. The invention was probably accidental, since it is easy to envisage its happening to anyone who had a number of lenses lying about. Galileo seized upon the discovery, made his own telescope, and began to make a series of discoveries—such as Jupiter's moons and Saturn's rings—that completely altered the subject of astronomy. Newton, dissatisfied with the colour defects in the image, invented the reflecting telescope (Fig. 1.5). Since then the telescope has not changed in essence, but it has changed in size and cost.

1.5.3 The microscope. The story of the microscope is quite different. Its origin is uncertain; many people contributed to its early development; new ways of using it are still being found; and it is possible that further developments may still be forthcoming.

The microscope originated from the magnifying glass. In the sixteenth and seventeenth centuries considerable ingenuity was exercised in making high-powered lenses; a drop of water or honey could produce wonderful results in the hands of an enthusiast.

Fig. 1.5. Newton's reflecting Telescope. (From Sir Oliver Lodge, *Pioneers of Science*, Macmillan, London.)

Hooke (1635–1703) played perhaps the greatest part in developing the compound microscope, and some of his instruments (Fig. 1.6) already showed signs of future trends in design. One can envisage the delight of such an able experimenter in having the privilege of developing a new instrument and of using it to examine the world of the very small, as described in his *Micrographia* (1665).

A particularly important use of the microscope was made by the botanist Brown (1773–1858) in 1827. Using only a single lens of about $\frac{1}{32}$ of an inch focal length (0·8 mm), he observed that particles of pollen suspended in water performed a random motion which he thought might be associated with sexual activity—a sort of mating dance! He found, however, that particles of long-dead plants showed the same effect, and later that inorganic materials—even particles taken from the Sphinx—also indulged in it. He was forced to conclude that it was a fundamental property of matter.

We now know the effect as Brownian motion, and that it is the result of the equipartition of energy: the submicroscopic molecules of water have a high energy which must mean that they are moving, on the average, with high velocity; although a larger particle—big

enough to be seen under the microscope—has a much smaller velocity, this velocity is still large enough to be observed. Brown's particles were about 5×10^{-4} cm in size, but he could describe their shapes in fair detail, even with his single lens. We now regard such particles as rather large for showing Brownian motion clearly.

Fig. 1.6. Hooke's microscope, from his *Micrographia*.

1.5.4   The spectrometer and diffraction grating.
Once the principles of the subject were known, instruments other than the obvious telescope and microscope arose. The most important were the spectrometer, which Fraunhofer invented for precise measurement of the optical properties of glass, and the diffraction grating.

The invention of the latter was apparently accidental; Fraunhofer was using a spectrometer to look at the diffraction pattern of a slit and was dissatisfied with the intensity. He therefore conceived the idea of increasing the intensity by using a number of slits. The intensity certainly increased, but so also did the number of patterns. Dissatisfaction can be a powerful ally to a physicist!

The diffraction grating, allied to the spectrometer, has proved to be one of the most useful tools in physics. It added, as it were, a new dimension to astronomy, for example. Lives have been devoted to making better and larger gratings, and their uses are considerable. Again, a chance discovery opened up new avenues in physics.

1.5.5 Geometrical optics. In order to put the theory of optical instruments on a sound basis, a new branch of optics—called geometrical optics—was founded. It was based entirely on the concept of rays of light, which travelled in straight lines in uniform media and bent abruptly on passing from one medium to another, obeying Snell's law (§ 1.3.2). For some time it seemed that geometrical optics and physical optics—that based upon the wave theory—were quite separate, but the two were reconciled by Fermat (1601–65) in 1665; he put forward the idea that a ray is simply the path that a wave traverses in minimum time. We can see that if the time is a minimum, waves traversing closely similar paths will arrive in phase and so produce an appreciable effect. We now know that Fermat's principle should be extended to include minimum and maximum times of traversal.

Based upon geometrical optics, rules for improving the performances of the microscope and telescope were found. Lenses were improved by the skilful shaping of surfaces and by combining lenses so that their errors cancelled. Newton knew how to correct for chromatic aberration, but did not know that glasses were available to put the correction into effect; Huygens devised a compound eyepiece that is still named after him. Progress seemed to be limited only by the ingenuity of designers and the skill of craftsmen.

1.6 Quantum theory

1.6.1 Shortcomings of wave theory. With all these successes it is remarkable that—as we now know—the wave theory will not account completely for all the properties of light. For some properties it is not even a close approximation. For example, in the middle

of the nineteenth century Kelvin (1824–1907) was concerned about the lack of any explanation of the distribution of energy in the spectrum of a hot body. Such spectra always show maximum intensity at a particular wavelength, the energy distribution falling off rapidly at shorter wavelengths and more slowly at longer wavelengths (Fig. 1.7). The wavelength of the maximum intensity decreases with temperature. This maximum is difficult to explain. If the principle of the equipartition of energy holds, each mode of vibration should contain the same energy and, since there are more short waves than long ones, the energy should increase progressively as the wavelength decreases (the so-called ultra-violet catastrophe). No solution of this problem seemed at all possible in terms of classical physics.

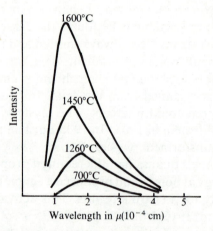

Fig. 1.7. Power spectrum of black-body radiation. (From F. C. Champion, *University Physics*, Blackie, 1960.)

Planck (1858–1947) in 1900 suggested an *ad hoc* solution: let the energy of a mode of vibration be proportional to the frequency. The production of the higher frequencies would then be inhibited, as the experimental results required. If a Boltzmann distribution of energies was assumed, then the spectral distribution curves came out correctly.

This idea was greeted with scepticism, even by Planck himself. It amounted to dividing energy into discrete packets (quanta), and this was too revolutionary for most physicists. It was therefore put into cold storage until a more acceptable theory could be produced. It might have remained there for many years had it not

been revived in 1905 by Einstein (1879–1955) to account for another effect in physics—the photoelectric effect. Here it fitted in so well that all scepticism was swept away.

1.6.2 Photoelectric effect. The effect had its origin in a chance observation by Hertz (1857–94) that a spark would pass across a gap more readily if it were illuminated by ultra-violet light. This apparently trivial fact was investigated more closely by Hertz and by other people, but it remained a mystery until the electron was discovered in 1895 by J. J. Thomson (1856–1940); then Thomson and Lenard (1862–1947) in 1899 both discovered that the discharge was caused by the emission of electrons under the influence of the ultra-violet light.

This discovery, of course, did not solve the problem. What caused the electron to be emitted? Lenard's experimental results were rather odd; in particular, he found that, however weak the radiation, some electrons were always emitted and that they would flow against a small potential gradient. They must therefore be emitted with appreciable energy—much more energy than they could possibly have gained from the small fraction of the wavefront that one atom could intercept. The mystery remained until it was solved by Einstein in 1905. (In 1905 Einstein published three papers which transformed physics; he was 26 years old!). He showed that Planck's quanta had the required property of concentrating their energy at points, and produced a simple equation which accounted clearly for Lenard's results. This activated the experimentalists and in 1916 Millikan (1868–1953) set up apparatus specifically for testing Einstein's equation and he found perfect agreement. Quanta *had* to be accepted.

1.6.3 Wave-particle duality. But the problem had not really been solved. We still cannot conceive the equivalence of waves and particles of energy. The energy of a wave is distributed through space; the energy of a particle is concentrated. Perhaps one of the closest analogies is that of the surf rider carried along and guided by a wave. If he had to pass through a narrow opening he would either miss it and be completely stopped or he would go completely through. The wave guiding him, however, would be curtailed and could no longer guide him with the same accuracy; this is equivalent to diffraction.

But no physical picture is quite adequate; we can accept Planck's

and Einstein's ideas and we can use them, but we do not understand them. This is not a depressing state of affairs; physics has developed in this way for three centuries, the difficulties of one generation being the stepping stones for the next. Perhaps someone will one day find a convincing physical picture—for those of us who like physical pictures—or perhaps we shall just accustom ourselves to the idea of the equivalence of waves and quanta, as we have accustomed ourselves to action at a distance. For those who do not need physical pictures, there is already no trouble.

1.6.4 Corpuscular waves. This history, however, is still not completely written; as usual in physics one idea leads to another and in 1924 a new idea occurred to de Broglie (born 1892), based upon the principle of symmetry. Faraday had used this principle in his discovery of electromagnetism; if electricity produces magnetism, does magnetism produce electricity? De Broglie asked, 'If waves are corpuscles, are corpuscles waves?'. By now physicists had learnt not to be sceptical, and within three years his question had been answered. Davisson (1881–1958) and Germer (born 1896) by ionization methods and G. P. Thomson (born 1892) by photographic methods, showed that fast-moving electrons could be diffracted by matter similarly to X-rays. Since then other particles such as neutrons and protons have also been diffracted. Schroedinger (1887–1961) in 1928 produced a general wave theory of matter, and the subject of wave mechanics is now a basic part of physics.

1.7 Resolving power

1.7.1 Wave limitations. The view that progress in optical instruments depended only upon the skill of their makers was suddenly brought to an end by Abbe (1840–1905) in 1873. He showed that the geometrical theory—useful though it was in developing optical instruments—was incomplete in that it took no account of the wave properties of light. Geometrically, the main condition that is necessary to produce a perfect image is that the rays from any point in the object should be so refracted that they meet together at a point on the image. Abbe showed that this condition is necessarily only approximate; waves spread because of diffraction and so cannot intersect in a point.

He put forward another view of image formation—that an image is formed by two processes of diffraction. The first occurs

when light is scattered by the object; the second occurs when the scattered beams are brought together again and combine to form an image. Limitations occur at both stages—at the first because light is diffracted through a finite angle (less than 180°) and at the second because only a finite part of the diffracted light passes through the instrument. The first is the fundamental limitation; in fact one cannot conceive of making use of radiation diffracted through more than 90°. The second is a practical limitation and places emphasis on making instruments which can accept as wide a cone of light as possible.

Abbe showed that one cannot resolve detail less than about half a wavelength, even with a perfectly corrected instrument. This simple result was greeted by microscopists with disbelief; many of them observed detail less than this with good rigidly-mounted instruments. Abbe's theory, however, proves that such detail is erroneous; it is a function of the instrument rather than of the object. Improving lenses further is not the right way to improve microscopes.

1.7.2   Resolving-power challenge. Any conclusion of this sort must not be considered as depressing; it must be regarded as a challenge. Until difficulties are clearly exposed no real progress is possible. Now that it was known where the limitations of optical instruments lay, it was possible to concentrate upon *them* rather than upon lens design. Since resolving power is a function of wavelength, we need to consider new radiations with shorter wavelengths rather than new lens combinations.

1.7.3   Shorter wavelengths. Ultra-violet light is an obvious choice but it is difficult to make microscopes that will work with this radiation; lenses must be made of material such as quartz that do not absorb these wavelengths, and testing of lenses and lens combinations can be carried out only by photographic methods. Ultra-violet microscopy has not made any great impact.

The radiations that *have* been effective are X-rays and electron waves; these have wavelengths about 10^{-3} or 10^{-4} of those of visible light. They have produced such revolutionary results that separate sections need to be devoted to them.

1.7.4   X-ray diffraction. For seventeen years after the discovery of X-rays in 1895, no one knew whether they were waves or corpuscles.

Their ionization properties suggested that they were corpuscles, but the belief that they were waves persisted. Ordinary diffraction experiments gave no convincing evidence, and indicated only that if they *were* waves their wavelengths were in the order of 10^{-8} cm (1 Ångstrom unit). Diffraction gratings would have helped, but gratings with spacing of this order of magnitude were thought to be impossible to obtain.

In 1912, however, Laue (1879–1960) had the inspiration to think of using a crystal as such a grating; it was known that crystals grew in the form of regularly repeated units (Fig. 1.8), and the

Fig. 1.8. Structure of a crystal. (From H. Lipson, *Memoirs of the Manchester Literary and Philosophical Society*, Session 1961–62, Vol 106.)

separation of these should be of the right order to diffract X-rays. Friedrich and Knipping successfully carried out the experiment (Fig. 1.9(*a*)) and were soon producing beautifully symmetrical diffraction patterns (Fig. 1.9(*b*)).

The proof that X-rays were a wave-motion opened up some completely new aspects of physics. Moseley's work on the wavelengths produced by different atoms began the new subject of

X-ray spectroscopy (Fig. 1.10) and its application to the electronic structures of atoms. The work of W. H. Bragg (1862–1942) and W. L. Bragg (born 1890) on the structure of crystals began a new phase in the study of matter; they called it 'Microscopy on the atomic scale'. Rarely has one discovery been so prolific in its results.

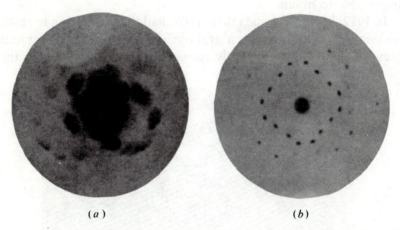

(a)   (b)

Fig. 1.9. X-ray diffraction patterns produced by a crystal. (From P. P. Ewald, *Fifty Years of X-ray diffraction*, published for I. U. Cryst. by N. V. A. Oosthoek's Uitgevesmaatschappij, Utrecht.)

This new microscopy is different from visual microscopy, for X-rays cannot be focused. In terms of Abbe's theory of image formation, only the first stage—diffraction by the object—is possible. The second stage—recombination of the diffracted beams—cannot be carried out experimentally, but it can, under certain circumstances, be carried out mathematically. We can then produce images with atomic resolution (Fig. 1.11). The results have been basic to our understanding of the behaviour of matter and have helped to found a new branch of physics—solid-state physics.

1.7.5   Electron microscopy. The realization that moving particles also have wave properties (§ 1.6.4) introduced a new factor into the subject. If such particles are charged they can be deflected electrostatically or magnetically, and so refraction can be simulated. It was found theoretically in 1926 by Busch (born 1884) that suitably shaped fields could produce focused beams so that image formation was possible.

Electrons have been used with much success for this work, and instruments with magnetic (or more rarely electrostatic) 'lenses' are available for producing images with very high magnifications; such instruments are called electron microscopes.

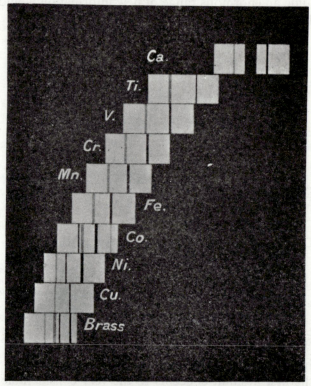

Fig. 1.10. X-ray spectroscopy. The relationship between wavelength of the *K* radiation from an atom and its atomic number. (After Moseley. *Phil. Mag.* Ser. 6, Vol. 26).

By using accelerating voltages of the order of 100 kV, wavelengths of the order of 0.1 Å can be produced, and thus a limit of resolution far better than that with X-rays should be obtainable. In practice, however, electron lenses are quite crude by optical standards and thus only small apertures are possible; the electron microscope developed rapidly in the 1930's, and the limit of resolution soon reached and then surpassed that of the light microscope. But now a limit of about 10 Å has been reached and does not seem likely to be easily surpassed.

This is a remarkable improvement on light microscopy. It has opened up new fields in many branches of science; biology, for

example, has been revolutionized. For physicists the limit of resolution is tantalizingly low; the electron microscope will show molecular detail (Fig. 1.8), but it will not reach down to atoms. If the limit of resolution could be taken down by another order of magnitude an enormous range of new information would become available.

Fig. 1.11. An electron-density map reconstructed from an X-ray diffraction pattern. (From J. M. Robertson, *J. Chem. Soc.* 1936.)

1.8 Summary

In this chapter we have tried to trace the development of optics from the first hesitant concepts to the very considerable body of knowledge that the subject now comprises. In addition to giving the reader an overall view of the way optics has advanced, we have also laid down a pattern for the succeeding chapters.

We start with waves in general (Chapter 2) and the extremely important treatment in terms of Fourier analysis (Chapter 3). We then deal with electromagnetic waves in particular (Chapter 4), and the effects—of which polarization is of outstanding importance —produced when they pass through anisotropic media (Chapter 5). The interaction of waves leads to the phenomena of diffraction and interference (Chapters 6 and 7). We have devoted more space than is usual to the concept of coherence (Chapter 8) because this is looming so large in present-day optics. On the basis of these chapters we are able to deal in detail with what is the most important

application of optics—image formation (Chapter 9). We then consider the comparison of the treatment of optics in terms of classical theory (Chapter 10) and quantum theory (Chapter 11). We conclude by taking a selection of topics and treating them in much more detail in terms of the concepts laid down in the intervening parts of the book.

The appendices contain matter—very briefly outlined—that is necessary for the understanding of the various chapters, but which we felt would interrupt the flow of ideas if they were inserted in appropriate places in the text.

We have included a number of questions that are designed to test the understanding of the textual matter, rather than to serve as examples of examination-type questions.

CHAPTER 2

WAVES

2.1 Introduction

Optics, as discussed in this book, is the study of wave propagation, and wave propagation is described mathematically in terms of wave equations. The exact definition of a *wave equation* is somewhat subject to personal taste, but for the purposes of this book it is defined as any equation which leads to a wave as a solution. This wave may be dispersive or nondispersive; it may be progressive, standing, attenuated or evanescent. Because of the variety of waves which can be involved, there is accordingly a large variety of wave equations. This chapter is devoted to the study of such equations, and how they arise as the result of the properties of media.

2.2 Non-stationary disturbances

To see the origin of a wave in a way which will lead to the understanding of wave equations, let us consider a simple experiment. We have a large stretched sheet of rubber and we press down on it at a certain point. An equilibrium state is reached, in which the elastic forces at the pressure-point exactly balance the applied force, and at all neighbouring points they exactly cancel out. Now remove the applied pressure. Instantaneously only the pressure-point is not in equilibrium; all the neighbouring points are unchanged. But as the rubber at the pressure-point moves to restore equilibrium, that at the neighbouring points is disturbed, and as a result they in turn move, and so the disturbance propagates outwards. To produce a quantitative theory of such an effect we therefore need to consider

(a) the equations governing the setting-up of an equilibrium state under the application of a steady applied force, and

(b) the equation of motion at a point in the medium when it is not in equilibrium.

2.2.1 The form of wave equations. As usual with physical problems, before attempting to produce an equation to describe an effect we should consider the type of result we expect to obtain.

Thinking in one dimension, we might expect that a wave should be basically a disturbance of some sort which can travel with a fixed velocity and be unchanged in form from point to point. In mathematical terms, the wave form at time t and position x is the same as that at time 0 and position $x - vt$, v being the velocity:

$$f(x, t) = f(x - vt, 0) = f(\xi_-, 0). \tag{2.1}$$

Alternatively, the wave can travel in the opposite direction with the same velocity giving

$$f(x, t) = f(x + vt, 0) = f(\xi_+, 0), \tag{2.2}$$

where $\xi_\pm = x \pm vt$.

Differentiating (2.1) by x and t respectively, we have

$$\frac{\partial f}{\partial x} = \frac{df}{d\xi_-}; \qquad \frac{\partial f}{\partial t} = -v \frac{df}{d\xi_-}, \tag{2.3}$$

and for (2.2)

$$\frac{\partial f}{\partial x} = \frac{df}{d\xi_+}; \qquad \frac{\partial f}{\partial t} = v \frac{df}{d\xi_+}. \tag{2.4}$$

Equations (2.3) and (2.4) can be reconciled to a single equation by a second similar differentiation followed by eliminating f'' between the pairs; either equation gives

$$\frac{\partial^2 f}{\partial x^2} = \frac{d^2 f}{d\xi^2}; \qquad \frac{\partial^2 f}{\partial t^2} = v^2 \frac{d^2 f}{d\xi^2},$$

whence

$$\frac{\partial^2 f}{\partial x^2} = \frac{1}{v^2} \frac{\partial^2 f}{\partial t^2}, \tag{2.5}$$

of which equations (2.1) and (2.2) are the most general solutions. Equation (2.5) is known as the '*non-dispersive wave equation*', because the solutions imply that the form of the wave does not alter as it progresses. This property, as the examples which follow in later sections will show, is not common to all waves; in practice it is quite rare.

Although equation (2.5) has a general solution given by (2.1) and (2.2), there is a particular solution to it which is more important because it is general for a large class of equations known as *wave equations*. This solution is a simple-harmonic wave of amplitude A in its complex exponential form:

$$f(x, t) = A \exp \left\{ 2\pi i \left(vt - \frac{x}{\lambda} \right) \right\},$$

where v is the frequency in cycles per unit time and λ is the wavelength. A more tidy expression can be written in terms of

$$\text{the wave number} \quad k = 2\pi/\lambda$$

$$\text{the angular frequency} \quad \omega = 2\pi v$$

which give

$$f(x, t) = A \exp\{i(\omega t - kx)\}. \tag{2.6}$$

It is easy to verify that this wave form satisfies equation (2.1), provided that the velocity is given by $v = \omega/k$. The importance of the wave form (2.6) is that it is by definition a solution of all wave equations; if a disturbance begins simple-harmonically in a medium satisfying such an equation, it will continue simple-harmonically and will not be distorted.

We shall define a general wave equation as that which has equation (2.6) as its solution. It can be produced by differentiating (2.6); we have in general:

$$\frac{\partial^n f}{\partial x^n} = (-ik)^n A \exp\{i(\omega t - kx)\} = (-ik)^n f \tag{2.7}$$

and

$$\frac{\partial^n f}{\partial t^n} = (i\omega)^n A \exp\{i(\omega t - kx)\} = (i\omega)^n f. \tag{2.8}$$

Notice that the use of the complex exponential in equation (2.6) has avoided the untidy alternation between cosine and sine which is involved if a cosine or sine function is used. The function f in equations (2.7) and (2.8) can always be eliminated; therefore, if there exists a polynomial relation between differentials of f, we can use the operator $(\partial/\partial x)^n$ to replace $\partial^n/\partial x^n$ (and similarly for t), when the general wave equation becomes:

$$g\left(\frac{\partial}{\partial x}, \frac{\partial}{\partial t}\right) f = 0, \tag{2.9}$$

where g is a polynomial function of the operators $(\partial/\partial x)$ and $(\partial/\partial t)$. For example, if

$$g = \left(\frac{\partial}{\partial x}\right)^2 - \frac{1}{v^2}\left(\frac{\partial}{\partial t}\right)^2$$

the equation becomes

$$\frac{\partial^2 f}{\partial x^2} - \frac{1}{v^2}\frac{\partial^2 f}{\partial t^2} = 0,$$

which is the non-dispersive equation (2.5).

Once the wave equation has been decided from the physics of the problem, we can immediately work out the dispersive properties of the wave—that is, the relationship between the angular frequency ω, the wave number k, and their quotient, the wave velocity ω/k. This is simply done. From equation (2.7) it will immediately be clear that the operation $\partial/\partial x$ is exactly equivalent to multiplying by $(-ik)$; equation (2.8) shows that $\partial/\partial t$ is equivalent to $(i\omega)$. Thus an equation relating ω and k can be obtained from the wave equation by these substitutions. This is called a *dispersion equation*; for example, equation (2.5) gives:

$$(-ik)^2 f = v^{-2}(i\omega)^2 f$$

or
$$\frac{\omega^2}{k^2} = v^2; \quad \frac{\omega}{k} = \pm v. \tag{2.10}$$

The velocity is $\pm v$, as expected. Thus we can see that any medium whose properties can be expressed by a polynomial equation in time and space derivatives

$$g\left(\frac{\partial}{\partial x}, \frac{\partial}{\partial t}\right) f = 0$$

must always have a solution of the form

$$f = A \exp\{i(\omega t - kx)\}.$$

The relationship between ω and k is entirely determined by the polynomial, which contains the physics of the problem.

An example of a complicated form of wave equation is

$$\frac{\partial^3 f}{\partial x^3} + \alpha \frac{\partial^3 f}{\partial x^2 \partial t} - \beta \frac{\partial f}{\partial t} = 0. \tag{2.11}$$

This would give a dispersion equation:

$$ik^3 - i\alpha k^2 \omega - i\beta\omega = 0. \tag{2.12}$$

The velocity ω/k is now dependent on wave number k:

$$\frac{\omega}{k} = \frac{k^2}{\alpha k^2 + \beta}.$$

This relationship is illustrated in Fig. 2.1. The disturbance is called a 'dispersive wave'. The concept is not new; it is an elementary fact that the refractive index of glass, or most materials, depends on the wavelength, and the refractive index is nothing more than the measure of the velocity of light in the medium.

2.2.2 Examples of wave equations.

The more common forms of wave equation should already be familiar to the reader. As examples we shall quote the following.

(i) Mechanical waves: for example, longitudinal sound waves in a compressible fluid. If the fluid has compressibility κ and density ρ, the equilibrium-state equation ((a) in § 2.2) is Hooke's law:

$$p = \kappa \frac{\partial \xi}{\partial x}, \tag{2.13}$$

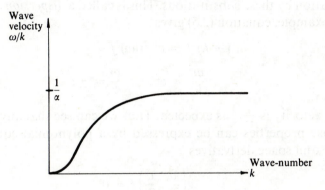

Fig. 2.1. The dispersion relation $\dfrac{\omega}{k} = \dfrac{k^2}{\alpha k^2 + \beta}$.

where p is the stress, the local pressure, and ξ the local displacement from equilibrium. The differential $\partial \xi / \partial x$ is thus the strain. The dynamic equation ((b) in § 2.2) is

$$\rho \frac{\partial^2 \xi}{\partial t^2} = \frac{\partial p}{\partial x}, \tag{2.13a}$$

leading to a wave equation

$$\frac{\partial^2 \xi}{\partial x^2} = \frac{\rho}{\kappa} \frac{\partial^2 \xi}{\partial t^2}. \tag{2.13b}$$

Thus the waves are non-dispersive, with wave velocity

$$c = \left(\frac{\kappa}{\rho}\right)^{\frac{1}{2}}.$$

Alternatively, the relationship between ω and k is:

$$k^2 = \omega^2 / c^2. \tag{2.13c}$$

(ii) Transverse waves on a rigid bar lead to a more complicated wave equation. Considering the couples exerted on a short length of bent rod (Fig. 2.2), we have that the equilibrium-state equation

relating applied couple G to curvature $\partial^2\xi/\partial x^2$ is

$$G = IE\frac{\partial^2\xi}{\partial x^2},$$

where I is the second moment of area and E is Young's modulus.

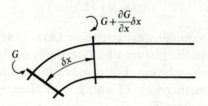

Fig. 2.2. Couple and force required to bend a bar.

This leads to a transverse force

$$F = -\frac{\partial G}{\partial x}$$

and the dynamic equation

$$\rho\frac{\partial^2\xi}{\partial t^2} = \frac{\partial F}{\partial x},$$

whence the wave equation follows:

$$\frac{\partial^2\xi}{\partial t^2} = -\frac{EI}{\rho}\frac{\partial^4\xi}{\partial x^4}. \tag{2.14}$$

The wave equation is dispersive, leading to an ω–k relationship

$$k^4 = \frac{\rho}{EI}\omega^2. \tag{2.14a}$$

(iii) The diffusion equation. Heat diffuses under steady-state conditions according to the equation

$$q = -K\frac{\partial\theta}{\partial x},$$

where q is the heat flow per unit area, K the thermal conductivity and θ the local temperature. The dynamic equation represents the rate of rise of temperature when heat flows into a region of specific heat s per unit volume:

$$s\frac{\partial\theta}{\partial t} = -\frac{\partial q}{\partial x},$$

whence the wave equation:

$$\frac{\partial \theta}{\partial t} = \frac{K}{s} \frac{\partial^2 \theta}{\partial x^2} \tag{2.15}$$

and the dispersion relation

$$\omega = i\frac{K}{s}k^2. \tag{2.15a}$$

(iv) **The Schroedinger wave equation.** One of the most important wave equations in the history of modern physics has been derived from its dispersion relation. For a moving particle, we know that the sum of its kinetic energy T and potential energy V is equal to a constant total energy E:

$$E = T + V. \tag{2.16}$$

Now the kinetic energy can be expressed in terms of the momentum p and mass m as

$$T = \frac{p^2}{2m} \tag{2.16a}$$

and thus

$$E = \frac{p^2}{2m} + V. \tag{2.16b}$$

We now resort to two hypotheses concerned with the diffraction of particle beams and the quantization of the energy in light waves. The first of these is due to de Broglie (§ 1.6.4), who suggested that an electron has a wavelength related to its momentum by Planck's constant h:

$$\lambda = hp^{-1}, \tag{2.17}$$

or

$$p = \hbar k, \tag{2.18}$$

where $\hbar$ is $h/2\pi$. The second relationship was invoked by Planck to explain the absence of the so-called ultra-violet catastrophe in black-body radiation (§ 1.6.1). He found it possible to explain the observed spectrum of a hot black body only by assuming that the total energy of radiation is quantized in units of $h\nu$, or equivalently $\hbar\omega$. Thus, extending the result to all particles,

$$E = \hbar\omega. \tag{2.19}$$

Substituting equation (2.18) and (2.19) in (2.16b) we have

$$\hbar\omega = \frac{\hbar^2 k^2}{2m} + V, \tag{2.20}$$

which is a dispersion relation, and arises from the one-dimensional wave equation

$$-i\hbar\frac{\partial\psi}{\partial t} = -\frac{\hbar^2}{2m}\frac{\partial^2\psi}{\partial x^2} + V\psi. \tag{2.21}$$

This is Schroedinger's equation. Discussion of the meaning of ψ, a dummy variable which has been introduced in order to write an equation from (2.20), will be deferred until Chapter 11.

2.3   Complex quantities: attenuation

2.3.1   Complex velocity of a wave. The reader may have noticed that the dispersion relations (2.14a), (2.15a) and (2.21) give rise to imaginary or complex velocities. Let us see what a complex velocity might mean by substituting it in equation (2.6). As the velocity is ω/k we can replace ω by vk, and since the complex velocity is

$$v = v_1 + iv_2 \quad (v_1 \text{ and } v_2 \text{ both real})$$
$$f = A\exp\{i(\omega t - kx)\}$$
$$= A\exp\{ik(v_1 t + iv_2 t - x)\}$$
$$= A\exp\{(-v_2 kt)\}\exp\{ik(v_1 t - x)\}. \tag{2.22}$$

In other words, the real part v_1 represents a true wave velocity—i.e. a phase progression with distance—whereas the imaginary part v_2 implies attenuation—a decay with time. It is more common to make ω real, when we have

$$f = A\exp(-s_2\omega x)\exp\{i\omega(t - s_1 x)\}, \tag{2.22a}$$

where we define $s = s_1 - is_2 = v^{-1} = k/\omega$.

A wave emitted at $x = 0$ with frequency ω and amplitude A is thus attenuated to amplitude $A\exp(-s_2\omega x)$ at a distance x away from the source. The complex velocity thus has a practical meaning (Fig. 2.3).

2.3.2   Imaginary velocity. Sometimes the velocity is calculated to be purely imaginary. The effect of this is to make s_1 or v_1 zero in equations (2.22) and (2.22a). In the latter expression the wave clearly has no harmonic space-dependence at all; it is a purely exponential function of x, but still oscillating in time with frequency ω (Fig. 2.4). It is then called an *evanescent wave*.

2.3.3   The diffusion equation. The diffusion equation leads to attenuated and evanescent waves and will be used as an example.

We had (equation (2.15))

$$\frac{\partial \theta}{\partial t} = D \frac{\partial^2 \theta}{\partial x^2} \quad \left(D = \frac{K}{s}\right),$$

for the evolution of the temperature distribution in a one-dimensional medium—say a straight rod. The $\omega : k$ dispersion relation is

$$i\omega = -Dk^2$$

giving

$$k = \left(\frac{\omega}{2D}\right)^{\frac{1}{2}}(1 - i). \tag{2.23}$$

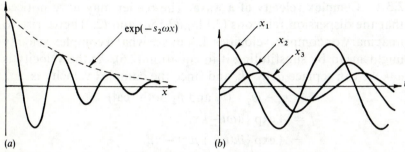

Fig. 2.3. An attenuated wave (k a complex function of ω). (a) as a function of distance at a fixed instant; (b) as a function of time at three positions $x_1 < x_2 < x_3$.

If one end of the bar is subjected to alternating heating so that its temperature θ varies as

$$\theta = \theta_0 \exp(i\omega t) \quad (\omega \text{ real}),$$

the wave is propagated along the bar in the form

$$\theta(x, t) = \theta_0 \exp\left[i\left\{\omega t - \left(\frac{\omega}{2D}\right)^{\frac{1}{2}}(1 - i)x\right\}\right]$$

$$= \theta_0 \exp\left\{-\left(\frac{\omega}{2D}\right)^{\frac{1}{2}}x\right\} \cdot \exp\left[i\left\{\omega t - \left(\frac{\omega}{2D}\right)^{\frac{1}{2}}x\right\}\right], \tag{2.24}$$

which is attenuated in distance along the bar with characteristic decay distance $(2D/\omega)^{\frac{1}{2}}$. This quantity is the distance in which θ decays by a factor e^{-1}. The propagated disturbance is still a wave, however; the phase of oscillation progresses regularly along the bar with a velocity $(2D\omega)^{\frac{1}{2}}$. Now suppose that the same bar has an initial temperature distribution

$$\theta = \theta_0 \exp(-ikx), \quad (k \text{ real}),$$

impressed upon it at time $t = 0$, and the temperature distribution is left to its own devices. We should expect, intuitively, that heat

would flow from hot to cold regions until the uneven distribution disappeared; we should not expect the temperature at any point to overshoot and oscillate, but simply to decay to its final value. To show that intuition is correct, we write down the subsequent temperature distribution:

$$\theta(x, t) = \theta_0 \exp\{i(\omega t - kx)\}$$
$$= \theta_0 \exp\{-(Dk^2 t)\} \cdot \exp(-ikx) \quad \text{from (2.24)}.$$

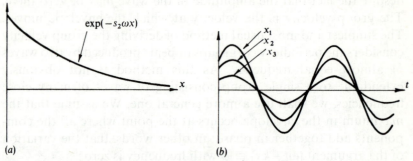

Fig. 2.4. An evanescent wave (k an imaginary function of ω). (a) as a function of distance at a given instant; (b) as a function of time at three positions $x_1 < x_2 < x_3$.

There is no oscillatory time-dependence; the phase of the distribution $\exp(-ikx)$ remains unchanged, but its amplitude decays to zero with time-constant $(Dk^2)^{-1}$. This is a wave evanescent in time. Thus the heat-diffusion equation illustrates both types of behaviour; it supports a wave attenuated in distance for a real frequency, or evanescent in time for a real wavelength.

To sum up, we have discovered three types of solution to wave equations, all of which can be represented by velocities of various types:

(i) real velocity: the wave is propagated at constant amplitude,

(ii) complex velocity: the wave is attenuated, either in distance or time,

(iii) imaginary velocity: the wave is evanescent.

2.4 Group velocity

The non-dispersive wave equation (2.5) is unique in that it leads to the propagation of disturbances of all frequencies with the same velocity, and as a result any wave travels unchanged. In general, provided that the dispersion is not very large, a disturbance which

is very like a wave of a single frequency ω_0 will travel with little distortion, but the velocity at which it moves is not the same as the velocity ω_0/k_0. Such a disturbance is called a 'wave group' (Fig. 2.5) and is discussed fully in Chapter 8; for the moment we need just accept the fact that it can be built up from waves of frequency close to ω_0 (see § 3.5.6). The obvious property we shall use, however, is that the position of the group is defined not by the individual waves in it, but by the envelope, which has its maximum point at P, despite the fact that the amplitude of the wave may be zero there. The group velocity is the velocity at which the envelope moves. The simplest and most usual method of deriving the group velocity considers the periodic wave groups or beats produced by two waves of almost equal frequency. As this method is not obviously extendable to a single group consisting of waves of many close frequencies, we shall use a more general one. We assume that the maximum in the envelope occurs at the point where all the components add together in phase; in other words, that the variation of the argument $(\omega t - kx) \equiv \phi$ with frequency is zero:

$$\frac{\partial \phi}{\partial \omega} = t - x\frac{\partial k}{\partial \omega} = 0. \tag{2.25}$$

The group velocity v_g is the relationship between the positions x and time t for which this is satisfied, i.e.

$$v_g = \frac{x}{t} = \frac{\partial \omega}{\partial k}. \tag{2.26}$$

This is the most useful expression for the group velocity. Notice that it has the same dimensions as the wave velocity ω/k. The equation (2.26) can be written in many other forms, one example being as follows. The wave velocity is given by $v = \omega/k$ whence the group velocity

$$v_g = \frac{\partial \omega}{\partial k} = \frac{\partial(kv)}{\partial k}$$

$$= v + k\frac{\partial v}{\partial k}$$

$$= v - \frac{2\pi}{\lambda}\left(\frac{1}{2\pi\lambda^{-2}}\right) \cdot \frac{\partial v}{\partial \lambda}$$

$$= v - \lambda\frac{\partial v}{\partial \lambda}. \tag{2.26a}$$

Other forms of the expression will be derived when necessary, for example in § 10.3.4.

2.4.1 The group velocity and energy transfer. Since the wave amplitude outside the wave group is zero (at points A and B in Fig. 2.5, for example) it is clear that any energy attached to the waves travels with the group, because a wave of zero amplitude cannot store any energy. If, however, a wave group becomes distorted on its passage through a medium, it becomes difficult to define exactly what velocity corresponds to the transfer of energy.

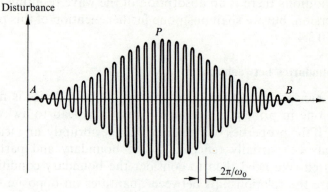

Fig. 2.5. A wave group.

Such conditions correspond to a highly frequency-dependent group velocity, and are discussed more fully in § 10.3.4 and 12.8.6, where they are considered as relevant to anomalous dispersion. The velocity of transfer of energy is called the *signal velocity*, and under conditions where a wave group does not become distorted the group velocity and signal velocity are equal.

The main importance of the group velocity, then, is that it is the velocity at which energy is transported by the waves. As a result of the theory of relativity we know that energy cannot be transported at a velocity greater than that of light in free space; this means that in no medium can the signal velocity be greater than the velocity of light. There is no such restriction on the wave velocity, however, so that a dispersion relation such as that for X-rays in a medium (§ 10.3.5)

$$v = \frac{\omega}{k} = c\left(1 + \frac{1}{2}\frac{\Omega^2}{\omega^2}\right) > c \qquad (2.27)$$

is quite permissible since the group velocity

$$v_g = \frac{\partial \omega}{\partial k} = c\left(1 + \frac{1}{2}\frac{\Omega^2}{\omega^2}\right)^{-1} \tag{2.28}$$

is then less than c. In fact, the relationship which occurs between equations (2.27) and (2.28),

$$vv_g = c^2, \tag{2.29}$$

is quite common, although not invariable. If this relationship (2.29) does hold, but v is less than c, it will follow that v_g is greater than c and the relativistic prediction will be violated. Fortunately, under such conditions there is an absorption of the wave resulting from its dispersion, but we shall postpone further mention of this point until § 10.3.4.

2.5   Boundaries between media

2.5.1   Boundary conditions. The problem of boundaries is not a difficult one in principle, although it may well lead to awkward algebra. If the properties of a medium change abruptly, an incident wave may be partially reflected at the boundary and partially transmitted. We need then to consider the boundary conditions, which are the relationships between quantities on opposite sides of the boundary. In the transmission of sound waves, for example, the displacement of the medium must remain continuous across the boundary (if it is well glued together!), otherwise either a crack or a region of infinite compression will occur. Similarly the pressure must be continuous otherwise the boundary layer, which is a mathematical plane containing zero mass of material, would accelerate at infinite rate under the action of a finite force. Since there exist three waves at the boundary—incident, reflected and transmitted—their relative amplitudes can be calculated consistently with these two boundary conditions. We shall not concern ourselves with more detail about the calculation here, as it is adequately illustrated by the discussion of reflexion and refraction characteristics for electromagnetic waves under many conditions in Chapter 4.

2.5.2   Impedance. The resistance or impedance of an electrical circuit is a useful concept because it indicates the relationship between the 'applied' quantity (voltage) and the 'induced' quantity (current). A similar definition can be applied to the propagation of

waves; in sound waves, for example (§ 2.2.2(i)), the two quantities are the stress, p, and the velocity of displacement $\partial\xi/\partial t$. Applying the relationships to the wave-form

$$\xi = \xi_0 \exp\{i(\omega t - kx)\} \tag{2.30}$$

we have
$$p = \kappa\frac{\partial\xi}{\partial x} = ik\kappa\xi_0 \exp\{i(\omega t - kx)\}$$

and
$$\frac{\partial\xi}{\partial t} = i\omega\xi_0 \exp\{i(\omega t - kx)\},$$

whence the impedance Z is given by

$$Z = p\left(\frac{\partial\xi}{\partial t}\right)^{-1} = \frac{-k\kappa}{\omega} = (\kappa\rho)^{\frac{1}{2}} = \rho v, \tag{2.31}$$

using the relationship that

$$v = \frac{\omega}{k} = \left(\frac{\kappa}{\rho}\right)^{\frac{1}{2}}.$$

The rate of energy flow in an electrical circuit is the product of current and potential difference IV; similarly in the mechanical circuit it is $p(\partial\xi/\partial t)$ (this gives a clue about what to look for in deciding the relevant quantities). In the mechanical 'circuit' it can be written alternatively as $Z(\partial\xi/\partial t)^2$ or $p^2 Z^{-1}$ analogously with the electrical case.

2.5.3 Complex impedance. Like the velocity, to which the impedance is usually related by a real property of the medium (equation (2.31)), the impedance can be complex. As the 'current' and 'voltage' are oscillating, the meaning of a complex impedance is clearly that the two are not oscillating in phase (the analogy with electric circuits is complete) and the power transfer is thus given by

$$\tfrac{1}{2}(VI^* + V^*I) = \tfrac{1}{2}II^*(Z + Z^*). \tag{2.32}$$

2.5.4 Impedance matching. The use of impedance in wave studies is most important when we try to maximize the power transfer across a boundary or a series of boundaries. If, in the electric circuit illustrated in Fig. 2.6, we have a source of impedance Z_1 feeding a load of impedance Z_2, electric-circuit theory shows that the power developed in the load

$$p = \tfrac{1}{2}II^*(Z_2 + Z_2^*) \quad \text{from (2.32)}$$

$$= \tfrac{1}{2}VV^*(Z_2 + Z_2^*)\left\{\frac{1}{Z_1 + Z_2} + \frac{1}{Z_1^* + Z_2^*}\right\}^2, \tag{2.33}$$

which is maximum when $Z_1^* = Z_2$. Similarly, the most efficient wave-power transfer occurs when the impedances are thus 'matched'. Usually we are dealing in such cases with real impedances, when the matching condition is simply

$$Z_1 = Z_2.$$

Further examples of this will be given in the chapter on interference (§ 7.9.1).

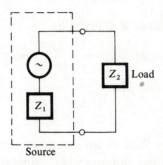

Fig. 2.6. Matching a source of impedance Z_1 to a load of impedance Z_2.

2.6   Summary

The intention of this chapter has been to give a short description of one-dimensional waves in general, and to introduce some of the concepts we shall need in a further study of electromagnetic waves and optics. The most important fact that should be retained is that we have defined a wave equation, by equation (2.9), to be a polynomial whose solution is of the form

$$f = A \exp \{i(\omega t - kx)\}$$

and all the properties of the waves can then be described in terms of the relationship between ω and k, the dispersion equation, which is a property of the medium.

2.6.1   Three-dimensional wave-form.

Although this discussion has been entirely in one dimension, nothing particularly striking arises from the transition to three dimensions, in which the analogous wave-form is a function of vector position $\mathbf{r} = (x, y, z)$ and time t:

$$\mathbf{f}(\mathbf{r}, t) = \mathbf{A} \exp \{i(\omega t - \mathbf{k} \cdot \mathbf{r})\}. \tag{2.34}$$

The vectors $\mathbf{f}$ and $\mathbf{A}$ represent the *polarization* of the wave, i.e. the direction in which the displacement takes place; the vector $\mathbf{k}$

represents the reciprocal of the wavelength along the direction of travel of the wave. For this reason it is known as the wave-vector, and it is **k**, and not λ, which can be resolved into components along different directions (Fig. 2.7). The dispersion equation is then a relationship between ω and the vector **k**, and the propagation properties come as a result of the equation.

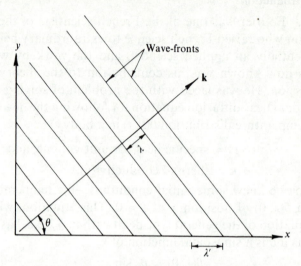

Fig. 2.7. A three-dimensional wave. The wave disturbance along the x-axis has wavelength $\lambda' = \lambda/\cos\theta$. Thus $k' = k\cos\theta$ and so **k**, not λ, is a vector which can be resolved.

A three-dimensional wave of the form (2.34) has a *wave-front*, which is a plane of constant phase

$$\mathbf{k} \cdot \mathbf{r} = \text{constant} \qquad (2.35)$$

and is clearly normal to the wave-vector **k**. The wave velocity is parallel to **k** and is therefore also normal to the wave-fronts. However, the group velocity is not necessarily parallel to **k** in an anisotropic medium, but we shall leave such considerations until Chapter 5, where the dependence of the propagation on both the magnitude and direction of **k** is of fundamental importance.

CHAPTER 3

FOURIER THEORY

3.1 Introduction

J. B. J. Fourier was one of the French scientists of the time of Napoleon who raised French science to extraordinary heights. He was essentially an applied scientist, and the work by which his name is now known was his contribution to the theory of heat transmission. He was faced with the problem of solving the one-dimensional heat-diffusion equation for following the development of the temperature distribution $\theta(x, t)$ in a body

$$\frac{\partial \theta}{\partial t} = \frac{\kappa}{s} \frac{\partial^2 \theta}{\partial x^2} \quad \begin{array}{l}(s = \text{specific heat per unit volume, and} \\ \kappa = \text{thermal conductivity})\end{array} \tag{3.1}$$

for which he knew some initial conditions—the temperature as a function $\theta(x, 0)$ of position x at $t = 0$. This equation, which is a wave equation of the general type dealt with in § 2.2.2, has analytic solutions if θ is a sinusoidal function of x,

$$\theta(x, 0) = \theta_0 \sin kx, \tag{3.2}$$

the solution then being an exponential with characteristic time related to k:

$$\theta(x, t) = \theta_0 \exp\left(-\frac{\kappa}{s} k^2 t\right) \sin kx. \tag{3.3}$$

As a sinusoidal initial distribution is a very artificial example, Fourier devised a method of expressing any periodic function, or any non-periodic function restricted to a body of regular shape, as the sum of a series of sinusoidal terms of various wavelengths for each of which the equation (3.1) could be solved individually. As the equation is homogeneous in θ, the solutions can then be added.

This principle of expressing an arbitrary function as the sum of a set of sinusoidal terms is called *Fourier theory* and has found applications far beyond the boundaries of heat-transmission theory. Since optics is concerned with light waves and their interactions with obstacles which represent regions in which the wave equations must be solved under different conditions from their

surroundings, Fourier theory is obviously a basic tool which we shall use repeatedly. The intention of this chapter is to make the theory familiar to readers, and to derive some of the more important results and ideas so that they can be used later without breaking the thread of an argument.

3.2   Analysis of periodic functions

3.2.1   Fourier's theorem.

Fourier's theorem states that any periodic function $f(x)$ can be expressed as the sum of a series of sinusoidal functions which have wavelengths which are integral sub-multiples of the wavelength λ of $f(x)$. To make this statement complete zero is counted as an integer, giving a constant leading term to the series:

$$f(x) = C_0 + C_1 \cos\left(\frac{2\pi x}{\lambda} + \alpha_1\right) + C_2 \cos\left(\frac{2\pi x}{\lambda/2} + \alpha_2\right) + \dots$$

$$+ C_n \cos\left(\frac{2\pi x}{\lambda/n} + \alpha_n\right) + \dots. \tag{3.4}$$

The n's are called the *orders* of the terms, which are harmonics. The theorem can be demonstrated as reasonable. If we cut off the series after the first term, the equation is satisfied only at a discrete number of points—at least two per wavelength. If we add a second term the number of points of agreement will increase; as we continue adding terms the number of intersections between the synthetic function and the original can be made to increase without limit (Fig. 3.1). This does not prove that the functions *must* be identical when the number of terms becomes infinite; there are examples which do not converge to the required function, but the regions of error must become vanishingly small.

This reasoning would, of course, apply to components other than sine waves. The sine curve, however, being the basic solution of all wave equations, is of particular importance in physics, and hence gives Fourier's theorem its fundamental significance.

3.2.2   Fourier coefficients.

Each term in the series (3.4) has an *amplitude* C_n and a *phase angle* α_n. The latter quantity provides the degree of freedom necessary for relative displacements of the terms of the series along the x-axis. The determination of these quantities for each term of the series is called *Fourier analysis*.

It is, however, not always convenient to specify an amplitude and phase; we can express each term in the form:

$$C_n \cos\left(\frac{2\pi n x}{\lambda} + \alpha_n\right) = A_n \cos\frac{2\pi n x}{\lambda} + B_n \sin\frac{2\pi n x}{\lambda}, \qquad (3.5)$$

where $A_n = C_n \cos\alpha_n$ and $B_n = -C_n \sin\alpha_n$. The series (3.4) is then written as

$$f(x) = A_0 + \sum_1^\infty A_n \cos\frac{2\pi n x}{\lambda} + \sum_1^\infty B_n \sin\frac{2\pi n x}{\lambda}. \qquad (3.6)$$

The process of Fourier analysis consists of evaluating the pairs (A_n, B_n) for each value of n.

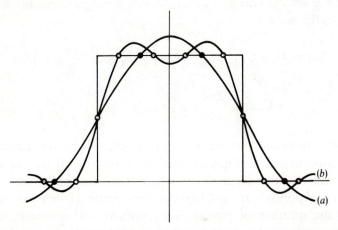

Fig. 3.1. Intersection between a square wave and its series terminated after (a) the first and (b) the third term.

3.2.3 Complex Fourier coefficients. The series can be still more simply specified in terms of complex quantities, A_n and B_n being regarded as the real and imaginary components of a complex quantity a_n. We then write

$$f(x) = A_0 + \sum_1^\infty a_n \exp\left(\frac{2\pi i n x}{\lambda}\right). \qquad (3.7)$$

This method of specification is useful because a complex a_n contains two items of information:

$$a_n = A_n - iB_n = -C_n \exp(i\alpha_n),$$

in terms of the two earlier pairs. For theoretical work we shall use the complex representation entirely, although the (A_n, B_n) pairs will be necessary for computation (Appendix V).

3.2.4 Range of summation for complex functions. Any real function $f(x)$ can be written in the manner above, but if the range of functions that can be dealt with is to be extended to include complex functions as well, we must increase the summation range to cover $-\infty$ to $+\infty$. The extra degree of freedom implied by allowing the $-n$ term as well as $+n$ makes it possible to express any function $f(x)$, real or complex, by such a series. For example, the real function $f(x) = \sin 5x$ can be written

$$\sin 5x = \frac{1}{2i} \exp(5ix) - \frac{1}{2i} \exp(-5ix),$$

for which $a_5 = 1/2i$ and $a_{-5} = -1/2i$, whereas the complex function $\sin 5x + (i/2) \cos 5x$ has $a_5 = -i/4$ and $a_{-5} = 3i/4$, all other a_n's being zero in both examples.

3.3 Fourier analysis

For certain functions Fourier analysis can be carried out analytically by a process that depends on an obvious property of a sinusoidal function—that its integral over a complete number of wavelengths is zero. Consequently, the integral of the product of two sinusoidal functions with integrally-related wavelengths over a complete number of cycles is also zero with one exception; when the two wavelengths are equal the product is always positive and the integral finite. Therefore, if we integrate the product of $f(x)$ (wavelength λ) with a sine function of wavelength λ/m, the result will be zero for all the Fourier coefficients of $f(x)$ except the mth, which has wavelength λ/m, and the value of the integral will then give the amplitude of the coefficient a_m.

To express this mathematically let us find the mth Fourier coefficient by multiplying the function $f(x)$ by $\exp(2\pi imx/\lambda)$ and integrating over a complete wavelength λ. It is convenient to take x in angular measure as $\theta = 2\pi x/\lambda = kx$ and then to take the integral I_m over the range $-\pi \leqslant \theta \leqslant \pi$, which is one wavelength. Then

$$I_m = \int_{-\pi}^{\pi} f(\theta) \exp(im\theta)\, d\theta$$

$$= \int_{-\pi}^{\pi} \sum_{-\infty}^{\infty} a_n \exp(in\theta) . \exp(im\theta)\, d\theta. \tag{3.8}$$

Every term in the summation is sinusoidal, with wavelength $\lambda/(m+n)$, with the exception of the one for which $n = -m$. The

sinusoidal terms, being integrated over $(m+n)$ wavelengths, do not contribute; so that

$$I_m = \int_{-\pi}^{\pi} a_{-m} \, d\theta = 2\pi a_{-m}. \tag{3.9}$$

Thus we have a general expression for the mth Fourier coefficient:

$$a_m = \frac{1}{2\pi} \int_{-\pi}^{\pi} f(\theta) \exp(-im\theta) \, d\theta. \tag{3.10}$$

Note that it includes the zero term, the mean value of $f(\theta)$:

$$a_0 = \frac{1}{2\pi} \int_{-\pi}^{\pi} f(\theta) \, d\theta. \tag{3.11}$$

3.3.1 Even and odd functions.

A function is said to be *even* if $f(\theta) = f(-\theta)$, and *odd* if $f(\theta) = -f(-\theta)$. See Fig. 3.2.

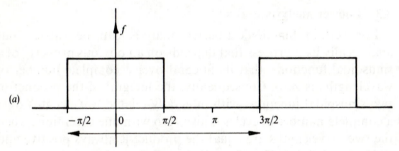

(a)

Function defined in this region

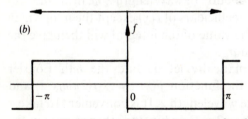

(b)

Fig. 3.2. A square wave (a) as an even function, (b) as an odd function.

Let us write a periodic even function $f_E(\theta)$ by its Fourier series. We have

$$a_m = \frac{1}{2\pi} \int_{-\pi}^{\pi} f_E(\theta) \exp(-im\theta) \, d\theta. \tag{3.12}$$

By replacing θ by $(-\theta')$ we can write this as

$$a_m = -\frac{1}{2\pi} \int_{\pi}^{-\pi} f_E(-\theta') \exp(im\theta') \, d\theta' \tag{3.13}$$

$$= \frac{1}{2\pi} \int_{-\pi}^{\pi} f_E(\theta') \exp(im\theta') \, d\theta' \qquad (3.14)$$

$$= a_m^*$$

having used the even properties of $f_E(\theta)$. Thus $a_m = a_m^*$, a_m^* being the complex conjugate of a_m, formed by replacing i by $(-i)$ in any complex expression for a_m.

Any function a_m for which $a_m = a_m^*$ must be completely real; hence the coefficients for an even function are purely real.

Analogously, a function $f_0(\theta)$ which is odd leads to the result $a_m = -a_m^*$, which shows that the coefficients for an odd function are purely imaginary.

3.3.2 The square wave. Mathematical textbooks contain many examples of Fourier analysis, and we shall therefore deal with only one here—the *square wave*. This has constant value over half its period $(-\pi/2$ to $\pi/2)$ and zero over the other half $(\pi/2$ to $3\pi/2)$ (Fig. 3.2(*a*)). (It corresponds to a diffraction grating of equal clear and opaque strips illuminated by light of uniform amplitude and phase.) The function as defined above is even; a_n is therefore real. If possible, it is often worthwhile choosing the position of the origin to make a function even, as the mathematics is usually simpler; if we had chosen to make the function a positive constant from 0 to π and an equal negative constant for π to 2π it would have been odd and its coefficients all imaginary (Fig. 3.2(*b*)). This effect—the altering of the phase of all coefficients together by a shift of origin— is often important; the form of the function determines the *relative* phases of the coefficients only.

For the even function (Fig. 3.2)

$$f(\theta) = 1 \quad (-\pi/2 \leqslant \theta \leqslant \pi/2); \quad f(\theta) = 0 \quad (\pi/2 \leqslant \theta \leqslant 2),$$

$$a_n = \frac{1}{2\pi} \int_{-\pi}^{\pi} f(\theta) \exp(-in\theta) \, d\theta$$

$$= \frac{1}{2\pi} \int_{-\pi/2}^{\pi/2} \exp(-in\theta) \, d\theta$$

$$= -\frac{1}{2\pi ni} [\exp(-in\theta)]_{-\pi/2}^{\pi/2} \quad \text{for} \quad n \neq 0$$

$$= \frac{1}{n\pi} \sin \frac{n\pi}{2}.$$

Thus we have, evaluating a_0 from (3.11),

$$a_0 = \tfrac{1}{2}, \qquad a_1 = \frac{1}{\pi}, \qquad a_2 = 0, \qquad a_3 = -\frac{1}{3\pi},$$

$$a_4 = 0, \qquad a_5 = \frac{1}{5\pi}....$$

3.3.3 Reciprocal space in one dimension.

We can think of the Fourier coefficients a_n as a function $a(n)$ of n. As $a(n)$ exists only for integral values of n, the function can be considered as being defined for non-integral values but as having zero value there; the function which represents the series for a square wave can therefore be drawn as in Fig. 3.3. Given this drawing, we could simply reconstruct the original square wave by summing the series it represents, except that it gives no information about the wavelength λ of the original wave. This defect can be simply remedied. Written in terms of x, the expression for a_n is

$$a_n = \frac{1}{\lambda} \int_{\text{one wavelength}} f(x) \exp\left(-\frac{2\pi i n}{\lambda} x\right) dx. \qquad (3.15)$$

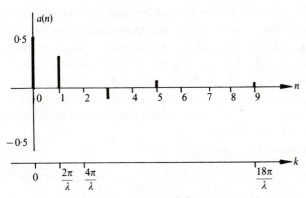

Fig. 3.3. Functions $a(n)$ and $a(k)$ for a square wave.

Information about the wavelength λ can be included in (3.15) by using the variable $2\pi n/\lambda$ rather than n; this is conventionally called k, and corresponds to a harmonic of wavelength λ/n. The extra information about the wavelength is included by re-labelling the abscissa in Fig. 3.3 (lower axis) and the function (3.15) becomes

$$a(k) = \frac{1}{\lambda} \int_{\text{one wavelength}} f(x) \exp\left(-ikx\right) dx. \qquad (3.16)$$

It is useful now to compare the functions $a(k)$ as λ changes. In Fig. 3.4 this comparison is carried out, the scales of k and x being the same in a, b, c. Clearly the scale of $a(k)$ is inversely proportional to that of $f(x)$. For this reason (k proportional to $1/\lambda$) the space whose co-ordinates are measured by k is called reciprocal space; real space has co-ordinates measured by x and reciprocal space by x^{-1}. So far, of course, we have discussed a purely one-dimensional space; the extension to two and three dimensions is simple, and will be discussed in Chapter 7.

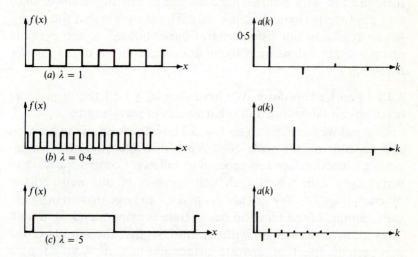

Fig. 3.4. Square waves of different scales and their Fourier coefficients $a(k)$.

3.3.4 Analysis of a general function.

In general, the integration involved in equation (3.16) is much more difficult than the example quoted. In many cases, even when $f(x)$ is a simple analytic function, the integral cannot be evaluated analytically and approximate or numerical methods must be used. The process, however, is the same in principle; the integral

$$\frac{1}{2\pi}\int_{-\pi}^{\pi} f(\theta)\exp(-in\theta)\,d\theta \tag{3.17}$$

has to be evaluated for a series of values of n, and because of the repetition involved techniques for reducing the work to a minimum are very valuable. An example to illustrate the calculation of Fourier coefficients appears as Appendix V.

3.4 Non-periodic functions

Periodic objects do not usually occur naturally; crystals, which have accurately repeated sets of atoms in three dimensions, are entirely periodic, but matter on the macroscopic scale is usually not so. Natural objects sometimes simulate periodicity in their growth, but this is never precise and most objects which we have to deal with optically (that is, on a scale greater than the wavelength of light) are completely non-periodic.

Since this book is concerned with light and real objects we may therefore ask why Fourier methods are of any importance, since they apply to periodic function only. The answer is that the theory has an extension, not visualized by Fourier himself, to non-periodic functions. The extension is based upon the concept of the *Fourier transform*.

3.4.1 Fourier transform.

We have seen in § 3.2.1 that a periodic function can be analysed into harmonics of wavelengths ∞, λ, $\lambda/2$, $\lambda/3$, ..., and we have shown by Fig. 3.4 how the form of the function $a(k)$ depends on the scale of λ. When our interest turns to non-periodic functions we can proceed as follows. Construct a wave of wavelength λ in which each unit consists of our non-periodic function (Fig. 3.5). We can always make λ so large that an insignificant amount of the function lies outside the one-wavelength unit. Now allow λ to increase without limit, so that the repeats of the non-periodic function separate further and further. What happens to the function $a(k)$? The spikes approach one another as λ increases, but the envelope of the tips of the spikes remains invariant; it is determined only by the unit, which is our non-periodic function. In the limit of $\lambda \to \infty$ the spikes are infinitely close to one another, and the function $a(k)$ has just become the envelope. This envelope is called the Fourier transform of the non-periodic function. The limiting process is illustrated in Fig. 3.5.

Admittedly, this demonstrates, rather than proves, that the Fourier series for a non-periodic function is a continuous function, rather than a set of spikes at discrete frequencies. The argument does not show that in the limit $\lambda \to \infty$ the set of spikes, now infinitely close together, does really become a continuous function, but physically the difference is unimportant. From the mathematical point of view it is better to work in reverse. We define the

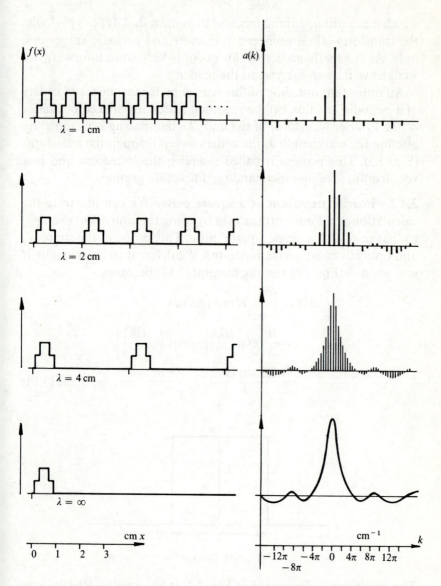

Fig. 3.5. Illustrating the progression from Fourier series to transform.

Fourier transform of a function $f(x)$ as

$$a(k) = \int_{-\infty}^{\infty} f(x) \exp{(ikx)} \, dx \qquad (3.18)$$

which is a continuous function, and then show that if $f(x)$ is periodic, the transform $a(k)$ is non-zero at discrete and periodic values of k only. As the mathematics of this proof is very straightforward we shall leave it as an exercise to the reader.

An important outcome of this reasoning is that the set of orders of a periodic function can be regarded as equally-spaced ordinates of the Fourier transform of the unit. As the spacing is changed by altering the wavelength λ, the orders sweep through the transform (Fig. 3.5). This process is called *sampling* the transform and is a very fruitful idea in understanding diffraction gratings.

3.4.2   Fourier transform of a square pulse. We can illustrate the calculation of a Fourier transform by using the equivalent example to that in § 3.3.2, a single square pulse. This is one of the simplest, and optically most useful, functions. We define it to have height H and width h (Fig. 3.6) and the integral (3.18) becomes

$$
\begin{aligned}
a(k) &= \int_{-h/2}^{h/2} H \exp{(ikx)} \, dx \\
&= \frac{H}{ik} \left[\exp\left(\frac{ikh}{2}\right) - \exp\left(-\frac{ikh}{2}\right) \right] \\
&= \frac{2H \sin{kh/2}}{k}.
\end{aligned}
\qquad (3.19)
$$

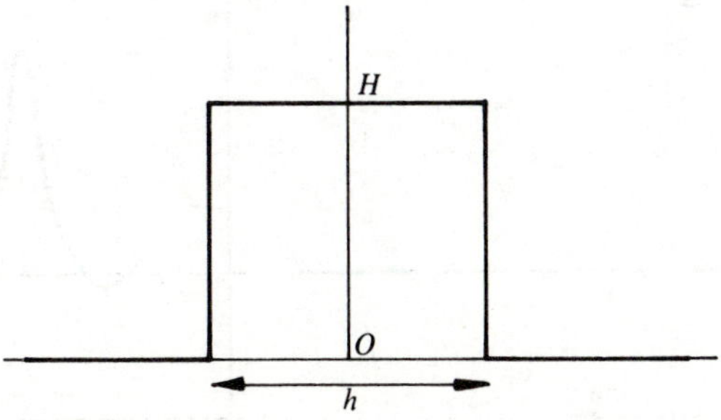

Fig. 3.6. A square pulse.

The transform is illustrated in Fig. 3.7. It has a value Hh (the area under the pulse) at $k = 0$ and decreases as k increases, reaching zero when $kh = 2\pi$. It then alternates between positive and negative values, being zero at $kh = 2n\pi$ ($n \neq 0$). It should be noted that the

transform is always real since we have made the function symmetrical about the origin; otherwise the transform would be complex, although the magnitude of its value would be unaffected by the displacement (§ 3.3.1).

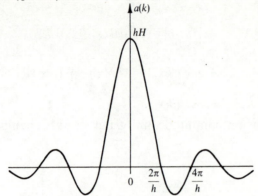

Fig. 3.7. Transform of a square pulse.

We can see the reciprocal property of the transform mentioned in § 3.3.3. As h is increased, the value of k at which the transform becomes zero decreases and the interval between successive zeros also decreases; the coarser the function, the finer is the detail of its transform. Conversely, as h decreases the transform spreads out, and when h reaches zero there is no detail at all in the transform, which has become a constant, Hh (see Fig. 3.8).

3.4.3　The δ-function. The limiting process above has introduced a new and very useful function, the δ-function. It is the limit of a square pulse as its width h goes to zero but its enclosed area Hh remains at unity. It is therefore zero everywhere except at $x = 0$, when it has infinite value, the particular value of infinity being $\lim_{h \to 0} 1/h$. The transform of the δ-function can be found by the limiting process above; we start with a square pulse of width h and height h^{-1}, which has transform

$$a(k) = \frac{2}{kh} \sin \frac{kh}{2}$$

and see that as $h \to 0$ the transform becomes unity for all values of k. The transform of a δ-function at the origin in one dimension is a constant.

To illustrate the change in phase, but not in amplitude, which occurs when the origin is shifted, we can calculate the transform of

the δ-function at $x = x_0$

$$f(x) = \delta(x - x_0) = \delta(x')$$

$$a(k) = \int_{-\infty}^{\infty} \delta(x - x_0) \exp{(ikx)} \, dx$$

$$= \int_{-\infty}^{\infty} \delta(x') \exp{[ik(x' + x_0)]} \, dx'$$

$$= \exp{(ikx_0)} \int_{-\infty}^{\infty} \delta(x') \exp{(ikx')} \, dx'$$

$$= \exp{(ikx_0)}. \tag{3.20}$$

This has constant amplitude, unity, but steadily changing phase.

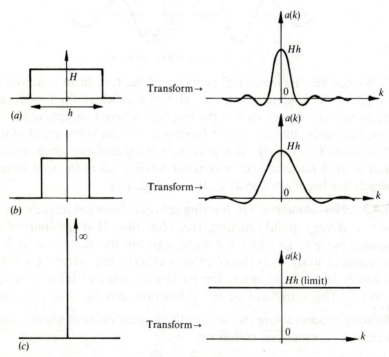

Fig. 3.8. Progression from a square pulse, (a) and (b), to a δ-function (c). The area hH remains constant throughout.

3.4.4 Multiple δ-function.
A collection of δ-functions at various values of x is another useful function:

$$f(x) = \sum_N \delta(x - x_N).$$

Its transform is clearly

$$a(k) = \sum_N \exp(ikx_N).\tag{3.21}$$

If there are two δ-functions, for example, at $x_n = \pm\alpha/2$ we have a transform

$$a(k) = 2\cos(k\alpha/2)\tag{3.22}$$

which is entirely real (even function) and is oscillatory (Fig. 3.9).

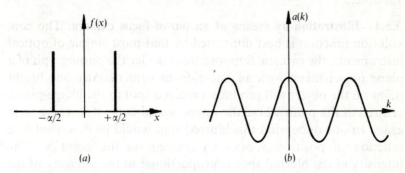

Fig. 3.9. (a) two δ-functions at $\pm\alpha/2$ and (b) their transform.

Its importance in discussing the optical experiment of Young's fringes will be evident in §7.4.1. The transform of a regular array of δ-functions

$$f(x) = \sum_{-\infty}^{\infty} \delta(x - n\alpha)$$

can be dealt with by two means.

(a) The expression above (equation (3.21)) gives

$$a(k) = \sum_{-\infty}^{\infty} \exp(ikn\alpha)$$
$$= \frac{1}{1 - \exp(ik\alpha)}\tag{3.23}$$

which consists of periodic δ-functions at $ka = 2\pi m$ (m integer).

(b) Alternatively, we can see that this is a periodic function consisting of one δ-function repeated, and the transform will thus be the transform of one δ-function (unity) sampled at intervals $2\pi/\alpha$—a series of spikes.

The two answers are, inevitably, the same.

3.5 Convolution

There is another particular type of operation which occurs very frequently in optics, and that is convolution. In its most general sense it is defined by the function

$$F(x) = \int_{-\infty}^{\infty} f(x')\phi(x-x')\,dx' \tag{3.24}$$

where F is called the convolution of f and ϕ, and x' is a dummy variable.

3.5.1 Illustration by means of an out-of-focus camera. The convolution function is best illustrated by that most simple of optical instruments, the camera. Suppose we consider the photograph of a plane object taken with an out-of-focus camera. Any one bright point on the object will produce a blurred spot in the image-plane, centred at the point where the image would come if focusing were exact. In one dimension this blurred spot would be described as a function of position $x, \phi(x-x')$ centred on the point x'. The intensity of the blurred spot is proportional to the intensity of the original point, which can be written as the intensity $f(x')$ that the sharp image would have at x'. The total intensity of the blurred spot is therefore

$$f(x')\phi(x-x') \tag{3.25}$$

and for the complete blurred image the total intensity observed at x is the integral

$$F(x) = \int_{-\infty}^{\infty} f(x')\phi(x-x')\,dx'. \tag{3.26}$$

This process, called *convoluting* the functions f and ϕ, is of great importance in optics and Fourier analysis. It is illustrated by the means described above in Fig. 3.10, where two dimensions have been employed and the function is written

$$F(x, y) = \iint_{-\infty}^{\infty} f(x', y')\phi(x-x', y-y')dx'\,dy'. \tag{3.27}$$

3.5.2 Convolution with an array of δ-functions. One of the most important applications of convolution in physical optics occurs when one of the functions is an array, regular or otherwise, of δ-functions. It can be illustrated in two dimensions by an infinite

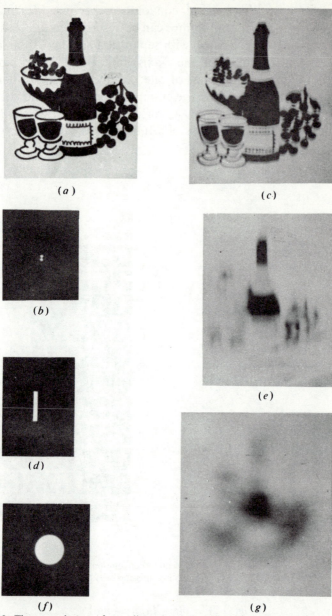

(a)

(c)

(b)

(d)

(e)

(f)

(g)

Fig. 3.10. The convolution of two-dimensional functions by the out-of-focus camera method described in § 3.5.1. The camera lens has been masked by three apertures, which can be observed by convoluting them with a δ-function, a pinhole, in (b), (d) and (f). The function (a) has been photographed through these apertures to give: (c) as the convolution of (a) and (b); (e) as the convolution of (a) and (d); (g) as the convolution of (a) and (f).

sheet of postage stamps (Fig. 3.11), and it will be seen that under these conditions the idea of convolution becomes particularly simple. Basically a sheet of stamps can be described as a rectangular lattice of points (Fig. 3.11(a)) with separation such as 2·5 cm along the y-axis and 2·0 cm along the x-axis, and at each lattice point is placed an identical unit, that of one postage stamp. We define a particular point on the postage stamp as the origin, and describe one stamp as a function $f(x', y')$ referred to this origin; we then describe the lattice by a series of δ-functions at the lattice points:

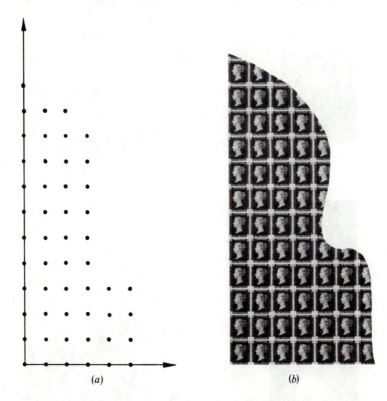

(a)   (b)

Fig. 3.11. Sheet of postage stamps, representing convolution of one stamp with a two-dimensional lattice of functions. (By kind permission of H.M. Postmaster-General.)

$$\phi(x, y) = \delta(x - la)\delta(y - mb), \qquad (3.28)$$

where $a = 2$ cm, $b = 2\cdot5$ cm and l and m are integers. The sheet of postage stamps can then be written as a composite function representing the density of ink at all points in the (x, y) plane (Fig. 3.11(b)).

$$F(x, y) = \int \int f(x', y')\phi(x - x', y - y') \, dx' \, dy' \qquad (3.29)$$

There is no reason why the integral should not be taken for $x', y' \to \infty$ to allow for a larger range of functions $f(x', y')$ which may be infinite in extent (unlike the postage stamp) and will overlap in the convolution function $F(x, y)$.

3.5.3 Physical convolution. The convolution function is important in optics because it can be used to represent two important objects: a crystal and a diffraction grating. A crystal clearly consists of a unit cell, containing a definite arrangement of atoms, convoluted with the crystal lattice, which is a set of δ-functions at lattice points. Clearly the example of a rectangular lattice given above is only one of many; a triclinic (oblique) lattice would have the function

$$\phi(x, y, z) = \prod_{i=1}^{3} \delta(l_i x + m_i y + n_i z - p_i a_i), \qquad (3.30)$$

where the three axes have direction cosines (l_i, m_i, n_i) and lattice constants a_i; p_i is any integer.

A diffraction grating with arbitrary line-shape is described as the convolution of a function representing the line-shape $\phi(x')$ with a regular series of δ-functions, one for each line. This is equivalent to a one-dimensional crystal.

A third important use of convolution occurs when the two functions f and ϕ (equation (3.24)) are identical. This is called self-convolution (Figs 3.12 and 3.13):

$$F_s(x) = \int_{-\infty}^{\infty} f(x')f(x - x') \, dx'. \qquad (3.31)$$

We shall see two uses for this in connexion with its transform, which will be shown to be the square of that of $f(x)$ (§3.5.7).

3.5.4 Fourier transform of a convolution. A mathematician would have introduced the subject of convolution the other way round. He would have asked: 'What is the transform of the product of two functions?', and then would have found the convolution function (equation (3.29)); he would have studied its properties, and found them to be what we have just discussed. Since the convolution itself is often important in physics, we shall now show that its transform is the product of the transform of the components. The

transform $A(k)$ of $F(x)$ (3.24) is

$$A(k) = \int_{-\infty}^{\infty} \left(\int_{-\infty}^{\infty} f(x')\phi(x-x')\, dx' \right) e^{ikx}\, dx$$

$$= \iint_{-\infty}^{\infty} f(x')\phi(x-x')\, e^{ikx}\, dx'\, dx. \qquad (3.32)$$

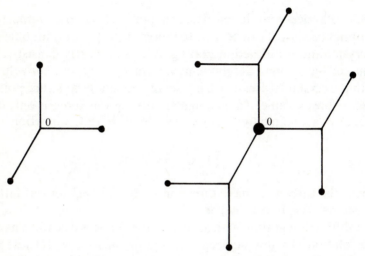

Fig. 3.12. Self-convolution of a two-dimensional function consisting of three δ-functions. Because $\phi(x-x', y-y')$ is involved in the integral, and not $\phi(x'-x, y'-y)$, at each δ-function we place the original function rotated through 180°. This inevitably leads to a strong δ-function at the origin.

By writing $y = (x-x')$ we can re-write the above as

$$\iint_{-\infty}^{\infty} f(x')\phi(y)\, e^{ik(x'+y)}\, dx'\, dy, \qquad (3.33)$$

which separates to

$$A(k) = \int_{-\infty}^{\infty} f(x')\, e^{ikx'}\, dx' \int_{-\infty}^{\infty} \phi(y)\, e^{iky}\, dy,$$

which is the product of the Fourier transform of $f(x)$ and $\phi(y)$. Thus the convolution theorem: *the Fourier transform of the convolution of two functions is the product of their individual transforms.*

3.5.5 The Fourier inversion theorem. We said in the preceding section that a mathematician would have approached the problem

of convolution by finding the transform of the product of two functions. That is not, in fact, the inverse of what we have just done; the inverse would be to find the function whose transform is the product of the two. That could be called *untransforming* the product function. But one very useful—certainly non-trivial—property of Fourier transforms is that transforming equals untransforming; in other words, the Fourier transform of the Fourier transform is the original function multiplied by 2π. The proof is not trivial, but is fairly straightforward: the original function is $f(x)$, so that we write the Fourier transform of its transform as

$$\Phi(x') = \iint_{-\infty}^{\infty} f(x)\, e^{ikx}\, dx\, e^{ikx'}\, dk$$

$$= \iint_{-\infty}^{\infty} f(x)\, e^{ik(x+x')}\, dx\, dk$$

$$= \int_{-\infty}^{\infty} f(x) \left[\frac{e^{ik(x+x')}}{i(x+x')} \right]_{k=-\infty}^{k=+\infty} dx. \tag{3.34}$$

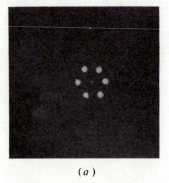   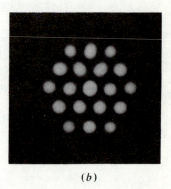

(a)   (b)

Fig. 3.13. A similar self-convolution to Fig. 3.12 has been constructed from (a) by photographing it through an aperture identical with itself (b). § 3.5.1 describes the method.

The function within the square brackets can be written as the limit:

$$\lim_{k\to\infty} \frac{2\sin ky}{y} \qquad \text{where } y = (x+x')$$

and is clearly the δ-function† $2\pi\delta(y)$. The transform $\Phi(x')$ is thus

$$\Phi(x') = \int_{-\infty}^{\infty} 2\pi\delta(x+x')f(x)\,dx = 2\pi f(x'), \qquad (3.35)$$

which is the Fourier inversion theorem.

The theorem can easily be demonstrated by many examples for which the transformation can easily be carried out in either direction. There are examples, however, in which the mathematics is more complicated for transformation in one direction than the other: for example, the square pulse. In such cases it is quite permissible to guess the answer and transform it to confirm its correctness.

3.5.6 Examples of the convolution theorem in action. There are many functions which can be most easily Fourier-transformed with the help of the convolution theorem. These functions are either

    (a) functions which can be expressed as the product of two simple functions, and whose transforms are therefore written as a convolution;

    (b) functions which are convolutions, usually with an array of δ-functions, and whose transforms are therefore products.

An example of the first type of function is the wave group (Fig. 3.14(a)):

$$f(x) = A \exp\left(\frac{-x^2}{2\sigma^2}\right) \exp\left(ik_0 x\right). \qquad (3.36)$$

The transform of the second function, $\exp(ik_0 x)$, is simply a δ-function at k_0. That of the first function is

$$g(k) = \int_{-\infty}^{\infty} \exp\left(\frac{-x^2}{2\sigma^2}\right) \exp\left(ikx\right)dx$$

$$= \int_{-\infty}^{\infty} \exp\left\{-\left(\frac{x}{(2\sigma^2)^{\frac{1}{2}}} - ik\left(\frac{\sigma^2}{2}\right)^{\frac{1}{2}}\right)^2\right\} \exp\left\{-k^2\left(\frac{\sigma^2}{2}\right)^{\frac{1}{2}}\right\}dx \qquad (3.37)$$

---

† That the function

$$\lim_{k \to \infty} \frac{2\sin ky}{y}$$

is a δ-function, can be justified by drawing the function out for a few values of k. That it has a value of 2π follows from the standard definite integral:

$$\int_{-\infty}^{\infty} \frac{\sin ky}{y}\,dy = \pi.$$

The magnitude of a δ-function is equal to the area underneath it.

by completing the square in the exponent. The integral is standard (it occurs frequently in statistical theory) and has the value

$$\int_{-\infty}^{\infty} \exp \frac{-\xi^2}{2\sigma^2} \, d\xi = (2\pi\sigma^2)^{\frac{1}{2}}$$

and therefore

$$g(k) = (2\pi\sigma^2)^{\frac{1}{2}} \exp\left\{-k^2\left(\frac{\sigma^2}{2}\right)^{\frac{1}{2}}\right\}. \tag{3.38}$$

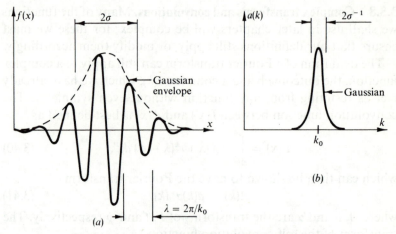

Fig. 3.14. (a) A wave-group; (b) transform of a wave-group.

The original function was a Gaussian of half width σ; the transform is a Gaussian of width σ^{-1}. The inverse relationship is important. The transform of the wave-group, equation (3.36), is therefore the convolution of δ-function at $k = k_0$ with a Gaussian centred on zero k (equation (3.38)). The convolution is therefore a Gaussian centred on $k = k_0$

$$a(k) = (2\pi\sigma^2)^{\frac{1}{2}} \exp\left\{-(k-k_0)^2\left(\frac{\sigma^2}{2}\right)^{\frac{1}{2}}\right\} \tag{3.39}$$

and is illustrated in Fig. 3.14(b).

Fig. 7.21, which illustrates the transform of a convolution with an array of δ-functions, is an example of the product nature of the transform of a convolution.

3.5.7   Self-convolution and self-coherence. One other important convolution function is the convolution of $f(x)$ with itself (§ 3.5.3).

Its transform is clearly $a^2(k)$. The quantity is always positive, and measures the intensity (amplitude squared) of the variations in the transform. If we replace x by t, so that the integral is taken over time, a is given in terms of frequency ω; and the transform of the self-convolution in time, otherwise known as the self-coherence function, is the intensity as a function of frequency ω, known as the *power spectrum*. The result that the power-spectrum is the Fourier transform of the self-coherence function is known as the Wiener–Khinchin theorem, which will be discussed in § 8.2.6.

3.5.8   Complex transforms and convolutions. Many of the functions we shall use in later chapters will be complex; for these we must ensure that our definitions still apply, or modify them accordingly.

The definition of a Fourier transform can still apply to a complex function, the outcome being a complex $a(k)$, which we have already met as resulting from any function without even symmetry. The convolution function between $f(x')$ and $\phi(x)$ is best defined as

$$F(x) = \int_{-\infty}^{\infty} f(x')\phi^*(x-x')\,dx', \tag{3.40}$$

which can then be shown to have the Fourier transform

$$A(k) = a(k)\alpha^*(k), \tag{3.41}$$

where A, a and α are the transforms of F, f and ϕ respectively. The transform of the self-convolution function

$$F_s(x) = \int_{-\infty}^{\infty} f(x)f^*(x-x')\,dx' \tag{3.42}$$

is then the intensity of the transform $a(k)$

$$A_s(k) = a(k)a^*(k) = |a(k)|^2. \tag{3.43}$$

The self-convolution is the only example in which the introduction of the complex conjugate into (3.40) makes any important difference, as it ensures that $A_s(k)$ is entirely real.

3.6   Three-dimensional transform

Nature exists in general in three dimensions, and all the above analysis can be carried out quite analogously for such cases. The variables are then $\mathbf{r} = (x, y, z)$ for real space and $\mathbf{k} = (k_1, k_2, k_3)$ for reciprocal space (§ 3.3.3). The Fourier transform of the three-dimensional function $f(\mathbf{r})$ is then

$$F(\mathbf{k}) = \int_{\text{all space}} f(\mathbf{r}) \exp{(i\mathbf{k} \cdot \mathbf{r})}\,d\mathbf{r}. \tag{3.44}$$

This transform is three-dimensional in reciprocal space. The convolution concept is still applicable (we started by describing it in two dimensions) and similarly that of self-convolution. These concepts are discussed more fully in Chapter 7.

CHAPTER 4

ELECTROMAGNETIC WAVES

4.1 Electromagnetism

In the previous chapters we have dealt with some of the general properties of waves without considering in detail any particular medium. This chapter will use Chapter 2 as a basis for understanding wave-like disturbances propagated in the electromagnetic field, both in free space and in the presence of material media. We shall not consider disturbances other than simple-harmonic waves, however, but we shall leave it to the reader to make his own synthesis of Chapters 3 and 4 when he needs it; he should find little difficulty in principle, although the mathematics may be complicated (e.g. problem 17).

The programme we shall follow starts with a description of some of the basic classical experiments on electromagnetism. The description is not detailed, and is intended as a reminder rather than an introduction. It is introduced mainly to illustrate the experimental basis for Maxwell's equations, which are the ingredients from which all the rest of the chapter is concocted. Once Maxwell's equations have been deduced, we shall show that they lead to wave equations, the simplest one being of the type of equation (2.5). The solutions of the wave equations will be discussed, in particular the transverse plane-wave solution.

In Chapter 2 the subject of boundary conditions was introduced but left without example. Here one of the most important sets of boundary conditions is used to deduce the reflexion and refraction coefficients that occur at plane boundaries between media, both dielectric and conducting. Following this discussion of sharp boundaries, we continue with consideration of very blurred boundaries in which the properties of the medium change gradually as the wave progresses. And finally we discuss two aspects of the theory of radiation, which will be important in some of our later work.

At this stage it will be appropriate to say something about the system of units we intend to use, since this can often be a serious stumbling-block in any discussion of electromagnetic theory. As far

as possible we shall try not to commit ourselves by introducing two constants:

μ, the magnetic permeability

ϵ, the dielectric constant (permittivity)

for any medium. These will take the values μ_0 and ϵ_0 for free space. On occasions when it is necessary to use some particular form of units we shall use the Gaussian electromagnetic system, since for these purposes they introduce the smallest number of unwanted constants. For practical comparisons we shall translate such absolute quantities into practical electromagnetic units.

4.1.1 Basic experiments in electromagnetism. The reader who is not already familiar with the material summarized in this section would do better to study some textbook on electromagnetism which considers the fundamentals in further detail (see Bibliography).

There are four basic experiments in electromagnetism which lead up to Maxwell's equations. The results of these experiments are as follows:

(a) The non-existence of free magnetic poles, and the magnetic inverse-square law.

(b) The inverse-square law in electrostatics.

(c) The observation and measurement of the magnetic field produced by an electric current.

(d) The observation of electromagnetic induction.

It is the quantitative formulation of the results of these experiments, together with what can be described as an inspired extrapolation to conditions that cannot be realized experimentally, which forms the basis of Maxwell's equations.

(a) and (b). There is a whole series of experiments, both electrostatic and magnetostatic, which confirm the existence of an inverse-square law in the electric and magnetic fields around free electric and magnetic poles. The evidence for the latter is indirect, since free magnetic poles do not exist in reality, and all experiments must be carried out on dipoles. The most significant experiment which confirms the electrostatic inverse-square law is Cavendish's observation of the complete absence of an electric field inside a closed conductor.

As a result of the inverse-square law of force between charges q_1 and q_2 with separation $\mathbf{r}$ in a material of dielectric constant ϵ

(defined by this equation):

$$\mathbf{F} = \frac{q_1 q_2 \mathbf{r}}{\epsilon r^3} = -\frac{q_1 q_2}{\epsilon} \nabla\left(\frac{1}{r}\right), \tag{4.1}$$

it is possible to define the *electric displacement*, $\mathbf{D}$, which is $\epsilon\mathbf{F}$ per unit charge q_2 and describes the field arising from the charge q_1 sampled by the test-charge q_2:

$$\mathbf{D} = -q_1 \nabla\left(\frac{1}{r}\right). \tag{4.2}$$

By a process which is entirely mathematical manipulation, this equation can be transformed to a more useful form applicable to a distributed charge of density ρ:

$$\nabla \cdot \mathbf{D} = 4\pi\rho. \tag{4.3}$$

The equivalent magnetic equation, taking into account the fact that the magnetic-pole density is always zero, is

$$\nabla \cdot \mathbf{B} = 0. \tag{4.4}$$

(c) The magnetic field due to a current element $id\mathbf{l}$ is observed to obey an inverse-square law also, but to be dependent on the angle between the vector $\mathbf{r}$ (separation of current element and point of observation) and the current element. The field is also observed to be along their mutual normal. Such a situation suggests a cross-product (or vector product) representation:

$$d\mathbf{H} = \frac{id\mathbf{l} \times \mathbf{r}}{r^3} = -id\mathbf{l} \times \left(\nabla\frac{1}{r}\right). \tag{4.5}$$

Once again this formula can be integrated and rearranged by purely mathematical procedures to give properties of the field $\mathbf{H}$. The most elementary of these is *Ampère's circuit theorem*:

$$\oint \mathbf{H} \cdot d\lambda = 4\pi I, \tag{4.6}$$

where I is the total current threading the closed loop λ (Fig. 4.1) around which the integral of $\mathbf{H}$ is performed. Expressed in terms of a distributed current density (current per unit area) $\mathbf{j}$, equation (4.6) becomes:

$$\nabla \times \mathbf{H} = 4\pi\mathbf{j}. \tag{4.7}$$

An interesting anomaly occurs in this equation as it stands. If the circuit carrying a current I (equation (4.6)) contains a condenser, through which no current passes, the loop integral round λ' must come to zero if taken round the condenser (Fig. 4.1). Such

a discontinuous change is physically unrealistic, and is taken into account by realizing that a changing charge on the condenser plates results in a changing field inside the condenser. The relationship between the two is that

$$I = \iint \frac{1}{4\pi} \frac{\partial \mathbf{D}}{\partial t} ds, \qquad (4.8)$$

the integration taking place across a cross-section of the condenser.

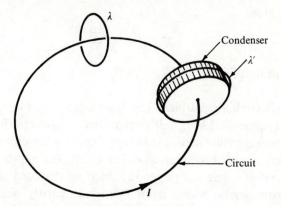

Fig. 4.1. Ampère's circuit theorem applied to a circuit containing a condenser.

In terms of the distributed current density

$$\mathbf{j} = \frac{1}{4\pi} \frac{\partial \mathbf{D}}{\partial t}$$

and therefore, because of this equivalence, equation (4.7) is written in its complete form

$$\nabla \times \mathbf{H} = 4\pi\mathbf{j} + \frac{\partial \mathbf{D}}{\partial t}. \qquad (4.9)$$

The term $\partial \mathbf{D}/\partial t$ is called the *displacement current*.

(d) Faraday stated his law of electromagnetic induction as: 'The e.m.f. generated in a circuit is equal to the rate at which it cuts magnetic lines of force.' This is almost complete, but does not explain how the e.m.f. is generated in a transformer, where lines of force never leave the iron core. The alternative statement, that e.m.f. is equal to the rate of change of flux through a loop (magnetic induction multiplied by area), fails to explain the unipolar-induction experiments in which a coil is unwound from an iron core. It is, however, the second of these formulations which is used as the

basis for Maxwell's equations, and we must be careful to think again if we come across any such 'unwinding experiments'.

In terms of the electric field produced in a region of changing **B** (which is equal to μ**H**) we have the e.m.f. round a loop λ

$$\oint \mathbf{E} . d\lambda = -\iint \frac{\partial \mathbf{B}}{\partial t} \cdot d\mathbf{s}, \tag{4.10}$$

the negative sign representing the fact that the e.m.f. tries to induce currents to oppose the change in flux, and by a simple transformation this gives

$$\nabla \times \mathbf{E} = -\frac{\partial \mathbf{B}}{\partial t} \tag{4.11}$$

for distributed fields.

4.1.2 Maxwell's equations. The four equations (4.3), (4.4), (4.9) and (4.11) are called Maxwell's equations and govern the behaviour of electromagnetic fields. Although vector differential operators give a very simple formulation of the equations, we should remark that Maxwell's original paper in which he deduced the existence of electromagnetic waves from them was hardly believed on its publication because the mathematics, in terms of components, was too complicated to follow. We shall reproduce the equations below so that their basic symmetry is clear; it would be complete if magnetic poles and hence magnetic currents existed leading to ρ_m in equation (4.13) and an additional $\mathbf{j}_m$ in equation (4.15)

$$\nabla \cdot \mathbf{D} = 4\pi\rho \tag{4.12}$$

$$\nabla \cdot \mathbf{B} = 0 \tag{4.13}$$

$$\nabla \times \mathbf{H} = \frac{\partial \mathbf{D}}{\partial t} + 4\pi\mathbf{j} \tag{4.14}$$

$$\nabla \times \mathbf{E} = -\frac{\partial \mathbf{B}}{\partial t}. \tag{4.15}$$

4.1.3 Potentials. The concept of a *potential*—a scalar quantity in terms of which a vector can be represented—is valuable in simplifying many calculations. The electric field **E** can be written in terms of a potential V, whose gradient is $-\mathbf{E}$:

$$\mathbf{E} = -\nabla V, \tag{4.16}$$

which is single-valued in electrostatic circumstances. When **E** and **H** are functions of time the concept is of little use, since its whole

value lies in its single-valuedness. Clearly from equation (4.16)

$$\nabla \times \mathbf{E} = -\nabla \times (\nabla V) \equiv 0; \qquad (4.17)$$

the identity can easily be proved by reference to the definitions of $\nabla \times$ and ∇. Hence a single-valued V is inconsistent with equation (4.15) unless the right-hand side is zero.

Another useful concept, although not so satisfying, is that of the *vector potential*, $\mathbf{A}$. This is used mainly for magnetic fields; where it is defined by

$$\mathbf{B} = \nabla \times \mathbf{A} \qquad (4.18)$$

and it immediately satisfies equation (4.13) because

$$\nabla \cdot \mathbf{B} = \nabla \cdot (\nabla \times \mathbf{A}) \equiv 0$$

for a single-valued $\mathbf{A}$. Hence a vector-potential for $\mathbf{D}$ would not be useful except in charge-free regions.

One drawback to the vector-potential $\mathbf{A}$ is that it is not defined uniquely by equation (4.18). We can add to $\mathbf{A}$ the ∇ of any single-valued scalar U, giving

$$\mathbf{A}' = \mathbf{A} + \nabla U \qquad (4.19)$$

whence

$$\nabla \times \mathbf{A}' = \nabla \times \mathbf{A} + \nabla \times (\nabla U)$$
$$= \nabla \times \mathbf{A}.$$

It is necessary to place a further restricting condition on $\mathbf{A}$; this operation is called *gauging* $\mathbf{A}$. The gauging condition is usually

$$\nabla \cdot \mathbf{A} = 0 \qquad (4.20)$$

together with boundary conditions, but there are examples where other conditions would be more appropriate. Whatever gauge is chosen, it is inconceivable that the result of a calculation should depend on it, since only the field $\nabla \times \mathbf{A}$ is observable. (Some nice problems in the theory of superconductivity, for example, have arisen because of apparently gauge-dependent solutions.)

Two examples of vector potential will be useful later. The first is for a uniform field

$$\mathbf{B} = (0, 0, B_z),$$

for which two vector potentials of different gauge are

$$\mathbf{A} = (0, B_z x, 0) \qquad (4.21)$$

and

$$\mathbf{A} = \tfrac{1}{2}\mathbf{B} \times \mathbf{r}. \qquad (4.22)$$

It is easy to confirm that both of these satisfy equation (4.18) and

(4.20), but they cannot both satisfy a complete set of boundary conditions.

The second example is the field due to a current element. Equation (4.5) leads to

$$dB = \nabla \times dA = \mu i d\mathbf{l} \times \left(\nabla \frac{1}{r} \right). \tag{4.23}$$

In the identity applying to vector $\mathbf{V}$ and scalar S

$$\nabla \times (\mathbf{V}S) \equiv S\nabla \times \mathbf{V} + \mathbf{V} \times (\nabla S) \tag{4.24}$$

we substitute $\mathbf{V} = d\mathbf{l}$ and $S = 1/r$, whence equation (4.23) becomes

$$dB = \nabla \times dA = \mu i \nabla \times \frac{d\mathbf{l}}{r} \tag{4.25}$$

since the second term, $(1/r)\nabla \times d\mathbf{l}$, is zero because $d\mathbf{l}$ is not a field variable. A solution to equation (4.25) is

$$dA = -\mu i \frac{d\mathbf{l}}{r} \tag{4.26}$$

which is a vector potential for the field due to a current element.

4.2 Electromagnetic waves

Having discussed at some length the evidence for Maxwell's equations we are now in a position to use them in a simple but important calculation which shows that they can lead to a wave equation. If we were pedantic, we should point out at this stage that the wave equation is valid only in the conditions under which Maxwell's equations have been experimentally verified, which are static or quasi-static. It is therefore completely unjustifiable to do what we shall proceed to do—that is, to apply them to very-high-frequency conditions; 10^{14} s^{-1} is a frequency so far removed from the stationary conditions of Gauss's theorem, of the *fast* withdrawal of a magnet from a coil implied in Faraday's law, that we have no right to expect Maxwell's equations to be accurate for light and X-rays. The only justification for their accuracy at such frequencies is that they do predict the subject of optics almost exactly. Quantization of the energy of the waves is the only aspect not included in Maxwell's equations.

4.2.1 Maxwell's wave equation. Maxwell deduced the existence of electromagnetic waves from the equations (4.12)–(4.15). In a uniform isotropic dielectric medium, in which there are no space-

charges ρ or currents $\mathbf{j}$, we can write these equations in the form:

$$\nabla \cdot \mathbf{D} = \epsilon \nabla \cdot \mathbf{E} = 0 \tag{4.27}$$

$$\nabla \cdot \mathbf{B} = \mu \nabla \cdot \mathbf{H} = 0 \tag{4.28}$$

$$\nabla \times \mathbf{H} = \frac{\partial \mathbf{D}}{\partial t} = \epsilon \frac{\partial \mathbf{E}}{\partial t} \tag{4.29}$$

$$\nabla \times \mathbf{E} = -\frac{\partial \mathbf{B}}{\partial t} = -\mu \frac{\partial \mathbf{H}}{\partial t}. \tag{4.30}$$

Taking $(\nabla \times)$ of both sides of equation (4.29) and replacing the resultant by the right-hand side of equation (4.30), we have

$$\nabla \times (\nabla \times \mathbf{H}) = \epsilon \frac{\partial}{\partial t}(\nabla \times \mathbf{E}) = \epsilon \mu \frac{\partial^2 \mathbf{H}}{\partial t^2}. \tag{4.31}$$

The quantity $\nabla \times (\nabla \times \mathbf{H})$ can be expanded:

$$\nabla \times (\nabla \times \mathbf{H}) = \nabla(\nabla \cdot \mathbf{H}) - \nabla \cdot (\nabla \mathbf{H}), \tag{4.32}$$

by virtue of which, and of equation (4.28), we write equation (4.31) as

$$\nabla^2 \mathbf{H} = \epsilon \mu \frac{\partial^2 \mathbf{H}}{\partial t^2}, \tag{4.33}$$

$\nabla^2 \mathbf{H}$ being the vector $\left(\dfrac{\partial^2 H_x}{\partial x^2}, \dfrac{\partial^2 H_y}{\partial y^2}, \dfrac{\partial^2 H_z}{\partial z^2} \right)$

in Cartesian coordinates, and equivalent expressions in other coordinates.

4.2.2 Velocity of the waves. This wave equation, which is of the non-dispersive type (equation (2.5)), gives rise to a well-defined and unique wave velocity:

$$v = (\epsilon \mu)^{-\frac{1}{2}}. \tag{4.34}$$

In free space, where ϵ and μ take on the values ϵ_0 and μ_0 we have the velocity in free space

$$c = (\epsilon_0 \mu_0)^{-\frac{1}{2}}, \tag{4.35}$$

which is an important physical constant. It is an important property of electromagnetic waves that they can be propagated through free space, since the forces between charges and between magnetic dipoles which serve to define ϵ and μ from equation (4.1) and its magnetic analogue, do not become zero if there is no material between them.

The numerical values of ϵ_0 and μ_0 depend on the system of units used to measure them. All sets of units begin by defining one or the

other of these, and then use equation (4.35) to evaluate the other; for example, in the electromagnetic absolute units (e.m.u.) we have

$$\mu_0 = 1 \quad \text{and therefore} \quad \epsilon_0 = c^{-2} \tag{4.36}$$

whereas in rationalized M.K.S. units:

$$\mu_0 = 4\pi \times 10^{-7} \quad \text{and therefore} \quad \epsilon_0 = 10^7/4\pi c^2.$$

It is possible to measure μ_0 and ϵ_0 in any particular set of units and hence to confirm equation (4.35). An example of an experiment to do this is illustrated in Fig. 4.2 in which the capacity of a geometrically simple condenser of capacity C is measured in a bridge circuit against a standard resistor. The switch oscillates at frequency n thus charging and discharging the condenser n times per second and passing a current

$$I = nCV$$

through the arm of the bridge. It can be seen that the condenser behaves as a resistor of magnitude nC, and C can thus be measured.

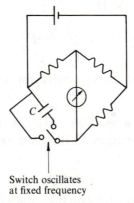

Switch oscillates
at fixed frequency

Fig. 4.2. Low-frequency experiment to determine the product $\epsilon_0\mu_0$.

Since the measurement is in terms of a resistor, it is an electromagnetic determination of C. Provided that the condenser is geometrically simple, its capacity can be calculated from its dimensions, giving C in electrostatic units. The ratio of the two measurements then leads to a value for the product $\epsilon_0\mu_0$. The estimate is essentially the static value of the product, since the frequency n is only of the order of 10^2 cycles per second. The value from this experiment and the observed velocity of light agree within experimental error. It should be pointed out that the experiment had already been carried

out by Kohlrausch and Weber in 1856 before Maxwell produced his explanation of the waves in 1865, but was subsequently repeated more accurately when its theoretical importance became apparent.

For optical purposes it is rarely necessary to consider media in which the magnetic susceptibility μ differs significantly from μ_0. As a result of this, we can combine equations (4.34) and (4.35) to give

$$\frac{c}{v} = \left(\frac{\epsilon}{\epsilon_0}\right)^{\frac{1}{2}}. \tag{4.37}$$

This quantity is, by definition, the refractive index μ. There follows the important relationship

$$\mu = \left(\frac{\epsilon}{\epsilon_0}\right)^{\frac{1}{2}} \tag{4.38}$$

which will be of importance in later chapters where the form of ϵ and hence of μ will be discussed.

4.2.3 Solutions of the wave equation. As pointed out in Chapter 2, the basic solution of the wave equation is sinusoidal. There are only two sinusoidal solutions of any importance:

(1) A radially propagating wave,

$$\mathbf{H} = \mathbf{H}_0 \frac{a}{r} \exp\{i(\omega t - kr)\} \tag{4.39}$$

which is a solution over a restricted solid angle. (The angle must be restricted because otherwise determination of the vector $\mathbf{E}$ leads to the topological conundrum of whether it is possible to comb a hairy ball flat without introducing singularities.) This solution is used in §§ 6.2.1 and 6.5 in which its vector form is not important.

(2) A plane wave,

$$\mathbf{H} = \mathbf{H}_0 \exp\{i(\omega t - \mathbf{k} \cdot \mathbf{r})\}, \tag{4.40}$$

is the most important solution. For such a wave-form we can replace the operators ∇ and $\partial/\partial t$ in Maxwell's equations by $-i\mathbf{k}$ and $i\omega$ respectively (§ 2.2.1), as a result of which equations (4.12) to (4.15) become, in the absence of charge and current densities ρ and $\mathbf{j}$,

$$\mathbf{k} \cdot \mathbf{D} = 0; \qquad \mathbf{k} \cdot \mathbf{B} = 0; \tag{4.41}$$

$$\mathbf{k} \times \mathbf{H} = -\omega\mathbf{D} = -\omega\epsilon\mathbf{E} \tag{4.42}$$

$$\mathbf{k} \times \mathbf{E} = \omega\mathbf{B} = \omega\mu\mathbf{H} \tag{4.43}$$

Thus the vectors $\mathbf{E}$, $\mathbf{k}$ and $\mathbf{H}$ are mutually orthogonal (Fig. 4.3) and the wave is transversely polarized. The relative magnitudes of $\mathbf{E}$ and $\mathbf{H}$ follow from (4.43); the wave velocity c is, of course, ω/k (§ 2.2.1) and therefore

$$\frac{E}{H} = \frac{k}{\epsilon\omega} = \frac{(\epsilon\mu)^{\frac{1}{2}}}{\epsilon} = \left(\frac{\mu}{\epsilon}\right)^{\frac{1}{2}} = Z. \tag{4.44}$$

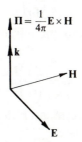

Fig. 4.3. Orthogonality of E, H and k in an electromagnetic wave.

This ratio is the impedance of the medium, and is further discussed in § 4.2.5.

For a transverse plane-wave, the *plane of polarization* is defined as the plane containing $\mathbf{E}$ and $\mathbf{k}$. We shall see in Chapter 5 that in an anisotropic medium the propagation depends on the orientation of this plane with respect to the crystal axes.

4.2.4 Flow of energy in an electromagnetic wave. It is an important feature of electromagnetic waves that they are able to transport energy, and our next problem is to find an expression for the energy flow associated with such waves.

The energy density in an electrostatic field is $(\mathbf{E} \cdot \mathbf{D})/8\pi$ and that in a magnetic field is $(\mathbf{H} \cdot \mathbf{B})/8\pi$; the total energy density is thus $(1/8\pi)(\mathbf{H} \cdot \mathbf{B} + \mathbf{E} \cdot \mathbf{D})$. The total energy contained inside surface S is

$$W = \iiint \frac{1}{8\pi}(\mathbf{E} \cdot \mathbf{D} + \mathbf{B} \cdot \mathbf{H})\, dV, \tag{4.45}$$

evaluated throughout the volume enclosed by S, and the rate of increase of W is

$$\frac{\partial W}{\partial t} = \iiint \frac{1}{8\pi}\frac{\partial}{\partial t}(\mathbf{E} \cdot \mathbf{D} + \mathbf{B} \cdot \mathbf{H})\, dV$$

$$= \iiint \frac{1}{4\pi}\left(\mathbf{E} \cdot \frac{\partial \mathbf{D}}{\partial t} + \mathbf{H} \cdot \frac{\partial \mathbf{B}}{\partial t}\right) dV. \tag{4.46}$$

To obtain the latter expression we have used the fact that $\mathbf{H}$ and $\mathbf{B}$, $\mathbf{E}$ and $\mathbf{D}$ are linearly related to each other to replace

$$\mathbf{E} \cdot \frac{\partial \mathbf{D}}{\partial t} + \mathbf{D} \cdot \frac{\partial \mathbf{E}}{\partial t} \quad \text{by} \quad 2\mathbf{E} \cdot \frac{\partial \mathbf{D}}{\partial t},$$

and similarly for $\mathbf{H}$ and $\mathbf{B}$. Using Maxwell's equations to substitute for the time-derivatives we get:

$$\frac{\partial W}{\partial t} = \iiint \frac{1}{4\pi} (\mathbf{E} \cdot \nabla \times \mathbf{H} - \mathbf{H} \cdot \nabla \times \mathbf{E}) \, dV = \iiint \frac{1}{4\pi} \nabla \cdot (\mathbf{H} \times \mathbf{E}) \, dV,$$

which, by a vector identity (Gauss's theorem)

$$= \iint_S \frac{1}{4\pi} \mathbf{H} \times \mathbf{E} \cdot d\mathbf{S}. \tag{4.47}$$

This must be the energy entering the surface; the amount leaving is

$$\frac{1}{4\pi} \iint_S \mathbf{E} \times \mathbf{H} \cdot d\mathbf{S}$$

and we can express this by saying that, locally, the energy flow through unit surface area is $(1/4\pi) \mathbf{E} \times \mathbf{H}$; the result has only been proved in integrated form, but there is no harm in expressing it for convenience in the form of a local vector, called *Poynting's vector*:

$$\mathbf{\Pi} = \frac{1}{4\pi} \mathbf{E} \times \mathbf{H}.$$

Reassuringly, the direction of this vector turns out to be along the direction of travel of the wave. It is shown above that in the simplest solution of Maxwell's equation $\mathbf{E}$ and $\mathbf{H}$ are transverse and normal to each other. The Poynting vector is therefore non-zero and along the direction of the wave (Fig. 4.3). The average value of $\mathbf{\Pi}$, $\langle \mathbf{\Pi} \rangle$, will depend on the phase of $\mathbf{E}$ and $\mathbf{H}$. If they are in phase,

$$\langle \mathbf{\Pi} \rangle = \frac{1}{4\pi} \langle E_0 \sin \omega t \, H_0 \sin \omega t \rangle$$

$$= \frac{1}{4\pi} E_0 H_0 \langle \sin^2 \omega t \rangle$$

$$= \frac{1}{8\pi} E_0 H_0 \tag{4.48}$$

but if they have components in quadrature, those components lead to the result that

$$\langle \mathbf{\Pi} \rangle = \frac{1}{4\pi} \langle E_0 \sin \omega t \, H_0 \cos \omega t \rangle = 0.$$

Thus electric and magnetic fields in quadrature lead to no transfer of energy. We shall shortly find that evanescent waves form an example of such behaviour.

4.2.5 Impedance of electromagnetic waves. That the Poynting vector is $\mathbf{\Pi} = (1/4\pi)\mathbf{E} \times \mathbf{H}$ gives a clue to the form of the impedance. We write it as

$$Z = \frac{E}{H} \tag{4.49}$$

H and E being the scalar magnitudes of $\mathbf{H}$ and $\mathbf{E}$; for plane waves $H = H_x, E = E_y$ for example. The power flow per unit area is then

$$\Pi = \frac{1}{4\pi}ZH^2 = \frac{1}{4\pi}E^2 Z^{-1}.$$

H and E, despite their being scalars, are time-dependent. If they oscillate with the same phase, Z will be real and the power transfer positive. If, however, H and E oscillate with a phase difference, Z will be complex and the power transfer will drop, becoming zero when the phase difference is $\pi/2$.

We have already deduced an expression (4.44) for E/H as

$$Z = \frac{E}{H} = \pm\left(\frac{\mu}{\epsilon}\right)^{\frac{1}{2}},$$

the sign depending on the direction of the energy flow. Clearly in non-magnetic media where $\mu = \mu_0$ we have

$$Z = \left(\frac{\mu_0}{\epsilon}\right)^{\frac{1}{2}} = \frac{1}{c}(\epsilon\epsilon_0)^{-\frac{1}{2}}. \tag{4.50}$$

In free space, where $\epsilon = \epsilon_0$ we have a well defined value for $Z = Z_0$. In electromagnetic units, where $\mu_0 = 1$ we have

$$Z_0 = 3 \times 10^{10} \text{ e.m.u.} = 30 \text{ ohms};$$

it is called the characteristic impedance of free space. In terms of the refractive index μ, $Z = Z_0/\mu$.

4.3   Reflexion and refraction

To determine the reflective and refractive properties of electromagnetic waves we need first to decide on the boundary conditions. These are fairly simple; we can immediately see that

(a) $\mathbf{E}$ parallel to the boundary surface must be continuous, because the potential V cannot have a discontinuity without causing breakdown;

(b) $\mathbf{H}$ parallel to the surface must be continuous; otherwise the

integral $\oint \mathbf{H} \cdot d\lambda$ round the loop in Fig. 4.4(a) would be non-zero, implying the existence of a surface current (a finite current in an infinitesimally small area—or infinite current density) because of equation (4.6);

(c) **B** normal to the surface must be continuous, because $\nabla \cdot \mathbf{B} = 0$ or $\iint B \, dS = 0$ over a closed surface, which implies $B_1 = B_2$ in Fig. 4.4(b);

(d) **D** normal to the surface must be continuous, similarly, unless there is a surface charge.

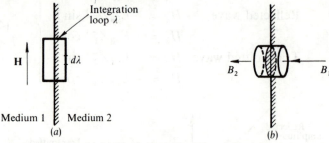

Fig. 4.4. (a) Continuity of **H**; (b) continuity of **B**.

4.3.1 Reflexion and refraction at a boundary.

We can now solve the problem of reflexion of a plane-polarized wave at the plane boundary between two media of impedances Z_1 and Z_2. Without loss of generality we need treat only the two polarizations in and perpendicular to the plane of incidence, any other plane of polarization being resolved into two components. In three-dimensional calculations of this sort it is very necessary to establish a rigorous sign-convention (§ I.2). We shall do this by allowing the light to be incident from the left on the plane $z = 0$, z being measured from left to right. Angles will be measured anticlockwise from the relevant normal, so that the reflected wave occurs at angle $\hat{\jmath} = -\hat{\imath}$. Fig. 4.5 shows the details. We shall first consider the plane of polarization normal to the plane of incidence, so that $\mathbf{E} = E_y$ only. We denote the wave numbers $2\pi/\lambda$ in the two media by k_1 and k_2.

Incident wave
$$E_y = E_{yI} = I \exp\{-i(k_1 z \cos \hat{\imath} + k_1 x \sin \hat{\imath})\}$$
Reflected wave
$$E_y = E_{yR} = R \exp\{i(k_1 z \cos \hat{\jmath} + k_1 x \sin \hat{\jmath})\}$$
Transmitted wave
$$E_y = E_{yT} = T \exp\{-i(k_2 z \cos \hat{r} + k_2 x \sin \hat{r})\}.$$

$$(4.51)$$

Any changes of phase occurring on reflexion and transmission will be indicated by negative or complex values of R and T. The magnetic fields are related by impedance $Z = E/H$ and are perpendicular to $\mathbf{k}$ and $\mathbf{E}$. The fact that the reflected wave travels in the opposite z direction to the others is represented by making its impedance equal to $-Z$, so that the Poynting vector, the energy flow, is reversed:

$$
\left.
\begin{aligned}
\text{Incident wave} \quad H_z &= E_{yI}Z_1^{-1}\sin\hat{\imath} \\
H_x &= -E_{yI}Z_1^{-1}\cos\hat{\imath} \\
\text{Reflected wave} \quad H_z &= -E_{yR}Z_1^{-1}\sin\hat{\jmath} \\
H_x &= E_{yR}Z_1^{-1}\cos\hat{\jmath} \\
\text{Transmitted wave} \quad H_z &= E_{yT}Z_2^{-1}\sin\hat{r} \\
H_x &= -E_{yT}Z_2^{-1}\cos\hat{r}.
\end{aligned}
\right\} \quad (4.52)
$$

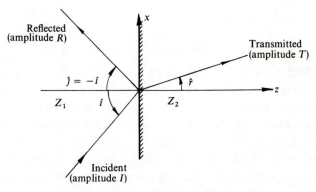

Fig. 4.5. Incident, reflected and transmitted rays.

Continuity conditions at $z = 0$ give equations as follows:

$$
\left.
\begin{aligned}
&E_\parallel \text{ at } x = 0,\, z = 0 \text{ gives } I + R = T, \\
&E_\parallel \text{ at } z = 0 \qquad \text{gives } k_1\sin\hat{\imath} = -k_1\sin\hat{\jmath} \\
&\qquad\qquad\qquad = k_2\sin\hat{r},
\end{aligned}
\right\} \quad (4.53)
$$

whence $\hat{\imath} = -\hat{\jmath}$ and

$$
\sin\hat{\imath} = \frac{k_2}{k_1}\sin\hat{r}
$$
$$
= \mu\sin\hat{r} \quad \text{(Snell's law).} \qquad (4.54)
$$

$H_\parallel$ at $z = 0$ gives

$$
-Z_1^{-1}\cos\hat{\imath} + RZ_1^{-1}\cos\hat{\jmath} = -TZ_2^{-1}\cos\hat{r}.
$$

Whence, for this polarization (denoted by subscript $\perp$)

$$\left.\begin{array}{c} R_\perp = \dfrac{Z_2 \cos \hat{\imath} - Z_1 \cos \hat{r}}{Z_2 \cos \hat{\imath} + Z_1 \cos \hat{r}} = \dfrac{\cos \hat{\imath} - \mu \cos \hat{r}}{\cos \hat{\imath} + \mu \cos \hat{r}} \\[4mm] T_\perp = \dfrac{2Z_2 \cos \hat{\imath}}{Z_2 \cos \hat{\imath} + Z_1 \cos \hat{r}}. \end{array}\right\} \qquad (4.55a)$$

The coefficients for the other plane of polarization (denoted by $\parallel$, since $\mathbf{E}$ is parallel to the plane of polarization) can be worked out similarly giving

$$\left.\begin{array}{c} R_\parallel = \dfrac{Z_2 \cos \hat{r} - Z_1 \cos \hat{\imath}}{Z_2 \cos \hat{r} + Z_1 \cos \hat{\imath}} = \dfrac{\cos \hat{r} - \mu \cos \hat{\imath}}{\cos \hat{r} + \mu \cos \hat{\imath}} \\[4mm] T_\parallel = \dfrac{2Z_2 \cos \hat{\imath}}{Z_2 \cos \hat{r} + Z_1 \cos \hat{\imath}}. \end{array}\right\} \qquad (4.55b)$$

The functions $R_\perp$ and $R_\parallel$ are illustrated in Fig. 4.6. The reflexion coefficients for normal incidence $\hat{\imath} = \hat{r} = 0$ are clearly the same:

$$R_\parallel = R_\perp = \frac{Z_2 - Z_1}{Z_2 + Z_1} = \frac{1 - \mu}{1 + \mu} \qquad (4.56)$$

which is negative when $\mu > 1$. Similarly

$$T_\parallel = T_\perp = \frac{2Z_2}{Z_2 + Z_1} = \frac{2}{1 + \mu}.$$

The constant μ refers, of course, to the relative refractive index between the two materials. If incidence is in the dense medium so that $\mu < 1$, it is clear that $T > 1$; this does not violate the principle of conservation of energy because the energy flow per unit area is $(1/4\pi)E^2 Z^{-1}$ and the proportion transmitted is thus

$$\left(\frac{2Z_2}{Z_1 + Z_2}\right)^2 \cdot \frac{Z_1}{Z_2} = \frac{4Z_2 Z_1}{(Z_2 + Z_1)^2} = \frac{4\mu}{(1 + \mu)^2}, \qquad (4.57)$$

which reaches a maximum value of 1 when $\mu = 1$. At non-normal incidence the fact that the areas of transmitted and reflected beams are in the ratio $\cos \hat{\imath} : \cos \hat{r}$ must also be taken into account when calculating total energy flows.

For the polarization-plane parallel to the incidence plane, Fig. 4.6 indicates that the reflexion coefficient is zero at a particular angle $\hat{\imath}_B$. For this condition we have

$$Z_2 \cos \hat{r} - Z_1 \cos \hat{\imath} = 0$$

$$\frac{\cos \hat{r}}{\cos \hat{\imath}} = \frac{Z_1}{Z_2} = \mu = \frac{\sin \hat{\imath}}{\sin \hat{r}},$$

which has the solution

$$\tan \hat{i} = \cot \hat{r} = \mu.$$

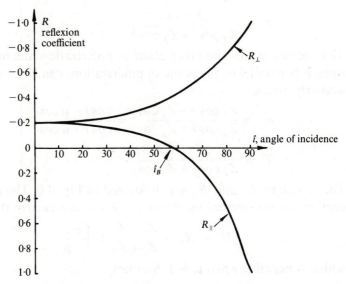

Fig. 4.6. Reflexion coefficient at the surface of a medium of refractive index $\mu = 1\cdot5$ for waves polarized in parallel ($\parallel$) and perpendicular to ($\perp$) the plane of incidence.

The angle $\hat{i} = \hat{i}_B$ which is the solution of this equation is *Brewster's angle*, and light of the parallel polarization is not reflected when incident at $\hat{i}_B$. Its origin can be seen physically as a result of the transverse nature of light. Consider the reflected ray of light as re-radiated by a plane of atoms in the surface layer of the medium, which are vibrating in a direction which is both in the plane of incidence and normal to the transmitted ray (Fig. 4.7). It is clear that no light can be re-radiated along the direction of vibration since light is a transverse and not a longitudinal wave, and when this direction coincides with the direction of the reflected ray it must have zero amplitude. Under these conditions, which are that the reflected and transmitted ray are perpendicular to each other, the reflexion coefficient is zero for this plane of polarization.

4.3.2 Incidence in the denser medium. Implicitly we have assumed $\mu > 1$ so far, in that we have drawn Fig. 4.6 with a real angle of refraction for all angles of incidence. If incidence occurs in the

denser medium, so that the equation

$$\frac{\sin \hat{i}}{\sin \hat{r}} = \mu \quad (\mu < 1) \tag{4.58}$$

cannot always be satisfied by a real angle $\hat{r}$, total internal reflexion occurs when $\hat{i}$ exceeds the critical angle $\hat{i}_c = \sin^{-1} \mu$. We can investigate this situation more closely as follows.

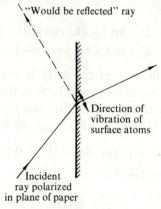

Fig. 4.7. Origin of the Brewster angle.

We postulate that a solution of equation (4.58) always exists, even if it leads to unreality. We shall then calculate the reflexion and transmission coefficients for all angles $\hat{i}$ and show that total reflexion does occur, and the disturbance on the far side of the boundary is an evanescent (§ 2.3.2) rather than a progressive wave. For the equation

$$\sin \hat{r} = \frac{1}{\mu} \sin \hat{i} > 1$$

we have $\cos \hat{r} = (1 - \sin^2 \hat{r})^{\frac{1}{2}} = \pm i\beta$ (β real and positive).

Substituting in the equations for R and T (4.55a, b) we obtain:

$$\left. \begin{array}{ll} R_\perp = \dfrac{\cos \hat{i} \mp i\mu\beta}{\cos \hat{i} + i\mu\beta}, & T_\perp = \dfrac{2\cos \hat{i}}{\cos \hat{i} \pm i\mu\beta} \\[3mm] R_\| = \dfrac{\pm i\beta - \mu \cos \hat{i}}{\pm i\beta + \mu \cos \hat{i}}, & T_\| = \dfrac{2\cos \hat{i}}{\mu \cos \hat{i} \pm i\beta}. \end{array} \right\} \tag{4.59}$$

As the reflexion coefficients are both of the form

$$R = \frac{u - iv}{u + iv} = \exp \left\{ -2i \tan^{-1} \left(\frac{v}{u} \right) \right\},$$

it is clear that they represent complete reflexion ($|R| = 1$) but with a phase-change α

$$\alpha_\perp = \mp\, 2\tan^{-1}\frac{\mu\beta}{\cos\hat{\imath}}; \qquad \alpha_\| = \pi\mp 2\tan^{-1}\frac{\beta}{\mu\cos\hat{\imath}}. \quad (4.60)$$

Neither of the transmission coefficients is zero, however, and so we must investigate the transmitted wave more closely.

We shall write the space-dependent part of the transmitted wave in full:

$$\begin{aligned}E &= E_0\exp\left\{-i(kz\cos\hat{r}+kx\sin\hat{r})\right\} \\ &= E_0\exp\left(\mp k\beta z\right)\exp\left\{-ikx(1+\beta^2)^{\frac{1}{2}}\right\}. \quad (4.61)\end{aligned}$$

The z-dependence shows that the wave is evanescent and decays rapidly to zero as z increases provided that the negative sign for β is chosen. The characteristic decay distance is $(k\beta)^{-1}$. For a critical angle of 45° ($\mu = 2^{-\frac{1}{2}}$) at an incident angle of 46°, for example,

$$\beta = (2\sin^2 46° - 1)^{\frac{1}{2}} = 0\!\cdot\!19$$

and the decay distance is thus

$$\frac{\lambda}{2\pi\beta} \doteqdot 0\!\cdot\!8\lambda.$$

The evanescent disturbance can be observed by putting a second parallel surface within the decay distance of the first boundary. The evanescent wave then gives rise to a real wave in the second medium (Fig. 4.8) which can be observed. To calculate the amplitude of the observed wave we need to solve the complete problem satisfying boundary conditions at the second surface as well; as this is complicated, although not difficult, we shall not go into the problem further.

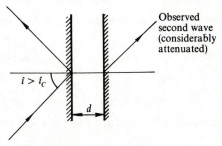

Fig. 4.8. 'Tunnelling' of an electromagnetic wave incident at an angle greater than the critical angle. The spacing d must be of the order of $(k\beta)^{-1}$.

4.3.3   An experiment to illustrate the evanescent wave. To demonstrate clearly the *frustration* of total reflexion by a second surface we make the separation d vary from zero upwards by replacing the second plane surface by a spherical one, that of a biconvex lens of focal length about 20 cm being adequate. The two surfaces are in contact at one point (Fig. 4.9). The intensity of the wave observed

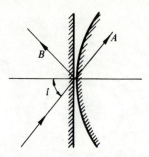

Fig. 4.9. Use of curved surface to observe tunnelling as a function of separation.

at A drops off—but not discontinuously—as we move away from the point of contact. Alternatively the intensity at B can be observed, in which case a dark spot is observed around the point of contact (Fig. 4.10(b)). To show that transmission occurs up to a separation of the order of one wavelength, the direction of illumination is altered to be non-critical so that a set of Newton's rings is observed at either A or B (Fig. 4.10(a)), and the separation between the surfaces can be estimated in terms of them. The observations shown in Fig. 4.10 indicate transmission over a region where the gap is up to about $\frac{3}{4}\lambda$.

4.3.4   Energy flow in the evanescent wave. Because the amplitude of the evanescent wave decays with z no energy can be transported away from the surface. The wave which was incident with perpendicular polarization has transmitted components which have space-variation.

$$\left.\begin{aligned} E_{yT} &\sim \exp\left(-k\beta z\right)\exp\left\{-ikx(1+\beta^2)^{\frac{1}{2}}\right\} \\ H_{zT} &\sim Z_2^{-1}(1+\beta^2)^{\frac{1}{2}}E_{yT} \\ H_{xT} &\sim Z_2^{-1}i\beta E_{yT}. \end{aligned}\right\} \tag{4.62}$$

The Poynting vector $\mathbf{\Pi} = (1/4\pi)\mathbf{E}\times\mathbf{H}$ thus has components

$$\left.\begin{aligned} \Pi_x &\sim (E_{yT})^2 Z_2^{-1}(1+\beta^2)^{\frac{1}{2}} \\ \Pi_z &\sim (E_{yT})^2 Z_2^{-1}i\beta. \end{aligned}\right\} \tag{4.63}$$

The former, being real, represents a real flow of energy along the x direction, parallel to the surface, but restricted to a layer of half the decay distance. The latter represents a wave in which **E** and **H** oscillate in quadrature with one another (the imaginary $i\beta$ indicates this) and the Poynting vector has zero time average. The evanescent wave thus transports no energy away from the surface.

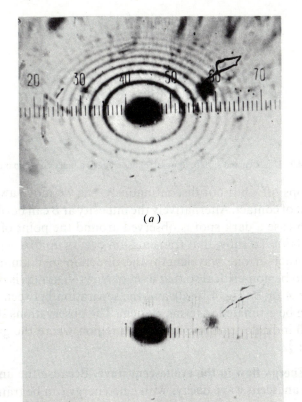

(a)

(b)

Fig. 4.10. Observations at B (Fig. 4.9) with (a) incidence just below critical angle ($\hat{\imath} < \hat{\imath}_c$), ($b$) incidence just greater than critical angle ($\hat{\imath} > \hat{\imath}_c$).

4.3.5   Phase changes on critical reflexion. The phase changes (4.60) for the two polarizations,

$$\alpha_\perp = 2\tan^{-1}\frac{\mu\beta}{\cos\hat{\imath}}; \qquad \alpha_\parallel = \pi + 2\tan^{-1}\frac{\beta}{\mu\cos\hat{\imath}} \qquad (4.64)$$

have somewhat different dependence on the angle $\hat{\imath}$ in the region between $\hat{\imath}_c$ and $\pi/2$. They have the values 0 and $-\pi$ respectively at $\hat{\imath} = \hat{\imath}_c(\beta = 0)$; at $\hat{\imath} = \pi/2$ they are π and 0. Although the difference $\alpha_\perp - \alpha_\parallel$ can be evaluated algebraically we can see it most easily by plotting $\tan \alpha/2$ against $\beta/\cos \hat{\imath}$ (straight lines of gradient μ and μ^{-1} for perpendicular and parallel polarizations respectively) and graphically evaluating the difference. The construction is shown in Figs. 4.11 and 4.12 for two values of μ, 1/1·5 and 1/2·5.

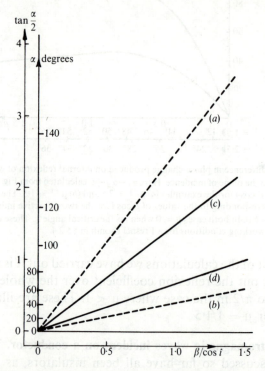

Fig. 4.11. The phase-change resulting from total internal reflexion. Here we have plotted $\tan \alpha/2$ against $\beta/\cos \hat{\imath}$ as suggested in § 4.3.5, the relationship being linear with gradient μ^{-1} for $\alpha_\parallel$ and μ for $\alpha_\perp$. The two examples are: $\mu^{-1} = 2\cdot5$—(a) is $\alpha_\parallel - \frac{1}{2}\pi$ and (b) is $\alpha_\perp$—and $\mu^{-1} = 1\cdot5$—(c) is $\alpha_\parallel - \frac{1}{2}\pi$ and (d) is $\alpha_\perp$. By reading the values of α from the scale on the left, Fig. 4.12 has been constructed.

The phase difference clearly goes through a maximum of about $\pi + 46°$ and $\pi + 94°$ respectively, and the value of $\hat{\imath}$ for which the maxima occur can be worked out from

$$\frac{\beta}{\cos \hat{\imath}} = [\mu^{-2} \tan^2 \hat{\imath} - \sec^2 \hat{\imath}]^{\frac{1}{2}} = [(\mu^{-2} - 1) \tan^2 \hat{\imath} - 1]^{\frac{1}{2}} \quad (4.65)$$

which gives $\hat{\imath} = 49°$ and $\hat{\imath} = 28°$ respectively for the two μ's. The steps in this calculation have been illustrated in some detail because it is used in the design of a *Fresnel rhomb*, a device which can be used to convert linearly-polarized into circularly-polarized light. It will be discussed in more detail in § 5.2.4.

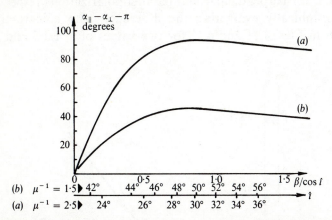

Fig. 4.12. The difference in phase-change produced on internal reflexion of waves polarized in and normal to the plane of incidence. Here $\alpha_{\parallel} - \alpha_{\perp} - \pi$, calculated from Fig. 4.11, is plotted as a function of $\beta/\cos\hat{\imath}$ for the examples (a) $\mu^{-1} = 2.5$ and (b) $\mu^{-1} = 1.5$. The lower abscissa scale shows $\hat{\imath}$ corresponding to the values of $\beta/\cos\hat{\imath}$ for the two refractive indices, calculated from equation (4.64). In both cases $\beta = 0$ when $\hat{\imath}$ is the critical angle $\hat{\imath}_c$. These curves are used to illustrate the working conditions for a Fresnel rhomb in § 5.2.4.

As a result of the calculations we have carried out it is now possible to work out the reflexion coefficient over the whole range of $\hat{\imath}$ from zero to $\pi/2$ in the case where $\mu < 1$. These are illustrated in Fig. 4.13 for $\mu = 1/1.5$.

4.3.6 Electromagnetic waves incident on a conductor. The media we have discussed so far have all been insulators, as a result of which we have been able to neglect the current term in the equation (4.14),

$$\nabla \times \mathbf{H} = \frac{\partial \mathbf{D}}{\partial t} + 4\pi\mathbf{j}. \tag{4.66}$$

If we wish to consider what happens to an electromagnetic wave incident on a conductor we must bring this term into play, as the electric field $\mathbf{E}$ will induce a non-zero current density $\mathbf{j}$ if the conductivity σ is appreciable;

$$\mathbf{j} = \sigma\mathbf{E}. \tag{4.67}$$

We can substitute (4.67) into (4.66) at the same time replacing **D** by ϵ**E** to give

$$\nabla \times \mathbf{H} = \epsilon \frac{\partial \mathbf{E}}{\partial t} + 4\pi\sigma\mathbf{E}.$$ (4.68)

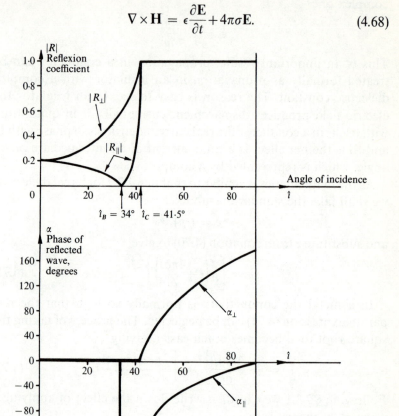

Fig. 4.13. Reflexion coefficient $|R|$ and phase-change α occurring with incidence in the denser medium, calculated for $\mu^{-1} = 1.5$. The complete reflexion coefficient is $R = |R| \exp(i\alpha)$.

Now, remembering that the wave is oscillatory with frequency ω, we replace the operator $(\partial/\partial t)$ by $i\omega$ (§ 2.2.1) and thus obtain the equation

$$\nabla \times \mathbf{H} = \mathbf{E}i\omega\left(\epsilon + \frac{4\pi\sigma}{i\omega}\right).$$ (4.69)

This equation can be seen to be formally identical with (4.66) without the current term if the real dielectric constant is replaced by a complex one

$$\epsilon_c = \epsilon + \frac{4\pi\sigma}{i\omega}. \tag{4.70}$$

This is an important result; propagation in a conductor can be treated formally as propagation in an insulator with a complex dielectric constant. The reason is easy to see. In an insulator the electric field produces displacement current $\partial\mathbf{D}/\partial t$ in quadrature with itself; in a conductor the real current density is in phase with $\mathbf{E}$, and thus the net effect is a total current at an intermediate phase angle, which is represented by a complex ϵ_c.

As the mathematics is similar to that in § 4.2.2 for a real dielectric, we shall take the standard result:

$$v = (\epsilon\mu)^{-\frac{1}{2}}$$

and substitute ϵ from equation (4.70) to give

$$v = \left[\mu\left(\epsilon - \frac{4\pi\sigma i}{\omega}\right)\right]^{-\frac{1}{2}}. \tag{4.71}$$

In a metal the conductivity is normally so high that the real part of expression (4.71) can be neglected. The process of taking the square root then becomes much easier, giving

$$\frac{1}{v} = \left[-\frac{4\pi\sigma i\mu}{\omega}\right]^{\frac{1}{2}} = \left[\frac{2\pi\sigma\mu}{\omega}\right]^{\frac{1}{2}}(1-i). \tag{4.72}$$

Following § 2.3.1 we can then write down the effect of applying a wave of frequency ω

$$E = E_0 \exp\{i(\omega t - kz)\},$$

normally to the surface $z = 0$ of a conductor; at depth z we have

$$E(z) = E_0 \exp\{-(2\pi\sigma\mu\omega)^{\frac{1}{2}}z\} \exp\{i[\omega t - (2\pi\sigma\mu\omega)^{\frac{1}{2}}z]\}. \tag{4.73}$$

This is an attenuated wave, with characteristic decay length

$$l = (2\pi\sigma\mu\omega)^{-\frac{1}{2}}$$

and wavelength inside the conductor:

$$\lambda = \left(\frac{\sigma\mu\omega}{2\pi}\right)^{-\frac{1}{2}}.$$

The decay per wavelength is thus independent of the frequency. The existence of a decay implies that a wave cannot travel any appreciable distance inside a conductor. As a result of this,

high-frequency alternating currents always travel in the surface layer of a conductor, the layer having depth about l. Stranded cables are therefore useful for such currents, as the ratio of surface to cross-sectional area is greater than in a solid wire. Table 1 shows some typical values of the *skin-depth* at various frequencies; it is clear that at optical frequencies the penetration into copper is almost negligible, even on an atomic scale, although admittedly the theory above is not applicable at such frequencies, where the skin-depth is less than the electronic mean free path in the metal.

Table 1. *Skin-depths in copper at various frequencies at $0°$C*

Frequency c/s	Free-space wavelength	Skin-depth
50		1·0 cm
1000		0·24 cm
10^6	300 m	0·001 cm
$1·6 \times 10^{15}$	5000 Å	17 Å

4.3.7   Reflexion by a metal surface. As a result of the above calculation it is possible to calculate the reflective properties of a metal. Since the reflexion and attenuation coefficients are functions of the conductivity at the particular frequency in question, measurements of the reflectivity is often a convenient way of measuring the conductivity, which is of great fundamental importance in the theory of metals.

We can calculate the reflectivity simply by the use of the complex dielectric constant again. The impedance

$$Z = (\mu/\epsilon)^{\frac{1}{2}} = \left(\frac{\mu\omega}{8\pi\sigma}\right)^{\frac{1}{2}} (1+i) \qquad (4.74)$$

gives the reflexion coefficient at the interface between the metal and free space as

$$R = \frac{Z-Z_0}{Z+Z_0} = \frac{\left(\frac{\mu\omega}{8\pi\sigma}\right)^{\frac{1}{2}}(1+i)-\left(\frac{\mu_0}{\epsilon_0}\right)^{\frac{1}{2}}}{\left(\frac{\mu\omega}{8\pi\sigma}\right)^{\frac{1}{2}}(1+i)+\left(\frac{\mu_0}{\epsilon_0}\right)^{\frac{1}{2}}} \qquad (4.75)$$

for normal incidence. For a non-magnetic metal, in which $\mu = \mu_0$ we then have

$$R = \frac{s(1+i)-1}{s(1+i)+1},$$

where $S = \epsilon_0\omega/8\pi\sigma$.

Perfect reflexion occurs, therefore, in both limits of frequency $\omega \to 0$ and $\omega \to \infty$ ($R \to \pm 1$ respectively). In between, there is clearly a phase change and partial reflexion; Fig. 4.14 shows the reflexion coefficient $|R|^2$ and the phase angle α.

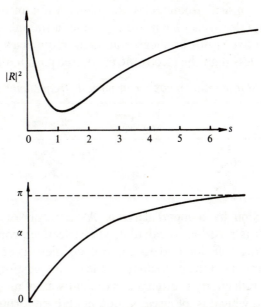

Fig. 4.14. Frequency dependence of the reflectivity and phase-change at the interface between a metal and free space.

4.4   Effects in non-homogeneous media

The results that we have discussed so far in this section are all concerned with sudden changes in properties at a plane boundary between one medium and another. It is well known that the reflective properties of a glass surface, for example, depend very much on the surface conditions, because it is very easy for a glass surface exposed to the air to accumulate a surface layer of grease or tarnish which is more than a fraction of a wavelength in thickness. In this particular example there is little point in trying to examine a physical model since the conditions are not reproducible, but there are other examples where a gradual change of the properties of the medium occur in a distance of the order of, or greater than, the wavelength. These are often important, for example, in the study of the reflexion of radio waves from a charged ionosphere,

which is one of the principal means of investigating the upper atmosphere (see § 12.7).

4.4.1   The W.K.B. method. The method of treatment is, of course, to try to solve Maxwell's equations under the given conditions; the difficulty arises in the mathematics because the value of μ, which has hitherto been a constant, is now a function of position. The easiest case to consider in general is the one in which the characteristic distance for a change of properties is very much larger than the wavelength, so that locally the disturbance can be well represented by a plane wave of amplitude $\mathbf{A}$:

$$\mathbf{E}(\mathbf{r}) = \mathbf{A}(\mathbf{r}) \exp \{i(\omega t - \mathbf{k}(\mathbf{r}) \cdot \mathbf{r})\}. \tag{4.76}$$

The reason that this is valid only for a slow change of conditions is that we should have difficulty in deciding exactly what we mean by the wavelength if the *constants* $\mathbf{A}$ and $\mathbf{k}$ change appreciably within that distance. We should also point out that the frequency must remain the same at all points in a time-independent system. The method of tackling the problem is quite adequately illustrated by a one-dimensional example. The refractive index is assumed to be a function of z only:

$$\mu = \left(\frac{\epsilon}{\epsilon_0}\right)^{\frac{1}{2}} = \mu(z) \tag{4.77}$$

and the wave equation for electric field becomes

$$\frac{\partial^2 E}{\partial t^2} = \frac{c^2}{\mu^2(z)} \nabla^2 E = \frac{c^2}{\mu^2(z)} \frac{\partial^2 E}{\partial z^2}, \tag{4.78}$$

which has a local solution of the form (4.76) with $k(r) = [\mu(r)\omega]/c$. The method of solution of the equation to find $\mathbf{A}(\mathbf{r})$ is called the W.K.B. method after its originators, Wentzel, Kramers and Brillouin. In a uniform medium the phase of the wave is $(\omega t - kz)$; in the non-uniform medium it will clearly be the integral $(\omega t - \int_0^z k(z)\, dz)$ as the phase is simply the number of cycles undergone by the wave along its path from $z = 0$. We thus take, for a trial solution of equation (4.78), the wave

$$E(z) = A(z) \exp \left\{ i \left(\omega t - \int_0^z \frac{\mu(z)\omega}{c}\, dz \right) \right\}. \tag{4.79}$$

Substituting this into the wave equation (4.78) leads to

$$-\omega^2 A = \frac{c^2}{\mu^2} \left\{ \frac{\partial^2 A}{\partial z^2} + 2\frac{i\omega\mu}{c}\frac{\partial A}{\partial z} - \frac{\omega^2\mu^2}{c^2} A + \frac{i\omega}{c}\frac{\partial \mu}{\partial z} A \right\} \tag{4.80a}$$

$$0 = \frac{c^2}{\mu^2}\frac{\partial^2 A}{\partial z^2} + 2\frac{i\omega c}{\mu}\frac{\partial A}{\partial z} + \frac{i\omega c}{\mu^2}\frac{\partial \mu}{\partial z}A. \qquad (4.80b)$$

The mathematics so far is exact. To make the equation tractable in general (for particular functions $\mu(z)$ there will no doubt be exact solutions) we use the fact that conditions are only varying slowly—$\partial\mu/\partial z$ is small—and so $\partial A/\partial z$ is small and $\partial^2 A/\partial z^2$ smaller still. We then neglect the last of these in equation (4.80b) giving

$$0 = \frac{2}{A}\frac{\partial A}{\partial z} + \frac{1}{\mu}\frac{\partial \mu}{\partial z}, \qquad (4.81)$$

which has the simple solution

$$A = B\mu^{-\frac{1}{2}}$$

where B is an arbitrary constant. The form of the wave is thus

$$E(z) = B\mu^{-\frac{1}{2}}(z)\exp\left\{i\left(\omega t - \int_0^z \frac{\omega\mu(z)}{c}\,dz\right)\right\}, \qquad (4.82)$$

provided that the refractive index μ varies slowly enough with distance and the amplitude A also varies slowly—which it will not do if $\mu \to 0$.

An example of the solution for a linear change of μ is shown in Fig. 4.15.

4.4.2   Energy flow. The continuity of energy flow is consistent with the above calculation. H is given, as before, by

$$H = E/Z$$

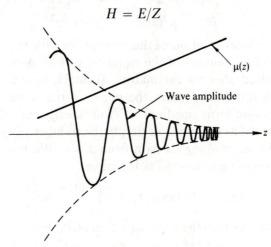

Fig. 4.15. Progression of a wave in a region where the refractive index μ is a linear function of position.

and as Z is proportional to μ^{-1} we have

$$\Pi = \frac{1}{4\pi} \mathbf{E} \times \mathbf{H} = \frac{1}{4\pi} \frac{E^2}{Z} \sim \mu^0,$$

which is independent of the position z. Thus energy is conserved. It is convenient here to consider one effect of the neglected $\partial^2 A/\partial z^2$ term. Without neglecting it, we have to solve the complete equation:

$$\frac{c}{\mu i\omega A} \frac{\partial^2 A}{\partial z^2} + \frac{2}{A} \frac{\partial A}{\partial z} + \frac{1}{\mu} \frac{\partial \mu}{\partial z} = 0, \qquad (4.83)$$

which must have a complex solution for A because of the complex coefficient of the first term. This, of course, leads to attenuation of the wave; in other words, the wave is dissipated in regions where $\partial^2 A/\partial z^2$ is not negligible, in particular close to the level where $\mu = 0$. Under such conditions, which rarely apply to optical phenomena, total internal reflexion can occur at normal incidence.

4.4.3 Reflexion of the wave.   Mirages.

When the wave is incident at an angle to the normal the same type of behaviour is observed, but the reflexion takes place at a positive value of μ. This is the situation which occurs when light is reflected by a temperature gradient in air, for example. We consider the same refractive conditions $\mu(z)$, but allow the wave vector to make an angle $\theta(z)$ with the z-axis (Fig. 4.16). We now write the wave as

$$E = A(z) \exp\left\{i\omega\left(t - \int_0^{x,z} \frac{\mu(z)}{c} (\sin \theta(z) \, dx + \cos \theta(z) \, dz)\right)\right\}. \quad (4.84)$$

(Compare equation (4.79), obtained by putting $\theta = 0$.) We can eliminate $\theta(z)$ by using Snell's law of refraction which states that

$$\mu(z) \sin \theta = K, \quad \text{a constant.} \qquad (4.85)$$

The value of K depends on the initial values of θ and μ at $z = 0$.

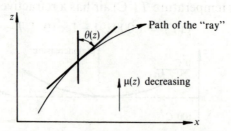

Fig. 4.16. Oblique ray in a region of changing μ.

Then (4.84) becomes

$$E = A(z) \exp\left\{i\omega\left[t - \int_0^x K \, dx/c - \int_0^z (\mu^2 - K^2)^{\frac{1}{2}} \, dz/c\right]\right\}. \quad (4.86)$$

We can substitute this value of E into the two-dimensional form of the wave equation (4.78),

$$\frac{\partial^2 E}{\partial t^2} = \frac{c^2}{\mu^2(z)}\left(\frac{\partial^2 E}{\partial x^2} + \frac{\partial^2 E}{\partial z^2}\right)$$

to give, in an identical manner to the previous calculation,

$$A(z) = C(\mu^2 - K^2)^{-\frac{1}{4}}. \quad (4.87)$$

The amplitude of the wave thus appears to become infinite at the height of critical reflexion where $\mu = K$; this part of the result is not to be trusted, however, as the W.K.B. approximation breaks down here, as explained earlier. In fact the wave disturbance travelling along the x-axis is progressive, since the wave can clearly be written as the product

$$E = C(\mu^2 - K^2)^{-\frac{1}{4}} \exp(i\omega t)$$
$$\times \exp\left(-\frac{i\omega Kx}{c}\right) . \exp\left\{\frac{i\omega}{c}\int_0^z (\mu^2 - K^2)^{\frac{1}{2}} dz\right\} .$$

Thus to conserve energy the light ray is bent to return downwards. Above the level where $\mu = K$ the wave becomes evanescent, as there $(\mu^2 - K^2)^{\frac{1}{2}}$ is imaginary. By comparing the values of the evanescent wave at the reflexion level and the necessarily standing wave below it we can in fact confirm that, to satisfy continuity of E, the amplitude of disturbance does not become infinite.

The practical results of this, as a mirage, is often observed above a black road during the summer. Because of the absorption of the sun's radiation by the road a layer of hot air is produced just next to the surface; the refractive index $\mu(z)$ thus increases with height, and a light ray proceeding downwards is turned round as in Fig. 4.17. At temperature $T(°C)$ air has a refractive index

$$\mu(T) = 1.000291 - 1 \times 10^{-6} \, T$$

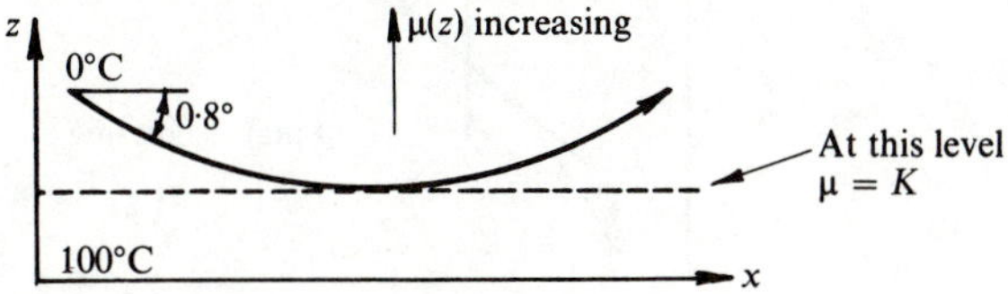

Fig. 4.17. A mirage.

so that if the road has a temperature of 100°C and the observer 0°C, the condition $\mu = K$ gives

$$\mu(100°\text{C}) = K = \mu(0°\text{C}) \sin \theta,$$

where θ is the angle of observation. This leads to $\pi/2 - \theta = 0.8°$; under these conditions mirages can be observed at angles smaller than this value.

4.4.4 Fermat's principle of stationary time.

Fermat's principle of stationary time is a result of the wave theory of light, and states that light will travel between two given points along such a path that small deviations in the path produce no first-order change in the time of transit. This ensures that light waves travelling by neighbouring paths arrive in phase and all interfere constructively at the final point. It is a very useful principle in dealing with transmission in inhomogeneous media, particularly if the variations are such that graphical or numerical calculation must be used. The phenomenon of a mirage, for example, can be treated by means of it, as we shall now show.

Consider two light rays starting from A in slightly different directions. As the lower one is always in a region of slightly lower refractive index the velocity there is larger, and therefore the upper ray must travel a shorter path to take the same time. The direction of travel at any point in the path is given by the normal to the wavefront which, from the definition in § 2.6.1, is the surface of constant phase—or time. Fig. 4.18 then illustrates why the path is curved. By the use of Lagrange's theory of minimizing or maximizing path-lengths as a function of the exact path taken this reasoning can be made quantitative.

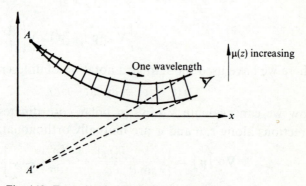

Fig. 4.18. Fermat's principle applied to the mirage.

4.5 Radiation

In this section we shall investigate two effects of importance in optics: the electromagnetics of radiation by multipoles, and radiation pressure.

4.5.1 Radiation by a dipole.

At what rate is radiation emitted from a dipole, and how is the radiation distributed in space? It is first pertinent to mention that in order to radiate at all a charge must be accelerating; a stationary charge does not radiate, because $\mathbf{E}$ is constant around it and $\mathbf{H}$ is zero; nor does a steady current, because $\mathbf{H}$ is then constant and $\mathbf{E}$ is zero. Only when the current is changing, or the charge accelerating, are $\mathbf{H}$ and $\mathbf{E}$ both non-zero.

Consider a dipole along the z-axis with moment $\mathbf{p}$ which can be imagined as charges $\pm q$ separated by distance l, so that $\mathbf{p} = q\mathbf{l}$. Then if q changes at rate dq/dt the current flowing between the two is dq/dt and the current element $\mathbf{l}(dq/dt)$ is thus equal to $d\mathbf{p}/dt$. Such a current element must produce a vector potential $\mathbf{A}$ at distance r:

$$\mathbf{A} = -\frac{\mu_0}{r} \cdot \frac{d\mathbf{p}}{dt} \qquad \text{(from § 4.1.3).} \qquad (4.88)$$

At distance r, however, the potential seen is not due to $\mathbf{p}$ at that instant, but due to $\mathbf{p}$ at a time r/c earlier; the value $\mathbf{p}(t-r/c)$ is written $[\mathbf{p}]$ and called the *retarded* value of $\mathbf{p}$. With this in mind we can work out $\mathbf{E}$ and $\mathbf{H}$. Because of the axial symmetry of the problem it will be easier to work in polar co-ordinates (r, θ, ϕ) (Fig. 4.19). Then, by differentiation, remembering that $[\mathbf{p}]$ is a function of r and needs to be treated as such, we get

$$\mathbf{H} = \frac{1}{\mu_0} \nabla \times \mathbf{A} = -\nabla \times \left(\frac{1}{r}[\mathbf{p}'] \right)$$

$$= \frac{1}{r} \nabla \times [\mathbf{p}'] + [\mathbf{p}'] \times \nabla \left(\frac{1}{r} \right),$$

where we have used the standard notation of differential calculus;

$$\mathbf{p}'(t-r/c) \equiv d\mathbf{p}/d(t-r/c).$$

Now we can evaluate $\nabla \times [\mathbf{p}']$ in polar co-ordinates. The vector directions along r, θ and ϕ are mutually orthogonal, so that

$$\nabla \times [\mathbf{p}'] = \left\{ \frac{1}{r \sin \theta} \frac{\partial [p'_\theta]}{\partial \phi} - \frac{1}{r} \frac{\partial [p'_\phi]}{\partial \theta}, \dots, \dots \right\}$$

the second and third components following in the usual manner.

The expressions are algebraically untidy, but are simplified considerably when $[\mathbf{p}]$ is $([p], 0, 0)$; they eventually lead to

$$\mathbf{H} = -\left(0, 0, \frac{\sin\theta}{r^2}[p'] + [p'']\frac{\sin\theta}{rc}\right). \tag{4.89}$$

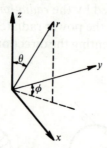

Fig. 4.19. Spherical polar coordinates.

Notice that $\mathbf{H} = H_\phi$ only; $\mathbf{H}$ circulates round the dipole axis. $\mathbf{E}$ can most easily be calculated by using

$$\frac{\partial \mathbf{E}}{\partial t} = \frac{1}{\epsilon}\frac{\partial \mathbf{D}}{\partial t} = \frac{1}{\epsilon}\nabla \times \mathbf{H}$$

in the outside region, where there is no current density. $\mathbf{E}$ is then found by integrating with respect to t:

$$\mathbf{E} = \left\{ \frac{[p]}{\epsilon r^3}(\cos\theta, 2\sin\theta, 0) + \frac{1}{\epsilon r^2 c}[p'] \cdot (\cos\theta, 2\sin\theta, 0) \right.$$
$$\left. + \frac{1}{\epsilon rc^2}[p''](0, \sin\theta, 0) \right\}. \tag{4.90}$$

The first term in $\mathbf{E}$ is clearly the electrostatic field from $[\mathbf{p}]$. In optics we are interested only in values of r very large compared with the wavelength; we can therefore neglect all but the lowest powers of r^{-1} in these expressions. The *storage field*, the higher-power terms in r^{-1}, which represent electromagnetic fields close to the dipole which do not contribute to the radiated energy (equation (4.92)), will not be discussed here. The *radiation field*, the r^{-1} term remaining, is thus

$$\mathbf{H} = \left(0, 0, \frac{\sin\theta}{rc}[p'']\right) \tag{4.91a}$$

$$\mathbf{E} = \left(0, \frac{\sin\theta}{\epsilon rc^2}[p''], 0\right). \tag{4.91b}$$

The power distribution is

$$\mathbf{\Pi} = \frac{1}{4\pi}\mathbf{E} \times \mathbf{H} = \frac{1}{4\pi}\left(\frac{\sin^2\theta}{\epsilon r^2 c^3}[p'']^2, 0, 0\right).$$

This is radially outwards, as we should expect radiated power to be. It has a maximum value in the equatorial plane, independent of ϕ, and this can be expressed by the *radiation polar diagram* (Fig. 4.20) in which OP represents the power radiated at angle θ. This is also a useful method of representing the directional properties of radiation from an aerial.

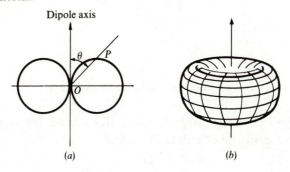

(a)   (b)

Fig. 4.20. Radiation polar-diagram for a dipole oscillator: (a) two-dimensional section; (b) three-dimensional sketch.

The total power radiated is then the integral of $\mathbf{\Pi}$ over a large surface S enclosing the dipole:

$$P_d = \iint_S \frac{1}{4\pi}\left(\frac{\sin^2\theta}{\epsilon r^2 c^3}[p'']^2, 0, 0\right) dS.$$

If S is a sphere of radius r the integral becomes:

$$P_d = \frac{1}{4\pi\epsilon c^3}[p'']^2 \int_{\theta=0}^{\pi} \int_{\phi=0}^{2\pi} \frac{\sin^2\theta}{r^2} r^2 \sin\theta\, d\theta\, d\phi \qquad (4.92)$$

$$= \frac{2}{3\epsilon c^3}[p'']^2.$$

Clearly if we included terms in $\mathbf{\Pi}$ with higher inverse powers of r than the second, they would have vanished in the integration provided r was taken large enough. At finite values of r, of the order of the wavelength λ, the integral would not have been independent of r, indicating that energy is stored in the field. Hence the term *storage field*. The stored power must oscillate with a time-average of zero if the total energy within the system is to remain within bounds.

Our main interest is with dipoles oscillating at a fixed frequency ω, in which case

$$P_d = \frac{2\omega^4 p^2}{3\epsilon c^3}. \tag{4.93}$$

This formula will be used later in the discussion of scattering and dispersion.

4.5.2 Radiation by higher-order multipoles. Calculation of the radiation by higher-order multipoles follows the same general pattern, the quadrupole, for example, being considered as two dipoles in very close proximity. Let us suppose that we have two opposed dipoles of strength $\mathbf{p}$ separated by a distance $\delta \mathbf{s}$. The quadrupole moment of this arrangement is

$$q = \mathbf{p}\,\delta\mathbf{s}$$

which is a second-rank tensor. The electric and magnetic fields are related to the fields $\mathbf{E}_p$ and $\mathbf{H}_p$, produced by dipole $\mathbf{p}$, by the relationships

$$\mathbf{E} = (\delta\mathbf{s} \cdot \nabla)\mathbf{E}_p, \tag{4.94}$$
$$\mathbf{H} = (\delta\mathbf{s} \cdot \nabla)\mathbf{H}_p. \tag{4.95}$$

If, for example, $\delta\mathbf{s}$ is along the z-axis (parallel to $\mathbf{p}$) we have

$$\delta\mathbf{s} \cdot \nabla = \cos\theta\,\delta s\frac{\partial}{\partial r} - \frac{\sin\theta}{r}\,\delta s\frac{\partial}{\partial\theta}; \tag{4.96}$$

whence the radiation field follows:

$$\mathbf{H} = \left(0, 0, \frac{\cos\theta\sin\theta\,\delta s}{rc^2}[p''']\right), \tag{4.97}$$

$$\mathbf{E} = \left(0, \frac{\sin\theta\cos\theta\,\delta s}{\epsilon rc^3}[p'''], 0\right), \tag{4.98}$$

from equations (4.91a) and (b), retaining only the lowest-order terms in r^{-1}. The radiation polar diagram is therefore as illustrated in Fig. 4.21, showing a $(\cos\theta\sin\theta)$ angular dependence. The total power radiated then comes to

$$P_q = \frac{\delta s^2}{2\epsilon c^5}[p''']^2\int_0^\pi \cos^2\theta\sin^3\theta\,d\theta$$

$$= \frac{2\,\delta s^2}{15\epsilon c^5}[p''']^2. \tag{4.99}$$

For harmonic time-variation, this can be written analogously to equation (4.93) as

$$P_q = \frac{2\omega^6 q^2}{15\epsilon c^5}. \tag{4.100}$$

To compare radiating powers of quadrupoles and dipoles it is necessary to take the relative dimensions of the wavelength and oscillator into account. Substituting k for ω/c we have

$$P_d = \frac{2ck^4 p^2}{3\epsilon} \quad \text{from (4.93)} \tag{4.101}$$

$$P_q = \frac{2ck^6 p^2 \, \delta s^2}{15\epsilon}. \tag{4.102}$$

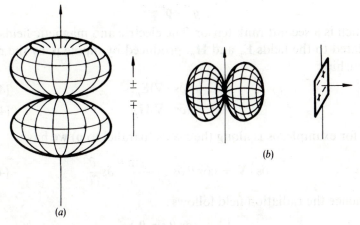

(a)

(b)

Fig. 4.21. Radiation polar-diagrams for two types of quadrupole. (a) zz; (b) zy.

These are of similar orders of magnitude only if

$$k \, \delta s \sim 1 \quad \text{or} \quad \lambda \sim \delta s.$$

If the wavelength λ is much longer than the dimensions of the quadrupole, it is a very poor radiator compared to a single dipole.

Calculation for the other quadrupole in which δs is perpendicular to $\mathbf{p}$ follows similarly, as also do calculations for octopoles and higher 2^n-poles.

4.5.3 Radiation pressure.

Electromagnetic radiation conveys momentum as well as energy, like all other methods of power transfer. When the direction or magnitude of the energy flow is

altered by interaction with a body, there is consequently a reaction equal to the rate of change of vector momentum in the wave, and this reaction is termed *radiation pressure*.

In terms of photons, a concept dealt with in more detail in later sections, the magnitude of radiation pressure is easily related to the radiation-energy density. In this section we shall show that it is not purely a particle property, but can be explained as a result of Maxwell's equations.

The electromechanical origin of radiation pressure as a surface effect is not difficult to see. If we consider reflexion by a metal surface, the wave induces electric currents in the surface-skin layer which are in phase with the electric and magnetic fields **E** and **H** and consequently there is a force with a non-zero time-average acting within the skin layer. This is simple to deal with quantitatively; the calculation is as follows.

4.5.4 Momentum in an electromagnetic wave. In the case of the complete normal reflexion of a wave by a metal surface it is easy to show that the radiation pressure is equal to the energy density of electromagnetic radiation at the surface, including both incident and reflected waves.

If the magnetic field in the combined waves at the surface is **H**, the surface current **J** in the metal is normal to **H**, and has magnitude:

$$J = \frac{H}{4\pi} \qquad (4.103)$$

and is distributed throughout the skin depth. This arises simply from the Ampère circuit integral (equation (4.6)). The wave-disturbance within the metal is evanescent, and therefore maintains the same phase as at the surface. The force per unit area is therefore given by

$$\mathbf{R} = \mathbf{J} \times \mathbf{H} = \frac{H^2}{4\pi}. \qquad (4.104)$$

This is twice the energy density $\mathscr{E}$ of the incident wave (§ 4.2.4), which is

$$\mathscr{E} = \frac{H^2}{8\pi}$$

since for a perfect conductor $\mathbf{E} = 0$ on its surface. The radiation pressure is thus equal to the combined energy density of incident

and reflected waves. The result can be explained in terms of momentum density in the wave

$$\rho_p = \frac{\mathscr{E}}{v} \qquad \left(= \frac{\mathscr{E}}{c} \text{ in free space} \right), \qquad (4.105)$$

which is reversed in the reflexion process. For a dielectric the same result holds, although it is not easy to prove as for a metal. If an incident wave is partially reflected and partly transmitted by a sheet of dielectric, the pressure is the difference between the energy density in the combined incident and reflected wave at the first surface and that in the transmitted wave at the second surface. The magnitudes of these energy densities are dependent on interference within the thickness of the sample.

One argument which seems to give the answer very simply, but is erroneous, is to consider the change in energy when the sheet of dielectric or metal is moved a distance δx normal to its surface. The change in energy per unit area is then $R\,\delta x$. However, although the magnitude of R is predicted correctly the direction is wrong, because moving the surface induces a Doppler shift in the reflected wave which alters its energy during the movement. Following this argument completely should give the correct answer.

4.5.5   Electromagnetic origin of radiation pressure in a dielectric. In the previous section we have seen that the radiation pressure on a dielectric is equal to the difference between the energy densities at its two surfaces. It is not immediately obvious in the dielectric why this is so, and in particular why radiation pressure is a surface effect and does not depend on the thickness of material.

In a transparent insulator the electric current density $\mathbf{j}$ must be replaced by the displacement current $\partial \mathbf{D}/\partial t$ and it is immediately obvious that, since in an insulator $\mathbf{B}$ and $\partial \mathbf{D}/\partial t$ are in phase quadrature, the vector product

$$\mathbf{F} = \mathbf{B} \times \frac{\partial \mathbf{D}}{\partial t}, \qquad (4.106)$$

which is the force per unit volume exerted on the material, will have zero time average. Only if we have two coherent waves, travelling in different vector directions, can the time-average be non-zero, $\mathbf{F}$ then arising from the interaction between $\mathbf{B}$ in one wave and $\partial \mathbf{D}/\partial t$ in the other.

Why then is the force a surface effect in such a case and not a

volume effect? The answer comes from a consideration of the space-variation of the force. In the simplest case we have, within the material, two waves travelling in $\pm z$ directions, the second being formed by reflexion of the first at the back surface. The second wave can thus be considered as the continuation of the first one at a distance 2ξ further on (Fig. 4.22), an amplitude reduction by a factor β having taken place *en route*. The force per unit volume at ξ is thus:

$$\mathbf{F}(\xi) = \beta\mathbf{B}(z)\times\frac{\partial\mathbf{D}}{\partial t}(z+2\xi)+\beta\mathbf{B}(z+2\xi)\times\frac{\partial\mathbf{D}}{\partial t}(z)$$

$$+\mathbf{B}(z)\times\frac{\partial\mathbf{D}}{\partial t}(z)+\beta^2\mathbf{B}(z+2\xi)\times\frac{\partial\mathbf{D}}{\partial t}(z+2\xi). \quad (4.107)$$

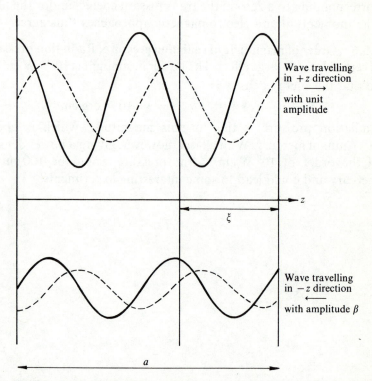

Wave travelling in $+z$ direction ⟶ with unit amplitude

ξ

Wave travelling in $-z$ direction ⟵ with amplitude β

a

Fig. 4.22. Wave disturbances leading to radiation pressure. Solid line is B; broken line is $\partial D/\partial t$.

The latter two terms have zero time average, as pointed out above. In the former two terms, the two fields in the product will have a phase difference $4\pi\xi/\lambda$, and on integration for all ξ from 0 to a

there will be exact cancellation between the positive and negative parts of **F** over any complete wavelength. The only net force arises when the thickness a is not an integral number of wavelengths, the radiation pressure then being related to δ where

$$a = (n+\delta)\lambda \qquad (0 \leqslant \delta < 1),$$

(n is an integer and λ the wavelength in the material). This is a surface effect, which will be periodically related to the thickness, but not proportional to it. If a is an exact number of wavelengths, no radiation pressure will be observed, but this is exactly the interference condition under which no reflexion of the beam occurs at the first surface, and so momentum considerations would lead to the same conclusion. Again, the maximum effect occurs when $\delta = \frac{1}{2}$, corresponding to a zero in the transmission coefficient for the film. The momentum and electromagnetic approaches thus agree.

4.5.6   Order of magnitude of radiation pressure. Radiation pressure is certainly not a large effect. The power in sunlight is 10^{-1} W cm^{-2}, so that the energy density is

$$\mathscr{E} = 10^6 \times (3 \times 10^{-10})^{-1} = 3 \times 10^{-5} \text{ erg cm}^{-3}.$$

Radiation pressure is thus of this magnitude, which is about 10^{-7} mm of mercury. With a laser, however, giving a power density of the order of 10^8 W cm^{-2}, the pressure would be 100 cm of mercury and could lead to some interesting experiments.

CHAPTER 5

POLARIZATION AND ANISOTROPIC MEDIA

5.1 Introduction

Wave propagation in anisotropic media is usually considered as a specialized topic, mathematically too complicated to be studied by the general physicist. To a certain extent this is true; a complete analysis of crystal optics usually involves a great deal of algebra and the gains in understanding seem very small compared to the cost. However, since dielectric crystals and light waves are not the only anisotropic media and wave-forms in existence, and since the study of such media by means of waves propagated in them is forming an increasing part of physical research, we feel that it is unwise to neglect this aspect of optics or even to present it in the usual algebraic manner.

As examples of the present importance of wave propagation in such media we can immediately offer the study of electron waves in metal crystals and radio waves in the ionosphere. We shall see that the latter of these, because the anisotropy is induced by an applied magnetic field (the earth's field), belongs to a different class of media from the crystal, and in order to make this chapter of the greatest general use we shall discuss both types, taking the ionosphere as an example of the second type in § 12.7.

The algebra of the subject is that of second-order equations in three dimensions and their simultaneous solution, and can be represented completely by ellipsoidal surfaces and their intersections. As a result of this, apart from an initial proof that the symmetric tensor can be represented by a certain ellipsoid, all the algebra can be dealt with by geometrical constructions, although we apologize in advance if some of the proofs of these constructions are not rigorous.

The chapter begins with a formal discussion of polarized light in terms of vectors and goes on to discuss the general formation of the problem of wave propagation in any medium. It shows that the complete propagation characteristics can be deduced from the construction of a refractive-index surface. Following this, we shall use the geometrical method mentioned above to calculate the

refractive-index surface for a dielectric crystal and hence to deduce its wave properties. In the final section we shall discuss some practical uses of crystal optics. We should also point out that in § 12.7 we outline a discussion along similar lines for a simple model of propagation of waves in the ionosphere, since this medium falls into a class in which the dielectric tensor is antisymmetric and leads to a completely different type of propagation. It is hoped that this line of attack will succeed in producing some measure of physical insight into the subject.

5.2 Polarized light

We shall discuss formally the main types of polarized radiation. All forms of polarization can be described as elliptical polarization of various degrees, and for some purposes this is a convenient specification. However, we shall here proceed in the usual fashion by describing linearly and circularly polarized light first and then absorbing the two into the more general description of elliptically polarized light.

5.2.1 Plane-polarized light.

In § 4.2.1 we showed that the simplest basic solution to Maxwell's wave equation was a plane-polarized transverse wave. If the wave-vector is $\mathbf{k}$, the electric and magnetic field vectors $\mathbf{E}$ and $\mathbf{H}$ are mutually perpendicular and lie in a plane normal to $\mathbf{k}$; they both oscillate in phase, so that :

$$\mathbf{E} = \mathbf{E}_0 \exp\{i(\omega t - \mathbf{k} \cdot \mathbf{r})\},$$
$$\mathbf{H} = \mathbf{H}_0 \exp\{i(\omega t - \mathbf{k} \cdot \mathbf{r})\},$$
$$\mathbf{E} \cdot \mathbf{H} = 0; \qquad \mathbf{E} \cdot \mathbf{k} = 0; \qquad \mathbf{H} \cdot \mathbf{k} = 0. \tag{5.1}$$

This solution was obtained for an isotropic medium, and in this section we shall restrict ourselves to that condition. It follows trivially from the orthogonality of $\mathbf{E}$, $\mathbf{H}$ and $\mathbf{k}$ that the direction of energy flow $\mathbf{\Pi}$ is parallel to $\mathbf{k}$;

$$\mathbf{\Pi} = \frac{1}{4\pi}(\mathbf{E} \times \mathbf{H})$$

$$\mathbf{\Pi} \times \mathbf{k} = \frac{1}{4\pi}\{(\mathbf{E} \times \mathbf{H}) \times \mathbf{k}\} = \frac{1}{4\pi}\{\mathbf{H}(\mathbf{E} \cdot \mathbf{k}) - \mathbf{E}(\mathbf{H} \cdot \mathbf{k})\} = 0. \tag{5.2}$$

Such a state of affairs is indicated by Fig. 5.1. In an anisotropic medium it will soon appear (§ 5.3.4) that matters are not quite so simple.

5.2.2 Circularly polarized light. There is a second form of polarized light that is just as important as plane-polarized light. It is the result of adding two equal plane-polarized waves with the same $\mathbf{k}$ but perpendicular electric vectors and a $\pi/2$ phase-difference between their oscillations. The two waves are respectively (suffices 1 and 2 which can represent x and y, $\mathbf{k}$ being along z)

$$\left.\begin{array}{l} \mathbf{E}_1 = \mathbf{E}_{10} \exp\{i(\omega t - \mathbf{k}\cdot\mathbf{r})\} \\[2mm] \mathbf{E}_2 = \mathbf{E}_{20} \exp\left\{i\left(\omega t - \mathbf{k}\cdot\mathbf{r} - \dfrac{\pi}{2}\right)\right\} \\[2mm] \mathbf{H}_1 = \mathbf{H}_{10} \exp\{i(\omega t - \mathbf{k}\cdot\mathbf{r})\} \\[2mm] \mathbf{H}_2 = \mathbf{H}_{20} \exp\left\{i\left(\omega t - \mathbf{k}\cdot\mathbf{r} - \dfrac{\pi}{2}\right)\right\} \end{array}\right\} \quad (5.3)$$

$$\left.\begin{array}{l} \mathbf{E}_1 \cdot \mathbf{E}_2 = 0 = \mathbf{H}_1 \cdot \mathbf{H}_2 \\[1mm] E_{10} = E_{20} = E_0; \qquad H_{10} = H_{20}. \end{array}\right\} \quad (5.4)$$

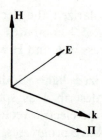

Fig. 5.1. Orthogonality of $\mathbf{E}$, $\mathbf{H}$ and $\mathbf{k}$ in an electromagnetic wave.

The combined wave represented by (5.3) and (5.4) consists of an electric field of magnitude E_{10} which rotates with frequency ω in the plane normal to $\mathbf{k}$. This is most easily shown by noting that the observed electric field is the real part of the wave-form in 5.3. We then have

$$E_1 = E_0 \cos(\omega t - \mathbf{k}\cdot\mathbf{r}), \qquad E_2 = E_0 \sin(\omega t - \mathbf{k}\cdot\mathbf{r})$$

whence $\mathbf{E} = \mathbf{E}_1 + \mathbf{E}_2$ has modulus E given by

$$\begin{aligned} E^2 = |\mathbf{E}_1 + \mathbf{E}_2|^2 &= E_1^2 + E_2^2 + 2|\mathbf{E}_1 \cdot \mathbf{E}_2| \\ &= E_0^2 \{\cos^2(\omega t - \mathbf{k}\cdot\mathbf{r}) + \sin^2(\omega t - \mathbf{k}\cdot\mathbf{r})\} \\ &= E_0^2 \quad \text{since} \quad \mathbf{E}_1 \cdot \mathbf{E}_2 = 0. \qquad (5.5) \end{aligned}$$

The angle θ at which this resultant lies in the plane normal to $\mathbf{k}$ is given by

$$\tan \theta = \frac{|E_2|}{|E_1|} = \frac{\sin(\omega t - \mathbf{k} \cdot \mathbf{r})}{\cos(\omega t - \mathbf{k} \cdot \mathbf{r})} = \tan(\omega t - \mathbf{k} \cdot \mathbf{r}),$$

$$\theta = (\omega t - \mathbf{k} \cdot \mathbf{r}). \tag{5.6}$$

The field is thus of magnitude E_0 and lies at an angle $(\omega t - \mathbf{k} \cdot \mathbf{r})$ to some constant direction in the plane. In a given plane normal to $\mathbf{k}$ (i.e. $\mathbf{k} \cdot \mathbf{r} = $ constant), the field therefore rotates in a clockwise direction. This is called right-handedly polarized light, and results if $\mathbf{E}_2$ lags in phase behind $\mathbf{E}_1$. If the reverse is true, so that $\mathbf{E}_2$ leads in phase giving

$$E_2 = E_0 \exp \left\{ i \left(\omega t - \mathbf{k} \cdot \mathbf{r} + \frac{\pi}{2} \right) \right\}, \tag{5.7}$$

in (5.3), the same calculation leads to

$$\theta = -(\omega t - \mathbf{k} \cdot \mathbf{r}), \tag{5.8}$$

which is left-handedly polarized, the electric vector rotating in an anticlockwise sense. Fig. 5.2 compares for plane and circularly polarized light the progress of $\mathbf{E}$ and $\mathbf{H}$ with time in a given plane.

5.2.3 Elliptically polarized light. Both circularly- and plane-polarized light can be described as special cases of *eliptically-polarized* light in which the electric vector rotates with a periodic change in length as the wave progresses, and can be thought of as describing an ellipse. Two quantities are necessary to describe elliptically polarized waves completely; these are the orientation of the axes of the ellipse and its eccentricity. The latter is defined as $(a_1 - a_2)/a_1$, where a_1 and a_2 are major and minor axes respectively. Plane-polarized light then corresponds to an eccentricity of unity, whereas circularly polarized light has an eccentricity of zero. In this special case the ellipse axes are degenerate.

We can combine the two quantities into one single complex measure of the degree of elliptical polarization, which introduces some simplifications into theories such as that of ionosphere propagation (§ 12.7). We must choose two reference axes, x and y, in the plane of polarization. We can then define

$$R = \frac{E_x}{E_y}, \tag{5.9}$$

where E_x and E_y are the time-dependent components of **E** resolved along the two axes.

The electric vector rotating round an ellipse of axes a_1 and a_2 can be written in terms of its principal components along a_1 and a_2:

$$(E_1, E_2) = (a_1, ia_2) \exp \{i(\omega t - kx)\}. \qquad (5.10)$$

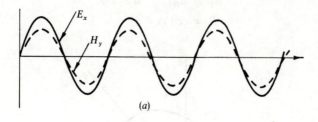

(a)

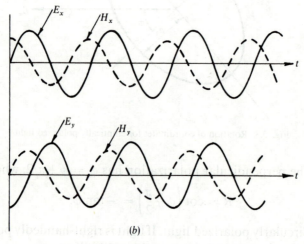

(b)

Fig. 5.2. (a) Plane and (b) circularly polarized waves.

Rotating this to axes (E_x, E_y) at angle ϕ to the principal axes (Fig. 5.3) we have

$$(E_x, E_y) = \begin{pmatrix} \cos \phi \; \sin \phi \\ -\sin \phi \; \cos \phi \end{pmatrix} \begin{pmatrix} E_1 \\ E_2 \end{pmatrix}$$

$$= (a_1 \cos \phi + ia_2 \sin \phi, \; a_1 \sin \phi - ia_2 \cos \phi) \cdot \exp\{i(\omega t - kx)\},$$
$$(5.11)$$

whence

$$R = \frac{E_x}{E_y} = \frac{a_1 \cos \phi + i a_2 \sin \phi}{a_1 \sin \phi - i a_2 \cos \phi}. \tag{5.12}$$

We can now look at one or two special cases.

(a) Plane-polarized light

$$a_1 = E_0, \qquad a_2 = 0,$$
$$R = \cot \phi. \tag{5.13}$$

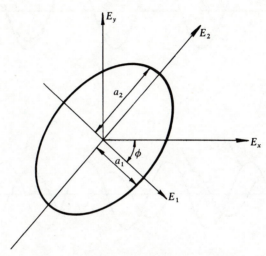

Fig. 5.3. Rotation of coordinates for elliptically polarized light.

The perpendicular polarization has $\phi = \phi + \pi/2$, whence

$$R = \cot \left(\phi + \frac{\pi}{2} \right) = -\tan \phi. \tag{5.14}$$

(b) Circularly polarized light. If light is right-handedly polarized, its vector can be represented by (5.10) if

$$a_1 = a_2 = E_0,$$
$$R = \frac{1+i}{1-i} = i. \tag{5.15}$$

Similarly, for left-handedly polarized light,

$$a_1 = -a_2 = E_0,$$
$$R = \frac{1-i}{1+i} = -i. \tag{5.16}$$

The type of polarization in a wave can be recognized from its R-value. We have the general rules:

R is real—plane polarized
R is complex—elliptically polarized
R imaginary—circularly polarized.

It is easy to see by rationalizing (5.12) that if R is pure imaginary it can only have the values $\pm i$. Only these two forms of circularly-polarized light can exist.

Two modes of polarization, represented by R_1 and R_2, can be termed *orthogonal* if their R-values satisfy

$$R_1 R_2^* = -1.$$

This is clearly satisfied for plane-polarized waves with orthogonal planes since, from (5.13) and (5.14),

$$R_1 R_2^* = -\cot \phi \tan \phi = -1 \qquad (5.17)$$

and also applies to left- and right-handedly polarized light;

$$R_1 R_2^* = i^2 = -1,$$

from (5.15) and (5.16). But every elliptically-polarized wave has an orthogonal conjugate too, and we shall see later in this chapter, and also in § 12.7.4, that pairs of characteristic waves are always orthogonal.

5.2.4 Production of polarized light by reflexion. We have already (§§ 4.3.1 and 4.3.5) studied the principle of two methods of producing polarized light, although neither is important from a practical point of view. The reflexion coefficient at the Brewster angle

$$i_B = \tan^{-1} \mu$$

is zero for polarization in the plane of incidence but not for the perpendicular polarization, so that all the light reflected at this angle is polarized normal to the incidence plane. Although in principle perfectly polarized radiation is produced, the exact surface conditions are rather critical and in practice the light is not completely polarized, although sufficiently so for many experiments. The most important property of light polarized by Brewster-angle reflexion is that its plane of polarization is exactly defined by the experimental arrangement (Fig. 5.4); polaroid materials and Nicol prisms need calibration (§ 5.6.3). The *Fresnel rhomb* is a device for producing circularly polarized light from plane-polarized by

using the phase changes on critical reflexion (§ 4.3.5). Light polarized at 45° to the plane of the paper is incident on the rhomb in Fig. 5.5 and is critically reflected twice. The angle of incidence i is arranged so that the two components of the light, polarized perpendicular to the paper and parallel to it, suffer phase-changes $\alpha_\perp$ and $\alpha_\parallel$ differing by $\pi/4$, so that after two reflexions a difference of $\pi/2$ in their phases is achieved. The compound wave is thus circularly polarized. In principle it would be possible to achieve this condition after one reflexion; $\alpha_\perp - \alpha_\parallel$ has a maximum value of 94° in the example $\mu = 1/2{\cdot}5$ illustrated in Fig. 4.12(a), but such a refractive

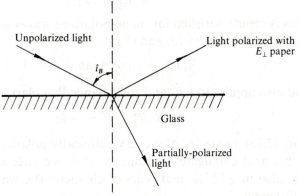

Unpolarized light

Light polarized with
$E_\perp$ paper

i_B

Glass

Partially-polarized
light

Fig. 5.4. Production of plane-polarized light by reflexion at the Brewster angle.

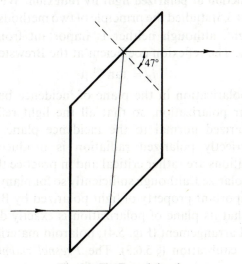

47°

Fig. 5.5. The Fresnel rhomb.

index is uncommon in transparent materials and it is easier to aim at 45° per reflexion, for which the example of $\mu = 1/1.5$ is adequate (the maximum value of $\alpha_\perp - \alpha_\parallel$ is 47°). The incidence angle for this refractive index should be either 47° or 51°, but it is clear from Fig. 4.12(b) that gross errors in i affect the phase difference imperceptibly. By altering the plane of polarization of the incident light any degree of elliptical polarization can also be created.

We shall leave further discussion of the production of polarized light until section 5.6.3, since crystal propagation affords much more convenient methods of production of both plane- and circularly-polarized light.

5.3   General problems of wave propagation in anisotropic media

5.3.1   The refractive-index surface. Before considering any anisotropic medium in detail, we shall discuss a general formation of the problem which we can then apply to any medium. In § 2.2.1 we showed that the wave velocity was given by

$$v = \omega/k \tag{5.18}$$

and the group velocity, the velocity at which energy is transported, by the relationship

$$v_g = \frac{\partial \omega}{\partial k}. \tag{5.19}$$

The study of anisotropic media immediately poses the question: how do we write these expressions to show their dependence on **k** as a vector, rather than a scalar? We cannot immediately replace k in (5.18) by **k**, as $(\mathbf{k})^{-1}$ is not a vector (see § 2.6.1); we can, however, make use of the refractive index μ instead of the velocity v, since

$$\mu = \frac{c}{v} = \frac{ck}{\omega} = \frac{k}{k_0}, \tag{5.20}$$

where k_0 is the value of k in free space, which is isotropic. Now let k be replaced by **k**, representing both the magnitude and direction of k; μ becomes **μ**, which is the refractive index for propagation in a particular direction. We have, then,

$$\boldsymbol{\mu} = \frac{1}{k_0}\mathbf{k}. \tag{5.21}$$

The vector of magnitude **μ** can be represented by a surface plotted as a function of its direction, and the surface has the simple meaning that its radius vector represents the refractive index for propagation

in that direction (Fig. 5.6). The surface is defined for a particular value of k_0, corresponding to a particular frequency ω; because of dispersion the shape and dimensions will change slightly with ω, but we shall ignore this effect by restricting our attention to some fixed frequency. The surface is thus to be regarded as dependent upon the frequency. The group velocity can also be expressed geometrically in terms of the surface. Writing k as $\mathbf{k}$ in 5.19 we can interpret $\mathbf{v}_g$ as

$$\mathbf{v}_g = \frac{\partial \omega}{\partial \mathbf{k}} = \left(\frac{\partial \omega}{\partial k_x}, \frac{\partial \omega}{\partial k_y}, \frac{\partial \omega}{\partial k_z} \right)$$

and substituting

$$\frac{\omega}{c} = k_0, \qquad \boldsymbol{\mu} = \frac{\mathbf{k}}{k_0},$$

we have

$$\mathbf{v}_g = \frac{1}{ck_0} \frac{\partial k_0}{\partial \boldsymbol{\mu}} = \frac{1}{ck_0} \left(\frac{\partial k_0}{\partial \mu_x}, \frac{\partial k_0}{\partial \mu_y}, \frac{\partial k_0}{\partial \mu_z} \right). \tag{5.22}$$

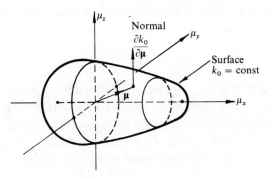

Fig. 5.6. Construction of a μ-surface.

This vector, which can alternatively be written as

$$\mathbf{v}_g = \frac{1}{ck_0} \operatorname{grad}_\mu k_0$$

is the normal to the μ-surface since $k_0 = $ constant. A rigorous proof of this is given in books on mathematical physics and a two-dimensional illustration in Fig. 5.7.

The general problem for anisotropic media can now be analysed. We must study the particular anisotropic system to calculate the form and features of the μ-surface, representing the refractive index

as a function of the direction of the wave vector. Then, given the wave-vector we can find the direction of the associated energy flow by constructing the normal to the surface at the point corresponding to the wave-vector direction.

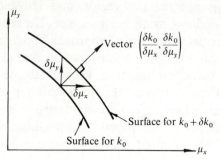

Fig. 5.7. Illustrating the fact that $\dfrac{\partial k}{\partial \boldsymbol{\mu}} = \left(\dfrac{\partial k}{\partial \mu_x}, \dfrac{\partial k}{\partial \mu_y}\right)$ is normal to the curve $k(\boldsymbol{\mu}) = \text{constant}$.

5.3.2   An isotropic medium as a special case. The application to an isotropic medium is simple. The refractive index μ is independent of direction and so the μ-surface is a sphere. The normal to the surface of the sphere is parallel to its radius vector, and therefore the energy is transported parallel to **k** (Fig. 5.8). In the terminology of crystal optics this is an *ordinary* ray; the ray vector (the direction along which energy travels, and which is therefore observed) is the same as the wave-vector **k**. The ray vector is identical with the Poynting vector **Π**, as both represent the energy flow.

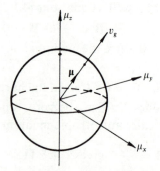

Fig. 5.8. The μ-surface for an isotropic medium.

5.3.3   Warning about μ-surfaces and wave-surfaces. We must give a warning about this approach. The μ-surfaces which we shall deduce are the reciprocals of the velocity surfaces, or wave-surfaces,

which are usually used in the theory of crystal optics. Superficially the two look similar. Both are fourth-order surfaces for a crystal, with two values corresponding to two orthogonal polarizations propagated along a particular direction. But the normal to the wave-surface is not the ray vector, and Huygens' construction cannot be carried out using the μ-surface. The μ-surface approach is, however, the usual method of approach in magnetoionic theory, to which § 12.7 is a simplified introduction, and also in most other problems of wave propagation in anisotropic materials. For example, the Fermi surface—the invaluable representation of the relationship between energy and $\mathbf{k}$ for electron waves in a metal—is the direct analogue of the μ-surface introduced above. It is with this general view in mind that a departure from the standard treatment has been made.

5.3.4   Electromagnetic waves in an anisotropic medium. The second general problem which we can discuss before approaching any particular medium is that of wave-propagation when the dielectric properties of the medium are anisotropic. We should expect Maxwell's equations to hold, and in view of their being applied immediately to waves of the form

$$\mathbf{E} = \mathbf{E}_0 \exp\{i(\omega t - \mathbf{k} \cdot \mathbf{r})\} = \mathbf{E}_0 \exp\{i(\omega t - xk_x - yk_y - zk_z)\},$$

we can use the operator substitutions (§ 2.2.1):

$$\frac{\partial}{\partial t} = i\omega, \qquad \nabla \equiv \left(\frac{\partial}{\partial x}, \frac{\partial}{\partial y}, \frac{\partial}{\partial z}\right) \equiv -i\mathbf{k}. \tag{5.23}$$

Then we can write Maxwell's equations (4.1.2) in the form:

(a) $$\nabla \cdot \mathbf{B} = -i\mathbf{k} \cdot \mathbf{B} = 0. \tag{5.24}$$

This implies $i\mathbf{k} \cdot \mathbf{H} = 0$, since the medium is assumed to be magnetically isotropic.

(b) $\nabla \cdot \mathbf{D} = i\mathbf{k} \cdot \mathbf{D} = 0$ (for an uncharged region).   (5.25)

This no longer implies $\nabla \cdot \mathbf{E}$ to be zero, since $\mathbf{D}$ and $\mathbf{E}$ are not parallel in an electrically anisotropic medium.

(c) $$\nabla \times \mathbf{H} = \frac{\partial \mathbf{D}}{\partial t} \quad \text{gives} \quad i\mathbf{k} \times \mathbf{H} = -i\omega\mathbf{D}. \tag{5.26}$$

(d) $$\nabla \times \mathbf{E} = -\frac{\partial \mathbf{B}}{\partial t} \quad \text{gives} \quad i\mathbf{k} \times \mathbf{E} = i\omega\mathbf{B} = i\omega\mu_0\mathbf{H}. \tag{5.27}$$

We have assumed here that the magnetic permeability differs negligibly from that of free space.

To derive a wave equation we proceed as before by operating $\nabla \times$, or $i\mathbf{k} \times$, on (5.27) giving

$$\mathbf{k} \times (\mathbf{k} \times \mathbf{E}) = \omega\mu_0(\mathbf{k} \times \mathbf{H}) = -\omega^2\mu_0\mathbf{D}. \qquad (5.28)$$

We can check that this equation is reasonable by applying it to an isotropic medium. Then a scalar dielectric constant ϵ applies, giving

$$\mathbf{k} \times (\mathbf{k} \times \mathbf{E}) = \mathbf{k}(\mathbf{k} \cdot \mathbf{E}) - k^2\mathbf{E} = -\omega^2\mu_0\epsilon\mathbf{E}. \qquad (5.29)$$

In such a medium, however, (5.25) does imply $\mathbf{k} \cdot \mathbf{E}$ to be zero, so that we have

$$\frac{\omega^2}{k^2} = v^2 = \frac{1}{\mu_0\epsilon},$$

which has already been deduced for an isotropic medium in § 4.2.2.

5.3.5 Characteristic waves and their velocity.

Now, however, equation (5.28) cannot be treated so simply, although one important fact emerges with no trouble. Equation (5.28) cannot have a solution unless the vectors $\mathbf{k} \times (\mathbf{k} \times \mathbf{E})$ and $\mathbf{D}$ are parallel. The direction of the former expression is perpendicular to both $\mathbf{k}$ and $\mathbf{k} \times \mathbf{E}$, and therefore lies in the plane of $\mathbf{k}$ and $\mathbf{E}$, normal to $\mathbf{k}$ (Fig. 5.9). From (5.25) $\mathbf{D}$ is also normal to $\mathbf{k}$, and so a condition for a solution of (5.28) to exist is that $\mathbf{k}$, $\mathbf{E}$ and $\mathbf{D}$ must be coplanar. It is the condition that defines the characteristic waves; if they are not coplanar the plane of polarization will rotate as the wave progresses, and the disturbance cannot be described by a single harmonic wave.

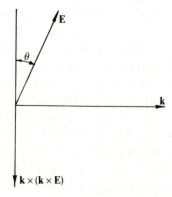

Fig. 5.9. The vectors $\mathbf{k}$, $\mathbf{E}$ and $\mathbf{k} \times (\mathbf{k} \times \mathbf{E})$.

Provided that **D**, **E** and **k** are coplanar, the equation (5.28) leads to an expression for the wave velocity. The vector $\mathbf{k} \times (\mathbf{k} \times \mathbf{E})$ has magnitude $-k^2 E \cos \theta$, **D** being defined as positive, and therefore we obtain

$$k^2 \mathbf{E} \cos \theta = \omega^2 \mu_0 \mathbf{D}$$

or
$$\frac{\omega^2}{k^2} = v^2 = \frac{E \cos \theta}{\mu_0 D}, \qquad (5.30)$$

θ being the angle between **D** and **E**. Fig. 5.10 shows the relative disposition of the vectors associated with the wave.

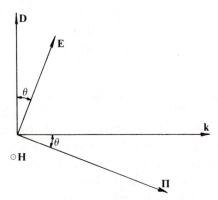

Fig. 5.10. The vectors **D**, **E**, **Π**, **k** and **H** for a wave in an isotropic medium.

5.3.6   Analysis of a particular medium.

To analyse the propagation properties of a medium the procedure is now straightforward in principle. Firstly we must find an expression for **D** as a function of **E**. As this depends on the direction of the vectors, it will be necessary to express the relationship by a tensor equation. Having done this, for every direction of **k** we must investigate all the transverse directions of **D** (since **D** and **k** are perpendicular, as a result of (5.25)) and choose those two for which **D**, **E** and **k** are coplanar as characteristic waves. Any arbitrary polarization can then be expressed as a linear combination of the two; it will turn out that their polarizations are orthogonal. Having chosen the characteristic waves, equation (5.30) will give a velocity for each one; the two velocities will generally be different, and can be used to construct a µ-surface having two sheets (which may intersect or touch). Finally, the wave propagation characteristics can be studied from the µ-surface.

5.4   Crystal Optics

5.4.1   The dielectric tensor. Crystals are anisotropic because of their crystal structure. Instead of defining a single dielectric constant for the material as a whole it is necessary to take into account the fact that the dielectric constant depends on the direction of the electric field and also that the resulting electric displacement $\mathbf{D}$ may then not be parallel to $\mathbf{E}$. The relationship between the two vectors will usually be a tensor equation† :

$$\mathbf{D} = \boldsymbol{\epsilon} \cdot \mathbf{E} \tag{5.31}$$

and the tensor

$$\boldsymbol{\epsilon} = \begin{bmatrix} \epsilon_{11} & \epsilon_{12} & \epsilon_{13} \\ \epsilon_{21} & \epsilon_{22} & \epsilon_{23} \\ \epsilon_{31} & \epsilon_{32} & \epsilon_{33} \end{bmatrix} \tag{5.32}$$

is called the dielectric tensor. In the absence of magnetic fields it can be shown that the tensor is symmetric:

$$\epsilon_{ji} = \epsilon_{ij} \tag{5.33}$$

so that the number of independent coefficients in (5.32) is six. The meaning of the tensor is straightforward. If an electric field

$$\mathbf{E} = (E_1, E_2, E_3)$$

is applied to the material, the resultant electric displacement is

$$\mathbf{D} = (D_1, D_2, D_3)$$

where $\qquad D_i = \epsilon_{1i}E_1 + \epsilon_{2i}E_2 + \epsilon_{3i}E_3 \qquad (i = 1, 2, 3).$

For particular directions of field the vectors $\mathbf{D}$ and $\mathbf{E}$ do turn out to be parallel:

$$\frac{D_1}{E_1} = \frac{D_2}{E_2} = \frac{D_3}{E_3} = \epsilon \tag{5.34}$$

and such directions are called *principal directions*; there are in general three of them, each having a characteristic value of ϵ in (5.34). The three principal directions for a tensor satisfying (5.33) are real and mutually orthogonal, and if the tensor is referred to these three axes as x, y and z axes it takes on the simpler form

$$\boldsymbol{\epsilon} = \begin{pmatrix} \epsilon_1 & 0 & 0 \\ 0 & \epsilon_2 & 0 \\ 0 & 0 & \epsilon_3 \end{pmatrix}. \tag{5.35}$$

† It does not follow simply from the fact that $\mathbf{E}$ and $\mathbf{D}$ are vectors that they are related by a tensor. For example, in optically active crystals (§ 5.5.4) the relationship is more complicated.

The process of referring it to its principal axes is called *diagonalizing the tensor*, and the details are dealt with quite thoroughly in most books on tensor analysis. For some materials two of the principal values ϵ_i are equal; such materials are called *uniaxial crystals* (§ 5.5).

5.4.2   Representation of the tensor by an ellipsoid. The possibility of a geometrical approach to the mathematics of crystal optics geometrically rests on the fact that a tensor of the form (5.34) can be represented as an ellipsoid. An ellipsoid in Cartesian coordinates can be written as the solution of a matrix equation:

$$(x, y, z) \begin{pmatrix} a_{11} & a_{12} & a_{13} \\ a_{21} & a_{22} & a_{23} \\ a_{31} & a_{32} & a_{33} \end{pmatrix} \begin{pmatrix} x \\ y \\ z \end{pmatrix} = 1, \tag{5.36}$$

where $a_{ij} = a_{ji}$. This equation can be expanded to give:

$$a_{11}x^2 + xy(a_{12} + a_{21}) + a_{22}y^2 + yz(a_{23} + a_{32})$$
$$+ a_{33}z^2 + zx(a_{31} + a_{13}) = 1$$

and is simplified in matrix notation to

$$\mathbf{x} \cdot \mathbf{A} \cdot \mathbf{x} = 1. \tag{5.37}$$

By referring the tensor A to its principal axes we obtain the equation

$$(x, y, z) \begin{pmatrix} a_1 & 0 & 0 \\ 0 & a_2 & 0 \\ 0 & 0 & a_3 \end{pmatrix} \begin{pmatrix} x \\ y \\ z \end{pmatrix} = 1, \tag{5.38}$$

or

$$a_1x^2 + a_2y^2 + a_3z^2 = 1 \tag{5.39}$$

in which the x, y, and z axes are clearly the symmetry axes of the ellipsoid. Thus the principal axes of the tensor are equivalent to the symmetry axes of the ellipsoid. The three semi-axes of the ellipsoid (5.38) have values $a_1^{-\frac{1}{2}}, a_2^{-\frac{1}{2}}, a_3^{-\frac{1}{2}}$.

To represent the dielectric tensor ϵ (equation (5.32)) by an ellipsoid we shall use its reciprocal tensor ϵ^{-1} referred to principal axes:

$$\xi = \epsilon^{-1} = \begin{pmatrix} \epsilon_1^{-1} & 0 & 0 \\ 0 & \epsilon_2^{-1} & 0 \\ 0 & 0 & \epsilon_3^{-1} \end{pmatrix} \tag{5.40}$$

and write the analogous equation to (5.37):

$$\mathbf{D} \cdot \xi \cdot \mathbf{D}' = 1. \tag{5.41}$$

This equation (5.41) represents an ellipsoid called the *optical*

indicatrix plotted on the axes D_1, D_2 and D_3 and clearly it has semi axes $\epsilon_1^{\frac{1}{2}}$, $\epsilon_2^{\frac{1}{2}}$, $\epsilon_3^{\frac{1}{2}}$. What does it represent? The vector **D** from the origin to a point on the ellipsoid is a solution of (5.41) which is

$$\mathbf{D} \cdot \boldsymbol{\xi} \cdot \mathbf{D}' = \mathbf{D} \cdot \mathbf{E} = 1 \tag{5.42}$$

from the definition of ξ. We therefore imagine both **D** and **E** to vary in magnitude and direction in such a way that (5.42) is always satisfied. For a given direction of **D**, the equation then determines both **D** and **E** completely, and the ellipsoid is the locus of the vector **D** drawn out from the origin (Fig. 5.11).

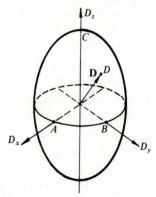

Fig. 5.11. The optical indicatrix.

5.4.3 Refractive index.

The refractive index then follows very simply from (5.30). We have

$$v^2\mu^2 = \frac{E\cos\theta}{\mu_0 D} = \frac{\mathbf{E} \cdot \mathbf{D}}{\mu_0 D^2} = c^2 \tag{5.43}$$

Since for all vectors from origin to the ellipsoid satisfy $\mathbf{E} \cdot \mathbf{D} = 1$ we have

$$\mu^2 = \frac{D^2}{\epsilon_0}$$

or

$$\mu = \frac{D}{\epsilon_0^{\frac{1}{2}}}. \tag{5.44}$$

The refractive index for polarization along the direction of **D** is thus given directly as the radius of the indicatrix in that direction. The indicatrix is the surface representing μ as a function of the polarization of the wave. To see that this is reasonable, consider the principal axes. It follows from (5.44) that the three principal refractive indices are $\epsilon_0^{-\frac{1}{2}} OA$, etc; from the value of the semi-axes

deduced above we then have

$$\mu_1 = \left(\frac{\epsilon_1}{\epsilon_0}\right)^{\frac{1}{2}}, \text{etc.}$$

which is clearly correct.

5.4.4 Characteristic waves. One part of the necessary calculation has thus been carried out. Provided a wave with polarization vector **D** is a characteristic wave (§ 5.3.5), it will have a refractive index given by the indicatrix in Fig. 5.11. This surface, it should be emphasized, is *not* the μ-surface of § 5.3.1, as it represents μ as a function of the polarization vector **D** and not the wave-vector **k**. We shall come to the μ-surface eventually. How do we decide what vector **E** corresponds to **D**, in order to judge the criterion for a characteristic wave, which is that **D**, **E** and **k** are coplanar? To determine the actual magnitude of **E** is slightly more difficult than to determine its direction, which is fortunately all that is necessary here. The construction to achieve the direction of **E** is to draw the tangent plane to the indicatrix at the end of the vector **D**; the direction of **E** is then given by the normal from the origin to this tangent plane (Fig. 5.12).† The construction is once again clearly correct for the principal axes, for which the plane-normal and **D** then coincide.

Now we can proceed to deduce the characteristic waves for a given wave-vector **k**. Since **k** is normal to **D** (equation (5.25)), it follows that all possible **D** vectors lie in a plane through O normal to **k** (Fig. 5.13(a)). This plane cuts an elliptical section $PQRS$ of the indicatrix. The characteristic polarizations are those **D** vectors

---

† This construction can easily be justified algebraically. The tangent to the ellipsoid

$$a_1 x^2 + a_2 y^2 + a_3 z^2 = 1 \quad (5.39)$$

at (x_1, y_1, z_1) is

$$a_1 x_1 x + a_2 y_1 y + a_3 z_1 z = 1.$$

A vector normal to this plane is proportional to

$$(a_1 x_1, a_2 y_1, a_3 z_1).$$

Translating this to the indicatrix (5.41) for which

$$a_1 = \epsilon_1^{-1}, \text{etc.}$$

the vector

$$\mathbf{D} \equiv (x_1, y_1, z_1)$$

and consequently the tangent-normal is

$$\left(\frac{x_1}{\epsilon_1}, \frac{y_1}{\epsilon_2}, \frac{z_1}{\epsilon_3}\right) = \left(\frac{D_1}{\epsilon_1}, \frac{D_2}{\epsilon_2}, \frac{D_3}{\epsilon_3}\right) \equiv \mathbf{E}.$$

whose associated **E** vectors lie in the **(D, k)** plane, and it is clear from the symmetry of the ellipse that they must correspond to the major and minor axes OP and OQ (Fig. 5.13(b)). There are two characteristic waves for each **k** vector. Thus to determine the μ-surface we must draw the ellipse $PQRS$ corresponding to each direction of **k** and measure its major and minor axes; these give the radii of the two branches of the μ-surface along each vector **k**.

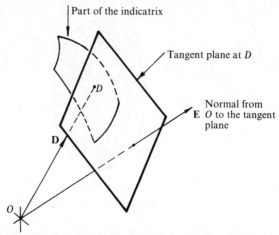

Fig. 5.12. Relationship between **D**, **E** and the optical indicatrix.

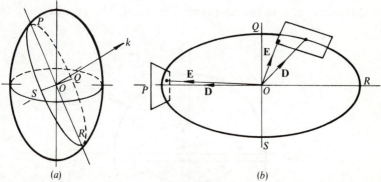

Fig. 5.13. Section of the indicatrix normal to **k**(a) and the axes of the section (b).

5.4.5   The μ-surface. A good idea of the form of the μ-surface results from considering its sections in the xy, yz and zx planes. We can standardize the indicatrix to have its major, intermediate and minor axes along z, y and x respectively.

We start with **k** along x and consider what happens as it rotates about z. When it is along OX the ellipse $PQRS$ has OZ and OY as major and minor axes, and therefore the two values of μ are μ_3 and μ_2 respectively. As **k** rotates about z, the section $PQRS$ still contains OZ as its major axis, but its minor axis shrinks from OY to OX, and μ from μ_2 to μ_1 (Fig. 5.14). The two refractive indices

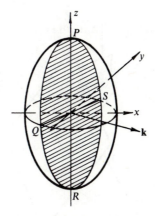

Fig. 5.14. Section of the indicatrix when **k** lies in the y–x plane.

for such directions are thus μ_3 and a value between μ_2 and μ_1, corresponding to polarization along z and in the perpendicular plane. We can therefore draw the horizontal section of the μ-surface for directions of **k** in the xy plane (Fig. 5.15). The symmetry of the

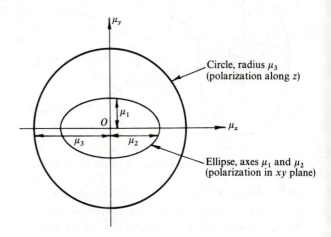

Fig. 5.15. Section of the μ-surface in the x–y plane.

section follows from the symmetry of the indicatrix. In the same way, by taking **k** from y to z by rotating about x we draw the section in the yz plane (Fig. 5.16). The zx section is similarly constructed by taking **k** from z to x; the two curves cross at A. For **k** in the directions OA, then, the two polarizations have the same refractive index; these directions are called *optic axes*, and there are in general two of them, at equal angles from z in the xz plane (Fig. 5.17).

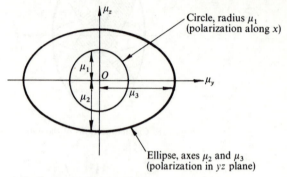

Circle, radius μ_1
(polarization along x)

Ellipse, axes μ_2 and μ_3
(polarization in yz plane)

Fig. 5.16. Section of the μ-surface in the y–z plane.

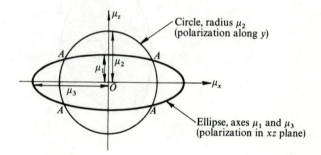

Circle, radius μ_2
(polarization along y)

Ellipse, axes μ_1 and μ_3
(polarization in xz plane)

Fig. 5.17. Section of the μ-surface in the z–x plane.

They are normal to the two circular diametric sections of the ellipsoid (Fig. 5.18). From this much information we can complete the surface by interpolation. The polarization of the two branches of it are not easily related to the axes except for the cases above; for example, in Fig. 5.19 the major and minor axes of the intersection ellipse are shown for a general **k**. One octant of the interpolated surface is sketched in Fig. 5.20(a). It is clear that it consists of two surfaces, which touch. The two complete surfaces touch at four points related by symmetry. They define the two optic axes.

5.4.6 Ray vectors from the μ-surface. Having constructed the μ-surface it is in principle a simple matter to deduce the direction of the normal **Π** at each point, which gives the ray-vector direction.

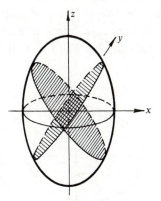

Fig. 5.18. Circular sections of the indicatrix.

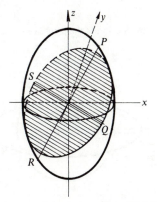

Fig. 5.19. For an arbitrary **k** the axes of the section-ellipse $PQRS$ bear no simple relation to the principal axes.

Using the definition of the two types of rays:

ordinary, for which the ray vector **Π** is parallel to the wave vector **k**,

extraordinary, for which **Π** is not parallel to **k**,

we can distinguish one general and two special cases (see Fig. 5.20(*b*)):

(a) for **k** in an arbitrary direction, $\mathbf{k}_1$, both surfaces give rise to extraordinary waves, as neither of the ray vectors $\mathbf{\Pi}_{i1}$ and $\mathbf{\Pi}_{o1}$ (from the inner and outer branches) is parallel to **k**.

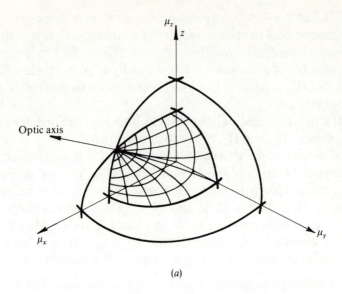

(a)

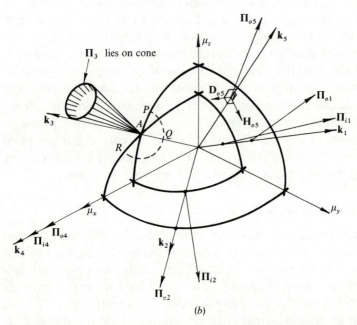

(b)

Fig. 5.20. (a) The μ-surface for a biaxial crystal; (b) the determination of propagation properties for various waves. The suffices *i* and *o* represent the inner and outer branches of the surface.

(b) If **k** lies in a symmetry plane xy, yz or zx, there is one ordinary ray corresponding to the section of the μ-surface which is a circle, and one extraordinary ray from the other branch. The ordinary ray always has a principal polarization: $\mathbf{k}_2$ is an example of this behaviour; $\mathbf{\Pi}_{o2}$ is parallel to $\mathbf{k}_2$ and corresponds to polarization in the z direction.

(c) If **k** lies in a principal direction $\mathbf{k}_4$ both rays are ordinary and the ray vectors $\mathbf{\Pi}_{i4}$ and $\mathbf{\Pi}_{o4}$ are both parallel to it.

Once the ray vectors have been determined it is easy to see the polarization direction of the extraordinary rays. We saw in § 5.4.4 that for a characteristic ray **k**, **D**, **E** and **Π** lay in the same plane normal to **H** and that **D**, **k** and **H** were mutually orthogonal. Since we can now construct **Π** for any given **k** vector, **H** is determined as normal to the plane defined by **k** and **Π**, and hence **D** can be deduced. This is illustrated for $\mathbf{k}_5$ on Fig. 5.20(b).

5.4.7 Conical propagation. A peculiar form of propagation occurs when the wave vector $\mathbf{k}_3$ is along the optic axis. The ray vector is then not unique, as both branches of the μ-surface are dimpled at the point A. The possible direction of **Π** then lies on a cone, one edge of which is along $\mathbf{k} = \mathbf{k}_3$. This gives rise to a phenomenon known as external conical refraction; if an unpolarized light wave is incident normally on the surface of a crystal cut perpendicular to an optic axis, the observed ray directions inside the crystal lie on a cone, one edge of which is parallel to the optic axis. The degeneracy of characteristic rays is also evident from Fig. 5.13(b) when the ellipse becomes a circle. A second form of conical propagation, known as internal conical refraction, occurs as a result of all points on the circle PQR (Fig. 5.20(b)) having parallel ray-vectors, although corresponding to wave-vectors lying on a cone.

5.5 Uniaxial crystals

The above analysis has been carried out for the most general type of crystal, which is known as a biaxial crystal since it has two optic axes. Uniaxial crystals, which have only one optic axis as a result of symmetry, frequently occur and have several important uses. They have the characteristic, already mentioned in § 5.4.1, that two of their principal dielectric constants are equal and their dielectric ellipsoids are spheroids. It follows that their optical indicatrices are also spheroids and therefore the one optic axis is

the axis of unique dielectric constant. The μ-surface for such a crystal is considerably simpler than for a biaxial crystal, and it is easy to see that it breaks into two branches, one a sphere and the other a spheroid touching it along the optic axis (Fig. 5.21).

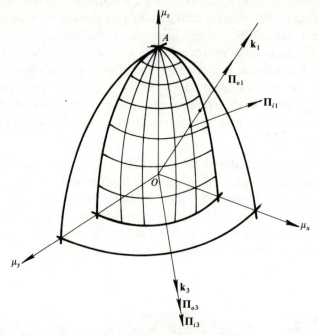

Fig. 5.21. The μ-surface for a uniaxial crystal.

5.5.1   Propagation in a uniaxial crystal. By following through an analysis of the ray-vector as a function of wave vector, the reader can easily see that

   (a) for a general $\mathbf{k}$ there is one ordinary and one extraordinary ray;

   (b) for $\mathbf{k}_2$ along the optic axis OA there are two identical ordinary rays, with equal refractive indices, so that propagation is the same as in an isotropic medium;

   (c) for a $\mathbf{k}_3$ normal to the optic axis there are two ordinary rays with different refractive indices;

   (d) conical propagation does not occur.

5.5.2   The Kerr effect. When an electric field is applied to a solid such as glass or a liquid such as nitrobenzene, the medium behaves as a uniaxial crystal, with optic axis along the electric field.

As a result, a beam of light passing across the electric field and polarized at about 45° to it will become elliptically polarized to a degree depending on the thickness of liquid in the same way as it does in a quarter- or half-wave plate (§ 5.6.3); this is known as the *Kerr effect*. The difference between the refractive indices varies as the square of the electric field E, and this dependence shows that the effect cannot be an inducement of optical activity (§ 5.5.4) which would reverse on reversing E and would therefore be proportional to an odd power of E. The *Kerr cell* is a shutter which consists of nitrobenzene between two crossed polaroids. By applying a suitable electric field the cell becomes transmitting, and can clearly be used as a fast non-mechanical shutter. Example of its use is given in § 11.7.2.

5.5.3 The photoelastic effect. In exactly the same way as the Kerr effect, the inducement of strain in a transparent plastic material such as perspex (polymethyl methacrylate) causes it to behave as a uniaxial crystal. The distribution of strains in a loaded beam, for example, can therefore be investigated in a plastic model by examining it between crossed polaroids (Fig. 5.22).

Fig. 5.22. An example of the photoelastic effect. A piece of strained perspex is observed in monochromatic light between crossed polaroids. The incident light is polarized at 45° to the edge of the strip.

5.5.4   Optical activity. The theory outlined so far is unfortunately not complete, in that it does not entirely fit the facts. On the basis of a dielectric tensor satisfying equation (5.33),

$$\epsilon_{ij} = \epsilon_{ji} \qquad (\epsilon \text{ real}),$$

we have shown that the characteristic waves in a crystal should be plane-polarized, and that μ-surfaces of the forms described should follow. In practice it is found that some materials, for example quartz, exhibit a phenomenon known as *optical activity*, whereby the plane of polarization of a wave along the optic axis is rotated as it passes through the crystal. Since the wave-velocities of the ordinary and extraordinary waves along this direction ought to be the same, and therefore no rotation of the plane should occur, the phenomenon does not fit into our present theory.

We must explain the process by assuming that the two sheets of the μ-surface do not quite touch along the optic axis, and for propagation in that direction the characteristic waves are circularly or elliptically-polarized, rather than plane-polarized. Restricting our attention to the uniaxial example of quartz (Fig. 5.23) symmetry arguments dictate right-handed and left-handed circularly-polarized characteristic waves, and if they have slightly different refractive indices μ_r and μ_l the plane of polarization of an incident plane wave will rotate by an angle

$$\theta = (k_r - k_l)x$$
$$= \frac{\omega x}{c}(\mu_r - \mu_l)$$

in a distance x. If $\mu_r > \mu_l$ the medium is called *laevorotatory*; that is, the plane of polarization rotates anticlockwise as seen by an observer whose eye the light is entering. A *dextrorotatory* medium has $\mu_r < \mu_l$. All living materials are laevorotatory. The phenomenon in quartz is explained by the helical structure of the crystal, which may have either a right-handed or left-handed character, giving rise to either laevorotatory or dextrorotatory wave propagation (Fig. 5.24). Optical activity can also occur in biaxial crystals.

5.6   Some practical procedures in crystal optics

5.6.1   General considerations. Although, in this book, we are mainly concerned with general principles, it is probably worth while clothing the preceding part of this chapter with some practical illustrations. These have always been of importance in the study of

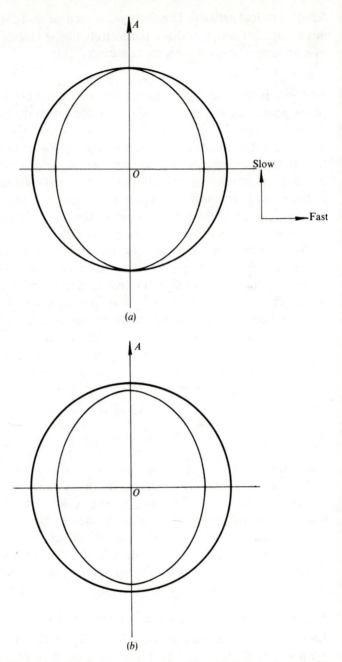

Fig. 5.23. (a) Section of the μ-surface in an inactive negative uniaxial crystal. *OA* is the optic axes. (b) Section of the μ-surface in an optically active negative uniaxial crystal, such as quartz.

solids, but have become particularly so since the discovery, by X-ray diffraction, of the ubiquity of the crystalline state. It is usually worth while beginning the study of a compound by an optical examination, even if only to discover fragments that are good single crystals.

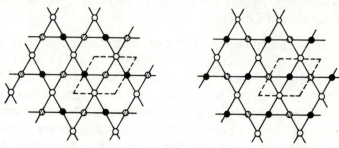

Fig. 5.24. Positions of the silicon atoms in right- and left-handed quartz (SiO$_2$) projected on a plane normal to the optic axis. The broken line outlines the unit cell, within which ● represents a Si atom at two-thirds of the cell dimension normal to the paper, ◍ at one-third and ○ at 0. Oxygen atoms are omitted. The Si atoms are seen to lie on helices, the senses of the helices being opposite in the two stereo-isomers. This structure of quartz (β) is stable above 573°C; below this temperature it is replaced by α-quartz which has a similar structure, the atoms being regularly displaced from the positions illustrated.

We shall attempt to explain only the general principles of the various procedures to be described; for full details books such as those by Hartshorne and Stuart and by Bunn should be consulted. There are, however, some basic terms that are in common usage and a knowledge of these will be a help in obtaining a grasp of practical procedures.

5.6.2   Nomenclature. The term birefringence is used both as an alternative to double refraction (§ 1.4.1) and as a measure of the difference between the two refractive indices of a principal section of the indicatrix (§ 5.4.2) of a crystal. As we have seen in § 5.4.6, when a beam of light is passed through a biaxial crystal it is split into two extraordinary beams and when it is passed through a uniaxial crystal it is split into an ordinary beam (o) and an extraordinary beam (e).

Uniaxial crystals are said to be positive if $\mu_e > \mu_o$ and negative if $\mu_e < \mu_o$; μ_e is not a constant, but it must always lie on one side of μ_o. There will be a direction in the crystal for which μ_e is maximum and a perpendicular direction for which it is a minimum. These directions are known as the slow and fast direction respectively (Fig. 5.23(a)).

Some crystals have quite different absorptions for the ordinary and extraordinary beams. Tourmaline, for example, even in thin sections, absorbs the ordinary ray almost completely and so can act as a means of polarizing light; it is very inefficient, however, because the extraordinary ray is also greatly absorbed. A biaxial crystal showing this effect is said to be pleochroic and a uniaxial crystal is said to be dichroic.

5.6.3   Some special devices. The most important devices are those that are used for producing plane-polarized light. The best known is the Nicol prism, which makes use of a crystal of Iceland Spar ($CaCO_3$) which is cut diagonally, the two parts being joined together with a film of Canada balsam (Fig. 5.25): the dimensions of the crystal are so chosen that the ordinary beam is totally internally reflected and is lost; the extraordinary beam emerges in a direction parallel to the incident direction.

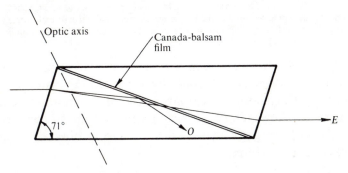

Fig. 5.25. Representation of a Nicol prism.

The Nicol prism has several disadvantages: large crystals are rare and so large areas—greater than a few square centimetres—of plane-polarized light cannot be produced; the process of cutting crystals is difficult as the cut is oblique to the planes of cleavage which are very pronounced indeed; and the complete device is rather bulky and not easy to insert in optical instruments such as microscopes.

A much simpler material—Polaroid—has now practically displaced the Nicol prism. This makes use of pleochroism, but obviously the use of single crystals would introduce some of the disadvantages associated with the Nicol prism. Instead, a stretched film of polyvinyl alcohol dyed with iodine is used; the oriented

polymeric chains absorb light whose electric vector lies along their length.

Polaroid works well, although polarization is not as complete as that produced by the Nicol prism; moreover, the transmitted beam is also appreciably absorbed. But it is *much* cheaper to produce than the Nicol prism, can be obtained in sheets of almost unlimited size, and is thin enough to be easily incorporated in scientific instruments.

Polarizers are usually used in pairs—a polarizer for producing plane-polarized light and an analyser for investigating the nature of such light after various adventures, to be discussed in the next section. Two polarizers set so that the vibrations that they transmit are perpendicular are said to be crossed and to produce extinction. The quality of polaroid can be tested by producing extinction with two pieces; usually the residual light is coloured, sometimes a dark purple.

Plane-polarized light is the raw material for producing other forms of polarized light. The Fresnel rhomb has already been described (§ 5.2.4). A simpler method is to use what is known as a quarter-wave plate—a plate of anisotropic crystal, such as mica, of a thickness such that the ordinary and extraordinary beams are transmitted with a phase difference of $\pi/2$. If a plane-polarized beam is incident so that its vibration makes an arbitrary angle ϕ with one of the vibrations that are transmitted by the plate (Fig. 5.26(a)) it can easily be seen that the resultant of the ordinary and extraordinary beams is elliptically polarized, with an axial ratio equal to tan ϕ.

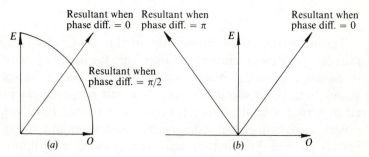

Fig. 5.26. Illustrating the action of (a) a quarter-wave plate and (b) a half-wave plate.

A half-wave plate—one that introduces a phase difference of π— is less useful; it would convert a plane-polarized beam at an angle ϕ

(Fig. 5.26(b)) into one at an angle $-\phi$, and can therefore be regarded as turning the plane of polarization through 2ϕ. It will reverse the sense of rotation of incident circularly polarized light.

Quarter-wave and half-wave plates can be correct only for particular wavelengths, since refractive index is frequency dependent. Although this dependence is small (~ 5–10 per cent) the relative phase shifts are much larger because λ varies by a factor of two over the visible spectrum. A quarter-wave plate of muscovite mica correct for $\lambda = 5900$ Å has a thickness of about $0{\cdot}026$ mm.

It is useful to be able to measure the phase difference between the ordinary and extraordinary beams by balancing it against a known phase difference. A device for producing such a phase difference to be used in this way is called a compensator. The simplest type is the quartz wedge, which has an angle of about $1°$; the phase difference is linearly related to distance, the constant of proportionality being obtained from knowledge of the principal refractive indices.

The quartz wedge suffers from the disadvantage of having non-parallel faces, and because no part of it has zero phase difference. This is overcome in the Babinet compensator by using two quartz wedges, the slow direction in one being perpendicular to the slow direction in the other (Fig. 5.27). By moving the compensator, a given phase difference can be produced in any part of the field of view.

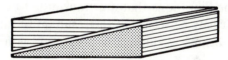

Fig. 5.27. Babinet's compensator. The parallel lines indicate the direction of the optic axis in the two wedges.

The most important instrument in this field is the polarizing microscope. Fundamentally it differs from the ordinary microscope in having a polarizer below and an analyser above the specimen stage; both these should be rotatable and it is convenient if the stage is rotatable also. Such a microscope should have both low-power and high-power condensers, corresponding to approximately parallel illumination and strongly convergent illumination respectively.

5.6.4 Practical applications.
It is easy to test whether a beam of light is polarized by passing it through a sheet of polaroid; if the

intensity changes, then some polarization is present. But this is far from a complete answer; if the intensity does not vary, the beam may be unpolarized, or circularly polarized or a mixture; if the intensity changes somewhat it may be elliptically polarized or a mixture of elliptically polarized light (including plane-polarized) and unpolarized light; only if the intensity is completely extinguished can one make a definite deduction—that it is plane-polarized.

For a complete answer, auxiliary equipment is needed, and this can take the form of the quarter-wave plate; by trial one can find an orientation that will convert elliptically polarized light into plane-polarized. The reader may like to amuse himself by devising a logical and systematic procedure whereby the distinctions mentioned in the last paragraph can be made. To specify a beam completely one would require to know what proportion is polarized and, if it is elliptically polarized, what are the orientations and the ratio of the axes of the ellipse.

To measure refractive indices of isotropic crystals, the most sensitive method is that which makes use of the apparent disappearance of a body when it is immersed in a liquid of the same refractive index. Laboratories that have to carry out such measurements have available standard liquids, which can be mixed to give intermediate values. If anisotropic crystals are to be studied, the refractive index depends upon direction and upon the plane of polarization; different results will therefore be obtained for crystals lying in different orientations in the liquid. Bunn, in his book *Chemical Crystallography*, gives an account of the determination of the principal refractive indices in these circumstances.

Of course, if a good single crystal is obtainable, large enough to handle and to orientate accurately, more direct results can be obtained. To begin with, one can find, with the polarizing microscope (§ 5.6.3), whether the extinction directions are simply related to the external form of the crystal; if the extinction direction is, for example, parallel to an edge, the extinction is said to be straight, but if it is not, and has no obvious relation to any symmetry that appears to be present, it is said to be oblique. Such results can distinguish between the different symmetries of biaxial crystals.

The most important use of the polarizing microscope is to obtain evidence of the symmetry of a crystal from what is known as its interference figure—the pattern obtained by interference of the

ordinary and extraordinary beams. At first sight, interference would seem to be impossible, since, although they are coherent, the ordinary and extraordinary beams are polarized at right angles; but if the two beams are passed through an analyser the components parallel to the vibration plane of the analyser *can* interfere.

If a high-power condenser is used to illuminate the crystal, convergent light is produced and quite beautiful interference patterns are obtained. These patterns represent a view of the crystal in terms of the direction of the light passing through it, and the pattern is in focus in the back focal plane of the objective where all rays parallel to a given direction intersect. An auxiliary lens—the Bertrand lens—enables the patterns to be seen on a larger scale through the eyepiece of the microscope.

It would take too long to describe the full implications of these patterns, but examples of figures for uniaxial and biaxial crystals are shown in Fig. 5.28(*a*) and (*b*). The uniaxial figure shows a dark cross which represents the two extinction directions of the polarizers used; the circular fringes are essentially similar to fringes of equal inclination (§ 7.1.6). The biaxial pattern is more complicated.

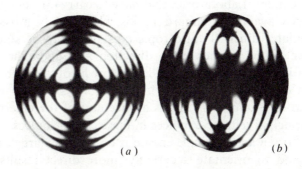

(*a*)   (*b*)

Fig. 5.28. Interference figures, (*a*) in a uniaxial crystal; (*b*) in a biaxial crystal.

It must not be assumed that figures as clear as these can be obtained for *any* crystal; often absorption makes the figures dark and indistinct, and the smallness of the birefringence may make the distinction between uniaxial and biaxial figures very small. Nevertheless, the polarizing microscope is a weapon of considerable utility in the preliminary investigation of any reasonably transparent crystal.

CHAPTER 6

DIFFRACTION

6.1 Meaning of diffraction

As we saw in Chapter 1, the wave theory of light was not at first generally accepted because light did not appear to have any obviously wave-like properties; for example, it did not bend round obstacles as water waves are clearly seen to do. The reason why this difficulty no longer prevents our acceptance of the wave theory is that we are now aware of the relative scales of the two sorts of waves: water waves are coarse and only bend round obstacles that have dimensions of the same order of magnitude as the wavelength; larger objects merely stop the waves in the sense that the waves bending round the edge produce negligible effects. But the wavelength of light is about 5×10^{-5} cm and an object of about a hundred waves in size—sufficient to stop a light wave—is still very small by ordinary standards.

Nevertheless some bending of the light waves round the edges of obstacles does occur and can be observed over a range of conditions. For particles of the order of a few wavelengths in size, no special apparatus is needed; for example, the water droplets that condense on a car window are surprisingly uniform in size and show beautiful haloes round the street lights as the car passes by. For objects that are much larger, special apparatus is needed; such an instrument is described in Appendix IV. The effects are called *diffraction* phenomena.

6.1.1 Interference and diffraction. There is another class of phenomena that is closely related to diffraction. For example, if we look at a distant source of light through our eyelashes we see odd patterns of light distribution. These are produced by the interaction of the waves passing through the spaces between the eyelashes; the effects are therefore called *interference* phenomena. It is sometimes claimed that the name is incorrect; the phenomena prove that waves can pass through each other unchanged and so do not interfere with each other. But this seems to be a pedantic

objection. The name is too firmly entrenched in physics to be changed.

A more awkward problem is that diffraction and interference are sometimes not clearly distinguishable, and different writers attach different meanings to the two words. We shall try to maintain the convention that interference involves the deliberate production of two or more separate beams and that diffraction occurs naturally when a single wave is limited in some way. We shall not always succeed in maintaining this convention because some names—the diffraction grating, for example—do not fit in with it and are too well established to change. But we shall try to preserve the distinction where we can. It is, in fact, identical with the distinction between the Fourier series (corresponding to interference) and the Fourier transform (diffraction), and it will be remembered from § 3.4.1 that the series can be deduced as a special case of the transform. In the same way all interference can be explained on the same basis as diffraction effects.

6.1.2 Approaches to the theory of diffraction. It is possible to produce a theory of diffraction on the basis of Huygens' principle of secondary emission, and by means of it to explain almost all observed diffraction phenomena. Before proceeding to do this, however, we ought to look at some of the assumptions implicit in such a theory. We can start by considering exactly how diffraction calculations should be carried out. An answer which must be correct can be obtained by writing down Maxwell's equations and solving them subject to the boundary conditions imposed by the diffracting obstacle. For example, diffraction of an incident plane wave by a perfectly conducting sphere can be tackled by this method which requires zero value for the component of $\mathbf{E}$ lying in the surface of the sphere. But even this simple example is too complicated for general understanding, and a considerably more naive approach has been evolved to explain almost all observed diffraction effects. It makes the basic approximation that light can be adequately described by a scalar variable, and that effects arising from the polarization of waves can be neglected.

6.1.3 The scalar-wave approximation. In principle, a scalar-wave calculation should be carried out for each component of the vector wave, but in practice this is rarely necessary. We can see the type of conditions under which the direction of polarization might be

important by considering how we would begin the problem of diffraction by a slit in a perfectly conducting sheet of metal. Considering each point on the plane of the sheet as a potential radiator, it will follow that

(a) points on the metal sheet will not radiate at all, because the field **E** must be zero in a perfect conductor;

(b) points well into the slit will radiate equally well in all polarizations, because the field can equally well be in any direction in free space;

(c) points close to the edge of the slit will radiate better when **E** is perpendicular to the edge of the slit than when **E** is parallel. This occurs because **E** (parallel) changes continuously from zero in the metal to a non-zero value in the slit, whereas **E** (perpendicular) is not continuous across a surface (§ 4.3).

The slit thus produces a diffraction pattern appropriate to a rather smaller width when the illumination is polarized parallel to its length.

The difference of effective slit-width is only going to be of the order of one wavelength; in practice differences of this order are rarely of importance when we are dealing with large obstacles and so we can use the scalar wave approximation with a fair degree of confidence.

The reader is therefore invited, for the time being, to forget that light consists of two oscillating vector fields, and imagine the vibration to be that of a single scalar variable ψ with angular frequency ω and wave-vector **k**, which is of magnitude $2\pi/\lambda$ in the direction of travel of the wave. This direction is assumed also to be the ray direction; we shall not concern ourselves with anisotropic media here. Because ψ represents both amplitude and phase we shall consider it as a complex quantity. The time-dependent factor $\exp(i\omega t)$ is of no importance in this chapter, since it is carried through all the calculations unchanged. It will therefore be omitted.

6.2   Fresnel and Fraunhofer diffraction

6.2.1   Diffraction under arbitrary conditions. Let us try intuitively to build a theory of diffraction based on the re-emission of scalar waves by points on a surface scanning the aperture. The reader who is not to be satisfied by this intuitive approach can be reassured that a more rigorous, but still scalar-wave, derivation of the same theory has been given by Kirchhoff and is discussed in § 6.5. But most of

the parts of the integral formulation can be written down intuitively, and we shall first derive it in such a manner.

We shall consider the amplitude observed at a point P arising from light emitted from a point source Q and scattered by a plane obstacle R (Fig. 6.1). We shall suppose that if an element of area dA at S on R is disturbed by a wave ψ_1 this same point acts as a coherent secondary emitter of strength $f_S \psi_1 \, dA$, where f_S is called the *transmission function* of R at point S. In the simplest examples we shall discuss f_S is zero where the obstacle is opaque and unity where it is transparent, but it is easy to imagine intermediate cases. The coherence of the re-emission is important; the phase of the emitted wave must be exactly related to that of the initiating disturbance ψ_1, otherwise the diffraction effects will change with time. The exact phase relation may vary over the screen, but so long as it is fixed at any one place it can be incorporated as a complex phase-factor in f_S. But such considerations can wait a while.

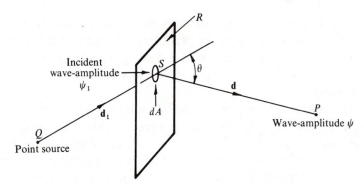

Fig. 6.1. Definition of quantities for the diffraction integral.

The scalar wave emitted from a point source Q of strength a_1 can be written as a spherical wave (§ 4.2.3),

$$\psi_1 = \frac{a_1}{d_1} \exp(-ikd_1), \qquad (6.1)$$

and consequently S acts as a secondary emitter of strength a,

$$a = f_S \psi_1 \, dA, \qquad (6.2)$$

so that the contribution of ψ received at P is

$$d\psi = f_S \psi_1 \, dA \cdot \frac{1}{d} \exp(-ikd)$$

$$= f_S \, dA a_1 \cdot \frac{1}{dd_1} \exp\{-ik(d+d_1)\}. \qquad (6.3)$$

The total amplitude received at P is therefore the integral of this expression

$$\psi = \int a_1 f_S \cdot \frac{1}{dd_1} \exp\{-ik(d+d_1)\}\, dA, \qquad (6.4)$$

remembering that f_S, d and d_1 are all functions of the position S. It is shown in §6.5.2 that expression (6.2) should really contain an inclination factor too; that is, the strength of a secondary emitter depends on the angle between the incident and scattered radiation θ in Fig. 6.1. We shall neglect this factor, except to consider its effect in general in §6.4.4.

Diffraction calculations involve integrating the expression (6.4) under various conditions. We shall consider first of all some simplifying conditions which may help to make the principles clearer. Firstly let us restrict our attention to a system illuminated by a plane wave. We do this by taking the source Q to infinity and making it infinitely bright; we therefore make d_1 and a_1 go to infinity while maintaining their ratio constant:

$$\frac{a_1}{d_1} = G.$$

Then we shall only consider plane obstacles R normal to the incident illumination (Fig. 6.2). The integral is then to be performed across the plane. If we denote position in the plane by a vector $\mathbf{r}$ from some origin O we write f_S as a function $f(\mathbf{r})$ and (6.4) becomes

$$\psi = \int_{\text{plane}} Gf(\mathbf{r}) \cdot \frac{1}{d} \exp\{-ikd\}\, d\mathbf{r}, \qquad (6.5)$$

where the factor $\exp(-ikd_1)$, being constant over the plane R as this is normal to the incident wave, has been omitted. The intensity observed at P is

$$I = |\psi|^2 = \psi\psi^*. \qquad (6.6)$$

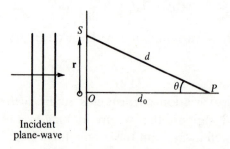

Fig. 6.2. Elements of a diffraction calculation.

6.2.2   Phase variation across the obstacle. The type of diffraction observed is mainly a function of the phase-variation across the obstacle. If this is linear, the diffraction is of the Fraunhofer type; if it is quadratic, it is Fresnel. No doubt further types of diffraction would occur for higher powers of **r** but they would not be of any practical importance; Fresnel diffraction itself is of little more than academic interest.

For convenience, we define the origin O of **r** so that OP is normal to the obstacle plane. This simplifies many of the calculations. Let us plot the variation of the phase

$$\phi = kd = k(d_0^2 + r^2)^{\frac{1}{2}} \tag{6.7}$$

of the integrand of (6.5) as a function of r as in Fig. 6.3. It can be seen that, near the origin, the variation is quadratic, but at large values of r it is linear.

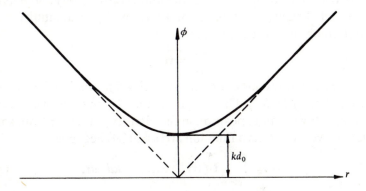

Fig. 6.3. Phase variation of contributions to the integral.

When $r \ll d_0$ we can expand (6.7) by the binomial theorem

$$\phi = kd_0\left(1 + \frac{r^2}{2d_0^2} + \cdots\right) \tag{6.8}$$

and the quadratic variation of ϕ with r is clear, provided that

$$\frac{r^2}{d_0^2} \ll 1. \tag{6.9}$$

This quadratic variation corresponds to *Fresnel diffraction*. On the other hand, suppose that we are looking at a restricted region of the screen well away from the origin, for which

$$\mathbf{r} = \mathbf{r}_0 + \delta\mathbf{r} \tag{6.10}$$

where $\delta r \ll r_0$ (Fig. 6.4). Then we can write (6.7) as

$$\phi = k\{d_0^2 + (\mathbf{r}_0 + \delta\mathbf{r})^2\}^{\frac{1}{2}}$$

$$\doteqdot k(d_0^2 + r_0^2)^{\frac{1}{2}} + \frac{k\mathbf{r}_0 \cdot \delta\mathbf{r}}{(d_0^2 + r_0^2)^{\frac{1}{2}}}$$

$$= k(d_0^2 + r_0^2)^{\frac{1}{2}} + k\xi \sin\theta_0$$

$$= \phi_1 + u\xi, \tag{6.11}$$

where $u = k \sin\theta_0$. In this expression ξ is the component of $\delta\mathbf{r}$ along $\mathbf{r}_0$ (as in Fig. 6.4) and we have taken θ_0 as the value of θ at the end of $\mathbf{r}_0$. In (6.11) the variation of phase with ξ is linear; this condition corresponds to *Fraunhofer diffraction*.

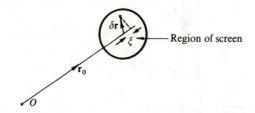

Fig. 6.4. Vectors for a small region of screen remote from 0.

Under some conditions it is impossible to distinguish between Fresnel and Fraunhofer diffraction. If we alter the phase of some of the contributors to the integral of ψ (6.4) by an amount considerably less than 2π, the value of $|\psi|^2$ will be affected very little (Rayleigh judged phase errors of less than $\pi/4$ to be insignificant), and if the difference between the quadratic variation shown in 6.8 and the linear variation shown in 6.11 is less than this amount, Fraunhofer and Fresnel diffraction effects become indistinguishable. This occurs when the size of the diffracting obstacle becomes small, when the distance d_0 becomes large, or when θ_0 becomes large. Because Fraunhofer diffraction is considerably easier to deal with than Fresnel, and is far more important, the term Fresnel diffraction is restricted to diffraction effects observed when the variation of phase kd across an obstacle deviates from a linear function of $\mathbf{r}$ by more than about π.

6.2.3   Experimental conditions for Fresnel diffraction. We can see the physical implications of the preceding statement best by drawing through the obstacle a hypothetical wavefront converging on the observation point P. This will be a sphere. The actual wave-front

through the obstacle is a plane, since it is that of the incident plane-wave illumination (Fig. 6.5). How large is the variation of the difference between the two? It will clearly depend on the obstacle; let us suppose it to be an opaque sheet ($f(\mathbf{r}) = 0$) containing a hole ($f(\mathbf{r}) = 1$) AB of diameter 2ρ in it. Only the hole will contribute to the diffraction integral (6.5), and we need only consider the difference between the sphere and the plane in this region. The Fresnel diffraction effects will be significantly different from the Fraunhofer effects if the distance

$$b \gtrsim \lambda. \tag{6.12}$$

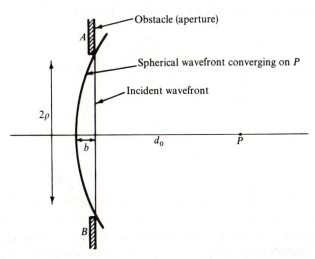

Fig. 6.5. Incident wave-front and spherical wave-front converging on P.

Now b is related to the radius ρ and distance d_0 by the sagitta relationship

$$b = \frac{\rho^2}{2d_0} \quad (\rho \ll d_0),$$

so that
$$d_0 \lesssim \rho^2/2\lambda.$$

For an obstacle of dimensions ρ of the order of 1 mm, characteristic Fresnel diffraction patterns can be observed with visible light when d_0 is of the order of 10 cm, which makes b equal to 5 wavelengths (see Fig. 6.15(a) and Fig. 6.16(a)). The condition 6.9 is also still satisfied:

$$\frac{r^2}{d_0^2} < 3 \times 10^{-5} \ll 1.$$

To return to Fig. 6.1, it is clear that the effects of a finite d_1 which is often the case, can easily be incorporated here. We replace the plane incident wavefront in Fig. 6.5 by a spherical wavefront diverging from Q, and it follows that the deviation b becomes

$$b = \rho^2 \left(\frac{1}{d_0} + \frac{1}{d_1} \right). \tag{6.13}$$

The whole of the mathematics of Fresnel diffraction can thus be modified for the condition of illumination by a point source by replacing d_0^{-1} by $(d_0^{-1} + d_1^{-1})$.

When the object is linear, for example, a slit or series of slits, it is common to replace the point source Q by a line or slit source. Each point of the line source produces a diffraction pattern from the obstacle, and provided these are identical and not displaced laterally they will lie on top of one another and produce an intensified version of the pattern from a point source. This requires the line source and slit obstacle to be accurately parallel. We shall deal in this chapter only with patterns produced by point sources; the experimental hazards of non-parallel slits must be left to fend for themselves.

6.2.4   Experimental conditions for Fraunhofer diffraction. Returning to Fig. 6.5 we can see that the condition for Fraunhofer diffraction is that both the incident and converging wave-fronts should be planar, or at least curved to the same radius. The allowable deviation from linearity in the separation of the two is less than one wavelength in the aperture.

This gives us, by the same arguments

$$b = \frac{\rho^2}{2d_0} \ll \lambda \tag{6.14}$$

and thus for the 1 mm hole and light waves,

$$d_0 \gg 100 \text{ cm}.$$

Thus Fresnel diffraction is seen to become Fraunhofer diffraction in the limit as $d_0 \to \infty$. The replacement of d_0^{-1} by $(d_0^{-1} + d_1^{-1})$ still applies.

To obtain an exactly linear deviation we can make d_0 infinite by employing an optical system. A plane wave-front is brought to a focus in the focal plane of a lens L in Fig. 6.6, and thus a system with lenses to produce parallel illumination (collimator) and to observe parallel diffracted light (telescope focused on infinity) is required.

This is called a spectrometer or diffractometer. Such an instrument is described in Appendix IV and is illustrated by Fig. 6.7.

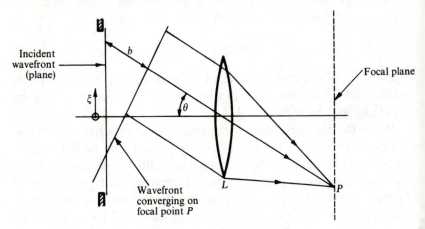

Fig. 6.6. Plane incident and converging wavefronts.

We can now see that the distance between the incident and diffracted wave-fronts is linearly related to distance along the obstacle. From Fig. 6.6

$$b = \xi \sin \theta \qquad (6.15)$$

and the angle θ is easily measured in the diffractometer. We shall leave further details of the consequences of this linear relationship (6.15) to Chapter 7, which is entirely concerned with Fraunhofer diffraction and its applications.

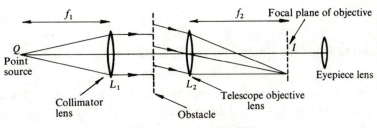

Fig. 6.7. Diffractometer (see Fig. IV.1).

The possibility of observing Fraunhofer diffraction patterns when the incident and diffracted wave-fronts are curved to the same radius indicate a simple manner of observing the patterns qualitatively. If we have a point source Q at a finite distance and a lens

producing a real image of it, at I, the insertion of the obstacle anywhere in the optical system will give rise to a Fraunhofer pattern surrounding I. One of the most important applications arises when the lens is the eye-lens; we then focus on a point source and insert the obstacle anywhere between the eye and the source to observe the pattern. It is best to place the object next to the eye, both to reduce the temptation to look at it directly and to make the best use of the restricted aperture of the lens (Fig. 6.8).

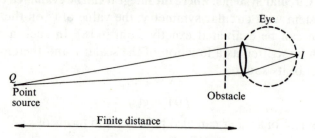

Fig. 6.8. Qualitative observation of Fraunhofer patterns.

6.3 Fresnel diffraction

This section and the next are to be devoted to a mathematical study of Fresnel diffraction in a few simple systems. Fraunhofer diffraction and its applications are a much more important subject, and are therefore given a chapter entirely to themselves (Chapter 7). The mathematics of Fresnel diffraction is more complicated, however, and as a result often receives much more attention than it deserves. The only real justification for this attention is that Fresnel diffraction affords an interesting example of the use of amplitude-phase diagrams, which form an important method of evaluating integrals of the form

$$I = \int f(x) \exp\{i\phi(x)\}\, dx, \qquad (6.16)$$

which occur frequently in many branches of physics. We do not, however, recommend any reader to spend a large amount of time simply in the mastering of Fresnel diffraction calculations once he has understood the principles.

The basic integral to be evaluated is therefore equation (6.5)

$$\psi = \int Af(\mathbf{r})\frac{1}{d}\exp(-ikd)\, d\mathbf{r}. \qquad (6.17)$$

We shall expand d in the exponent by the binomial theorem, as in

§ 6.2.2, but we shall not do so in the reciprocal since it has relatively little effect there:

$$\psi = \int_{\text{plane } R} A f(\mathbf{r}) \frac{1}{d_0} \exp\left[-ik\left(d_0 + \frac{1}{2}\frac{r^2}{d_0} + \cdots\right)\right] d\mathbf{r}$$

$$= \frac{A}{d_0} \exp\left(-ikd_0\right) \int_R f(\mathbf{r}) \exp\left(-ik\frac{r^2}{2d_0}\right) d\mathbf{r}. \tag{6.18}$$

It will be clear that (6.18) is the same type of integral as (6.16).

6.3.1 Circular systems, where the integral can be evaluated exactly.
In a system with circular symmetry, the value of ψ on the axis of rotation can be evaluated exactly from (6.18). In such a system, $f(\mathbf{r})$ can be written as a function of the scalar r and therefore as a function of its square

$$s = r^2, \tag{6.19}$$

$$f(r) = g(s). \tag{6.20}$$

The element of area $d\mathbf{r}$ can also be written in terms of s

$$d\mathbf{r} = 2\pi r\, dr = \pi\, ds \tag{6.21}$$

and therefore the integral (6.18) becomes (omitting the $\exp(-ikd_0)$ which will be eliminated when we observe the intensity $\psi\psi^*$)

$$\psi = \frac{A\pi}{d_0} \int_R g(s) \exp\left(-\frac{iks}{2d_0}\right) ds. \tag{6.22}$$

This is a Fourier-transform integral (§ 3.4.1), in which ψ is a function of the variable $k/2d_0$, which is related to the position along the symmetry axis of the system. We cannot calculate the pattern off this axis—although we can observe it quite easily (Fig. 1.2).

There are three systems of importance in this class:

(a) the circular hole of radius ρ, $g(s) = 1, s < \rho^2$
$$g(s) = 0, s > \rho^2$$

(b) the circular disc of radius ρ, $g(s) = 0, s < \rho^2$
$$g(s) = 1, s > \rho^2$$

(c) the zone plate, for which $g(s)$ is periodic.

We can see that with this condition the Fourier integral (6.22) must lead to some interesting results.

6.3.2 The circular hole.
The integral becomes, under the conditions (a) above,

$$\psi = \frac{A\pi}{d_0} \int_0^{\rho^2} \exp\left(-\frac{ik}{2d_0}s\right) ds \tag{6.23}$$

$$= \frac{A\pi}{d_0} \cdot \frac{2d_0}{ik} \left[\exp\left(-\frac{ik}{2d_0}\rho^2\right) - 1\right]. \tag{6.24}$$

The observed intensity along the axis then becomes

$$\psi\psi^* = \frac{A^2\pi^2}{k^2} \cdot 2\left(1 - \cos\frac{k\rho^2}{2d_0}\right). \tag{6.25}$$

As the point of observation moves along the axis, the intensity at the centre of the pattern alternates between zero and $4A^2\pi^2/k^2$ periodically with d_0^{-1}.

6.3.3 The circular disc.

In a similar way, we must evaluate the integral for (b):

$$\psi = \frac{A\pi}{d_0} \int_{\rho^2}^{\infty} \exp\left(-\frac{ik}{2d_0}s\right) ds \tag{6.26}$$

$$= \frac{A\pi}{d_0} \cdot \frac{2d_0}{ik}\left[e^{-i\infty} - \exp\left(-\frac{ik}{2d_0}\rho^2\right)\right]. \tag{6.27}$$

The exponential $e^{-i\infty}$ can safely be taken as zero. We have, it will be remembered, approximated the d^{-1} term in (6.17) by d_0^{-1}; this approximation will be invalid in the limit $s \to \infty$, and the fact that in this limit $d \to \infty$ and $d^{-1} \to 0$ makes it permissible to neglect the $e^{-i\infty}$ term. Thus the intensity

$$\psi\psi^* = 4\frac{A^2\pi^2}{k^2} \tag{6.28}$$

for all values of d_0. This surprising result, that there is always a bright spot at the centre of the diffraction pattern of a disc (Fig. 1.2), was the argument used finally to overthrow the opponents to the wave theory of light (§ 1.2.4). To this extent Fresnel diffraction has been of vital importance to the development of optics.

6.3.4 The zone plate.

The zone plate is little more than an amusing physical toy to illustrate Fresnel diffraction, although its significance is now enhanced as providing an approach to the understanding of holograms (§ 9.7.3). It is usually made by photographing down a large drawing of alternate black and white rings of diameters such as to make $g(s)$ a periodic function (Fig. 6.9) with periodicity a_0^2.

$$g(s) = 0 \quad \text{from} \quad s = 0 \text{ to } a_0^2$$
$$2a_0^2 \text{ to } 3a_0^2$$
$$4a_0^2 \text{ to } 5a_0^2, \text{ etc.}$$
$$= 1 \quad \text{from} \quad s = a_0^2 \text{ to } 2a_0^2$$
$$3a_0^2 \text{ to } 4a_0^2$$
$$5a_0^2 \text{ to } 6a_0^2, \text{ etc.}$$

If there is an infinite number of rings, the Fourier integral (6.22) for ψ will be zero except at discrete values of d_0 satisfying

$$\frac{k}{2d_0} = \frac{n2\pi}{2a_0^2} \quad (n \text{ integral}).$$

Fig. 6.9. Zone plate.

The wave-form of $g(s)$ dictates the amplitude of ψ at its various peaks. In the case of the square-wave illustrated in Fig. 6.10 we have a Fourier series with amplitude $1/n$ for odd n and zero for even n (§ 3.3.2), so that ψ has values proportional to

$$\frac{A\pi}{d_0} \cdot \frac{1}{n} = \frac{A\pi}{d_0} \cdot \frac{2d_0\pi}{ka_0^2}$$

$$= \frac{2A\pi^2}{ka_0^2},$$

at values of $d_0 = ka_0^2/2\pi n$ for odd integers n (Fig. 6.11). Notice that the amplitude reduction of the orders of the Fourier series has been cancelled exactly by the $1/d_0$ before the integral.

The zone plate can be used in a similar way to a lens. If we concentrate on one particular order of diffraction, $n = 1$ say, we can see that if illumination is provided by a point source at distance d_1 (Fig. 6.1), the position of the image moves out to satisfy

$$\frac{1}{d_0} + \frac{1}{d_1} = \frac{2\pi}{ka_0^2}$$

which is equivalent to a lens of focal length

$$f = \frac{ka_0^2}{2\pi} = \frac{a_0^2}{\lambda}.$$

It clearly suffers from serious chromatic aberration (see Problem 31).

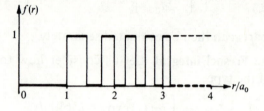

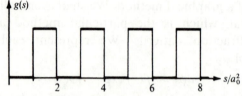

Fig. 6.10. Functions $f(r)$ and $g(s)$ $(s = r^2)$ for a zone plate.

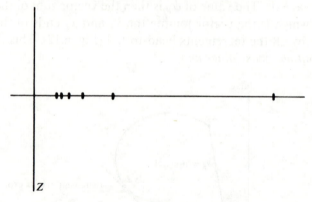

Fig. 6.11. Positions of the 'foci' of a zone plate, Z.

6.4   Fresnel diffraction by linear systems

The Fresnel integral (6.18) must be evaluated graphically for systems without circular symmetry. We can write it in Cartesian co-ordinates, for example:

$$\psi = \frac{A}{d_0} \iint_{\text{plane } R} f(x, y) \exp \left\{ -\frac{ik}{2d_0} (x^2 + y^2) \right\} dx dy. \qquad (6.29)$$

In this section we shall consider only systems in which $f(x, y)$ can be separated into the product of two functions

$$f(x, y) = g(x)h(y)$$

so that the integral is separable:

$$\psi = \frac{A}{d_0} \int_{-\infty}^{\infty} g(x) \exp\left\{-\frac{ik}{2d_0}x^2\right\} dx \int_{-\infty}^{\infty} h(y) \exp\left\{-\frac{ik}{2d_0}y^2\right\} dy. \quad (6.30)$$

The two parts can then be evaluated separately.

6.4.1 The Fresnel integral. Let us consider how to evaluate an integral of the type

$$\psi_P = \int_{x_1}^{x_2} f(x) \exp\left\{-i\phi(x)\right\} dx \quad (6.31)$$

by means of a graphical method. We shall eventually be led to the Cornu spiral, which is the particular method appropriate to Fresnel diffraction patterns. We represent each infinitesimal increment of ψ_P

$$d\psi_P = f(x) \exp\{-i\phi(x) \, dx\}, \quad (6.32)$$

by a vector in the Argand diagram of length $f(x) \, dx$ and at angle $\phi(x)$ to the real axis. The value of ψ_P is then the vector sum of the increments, which is the vector joining the x_1 and x_2 ends of the curve formed by all the increments head-to-tail (Fig. 6.12). This is called an *amplitude-phase diagram*.

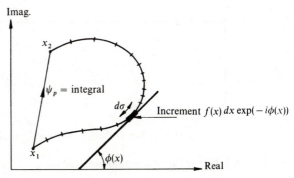

Fig. 6.12. Argand diagram of the integral $\int_{x_1}^{x_2} f(x) \exp\{-i\phi(x)\} \, dx$.

The problem is to calculate the form of the curve which is drawn schematically in Fig. 6.12. If we move a length $\delta\sigma$ along the curve, and the angle ϕ changes by $\delta\phi$ as a result, the radius of curvature of the curve is clearly

$$\rho = \frac{\delta\sigma}{\delta\phi} \to \frac{d\sigma}{d\phi} \quad \text{as} \quad \delta\sigma \quad \text{and} \quad \delta\phi \to 0$$

and if we know ρ as a function of σ the complete curve can be drawn out. Now σ, being the length along the curve, is simply $\int_0^x f(x)\, dx$ and therefore the functions necessary to plot the curve are

$$\sigma = \int_0^x f(x)\, dx \quad \text{and} \quad \rho^{-1} = \frac{d\phi}{d\sigma} = \frac{1}{f(x)} \frac{d\phi}{dx}.$$

6.4.2 Diffraction by a slit. In the example of the Fresnel diffraction pattern we proceed as follows. Let us consider the problem of diffraction by a single slit, so that

$$g(x) = 1 \qquad x_1 < x < x_2,$$
$$g(x) = 0 \quad \text{otherwise.}$$

The integral then gives the amplitude and phase of the disturbance at P, which is opposite $x = 0$ (Fig. 6.13). To build up to the whole of the pattern we must repeat the calculation for P opposite various points on the slit by varying x_1 and x_2 so that $(x_1 - x_2)$ remains constant. The integral is therefore

$$\psi_P = \int_{x_1}^{x_2} \exp\left\{-i\left(\frac{kx^2}{2d_0}\right)\right\} dx.$$

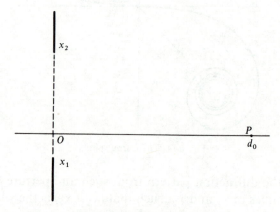

Fig. 6.13. Parameters of a slit.

The amplitude and phase are given by the vector between the points representing x_1 and x_2 on the curve defined by

$$\sigma = \int_0^x dx = x,$$

$$\rho^{-1} = \frac{d\phi}{dx} = \frac{d}{dx} \frac{(kx^2)}{2d_0} = \frac{kx}{d_0} = \beta^2 x.$$

Thus x is the distance from the origin measured along the curve, and the curvature at that point is $\beta^2 x$, proportional to x. This curve is a function of β, which is inconvenient, but it can be written in terms of the dimensionless quantities;

$$x' = \beta x, \qquad \rho' = \beta\rho$$

(which simply involves increasing the scale of the drawing by a factor β); then we have:

$$\frac{1}{\rho'} = x'.$$

The curve in terms of ρ' and x' is thus independent of β. It is called the *Cornu spiral* and is illustrated in Fig. 6.14. To calculate the

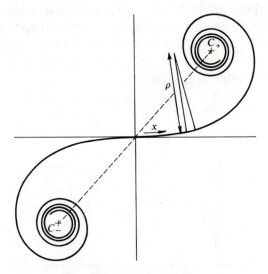

Fig. 6.14. The Cornu spiral.

whole of the diffraction pattern from such an aperture we take a series of values of x_1 and x_2, such that $(x_1 - x_2)$ is the width of the slit, and measure the vector length between the points on the spiral representing x_1 and x_2. This corresponds to the amplitude of the wave at P, which is opposite zero, or a distance x_1 from the x_1-end of the slit. To allow for the factor β, when using the dimensionless curve in Fig. 6.15, distances measured along the curve are βx rather than x. It will be seen, then, that diffraction patterns become rather complicated when both βx_1 and βx_2 are in the horns of the spiral—that is, when βx is typically of the order of, or greater than,

10. As an example, we have calculated the diffraction pattern for a value of $\Delta x' = 8.5$. Using light of wavelength 6×10^{-5} cm we then have

$$\Delta x' = \left(\frac{k}{d_0}\right)^{\frac{1}{2}} \Delta x = \left(\frac{2\pi}{\lambda d_0}\right)^{\frac{1}{2}} \Delta x = 8.5,$$

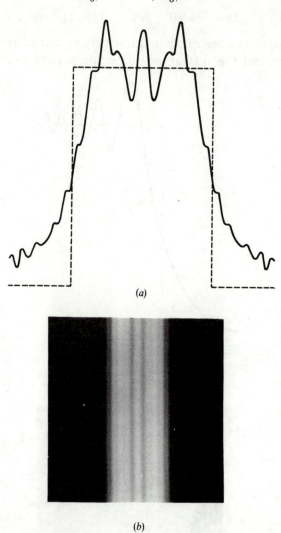

(a)

(b)

Fig. 6.15. (a) Amplitude of the Fresnel diffraction pattern calculated for a slit of width 0·9 mm observed with $d_0 = 20$ cm, $d_1 = 28$ cm and $\lambda = 6 \times 10^{-5}$ cm. The geometrical shadow is indicated by the broken lines. (b) Photograph of the diffraction pattern observed under the same conditions as (a).

whence $\qquad \dfrac{(\Delta x)^2}{d_0} = \dfrac{72 \times 6 \times 10^{-5}}{2\pi} \doteqdot 7 \times 10^{-4}$ cm.

The same pattern is observed for all slit widths Δx at distance d_0 from the observation point which satisfy this equation; for example,

$$\Delta x = 9 \times 10^{-2} \text{ cm}, \qquad d_0 = 11 \cdot 7 \text{ cm}$$

Fig. 6.15(a) shows the calculated intensity variation as a function of distance, and Fig. 6.16(a) the diffraction pattern as observed.

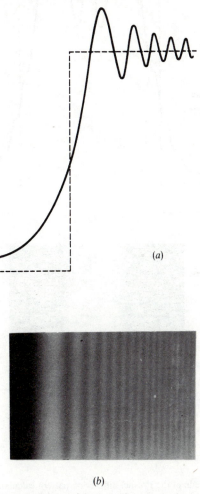

(a)

(b)

Fig. 6.16. (a) Amplitude of the Fresnel diffraction pattern for a single straight edge. The geometrical shadow is indicated by the broken lines. (b) Photograph of the pattern from a single straight edge.

We must not, however, neglect the y integral in (6.30). In this example of a long slit, $h(y)$ is always unity and the Cornu spiral gives the integral

$$\int_{-\infty}^{\infty} h(y) \exp\left\{-\frac{ik}{2d_0}y^2\right\} dy$$

$$= \int_{-\infty}^{\infty} \exp\left\{-\frac{ik}{2d_0}y^2\right\} dy = \text{vector } C_+ C_-. \tag{6.33}$$

This vector is of constant fixed length, and is therefore rather irrelevant, but it does alter the phase of the whole pattern by $\pi/4$ since $C_+ C_-$ is at $45°$ to the axes of the diagram. The phase is, of course, unobservable, but as a mathematical curiosity it is interesting to notice that the diffraction pattern of an infinite aperture, for which the integrals in both x and y are like (6.33), is the incident wave shifted in phase by $\pi/4$ twice, or $\pi/2$. But since an infinite aperture should not affect the wave at all, it is hard to understand this phase shift. It is explained by the Kirchhoff diffraction integral in § 6.5.2.

6.4.3   Diffraction by a single edge: the edge wave. Some diffraction patterns have certain characteristics which can easily be recognized as geometrical properties of the Cornu spiral. The most characteristic property of the spiral is that for large values of x it becomes almost circular and converges very slowly towards its limits; over a considerable range of x it can be considered as a circle of radius x^{-1}.

The diffraction pattern of a straight edge, which can be considered as an aperture extending from a finite value of x to infinity, can be expressed in terms of the Cornu spiral similarly to the previous example (Figs. 6.16(a) and 6.16(b)). But the vector that joins the point βx to ∞ on the spiral can be investigated qualitatively with little difficulty.

When the point x representing the edge of the aperture is at a value so that $x = 0$ is in the geometrical shadow, the vector simply rotates about the centre of the horn, becoming slowly shorter as $\beta x \to \infty$. There are no oscillations in its length so that there are no dark and light bands, and its phase changes steadily:

$$\frac{d\phi}{dx} = \beta x \qquad \text{(Fig. 6.17)}.$$

This is identical with the wave coming from a line source, since the phase variation for such a wave is (Fig. 6.18)

$$\psi_P = \exp\left\{-ik(x^2+d^2)^{\frac{1}{2}}\right\}$$

$$\doteq \exp\left\{-ik\left(d+\frac{1}{2}\frac{x^2}{d}\right)\right\}$$

$$= \exp\left\{-i\phi(x)\right\},$$

Fig. 6.17. Cornu-spiral construction for the edge-wave observed in the shadow region.

for which $d\phi/dx = kx/d = \beta x$ also. The amplitude is almost independent of x. As the phase and amplitude variations in the geometrical shadow are thus almost identical with those that would arise from a line source coincident with the edge, the appearance of

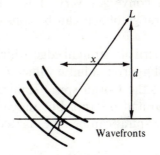

Fig. 6.18. Wave emanating from a line-source normal to the paper at L.

the aperture is that of a line source, and this is known as the *edge wave*. Well into the bright part of the pattern a similar analysis can be applied, by representing the vector between $x = \infty$ and $x < 0$ by the sum of the two vectors C_+C_- and C_-x (Fig. 6.19). The appearance is thus of uniform illumination (C_+C_-) and a bright

edge again. Interference between these two waves, plane and diverging, gives rise to a set of light and dark bands with a spacing which
decreases as $x \to -\infty$. The edge wave is not observable in the
region near $x = 0$.

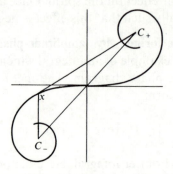

Fig. 6.19. Cornu-spiral construction for the edge-wave observed in the bright region.

6.4.4   The effect of the approximation on the Cornu spiral.

Having derived the Cornu spiral as the amplitude-phase diagram for
Fresnel-diffraction calculations, we can see qualitatively what
effect the various approximations might have.

The inclination factor and the inverse-square law can be included
by a reduction of $g(x)$ below its value of unity at large x. This will
make the spiral wind into its horns rather more quickly than in the
uncorrected case (Fig. 6.20). Unfortunately these effects are not
proportional to the dimensionless βx, and so the spiral would have
to be recorrected for each calculation. The correction is of no
practical importance.

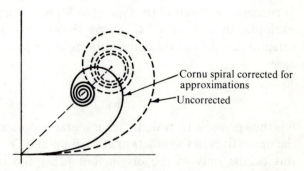

Fig. 6.20. Schematic corrections to the Cornu spiral.

The neglect of higher powers of x than the second in the binomial expansion of the exponent

$$ik(d_0^2 + x^2)^{\frac{1}{2}} \doteqdot ik\left(d_0 + \frac{1}{2}\frac{x^2}{d_0} + \cdots\right)$$

would have a similar effect on the spiral. Once again, experimental conditions are usually such that this effect is negligible also.

6.4.5 Integrals performed by amplitude-phase diagrams.

The Cornu spiral is one example of an integral which can be carried out using an amplitude-phase diagram. The method is applicable to any integral of the form

$$\int_{x_1}^{x_2} f(x)\exp\{-i\phi(x)\}\,dx, \tag{6.34}$$

which includes the Fourier integral. Here the phase

$$\phi(x) = kx\sin\theta = ux.$$

The Fourier integral for a slit is therefore simple, since $f(x)$ is unity across the slit; thus

$$\sigma = \int_0^x f(x)\,dx = x$$

and the curvature of the amplitude phase diagram

$$\rho^{-1} = \frac{d\phi}{ds} = u,$$

which defines an arc of length x of a circle, the diameter of which is determined by the value of u or $k\sin\theta$.

The theory of integration by the method of stationary phase, or steepest descent, is another outcome of amplitude-phase diagrams. It concerns integrals of the type of (6.34) between infinite limits (for example, the vector C_+C_-) and shows that almost the entire integral comes from the contributions of the parts where the curvature

$$\frac{d\phi}{ds} = 0;$$

it is then possible to evaluate the integral approximately in terms of the derivatives of the function at such points. For the Cornu spiral this occurs only at the origin, but other functions may give a number of points of stationary phase.

6.5 The Kirchhoff diffraction integral

As an electromagnetic field everywhere in a bounded region of space can be uniquely determined by the boundary conditions around this region, it is of interest to see to what extent such an approach is consistent with the idea of re-radiation by points on a wave-front through the aperture. As a result of solving the scalar wave equation:

$$\nabla^2 \psi = -\frac{\omega^2}{c^2} \psi = -k^2 \psi, \tag{6.35}$$

which refers to any component of the electric or magnetic wave-field, we shall see that the disturbance ψ_0 at a point inside the bounded region can be written in terms of the disturbances and its derivatives on the boundary of the region. In simple cases where these are determined by external waves originating from a point source the result is very similar to the one which we have already used intuitively.

6.5.1 The exact mathematics for the diffraction integral.

In many mathematical methods it is convenient to study the properties of the differences between two solutions of an equation rather than of one solution alone, since the functions to be dealt with may be simpler to handle. The diffraction integral provides one such example, and we shall compare the required solution of (6.35) with a *trial solution*

$$\psi_1 = \frac{1}{r} \exp{(ikr)}, \tag{6.36}$$

which is a spherical wave converging on the origin $\mathbf{r} = 0$ (see § 4.2.3). This wave satisfies (6.35) except at $\mathbf{r} = 0$. This origin we shall define as the point of interest inside the bounded region, and ψ_0 is then the disturbance there:

$$\psi_0 = \psi(0). \tag{6.37}$$

The two wave-fields ψ (to be calculated) and ψ_1 (the convergent reference wave) satisfy the equation

$$\psi \nabla^2 \psi_1 - \psi_1 \nabla^2 \psi = 0 \tag{6.38}$$

at all points except $\mathbf{r} = 0$, because both ψ and ψ_1 are solutions of (6.35). This expression (6.38) can be integrated throughout the bounded region of space that we are considering, which is a volume V bounded by a surface S, and the integral changed by Green's

theorem to a surface integral:

$$\iiint_V (\psi \nabla^2 \psi_1 - \psi_1 \nabla^2 \psi)\, dV = \iint_S (\psi \nabla \psi_1 - \psi_1 \nabla \psi) . \mathbf{n}\, ds, \quad (6.39)$$

$\mathbf{n}$ being the normal to the surface S at each point. Because the integrand (6.38) is zero, the integrals (6.39) are also zero, provided that the region V does not include the origin $\mathbf{r} = 0$. The surface S is therefore chosen to be as illustrated in Fig. 6.21 consisting of an arbitrary outer surface S_1 and a small spherical surface S_0 of radius δr surrounding the origin. Volume V lies between the two surfaces, and $\mathbf{n}$ is the outward normal from V, which is therefore inward on S_0 and outward on S_1.

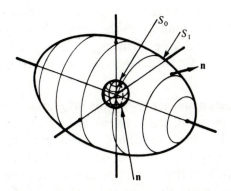

Fig. 6.21. The surface for integration. V lies between S_0 and S_1.

Over this two-sheet surface we thus have, for (6.39) and (6.38)

$$\iint_{S_1} (\psi \nabla \psi_1 - \psi_1 \nabla \psi) . \mathbf{n}\, ds + \iint_{S_0} (\psi \nabla \psi_1 - \psi_1 \nabla \psi) . \mathbf{n}\, ds = 0. \quad (6.40)$$

We can evaluate the functions of ψ_1:

$$\psi_1 = \frac{1}{r} e^{ikr}$$

$$\nabla \psi_1 = \frac{\mathbf{r}}{r^2} ik\, e^{ikr} - \frac{\mathbf{r}}{r^3} e^{ikr} = \frac{\mathbf{r}}{r^3} e^{ikr}(ikr - 1) \quad (6.41)$$

and substitute in (6.40) to obtain

$$\iint_{S_1 + S_0} \frac{e^{ikr}}{r^3} [\psi(ikr - 1)\mathbf{r} + r^2 \nabla \psi] . \mathbf{n}\, ds = 0. \quad (6.42)$$

The S_0 contribution can be evaluated, since over the small sphere of radius δr we can consider ψ to be constant (equal to ψ_0). Also since $\mathbf{n}$ is then the unit vector parallel to $-\mathbf{r}$, we can write $\mathbf{r} \cdot \mathbf{n}$ as

$-r$ and substitute $r^2 \, d\Omega$ for ds; thus

$$\iint_{S_0} \frac{e^{ikr}}{r^3} [\psi_0(ikr-1)\mathbf{r} + r^2\nabla\psi(0)] \cdot \mathbf{n} \, ds$$

$$= \int_{S_0} \frac{-e^{ikr}}{r^3} [\psi_0(ikr-1)r - r^2\nabla\psi(0) \cdot \mathbf{n}]r^2 \, d\Omega,$$

evaluated at $r = \delta r$, $d\Omega$ being the element of solid angle. In the limit as $\delta r \to 0$ there is only one term which does not approach zero and that is

$$\int_{S_0} e^{ikr}\psi_0 \, d\Omega \to 4\pi\psi_0 \tag{6.43}$$

since the maximum value of $\nabla\psi(0) \cdot \mathbf{n}$ is finite, being $|\nabla\psi(0)|$ and occurring when $\nabla\psi$ is parallel to $\mathbf{n}$. Equation (6.42) therefore gives

$$\iint_{S_1} \frac{e^{ikr}}{r^3} [\psi(ikr-1)\mathbf{r} + r^2\nabla\psi] \cdot \mathbf{n} \, ds = -4\pi\psi_0. \tag{6.44}$$

This expression is the analytical result of the wave equation (6.35) and applies to any solution of ψ and to any surface S_1 which surrounds the origin. For a surface not enclosing the origin the introduction of S_0 was unnecessary and the right-hand side of (6.44) would be zero. To make calculation of ψ_0 possible in a practical case we shall now consider a particular system which gives rise to a ψ that can be calculated approximately at all points on the surface S_0.

6.5.2 Illumination by a point source.
If the disturbance on the surface originates from a point source, the value of ψ can be easily calculated at each point. We consider a point on the surface S_1 to lie a distance $\mathbf{d}$ from the origin, as before, and $\mathbf{d}_1$ from the point source (Fig. 6.22 and also 6.1). The value of ψ is then

$$\psi = \frac{1}{d_1} \exp(ikd_1) \tag{6.45}$$

and its gradient

$$\nabla\psi = \frac{\mathbf{d}_1}{d_1^3} e^{ikd_1}(ikd_1-1), \tag{6.46}$$

which is the analogue of (6.41). Substituting these values into (6.44) gives

$$\iint_{S_1} e^{ik(d+d_1)} \left\{ \frac{\mathbf{d} \cdot \mathbf{n}}{d_1 d^3}(ikd-1) + \frac{\mathbf{d}_1 \cdot \mathbf{n}}{d_1^3 d}(ikd_1-1) \right\} dS = -4\pi\psi_0.$$

When d and d_1 are both very much greater than the wavelength, which is not at all difficult to achieve, we can neglect 1 with respect to kd and therefore, substituting for the scalar products $\mathbf{d} \cdot \mathbf{n}$ and $\mathbf{d}_1 \cdot \mathbf{n}$ in terms of the angles θ and θ_1 in Fig. (6.22), we have

$$4\pi\psi_0 = \iint_{S_1} e^{ik(d+d_1)} \frac{ik}{dd_1}(\cos\theta_1 + \cos\theta)\, ds. \qquad (6.47)$$

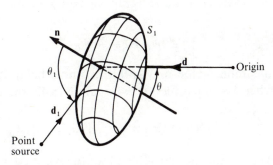

Fig. 6.22. Part of the surface S_1 showing normal and vectors.

This is the justification for the expression (6.4) which we have already used in our diffraction calculations. But it contains three extra pieces of information. The first is a definite form $(\cos\theta_1 + \cos\theta)$ for the inclination factor; the second is a phase-factor i; and the third a proportionality to k. The latter two, if introduced at the beginning, would have removed two slight inconsistencies that have been running through the calculations. The anomaly pointed out in § 6.4.2, in which diffraction by an infinite aperture appears to lead to a phase lagging $\pi/2$ behind the incident wave, is now resolved, since this factor of i produces a forward phase shift of $\pi/2$ to cancel it. The factor k has also appeared incongruously in the denominator of expressions such as (6.24) and (6.27); although it is not completely self-evident that the diffracted amplitudes should not depend on wavelength, it is reassuring to find the dependence to be a fiction. The inclination factor is more interesting, and is discussed in § 6.5.3 below.

We have, of course, omitted the variable transmission function f_S from this discussion, which is a serious omission in that it prevents us from calculating diffraction patterns. However it is easily remedied, and we have carried out our main purpose, which is to justify the intuitive expression already used.

6.5.3   The inclination factor.

The form of the inclination factor

$$f(\theta_1, \theta) = (\cos \theta_1 + \cos \theta) \qquad (6.48)$$

is of considerable interest. If we assume that the surface S_1 is normal to the incoming radiation—that is, that it lies in a wavefront—we have

$$f(\theta) = 1 + \cos \theta, \quad \text{since} \quad \theta_1 = 0.$$

This condition is the one which we have used in our discussion of Fresnel diffraction, where $d_1 \to \infty$ and S_1 is a plane. In Fig. 6.23 $f(\theta)$ is sketched as a polar plot of θ; it has value 2 in the forward direction, 1 at right angles, and zero backwards. It is therefore consistent with the simple Huygens construction, which always neglects back-radiation.

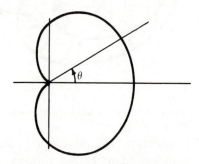

Fig. 6.23. The inclination factor $f(\theta)$ plotted in polar coordinates.

But why does the inclination factor depend on θ_1 and θ separately, so that $f(\theta_1, \theta)$ depends on the direction of the particular surface S that has been chosen? It would seem reasonable at first for it to depend on $(\theta - \theta_1)$, so that the direction of the surface would not matter, but on closer inspection we see that this is not so. The whole picture of *re-radiation* is a fiction of course; it is not as if we have a real screen of material at S which is scattering light uniformly in all directions. The important property of the integral is not that any one bit of the integrand

$$e^{ik(d+d_1)} \frac{ik}{dd_1} (\cos \theta_1 + \cos \theta)$$

should be independent of S, but that the whole should be, and that has already been assured. Suppose we were to change the surface S_1 to another surface S_2, also satisfying the conditions that it

surrounds the origin. Then the value of ψ_0 is given by

$$4\pi\psi_0 = \iint_{S_2} = \iint_{S_1} + \left\{ \iint_{S_2} - \iint_{S_1} \right\}, \qquad (6.49)$$

where the integrals are of the exact form of (6.44). The last term (bracketed) in (6.4) is the surface integral over a surface not enclosing the origin; its surface normals are outward over the part which is S_2 and inward over S_1, and thus the volume V lies between the two (Fig. 6.24). The integral over such a surface is zero, as

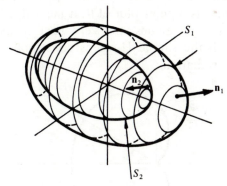

Fig. 6.24. Surface consisting of two neighbouring surfaces S_1 and S_2.

explained in § 6.5.1. Therefore the value of ψ_0 calculated from any surface S_1 or S_2 is independent of the surface. The variation of inclination factor $f(\theta, \theta_1)$ with the surface is necessary to maintain the total integral invariant, despite the fact that the integrand itself changes. In practice, the surface is usually chosen to span the aperture lying in a single wave-front, so that θ_1 is zero. Only the aperture itself is included in the integral, as the disturbance is zero everywhere else on the surface and evaluation of (6.47) is not difficult. We are then faced with integrals exactly of the type we have already studied.

CHAPTER 7

FRAUNHOFER DIFFRACTION AND INTERFERENCE

7.1 Significance of Fraunhofer diffraction

The difference between Fresnel and Fraunhofer diffraction has been discussed in the last chapter. In § 6.2.2 we showed that Fraunhofer diffraction is characterized by a linear change of phase over the diffracting obstacle; in practice this linear change is achieved only in special circumstances, since it involves illuminating the obstacle in a beam of parallel light. It is therefore necessary to use lenses, both for the production of the parallel beam and for observation of the resultant diffraction pattern (Appendix IV). The more usual statement is that Fraunhofer diffraction is the limit of Fresnel diffraction when the source and the observer are infinitely distant from the obstacle.

7.1.1 Interference. We stated in § 6.1 that we would try to draw the distinction that diffraction corresponds to the effects produced by limiting a beam of radiation, and interference to the effects produced when a finite number of beams overlap. Interference can take place under both Fresnel and Fraunhofer conditions, but all the important aspects of the phenomena are closely related to Fraunhofer conditions and we shall treat them solely in this way in this chapter.

7.1.2 Elementary treatment of interference. If we have two point sources of radiation (Fig. 7.1) we can see that, at a particular instant in time, the crests and troughs reinforce each other. So long as the waves remain perfect, the loci of the points where the waves cancel are time-invariant, and therefore what we see on a screen intercepting the waves is a set of dark bands with illumination in between; these are called *interference fringes*, and their first production by Young (§ 1.2.3) was of importance in establishing the wave nature of light.

7.1.3 Coherence. It is a necessary condition for the production of interference fringes that the sets of waves remain perfect over a

period of time. If one wave changes in phase, the positions of the fringes on the observing screen—which may of course be the retina of the observer's eye—will change with time, and if the change is rapid, as it is if natural sources of light are used, then the effects average out and no interference fringes are seen.

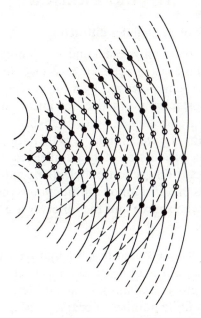

Fig. 7.1. Interference of two sets of spherical waves. Black spots show coincidences of troughs and of crests, small circles show coincidences of troughs of one wave and crests of the other.

Interference effects can be seen with water waves because reasonable perfection of these waves can be preserved over a period of time; such waves are said to be *time-coherent*. Sound waves, such as those produced by a tuning-fork, are also time-coherent, and interference phenomena such as beats can easily be observed with two separate sources. But light pulses from an ordinary source last only for about 10^{-9} s (§ 8.2.4) and so two such light sources could not produce observable effects; they are said to be *incoherent*. To produce interference fringes with light special means must be used to produce some sort of time-coherence.

The laser (§ 11.7) does produce waves of much greater time-coherence than any other source, but even with two lasers it is difficult to keep conditions steady for more than a fraction of a

second. The only practicable way of producing two time-coherent light sources for accurate interference work is to use one source as the originator of two separate sources; then as the pulses succeed each other the phase relationships remain constant and interference effects can be observed. Young achieved this condition by using the light from one slit to illuminate the two others (Fig. 7.2), and this is the simplest way of producing time-coherent light sources. But it will be noted that another condition is also necessary: the first slit must obviously be finer than the fringes to be observed, other-wise the interference fringes produced by the different parts of the width of the slit will overlap and tend to give uniform illumination. The slit must be fine enough to give what is called *space-coherent* illumination.

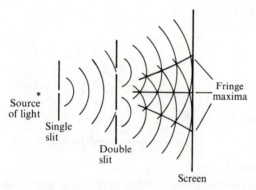

Fig. 7.2. Set-up for Young's fringes. Each of the pair of slits behaves as a separate source (cf. Fig. 7.1).

For the purpose of the present chapter we shall assume that waves are either completely coherent or incoherent with respect to each other. But there is in fact an infinite gradation of coherence, of both space and time, and in Chapter 8 we shall discuss the impli-cations of the degree of coherence on optical phenomena.

7.1.4 Some simple devices for producing time-coherent light.
Three general methods are available for producing two coherent beams: we can use the wave-front of a single wave (Young's fringes); we can use a source and its image; we can use two images of the same source. The last is the most popular and several devices—the biprism, the double mirror, and the split lens, for example—are fully described in most textbooks on optics. These

can all be used for measurements of wavelengths to an accuracy of a few per cent.

Interference between a source and its image is best illustrated by Lloyd's single mirror, with which interference occurs between the direct source and its image produced in a plane mirror (Fig. 7.3); if the source is nearly in the plane of the mirror the separation of the source and its image is quite small, and well-separated interference fringes can be produced. Obviously, however, the zero fringe—that which is equidistant from the two sources—cannot be produced by this method; but if one extrapolates back to the position where it should occur, one finds that there is a minimum of intensity there, not a maximum. There is therefore some asymmetry between the source and its image; this can be traced to the change of phase that occurs when light is reflected from a medium of higher refractive index (§ 4.3.5).

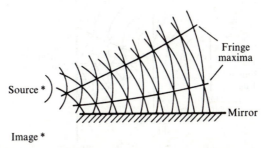

Fig. 7.3. Set-up for Lloyd's single-mirror fringes. The phase change on reflexion is simulated by making the radii of the circles representing the reflected wave interleave those representing the direct wave.

7.1.5 Naturally occurring interference phenomena. The coherence conditions described in § 7.1.3 sometimes arise naturally and produce interference patterns in quite simple conditions, as, for example, the colours produced by a thin film of oil on a wet road. Here, the interference takes place between the light reflected from the top and bottom of the film.

Such effects, however, are not interpretable in detail because they are too imprecise: the illumination is white, not monochromatic; the source (usually the sky) is large; and the film is nonuniform. For precise work all these variables must be controlled.

7.1.6 Interference measurements. We must first consider how these variables are related. Fig. 7.4 shows a ray incident upon the

surface of a film of refractive index μ; it divides into a reflected ray and a transmitted ray AB, which is incident at angle θ on the lower surface of the film and is then reflected along the path BC. We require to find the path difference between the directly reflected ray and that reflected at the lower surface.

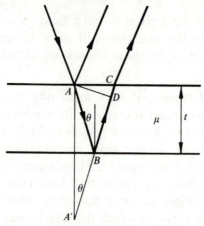

Fig. 7.4. Path differences for rays reflected from top and bottom of plane film.

Let A' be the mirror image of A in the lower surface, and let AD be the perpendicular from A on to $A'C$. Then the optical path difference required is obviously $\mu(AB+BD)$, which is equal to $\mu A'D$ or $2\mu t \cos \theta$, where t is the thickness of the film. Thus for interference minima (not maxima, since the ray reflected at A suffers a phase change of π, as we noted in § 7.1.4),

$$2\mu t \cos \theta = m\lambda, \qquad (7.1)$$

where m is an integer. This is the basic equation on which all thin-film interference theory is based.

If we illuminate a non-uniform film with parallel monochromatic light, a system of interference fringes is produced that follow the lines of constant t; such fringes are called *fringes of equal thickness* and are discussed further in § 12.2.2. If we illuminate a uniform film with an extended source of monochromatic light, fringes are seen that trace out lines of constant θ; these are called *fringes of equal inclination* and form the basis of most precise work in optics, as we shall show in § 7.8.3. Finally, if we allow a beam of white light to fall at a fixed angle of incidence on a uniform film, the values of λ that satisfy equation (7.1) will be absent from the reflected light

and so the film will be uniformly coloured; the colour can give a rough indication of the thickness of the film.

Variations on these three themes are possible. For example, if both t and λ vary we may write

$$\frac{t}{\lambda} = \frac{m}{2\mu \cos \theta}, \tag{7.2}$$

which is constant for a given m and a fixed value of θ. If the light is then dispersed, the spectrum will show fringes corresponding to different values of m; these fringes are called *fringes of equal chromatic order*.

7.1.7 Localized fringes. It may seem odd that fringes can be observed when extended sources of illumination are used. From our understanding of Young's fringes (§ 7.1.3) we should expect that space-coherent illumination would always be necessary. The answer is that if we require a fringe system throughout space, then space-coherence *is* necessary; but, even without space-coherent illumination we may find that there is some closely defined region in space in which the interference effects from the various time-coherent points all coincide. Fringes are then observed, and are said to be *localized*.

We can find the surface of localization for fringes of equal thickness (§ 7.1.6) by means of a simple construction (Fig. 7.5(a)). Let OP_1 and OP_2 represent the two reflecting plane surfaces. With centre O draw a circle—representing a cylinder—cutting the plane of illumination in the points A and B; the two chords A_1B_1 and A_2B_2 are the images of AB in OP_1 and OP_2 respectively. Therefore the points A_1A_2 are time-coherent and so are B_1 and B_2. Thus the fringe system produced by A_1 and A_2 has its zero-order along a radius bisecting the chord A_1A_2 and that produced by B_1 and B_2 along the bisector of B_1B_2. These two fringes will intersect at O. This is the position where the fringes will be localized.

As shown in Fig. 7.5(b), the orders other than the zero cannot be treated so simply, but we can see from this figure that the composite fringe system is recognizable only on one plane. The set of fringe maxima from A_1 and A_2 lie upon hyperbolae (cf. Fig. 7.1) that approximate to a set of straight lines diverging from a point midway between A_1 and A_2; the superposition of fringes from other coherent pairs of points leads to an unintelligible mixture except in the plane of localization.

If the illumination is roughly normal to the film, the fringes will be localized in the plane of the film. If the film surfaces are not both plane—as, for example, in the formation of Newton's rings—the construction does not apply; but we can assume that it applies approximately to successive portions of the film by taking tangents to the surfaces. For Newton's rings, this would lead to fringes localized in the plane surface of the film.

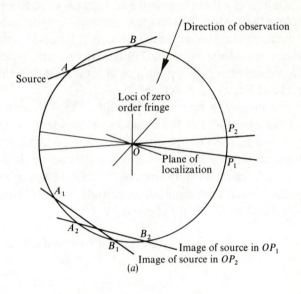

(a)

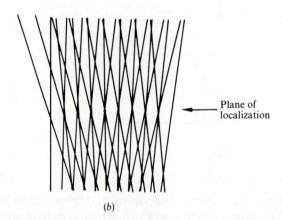

(b)

Fig. 7.5. (a) Construction for finding plane of localization for fringes from wedge-shaped film; (b) three sets of fringe maxima from three pairs of time-coherent point images, showing that only in one position is a recognizable fringe system produced.

7.2 Fourier theory of Fraunhofer diffraction

The whole of Fourier diffraction theory can be summed up in one statement: 'The Fraunhofer diffraction pattern of an object is the Fourier transform (§ 3.4.1) of that object.' This is true in the sense that the amplitude and the phase of the radiation at any point in the diffraction pattern are the amplitude and phase (§ 3.2.2) at the corresponding point in the Fourier transform.

We shall justify this statement and then proceed to use it in some examples; the reason for the great practical importance of Fraunhofer diffraction is contained in it, because the operation of deriving a Fourier transform is a mathematical operation and does not involve constants of the apparatus. A similar statement cannot be made about Fresnel diffraction.

Let us consider two points, A_1 and A_2 (Fig. 7.6), scattering radiation of wavelength λ. If the radiation is incident normally to the line separating the two points, which are at a distance x apart, the phase difference for waves diffracted at an angle θ is equal to $(2\pi x/\lambda) \sin \theta$, which we may write as $kx \sin \theta$. If we have a collection of points A, each scattering an amplitude $f(x)$, the complete wave diffracted in the direction θ is given by

$$\psi = \int_{-\infty}^{\infty} f(x) \exp\left(-ikx \sin \theta\right) dx. \tag{7.3}$$

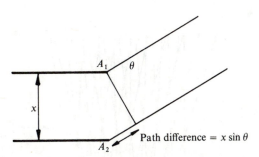

Fig. 7.6. Path difference for rays scattered at angle θ from two points A_1 and A_2.

Thus, ψ is the Fourier transform of $f(x)$ in terms of the variable $k \sin \theta$ (compare equation (3.18)), which we shall call u.

This treatment is one-dimensional. We shall consider later in this chapter transforms in two and three dimensions.

7.2.1 Diffraction by a uniform slit. The most important diffraction pattern is that of a uniform slit. If the width is a, the transform is

$$\psi(u) = \int_{-a/2}^{a/2} \exp(-iux)\, dx$$

$$= -\frac{1}{iu}[\exp(-iux)]_{-a/2}^{a/2}$$

$$= a\frac{\sin\frac{1}{2}au}{\frac{1}{2}au}. \tag{7.4}$$

This, of course, is the same result as we obtained for the square pulse considered in § 3.4.2.

The form of this function (Fig. 7.7) is important; it has a maximum of unity at $\theta = 0$, and is zero at regular intervals where $\frac{1}{2}ka\sin\theta = m\pi$, where m is a finite integer. The heights of the resulting maxima are approximately proportional to $1/(2m+1)$: this result arises if we assume that these maxima lie half-way between the zeros; their *exact* positions are not easy to find.

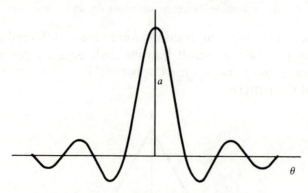

Fig. 7.7. Form of function $\sin\frac{1}{2}au/\frac{1}{2}u$.

The square of the function (Fig. 7.8) gives the observed intensity, which may be compared with the diffraction pattern shown in Fig. 7.9. The zeros in this pattern occur at angles given by

$$\frac{1}{2}ka\sin\theta = m\pi$$

or

$$\frac{\pi}{\lambda}\sin\theta = m\pi/a$$

i.e.

$$\sin\theta = m\lambda/a. \tag{7.5}$$

7.2.2 Diffraction by a tapered slit. If the slit is tapered we can represent it by a triangular function (Fig. 7.10) given analytically by

$$f(x) = \frac{1}{a}(a - |x|) \quad \text{for} \quad -a < x < a \qquad (7.6)$$

$$f(x) = 0 \quad \text{elsewhere.}$$

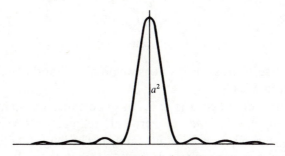

Fig. 7.8. Form of function $[\sin \frac{1}{2}au/\frac{1}{2}u]^2$.

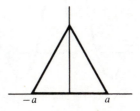

Fig. 7.9. Fraunhofer diffraction pattern of a slit, with a *slit* source.

This makes the slit of unit transmission in the middle, and gives its base width as $2a$. The result that we shall obtain represents the diffraction pattern only along a line parallel to the base through the centre of the pattern.

Fig. 7.10. Triangular function.

We have that

$$\psi = \frac{1}{a}\int_0^a (a - x)\exp(-iux)\,dx + \frac{1}{a}\int_{-a}^0 (a + x)\exp(-iux)\,dx. \qquad (7.7)$$

We need the integral

$$\int_0^a x\exp(-iux)\,dx = -\frac{a\exp(-iua)}{iu} + \frac{\exp(-iua)-1}{u^2}. \qquad (7.8)$$

Thus
$$\psi = \frac{1}{a}\left\{\frac{\exp(iua)-2+\exp(-iua)}{u^2}\right\}$$

$$= 4\frac{\sin^2 ua/2}{u^2 a}. \tag{7.9}$$

The form of this expression shown in Fig. 7.8 is, at first sight, rather surprising; it is everywhere positive, reaching zero at values of u given by

$$ua/2 = m\pi$$

or
$$a\sin\theta = m\lambda.$$

The angular positions of these zeros are thus exactly the same as for the uniform slit; since the average width of the wedge is the same as that of the slit, this result is not surprising. But the maxima of the side bands produced (Fig. 7.11) are much less; their intensities are proportional to $(2m+1)^{-4}$.

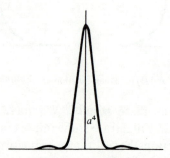

Fig. 7.11. Form of function $[\sin\frac{1}{2}au/\frac{1}{2}u]^4$, the intensity along the equatorial line of the diffraction pattern of a tapered slit.

It will also be seen that the *amplitude* function for the wedge-shaped slit is the same as the *intensity* function for the uniform slit. The physical significance of this fact will be seen when we consider two-dimensional diffraction in § 7.3.

7.2.3 Diffraction by a Gaussian distribution.

Let us suppose that the wedge-shaped slit is replaced by a Gaussian function (Fig. 7.12(a)) of the same half width and enclosed area;

$$f(x) = \frac{1}{a}\sqrt{\frac{2}{\pi}}\exp\left(-\frac{2x^2}{a^2}\right). \tag{7.10}$$

Then $\psi = \dfrac{1}{a}\sqrt{\dfrac{2}{\pi}} \displaystyle\int_{-\infty}^{\infty} \exp\left(-\dfrac{2x^2}{a^2} - iux\right)dx$

$\qquad = \dfrac{1}{a}\sqrt{\dfrac{2}{\pi}} \displaystyle\int_{-\infty}^{\infty} \exp\left\{-\left(\dfrac{\sqrt{2}x}{a} + \dfrac{iua}{2\sqrt{2}}\right)^2\right\} \exp\left(-\dfrac{u^2a^2}{8}\right)dx$

$\qquad = \dfrac{1}{a}\sqrt{\dfrac{2}{\pi}}\sqrt{\dfrac{a^2\pi}{2}} \exp\left(-\dfrac{u^2a^2}{8}\right)$

$\qquad = \exp\left(-u^2a^2/8\right).$ \hfill (7.11)

This is another Gaussian function (Fig. 7.12(b)), of half-width $2/a$, and thus has no side bands at all.

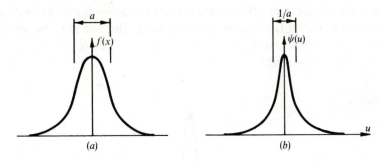

Fig. 7.12. (a) and (b) Gaussian function and its diffraction pattern.

7.2.4 Discussion of these results. We have taken these three examples because they illustrate some important general principles. The two finite functions have Fourier transforms with side-bands; this result follows because, if we sum a Fourier series with a finite number of terms—the Fourier transform can be regarded as the limit of a Fourier series (§ 3.4.1)—there are bound to be ripples with periodicity of the same order of magnitude as that of the highest term introduced. If, however, we take an infinite function, such as a Gaussian, there is the possibility that the Fourier transform can be smoothed out by the inclusion of the higher-order terms.

Secondly, the widths of all the three central diffraction peaks is inversely proportional to the widths of the diffracting objects. And, finally, the scale of detail in the diffraction patterns of the two finite slits is also inversely proportional to the widths of the slits.

7.2.5 Diffraction by an object with phase-variation only. There are many objects, particularly natural ones, that do not absorb light

appreciably but change its phase on transmission. Any ordinary piece of window glass will do this; it is transparent, but its thickness is not uniform and light passing through different parts of it suffers a varying amount of phase retardation. If the refractive index of the glass is μ, the optical difference between two paths of different thicknesses t_1 and t_2 is

$$(\mu - 1)(t_1 - t_2)$$

and consequently the wave-front emerging from the glass sheet is no longer a plane as it was when incident (Fig. 7.13). Since waves of different phases but the same amplitudes are represented by complex amplitudes with the same modulus, such a state of affairs as this 'phase object' is represented by a complex transmission function $f(x)$ with constant modulus. We shall take as an example of this behaviour a thin prism, of angle α and refractive index μ.

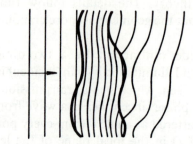

Fig. 7.13. Distortion of plane wave front by non-uniform glass plate.

The thickness of the prism at position x is αx (Fig. 7.14) and the phase lead introduced is thus

$$f(x) = \exp\{ik(\mu - 1)t\}$$
$$= \exp\{ik(\mu - 1)\alpha x\}. \tag{7.12}$$

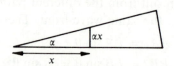

Fig. 7.14. Thickness of prism of angle α.

The prism is assumed to be infinite in extent along both x and y directions. The diffraction pattern corresponding to $f(x)$ is then

$$\psi(u) = \int_{-\infty}^{\infty} \exp\{ik(\mu - 1)\alpha\}\, e^{-iux}\, dx = \delta\{u - k(\mu - 1)\alpha\}, \tag{7.13}$$

the expression $\delta(\ )$ representing a δ-function. The diffracted wave thus travels in the direction represented by

$$u = k(\mu - 1)\alpha. \tag{7.14}$$

Substituting for u, (§ 7.18)

$$\left.\begin{array}{l} u = k \sin \theta = k(\mu - 1)\alpha, \\ \theta = (\mu - 1)\alpha \quad \text{for small } \theta. \end{array}\right\} \tag{7.15}$$

The light thus remains concentrated in a single direction, but is deviated from the incident by the same angle as deduced from geometrical optics.

7.3 Two-dimensional diffraction

Having established the principles of Fraunhofer diffraction in one dimension, we can now proceed to the much more important two-dimensional theory. The details follow those given in the previous section, but the geometry is more complicated as Fig. 7.15 shows.

We shall consider diffraction by a two-dimensional screen, lying in the plane and illuminated by light incident in the z-direction. All parts of the screen, which has a transmission function $f(x, y)$, are illuminated in phase since it lies in a wave-front of the incident light. The light scattered at angle θ from every point on the screen is concentrated at Q in the focal plane of the lens L (Fig. 7.15). A lens is a device which focuses a plane wave-front to a point focus in its focal plane; there is no optical path difference between points on the plane wave-front and the focus (Appendix I). Now all the light scattered from points on a diffracting obstacle in a particular direction, parallel to AA_2 in Fig. 7.15, is brought to a focus at point Q: the path difference between the various rays AQ, BQ, CQ must all therefore result from the different paths AA_1, BB_1, CC_1, since $A_1B_1C_1$ lie in the same wave-front. These paths are clearly

$$\begin{aligned} AA_1 &= LA \sin \theta = x_a \sin \theta, \\ BB_1 &= LB \sin \theta = x_b \sin \theta, \\ CC_1 &= MC \sin \theta = x_c \sin \theta, \end{aligned} \tag{7.16}$$

if the points A, B, C have coordinates (x_a, y_a), etc. in the plane of the screen. Now if we integrate the total amplitude ψ at Q arising from all points such as A, B, C in the obstacle, remembering that each point scatters a wave with amplitude $f(x, y)$ corresponding to the

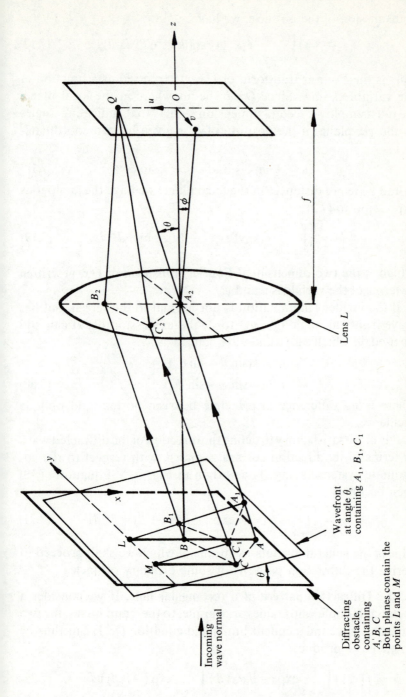

Fig. 7.15. Illustrating Fraunhofer diffraction in two dimensions.

transmission of the obstacle, we have

$$\psi = \iint_{\text{obstacle}} f(x, y) \exp(ikx \sin \theta) \, dx \, dy. \tag{7.17}$$

This is the Fourier transform of $f(x, y)$ expressed as a function of the variable $k \sin \theta$. Since Q can be anywhere in the focal plane, we must employ a second dimension similar to θ, indicating angles in the y-z plane; if the position of Q is given by two coordinates (u, v):

$$u = k \sin \theta \quad \text{and} \quad v = k \sin \phi \tag{7.18}$$

(u and v are *not* distances in the focal plane) we have the analogous expression to (7.3):

$$\psi = \iint_{\text{screen}} f(x, y) \exp\{-i(ux + vy)\} \, dx \, dy, \tag{7.19}$$

which is the two-dimensional Fourier transform of $f(x, y)$ written in terms of the variables u and v.

If the incident illumination is not normal to the screen, but has wave-fronts at angle (θ_1, ϕ_1) to it, the expression (7.19) can still be used, in which case u and v are defined as:

$$\left. \begin{array}{l} u = k(\sin \theta - \sin \theta_1), \\ v = k(\sin \phi - \sin \phi_1). \end{array} \right\} \tag{7.20}$$

There is no difference in principle between normal and oblique incidence.

It is more satisfactory to define the direction of the diffracted wave in terms of its direction cosines, α and β, with respect to the co-ordinate system having A_2 as origin in Fig. 7.15. Equation (7.19) then becomes

$$\psi = \iint_{\text{screen}} f(x, y) \exp\{-ik(\alpha x + \beta y)\} \, dx \, dy. \tag{7.21}$$

This is the general formula by means of which we shall proceed to derive the diffraction patterns of some ordinary obstacles.

7.3.1 Diffraction pattern of a rectangular hole. If we consider a rectangular hole whose sides are parallel to the x and y axes, the two variables have independent limits and equation (7.21) can thus be written as a product

$$\psi = f(x, y) \int_{-a/2}^{a/2} \exp(-ik\alpha x) \, dx \int_{-b/2}^{b/2} \exp(-ik\beta y) \, dy, \tag{7.22}$$

the function $f(x, y)$ being constant (we may take it as unity) over the area of the aperture, of sides a and b. As usual, we take the origin to be at the centre of the aperture so that it represents an even function and thus has a real transform.

Thus
$$\psi = \frac{\sin \tfrac{1}{2}k\alpha a}{\tfrac{1}{2}k\alpha} \cdot \frac{\sin \tfrac{1}{2}k\beta b}{\tfrac{1}{2}k\beta} \qquad (7.23)$$

each factor being similar to that derived for a uniform slit (equation (7.4)).

The diffraction pattern has zeros at values of α and β given by $k\alpha a$ and $k\beta b = 2m\pi$, except for $m = 0$, for which the value of ψ is unity. Thus the zeros lie on lines parallel to the edges of the slit, given by the equations

$$\alpha a = m_1 \lambda \quad \text{and} \quad \beta b = m_2 \lambda. \qquad (7.24)$$

Thus the centre peak (Fig. 7.16), for example, is bounded by lines, given by $m_1 = \pm 1$ and $m_2 = \pm 1$, which form a rectangle whose dimensions are inversely proportional to those of the diffracting aperture.

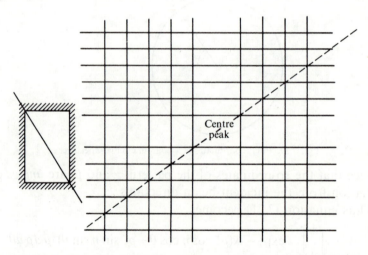

Fig. 7.16. Lines of zero intensity in diffraction pattern of aperture shown at left of diagram. The aperture can be considered as made of two triangles.

It can be seen that the value of ψ at any point (α, β) in the diffraction pattern can be considered as the product of $\psi(\alpha, 0)$ and $\psi(0, \beta)$. In this way it is possible easily to derive the value of ψ from the expression given in § 7.2.1. In particular, the value of ψ along the

diagonal line shown in Fig. 7.16, which is such that $\alpha a = \beta b$, is

$$\psi = ab\frac{\sin^2 \frac{1}{2}k\alpha a}{(\frac{1}{2}k\alpha a)^2} \qquad (7.25)$$

With respect to this line as axis, the aperture can be considered as composed of two triangles placed base to base. This is a physical explanation of the expression for ψ for a tapered slit along the equator of the diffraction pattern (§ 7.3.2).

7.3.2 Diffraction pattern of a circular hole. For a circular hole the integral (7.21) is more difficult to evaluate since the limits are not now independent. It is best to use polar coordinates (Fig. 7.17) for points in the aperture and in the diffraction pattern. If (ρ, θ) are the polar coordinates in the aperture

$$x = \rho \cos \theta \quad \text{and} \quad y = \rho \sin \theta, \qquad (7.26)$$

and if (ζ, η) are the polar coordinates in the diffraction pattern

$$\zeta \cos \eta \equiv \alpha, \qquad \zeta \sin \eta \equiv \beta. \qquad (7.27)$$

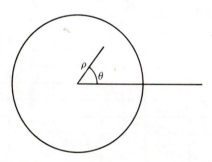

Fig. 7.17. Polar coordinates of a point in circular aperture.

Notice that the co-ordinates of the pattern, α and β, are *angles* of deviation from the incident-beam directions.

Thus equation (7.21) becomes

$$\psi = \int_0^a \int_0^{2\pi} \exp\{-ik(\rho\zeta \cos \eta \cos \theta + \rho\zeta \sin \eta \sin \theta)\}\rho \, d\rho \, d\theta$$

$$= \int_0^a \int_0^{2\pi} \exp\{-ik\rho\zeta \cos(\theta-\eta)\}\rho \, d\rho \, d\theta. \qquad (7.28)$$

To evaluate this expression we can make use of the properties of Bessel functions. A Bessel function $J_n(z)$ of order n can be defined as

$$J_n(z) = \frac{i^{-n}}{2\pi} \int_0^{2\pi} \exp(iz \cos x') \exp(inx') \, dx' \qquad (7.29)$$

(where x' is a dummy variable), whence

$$J_0(z) = \frac{1}{2\pi} \int_0^{2\pi} \exp(iz \cos x') \, dx'. \tag{7.30}$$

If we put $\qquad z = -k\rho\zeta \quad$ and $\quad x' = \theta - \eta$

$$J_0(k\rho\zeta) = \frac{1}{2\pi} \int_0^{2\pi} \exp\{ik\rho\zeta \cos(\theta - \eta)\} \, d\theta. \tag{7.31}$$

Therefore $\qquad \psi = 2\pi \int_0^a J_0(k\rho \zeta)\rho \, d\rho. \tag{7.32}$

Now from a recurrence relation for Bessel functions,

$$xJ_1(x) = \int_0^x x'' J_0(x'') \, dx'', \tag{7.33}$$

if we put

$$x'' = k\zeta\rho \quad \text{and} \quad x = k\zeta a$$

$$k\zeta a J_1(k\zeta a) = \int_0^{k\zeta a} k\zeta\rho J_0(k\zeta\rho) \, dk\zeta\rho$$

$$= k^2\zeta^2 \int_0^a J_0(k\zeta\rho)\rho \, d\rho$$

$$= \frac{k^2\zeta^2}{2\pi} \psi. \tag{7.34}$$

Thus $\qquad \psi = \frac{2\pi a J_1(k\zeta a)}{k\zeta}$

$$= \pi a^2 \left[\frac{2J_1(k\zeta a)}{k\zeta a} \right]. \tag{7.35}$$

Since $k = 2\pi/\lambda$, we have that

$$\psi = \pi a^2 \left[\frac{2J_1(2\pi a\zeta/\lambda)}{2\pi a\zeta/\lambda} \right]. \tag{7.36}$$

The form of the function $2J_1(x)/x$ is interesting. $J_1(x)$ is zero at $x = 0$, but—like $\sin x/x$—the function has a finite value of unity there. It then decreases to zero, becomes negative and continues to oscillate with a gradually decreasing period that tends to a constant (Fig. 7.18(a)).

The diffraction pattern is shown in Fig. 7.18(b). The centre maximum is known as the Airy disc, and it extends to the first zero, which occurs at $x = 3\cdot832$, or $\zeta = 0\cdot61\lambda/a$. We see, therefore, as we

expect, that the radius of the Airy disc is inversely proportional to the radius of the hole.

It should also be noted from equation (7.36) that the amplitude—not the intensity—at the centre of the diffraction pattern is proportional to the *area* of the hole. This odd result makes sense when we realize that the linear dimensions of the diffraction pattern are inversely proportional to those of the hole, and thus that the total intensity in the diffraction pattern is proportional to the area of the hole, as it should be. As the hole varies in size, the intensity at the centre varies proportionately to the square of the area.

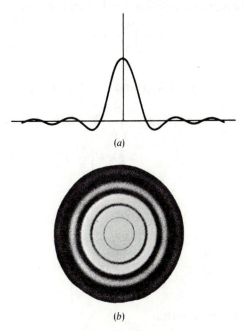

(a)

(b)

Fig. 7.18. (a) Form of function $J_1(\xi)/\xi$ the diametral amplitude distribution in the diffraction pattern of a circular aperture; (b) Fraunhofer diffraction pattern of circular hole.

7.3.3 A crude derivation of the size of the Airy disc.

The derivation of the form of the diffraction pattern in terms of a Bessel function does not really throw any light upon the physics of the problem. If it had not been that Bessel functions appear in other physical problems, the function $J_1(\xi)$ would not have been worth tabulating and we should be no nearer an acceptable solution when the equation (7.36) had been derived. It is, however, possible to see a rough solution in terms of the concepts discussed in §§ 7.2.1–4, where we

derived the diffraction patterns of a uniform slit, a tapered slit and a Gaussian function.

We saw that the diffraction patterns of the first two had side-bands, and that that of the last had not; we therefore deduced that the side-bands were the result of the sudden termination of the diffracting object. We also saw that the positions of the first minimum of the diffraction pattern of the uniform slit and the tapered slit were equal if the areas were equal. Let us extend this idea to a circular hole. If a hole has radius r, the side of a rectangle of equal area, of which the other side is $2r$, must be $\pi r/2$ (Fig. 7.19).

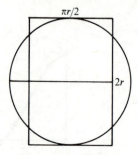

Fig. 7.19. Rectangle and circle of equal area.

The position of the first minimum in the diffraction pattern of this slit is, as we can see from equation (7.4), given by

$$\sin \theta = 2\lambda/\pi r, \tag{7.37}$$

which is a factor of $4/\pi$ greater than is given by a slit of width $2r$. This factor is $1\cdot27$—a fair approximation to the correct value $1\cdot22$.

This idea is included here because, although it cannot be quantitatively justified, it gives some impression of the way a crude approximation can sometimes give a reasonably good value for a physical quantity much more quickly than elaborate mathematics.

7.3.4 Derivation of the diffraction pattern of a circular aperture by Fourier methods.

The mathematics carried out in § 7.3.2 appears to have no physical significance, and thus provides an excellent example of the way in which an extensive knowledge of mathematics can help the physicist. But to those physicists who do not have such an extensive knowledge, and who are not capable of realizing that the solution of equation (7.28) can be found in terms of a Bessel function, the more general approach through Fourier series is more helpful. Every physicist is familiar with a cosine curve!

The general statement in § 7.2 is applicable; we need to find the Fourier transform of a circle. This we can do by the numerical methods described in Appendix V. The circle (Fig. 7.20(*a*)) must be represented by a series of ordinates; the number taken will depend upon the amount of work that the calculator is prepared to do. Each ordinate is taken as the coefficient of a Fourier summation, and the sum of the series should give the required result. The exercise will be left to the reader, but the result for six ordinates, compared with the curve given by the Bessel-function approach, is shown in Fig. 7.20(*b*).

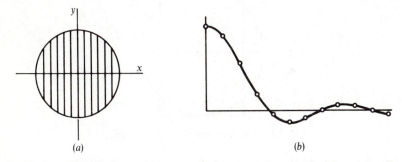

(*a*)   (*b*)

Fig. 7.20. (*a*) Representation of circular aperture by series of ordinates; (*b*) result of Fourier method of derivation of diffraction pattern of circular aperture. The small circles represent the Fourier results and the curve is $J_1(\xi)/\xi$.

7.3.5   Addition of diffraction patterns. The additive property of transforms sometimes enables the diffraction patterns of relatively complicated objects to be derived, if their shapes can be expressed in terms of simpler ones. The separate transforms must be expressed with respect to the same origin, and the real and imaginary parts of the complete transform are then obtained by adding the real parts and the imaginary parts, respectively, of the separate components of the object.

The process is particularly simple if the separate components are centro-symmetric about the same point; then the separate transforms merely add algebraically. For example, it is possible to derive the diffraction pattern of three slits by adding the transform of the two outer ones to that of the inner one; the diffraction pattern of four slits can be obtained by regarding them as two pairs, one with

three times the spacing of the other. Some examples of this sort are included in the problems.

An opaque obstacle can be regarded as giving a negative transform. For example, a thick rectangular frame may be regarded as the difference between the outer rectangle and the inner one. (Note in working out such an example that the height of the central peak of the transform of a rectangle is proportional to the area, as shown in § 7.3.1.) The diffraction pattern of an annular ring is given by the difference between the diffraction patterns of the outer and inner circles; the result has practical implications that will be discussed later in § 9.6.4.

7.3.6 Three-dimensional diffraction. The principles so far enunciated can be extended to three-dimensional objects, although there are extra difficulties involved because all the points in an object cannot lie in a single wave-front of the incident light. In fact, three-dimensional diffraction is not of importance in its own right; it becomes important, in the study of crystals, only when allied to the phenomenon of interference, which forms the next part of this chapter.

7.4 Interference

We have so far considered only the effect of limiting wave-fronts; we now wish to consider the effects occurring when two or more wave-fronts interact. These effects are called interference. We shall concern ourselves only with wave-fronts from identical objects; any other cases are extremely difficult to deal with theoretically and are of little practical importance.

For identical apertures we can make use of the principle of convolution (§ 3.5.2). For example, two similar parallel apertures can be considered as the convolution of one aperture with a pair of δ-functions representing the separation. The interference pattern is therefore the product of the diffraction pattern of one aperture and that of the pair of δ-functions (§ 3.5.4). We can therefore always divide an interference problem into two parts—the derivation of the Fourier transform of the single aperture and that of the set of δ-functions.

The transform of the single aperture is called the diffraction function and that of the set of δ-functions is called the interference function; the complete diffraction pattern is the product of the two (Fig. 7.21).

7.4.1 Interference pattern of two pin-holes. We can regard a pair of pin-holes, with separation a, as the result of convoluting a single pin-hole with a pair of δ-functions. Now we have seen in § 3.4.4 that the transform of two δ-functions is given by

$$\psi(u) = 2\cos(ua/2). \tag{7.38}$$

Thus the diffraction pattern of the two pin-holes is the diffraction pattern of one of them multiplied by a cosinusoidal function, varying in a direction parallel to the separation a. A practical illustration for a hole of finite size is shown in Fig. 7.22.

The zeros of the function occur at values of θ given by

$$ua/2 = (m+\tfrac{1}{2})\pi, \tag{7.39}$$

where m is an integer and $u = k\sin\theta = 2\pi\sin\theta/\lambda$.
Thus

$$\frac{2\pi\sin\theta}{\lambda}\cdot\frac{a}{2} = (m+\tfrac{1}{2})\pi,$$

or
$$a\sin\theta = (m+\tfrac{1}{2})\lambda. \tag{7.40}$$

It will be realized that what we have achieved is a rather round-about method of deriving an expression for Young's fringes (§ 1.2.4). There are, however, several reasons for using this approach: first, we have derived the full expression for the profile of the fringes, not just the spacing; secondly, we have demonstrated that the convolution method gives the correct result for a simple example; and, thirdly, we have prepared the ground for more complicated systems, such as that which follows.

7.4.2 Interference pattern of a linear regular array of pin-holes. An array of pin-holes can be regarded as the convolution of a set of δ-functions with one pin-hole. In § 3.4.4 we showed that, if the δ-functions form a regular one-dimensional lattice with spacing d, the transform is

$$\psi(u) = \sum_{n=1}^{N} \exp(-iund), \tag{7.41}$$

where N is the number of pin-holes. The sum of this geometrical series is

$$\psi(u) = \exp(-iud)\cdot\frac{1-\exp(iuNd)}{1-\exp(iud)}.$$

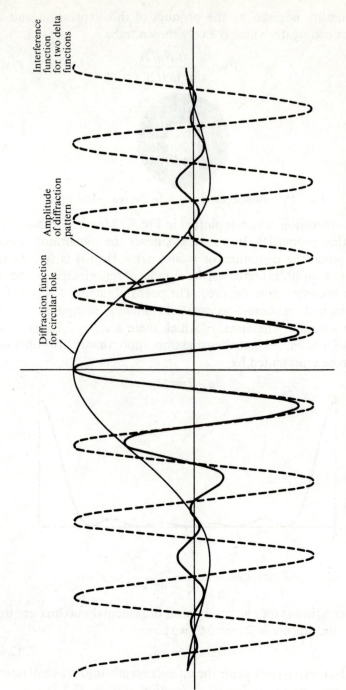

Fig. 7.21. Product of diffraction function and interference function gives amplitude of complete diffraction pattern of two circular holes.

The intensity is given by the product of this expression and its complex conjugate, which is easily shown to be

$$I = \frac{\sin^2(uNd/2)}{\sin^2(ud/2)} \tag{7.42}$$

Fig. 7.22. Fraunhofer diffraction pattern of two circular holes.

This expression, which is plotted in Fig. 7.23 for $N = 6$, has some interesting properties. It is zero whenever the numerator is zero except when the denominator is also zero; then it is N^2. As the number of pin-holes increases, the number of zeros increases and the pattern becomes more detailed. The peaks of intensity N^2—called the principal maxima—become outstanding compared to the smaller subsidiary maxima, of which there are $N-2$ between the principal maxima. In fact, these maxima approximate to δ-functions and can be represented by

$$\delta(u - 2m\pi/d).$$

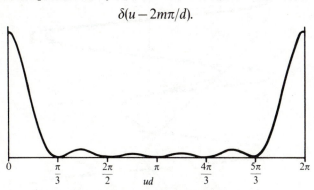

Fig. 7.23. Form of function $\dfrac{\sin^2 uNd/2}{\sin^2 ud/2}$ for $N = 6$.

The conditions for the production of principal maxima are that $ud/2 = m\pi$. Since $u = 2\pi \sin \theta/\lambda$, we have

$$d \sin \theta = m\lambda, \tag{7.43}$$

the well-known equation for the diffraction grating. We shall return to this later, when we discuss diffraction gratings (§ 7.7).

7.4.3 Interference pattern of a lattice of pin-holes. We can now extend our results to a regular array of pin-holes, which we may call a two-dimensional lattice. We can approach this through a set of four pin-holes, at positions $\pm(x_1, y_1) \pm (x_2, y_2)$ (Fig. 7.24). We have to evaluate the expression

$$
\begin{aligned}
\psi &= \sum \exp\{-i(ux+vy)\} \\
&= 2[\cos(ux_1+vy_1)+\cos(ux_2+vy_2)] \\
&= 4\cos\left(u\frac{x_1+x_2}{2}+v\frac{y_1+y_2}{2}\right)\cos\left(u\frac{x_1-x_2}{2}+v\frac{y_1-y_2}{2}\right). \quad (7.44)
\end{aligned}
$$

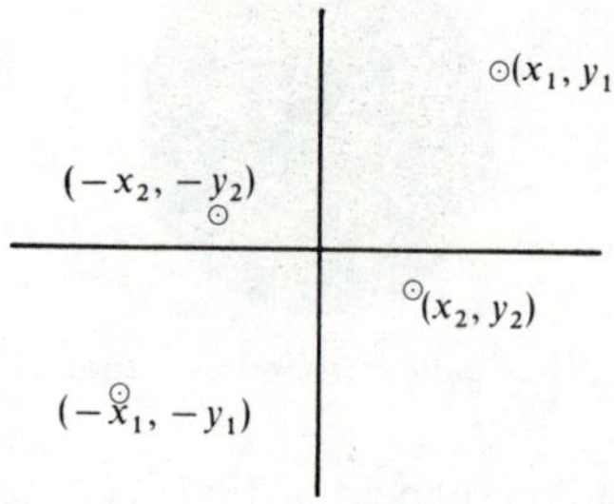

$\circ(x_1, y_1)$

$(-x_2, -y_2)$
$\circ$

$^{\circ}(x_2, y_2)$

$(-x_1, -y_1)$

Fig. 7.24. Two pairs of pin-holes.

As in § 7.4.1, we see that this function has maxima at values of u and v given by the equations

$$
\left.
\begin{aligned}
u\frac{x_1+x_2}{2}+v\frac{y_1+y_2}{2} &= h\pi \\
u\frac{x_1-x_2}{2}+v\frac{y_1-y_2}{2} &= k\pi,
\end{aligned}
\right\} \quad (7.45)
$$

and

where h and k are integers. The interference pattern is therefore the product of two sets of linear fringes, each set being perpendicular to the separation of the pairs of holes (Fig. 7.22). Such fringes are called *crossed fringes* and are shown in Fig. 7.25.

Fig. 7.25. Diffraction pattern of four holes at corners of parallelogram, showing crossed fringes.

By reasoning analogous to that of § 7.4.2, and which we do not therefore need to reproduce here, we can see that as the lattice of pin-holes, with these four points providing the unit cell, increases in extent, the conditions for constructive interference become more precisely defined, and in the limit the interference pattern becomes a collection of points, also arranged on a lattice (Fig. 7.26). This is called the *reciprocal lattice* of the original lattice, because u and v are reciprocally related to the separations of the pairs of holes in Fig. 7.24.

Fig. 7.26. Diffraction pattern (reciprocal lattice) of lattice of holes.

This concept of the reciprocal lattice becomes more important in connexion with three-dimensional interference which we shall discuss in § 7.6.

7.4.4 Interference pattern of two parallel apertures of arbitrary shape. We can regard a pair of similar parallel apertures (Fig. 7.27) as the convolution of a single aperture with two δ-functions. The interference pattern is therefore the product of the diffraction pattern of a single aperture and a set of sinusoidal fringes. This is illustrated in Fig. 7.28, and is one of the most important results in diffraction theory.

 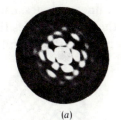 

(a) (b)

Fig. 7.27. Pair of parallel apertures.   Fig. 7.28. Diffraction pattern of Fig. 7.27.

If we have an extended lattice of similar apertures (Fig. 7.29), we may consider it as the convolution of a single aperture by the lattice

translations, *a* and *b*. Then the diffraction pattern (Fig. 7.30) is the product of the diffraction patterns of the single aperture and that of the lattice. In other words, the reciprocal-lattice pattern is multiplied by the diffraction pattern of the unit.

Fig. 7.29. Lattice of parallel apertures.

Fig. 7.30. Diffraction pattern of Fig. 7.29.

If the unit is a circular hole, fairly small with respect to the lattice spacings, then the influence of the diffraction pattern is easily seen (Fig. 7.26); if the pattern is more complicated (Fig. 7.31), such as a set of holes representing a chemical molecule, the result is less clear (Fig. 7.32) but the correspondence is quite definite.

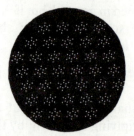

Fig. 7.31. Set of holes representing lattice of chemical molecules.

We may look upon the diffraction pattern in another way. A single unit of Fig. 7.31 gives a particular diffraction pattern (Fig. 7.33); the effect of putting the units on a lattice is, apart from making the pattern stronger, to make the diffraction pattern observable only at the reciprocal-lattice points. This process is called 'sampling' and is particularly important in dealing with diffraction by crystals.

Fig. 7.32. Diffraction pattern of Fig. 7.31.

Fig. 7.33. Diffraction pattern of unit of Fig. 7.31.

If we regard the set of apertures as a two-dimensional diffraction grating, the reciprocal lattice represents the set of orders that it gives. Each reciprocal-lattice point is an order of diffraction, specified now by *two* integers, h and k, instead of one. In three dimensions (§ 7.6) we shall see that *three* integers are needed.

7.4.5 Diffraction by a random collection of parallel apertures.
Suppose that the diffracting object consists of a collection of parallel apertures arranged randomly. We can regard the collection as the convolution of the single aperture with a set of delta functions representing the aperture positions. We therefore require to determine the diffraction pattern of a set of randomly-arranged delta functions.

The relevant expression is

$$\psi = \sum A(u, v) \exp\{-i(ux+vy)\}, \tag{7.46}$$

where (x, y) is the position of any one of the apertures (Fig. 7.34) and A represents the diffraction pattern of a single aperture. This, of course, cannot be summed in general, but if the number of apertures is large we can make some deductions about the form of the intensity distribution; this is given by

$$I = A^2 \sum_{xy} \sum_{x'y'} \exp\{-i(ux+vy)\} \exp\{i(ux'+vy')\}, \tag{7.47}$$

the two sets of co-ordinates indicating that the expression for the intensity involves multiplying each term by the complex conjugate of *all* the others.

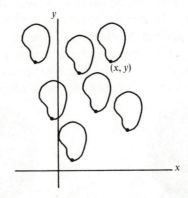

Fig. 7.34. Random set of similar apertures, showing representative points (x, y) on the separate apertures.

Over a large number of apertures we should expect the summation to be zero, since each term can have any value of phase angle. But for the particular case $x = x'$, $y = y'$ the terms are all $+1$, and the total summation is NA^2 where N is the number of apertures. We have therefore arrived at the result that the intensity distribution of the interference pattern of a number of similar parallel apertures is the diffraction pattern of a single aperture multiplied by the number of apertures.

This statement, which appears in many optics textbooks, is not however completely true; we have not considered the other special case, $u = v = 0$. Then (7.46) becomes $\psi = NA$, and the intensity at zero angle of scattering becomes N^2 times that for a single aperture. Thus the complete interference pattern consists of the diffraction pattern of the single aperture, with a much brighter spot at the centre. This is illustrated in Fig. 7.35. If the number of apertures is *very* large, the bright spot would be the only observable feature.

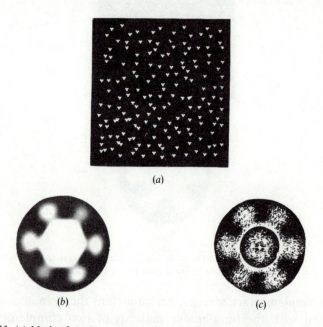

(a)

(b)   (c)

Fig. 7.35. (a) Mask of random parallel apertures; (b) diffraction pattern of one unit of Fig. 7.35a; (c) diffraction pattern of Fig. 7.35a; the centre inset is an under-exposed part of the diffraction pattern showing the strong spot at the centre.

7.4.6 Effects of coherence. It is important to remember that these results are true only if the apertures are coherently illuminated; if

the illumination is incoherent no interference effects will arise. In practice it is difficult to attain either complete coherence or complete incoherence, and the results will depend upon the degree of coherence (§ 8.4.1) that exists in the incident beam. An important intermediate case exists when the mean separation of the apertures —either randomly or regularly arranged—is great enough with respect to the size of the apertures for the illumination to be reasonably coherent over each aperture, but incoherent from one aperture to another. Then the complete diffraction pattern is simply the diffraction pattern of the single aperture multiplied in intensity by the number of apertures. This is illustrated in Fig. 7.36. See also §8.6.2.

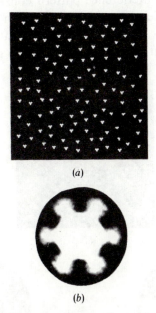

(a)

(b)

Fig. 7.36 (a) Mask of parallel apertures at roughly equal separations; (b) diffraction pattern of Fig. 7.36a with coherence only over individual apertures.

7.4.7 Complementary screens. An important theorem in optics is concerned with the interference patterns of two complementary screens. This theorem was first stated by Babinet and has some practical applications.

Two screens are said to be complementary if they each consist of openings in opaque material, the openings in one corresponding exactly to the opaque parts of the other (Fig. 7.37). Babinet's

theorem says that the interference patterns of two such screens are exactly the same except for a small region near the centre. For example, the pattern of a set of spheres should be the same as that of a set of equally-sized holes similarly arranged. The theorem is illustrated by the diffraction patterns shown in Fig. 7.38.

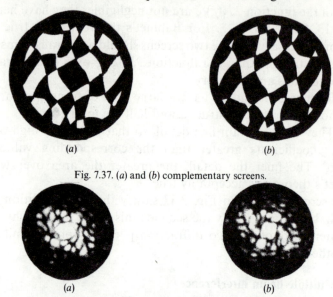

(a)   (b)

Fig. 7.37. (a) and (b) complementary screens.

(a)   (b)

Fig. 7.38. (a) and (b) diffraction patterns of Fig. 7.37.

The theorem can be proved on general grounds. Suppose that the amplitude function for the interference function of two screens are ψ_1 and ψ_2. Now, the interference (or diffraction) function for a combination of apertures can be obtained by adding the separate (complex) functions. If we add ψ_1 and ψ_2 we should obtain the diffraction function for the complete opening. If this is circular, the sum of ψ_1 and ψ_2 is thus the Airy disc pattern, which is confined to a small region round the centre; the rest is blank. Therefore the sum of ψ_1 and ψ_2 must be zero everywhere except over the region of the Airy-disc pattern. The moduli of ψ_1 and ψ_2 must therefore be equal, their phases differing by π. The intensity functions are therefore the same.

This reasoning, however, is deceptively simple; experiments show that Babinet's theorem is not even approximately obeyed for simple screens, and certain extra conditions are necessary to produce results such as those shown in Fig. 7.38.

Screens can be complementary only over a limited area, which is most simply taken to be circular. Babinet's theorem assumes that we can ignore all but the centre part of the diffraction pattern of this circle—that is, that the transform tends to a delta function. This is not so; as we can see from Fig. 7.18(a), the non-origin troughs and peaks of the function $2J_1(\xi)/\xi$ are not negligible: they have heights of -0.13, 0.06, -0.04, ... For Babinet's theorem to be true it is therefore necessary that the two screens should have transforms that are much stronger than the function $2J_1(\xi)/\xi$ over a large range. Two conditions are necessary.

(a) Both screens should have a large area of transmission, and they should therefore obstruct about half the total area.

(b) They must contain fine detail, so that they have high-order Fourier coefficients greater than the corresponding values of $2J_1(\xi)/\xi$. The finer the detail, the greater the area over which Babinet's theorem is acceptably true.

The screens shown in Fig. 7.37 satisfy the first condition well enough, but barely satisfy the second; this is the reason why only the outer parts of the two diffraction patterns appear similar to each other.

7.5 Multiple-beam interference

Two-beam interference provided both an initial verification of the wave theory of light and a method of measuring wavelengths with an accuracy of a few per cent. Because, as we showed in § 7.4.1, the intensity distribution in two-beam interference is sinusoidal, the positions of the maxima and minima cannot be located with any great accuracy. Multiple-beam interference overcomes this difficulty; it is possible to arrange the conditions for reinforcement of several beams to be much more precise than those for the reinforcement of two, and thus very sharp maxima can be obtained.

The first discovery of this sort arose when Fraunhofer was investigating diffraction effects with his newly-invented spectroscope; he wanted to increase the intensity of the pattern that he was observing and decided to use a row of apertures instead of one. To his surprise, he found that he obtained several diffraction patterns. He had invented the diffraction grating.

Other devices for producing multiple beams are now also in use. Chief amongst these are the accurately-made highly-reflecting surfaces which reflect waves backwards and forwards a large

number of times. Such instruments can attain a great precision which makes optics the most highly accurate branch of physics.

7.5.1 Multiple reflexions. We have seen in § 7.1.5 that interference fringes can be obtained with light reflected from the top and bottom of a thin film but obviously there are in practice more than two beams interfering; some light will continue to be reflected within the film as shown in Fig. 7.39. But the two-beam approximation is adequate because after the first reflexion there is a rapid reduction in the amplitude of successive reflexions; therefore the observed fringes are approximately sinusoidal. How can we increase the sharpness?

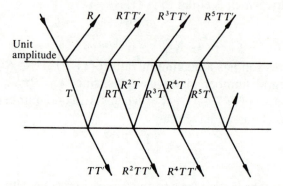

Fig. 7.39. Multiple internal reflexions in a glass plate.

Clearly, we must reduce the rate of fall-off of amplitude; we can, if the film is solid, deposit a highly-reflecting metal such as silver on the surface. The more highly-reflecting the deposit, the sharper the fringes, but the weaker the light that will go to form them. Therefore we must try to see theoretically what practical conditions are to be aimed at.

Fig. 7.39 shows a film at the surfaces of which a fraction R of the incident amplitude is reflected and fractions T, T' transmitted. By reflexion and by transmission we have a succession of waves whose phases change by constant increments in a similar way to the operation of the diffraction grating (§7.4.2). The difference now, however, is that the amplitudes of the waves also vary. We can see, with reference to Fig. 7.39, that the series which we have to sum has reflected terms R, $- RTT'$, $- R^3 TT'$,..., and transmitted terms

TT', $R^2 TT'$, $R^4 TT'$,.... The minus sign in the first set expresses the change of phase that takes place at one of the reflexions (§ 4.3.5).

Let us consider the transmitted light. By comparison with § 7.4.2, we see that the series that we have to sum is

$$TT' \sum_{p=0}^{\infty} R^{2p} \exp(-ikps), \qquad (7.48)$$

where p represents the number of the transmitted beam, and s is the optical path difference between successive reflexions at the same surface. This is a geometric series and its sum to infinity is

$$A = \frac{TT'}{1 - R^2 \exp(-iks)}. \qquad (7.49)$$

The intensity, which is equal to AA^*, is

$$I = \frac{(TT')^2}{1 + R^4 - 2R^2 \cos ks}. \qquad (7.50)$$

This expression has a maximum value of $(TT')^2/(1 - R^2)^2$ when s is an integral number of wavelengths, since $k = 2\pi/\lambda$; it has a minimum value of $(TT'^2)/(1 + R^2)^2$ when s is an odd number of half-wavelengths. Thus we have that

$$\frac{I_{\max}}{I_{\min}} = \left(\frac{1 + R^2}{1 - R^2}\right)^2, \qquad (7.51)$$

which shows that the contrast in the fringes increases with R, as we should expect.

Sharpness is more important than contrast, however, and it is instructive to plot the curves of variation of I with s; s varies with the angle of incidence, being equal to $2\mu t \cos \theta$ (§ 7.1.6), and thus if the film is illuminated with a broad source of monochromatic light fringes of equal inclination (§ 7.1.6) appear.

The forms of the curves of I against s are shown in Fig. 7.40 for several different values of R, and we can see how sharp the fringes become as R increases. But as R increases T and T' decrease, so that we obtain sharpness only at the expense of total intensity. At least, this result applied before the invention of the laser (§ 11.7); since this is capable of amplifying the intensity as the light is transmitted through the medium, we obtain the very considerable sharpness *and* intensity which the laser is capable of producing.

Since, as we can see from Fig. 7.40, we cannot specify the width of a fringe by the positions of neighbouring minima, we must use

another sort of definition—the half-peak width; in general, this is the amount of variation of a parameter between the two values at which the intensity reaches half of its maximum (Fig. 7.41).

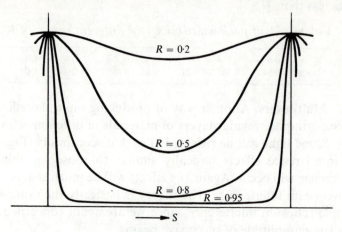

Fig. 7.40. Form of curves of I/I_{max} for different values of R.

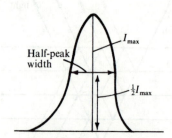

Fig. 7.41. Definition of half-peak width.

For curves of the form given by equation (7.50), we have that

$$\frac{I}{I_{max}} = \frac{1 + R^4 - 2R^2}{1 + R^4 - 2R^2 \cos ks} \tag{7.52}$$

and thus the value s_1 for which this quantity is $\frac{1}{2}$ is given by

$$2(1 + R^4 - 2R^2) = 1 + R^4 - 2R^2 \cos ks_1,$$

which gives

$$\cos ks = -\frac{1 + R^4 - 4R^2}{2R^2}. \tag{7.53}$$

The following table gives the values of $2ks$ (that is $4\pi s/\lambda$) corresponding to different values of R. For comparison it should be noted

that the corresponding value for Young's fringes is 0·50, so that until we attain a value of R greater than 0·6 no improvement in sharpness is obtained. (For values of R less than about 0·5, I does not reach values less than $\frac{1}{2}I_{max}$).

Values of half-peak width $(2ks_1)$ for different values of R

R	0·5	0·6	0·7	0·8	0·9	0·95	0·98
$2ks_1$	0·54	0·36	0·24	0·15	0·07	0·03	0·01

7.5.2 Multilayers. Another way of producing multiple reflexions is to superimpose regular layers of materials of different refractive index. Some light will be reflected at each discontinuity (Fig. 7.42) and interference effects basically similar to those for thin-film interference will occur. Again, the effects will be much sharper than for two-beam interference. The theory is basically the same as for multiple-reflexion interference, since we are again concerned with decreasing amplitude of successive beams.

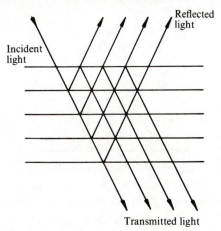

Fig. 7.42. Reflected and transmitted beams from a multilayer. Effects of refraction have been ignored.

Multilayer interference has been applied to an important practical device—the interference filter. The purpose of this and some practical details are given in § 7.9.2.

7.6 Three-dimensional interference

It might be thought that there is no need to extend the subject to three dimensions, since diffraction and interference patterns can

exist only on two-dimensional screens. The need arose, however, when the diffraction of X-rays by crystal was discovered; crystals are three-dimensional diffraction gratings, and if we wish to investigate crystal structures we must make use of three-dimensional diffraction.

A crystal is a collection of atoms. For simplicity let us consider a crystal composed of identical atoms only. From the point of view of X-ray diffraction, since X-rays are scattered only by electrons, a crystal can be considered as a set of atomic positions—delta functions—convoluted by the electron density function for one atom. The atomic positions repeat on a lattice; that is, a small group of atoms—the unit cell—is repeated regularly in three dimensions. Therefore we can regard the crystal as composed of the single group convoluted with the lattice positions. These ideas are illustrated in two dimensions in Fig. 7.43. (It should be noted that the

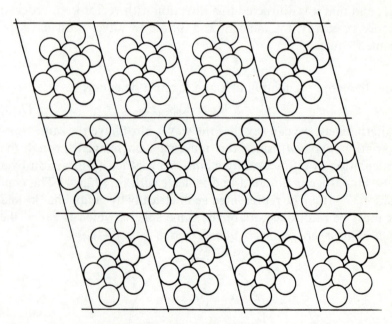

Fig. 7.43. Two-dimensional representation of a crystal structure.

lattice is not synonymous with the structure; it is merely a name for the framework upon which the structure is built.) This would lead to an infinite crystal. We limit it therefore by multiplying the convolution by the shape function—the external boundary.

From the convolution theorem, therefore, we see that the diffraction pattern is the product of the transform of the atom, the transform of the set of delta functions representing the atomic positions in the unit cell, and the transform of the crystal lattice; this product must then be convoluted with the transform of the shape function of the crystal.

This is a *complete* outline of the theory of X-ray diffraction. All that remains is to fill in the details. Unfortunately, this would require several textbooks since each aspect is complicated. We shall deal fully, therefore, only with the third aspect—the transform of the lattice—since this is directly related to the previous parts of this chapter.

7.6.1 Diffraction by a three-dimensional grating. We are concerned with the diffraction pattern produced by a three-dimensional lattice of δ-functions. Suppose we have an incident wave with wave-vector $\mathbf{k}_0$, and that it is diffracted to a direction with vector $\mathbf{k}$. In order to conserve energy, the incident and diffracted waves must have the same frequency

$$\omega = ck$$

and therefore the moduli of $\mathbf{k}$ and $\mathbf{k}_0$ must be equal;

$$|\mathbf{k}| = |\mathbf{k}_0|. \tag{7.54}$$

Alternatively, we can say that the waves must have the same time-variation, $\exp(i\omega t)$, since this must pass unchanged through the calculation of diffraction by a *stationary* lattice. (Diffraction by a moving lattice is different and is dealt with in § 12.4.4.) The condition (7.54) can be represented geometrically by saying that $\mathbf{k}_0$ and $\mathbf{k}$ must be radius-vectors of the same sphere, which is called the *reflecting sphere* or *sphere of observation* (Fig. 7.44).

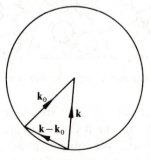

Fig. 7.44. Sphere of observation.

Let us proceed with the calculation of the amplitude of the wave diffracted in the direction of $\mathbf{k}$. The δ-function of the lattice point $\mathbf{r}'$ acts as a secondary source of strength equal to the value of the incident wave at the point,

$$\exp\left[-i(\mathbf{k}_0 \cdot \mathbf{r}')\right], \tag{7.55}$$

and this scatters a wave in the direction $\mathbf{k}$ which can be written as

$$\psi(\mathbf{k}) = \exp\left\{-i[(\mathbf{k}\cdot\mathbf{r}) + \alpha]\right\}, \tag{7.56}$$

where α is, as yet, an arbitrary phase. But this wave originates from $\mathbf{r}'$ as (7.55), so that

$$\exp\left\{-i[\mathbf{k}\cdot\mathbf{r}' + \alpha]\right\} = \exp\left\{-i[\mathbf{k}_0\cdot\mathbf{r}']\right\}. \tag{7.57}$$

Thus

$$\alpha = (\mathbf{k}_0 - \mathbf{k})\cdot\mathbf{r}'$$

and

$$\psi(\mathbf{k}) = \exp\left\{-i[(\mathbf{k}\cdot\mathbf{r}) + (\mathbf{k}_0 - \mathbf{k})\cdot\mathbf{r}']\right\}. \tag{7.58}$$

The total diffracted beam with wave-vector $\mathbf{k}$ is therefore given by integrating (7.58) over all space $\mathbf{r}'$, which for the lattice of δ-functions with unit-cell vectors $\mathbf{a}, \mathbf{b}, \mathbf{c}$ (Fig. 7.45(a))

$$f(r) = \delta(\mathbf{r} - l\mathbf{a} - m\mathbf{b} - n\mathbf{c}) \qquad (l, m, n \text{ integers}) \tag{7.59}$$

reduces to the summation

$$\psi(\mathbf{k}) = e^{-i\mathbf{k}\cdot\mathbf{r}} \sum_{-\infty \to l,m,n \to \infty} \exp\left[-i\{(\mathbf{k}-\mathbf{k}_0)\cdot(l\mathbf{a}+m\mathbf{b}+n\mathbf{c})\}\right]. \tag{7.60}$$

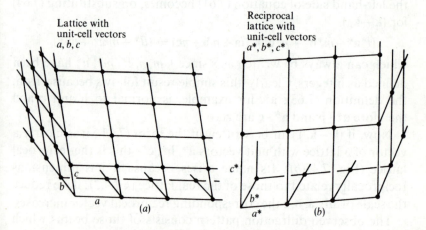

Lattice with unit-cell vectors a, b, c

Reciprocal lattice with unit-cell vectors a^*, b^*, c^*

(a)

(b)

Fig. 7.45. Reciprocal lattice with unit-cell vectors.

The summation is clearly zero unless the phases of all the terms are multiples of 2π:

$$(\mathbf{k}-\mathbf{k}_0)\cdot(l\mathbf{a}+m\mathbf{b}+n\mathbf{c}) = 2\pi s \qquad (s \text{ is an integer}). \tag{7.61}$$

One trivial solution to this equation is

$$\mathbf{k} - \mathbf{k}_0 = 0 \qquad (s = 0), \tag{7.62}$$

which also satisfies (7.54). But there is also a host of other solutions.

7.6.2   Reciprocal lattice. These other solutions to (7.61) can be derived by means of a reciprocal lattice (§ 7.4.3). The vectors between points in the reciprocal lattice are then solutions of (7.61), and in order to represent observable diffracted beams must also satisfy (7.54).

We define three vectors $\mathbf{a}^*$, $\mathbf{b}^*$ and $\mathbf{c}^*$ in terms of the real-lattice constants by means of the equations

$$\left. \begin{aligned} \mathbf{a}^* &= V^{-1}\mathbf{b} \times \mathbf{c}, \\ \mathbf{b}^* &= V^{-1}\mathbf{c} \times \mathbf{a}, \\ \mathbf{c}^* &= V^{-1}\mathbf{a} \times \mathbf{b}, \end{aligned} \right\} \tag{7.63}$$

where V is the volume of the unit cell in real space:

$$V = \mathbf{a} \cdot \mathbf{b} \times \mathbf{c}.$$

It now follows that if $(\mathbf{k} - \mathbf{k}_0)/2\pi$ can be written as the sum of integral multiples of $\mathbf{a}^*$, $\mathbf{b}^*$ and $\mathbf{c}^*$:

$$(\mathbf{k} - \mathbf{k}_0)/2\pi = l^*\mathbf{a}^* + m^*\mathbf{b}^* + n^*\mathbf{c}^* \qquad (l^*, m^*, n^* \text{ are integers}), \tag{7.64}$$

the left-hand side of equation (7.61) becomes, on substituting (7.64) for $(\mathbf{k} - \mathbf{k}_0)$,

$$(l^*\mathbf{a}^* + m^*\mathbf{b}^* + n^*\mathbf{c}^*) \cdot (l\mathbf{a} + m\mathbf{b} + n\mathbf{c}) = (ll^* + mm^* + nn^*),$$

which can always be written as s since l, m, n, l^*, m^*, n^* have been defined as integers. Clearly, this simple result follows because, from the definition (7.63), $\mathbf{a}^*$, for example, is normal to $\mathbf{b}$ and $\mathbf{c}$ and therefore $\mathbf{a}^* \cdot \mathbf{b}$ and $\mathbf{a}^* \cdot \mathbf{c}$ are zero.

Now, if $(\mathbf{k} - \mathbf{k}_0)$ can be written in the form (7.64), it is clearly a vector of a lattice with unit vectors $\mathbf{a}^*$, $\mathbf{b}^*$, $\mathbf{c}^*$; this is the reciprocal lattice (Fig. 7.45(b)). Its name arises because it has dimensions reciprocally related to those of the real lattice (§ 7.4.3); if we reduce the scale of any $\mathbf{a}, \mathbf{b}, \mathbf{c}$ the corresponding reciprocal vector increases.

The observed diffraction pattern consists of those beams which satisfy both (7.54) and (7.64). The two conditions are represented geometrically by

(a) the observation sphere,

(b) the reciprocal lattice,

and where the two intersect, a diffracted beam can occur (Fig. 7.46).

Mathematically, the exact intersection of a sphere and a set of discrete points is negligibly probable; but because neither an exactly parallel beam nor a purely monochromatic source of X-rays exists, diffraction by a crystal does in fact occur. (One important point is the trivial solution (7.62) which ensures that at least one 'diffracted' beam (the undeflected one) exists to carry away the incident energy.) By controlling k_0—the direction of the incident beam—and moving the crystal and recording screen in appropriate ways, it is possible to produce a section of the reciprocal lattice with, say, one index constant. Such a photograph is shown in Fig. 7.47.

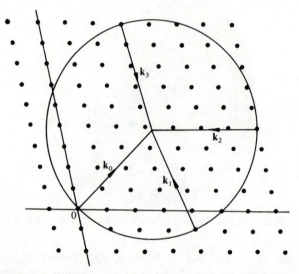

Fig. 7.46. Two-dimensional representation of intersection of sphere of observation with reciprocal lattice, showing directions of incident beam k_0 and of three possible diffracted beams k_1, k_2 and k_3.

7.6.3   Diffraction by a complete crystal.

We can see from Fig. 7.47 that the patterns cover a circular patch; the reason for this is that the atomic scattering factor, or the transform of the electron density, falls off with increasing angle of diffraction, producing negligible intensities at a fairly definite angle. The product of the transform and the reciprocal lattice therefore covers a spherical volume and Fig. 7.47 shows a circular section.

We can see also that the intensities within the observed reciprocal lattice vary in unpredictable ways; some orders of diffraction are

strong and some weak. This variation is a result of multiplying by the transform of the atomic positions.

Finally, the spots in Fig. 7.47 are of finite size. This is caused by the geometry of the apparatus—finite size of X-ray focus, angular divergence of beam and so on. Even if these factors could be allowed for however, the spots would still have a finite size; because of the size of the crystal the complete diffraction pattern convolutes the shape transform of the crystal, and thus each diffraction spot would have a shape corresponding to this transform.

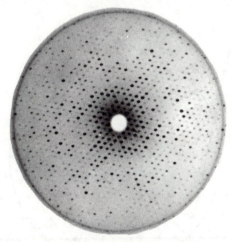

Fig. 7.47. Precession photograph of haemoglobin. (By courtesy of Dr M. F. Perutz.)

This statement is exactly equivalent to the result that each of the principal maxima from a diffraction grating has the same shape. This effect cannot be observed directly in practice, because a crystal small enough to scatter X-rays with appreciable broadening of the orders of diffraction would not scatter enough radiation to be observed. But the broadening can be observed from an agglomeration of small crystals.

7.7 Diffraction gratings

7.7.1 Production of diffraction gratings. Although this book is concerned primarily with general principles and not with practical details, methods of production of diffraction gratings must be briefly described because some of the succeeding theory depends upon acquaintance with them.

The theory outlined in § 7.4.2 is based upon a grating constructed of a large number of slits at regular intervals. This would be impossible to make on the scale of a few wavelengths of light, but fortunately it is not necessary; any repeated discontinuity that will scatter light will suffice. We have seen, for example, in §7.4.4 that the interference pattern of a grating can be expressed as the product of two parts, which we called the interference function and the diffraction function (§ 7.4), and that it was the former that decided the basic properties of the grating. If we use elements other than slits the diffraction function will change, but the essential function of the grating will be unaltered.

The first serious gratings were therefore made by scratching lines on glass or metal with a fine diamond. Rowland used an accurate screw to translate the diamond through a small distance after a short line of two or three centimetres had been ruled. Obviously much is implied in this sentence: the diamond and the flat upon which the grating is to be ruled must be carefully chosen; the screw and flat must be accurately adjusted relatively to each other; the diamond point must not change during the ruling operation; and the temperature of the whole apparatus must be kept constant so that no irregular expansions occur. Thus devices— which are called ruling engines—for ruling gratings are extremely complicated and costly.

Since damage to the diamond point is most likely to happen when it is brought into contact with the ruled surface, a more recent method has been devised that is continuous; the grating is ruled on a cylinder in the same way that a screw is cut on a lathe, and, in fact, the result is a very-fine-pitched screw. To make flat gratings an accurate replica is obtained by depositing a layer of plastic material upon the screw and removing it when it has set; it can then be mounted on an optical flat, and protected by a vacuum-deposited layer of aluminium.

7.7.2   Resolving power. One of the important functions of a diffraction grating is the measurement of the wavelengths of spectral lines; since we know the spacing of the grating we can use equation (7.43) to measure wavelengths absolutely. The first question we must ask about a grating is 'What is the smallest separation between two wavelengths that will result in two separate peaks in the spectrum?' In other words, what is the limit of resolution?

This problem can be considered in terms of equation (7.42), which gives the shapes of the principal and secondary maxima. In § 7.4.2 we showed that there were $N-1$ zero values of the intensity lying between the principal maxima produced by a grating containing N lines. If two different wavelengths are present in the radiation falling on a grating, the intensity functions will add together; we require to find the conditions that decide whether single or double principal maxima are produced. We therefore require to consider in more detail the exact shape of the interference function.

First of all there are the heights of the secondary maxima. It is difficult to find the values precisely but a close approximation can be made by assuming that they lie exactly half-way between the minima. From equation (7.42),

$$I = \frac{\sin^2(uNd/2)}{\sin^2(ud/2)}$$

we can see that the maxima lie close to positions given by

$$\frac{ud}{2} = \left[m + \frac{2p+1}{2N}\right]\pi, \qquad (7.65)$$

where m denotes the principal maxima and p the secondary maxima. If we substitute these values in equation (7.42), we find that

$$I = \frac{\sin^2\{(2p+1)/2\}\pi}{\sin^2\{(2p+1)/2N\}\pi}$$

$$= \frac{1}{\sin^2\{(2p+1)/2N\}\pi}. \qquad (7.66)$$

This result indicates a series of gradually decreasing maxima as p increases from unity. If p is small compared with N, the first subsidiary maxima have heights, relative to the principal maxima, of

$$\left(\frac{2}{3\pi}\right)^2, \quad \left(\frac{2}{5\pi}\right)^2, \quad \left(\frac{2}{7\pi}\right)^2, \dots$$

which are equal to 0·045, 0·016, 0·008, ... These values, particularly the first, are by no means negligible.

We can plot a graph (Fig. 7.48) showing these maxima, and we can find the effect of adding to it another graph on a slightly different scale. If we adopt the Rayleigh criterion for resolution, that the maxima for one curve should lie on the first minimum of

the other, the resultant shows a definite dip (Fig. 7.48). If we reduce the separation to 0·9 of that given by Rayleigh (Fig. 7.49(a)), the dip is still present but at 0·8 (Fig. 7.49(b)) it has almost disappeared. Since resolution is never as clear-cut as the precise equation would seem to indicate, the Rayleigh criterion is seen to be a reasonable one to use.

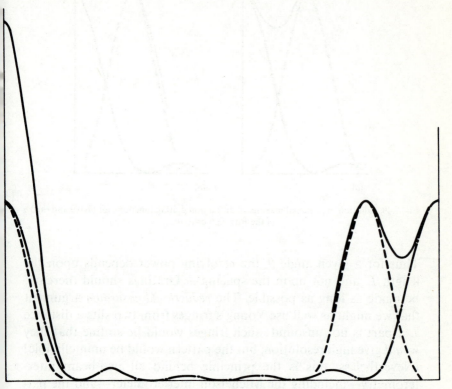

Fig. 7.48. The addition of two diffraction-grating functions (Fig. 7.23) for different wavelengths, showing resolution of the two wavelengths according to the Rayleigh criterion.

If Fig. 7.48 represents the first order, we can see that the limit of resolution, represented by $\delta\lambda/\lambda$, is equal to $1/N$, since $1/N$ is the fractional displacement of the first minimum for the principal maximum. For the order n, the fractional displacement is $1/nN$. We therefore arrive at the result that the resolving power—the reciprocal of the limit of resolution—of a grating is equal to nN.

This result shows that the resolving power obtainable does not depend solely upon the number of lines; if a coarse grating is

made, a higher order can be used and the resolving power may be as good as that of a finer grating. If L is the total length of the grating the spacing is L/N, and the resolving power is equal to

$$Nn = L\sin\theta/\lambda. \qquad (7.67)$$

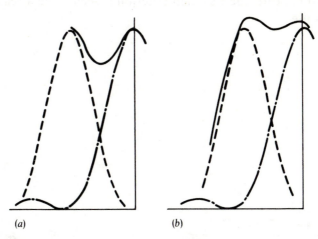

(a)   (b)

Fig. 7.49. Addition of principal maxima of diffraction grating functions for (a) 0·9 and (b) 0·8 of the Rayleigh criterion.

Thus for a given angle θ, the resolving power depends upon the length L, and not upon the spacing d. Gratings should therefore be made as long as possible. The *reductio ad absurdum* argument that we might as well use Young's fringes from two slits a distance L a part is not unsound; such fringes would be so fine that they *would* give high resolution, but the pattern would be unintelligible! (Nevertheless, this is the principle behind all two-beam inter-ferometry—including the Michelson interferometer—and the patterns *can* be interpreted by means of a computer.)

In practice, it is rare for a grating to have a resolving power equal to the theoretical value; errors in ruling are inevitably present and they can affect the performance considerably. With a very good grating and well-corrected (Appendix II) optical components, resolving power of over half the theoretical value can be obtained, but this is unusual.

7.7.3 Effects of periodic errors. There is one type of error that does not affect the resolving power but is nevertheless undesirable for other reasons; this is a periodic error in line position. It can

arise from a poor screw or by a badly designed coupling between the screw and the table carrying the grating (§ 7.7.1), and has the effect of enhancing some of the secondary maxima.

One possible treatment is to consider that an error in line position is repeated every qth line; the true spacing is qd, and therefore q times as many orders will be produced. Most of them will be very weak, but some may be strong enough to be appreciable compared with the main orders. More generally, we may deduce the interference pattern of a grating in which the positions of the lines vary sinusoidally; this is the method that we shall use here.

Let us suppose that the position of the pth line is

$$pd + \varepsilon \sin 2\pi p/q,$$

where ε is small compared with d. Then the series that we require to sum (see equation (7.3)) is

$$\sum_p \exp\{-iu(pd + \varepsilon \sin 2\pi p/q)\}$$
$$= \sum_p [\exp\{-iupd\} \exp\{-iu\varepsilon \sin 2\pi p/q\}]. \tag{7.68}$$

If ε is small compared with d, this summation is equal to

$$\sum_p [\exp\{-iupd\} . \{1 - iu\varepsilon \sin 2\pi p/q\}]. \tag{7.69}$$

The first term represents the ordinary diffraction-grating summation (7.41); the second term, which of course represents the effect of the sinusoidal error, can be written as

$$\sum_p \exp\{-iupd\}\left\{-\frac{u\varepsilon}{2}[\exp(2\pi ip/q) - \exp(-2\pi ip/q)]\right\}$$
$$= \frac{u\varepsilon}{2}\sum_p [\exp(-iupd + 2\pi ip/q) + \exp(-iupd - 2\pi ip/q)]$$
$$= \frac{u\varepsilon}{2}\sum_p \left[\exp\left\{-ip\left(\frac{2\pi \sin \theta d}{\lambda} + \frac{2\pi}{q}\right)\right\} + \exp\left\{-ip\left(\frac{2\pi \sin \theta d}{\lambda} - \frac{2\pi}{q}\right)\right\}\right]$$
$$= -\frac{u\varepsilon}{2}\sum_p \left[\exp\left\{-2\pi ip\left(m + \frac{1}{q}\right)\right\} + \exp\left\{-2\pi ip\left(m - \frac{1}{q}\right)\right\}\right], \tag{7.70}$$

where m is the order of diffraction defined by equation (7.43).

The summations show that, in addition to the principal maxima given by the first part of expression (7.69), there are also maxima at angles given by the two quantities $m + 1/q$ and $m - 1/q$. That is, each order m is flanked by two lines (satellites) at a separation of

$1/q$th of the orders in reciprocal space (Fig. 7.50(a)). The intensities of these lines are proportional to ε^2, and to $\sin^2\theta$; thus they should increase rapidly with order. They should not exist around the zero order.

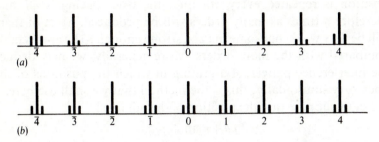

Fig. 7.50. Representations of side-bands from periodically deformed gratings. (a) Result of periodic error in line position; (b) result of periodic error in line intensity.

If ε is not small compared with d, we should have to include further terms in expression (7.70); we should find that further satellites at $2/q$, $3/q$, ... would appear. But since we are concerned here only with basic principles, it is not worth while taking the theory further.

Another type of periodic error can occur if the scratches on the grating are made in the correct places but have periodically varying intensity. The quantity A in equation (7.46) is then no longer a constant, but has to be replaced by such an expression as $A + B \sin 2\pi p/q$. The manipulation of the summation will be left to the reader, who should find that satellites again arise, but they do not now depend upon $\sin\theta$. Thus all the orders, including the zero order, are flanked by satellites (Fig. 7.50(b)).

Further complications can arise if both the effects co-exist; then the satellites become of unequal intensity on each side of the order that they accompany. Effects of this sort might seem to be of purely academic interest, but they can in fact arise in alloys, where heavier and larger atoms may upset the regularity of a matrix of lighter atoms. The effect may not be periodic, but the analysis of the periodic problem provides a useful start for the more general one.

A natural question for a physicist to ask is 'Where does the energy contained in the satellites come from?' The analysis shows no reduction in the intensity of the principal maxima as the satellites appear. The answer is that the principal maxima *are* reduced in

intensity, but the effect is only a second-order one that is not apparent in expressions such as the first term of (7.69). The intensity of the satellites depends upon ε^2, and the effect on the principal maxima is negligible. More detailed analysis would show a reduction, and this would increase with θ.

The effects of periodic error of various types are shown in the illustrations for problem 7; it is hoped that the reader will be able to recognize the diffraction patterns of the diffraction gratings shown.

7.7.4   Effects of random errors. Random errors must, of course, always exist in gratings and with fine gratings they must always be appreciable. A spacing of 6000 lines to the centimetre is equivalent to about 10^4 atomic diameters, so that an error of $0 \cdot 1 \%$ is equal to about only 10 atoms! To consider precisely the effects of such errors would take us into branches of mathematics that would be inappropriate for this book, and so we shall consider the problem in terms of the theory of periodic errors in the last section.

There are two basically different types of error that we have to consider. First, we may assume that we know the *position* of each element, and try to attain it as closely as possible; secondly, we may try to reproduce the correct *spacing*, so that, having ruled one element, we try to rule the next at the correct distance from it.

Let us consider these two possibilities in general terms. In one sense, the errors in the former are limited; if we know the position of one line, we know that the pth line will lie at a distance pd from it within defined limits. In other words, there is no accumulation of error, and the grating retains a degree of perfection over its whole length. We would therefore expect that such a grating would have undiminished resolving power, but that some effects such as decreased intensity and increased background might arise.

The latter type of error is obviously cumulative; if one line is in error the next line must add its error to that one. Nevertheless, there appears to be an inconsistency; can we define the spacing as the total length of the grating divided by $N-1$? Then the final accuracy is as precisely known as for the previous type of error. The answer is that the errors in the intermediate lines will still be cumulative, and to pin down the last line does not materially affect the problem. In general, the error in the position of the pth line increases with p, and this must affect the performance of the

grating. If we accept, for example, that a line is correctly placed if its error is less than a given fraction of d, the region over which the grating is perfect will be less than the length; the resolution is therefore decreased (§ 7.4.2) and so we should find that the lines are broadened. Since the fraction of d that we must choose decreases with order, the length of perfection is less and therefore the broadening increases with order.

These ideas can be dealt with more objectively by using Fourier ideas. We shall not deal with the problem rigorously but shall give an outline of the basic principles. Fig. 7.51(a) gives a plot of a succession of random numbers which we may take to represent the errors in successive lines in a grating. To find the Fourier transform of this set we must multiply the curve successively by sinusoidal curves of different wavelengths; it is clear that there is no favoured wavelength in the set and therefore the Fourier coefficients are all likely to be equal, even down to a wavelength of twice the separation between the points. (For shorter wavelengths the analysis is meaningless.) Thus the Fourier transform is essentially a constant function.

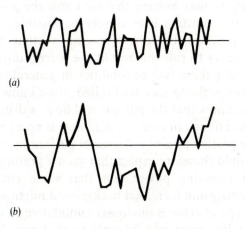

(a)

(b)

Fig. 7.51. (a) Plot of random numbers; (b) plot of cumulative distribution of the same set of random numbers.

Physically, in terms of the treatment in the previous section, this means that between the principal maxima there will be many satellites, filling the whole of the space between the principal maxima, and these form a continuous background. This background increases with θ, but the sharpness of the principal maxima

is not affected. Thus the resolution of the grating is not dependent upon this random error. This rather unsuspected result can be looked at in another way; the grating can be regarded as perfect with each element corresponding to the error function of the separate lines.

There is an important application of these ideas in X-ray diffraction. At ordinary temperatures the atoms are vibrating, with periods much lower than those of pulses of X-rays. Therefore to a coherent pulse of X-rays the atoms appear 'frozen-in' with random displacements; it is well known (§ 12.4.3) that the sharpness of X-ray lines is not affected by temperature, although the intensities of the higher orders are weakened.

For the second type of error—randomly distributed errors in spacings—the result is quite different. Fig. 7.51(b) gives a plot of the cumulative addition of the numbers in Fig. 7.51(a), and this shows that there are now much longer waves present. Thus the Fourier transform will show maxima ordinates close to the origin; in the diffraction pattern, therefore, satellites will be bunched around the principal maxima and so will give the effect of broadened peaks.

This type of error again has a counterpart in X-ray diffraction; when a metal is cold-worked the atoms are displaced in a continuous way, so that the displacement of one atom depends upon its neighbour. A photograph of a conglomeration of small crystals (a powder photograph) shows the effect of broadening of successive orders very well (Fig. 7.52).

(a)

(b)

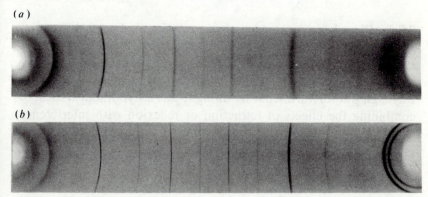

Fig. 7.52. X-ray powder photograph of (a) cold-worked niobium; (b) annealed niobium, showing the broadening due to the imperfections in the lattice. (Photographs kindly supplied by Dr W. J. Kitchingman, Dr W. D. Hoff and Mr D. Wooding.)

The real effect of temperature in crystals is a mixture of these two. The temperature vibrations in a crystal proceed in waves governed by its elastic properties, and often X-ray photographs show sharp spots with symmetrical diffuse backgrounds reaching maximum values around these spots (Fig. 7.53). Analysis of these photographs has provided a means for the determination of the elastic constants of a crystal—a quite unexpected development of X-ray optics!

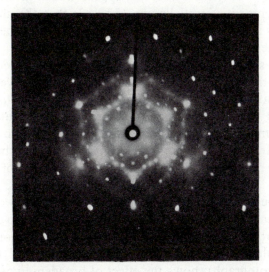

Fig. 7.53. X-ray diffraction photograph of benzil $(C_6H_5CO)_2$. (By courtesy of Professor K. Lonsdale.)

7.7.5 Blazed gratings. Any physicist using ordinary diffraction gratings must be concerned about the great inefficiency of the system that he is using; most of the light is undeviated and very little goes into the order of diffraction that is being used. Lord Rayleigh put forward what he thought was a hypothetical idea, of combining the effects of refraction or reflexion with interference to make a grating in which most of the intensity is concentrated in one particular order. The principle is illustrated by Figs. 7.54 and 7.55. Each element in the transmission grating shown in Fig. 7.54 is made in the form of a prism, of which the angle is such that the deviation produced is equal to the angle of one of the orders of diffraction; correspondingly, in Fig. 7.55 a reflexion grating is shown in which each element is a small mirror.

Such gratings can now be made and are used very considerably. Instead of using any available sharp diamond edge for ruling a grating, a special edge is selected that can make optically-flat cuts at any desired angle. Gratings so made are called 'blazed gratings'. It should be noted that a transmission grating can be blazed only for one particular order and one wavelength, and it can therefore be used only if a particular wavelength is being studied.

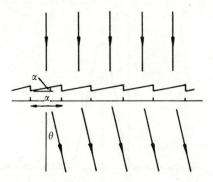

Fig. 7.54. Blazed transmission grating. The value of θ must satisfy the two equations
$$\lambda = d \sin \theta \text{ and } \theta = (\mu - 1)\alpha.$$

A reflexion grating is more versatile, essentially because the process of reflexion is not dependent upon wavelength; a spectrum of a particular order can be scanned by varying the angle of incidence.

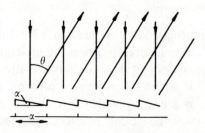

Fig. 7.55. Blazed reflexion grating. The value of θ must satisfy the two equations $\lambda = d \sin \theta$ and $\theta = 2\alpha$.

It is instructive to consider blazing of gratings from the Fourier-transform point of view. Suppose that we make a grating of slits whose width is equal to the spacing of the grating; obviously, we have merely made a large rectangular aperture, whose diffraction

pattern is confined to small angles—the zero order of diffraction. This result arises because the other orders of diffraction must all fall at zero positions on the transform of the single slit. But if we now introduce a phase variation (compare § 7.2.5) along the width of each slit—either by reflexion or transmission—then the transform will be displaced. Blazing consists in displacing the transform so that its peak coincides with a particular order, usually the first (Fig. 7.56).

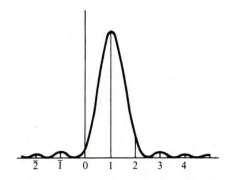

Fig. 7.56. Diffraction function for blazed grating, showing transform displaced so that first order is at the peak.

The matching cannot be exact because the width of each element cannot be exactly equal to the spacing. Moreover, the shift of the transform depends upon the wavelength of the radiation, as we saw in the last paragraph.

7.7.6   Echelon gratings. We have seen in § 7.7.2 that the resolving power does not depend directly upon the spacing of a grating or upon the number of lines; it depends on their product—the length L of the grating. It should therefore be possible to obtain a high resolving power by a grating with relatively few elements of large spacing. At the same time we can, in effect, make use of the 'blazing' technique described in the last section.

Michelson first made such gratings, and now they are in common use. A typical construction is shown in Fig. 7.57; this is a reflexion grating made from precisely equal flat plates, accurately stepped back in sequence. A typical construction would have a step depth of the order of 1 mm and 'treads' somewhat less. Such a grating can give orders of diffraction up to about 2000. Resolving powers

of the order of 10^5 are attainable. Echelon gratings can also be used in transmission.

Echelon gratings are useful in investigating fine structures, but not as primary means of investigating spectra; the various orders of diffraction are very close together, and consequently the patterns obtained are rather complicated. In the visible region, of course, the colours of the lines establish their identities, but in the infra-red, where echelon gratings are of most use, the patterns have to be photographed, and the spectral lines are not easily recognized.

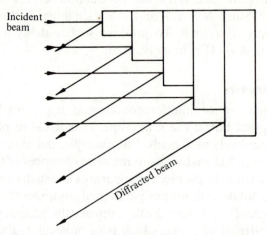

Fig. 7.57. Echelon grating.

7.7.7 Talbot's bands. Talbot's bands were discovered by Fox-Talbot, one of the pioneers of photography; he discovered that, if a glass plate were placed over half the length of a grating, fringes appeared in the spectra. Rather mysteriously, the effect was produced only if the plate were inserted from the high-angle side of the diffraction pattern, and the thickness of the plate was rather critical. Several explanations were put forward; for example, it was suggested that they might be Young's fringes from the two parts of the grating. But this explanation will not fit the facts. The true explanation is rather interesting, and is thought worth while including here although it can hardly be considered as being of fundamental importance.

The accepted explanation can best be expressed in terms of optical paths. For the first order of diffraction, each element produces a wave one wavelength ahead of its neighbour. Thus for a

grating of N lines, the middle element produces a wave $\frac{1}{2}N\lambda$ ahead of the first, and therefore the average wave-train from one half of the grating is this amount ahead of that from the other half. If, therefore, we delay this half by $\frac{1}{2}N\lambda$, the two wave-trains will superpose in time, and so can interfere. Destructive interference takes place for particular λ's, and so fringes appear in the spectrum. If the plate is inserted over the other side of the grating, the two wave-trains will be further separated in time and so interference will not take place.

The optical path necessary for production of the bands is obviously $\frac{1}{2}N\lambda$. Since $N = L/d$ and $\lambda = d \sin \theta$ for the first order, the optical path is $\frac{1}{2}L \sin \theta$. To produce such a delay a plate of thickness $\frac{1}{2}L \sin \theta(\mu - 1)^{-1}$ must be used.

7.8 Interferometers

The phenomenon of interference cleared up a fundamental problem in optics, but at the same time, as is usual in physics, it opened up completely new fields. For example, the experiment of Young's fringes (§ 7.1) enables us to measure distances of the order of 10^{-5} cm. If such a simple piece of apparatus has such capabilities, what could we not do with properly-designed equipment? Multiple-beam interference (§ 7.5) can radically improve the accuracy obtainable, to the order of 10^{-7} cm, which is of molecular dimensions. Diffraction gratings can have resolving power of the order of 10^6 (§ 7.7.2); thus wavelengths differing by 10^{-10} cm can be separated, and measured perhaps to 10^{-11} cm. Thus the simple experiments opened up a world of accuracy, and of measurements of small dimensions, that was unthinkable before the nature of light was understood.

These great steps forward could not, however, be accomplished without careful work and minute attention to experimental detail, resulting in instruments known generally as interferometers. In the next few sections we shall discuss the basic principles of these instruments, giving only the essential minimum of practical detail. Their uses, and the influence that they have had on the rest of physics, will be discussed in Chapter 12.

7.8.1 Rayleigh refractometer. Since the Young's slit experiment produces interference fringes from two separate beams, it should be possible to vary the conditions in one of the beams and to observe

the change in the fringe pattern. Lord Rayleigh, for example, showed that it was possible in this way to compare refractive indices that are very close to unity—for example, the refractive indices of gases.

Since the two beams must be separated over appreciable distances, it is first of all necessary to have a rather large slit separation—of the order of 1 cm; also, the beams must be parallel and so a lens (Fig. 7.58) has to be used to give parallel light from the source. The two beams then pass through separate tubes and are caused to interfere in the focal plane of a second lens.

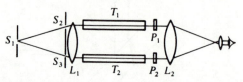

Fig. 7.58. Rayleigh refractometer. S_2 and S_3 are slits illuminated by light from the slit S_1, L_1 is the collimating lens, T_1 and T_2 are the two tubes, P_1 and P_2 are compensating plates which can be tilted in order to adjust the positions of the fringes, L_2 brings the two beams to a focus. (From *The Dictionary of Physics*, Vol. 3, p. 889, Pergamon Press.)

With a large separation of the slits, the fringes are very fine; if the maxima are separated by 5×10^{-5} radians, with a second lens of focal length 20 cm the fringes are only 10^{-3} cm apart. Their measurement therefore requires a high-power microscope, with correspondingly small intensity. Moreover, the centre fringe is not easily identified, and the use of white light as a preliminary is helpful; the centre fringe is white and the others are coloured.

With this instrument Rayleigh was able to show that the refractive index of a gas varied linearly with pressure, and measured refractive indices of gases to about 1 in 10^6. Variations on the apparatus have been made by Jamin, who produced two beams by internal and external reflexion from a glass plate (Fig. 7.59), and by Mach and Zehnder, who used separate reflexions from mirrors (Fig. 7.60). In some ways, the last interferometer is more akin to the Michelson interferometer, which will be described in the next section.

7.8.2 Michelson interferometer. The Michelson interferometer differs from the others so far described in that it produces beams that are not only widely separated but are also directed into

directions at right angles. These two features make it a very versatile instrument and, with its modifications, it is the best known of all the interferometers. It should not be confused with the Michelson stellar interferometer, which is described in § 8.4.4.

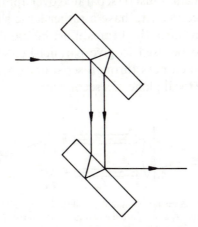

Fig. 7.59. Jamin interferometer.

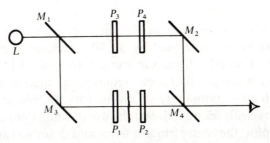

Fig. 7.60. Mach–Zehnder interferometer. L is the source, M_1, M_2, M_3, M_4 are the mirrors, P_1, P_2, P_3, P_4 are plates enclosing spaces in which the optical paths are to be compared. (From *The Dictionary of Physics*, Vol. 3, p. 891, Fig. 4, Pergamon Press.)

The principle is illustrated in essence in Fig. 7.61. Light enters from the left and is partly reflected and partly transmitted by the semi-silvered mirror S; the two beams are reflected from the mirror M_1 and M_2, and the resultant interference fringes are observed by the eye at E. Since the rays reflected from M_1 have to pass through three thicknesses of the mirror S, whereas those reflected from M_2 have to pass through only one (Fig. 7.61), an extra plate at P is inserted to give equality between the two paths. This plate is needed because glass is dispersive and so only by having the same amount

of the same glass in both beams can the optical paths be made equal at *all* wavelengths. This compensating plate must be of the same thickness as S and placed at the same angle.

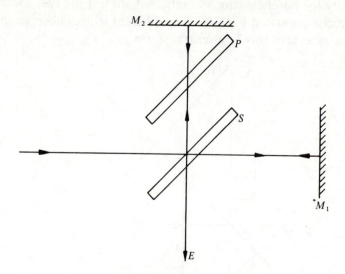

Fig. 7.61. Michelson interferometer.

With the Michelson interferometer many different sorts of fringes can be obtained—straight, curved, or completely circular, in monochromatic or white light. These can all be understood in terms of a single theory if we regard the problem as a three-dimensional one, the different sorts of fringes resulting from looking at the same pattern from different directions.

The source must be a broad one, but we can simplify the understanding of the interferometer by considering one 'ray' at a time, coming from one point on the source. If we ignore the finite thickness of the components, we see from Fig. 7.62 that O has an image in S at O_s and an image at O_2 in M_2. O_s has an image O_{s1} in M_1, and O_2 has an image O_{2s} in S. O_{s1} and O_{2s} are the two virtual sources that give rise to interference.

It can easily be seen that O_{s1} and O_{2s} can be brought as closely together as we require. Small adjustments in M_1 and M_2 can change their relative positions, and it is even possible to have one behind the other. The different sorts of fringes arise from the relative positions of O_{s1} and O_{2s}, and the scales of the fringes depend upon their separation.

All these facts can be understood by considering the Fourier transform (§ 3.4.1) of the two points; this is a set of planar sinusoidal fringes, represented with artificial limits (they would extend to infinity for purely monochromatic radiation if the two sources were precise points) in Fig. 7.63. The different fringes observed are different aspects of this Fourier transform.

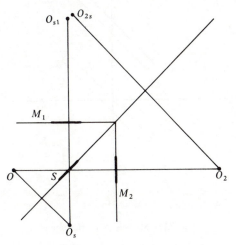

Fig. 7.62. Principle of Michelson interferometer.

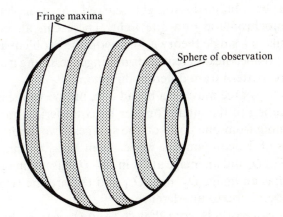

Fig. 7.63. Representation of Fourier transform of two points—plane sinusoidal fringes—cutting sphere of observation.

To understand this statement we make use of the concepts introduced in § 7.6.1—particularly the sphere of observation. Now, however, we are dealing with coherent *sources* and not

scatterers so that their phase difference is always zero and does not depend upon an incident beam $\mathbf{k}_0$. The only vector that is involved is $\mathbf{k}$, and this, being of constant length $2\pi/\lambda$, describes a sphere with the origin of reciprocal space at its centre. The sphere of observation therefore penetrates the Fourier transform, with its centre on a maximum (Fig. 7.63).

As the points O_{s1} and O_{2s} become closer, the scale of the fringes becomes larger, and as the disposition of the points changes the transform rotates into different orientations. Fig. 7.64 shows how different types of fringes arise. If white light is used, the sphere of observation must be considered as having a finite thickness; as we can see from Fig. 7.64(d), the centre fringe only is sharp and the others are coloured and soon merge together. Such coloured fringes are the best way of identifying the zero-order interference.

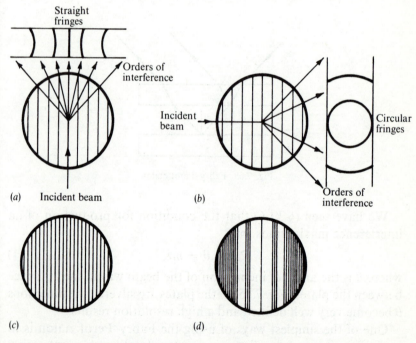

Fig. 7.64. Different types of fringes from the Michelson interferometer: (a) and (b) show how straight and circular fringes are produced, and obviously intermediate types of fringes are possible; (c) shows how the fringes become finer as O_{s1} and O_{2s} move further apart; (d) shows how broadened fringes are produced if a range of wavelengths (e.g. white light) is used.

So far we have considered only point O on the source, and it might be thought that we have shown that fringes are produced from this one point. In fact, what we have shown is that different intensities are produced in different directions of **k**; and each point on the observer's retina, or on a photographic plate, corresponds to such a direction. But the ray from O to the eye or camera lens also selects a well-defined direction, and so what one sees is an image of the source with each point giving its own contribution to the interference pattern. The fringes are therefore localized in space (§ 7.1.7) in the image of the source produced by reflexion in S and M_1 or M_2 and S.

7.8.3 Fabry–Pérot plate. In complete contrast to the Michelson interferometer is the Fabry–Pérot plate or etalon which, instead of versatility, aims only at high resolution. It achieves this by using multiple reflexion (§ 7.5.1). The interferometer consists simply of two optically worked, precisely parallel, glass plates (Fig. 7.65).

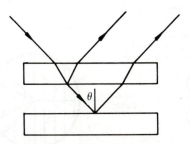

Fig. 7.65. Fabry–Pérot etalon.

We have seen (§ 7.1.6) that the condition for production of an interference maximum is that

$$2t \cos \theta = m\lambda, \qquad (7.71)$$

where θ is the angle of inclination of the beam within the air space between the plates (Fig. 7.65). If the plates are silvered the directions θ become very well defined and a high resolution results.

One of the simplest ways of using the Fabry–Pérot etalon is to insert it in front of the dispersing system (grating or prisms) on a spectrometer (Fig. 7.66). The spectral lines are then crossed by circular fringes that satisfy equation (7.71) and thus any fine structure becomes evident. If only one wavelength is present, only one set

of fringes is observed, but if there are two or more wavelengths— too close together of course to be resolved by the dispersing system—more complicated groupings are observed, as shown diagrammatically in Fig. 7.67.

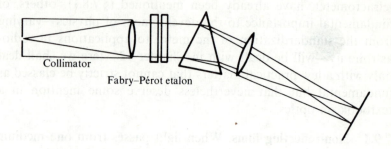

Collimator

Fabry–Pérot etalon

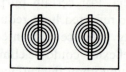

Photographic plate showing two spectral lines crossed by circular fringes

Fig. 7.66. Use of Fabry–Pérot etalon for high-resolution spectroscopy.

Fig. 7.67. Diagrammatic representation of pattern produced by Fabry–Pérot etalon for a close doublet. The faint lines represent the images of the edges of the slit of the spectrometer.

7.9 Some practical applications

Interferometry is one of the most useful branches of optics, in both pure and applied physics. Some applications, such as the determination of the refractive indices of gases by the Rayleigh refractometer, have already been mentioned (§ 7.8.1); others, of fundamental importance to the development of physics—varying from the standardization of the metre to applications in radio-astronomy—will be dealt with in Chapter 12. Here we shall deal only with a few practical matters that cannot strictly be classed as fundamental but that nevertheless deserve some mention in a textbook on optics.

7.9.1 Non-reflecting films.

When light passes from one medium to another, a certain amount of light is reflected, depending upon the refractive indices of the two media. For certain purposes— notably in image formation, where the reflected light reduces the intensity of the image and also may produce unwanted light elsewhere—it would be helpful if the reflexion could be eliminated. This can be done fairly well by depositing upon the surface a thin layer with appropriate refractive index and of a thickness such that it produces reflected beams from its two surfaces that are roughly equal in intensity and have a phase difference of π.

There is obviously no general solution that is appropriate to all wavelengths and all angles of incidence. We therefore concentrate upon the middle of the visible spectrum—say, 5500 Å—and normal incidence. To produce beams of equal intensity, equation (4.56) shows that the refractive index of the film must be $\sqrt{\mu_1\mu_2}$, where μ_1 and μ_2 are refractive indices of the two media. For a glass lens in air we therefore require a medium of refraction index of about 1·25. Its optical thickness must be $\lambda/4$—about 1600 Å—and its actual thickness about 1300 Å.

It is impossible to find a material that has the required general properties—hardness, stability, adhesion to glass—with such a low refractive index, and materials such as magnesium fluoride ($\mu = 1\cdot38$) are the best that can be obtained.

The process of depositing such a film is called 'blooming'; it is an example of impedance-matching (§ 4.2.5). It is carried out by evaporating the material *in vacuo* on to the glass surface, continuing until a characteristic purple coloration is seen; this colour

results from the combination of blue and red resulting from the elimination of the middle of the spectrum.

7.9.2   Interference filters. We often require in optics to isolate one particular line from a spectrum—in other words, to transmit the given line with as little decrease in intensity as possible while reducing the intensities of all the other lines to zero. This operation can be carried out approximately with coloured filters, but they are not very efficient and their production for any particular wavelength is not very easy to carry out.

A more precise filter can be made by depositing alternate layers of material on a glass surface to produce the multilayer effect described in § 7.5.2; we saw that the reflected light from such a device consisted of a general background with dark lines superposed upon it. The transmitted light is the opposite; it is zero except around specific wavelengths that satisfy the equation (7.1). An interference filter is designed so that one of the transmitted wavelengths coincides with the required emission line from the source. The other transmitted wavelengths can be put into the infra-red and the ultraviolet.

In practice, interference filters are made by vacuum deposition of successive films of optical thickness $\lambda/4$ of material such as zinc sulphide and sodium aluminium fluoride (cryolite) on to a glass substrate (Fig. 7.68). It is better to use materials of this sort than metals such as silver because of the lower absorption that they produce.

Fig. 7.68. Interference filter consisting of alternate layers of materials of different refractive index.

7.9.3   Twyman–Green interferometer. The Michelson interferometer can be adapted for use as a testing device for optical components. Two lenses L_1 and L_2 (Fig. 7.69) are inserted in the position shown so that the incident light is parallel and the emergent light is observed in only one direction. Under these conditions, as we have seen in § 7.8.2, only a uniform field will be seen in the ordinary Michelson interferometer. If an optical component such as

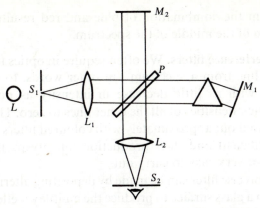

Fig. 7.69. Twyman–Green interferometer. (From *The Dictionary of Physics*, Vol. 3, p. 891, Fig. 3, Pergamon Press.)

a prism is introduced, the field will remain uniform if the prism is perfect, but otherwise defects will show up as variations of light intensity. Usually, however, the instrument is adjusted to give a moderate number of fringes and the defects of the prism show up as a bending of the fringes.

CHAPTER 8

COHERENCE

8.1 Introduction: coherence

The coherence of a wave describes the accuracy with which it can be represented by a pure sine wave. So far we have discussed optical effects in terms of waves whose wave number k and frequency ω can be exactly defined; in this chapter we intend to investigate the way in which uncertainties and small fluctuations in k and ω can affect the observations in optical experiments. Waves which appear to be pure sine waves if they are observed only in a limited space or for a limited period of time are called *partially coherent waves*, and we shall devote a considerable amount of our effort in this chapter to developing measures of the deviations of such impure waves from their pure counterparts. These measures of the coherence properties of the waves are functions of both time and space; we shall therefore define two distinctly different criteria of coherence. The first criterion expresses the correlation to be expected between a wave now and a certain time later; the other between here and a certain distance away. The two measures are in general completely unconnected—as is illustrated schematically by Fig. 8.1. Then we shall look at the effects that an extended partially coherent source (using the latter criterion above) has on the simplest of all interference systems, Young's double-slit experiment, and see how such an experiment is used in the Michelson stellar interferometer and the Brown–Twiss interferometer for measurements of the angular diameter of stars. In a short final section we shall very briefly introduce the growing subject of photon statistics. We shall show that the simple ideas introduced in the earlier sections, about the way in which partially coherent waves are produced, are somewhat inaccurate, and that a more complicated approach—on which we shall not elaborate—is needed.

8.2 Wave-trains of finite length

Electromagnetic waves are quantized in energy, and are generally emitted in units of one quantum on random occasions. The wave can therefore exist only for a finite time before the energy of the

quantum disappears in some way. The quantum is thus emitted as a finite wave-train. Except in high-intensity devices like lasers (§ 11.7), the emission of the next quantum is an event which is uncorrelated with its predecessor and there is therefore no phase relation between them. The quantity that we can define is the average number N of quanta emitted per second; the distribution of emissions with time will then follow a Poisson distribution (the standard deviation is therefore $N^{\frac{1}{2}}$) resembling emissions from a radioactive nucleus. For the moment this description of wave-packet emission will be adequate for our purpose, although later on (§ 8.7) we shall consider the statistics of photon emission more

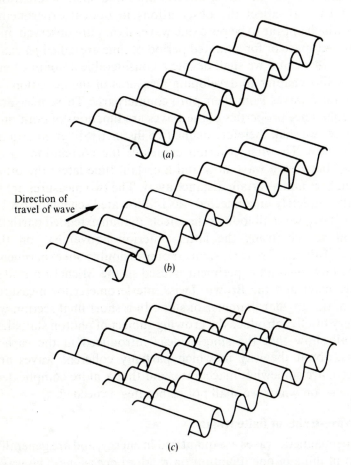

Direction of
travel of wave

Fig. 8.1. Partially coherent waves: (a) perfectly coherent wave; (b) wave with space-coherence only; (c) wave with time-coherence only.

carefully and show that the description is true only in the limit of very low intensities.

8.2.1   Emission of a single wave-packet.

The basic unit of emission, then, is a finite wave-train which we can define as having frequency ω_0 and lasting for a time 2τ. This can be described by its Fourier transform (§ 3.4.1) as composed of a number of waves of frequency approximately ω_0 and lying in the range $(\omega_0 \pm 1/\tau)$ (Fig. 8.2).

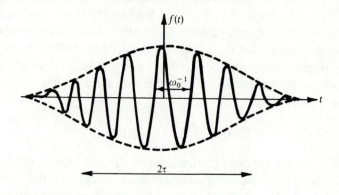

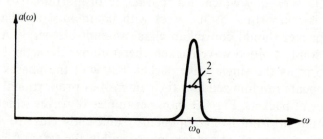

Fig. 8.2. Wave-packet of frequency ω_0 and half-width τ, and its Fourier transform.

Clearly the longer the wave-train exists, the closer is the approximation to a simple harmonic wave, and the smaller the spread of its component frequencies about ω_0. The relation between the phases of the various components is exactly defined. If we write the wave-train as

$$f(t) = A \exp\left(i\omega_0 t\right) \exp\left(\frac{-t^2}{2\tau^2}\right),$$

officially described as a *Gaussian wave-packet of frequency ω_0 and half-width τ*, we reach a Fourier transform:

$$a(\omega) = B \exp\left(\frac{-\tau^2(\omega_0 - \omega)^2}{2}\right),$$

which is a Gaussian centred on $\omega = \omega_0$ and half-width $1/\tau$ (hence the *range* $\omega_0 \pm 1/\tau$). All the components are real and therefore in phase at time $t = 0$, the centre point of the original wave-packet.

8.2.2   A series of wave-packets emitted at random. Such are the properties of a single wave-packet. Suppose that we now consider a random series of such packets. Each one is built up from waves of the same frequencies in the same proportions, but each requires them to be in phase at its own centre point. The total amplitude of component ω that is needed for a random series of n wave-packets is thus

$$C(\omega) = a(\omega) \sum_{m=1}^{n} \exp(i\omega t_m),$$

where t_m is the random centre time of the mth wave-packet. The summation involved is a random-walk problem; the result is therefore of indeterminate phase, and amplitude proportional to $n^{\frac{1}{2}}$ for large n. It follows that the intensity at frequency ω in the range $\omega \to \omega + d\omega$ which is $C^2(\omega)\,d\omega$, is proportional to n; the result is comforting, as it agrees with common-sense that each wave-packet should convey an equal amount of energy. A series of randomly emitted wave-packets therefore has the same Fourier transform as the single wave-packet, but with the phases of the components randomized and their intensities proportional to the number of packets. Fig. 8.3 shows examples of waves which have been built up from five components (sufficiently close to infinity for these purposes!) of random phase within the stated frequency ranges. The structure, consisting of a random series of wave-groups whose lengths are inversely proportional to the range of frequencies used, is clearly visible; it is obvious that some of the groups overlap.

8.2.3   White light. One limiting case is of interest; if we make the wave-packet shorter, so that it eventually becomes a δ-function pulse, the function $a(\omega)$ becomes a constant, independent of ω. Thus a series of δ-pulses emitted at random times transforms to a set of all frequencies occurring with random phases. This is white

light; it contains all frequencies in equal amounts, and they are again completely uncorrelated in phase.

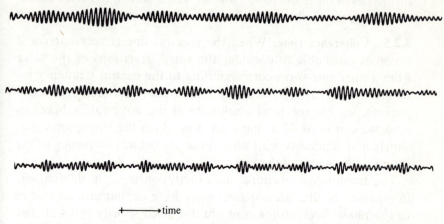

Fig. 8.3. Three impure sine waves, showing the amplitude fluctuations resulting from a spread in component frequencies. Each is generated from five components randomly distributed in the range $\pm\frac{1}{2}\varepsilon$ about ω_0, where the values of ε/ω_0 are as follows: (a) 0·08, leading to groups containing about $1/0·08 = 12$ waves; (b) 0·16, leading to groups containing about 6 waves; (c) 0·25, leading to groups containing about 4 waves. As can be seen, the definition of a group containing so few waves is very hazy.

8.2.4 Measures of coherence.

The preceding discussion has provided two descriptions of light as wave-trains. One of them is in terms of the individual wave-packets and the other is its Fourier transform, the spectral analysis. Which description we use is entirely dependent on the questions asked about light; in the example of white light the interference patterns produced can best be described in terms of superimposition of interference patterns from each wavelength component (we use the spectral analysis), whereas an experiment like Talbot's bands (§ 7.7.7) is most easily understood as the result of a random series of δ-pulses. For *mono-chromatic* light, as the term is usually understood, the dual-description question still arises. Such light, used for ordinary optical experiments, usually consists of a single spectral line or unresolved multiplet; an example is the krypton yellow line $\lambda = 5570$ Å which has a half-width of 0·003 Å. This description, of course, is the spectral description; its Fourier transform is the actual wave-structure, which therefore consists of a random series of wave-trains each of length $5570 \div 0·003 \doteq 2 \times 10^6$ waves, therefore lasting for a time of order 4×10^{-9} s at one point and having length

about 120 cm. For many experiments it turns out that the description in terms of wave-packets conveys a clearer picture of the properties of the disturbance, and we shall proceed to derive one or two measures of what are called the coherence properties.

8.2.5   Coherence time. When the spectral line is very narrow it becomes justifiable to consider the small deviations of the wave from a pure sine-wave corresponding to the central frequency ω_0 in the line. If there is considerable overlap between the wave-packets, so that the total amplitude of the wave rarely becomes zero, we can think of a single wave in which the frequency varies slowly and randomly with time about the central frequency to the extent of the width of the line.

The amplitude is, of course, not exactly constant; the fluctuations in intensity of this 'almost-sine' wave have similar characteristics to the phase fluctuations, and are discussed shortly (§ 8.4.5). The examples in Fig. 8.3 show the amplitude variations quite clearly. Over a short interval of time T, considerably less than the duration of one wave-packet, the wave will appear to be a pure sine-wave of frequency ω_0, since in that short time we cannot measure the frequency accurately enough to determine it to better than

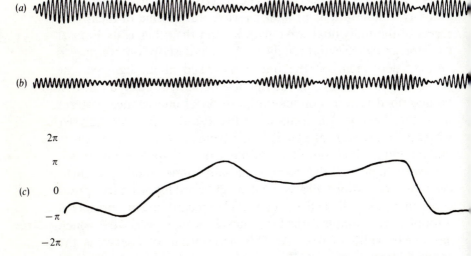

Fig. 8.4. Correlation between two impure sine waves. (a) Section of a sine wave with frequency components over a range of about $\pm 0\cdot 04$ about the mean frequency (Fig. 8.3a); (b) a later section of the same wave; (c) phase difference between the two samples. Notice that the phase changes by about π in a time approximately the period of a wavegroup. Phase and amplitude fluctuations are thus related.

$\delta\omega = 1/T$. But if T is made long enough we eventually discover that the phase difference between the ends has wandered by more than one cycle from that corresponding to ω_0 (i.e. from $\omega_0 T$) and any correlation between the phases at the beginning and end of the interval vanishes. The time T at which this happens is clearly the time for which the wave-trains exist, since the two ends of the interval will then almost certainly lie in different wave-packets which have completely arbitrary phases. Fig. 8.4 shows this effect. We have taken a wave generated in the same way as those of Fig. 8.3 and compared two consecutive sections of it (a and b). The phase difference between the two curves is plotted in the lowest curve (c) and it is clear that the phase difference wanders by a substantial amount (of the order of π) in the length of one wave-group.

To describe this mathematically we define a correlation coefficient $\gamma(\tau)$ between the waves at t and $(t+\tau)$ averaged over all t and normalized to be unity for a pure sine-wave. The complex form of it is designed to eliminate the phase lag $\omega_0\tau$ which would be present for the pure wave:

$$\gamma(\tau) = \left[\frac{\left|\int_0^\infty f(t)f^*(t+\tau)\,dt\right|}{\left\{\int_0^\infty f(t)f^*(t)\,dt\right\}}\right] = \frac{|c(\tau)|}{|c(0)|}. \qquad (8.1)$$

The quantity $c(\tau)$ as defined above is the 'self-correlation function' which does have an $\exp(i\omega_0\tau)$ dependence at small τ. The time τ_c, which is the length of time for which the average wave-packet exists, is the value of τ at which $\gamma(\tau)$ becomes zero and is called the *coherence time*; after τ_c there is no correlation between the phases of the waves at the ends of the interval. The corresponding train-length $c\tau_c$ is the *coherence length* of the light.

8.2.6   The Wiener–Khinchin theorem. The Fourier transform of the self-correlation function $c(\tau)$ is easily calculated by using the convolution theorem (see § 3.5.3) to be the intensity $|a(\omega)|^2$ of the Fourier components of the original wave, known as the power spectrum. This does in fact contain complete information about the light, as the phases of the components are all random. It follows that the self-correlation function (and therefore $\gamma(\tau)$) contains complete information about the properties of the light, and we should therefore aim to express all results peculiar to experiments on partially-coherent light in terms of the correlation coefficient. The

Wiener–Khinchin theorem states that the 'power spectrum is the Fourier transform of the self-correlation function' and has many applications in electronics and electromagnetic theory. As $c(\tau)$ has the form shown in Fig. 8.5(a), it follows that the power spectrum has the form Fig. 8.5(b), which is observed through a spectrometer.

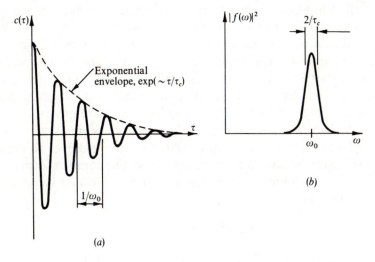

(a)

(b)

Fig. 8.5. Illustrating the Wiener–Khinchin theorem for a wave-group of coherence time τ_c. (a) The correlation-function $c(\tau)$; (b) the power spectrum $|a(\omega)|^2$.

8.3 Physical origins of line-widths

So far we have introduced the width of a spectral line, or the finiteness of a wave-train, simply as a parameter to be reckoned with; now we shall enquire briefly into the physical causes of line-broadening. A spectral line has its origin in a quantum transition in which an atom changes its stationary state from level A to level B, of energies E_A and E_B; a photon, or wave-packet, of total energy $E_A - E_B$ is emitted at the same time. The causes of line-width can be either processes to do with the actual emission, or details of the state of the atom while the emission process is occurring, such as its velocity.

8.3.1 Pressure and temperature effects. The second cause can be treated quite easily. If the atom of mass m has a velocity along the line of sight while the transition is taking place, the spectral line will appear shifted by the Doppler effect. The distribution of

velocities along a particular axis (x) in a perfect gas is in fact Gaussian

$$f(v_x)\, dv_x = C \exp\left(\frac{-mv_x^2}{2kT}\right) dv_x$$

and the Doppler shift in the observed frequency is $v_x/c = \delta\lambda/\lambda$ so that

$$f(\lambda)\, d\lambda = C' \exp\left(\frac{-m(\delta\lambda)^2 c^2}{2\lambda^2 kT}\right) d\lambda,$$

giving a half-width for the line of $(\lambda^2 kT/mc^2)^{\frac{1}{2}}$. As an example we can take the krypton line mentioned previously for which $\lambda = 5\cdot6 \times 10^{-5}$ cm, $m = 84 \times 1\cdot7 \times 10^{-24}$ g, $T = 80°K$, giving a half-width of $1\cdot6 \times 10^{-11}$ cm $\simeq 0\cdot002$ Å. This agrees reasonably with the observed half-width of $0\cdot003$ Å.

The above is the effect of temperature and is calculated for a perfect gas. Gases suffer collisions between molecules, and if such a collision occurs while emission of a wave-train is in progress it is reasonable to expect that the phase of the train will be altered in an unpredictable manner, equivalent to a premature ending of the train. If the atoms were emitting continuously this would break the continuous wave into wave trains of mean duration t_c, the mean interval between collision, and lead to a half-width of

$$\frac{\delta\lambda}{\lambda} = \frac{2\pi}{\omega t_c}; \qquad \delta\lambda = \frac{\lambda^2}{ct_c}.$$

Admittedly, the distribution will be Poisson, since collisions are random, but this is close enough to Gaussian if the collision rate is large. At low pressure the mean free time t_c may be determined by the dimensions of the apparatus; at higher pressures it is dependent on the collision rate with other molecules. In air at N.T.P. the mean free time is of the order of 5×10^{-9} s, leading to a half-width $\delta\lambda \simeq 10^{-10}$ cm $= 0\cdot01$ Å. The effect can therefore be quite considerable.

A further pressure effect that is observable under special conditions occurs when the excited atoms are in a very high quantum state. The electronic wave-function then extends over a very large region which may include several other atoms, the number depending on the pressure. This number will fluctuate, and, as there will be an interaction between the electron and the foreign atoms, the

energy of the electronic level will fluctuate too. The effect has been calculated and fits experimental determinations of pressure effects in highly-excited alkali vapours.

8.3.2 Natural widths. If neither pressure nor temperature effects were present emission lines would still not be absolutely sharp; from the quantum point of view the uncertainty principle (§ 11.4.3) must be reckoned with. If the atom has been in state A only for time t_A before emission occurs, then the energy of level A will be uncertain to an extent $\pm h/t_A$. So will the energy of the lower level, so that the energy difference between the two will be uncertain to the extent of $\pm h(1/t_A + 1/t_B)$. Note that the time taken for the emission is therefore determined by the times the atom spends in both of the energy levels. If, for example, t_A is very short (very much less than t_B) it follows that the time the atom takes to make the transition is also t_A. It seems odd, also, that t_B is involved as the stay in level B occurs *after* the emission of the photon. However, if the energy of the photon is measured at a time less than t_B after the transition, it will be uncertain because of the finite time taken for measurement, and it cannot be measured in a time longer than t_B because the change of state occurring at the end of t_B will make further observation of the previous transition impossible.

The lifetimes of energy levels vary widely in magnitude. Very intense lines will originate from levels of short life much less than 10^{-8} s, but states which can emit only by quadrupole radiation (i.e. *forbidden* transitions as discussed in § 11.4.5) can exist for perhaps 0·1 s. The 21 cm hydrogen line, for example, has a lifetime of about 10^6 years.

8.3.3 Reduction of observed line-widths. To carry out accurate spectroscopic experiments it is desirable to reduce the line-widths as far as possible. Clearly, pressure-broadening can be reduced by working at the lowest pressure that is necessary for a discharge of sufficient intensity; thermal-broadening can, in the first place, be reduced by working at low temperature. However, the temperature of the excited atoms is often high compared with the average, and it is difficult to obtain Doppler temperatures much less than 100°K by cooling the surrounds. But Doppler-broadening can be reduced almost without limit by ensuring that the atoms are not in thermal equilibrium by collimating them into a beam and observing the emission at right-angles.

8.3.4   Inversion of spectral lines. One interesting point in connexion with the Doppler-broadening occurs when the emission tube is artifically cooled to reduce the line-width. The shape and width of absorption lines of a gas are exactly the same as emission lines under the same conditions; since light emitted from the centre of the tube by hot atoms can be absorbed by those at the tube edges which are colder, and therefore have narrower absorption lines, the observed emission line may appear to be clear doublet (Fig. 8.6). This process also takes place when emission occurs in the sun and absorption in the outer atmosphere of either the sun or the earth.

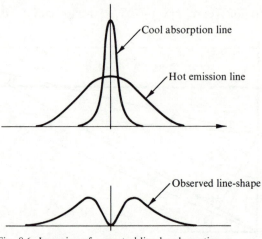

Fig. 8.6. Inversion of a spectral line by absorption.

8.4   Partial-coherence experiments

Two waves are said to be *partially coherent* when their correlation function lies between zero and unity—typically one half. The patterns resulting from interference between such waves are less-clear versions of their fully coherent equivalents, but a study of their visibility is useful in that it is a direct measure of the degree of coherence of the incident waves and can lead to useful measurements of their original source, which may well be inaccessible. We shall start by defining a measure of the spatial coherence of a light wave.

8.4.1   Partially-coherent light from an extended source; coherence area. Let us consider very simply the disturbance E in the observation plane of Fig. 8.7, illumination being derived from an incoherent

source S of extended dimensions. At some point P in the observation plane we shall have contributions to E originating from all points on S; we shall consider the extreme points S_1 and S_2. Each point on S radiates incoherently; the disturbances at S_1 and S_2 are

$$f(S_1) = \exp\{i(\omega t + \phi(S_1))\},$$
$$f(S_2) = \exp\{i(\omega t + \phi(S_2))\}, \qquad (8.2)$$

where $\phi(S_1) - \phi(S_2)$ fluctuates irregularly with time. At P, the contributions to E are summed

$$E_P = f(S_1)\exp(-ikS_1P) + f(S_2)\exp(-ikS_2P)$$
$$= \exp(i\omega t)[\exp\{\phi(S_1) - ikS_1P\} + \exp\{\phi(S_2) - ikS_2P\}]. \qquad (8.3)$$

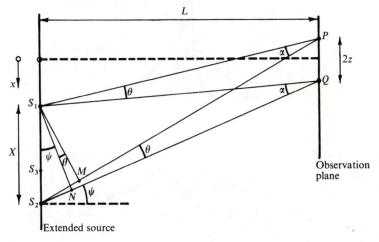

Fig. 8.7. Coherence area of an extended source. When the angles ψ, α and θ are all small we have:

$$S_1P - S_2P = S_2M$$
$$S_1Q - S_2Q = S_2N$$

and

$$S_2M - S_2N = X\theta = L\alpha 2z/L = 2\alpha z.$$

For the radiation at P and Q to be coherent, the path difference $S_2M - S_2N$ must be less than λ; thus the dimensions of the coherence region are given by $2z = \lambda/\alpha$.

Similarly at Q we shall observe

$$E_Q = \exp(i\omega t)[\exp\{\phi(S_1) - ikS_1Q\} + \exp\{\phi(S_2) - ikS_2Q\}]. \qquad (8.4)$$

All contributions from points such as S_3 between S_1 and S_2 will produce similar effects of phase lying between those of E_P and E_Q.

If ikS_1P and ikS_1Q were equal, and also ikS_2P and ikS_2Q, the disturbances E_P and E_Q would obviously be identical and coherent (since P and Q would coincide); we may now ask how far apart P and Q can be separated before this coherence disappears. Separating P and Q will make negligible difference provided that

$$ik(S_1P - S_2P) - ik(S_1Q - S_2Q) \ll 2\pi i$$

or
$$(S_1P - S_2P) - (S_1Q - S_2Q) \ll \lambda. \tag{8.5}$$

When the sign $\ll$ is replaced by equality as P and Q move apart, all coherence disappears; this will occur at a distance PQ given by $PQ = \lambda/\alpha$ when α is very small (Fig. 8.7). If the argument is extended to two dimensions, we can define an area around P of diameter λ/d within which all points Q receive illumination which is partially coherent with that at P; this region is called the *coherence area*. If the source S is circular, the coherence area is a circle of radius $0.61\lambda/\alpha$; it is circular because the source is circular, in general being the reciprocal area to the source.

The relationship between the coherence area, or strictly the coherence function, and the source dimensions turns out to be that between Fourier transforms, at least when the source has a small angular diameter α. This relationship can be very useful in practice, as is illustrated in § 12.6.7, because the measurement of a correlation function requires considerably less costly apparatus than a telescope suitable for the observation of very fine detail. The disadvantage is the necessity for an electronic computer to understand the results.

We can prove this useful Fourier relationship quite easily. The proof below is one-dimensional, but it is readily extended to two dimensions. We measure the signals E_P and E_Q arising from the whole of the source, not just from two points as in equation (8.2), and evaluate the spatial correlation function which is defined analogously to equation (8.1) as

$$\gamma(z) = \frac{|c(z)|}{|c(0)|}, \tag{8.6}$$

$$= \left[\frac{\left| \int_0^\infty E_P E_Q^* \, dt \right|^2}{\left\{ \int_0^\infty E_P E_P^* \, dt \int_0^\infty E_Q E_Q^* \, dt \right\}} \right]^{\frac{1}{2}}. \tag{8.7}$$

Now E_P and E_Q, arising from the complete source S, are written in integral form

$$E_P = \int_{-\infty}^{\infty} f(x) \exp\left[\frac{-ik(x-z)^2}{2L}\right] dx, \tag{8.8}$$

$$E_Q = \int_{-\infty}^{\infty} f(x) \exp\left[\frac{-ik(x+z)^2}{2L}\right] dx. \tag{8.9}$$

The infinite limits of the integral are a mathematical formality; a finite source gives rise to an emission amplitude $f(x)$ which becomes zero outside some finite limits of x. The form of E_P or E_Q is clearly similar to that derived for Fresnel diffraction (equation (6.18)), except that we have neglected the inverse-square law because the difference between SP and SQ is only of the order of λ (compared with SP of the order of 10^3 light years!). Thus $\gamma(z)$ can be written

$$\gamma(z) = \frac{\iint_{-\infty}^{\infty} \overline{f(x)f(y)^*} \exp\left[(-ik/2L)\{(x+z)^2 - (y-z)^2\}\right] dx \, dy}{\iint_{-\infty}^{\infty} \overline{f(x)f(y)^*} \, dx \, dy} \tag{8.10}$$

where $\overline{f(x)f(y)^*}$ means the time-average of $f(x)f(y)^*$. The integrals have been assumed to be real, so that the square modulus and square-root signs in (8.7) can be mutually eliminated. The symbol y has been introduced as a dummy variable to replace x and write the product of two integrals as a double integral.

Now it is clear that for an incoherent source, the mean value $\overline{f(x)f(y)^*}$ becomes zero unless x and y refer to the same point, that is, $x = y$, whence $\gamma(z)$ in equation (8.10) becomes

$$\gamma(z) = \frac{\int_{-\infty}^{\infty} f(x)f(x)^* \exp\left[(-2xz/L)ik\right] dx}{\int_{-\infty}^{\infty} \overline{f(x)f(x)^*} \, dx}$$

$$= \frac{\int_{-\infty}^{\infty} I(x) \exp\left[-ik\phi 2z\right] dx}{\int_{-\infty}^{\infty} I(x) \, dx}. \tag{8.11}$$

This is clearly a normalized value of the Fourier transform, with respect to the variable $2kz$, of the source intensity I as a function of the angle $\phi = x/L$,

$$I(\phi) = f(\phi)f(\phi)^*, \tag{8.12}$$

with respect to the variable $2z$.

The effect of the normalization is to ensure that when z is zero, $\gamma(z)$ is unity. Thus, the correlation between the disturbances at two points separated by the distance $2z$ is the Fourier transform of the intensity distribution in the source, written as a function of ϕ. This is the spatial analogue of the Wiener–Khinchin theorem (§ 8.2.6).

Consider a circular star as an example. The intensity is unity within a circle of angular radius α and zero outside it. The correlation function is therefore the Fourier transform which is (§ 7.3.2)

$$\gamma(z) = \frac{J_1(2k\alpha z)}{(2k\alpha z)}, \tag{8.13}$$

which has its first minimum at a separation

$$2z = \frac{1 \cdot 2\pi}{k\alpha}. \tag{8.14}$$

For a star of angular diameter 1 second, or about $0 \cdot 5 \times 10^{-5}$ radians, coherence exists over a circle of radius about 5 cm (Fig. 8.8).

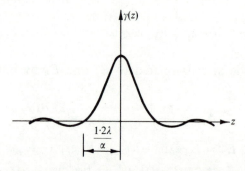

Fig. 8.8. Correlation function between P and Q as a function of their separation, $2z$, when illumination is by a circular source of angular radius α.

Admittedly, after the first zero there are further regions of correlation, both negative and positive, but these result from the sharp cut-off at the edges of the star and are rarely observed except in academic experiments.

8.4.2 Visibility. The visibility of a set of fringes can be defined quantitatively as

$$V = \frac{I_{max} - I_{min}}{I_{max} + I_{min}},$$

I being the intensity of illumination at any particular point in the

interference pattern. Clearly, if I has a minimum value of zero (it cannot be negative) $V = 1$; If $I_{max} = I_{min}$ (as for uniform illumination) $V = 0$. If an interference pattern is produced between two equally intense partially-coherent sources A and B, with correlation γ_{AB} between their disturbances, we can show that the visibility V is equal to γ and forms a convenient measure of it.

We have the simple set-up shown in Fig. 8.9; γ_{AB} is defined in terms of the disturbances E_A and E_B at A and B respectively as

$$\gamma_{AB} = \frac{\overline{E_A E_B^*}}{(|\bar{E}_A|^2 |\bar{E}_B|^2)^{\frac{1}{2}}} = \frac{\overline{E_A^* E_B}}{(|\bar{E}_A|^2 |\bar{E}_B|^2)^{\frac{1}{2}}}.$$

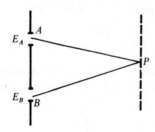

Fig. 8.9. Disturbance at P resulting from two disturbances E_A and E_B.

The amplitude at P is related to E_A and E_B by introducing the phase lags

$$\phi_{AP} = \frac{2\pi AP}{\lambda}, \qquad \phi_{BP} = \frac{2\pi BP}{\lambda},$$

giving
$$E_P = E_A \exp(-i\phi_{AP}) + E_B \exp(-i\phi_{BP})$$
$$= \exp(-i\phi_{AP})(E_A + E_B e^{i\phi}),$$
where
$$\phi = \phi_{AP} - \phi_{BP}.$$
The intensity
$$I_P = E_P E_P^* = |E_A|^2 + E_A E_B^* e^{i\phi} + E_B E_A^* e^{-i\phi} + |E_B|^2.$$

Its time average $\overline{I_P}$ therefore equals

$$|\bar{E}_A|^2 + 2\gamma_{AB}(|\bar{E}_A|^2 |\bar{E}_B|^2)^{\frac{1}{2}} \cos\phi + |\bar{E}_B|^2$$

and as the maximum and minimum values of $\overline{I_P}$ correspond to $\cos\phi = \pm 1$ respectively, it follows that

$$V = \frac{2\gamma_{AB}(|\bar{E}_A|^2 |\bar{E}_B|^2)^{\frac{1}{2}}}{(|\bar{E}_A|^2 + |\bar{E}_B|^2)}.$$

Where the intensities of the two sources are equal, i.e. $|\bar{E}_A^2| = |\bar{E}_B^2|$, it follows that

$$V = \gamma_{AB}.$$

Obviously, the visibility for two sources of unequal intensities is never unity, even if they are perfectly coherent. The measurement of the visibility is therefore a convenient determination of the correlation only between two equally intense sources.

8.4.3   An academic partial-coherence experiment. The manner in which the visibility of the interference pattern in a Young's slit experiment varies with the coherence between the sources can be investigated in the simple experiment illustrated in Fig. 8.10, which serves to define the quantities involved. The set-up is one-dimensional, and the form of the correlation function between pairs of points in the plane T resulting from a wide slit A is the familiar $\sin \beta/\beta$ function (§ 7.2.1), where

$$\beta = \frac{2kaz}{L} = \frac{4\pi az}{\lambda L},$$

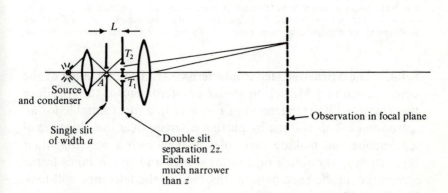

Fig. 8.10. Young's fringes experiment to illustrate partial coherence.

this function being the Fourier transform in equation (8.11). As a is increased from zero, the correlation between slits T_1 and T_2 begins at unity, becomes zero when

$$a = \frac{\lambda L}{4z}$$

and has the usual series of maxima and minima as a is increased beyond this value. The interference patterns observed for various

values of a are illustrated in Fig. 8.11, in which the visibility clearly follows the same pattern. Notice that the effect of negative values of γ is to shift the pattern by half a fringe.

This experiment is the basis of two fundamentally important interferometers which are used to determine the angular diameters, $\alpha = a/L$, of inaccessible sources such as stars. As in the Young's slit experiment, the *Michelson stellar interferometer* measures the coherence between the illuminations at T_1 and T_2 by observing the visibility of the fringes formed by their interference; the *Brown–Twiss interferometer* carries out the correlation directly by electronic means.

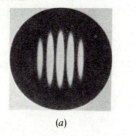

| (a) | (b) | (c) |

Fig. 8.11. Young's fringes with different degrees of spatial coherence. (a) $\gamma = +0.70$; (b) $\gamma = -0.132$; (c) $\gamma = +0.062$. Note particularly the minimum at the middle of (b), produced by the negative coherence. (From B. J. Thompson, *J. Opt. Soc. America*, 1958, **48**, 95.)

8.4.4. The Michelson stellar interferometer.

The first stage of the construction of a Michelson stellar interferometer is to reproduce the Young's slit arrangement in Fig. 8.10 in a form suitable for an astronomer. This is done by putting a screen over the objective of a telescope and making two holes in it in such a way that their separation is variable. For a point source and round holes in the screen the interference pattern observed in the telescope will look like Fig. 7.22; this is the diffraction pattern of two holes (producing a circular ring pattern crossed by fringes representing the *two* in the problem). This should be compared to the *Airy disc* normally observed, which is the circular ring pattern corresponding to the finite aperture of the objective (Fig. 7.18(b)).

When a source of finite diameter replaces the point source the continued existence of the fringes depends upon the coherence between the illumination of the two circular holes. The circular pattern is produced by each hole separately, but the straight fringes are joint property of the two. If the separation of the holes is

increased, the fringes will become less and less clear, disappearing completely when the separation is $1·22\lambda/\alpha$; this property can be used to measure α.

If the angular diameter α of the star is very small, the separation of the holes may need to be very large before disappearance of the fringes is observed. This has two disadvantages. First, the fringes become extremely closely-spaced when the holes are well apart, and secondly, a telescope of very large aperture is needed, although the greater part of the expensive lens is never used. These difficulties were overcome in an ingenious manner by a mirror system illustrated in Fig. 8.12. The coherence measured is clearly that between the light at A and A', which can conveniently be mounted on racks to alter their separation. The interference pattern observed is that arising from the two apertures B and B', and can therefore be made conveniently large by making the holes B and B' small and close together. Moreover, the dimensions of the pattern do not change as A and A' are separated. As an example, a star of diameter 1

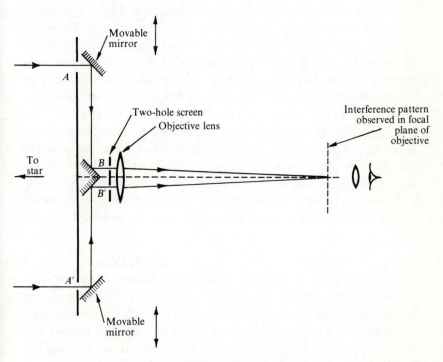

Fig. 8.12. The Michelson stellar interferometer.

second of arc could require separation

$$AA' = 1{\cdot}2\lambda/(6 \times 10^{-6}) = 2 \times 10^5 \lambda;$$

for $\lambda = 5 \times 10^{-5}$ cm this makes $AA' = 10$ cm. Unfortunately, the small intensity of starlight limits the use of this instrument to a few stars of exceptional brilliance; the original experiments on it were confirmed on the star Betelgeuse in the Orion constellation.

8.4.5 Electronic means of correlation: the Brown–Twiss stellar interferometer.

Brown and Twiss have improved the efficiency of the Michelson stellar interferometer by carrying out the correlation between P and Q directly, using electronics, instead of by means of an optical system. The interferometer consists simply of two photomultipliers backed by reflectors which are focused on the star in question and separated by the variable distance. The outputs from the photomultipliers are then correlated directly by electronic means, and the correlation coefficient evaluated as a function of z.

As a practical problem, it would seem impossible to correlate two waves oscillating with frequencies of about 10^{15} c/s, since no electronic system could respond to such a high frequency. However, this is a wrong approach to the Brown–Twiss interferometer. Referring back to § 8.2.2, and in particular to Fig. 8.3, we see that the fluctuations in phase resulting from a coherence time τ_c give rise to fluctuations in envelope amplitude with the same coherence time. If the two partially-coherent waves which interfere to form fringes in the Michelson stellar interferometer are examined in detail therefore, we find that their intensities fluctuate, and the intensity fluctuations of the waves are correlated only under the same conditions as give rise to correlation between the individual wave disturbances. The intensity fluctuations occur with a characteristic frequency of τ_c^{-1}, and for the krypton line in § 8.2.4

$$\tau_c = 10^{-9} \text{ s},$$

giving a characteristic fluctuation frequency of about 10^9 rad/s^{-1} or about 100 Mc/s. This is not too difficult a frequency to deal with.

To establish definite correlation it is necessary to observe the fluctuations over a period of many cycles, which in this case may mean only for a millisecond or so. If, however, we come to deal with sources of much longer coherence times, the time involved for establishing correlation may be considerable. This is apart from

consideration of signal-to-noise ratios, which are not relevant to the discussion here. It should be pointed out that the operation of the Michelson stellar interferometer, in contrast to the Brown–Twiss instrument, does not involve the existence of a coherence *time* at all.

8.5   Beats between light waves

The sum of two waves with different frequencies can always be written as the product of oscillations with the sum and difference frequencies:

$$\sin \omega_1 t + \sin \omega_2 t = 2 \sin \left(\frac{\omega_1 + \omega_2}{2} \right) t \cos \left(\frac{\omega_1 - \omega_2}{2} \right) t.$$

If the difference between ω_1 and ω_2 is small compared with either of them the right-hand side of the above expression is best described as a continuous train of the mean frequency $(\omega_1 + \omega_2)/2$ modulated in intensity at frequency $(\omega_1 - \omega_2)$. The observation of this beat effect in acoustics is very common; the question here is whether it can be observed with light waves. The major problem is one of the accuracy of the frequencies. Although the basic frequencies ω_1 and ω_2 may be defined to better than one part in 10^5, the uncertainties will be additive in the beat frequency, and if the proportional difference between ω_1 and ω_2 is only 10^{-4} the beat frequency will have an uncertainty of at least one part in 10. It can only just be defined as having a recognizable frequency at this level of uncertainty. It is therefore necessary to look for beats between light waves with greater frequency difference than this limit.

Looked at from the wave-group point of view the problem is a little clearer. We are presented with two wave groups, each consisting of some 10^5 waves and therefore lasting only for a finite time. If we want to observe beats between them we must have a beat frequency which goes through a reasonable number of cycles during the coherence time, the lifetime of the wave group. If we make this 'reasonable number' ten we arrive at exactly the same criterion as before. Every pair of wave-groups will, of course, interfere, and will produce beats of random phase, so the total beat disturbance has the same coherence time as the original wave, but of course a much lower frequency, and so the relative uncertainty in the beat frequency is much larger.

8.5.1 Beats between discharge-tube sources. Beats between light sources of standard type have been observed, but with some difficulty. The two frequencies used were Zeeman components of a single spectral line, and the compound disturbance was picked up by a photocell and analysed in the expected frequency range of the beats. The use of a non-linear device, the photocell—compared with the ear in the observation of audible beats—to produce a separate beat component is a necessary part of the experiment. Sufficient magnetic field was applied to give a Zeeman splitting an order greater than the width of the spectral line to satisfy the uncertainty criterion, but even so the signal-to-noise ratio was very poor. This was improved sufficiently to make the observations possible by switching the magnetic field on and off at a low frequency and looking for beats appearing and disappearing at the same frequency. This principle of improving signal-to-noise ratio by modulation of the experimental conditions is a widely used technique; its value arises because at a given temperature random noise is equally distributed throughout the frequency spectrum (it is therefore equivalent to a random series of δ-pulses, and is called *white noise* because of its similarity to white light). By selecting a particular frequency range (that around the modulation frequency) for observation the only troublesome noise is that within this range.

8.5.2 Beats between lasers. Because continuous lasers have very long coherence times, of the order of seconds, it is considerably easier to observe beats between them. The experiment can easily be done by using two nominally identical lasers, which will have slightly different frequencies because the interference systems which make the selection will not be exactly identical, and shining them simultaneously on to a photocell (which will produce electrical beat oscillations) or an electrostrictive crystal (which will produce sound, possibly audible).

8.5.3 Measurement of very long coherence times. What is essentially a beat method can be used to measure the very long coherence times observed with gas lasers. If, for example, we had two gas lasers, emitting frequencies ω_1 and ω_2 and simultaneously shining on a photocell, frequency analysis of the photocell output would show the beat frequency $\omega_1 - \omega_2$. If finite coherence times exist for both lasers, giving rise to line-widths $\delta\omega_1$ and $\delta\omega_2$, the $\omega_1 - \omega_2$ line

in the photocell output will have width $\delta\omega_1 + \delta\omega_2$ which may be quite measurable compared with $\omega_1 - \omega_2$. This would be an appropriate method for two lasers; it is not immediately obvious that one laser, making $\omega_1 = \omega_2$, will supply a band of breadth $2\delta\omega$ around zero frequency, because the fluctuations of the *two* lasers are now correlated, being identical. But in fact we can see that this will be so, because a spectral analysis of the photocell output is then a spectral analysis of the square of a wave-group of length $1/\delta\omega$ (Fig. 8.13), and if this is broken down in the form indicated in the figure it obviously contains a band of width $\delta\omega$ at zero frequency amongst its Fourier components. For a laser with a coherence time of one second this band is of width $1\ \mathrm{s}^{-1}$.

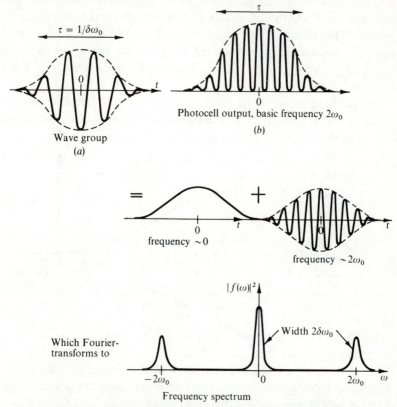

Fig. 8.13. Photocell used to measure the length of a wavegroup.

8.6 Coherence and optical instruments

8.6.1 The Michelson interferometer as a spectral analyser. The interference pattern observed in a Michelson interferometer

(§ 7.8.2) is compounded from two coherent beams derived from the same source. A relative phase lag is introduced between the two disturbances, its size depending on the position of the mirrors. Now we have noted that the visibility of the fringes produced by two beams is a measure of the correlation between them; the visibility of the Michelson fringes is thus a measure of the self-correlation of the initial source:

$$C_S(\tau) = \langle f(t)f^*(t+\tau) \rangle,$$

where the time interval τ is the time-lag introduced by the separation of the two mirrors. The Fourier transform of the self-correlation function is the power spectrum (Wiener–Khinchin theorem, § 8.2.6) and so a measurement of the fringe-visibility as a function of mirror position is all that is necessary to make a spectral analysis of the source. The method is particularly useful when only a very small range of wavelengths is involved, so that the mirror movements necessary to change the visibility appreciably are quite large. Some obvious examples are as follows:

(a) A *broad* spectral line produces fringes which become invisible when the mirror separation reaches the coherence distance, about 40 cm in the example quoted earlier (Fig. 8.14).

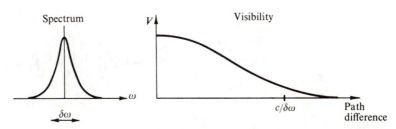

Fig. 8.14. Visibility of the fringes in a Michelson interferometer when illumination is by a single wide spectral line.

(b) A doublet produces fringes which appear and disappear periodically as the separation is steadily increased (Fig. 8.15).

(c) A source exhibiting the anomalous Zeeman effect in a magnetic field would have highly-visible fringes only over short periodically-occurring regions (Fig. 8.16).

This method of spectral analysis, which was originally invented by Michelson and is described in detail in *Studies in Optics*, was never very popular because of the necessity for a Fourier transform in order to convert the observations into a conventional

spectrum. The advent of electronic computers has now changed the situation. Because of the basic simplicity of construction of a Michelson interferometer, and its ease of application to wavelengths other than the visible (in particular infra-red), the method of 'two-beam interference' is becoming of considerable practical importance in modern physics and chemistry.

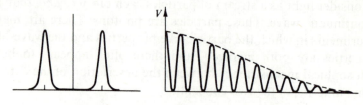

Fig. 8.15. As Fig. 8.14, illumination by a doublet.

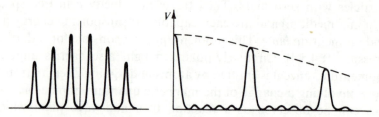

Fig. 8.16. As Fig. 8.14, illumination by a Zeeman multiplet.

8.6.2   Can the use of incoherent illumination solve the phase problem?

If an object periodically repeated on a lattice is illuminated in such a way that the coherence area is of the order of the lattice period, the diffraction pattern observed will be that of the object alone, since the visibility of the contribution to the pattern produced by the regular lattice will be zero. By the intelligent use of symmetry considerations, this observation of the transform of the object alone could be used to derive its structure unambiguously, the effect of the periodic repetition no longer being to sample the transform only at the reciprocal-lattice points (§ 7.6.3). Unfortunately, this principle, which can be used for artificial *optical crystals* (which can be studied quite satisfactorily under a microscope anyhow), cannot be extended to X-ray work because coherence areas with dimensions as small as 1 Å cannot be achieved. A source of extremely large diameter would be needed.

8.7 Waves and photons

In Chapter 4 we pointed out that Maxwell's equations were sufficient to explain the properties of light completely, with the exception of the quantization of energy in the waves. The existence of energy only in units of $\hbar\omega$ is of fundamental importance in certain types of problem, such as the photoelectric effect and atomic transitions (Chapter 11), and in such problems it is more realistic to consider light as a stream of particles each of energy $\hbar\omega$ than as a continuous wave. These particles are photons. There are many experiments in which the particle-like properties and the wave-like properties are both involved, and there often appears to be a philosophical inconsistency between the description of the experiments in terms of the two concepts.

8.7.1 The properties of photons. As particles, photons have the following characteristics. They can be considered as elementary particles with zero mass. They travel at velocity c in free space (c/μ in a medium) and are each capable of transporting energy $\hbar\omega$ and momentum $\hbar\omega/c$. This momentum is responsible for radiation pressure (§ 4.5.4). Circularly-polarized light also carries angular momentum, since it is emitted by atoms undergoing Zeeman transitions involving a change of the magnetic quantum number m, and this can be observed as a reaction in a half-wave plate which reverses the sense of polarization (problem 28). The quantum of angular momentum must be $\hbar$, in order to conserve it in Zeeman transitions, and this can be resolved along the direction of motion to be $\pm\hbar$ (or zero) corresponding to left-handed, right-handed (and linearly-) polarized waves. Consequently, photons obey Bose–Einstein statistics (§ 8.7.3).

8.7.2 Wave–particle inconsistencies. The inconsistency between wave and particle approaches to certain experiments, such as an *observed* interference experiment, is mainly a result of the inadequacy of the human brain to appreciate a particle which is a wave at the same time. For it always appears that we can never carry out an experiment in practice to distinguish between wave- and particle-like behaviour. One of the most important experiments in this field was the low-intensity diffraction experiment of G. I. Taylor in 1909, in which a diffraction pattern was observed at an intensity such that there was a negligible probability of the simultaneous presence of two photons in the system. It would therefore

be impossible to talk in terms of interference between two photons; the interference must occur between a photon and itself.

To see the impossibility of distinguishing between a wave and a particle we can discuss this experiment in terms of a Young's slit set-up. It is necessary to have two slits illuminated from the same source, and in the wave theory we consider the waves passing through the two slits to interfere and produce fringes. But in the low-intensity experiment, the single photon must have passed through either one slit *or* the other; the essence of a particle is that it cannot be split into two halves. In principle we might try to find out which of the two slits the photon went through. But in order to observe a photon we must destroy it, or at least change it irreversibly, and if we put a photocell in the way of one of the slits to observe photons passing through it we destroy the interference pattern by blocking one slit. We can try to be more subtle in our observations and observe the temporary momentum transfer to a glass plate through which the photon passes. While the photon is passing through the plate its momentum is reduced from $\hbar\omega/c$ to $\hbar\omega/\mu c$, the excess being transferred to the plate. Since we know the time for which the photon is travelling in the plate we can deduce how far the plate moves in this time, and measurement of the positions of the plate before and after the admission of a photon to the interference system will tell us which slit the photon passed through. Of course, the glass plate will introduce a phase lag to the photon that passes through it, but this will only shift the fringes and not destroy them. The fringes *are* destroyed, however, by the mere fact of *observing* the position of the glass plate. It is left as a problem (39) to show that measurement of the position of the plate, to an accuracy sufficient to discover subsequently whether it has moved or not, leads to sufficient momentum and velocity uncertainty to destroy completely the fringe pattern by the introduction of a phase uncertainty of 2π. Here we have been beaten by the uncertainty principle. And so it continues; it never turns out to be possible to discover anything positive about photons as particles without destroying evidence of their wave-like properties.

8.7.3 The statistics of photon emission.

8.7.3 The statistics of photon emission. Another aspect of photon theory is concerned with their statistics, particularly in view of their being Bose–Einstein particles of zero mass. Suppose photons are emitted at random intervals, but on a scale such that the number

of photons emitted in unit time is on the average less than the reciprocal of the lifetime of the photon. We should then expect the corresponding wave to consist mainly of zero, but with occasional discrete, wave-packets. On the other hand, if the lifetime is greater than the average time between photon emissions the wave-packets will overlap. Taking this argument to its limit, for a very intense beam we might expect that the overlapping should be so great that the fluctuations in number of wave-packets contributing to the wave at a given instant would be so small compared to the total that the wave would have an almost constant total amplitude. We shall investigate these ideas more carefully.

Consideration of photon emissions as random events, each one uncorrelated with its predecessors, leads one to the following conclusion mathematically. To reduce the problem to its simplest level, we assume that a photon contributes a constant amount of the total amplitude at time t if its centre point lies in the range $t \pm \tau$, τ being the half-width of the wave-packet (Fig. 8.2), and nothing if it lies outside this range. The random-emission process indicates a Poisson distribution for the emission of individual photons, and if the mean rate of emission is N per unit volume the mean number contributing at time t is $2N\tau$, giving intensity $I = 2N\tau\varepsilon$ where εc is the photon energy. The standard deviation of the number will therefore be $(2N\tau)^{\frac{1}{2}}$. The latter term indicates the size ΔI of fluctuations in intensity, giving

$$\frac{\Delta I}{I} = \frac{1}{(2N\tau)^{\frac{1}{2}}} = \left(\frac{\varepsilon}{I}\right)^{\frac{1}{2}}. \tag{8.15}$$

This shows that the relative size of fluctuation in intensity goes down as the intensity goes up, as suggested above. The basic point that has contributed to this result is that the emission of individual photons occurs randomly, leading to a Poisson distribution. Now in § 8.2.1 we showed that a series of randomly-emitted photons can be represented by the Fourier transform consisting of waves in the range $\omega_0 \pm 1/\tau$ with random phases. On this basis we can again calculate the fluctuations in intensity which should be expected. At a given instant we must add together a number of vectors, representing each Fourier component together with its phase, the phases of which are random. This is a two-dimensional random-walk problem, and the theory of such a process shows that

$$\frac{\Delta I}{I} \simeq 1. \tag{8.16}$$

The two approaches do not agree in form.

The discrepancy can be removed in two possible ways. At very low intensities it is inconsistent to consider the photon lifetime 2τ as much shorter than the interval between emissions because this would imply knowledge of the approximate time of emission. And so we should write

$$2\tau \simeq \frac{1}{N}$$

in this limit. The two results then agree; in other words, the random-emission hypothesis now gives consistent results at low intensities. However, as there is no bar against two atoms emitting simultaneously, the same argument cannot apply at high intensities, and we are forced to admit then that emissions of photons cannot be random but must be correlated. This suggests that very intense sources will have a high degree of coherence, as is observed in lasers (§ 11.7).

It is interesting that a trial function consisting of the sum† of (8.15) and (8.16), which is satisfactory in limits of both large and small intensity

$$(\Delta I)^2 = \varepsilon I + I^2$$

can be shown by statistical-mechanical arguments to lead directly to a distribution function for the photon energies:

$$n(\varepsilon) = [\exp(\alpha + \beta\varepsilon) - 1]^{-1},$$

indicating that photons obey Bose statistics. The reason for the high correlation observed in very intense beams is then clear. A source of finite dimensions will have discrete quantum states available, of which the highest energy ones will be very unlikely to be filled. If, as a result of the high intensity, we have many photons present, it is necessary to put a considerable number of them into the same quantum state, and these will necessarily be correlated.

This opens up the whole subject of photon statistics, a subject which has grown as a result of the invention of lasers and involves detailed consideration of photons as an assembly of Bose–Einstein particles not in thermal equilibrium. It is outside the scope of this book, and we shall leave it to rest at that.

---

† There is a statistical theorem which says that mean-square fluctuations arising from independent causes are additive.

CHAPTER 9

OPTICAL INSTRUMENTS AND IMAGE FORMATION

9.1 Geometrical theory

As we have seen in Chapter 1, one of the first applications of the newly discovered physics of the seventeenth century was the use of lenses for the production of magnified images of objects. At first single lenses were used, but soon the advantages of lens combinations were discovered and the microscope and telescope were invented.

In the following sections we shall deal briefly with the principles of these instruments; since they are dealt with thoroughly in elementary textbooks we shall give only enough detail for the more important practical and theoretical aspects to be properly appreciated.

9.1.1 Magnifying glass. The magnifying glass—or its more elaborate form, the eyepiece—is an important component of most optical instruments and its function should be clearly understood. Its main purpose is to allow us to bring an object well within the near point by throwing an image to a distance at which the eye can produce a sharply focused image. This is illustrated in Fig. 9.1 in terms of paraxial rays—that is, rays that are near to, and nearly parallel to, the axis.

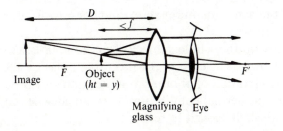

Fig. 9.1. Ray diagram of magnifying glass. In practice, $f \ll D$ and the object distance would be nearly equal to f.

The magnifying power is a more useful quantity than the magnification; it can be defined in two equivalent ways:

(a) the ratio of the angle subtended at the eye by the image formed by the instrument to the angle subtended at the eye by the object when viewed directly;

(b) the ratio of the linear dimensions of the retinal image produced with the lens to those of the largest clear retinal image produced without the lens. Since the latter image is produced when the object is at the near point—a distance D, say, from the eye—the magnifying power can easily be seen (Fig. 9.1) to be about

$$\frac{y}{f} \bigg/ \frac{y}{D} = \frac{D}{f}.$$

Therefore Brown's lens (§ 1.5.3) would have produced a magnifying power of $10/\frac{1}{32}$ or about 300.

The single lens is now used only for informal purposes. For precise work eyepieces are generally used and the general principles upon which these are based are described in Appendix III.

9.1.2 Microscope. The essential principle of the microscope is that a lens (called the objective) of high power is used to form a highly magnified real image of the object; this object must therefore be placed just outside the focus of the lens: an eyepiece is then used to examine this image. A ray diagram of the formation of the image is shown in Fig. 9.2. It will be seen that the final image is virtual and inverted.

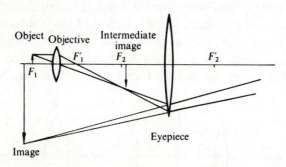

Fig. 9.2. Ray diagram of microscope.

9.1.3 Telescope. The principle of the telescope is similar to that of the microscope, except that, of course, the object is not accessible

and must therefore be considered as being infinitely distant from the lens, which is again called the objective. The intermediate image is thus formed in the second focal plane of the objective and is very small. This image is then viewed by means of an eyepiece and is again virtual and inverted.

The geometrical theory of image formation in the microscope and telescope is straightforward and will not be dealt with here.

9.2 Practical considerations

9.2.1 Extrance and exit pupils.
The elementary theory outlined in the previous sections says nothing about the sizes of the lenses, although in practice their dimensions are very important. It is wasteful to use large lenses if the outer parts do not contribute to the production of the image; it is wrong to use a lens that is so small that it reduces the efficiency of the others in the combination. The systematic study of these considerations is called the theory of stops, and a brief résumé of some of its aspects will be given here.

Three considerations are of importance. First, for efficiency we should try to see that each lens plays its full share in producing the image; secondly, the brightness of the image shall be as high as possible and of reasonable uniformity; and thirdly, the image should not, over the field of view, have any appreciable distortion or loss of sharpness. None of these requirements can be *exactly* realized; we therefore design optical equipment around the most expensive item—the objective of a microscope or of a telescope—and make the other components match it as well as possible.

A stop—despite its name—is an opening in a coaxial system of lenses, a coaxial system being one for which the centres of curvature of all the refracting surfaces lie on a straight line—the axis. A stop may be an actual hole, such as the iris diaphragm of a camera, or it may be a lens itself. For a particular object point on the axis *one* stop must limit the cone of light forming the image (Fig. 9.3); this

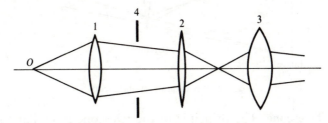

Fig. 9.3. System of three lenses with an object at O; lens 1 is the aperture stop. If the stop 4 is reduced in size, it could replace 1 as the aperture stop.

is called the *aperture stop*. The aperture stop is not necessarily the same component for different positions of the object, but since most optical instruments are used without much drastic variation, the aperture stop does not usually vary.

The image of the aperture stop in the lenses preceding it is called the *entrance pupil*. In the telescope or microscope this should be the objective itself, but in the camera it is the image of the iris diaphragm in the lens or in that part of the lens system that precedes it. The image of the aperture stop in the lenses that follow it is called the *exit pupil*. In the telescope or microscope this is the image of the objective in the eyepiece, and, as we can see from Fig. 9.4, it is the plane where there is the greatest density of light. It is thus the place where the entrance pupil of the eye should be located. An optical system should therefore be designed so that its exit pupil is accessible; some instruments, such as the Galilean telescope (Fig. 9.5), do not satisfy this condition.

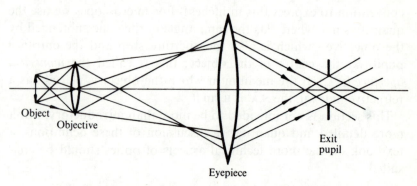

Fig. 9.4. Ray diagram for microscope showing position of exit pupil.

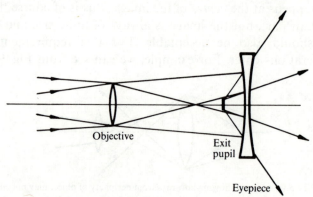

Fig. 9.5. Galilean telescope showing position of exit pupil.

It must be remembered that the eye also forms part of any optical system that is used for direct viewing, and it is no use designing a system that is wasteful by under-using either the abilities of the eye or those of the instrument. The condition to be satisfied is that the exit pupil of the instrument should match the entrance pupil of the eye in both size and position but, as we have seen, this is not always possible.

9.2.2   Definitions of aperture. The cone of light that goes to form the centre of the image decides the brightness of the image. More precisely, the brightness depends upon the angle subtended by the entrance pupil at the centre of the object; for a camera lens this quantity is defined by the f-number—the ratio of the focal length to the diameter of the entrance pupil. For the telescope, since all objects are effectively at infinity, the diameter of the objective —which is also the aperture stop and the entrance pupil—is usually given. (In spite of the metric system, it seems to be an international convention to express this in inches!) For microscopes we use the quantity $\sin \theta$, where θ is the semi-angle of the cone subtended by the objective—which is also the aperture stop and the entrance pupil—at the centre of the object; this is called the *numerical aperture* (N.A.). If the medium in which the object is placed has a refractive index μ, the N.A. is $\mu \sin \theta$.

This section is not intended to be more than introductory. For a more detailed and quantitative discussion of these definitions, a textbook on the more technical aspects of optics should be consulted.

9.2.3   Entrance window. The entrance and exit pupils decide only what happens at the *centre* of the image; this is of course the most important part, but the image is always of finite size and off-axis parts should also be acceptable. For this requirement, other considerations enter. For example, we can see from Fig. 9.6 that,

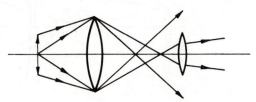

Fig. 9.6. Two-lens system showing how rays from periphery of object may not enter second lens.

although the first lens of the system is obviously the aperture stop, some of the off-axis rays passing through it will not pass through the second lens. In other words, the second lens decides *how much* of the object is seen. The stop that decides the visible area of the image is called the *field stop*.

The field stop is almost always an actual aperture inserted in the system. In its simplest form, in the camera, it is simply the edge of the plate or film holder, but in the microscope a special stop is inserted so that its image is in focus together with that of the object. This merely satisfies the aesthetic requirements that the image field shall have a sharp edge.

We can therefore see that the image of the field stop is important. The image in the lenses preceding it is called the *entrance window*, since this defines the area of the object that we are looking at; and the image in the lenses following it is called the *exit window*, since this defines the area of the image seen. The entrance window of a camera is thus the image of the plate-holder in the lens. The view-finder of a camera attempts to show the user a close approximation to the entrance window; it cannot of course be precise because the lens of the view-finder is not in the same place as that of the camera (except, of course, in a reflex camera).

We may now ask how the field stop is chosen. As we have already pointed out, it gives a sharp edge to the field of view. The choice of the position of this boundary is based upon two considerations: the simpler is that we do not want to have obvious variation in the brightness of the image, and it is usual to limit the field so that the brightness does not fall, at the edges, to less than half the value at the centre; the other is that the aberrations (Appendix II) necessarily increase with distance from the centre, and the image should be cut off before these aberrations become apparent.

There are other aspects also of the theory of stops—such as depth of field and of focus—but we shall not deal with them since they do not enter into the subsequent topics dealt with in this book.

9.2.4 Illuminating systems. For microscopes, the object must be illuminated in some way, either naturally or artificially. If the latter, the intensity of illumination must usually be as great as possible and therefore a condensing lens is used to focus light from a source on to the object. From the geometrical-optics point of view, the design of this component of a microscope may seem quite trivial;

from the physical-optics point of view, however, we shall see later (§ 9.5.1) that a condenser can be comparable in complexity with a microscope objective if the highest possible resolution is to be obtained.

9.3 Diffraction theory of image formation

9.3.1 Image of a periodic object. We know that the theory in the first two parts of this chapter cannot be complete; the description of image formation in terms of rays can be only an approximation, since light is a wave motion and cannot adequately be described in terms of rays. We must now ask 'What difference does the wave nature of light make to our conclusions?'

The answer can be most simply given if we first consider the object to have a periodic structure and thus to behave as a diffraction grating (§ 7.4.2). It must be emphasized, however, that this type of object is considered first merely for simplicity; we shall show later that the resulting theory is applicable to *all* objects.

We have seen in § 7.4.2 that if parallel light falls normally upon a diffraction grating several orders of diffraction are produced (Fig. 9.7). Each order can be considered as a plane wave and the set of plane waves can be refracted by a lens so that they converge individually to a set of points S in the focal plane F of the lens and then continue so that they all overlap in the plane I. Here they form a complicated interference pattern; this pattern is the image.

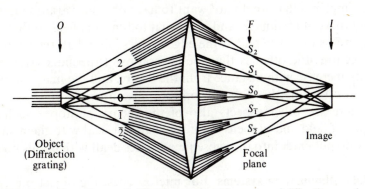

Fig. 9.7. Formation of image of diffraction grating. Five orders of diffraction are shown, producing five foci S in the plane F.

The advantage of taking a diffraction grating as an object is that we can consider the process of image formation in discrete steps. Each pair of equal orders of diffraction produces a set of

Young's fringes in the plane I and these fringes form one component of the image. The zero order (Fig. 9.7) is an exception; it produces no fringes and therefore gives no information about the structure of the object. The first orders from a grating of spacing d will be produced at angles θ_1 given by the equation

$$\lambda = d \sin \theta_1. \tag{9.1}$$

After refraction the waves meet at angles $\pm\theta_1'$, where $\theta_1' = l\theta_1/l'$, l' being the image distance. Here, as shown in Fig. 9.8, they produce fringes of spacing $d' = \lambda/\theta_1'$. Thus

$$d_1' = \frac{\lambda}{\theta_1} \cdot \frac{l'}{l}$$

$$= \frac{m\lambda}{\theta_1}, \tag{9.2}$$

where m is the magnification. But from equation (9.1)

$$\lambda/\theta_1 = d$$

for small values of θ_1. Thus $\quad d_1' = md.$

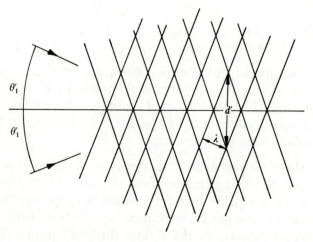

Fig. 9.8. Interference of two plane waves. The lines indicate crests of the waves and the points of intersection are maxima in the interference pattern.

In other words, the information contained in the first orders is that the object is periodic, and the period is obtained by dividing the spacing of the fringes by the magnification deduced from l and l'.

This is not quite true, since we cannot distinguish between positive and negative parts of a sine curve; the Young's fringes

produced by the two orders ± 1 would appear to have only half the spacing given in equation (9.2). Here the importance of the zero order emerges; it gives, in effect, a positive component to be added to the fringes and causes the crests to give maximum intensity and the troughs to give minimum (Fig. 9.9).

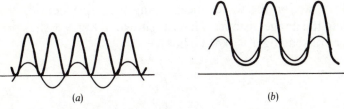

(a)   (b)

Fig. 9.9(a) Square of sine curve showing function of half the wavelength; (b) square of the sum of a sine curve and a constant, showing a function of the same wavelength (not to the same scale as (a)).

The effects of the higher orders can now be considered. The second orders have angles given by the equation

$$2\lambda = d \sin \theta_2. \tag{9.3}$$

These can be seen to give fringes with spacing

$$d'_2 = \tfrac{1}{2}md. \tag{9.4}$$

In other words they add finer detail to the interference pattern. In general the orders $\pm n$ give detail of fineness $1/n$th of the spacing of the grating. The complete image is produced by adding together all the fringes produced by the separate orders. Several important results follow from this approach.

9.3.2 Abbe's sine condition. The theory in the last section would suggest that an accurate image would be built up only if the angles of diffraction were kept small. This would be an intolerable condition for an efficient optical instrument and Abbe realized that the image would be accurate if the ratio $\sin \theta / \sin \theta'$ rather than θ/θ' were constant for all zones of a lens; this is obvious from Fig. 9.8. One important system having this property is described in Appendix III and forms the basis of high-powered microscope objectives.

9.3.3 Diffraction as Fourier analysis. The plane F and the points S (Fig. 9.7) are of extreme importance in the theory of image formation. The image would be produced even if an opaque screen were

placed in F with openings only at the points S. That is, these points contain all the information about the object in condensed form. In fact, we can see, from the reasoning in equations (9.1) to (9.4), that each pair of points S_n provides the nth Fourier components (§ 3.2.2) of the image. Thus the orders of diffraction can be regarded as providing, in the plane F, a natural Fourier analysis of the object.

What information is contained in this plane? First, there is obviously the relative intensities of the orders. Secondly, there is less obviously the relative phase of the waves at the points S. To form an accurate image not only must the relative intensities of the Fourier components be correct, but they must interfere with each other in the correct relative phases. These phases are decided by the object and they must not be changed in any subsequent process of refraction. An accurate lens must obey the condition that the optical path is independent of the route between object and image, not merely for small angles—which is easy—but for angles which, in a microscope, may be as much as 60°.

9.3.4   Image formation as a double process of diffraction. The ideas in the last section help us to generalize the process of image formation in a way that has had important practical consequences. We have seen that the plane F can be considered as containing the diffraction pattern of the object, and that the image can be considered as the pattern resulting from the interference of the separate components of this diffraction pattern. If we ignore the difference between interference and diffraction—never an easy matter to define (§ 7.1)—we may say that the image is the result of a double process of diffraction. This is the approach put forward by Zernicke, and on the basis of it he has been responsible for some considerable advances in the practice of optics as we shall see later.

9.3.5   Extension to non-periodic objects. The Abbe theory outlined in § 9.3.1 is a special case of a general theory. It has made use of a diffraction grating as an object because this gives discrete orders of diffraction that can be clearly visualized. These discrete orders, however, are not essential to the theory; a non-periodic object gives a pattern of scattering that is not limited to specific directions, but each pair of scattered beams, at angles $\pm\theta$, can still be regarded as giving rise to a set of fringes and the addition of these fringes produces the image. *All* spacings of fringes are now possible, and

obviously much more complicated images can be built up; this we should expect, since a periodic object is normally simpler than a non-periodic object.

We can see that the process of scattering by a non-periodic object bears to that by a periodic object the same relation as the Fourier transform (§ 3.4.1) bears to the Fourier series. We saw in § 9.3.3 that the process of diffraction could be regarded as Fourier analysis: for a periodic function (a grating) we have a series of orders of diffraction (the Fourier coefficients); for a non-periodic object we have a general pattern of diffraction (the Fourier transform). The diffraction pattern that we observe is the square of the modulus of the Fourier transform; from it we can derive the relative amplitude of the light diffracted in different directions, but we have no knowledge of the relative phases.

The theory of § 7.3.1 now assumes a more general significance; the image that is finally produced can be regarded as the diffraction pattern of the diffracted light. Thus Zernicke's statement that an image is formed by a double process of diffraction is equivalent to the mathematical statement that the Fourier transform of a Fourier transform is the original function (§ 3.5.5). This is the key statement in this way of looking at the process of image formation.

These ideas can be illustrated by using a diffraction grating as an object. We have constructed one with slits 1 mm wide, with a spacing of 5 mm, and this gives the diffraction pattern shown in Fig. 9.10(a); we can see the regular array of orders, with the 5th and 10th of zero intensity. If we now limit the number of orders that continue to form the image, we produce an image that is essentially a Fourier synthesis of this limited number of coefficients.

From § 3.3.2 we know that the Fourier coefficients of a square-wave function representing the grating have the values of $(\sin nx)/x$, where x is equal to $2\pi/10$. Thus the coefficients are successively 1, 0·94, 0·76, 0·50, ... Fourier syntheses with the appropriate numbers of terms are also shown in Fig. 9.10 and it will be seen that they correspond closely to the observed images.

9.3.6 Extension to two dimensions. So far we have confined ourselves to one dimension for the sake of simplicity, but there is no difficulty in extending the theory to two dimensions. We must envisage a point source of illumination instead of a slit, so that we can now consider the diffraction of light in two dimensions. An

object such as a set of holes in an opaque screen (Fig. 9.11(a)) has the general diffraction pattern shown in Fig. 9.11(b). Each pair of elements in the latter produces a set of fringes whose spacing is inversely related to the angular separation of the elements, and whose direction is perpendicular to the direction of this separation. This latter gives the extra variable necessary for the production of a two-dimensional image; the combination of fringes varying in intensity, spacing and direction can obviously be used to build up extremely complicated patterns.

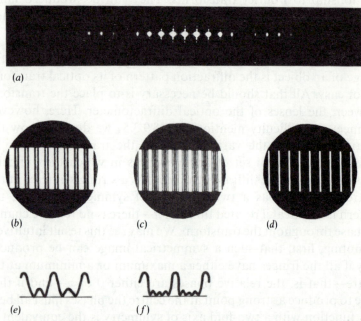

Fig. 9.10. (a) Diffraction pattern of grating; (b) image formed with three central orders; (c) image formed with five central orders; (d) image formed with all orders; (e) rough representation of square of Fourier synthesis with three central terms; (f) rough representation of square of Fourier synthesis with five central terms.

Fig. 9.11. (a) Set of holes in opaque screen; (b) diffraction pattern of (a).

The process is perhaps most easily visualized in connexion with a periodic object—a lattice of holes; the diffraction pattern of this is a lattice of orders of diffraction (Fig. 7.26)—the reciprocal lattice (§ 7.4.3). The diffraction pattern of this is again a reciprocally related periodic function and is therefore the original function—the image.

9.3.7 Optical transforms. Because of the important part that two-dimensional diffraction patterns play in image-formation theory, they are called optical transforms; the name also emphasizes their relationship to Fourier transforms. They can be produced fairly simply in the piece of apparatus called the optical diffractometer, which is described in detail in Appendix IV.

9.3.8 Image recombination. To show experimentally that the image of an object is the diffraction pattern of its optical transform is not easy. All that should be necessary is to place the transform between the lenses of the optical diffractometer. Here, however, we meet the difficulty mentioned in § 9.3.5; we do not know the relative phases of the various parts of the transform. There is, however, one special set of circumstances in which the difficulty does not arise; if the diffracting object has a strong scatterer at the centre, and if it has a two-fold axis of symmetry—that is, the pattern is identical if rotated through π—there is no relative change of phase throughout the transform. We may see this result intuitively by noting, first, that such a symmetrical image can be produced only if all the fringes have either a maximum or a minimum at the centre—that is, the relative phases are either 0 or π—and if they have to produce a strong point at the centre the phases must all be 0.

A function with a two-fold axis of symmetry is the equivalent in two dimensions of an even function (§ 3.3.1) in one dimension. The Fourier coefficients are all real; that is, they consist of cosine terms only. If the function has a strong maximum at the centre, then these cosine terms must all be positive at the centre.

These conditions may be produced artificially by making a symmetrical arrangement of holes with a larger one at the centre (Fig. 9.12(a)) and covering the smaller ones with gauze to reduce their contributions to the optical transform. The resulting transform is shown in Fig. 9.12(b). This is placed between the lenses of the optical diffractometer, sandwiched between optical flats and immersed in cedarwood oil which has the same refractive index as

the film emulsion; the resulting diffraction pattern (Fig. 9.12(c)) can be seen to be a good image of the object.

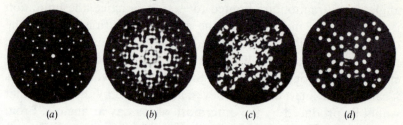

(a)   (b)   (c)   (d)

Fig. 9.12. (a) Mask representing chemical molecule with heavy atom at centre; (b) transform of (a); (c) transform of (b) without precautions to eliminate phase changes. The pattern of (a) is quite recognizable; (d) transform of (b) placed between optical flats with cedar-wood oil to eliminate phase changes. The pattern of (a) is quite clear.

9.3.9   Extension to three dimensions. Although it is always easy in principle to extend a theory to any number of dimensions, it might be thought that two dimensions are all that are necessary in optics, since all images ultimately are formed on the retina of the eye. This, however, is not the full story; matter is three-dimensional and any attempts to describe it fully must also be three-dimensional. In particular, crystals can be described only in this way. A crystal is a diffraction grating since it contains groups of atoms regularly arranged; its transform is therefore a set of orders of diffraction regularly arranged on a three-dimensional lattice—the reciprocal lattice (§ 7.6.2) of the crystal. The transform of this set of orders is the crystal structure.

There is now no real alternative to using this description of the process of image formation of a crystal. Because atoms are of about 1 Å in diameter, a wavelength of the same order of magnitude must be used to investigate them. X-rays are the most convenient radiation to use (§ 1.7.4), but they cannot be refracted and so an image cannot be formed practically. An image can be formed only by the mathematical method of Fourier transformation, and thus there is no reason why three dimensions should not be adopted. This is now the usual practice in this work, which will be discussed in more detail in § 12.3.2.

9.4   Effects of finite apertures

9.4.1   Limit of resolution. We are now in a position to appreciate the consequences of the Abbe theory of image formation. An image is the diffraction pattern of the diffraction pattern of the object.

A perfect image can result only if the transformation at each stage is complete. But the first step of diffraction *cannot* be complete; angles of diffraction are limited to $\pm \pi$. In practice, the limitation is considerably more severe; the cone of radiation entering the objective of a microscope cannot exceed $\pi/2$ and is unlikely to be much greater than $\pi/3$. If all the light scattered by the object is effectively included in this cone, then the image will be as good as it can be. The finest detail, however, is measured by the fringes that would be produced by the outermost waves, say at angle α. From the reasoning in § 9.3.1 we can see that these fringes will have a spacing d' given by

$$d' = m\lambda/\sin \alpha.$$

Thus the finest detail in the image corresponds to a distance $\lambda/\sin \alpha$ in the object. This is the *limit of resolution* of the microscope and is equal to λ/numerical aperture (§ 9.2.2).

A more detailed treatment, taking into account the whole of the diffraction pattern (§ 9.3.4) and not merely the extreme parts, leads to a rather coarser limit. Suppose that we are trying to produce the image of two adjacent independent points of light. What in fact we see is the sum of two diffraction patterns of the aperture stop (§ 9.2.1), which is the objective of the instrument. If the two points are so close together that the total pattern is indistinguishable from a single pattern, the two points are completely unresolved. If we use the Rayleigh criterion that for complete resolution the maximum of one pattern should lie on the minimum of the other (§ 7.7.2), then from § 7.3.2 we see that the angular resolution is given by $1\cdot22\lambda/d$ where d is the diameter of the objective.

This result applies directly to the telescope. For the microscope, we have that the linear limit of resolution is given by $1\cdot22\lambda f/d$, where f is the focal length of the objective. This is $1\cdot22\lambda$/numerical aperture, slightly larger than that given by the previous simplified argument.

We shall show later that this result is not generally true; it applies only if the two points are independent, as when a telescope is used for observing a double star. When a microscope is used, the illumination on the object usually has some coherence (§ 9.5) and the resolution then becomes less.

Nor does this reasoning imply that a double star can be detected only if the two components are resolved. The eye is sensitive to

departures from circular symmetry, and can detect the presence of
two components when they are separated by much less than the
limit of resolution.

This theory may be illustrated by using a simple extension of the
optical diffractometer; as shown in Fig. 9.13, an extra lens is used
to form a direct image of the diffracting object. We can now
investigate the changes that occur in this image if the optical
transform is limited in some way.

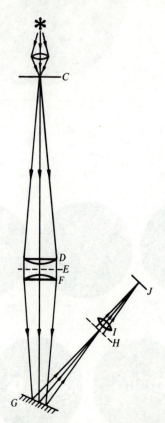

Fig. 9.13. An image of the pin-hole *C* is formed in the plane *H* by the optical system *DFG*.
The diffraction pattern of an object in the plane *E* is formed in the plane *H* and its image *J*
is formed by the auxiliary lens *I*. (From C. A. Taylor & H. Lipson, *Optical Transforms*,
Bell, 1964.)

For example, suppose that we have a general object as shown in
Fig. 9.14(*a*); its transform is shown in Fig. 9.14(*b*). We may place a
series of successively smaller holes over the transform, and we can

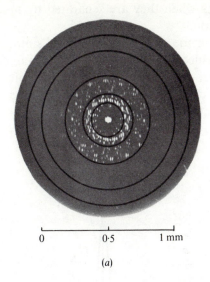

(a)

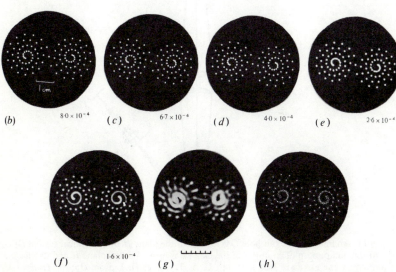

(b) 8.0×10^{-4} (c) 6.7×10^{-4} (d) 4.0×10^{-4} (e) 2.6×10^{-4}

(f) 1.6×10^{-4} (g)   (h)

Fig. 9.14. (a) Diffraction pattern of set of holes shown in 9.14(b). The circles indicate the apertures used to limit the transform. (b)–(g) Images of object shown in (b), with different numerical apertures. The apertures used are shown as circles superimposed on the diffraction pattern shown in 9.14(a). The divisions of the line below (g) show the Rayleigh limit of resolution. (h) is the image formed by the part of the diffraction pattern between the second and third circle from the centre. This illustrates apodization (§ 9.6.4). The image is sharper than the object, but it contains false detail.

then see how the image is affected. The succession of diagrams is self-explanatory.

The resolution limit imposed by a finite aperture can also be considered as an application of the convolution theorem (§ 3.5.4). As far as the reconstruction of the image is concerned, the optical transform of the object has been limited in extent by multiplying it by a finite aperture, a function which is zero outside certain limits. The reconstruction, which is the transform of the limited transform of the object, is therefore the convolution of the original object with the transform of the aperture. The latter transform exists for a certain region around zero, and therefore the convolution can be described roughly by saying that each point in the original sharp object is blurred into a region of this size.

This theory is intended to illustrate the principles of limit of resolution, but it is quite inadequate in practice since the type of illumination—a completely coherent plane wave—should not be used for image formation. The reasons for this statement will appear in § 9.5.

9.4.2   False detail. It is often thought that the sole effect of reducing the aperture of an optical system is to reduce the resolution by blurring fine detail. There can be, however, a more serious defect —the production of false detail, which may be finer than the limit of resolution: for example, in Fig. 9.10 we have seen that the reduction in the number of orders of diffraction leading to an image does not only blur the images of the slits forming the object; it also produces sets of intermediate maxima which, because they are weak, may appear as fine lines. The use of an optical instrument near to its limit of resolution is always liable to produce effects of this sort; when Abbe's theory (§ 1.7.1) was first announced, many microscopists adduced such effects as evidence that the theory was unacceptable. Even now, when the theory is fully accepted, it is sometimes forgotten in dealing with images produced by, for example, the electron microscope.

9.5   Effects of coherence

9.5.1   Importance of condenser. As far as geometrical optics is concerned, the condenser in a microscope merely serves to illuminate the specimen strongly. According to the wave theory, however, the conditions of scattering of the incident light are important, and

thus the condenser has as much importance as any other part of the optical system. In practice, for producing the best results from a microscope used to its limits, the condenser must be as good as the objective, and usually has exactly the same design.

The reason for this requirement can best be expressed in terms of coherence. Ideally, as we shall show in § 9.5.2, the object should be illuminated in completely incoherent light, which we could obtain by a general external illumination from a large source such as the sky. But this would be very weak, and we increase it by using a lens to focus a source of light on to the object; an image, however, cannot be perfect, and each point on the source is represented by an area of finite size on the object. In other words, neighbouring points on the object are illustrated by partially coherent light. What effect will this have?

9.5.2 Coherence and resolution. We can consider two extreme cases—complete coherence and complete incoherence. Suppose that we take as an object a pair of identical holes, over each of which the incident light is coherent. In the first case, we suppose that the coherence extends over the pair of holes. The transform is the diffraction pattern of a single hole, crossed by fringes, and the re-transformation of this is the image. In the second case we suppose that there is no coherence between the illumination of the two holes; the transform is then that of a single hole, blurred because a larger source has been used to give incoherence. The re-transformation again is the image.

To see the difference in the two image-producing processes we make use of the result (§ 7.4.6) that for coherent illumination we add the two vector amplitudes at each point in the combined diffraction pattern and then square the result to obtain the intensity; for incoherent illumination we square the amplitudes first to obtain intensities and then add them. But the curve formed by squaring each ordinate of a peak is always sharper than the peak itself; therefore for incoherent illumination the resolution must be better than for coherent illumination.

This difference can be shown by taking the results for the pair of holes that has just been considered. Fig. 9.15 shows sections through the amplitude-distribution curves in the images of two holes; these are the Bessel functions mentioned in § 7.3.2. The sum of these curves, which are within the Rayleigh-specified distance

for resolution, shows no dip which would correspond to resolution and therefore neither would its square. But if we square the curves first and then add them, Fig. 9.16 shows that there is now a dip.

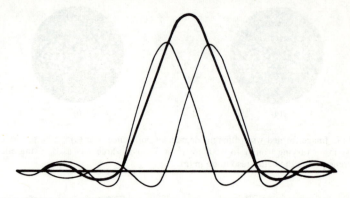

Fig. 9.15. Addition of the diffraction patterns of two holes coherently illuminated. The thin lines show the amplitude curves and the thick line their sum.

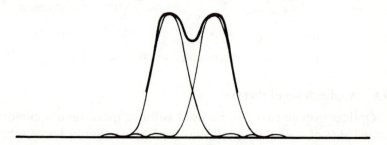

Fig. 9.16. Addition of the diffraction patterns of two holes incoherently illuminated. The thin lines show the intensity curves and the thick line their sum.

9.5.3 Practical illustration.
We have investigated these conclusions by forming an image of an object in the optical diffractometer, using different areas of transforms to obtain different resolutions, and different sizes of pin-hole for illumination to vary the coherence. The results are shown in Fig. 9.17.

In practice, incoherent illumination—called critical illumination—is obtained by forming an image of a source (Fig. 9.18(a)) directly on the object by means of a condenser. This arrangement, however, has the defect that irregularities of the source can affect the image formed. An arrangement that does not have this defect is called Kohler illumination and is shown in Fig. 9.18(b); an extended source is used and any one point on it gives parallel

coherent illumination of the object. For this reason it is sometimes called coherent illumination, but it is not so because different points on the source give different angles of incidence.

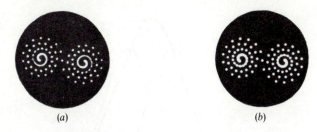

(a)   (b)

Fig. 9.17. Image formed with different degrees of coherence. For (a) a 12 μ pin-hole was used, giving γ varying from 1 to 0·50; for (b) a 370 μ pin-hole was used, giving effective incoherence. Note the better resolution in (b).

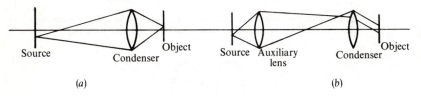

(a)   (b)

Fig. 9.18. Types of illumination. (a) Critical; (b) Kohler.

9.6 Applications of theory

Optical instruments can be used without more than a cursory knowledge of how they work, but a physicist should know more than this. He can then fully appreciate their limitations, can find the conditions under which they can be best used, and—most important—may find ways of extending their use to problems that cannot be solved by conventional means. Examples of these procedures will be described in the following sections. Four topics will be discussed—dark-ground illumination, Schlieren methods, phase-contrast microscopy and apodization of lenses for increased resolution. These topics are normally treated separately, but from the point of view of the transform treatment of image formation they can be seen to be simply related: they all involve some disturbance of the transform. Dark-ground illumination—the elimination of the direct light—is equivalent to removing the central peak of the transform; the Schlieren method is equivalent to cutting off half the transform including the central peak; phase contrast involves changing the phase of the central peak with respect to the rest of

the transform; apodization involves cutting out all but the extreme edge of the transform. In addition, we shall also give a brief description of the interference microscope.

9.6.1　Dark-ground illumination.

Suppose that we wish to observe a very small non-luminous object. If we use the ordinary method of illumination, in which the incident light bathes the specimen and enters the objective, it is likely that the amount of light scattered will be so small that it will be negligible compared with that contained in the incident beam and the object will not be seen. We can avoid this difficulty by arranging that the incident light is directed obliquely at the specimen so that it does not enter the objective; for observation of Brownian motion (§ 1.5.3), for example, it is usual to direct the incident light perpendicularly to the axis of the microscope.

The method is adequate if we merely want to know whether a scattering object is present or not; it is equivalent to forming an image by using only a small, off-centre, part of the transform, and this will not give much information about the nature of the object. For a reasonable image of the object we must use as much as possible of the transform, and this is achieved in practice by cutting out the incident beam precisely and using as much of the scattered light as possible (Fig. 9.19). This procedure is useful for an object

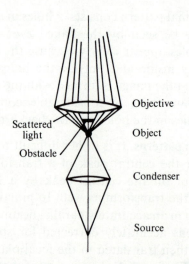

Fig. 9.19. Principle of dark-ground illumination.

that produces little absorption, but because of variations in thickness or refractive index, introduces appreciable phase differences into the waves transmitted by various parts—a phase object (§ 7.2.5).

The method can be illustrated quite simply by producing the transform of an object and placing a small black spot over the central peak. We have chosen as object a pattern of holes punched in a thin transparent film (Fig. 9.20(*a*)); since the film is not optically uniform the transform (Fig. 9.20(*b*)) is rather diffuse. A *very* small ink-spot on a piece of glass—it need not be optically flat since only a small area is used—is then placed over the centre of the transform (Fig. 9.20(*c*)) and the final image (Fig. 9.20(*d*)) compared with that obtained when the ink-spot is absent.

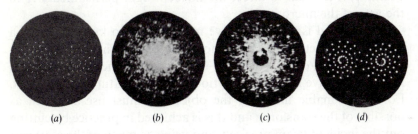

(*a*)   (*b*)   (*c*)   (*d*)

Fig. 9.20. (*a*) Pattern of holes in cellophane sheet; (*b*) diffraction pattern of (*a*); (*c*) as (*b*) with small spot over centre; (*d*) image formed from (*c*).

Since the original pattern consists of holes in a transparent sheet, it cannot easily be seen by the naked eye; in the instrument, however, the holes appear clearly because the edges scatter light, but the *intensity* inside and outside the holes is the same (Fig. 9.20(*a*)). But when the image is formed with the centre of the transform blacked out, there is considerable contrast (Fig. 9.20(*c*)) between intensities in the holes and the background.

9.6.2   Schlieren patterns. It is rather difficult to place a small spot ($\sim 0 \cdot 1$ mm) over the central peak of a transform. An alternative method is to cut off the central peak by a knife-edge, thereby cutting off half the transform as well. In practice the object to be studied is placed in an accurately parallel beam which is brought to a focus by a lens accurately corrected for spherical aberration. A knife-edge is then translated in the focal plane of the lens until it just overlaps the focus. A clear image of the object can then be

seen (Fig. 9.21). We have illustrated this method by the same object that we used for dark-ground illumination (Fig. 9.20(a)); the image now has some defects that will be discussed later.

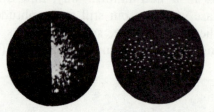

Fig. 9.21. Image formed by cutting out half the diffraction pattern in 9.20(b).

The Schlieren method has two other by-products. First, it can be used to test a lens—the Foucault knife-edge test—for if a lens suffers from spherical aberration it will not be possible to put the knife-edge in a position to cut off only half the transform. Thus, if we observe the lens with the eye close to the knife-edge as it traverses the focal plane, the intensity of illumination across the surface will appear to change (Fig. 9.22); we can then deduce what modifications to make to the lens. The Foucault method can also be used to locate the focus of a lens extremely accurately.

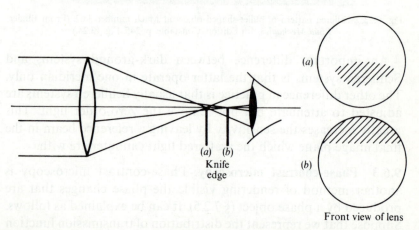

Fig. 9.22. Appearance of lens suffering from spherical aberration when subject to Foucault knife-edge test. (a) When knife edge is in paraxial focal plane; (b) when knife-edge is in marginal focal plane.

A second use of the Schlieren method is important in fluid dynamics. A wind tunnel in which the density of air is constant

(and hence the refractive index is constant too) is an object with neither phase nor amplitude variations. The existence of waves or other disturbances in the tunnel will modify the density and refractive index in a non-uniform way, and thus produces an object with phase variation but still no amplitude variations. By using the Schlieren technique, such variations can be studied visually as changes in intensity in the final image (Fig. 9.23).

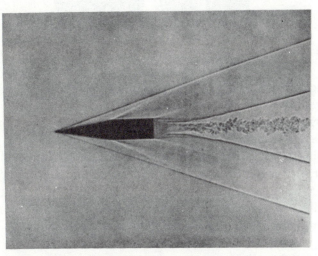

Fig. 9.23. Schlieren pattern of bullet-shaped object at Mach number 3.62. (From Binder, *Fluid Mechanics*, 4th Edition, Constable, p. 245, Fig. 13.24.)

An important difference between dark-ground systems and Schlieren systems is that the latter operate in one meridian only. The other difference in practice is that usually Schlieren systems are adjusted to attenuate but not remove the zero-order light. This greatly increases the sensitivity by leaving a reference beam in the final image plane which the scattered light can interfere with.

9.6.3 Phase-contrast microscopy. Phase-contrast microscopy is another method of rendering visible the phase changes that are produced by a phase object (§ 7.2.5). It can be explained as follows. Suppose that we represent the distribution of transmission function in the image by the expression $Ae^{i\phi}$, where A is the amplitude and ϕ is the phase angle. In the type of image that we are considering A is constant but ϕ varies from point to point. An object with varying ϕ will produce a diffraction pattern and we can envisage the production of the image from this pattern in terms of an Argand diagram;

two examples are shown—for a positive value of ϕ (Fig. 9.24(a)) and a negative value (Fig. 9.24(b)). The length of the vector is the same for each.

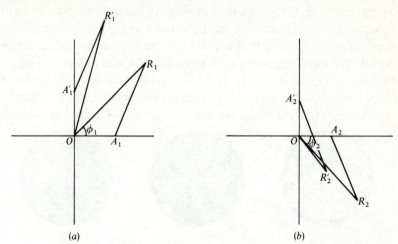

Fig. 9.24. Principle of phase contrast. (a) Positive phase angle; (b) negative phase angle.

Each vector, OR_1 or OR_2, can be considered as having two components—a real one, OA_1 or OA_2 from the central peak, and a complex one, A_1R_1 or A_2R_2 from the rest of the transform. OA_1 and OA_2 are, of course, equal. If the real components are changed by $\pi/2$ they are represented, OA'_1 and OA'_2, on the imaginary axis, and combined with the same complex components as before produce resultants OR'_1 and OR'_2, which are of quite different lengths. In other words, the change in phase ϕ has been translated into a difference of intensity.

An algebraic method of explaining the process, which clearly points out its exactitude only for small values of ϕ, expands the transmission function to

$$Ae^{i\phi} \doteqdot A + iA\phi.$$

Changing the phase of the zero-order term by $\pi/2$ gives the function

$$iA + iA\phi \doteqdot iAe^{\phi},$$

which has a real variation of amplitude.

It is difficult to illustrate this device in any primitive way; putting a very thin plate of about 0·1 mm diameter over the centre of a transform is too difficult. We can, however, produce an arbitrary

phase difference by putting a transparent sheet with a small hole in it over the transform, and the results of this are shown in Fig. 9.25.

In practice, the device is not so simple as we have described. As we have seen in § 9.5.1, we do not want to use completely coherent light, and if we use incoherent light there is no precise transform over the centre of which a thin plate—the phase plate—can be introduced. We must use a beam of finite angular dimensions in order to have sufficient intensity and also to produce a small depth of focus; otherwise the out-of-focus parts of the image will be disturbing. A compromise is therefore necessary, and is effected as follows.

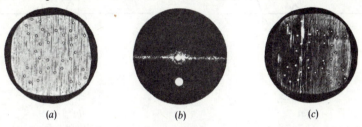

(a) $\qquad\qquad\qquad\qquad$ (b) $\qquad\qquad\qquad\qquad$ (c)

Fig. 9.25. (a) Pattern of holes punched in cellophane. (Note the irregularities produced by the method of production of the sheet). (b) Fraunhofer diffraction pattern of (a). The white spot shows the size of hole in the thin transparent sheet placed over the centre of the pattern. (c) Image of (a) formed with hole in position. Note the contrast between the holes and the background.

The beam from the source of light is limited by an annular ring (Fig. 9.26) placed between the source and the condenser; the condenser and the objective form a lens system which produces a real image of the ring above the objective. A phase plate is then inserted in the plane of this image to match its dimensions exactly. All undeviated light from the specimen must therefore pass through this plate. The final image is formed by interference between the undeviated light passing through the phase plate and the deviated light which passes by the side of it. The ideal conditions are only approximately obeyed, for some of the deviated light will also pass through the phase plate. The phase plate is constructed by the vacuum deposition of a dielectric material such as cryolite (Na_3AlF_6) on to an optically parallel glass support. The techniques of vacuum deposition have reached a level of perfection which makes control of the dimensions and thickness of such a plate a fairly simple process.

If the object produces only small differences of phase, the centre spot of the diffraction pattern is outstandingly strong and changing

its phase produces too great a difference in the image. Therefore the phase plate is made to transmit only about 10–20 per cent of the light. It looks like a small dark ring on a clear background.

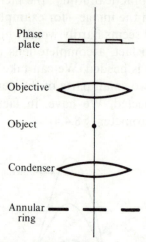

Fig. 9.26. Principle of phase-contrast microscope. The phase plate is coincident with the image of the annular ring formed in the condenser-objective lens system.

9.6.4 Enhanced resolution.

It might be thought that the theory outlined in § 9.4.1 would give the maximum resolution of which a lens of given aperture was capable. In fact, we can, if we wish, increase resolution at the expense of other image-forming properties merely by placing an opaque circular screen over the centre of the aperture stop—the lens of a telescope for example. We can see how this increased resolution arises by using the theorem that the diffraction pattern of two objects is the vector sum of the two separate diffraction patterns computed with respect to the same origin (§ 7.3.5). Thus the diffraction pattern of an annular ring is the diffraction pattern of the whole aperture up to the outer circumference minus that of the inner, opaque, part. From Fig. 9.27 we can see that the first minimum of this diffraction pattern occurs at a smaller angle than that of the outer aperture. The Rayleigh criterion thus indicates a better resolution.

Fundamentally, what we have done is to make use only of the outer part of the transform—the part that gives the finest detail in the image. Because the information is not confused by that from the inner part of the transform, increased resolution results. But the image itself is obviously unsatisfactory.

The device can be used for telescope objectives by depositing a thin layer of metal on the surface; it is best to shade it off gradually rather than to produce a sharp cut-off. It is doubtful, however, whether the device is of practical utility; the increase in resolution is appreciable only when the image—for example, a double star—is barely recognizable. It seems hardly worthwhile spoiling a good lens for this purpose. In fact, a complete lens need not be used, since only the periphery is needed. We can take the method to its extreme, and use only two small parts of the periphery, and these need not even be connected. We have, in fact, re-invented the Michelson stellar interferometer (§ 8.4.4)!

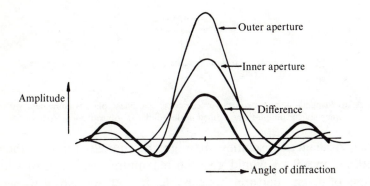

Fig. 9.27. Diffraction pattern of annular aperture of which the inner radius is 0·8 of the outer radius. The curve shown by the heavy line is the difference of the other two.

9.6.5 Interference microscope.

It is possible to adapt an ordinary microscope to view a transparent specimen in terms of the distortion that it produces in an interference pattern. The general principle is to form a pattern of two-beam interference fringes by some sort of interferometer (§ 7.8), and to place the object in the path of one of the beams. The microscope enables objects to be studied on a very small scale.

One of the most sensitive devices is the Michelson interferometer (§ 7.8.2); if the fringes are very broad, the specimen can cover only a fraction of one of them, and then quite small differences of optical paths are shown. A more conventional type of interference microscope, devised by Dyson, is as follows.

The specimen O is placed between two optical flats, G_1 and G_2 (Fig. 9.28), of which the lowest face is heavily silvered on a small

patch C_1 at the centre and the other faces are semi-silvered. The specimen is illuminated by a converging cone of light, of which the middle is obstructed by the patch C_1. Let us trace the path of one oblique ray AO, ignoring any refraction that takes place. This ray will be partially reflected at the upper surface of G_1, will be reflected from C_1 and will interfere with the ray through O that has undergone similar reflexions in G_2. It can be seen that, if we consider the whole cone of light, the resultant will be a divergent interference pattern. To bring the pattern to the entrance window of the microscope, Dyson uses a spherical reflector, with a clear patch in the centre, which behaves as shown in Fig. 9.28.

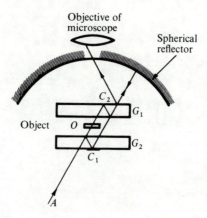

Fig. 9.28. A form of interference microscope.

9.7 Holograms

Since all the information concerning the image of an object is contained in its diffraction pattern, it is tempting to ask whether this information can be recorded on a photographic plate and then used to reconstruct the image. The germ of this idea was suggested in 1948 and had some limited success; but the invention of the laser has now enabled the operation to be carried through completely successfully.

The difficulty involved is the recording of the relative phases of the different parts of the optical transform (§§ 9.3.5 and 9.3.8);

photographic film can record only intensities, and a direct diffraction pattern of the intensity distribution, although it has some relation to the object, is not an image of it.

Fig. 9.29. Gabor hologram. (From *Nature* (1948), **161**, 778.)

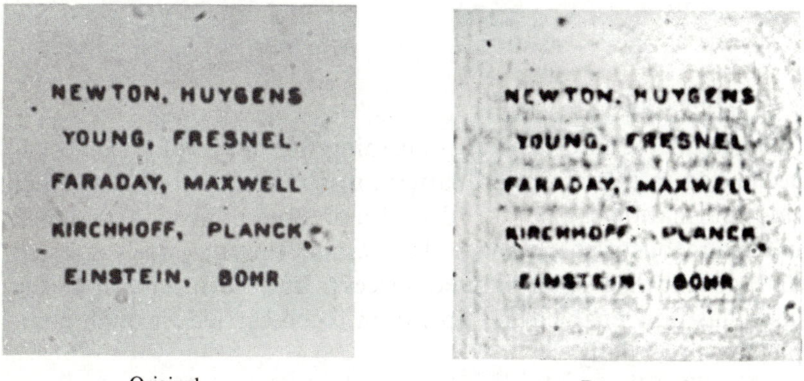

NEWTON, HUYGENS	NEWTON, HUYGENS
YOUNG, FRESNEL.	YOUNG, FRESNEL
FARADAY, MAXWELL	FARADAY, MAXWELL
KIRCHHOFF, PLANCK	KIRCHHOFF, PLANCK
EINSTEIN, BOHR	EINSTEIN, BOHR
Original	Reconstruction

Fig. 9.30. Image reconstituted from Gabor hologram.

9.7.1 Gabor's method. A reason for trying to overcome this difficulty was an attempt by Gabor to solve the problem of image formation in the electron microscope. As we shall see later (§ 12.3.3), the resolution obtainable in the electron microscope is not limited by the wavelength (~ 0.1 Å) but by the aberrations (Appendix II) of the electron lenses; these cannot be corrected and therefore a very small aperture has to be used. This aperture is so small that the resultant image can be considered effectively as a Fresnel diffraction pattern (§ 6.3) of the object. Gabor thought that a better image might be reconstructed from this pattern with visible light, using a lens system that could correct for the aberrations of the electron lenses.

To demonstrate this idea, he made some optical diffraction patterns and reconstructed images from them. The phase problem was solved by using an object that consisted of a small amount of black detail on a large transparent background; the background would produce a uniform phase and the variation in phase of the diffraction pattern would be recorded as differences in intensity. The intensity would be greatest where the phase of the diffraction pattern was the same as that of the background and least where there was a phase difference of π.

The method did not work very well, even for optical patterns, as we can see from Fig. 9.30, and was never applied to electron-microscope pictures. But it had an idea in it that was later developed with complete success in another approach, which will be described in § 9.7.3.

9.7.2 X-ray microscope. A more successful approach in a limited field was made by Bragg in 1939; he used the fact that if a crystal had an atom of preponderant weight in the unit cell, its diffraction pattern would decide the phases of the diffracted radiation; in particular, if the atom were at the origin of the unit cell the phases would all be the same and could be taken as zero. Therefore if one made a representation of a section of the X-ray diffraction pattern of a crystal in the form of holes in an opaque plate (Fig. 9.31(a)), the sizes of the holes being related to the corresponding order of X-ray diffraction, then the Fraunhofer diffraction pattern of the plate should be an image of the structure (Fig. 9.31(b), (c)).

Other workers have taken the subject further, by extending the scope of the method to crystals that do not contain a heavy atom

and for which the relative phases of the orders of diffraction can adopt general values between 0 and π. The resulting diffraction patterns, of which Fig. 9.32 is an example, can be regarded as photographs of atomic arrangements with magnification of the order of 10^8. It must be pointed out, however, that these are not images in the proper sense of the word since extra information —the relative phases of the waves—has to be supplied artificially.

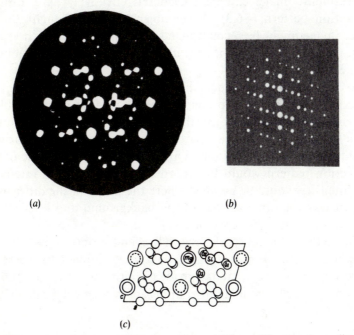

(a)   (b)

(c)

Fig. 9.31. (a) Set of holes representing orders of X-ray diffraction from diopside, $CaMg(SiO_3)_2$; (b) diffraction pattern of (a) representing atoms in crystal structure; (c) diagram of structure to compare with (b). (From *Nature* (1939), **143**, 678.)

9.7.3 Application of the laser.

The hologram approach has now been applied successfully, by Leith and Upatnieks, because of the intense beams of spatially coherent light (§ 8.4.1) that can be produced by a laser (§ 11.7). In 'principle, the same method can be used with ordinary sources of light, but the production of spatially coherent sources in this way usually results in such a small intensity that the experiments would hardly have been practicable.

The experimental set-up is surprisingly simple (Fig. 9.33(a)). A beam from the laser is reflected so that it impinges obliquely on an optically flat photographic plate. At the same time, some light from

the laser beam falls directly upon the object, which must be firmly sited and not subject to any vibration; scattered light from the object also falls on the photographic plate. A pattern of light and shade is recorded, resulting from the interference between the incident wave and the scattered light. This is the hologram.

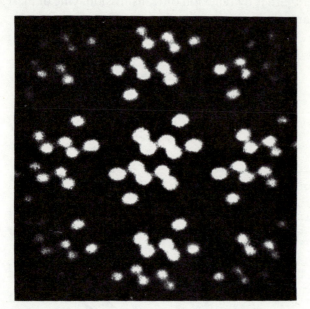

Fig. 9.32. Image of hexamethylbenzene crystal.

To observe the image, light from a laser is allowed to fall on the hologram, and two images can be seen—a real one formed by convergent light and a virtual one formed by divergent light. The images are both three-dimensional in the sense that as the direction of observation changes the relative positions of the various parts of the image change exactly as in a three-dimensional object. Apart from the fact that the image is in monochrome, the illusion of reality is complete.

The theory of the process, since it makes use of Fresnel diffraction, is rather complicated, but if we reduce it to Fraunhofer terms (§ 7.1) it can be reasonably simply understood. Suppose that the beam directly incident upon the hologram plate is parallel, and that the object consists of a single point scatterer, a long distance from the plate. The direct beam produces a uniform illumination with a linear change of phase along it (Fig. 9.34): but this change of phase

becomes apparent only when the scattered beam is also present; then a set of interference fringes is formed with a sinusoidal variation of intensity similar to that in Young's fringes (§ 7.1.4). This hologram behaves as a diffraction grating, and because it has a sinusoidal distribution of intensity it will produce only a zero order and two first orders, either by reflexion or transmission. One of these orders is the image of the point scatterer.

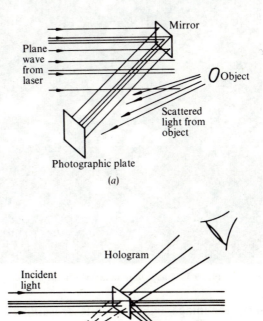

Fig. 9.33. (a) Set-up for producing holograms; (b) set-up for producing real image I_R and virtual image I_V.

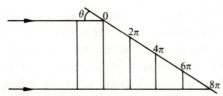

Fig. 9.34. Plane wave falling on oblique plate showing linear variation of phase on plate at particular instant of time.

It is most surprising that the same result applies if the object produces a complicated diffraction pattern. The basic periodicity is that produced by the obliquity of the direct beam on the hologram plate; if the angle of incidence is θ, the periodicity has a spacing of $\lambda/\sin\theta$ (Fig. 9.34). If a pattern with varying phase falls upon this, a maximum of a given phase will be displaced towards the region of the plate for which the phase is more nearly the same, for the two waves will tend to add on that side more than on the other. Thus the effect is to produce a grating in which the elements are somewhat displaced.

Now we have seen (§ 7.7.3) that such a grating produces satellites or ghost lines. If we look along the direction of the first order we see this collection of ghosts, and it is these that form the image. The grating is so imperfect that the precise order of diffraction is not produced; otherwise there would be a strong spot at the centre of the image.

Another approach can be made in terms of Fresnel diffraction. The scattering from a point interferes with the reference wave to produce something like Newton's rings, which—after development of the plate—can act like a zone plate with sinusoidal variation. From the theory of § 6.3.4 it can be shown that such a zone plate gives only first orders of diffraction in addition to the zero order, and so produces only two foci—one real and one virtual. These are the two images of the point scatterer.

Nevertheless, it is difficult to see any important applications for the device; its only advantage over an ordinary photograph is its three-dimensional quality, and this can be simulated by stereo-scopic photographs. There have been some suggestions that the method might be used with X-rays; by taking a hologram with X-rays and viewing it with visible light from a laser, one might be able to 'see' an image of a crystal structure directly. This project seems unlikely; making an X-ray laser is several orders of magnitude more difficult than making an optical laser, and controlling an object to a fraction of an X-ray wavelength would appear to be impossible. Moreover a crystal does not give all its diffraction pattern at one setting (§ 7.6), and a three-dimensional pattern cannot be recorded on a plate. The method would therefore be applicable only to non-crystalline matter. Success in this field would indeed be of inestimable value, but the problems of producing spatial coherence on the X-scale seem to be remote.

CHAPTER 10

THE CLASSICAL THEORY OF DISPERSION

10.1 Why classical theory is usually adequate

Long before the advent of quantum theory, which is necessary for a complete description of the interaction between radiation and matter, many of the more striking dispersion effects in materials had been explained on very simple and non-too-unrealistic classical models of the structure of matter. Since the mechanisms involved are simpler and easier to grasp than those of quantum mechanics, we shall discuss the classical theory first. The reason why classical and quantum results do not diverge much is that most of the interesting results are the effect of resonances, and it turns out that the classical description of a resonance is very similar in almost all respects to the quantum description. Where the classical theory is at its weakest is in the explanation of the sub-atomic processes that are responsible for the atom's behaving in a resonant manner at all. This question will therefore have to await the next chapter for its answer.

We shall discuss dispersion effects arising from two distinct causes. The first effects, which result from sub-atomic processes, and whose explanation involves postulating a model of the structure of an atom, are resonance phenomena and occur at frequencies in and around the optical region; in quantum theory they are transitions between atomic energy levels. The second group of effects arises from interactions between neighbouring atoms or molecules and are generally characterized by being relaxation rather than resonance phenomena. Those we shall discuss are typical in having their greatest effects at frequencies lower than optical, extending over a band very broad compared with the resonance effects.

10.1.1 The classical atom. To discuss the internal structure of an atom or molecule we shall use a model consisting of two parts of opposite charge connected by springs (Fig. 10.1). If the two parts have non-zero masses this system will have a resonance frequency; it is a weakness of the model that only one resonant frequency

results, since we know that any one atom has a large number of frequencies, observed as spectral lines. The atom may or may not have a static dipole moment when it is in its equilibrium state; if it has, it becomes eligible for study from the point of view of relaxation processes, and it can then respond by bodily rotation to a static electric field. Such effects are discussed in the fourth part of this chapter.

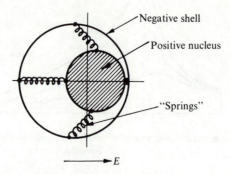

Fig. 10.1. The model 'classical atom'.

10.1.2 Properties of a forced harmonic oscillator.
The electric field in an electromagnetic wave will exert forces and couples on a molecule such as we have described, and since it has a resonant frequency we shall first give a brief résumé of the properties of a damped simple-harmonic oscillator subject to a periodic force.

Suppose that the oscillator has a natural frequency η and damping constant κ, so that its equation of motion when the driving force has frequency ω is

$$\ddot{x} + \kappa \dot{x} + \eta^2 x = \frac{F}{m} \exp(i\omega t). \tag{10.1}$$

The equation has two solutions; the first is a transient oscillation of frequency η which dies away in a time κ^{-1} and is rarely of interest. The second is the forced solution, which has time variation $\exp(i\omega t)$ and settles down to a constant amplitude and phase during a time considerably longer than κ^{-1} from the beginning of the force. The amplitude and phase of the forced oscillations are found by substituting $x = A \exp(i\omega t)$ into (10.1). We shall allow A to be complex, thereby indicating that the amplitude x does not always oscillate in phase with the driving force. The phase difference between x and F is the *argument* of A (arg A). We obtain a family of

(A, ω) curves depending on the parameter κ/η. The curves are illustrated in Fig. 10.2.

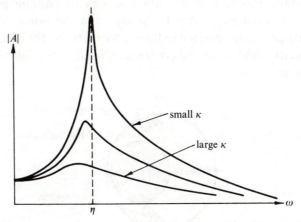

Fig. 10.2. Amplitude of response of a simple harmonic oscillator for various degrees of damping.

The important facts to notice are as follows:

(1) The lightly damped oscillator has a large amplitude only in a band with a width of the order of κ about the resonant frequency η (Fig. 10.2). At frequencies below η, arg $A = 0$, implying that the oscillator moves in phase with the force, whereas above the resonant frequency the oscillator moves out of phase with the force (Fig. 10.3). At the resonant frequency η, the oscillator and force are in phase quadrature (arg $A = \pi/2$).

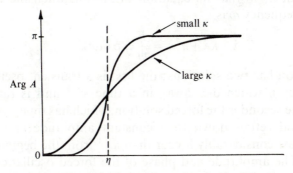

Fig. 10.3. Phase of the response in Fig. 10.2.

(2) The heavily damped oscillator responds to the force over a very much larger frequency range, again $\pm \kappa$ about η, but never

reaches as large an amplitude as the lightly damped one. The phase relations are the same as in (1), the transition being spread out over the larger frequency band.

(3) The maximum amplitude is not achieved exactly at the resonant $\eta = \omega$, but always at a slightly lower value of ω, depending on κ:

$$\omega \, (\text{max. amplitude}) = \left(\eta^2 - \frac{\kappa^2}{2}\right)^{\frac{1}{2}}.$$

10.1.3 Radiation from an oscillating dipole.

It will also be useful to remember the rate at which an oscillating dipole radiates energy, as we are concerned here with simple harmonic oscillators whose elements are charged. A changing dipole moment radiates energy at rate

$$W = \frac{2[\ddot{p}]^2}{3\epsilon_0 c^3} \tag{10.2}$$

(§ 4.5.1); if the dipole is oscillating, $p = p_0 \exp(i\omega t)$, and (10.2) becomes

$$W = \frac{2\omega^4 p^2}{3\epsilon_0 c^3}. \tag{10.3}$$

This power radiation, with its strong frequency dependence, is one of the reasons for the existence of damping.

10.2 Rayleigh scattering

The simplest interaction between radiation and matter is Rayleigh scattering, in which the frequency of the light is well removed from a resonance in the atom. Application of an electric field **E** to the hypothetical atom (Fig. 10.1) separates the positive and negative charges by forcing them in opposite directions and thus produces a dipole moment proportional to **E**, at least to the first order; i.e.

$$\mathbf{p} = \alpha \mathbf{E}$$

where α is called the polarizability of the atom. The effect of a breakdown in this relationship at high value of **E** is discussed in § 11.8.1. When a light wave falls on the atom the electric field **E** oscillates, and so the atom radiates energy at rate

$$W = \frac{2\omega^4 \alpha^2 E^2}{3\epsilon_0 c^3},$$

the energy being entirely derived by absorption from the incoming radiation. Since the rate of energy incidence in the incoming beam is

$$\mathscr{E} = \frac{\epsilon_0 E^2 c}{4\pi} \quad (\S 4.2.4), \tag{10.4}$$

we can write the rate of loss of energy with distance as equal to the rate of loss of energy per atom multiplied by the number, N, of atoms per unit volume:

$$\frac{\partial \mathscr{E}}{\partial x} = -NW = -N \cdot \frac{2\omega^4 \alpha^2 E^2}{3\epsilon_0 c^3}$$

$$= -\frac{8\pi\omega^4 \alpha^2 N \mathscr{E}}{3\epsilon_0^2 c^4}. \tag{10.5}$$

Thus $\mathscr{E}$ can be deduced from the equation

$$\frac{1}{\mathscr{E}} \frac{\partial \mathscr{E}}{\partial x} = -\frac{8\pi\omega^4 \alpha^2 N}{3\epsilon_0^2 c^4},$$

to be

$$\mathscr{E} = \mathscr{E}_0 \exp(-\gamma x),$$

where

$$\gamma = \frac{8\pi\omega^4 \alpha^2 N}{3\epsilon_0^2 c^4}.$$

There are two assumptions here: first, that each scattering centre behaves independently—that is, that there are no interference effects between the scattered waves—and, secondly, that a negligible proportion of the scattered radiation continues in the forward direction to contribute to the main beam. The first assumption is valid if the scattering centres are separated by distances of the order of, or greater than, one wavelength, because the phases of the scattered waves are then random and they will not interfere. The validity of the second assumption depends on the geometry of the experiment; in a very narrow beam it will be true, whereas in an infinitely wide beam half the scattered light will be travelling onwards and remain part of the initial beam. The effect of such considerations forms the substance of the following sections.

10.2.1 Polarization of the scattered waves. The dipole moment produced in the atom is parallel to the electric vector in the incident light and will re-radiate with a radiation polar diagram as described in §4.5.1 (Fig. 4.20). The intensity radiated along the axis of the dipole is zero. It therefore follows that scattered radiation along

a line perpendicular to the incident light is plane-polarized normal to the plane containing the incident and scattered light. In other directions the light will appear incompletely polarized. With the aid of a single polaroid sheet (§ 5.6.3), these conclusions can easily be tested using ordinary sunlight (Fig. 10.4), although polarization is far from complete because of multiple scattering.

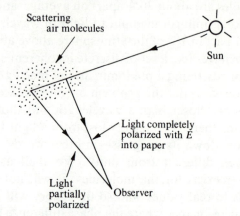

Fig. 10.4. Polarization of atmospherically scattered sunlight.

10.2.2 Frequency dependence. The most striking part of formula (10.5) is the fourth-power dependence on frequency: blue light is scattered about ten times more intensely than red light; this is the reason for the common observation that the sky is blue (weather permitting) during most of the day, but can appear red when one looks directly towards the sun at dawn or sunset. The mid-day appearance involves radiation scattered by air molecules at all heights and is therefore predominantly blue; the redness occurs at daybreak and sundown because at those times the sun's light passes horizontally through the atmosphere, and the very long air-passage results in the scattering away of a much greater fraction of the blue light than of the red.

A little thought, however, will show that this explanation is far from being a complete answer to the question.

10.3 Coherent scattering by a dense medium

If the atmosphere were all condensed to atmospheric pressure it would exist for a height of about 7 miles, and we know that—on a

clear day at least—a path of seven miles of air is quite transparent; there is certainly very little bluish tinge in view at this distance. However, in the atmosphere the pressure decreases with height and the molecules separate further; the stage is eventually reached when the mean separation becomes of the order of the wavelength of light, and then incoherent scattering from the air molecules takes the place of coherent scattering at lower levels. At sea level the air molecules are about 30 Å apart on average, and thus appear very much like a uniform medium to light of wavelength 5000 Å; it is only the 1 part in 10^6 of the atmosphere above about 100 miles which really behaves like a set of discrete incoherent scatters and is responsible for scattering a predominance of blue light towards us.

We shall now consider the problem of coherent scattering when the molecules are closer than a wavelength and show that under these conditions there is no energy lost from a light beam, but the effect is to slow down its progress—in other words, to produce a refractive index different from unity. We shall assume that a polarizability α exists for the molecules; it will not be necessary to restrict this to real values, and so the theory will be applicable to regions near resonance where the phase difference between force and response of the simple harmonic oscillator can be represented by a complex value of α.

Consider scattering by a thin slab δx in the yz plane, the incident radiation travelling in the x direction. There are N molecules per unit volume, each of polarizability α. The scattered amplitude at point Q (Fig. 10.5) is calculated by a Fresnel integral (§ 6.4). In this integral we can use the explicit form $(4.9(b))$ for the electric field at a large distance from an oscillating dipole, remembering to

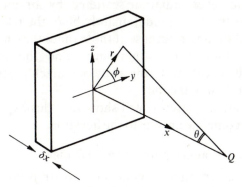

Fig. 10.5. Coherent scattering by a dense medium.

replace $[\ddot{p}]$ by $-\omega^2\alpha E_0$; we obtain a contribution to δE_Q to the field at Q arising from this slab given by

$$\delta E_Q = -\int_{r=0}^{\infty} \frac{N\alpha E_0 \omega^2\, \delta x}{\epsilon_0 c^2 (x^2+r^2)^{\frac{1}{2}}} \exp\{-ik(r^2+x^2)^{\frac{1}{2}}\}2\pi r\, dr. \quad (10.6)$$

There should also be an inclination factor resulting from the polarization of the incident wave but, as in other Fresnel diffraction calculations (§ 6.4.5), this has negligible effect. The integral (10.6) has the value

$$\delta E_Q = -\frac{N\alpha E_0 \omega^2}{\epsilon_0 c^2} \exp(-ikx) i\lambda\, \delta x$$

$$= -2\pi i E_0 k N\alpha \epsilon_0^{-1} \exp(-ikx)\, \delta x \quad (k = \omega/c).$$

If α is real, the scattered amplitude is in phase quadrature with the direct wave (that is the meaning of the i factor) and therefore does not alter its magnitude, but only its phase; in other words, the velocity of the wave is modified, but there is no attenuation (Fig. 10.6).

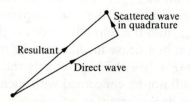

Scattered wave in quadrature

Resultant

Direct wave

Fig. 10.6. Amplitude-phase diagram for coherent scattering when there is no absorption.

We now have

$$E\,(\text{total}) = E\,(\text{direct}) + E\,(\text{scattered}),$$

of which $E\,(\text{direct})$ is $E_0 \exp(-ikx)$. Thus, differentiating,

$$\frac{dE}{dx} = -ikE - i2\pi N\alpha\epsilon_0^{-1}kE,$$

to which equation the wave solution

$$E = E_0 \exp\left\{-ikx\left(1+\frac{2\pi N\alpha}{\epsilon_0}\right)\right\}$$

is appropriate. The medium has refractive index $\mu = 1+2\pi N\alpha/\epsilon_0$ which is the binomial approximation to what we should expect from Maxwell's equations

$$\mu^2 = \frac{\epsilon}{\epsilon_0} = 1+\frac{4\pi P}{\epsilon_0} = 1+\frac{4\pi N\alpha}{\epsilon_0}.$$

Thus the *bulk continuum* approach of Maxwell's equations is justified by integrating the microscopic scattering produced by individual coherent scatters. We can therefore restrict our attention to determining the value of α for individual molecules and know that, providing they are arranged closely enough and uniformly enough to scatter coherently, the bulk refractive index and dielectric constant can be written down immediately.

10.3.1   Dipole interaction in a dense medium. If the medium is dense, the field that produces the dipole moment in an atom may be appreciably different from that applied by the external wave because of interactions with neighbouring molecules. The polarization is produced by a local field

$$E_{\text{loc}} = E_{\text{app}} + \frac{4\pi}{3\epsilon_0}P,$$

(a proof of this formula, which is true for cubic or random arrangements of molecules, is given in most textbooks on electricity). If we use E_{loc} instead of E_{app} in the analysis which follows, slight differences will arise because dielectric constant is defined and measured as D/E_{app} and the refractive index is the square root of this. The correction in a dense medium can be made by replacing $E-1$ by $3\{(E-1)/(E+2)\}$ (which are clearly the same in the limit $E \to 1$), but we shall not be concerned with such corrections here, although they may be important in practice.

10.3.2   Resonance and anomalous dispersion. Near the resonance frequency α is not real, and as a result the statement that the scattered wave is in quadrature with the direct wave is no longer correct. The refractive index is still modified, but absorption may also occur (Fig. 10.7).

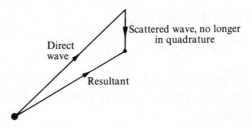

Fig. 10.7. Absorption occurs when the scattered wave is no longer in quadrature with the direct wave.

The atom, it will be remembered, is considered as a charged mechanical system with natural frequency η and damping constant κ like the oscillator in § 10.1.1. Under the action of an oscillating field $E_0 e^{i\omega t}$ the light electron shell receives a force

$$E_0 e \exp(i\omega t)$$

and its equation of motion is therefore

$$\ddot{x} + \kappa\dot{x} + \eta^2 x = \frac{E_0 e}{m} \exp(i\omega t). \tag{10.7}$$

This equation has a steady solution

$$x = \frac{E_0 e}{m} \cdot \frac{1}{\eta^2 - \omega^2 + i\kappa\omega} \exp(i\omega t). \tag{10.8}$$

Using the relationship that the dipole moment of the atom is

$$p = ex$$

and that the polarizability α is the ratio p/E, we obtain

$$\alpha = \frac{e^2}{m}(\eta^2 - \omega^2 + i\kappa\omega)^{-1}. \tag{10.9}$$

The dielectric constant ϵ, arising from N such molecules per unit volume, is thus

$$\epsilon = 1 + 4\pi N\alpha\epsilon_0^{-1} = 1 + \Omega^2(\eta^2 - \omega^2 + i\kappa\omega)^{-1}, \tag{10.10}$$

where Ω is the plasma frequency (§§ 12.7.1 and 10.3.6),

$$\Omega = \left(\frac{4\pi Ne^2}{\epsilon_0 m}\right)^{\frac{1}{2}}.$$

The complex refractive index is

$$\mu = \epsilon^{\frac{1}{2}}$$

and, when ϵ is approximately unity, can be expanded by the binomial theorem. If μ has real and imaginary parts μ_1 and μ_2

$$\mu_1 = 1 + \frac{\frac{1}{2}\Omega^2(\eta^2 - \omega^2)}{(\eta^2 - \omega^2)^2 + \kappa^2\omega^2},$$

$$\mu_2 = -\frac{1}{2}\Omega^2 \frac{\kappa\omega}{(\eta^2 - \omega^2)^2 + \kappa^2\omega^2}.$$

It should be pointed out, however, that in practice this approximation is often invalid, and the square root of ϵ must be evaluated properly. It is quite possible for ϵ to become negative in this region. and then only evanescent propagation (§ 2.3.2) is possible. As

implied in § 2.3.1 the real and imaginary parts of μ represent refractive index and absorption coefficient respectively.

These two quantities, μ_1 and μ_2, are illustrated in Figs. 10.8 and 10.9 which show two important features:

(1) The refractive index becomes large at frequencies just below resonance, and sharply drops to a value less than unity just above the resonance. The region of sharp change, where $d\mu_1/d\omega$ is negative, is called the *anomalous dispersion region*, because dispersion usually gives rise to positive $d\mu_1/d\omega$.

(2) The anomalous dispersion region is accompanied by absorption. We shall show that this is necessary from very general considerations (§ 12.8.5).

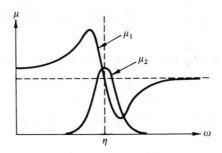

Fig. 10.8. Anomalous dispersion.

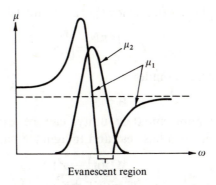

Evanescent region

Fig. 10.9. Anomalous dispersion by a strong spectral line, which can lead to evanescent propagation.

This absorption is, of course, the absorption line corresponding to an emission line in the atomic spectrum. If the atom is excited, its oscillations at its natural frequency will be radiated and die away in the decay time κ^{-1} (the transient of § 10.1.1). Such a decaying oscillation gives rise to a spectral line of width κ corresponding

to the absorption line at the same frequency and of the same width
as that which we have calculated above. In fact, the correspondence
between the emission and absorption line characteristics is sufficiently complete for it to lead to a convenient method of measuring
line-widths which will be discussed shortly (§ 10.3.3).

A real atom has a series of spectral lines at various frequencies,
and anomalous dispersion takes place in the region of each one of
them. The classical theory cannot explain this multitude of resonances, but takes them into account by assigning a number N_j of
model atoms to the jth resonance so that the refractive index is
written

$$\mu_1 - 1 = \frac{2\pi e^2}{\epsilon_0 m} \sum_{j=1}^{\infty} \frac{N_j(\eta_j^2 - \omega^2)}{(\eta_j^2 - \omega^2)^2 + \kappa_j^2 \omega^2}.$$

The N_j's are called *oscillator strengths* and are related to the matrix
elements derived from the quantum-mechanical description
(§ 11.4.5). Fig. 10.10 shows a typical refractive-index curve through
three spectral lines.

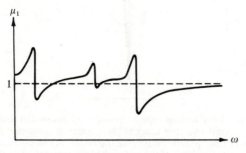

Fig. 10.10. A typical refractive-index curve through three weak spectral lines.

10.3.3 Experimental investigation of anomalous dispersion. The
refractive index and absorption coefficient in an anomalous region
can be determined by a number of methods, the common property
being that they must all be sensitive to small changes in wavelength. For example, the reflectivity of a surface for oblique incidence and various polarizations can be used to calculate the real
and imaginary parts of the refractive index. The method has been
used to study dispersion in the region of the infra-red rotation-
spectral lines in water.

R. W. Wood used a double spectrometer to show dispersion in
sodium vapour in the region of the sodium D-lines. His first 'prism'

was a horizontal glass-ended tube containing sodium vapour, across which there was a temperature gradient and therefore a density gradient. This prism produced an angle of deviation in a vertical plane which depended on the refractive index of the sodium vapour. A second glass prism produced normal deviation related to wavelength in the horizontal plane, and so the observer saw the collimator pinhole spread into a curve of refractive index of sodium against wavelength (Fig. 10.11).

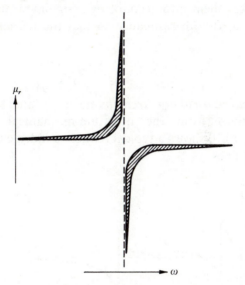

Fig. 10.11. Dispersion by a sodium-vapour 'prism'. The horizontal scale has distance proportional to the normal refractive index of glass, which is monotonic in frequency ω; the vertical scale has distance proportional to the real refractive index of the sodium vapour. The broken line shows the position of the sodium D-lines (unresolved in this experiment).

Probably the most attractive of the methods that can be used in the visible region is the interference method due to Roschdestwenski. Sodium vapour with uniform density is introduced into one tube of a modified Jamin interferometer (§ 7.8.1) illuminated by white light. The resulting interference pattern is analysed on a spectrometer so that the components at various wavelengths are separated, and since a fringe shift proportional to the refractive index occurs in the interferometer the analysed interference pattern is bent into *hooks* (Fig. 10.12). This method has been used to investigate the shape of the absorption line, and hence the width of the corresponding emission line, the pattern being calibrated by the fringe separation. The line shape can therefore be reliably measured.

10.3.4 Group velocity in the anomalous region. The group velocity arising from equation (2.26) poses an interesting problem. It can be written in terms of the real part μ_1 of the refractive index,

$$v_g = \frac{\partial \omega}{\partial k} = \frac{c}{\mu_1}\left(1 - \frac{\partial \log \mu_1}{\partial \log k}\right).$$

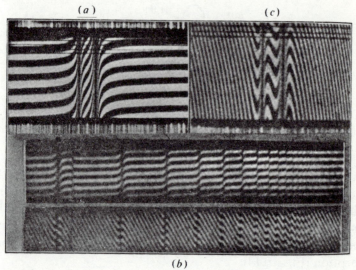

Fig. 10.12. Roschdestwenski's hooks, observed in sodium vapour. (From R. W. Wood, *Physical Optics*, Dover Publications Inc., New York, 1967. Reprinted through permission of the publisher.)

Under normal dispersion conditions μ_1 increases with k so that v_g is definitely less than c and the theory of relativity is not disputed on that account; however, in the anomalous-dispersion region it is quite possible for v_g to be greater than c provided that the damping constant κ is small enough (Fig. 10.13). Is there any way of resolving this confrontation between classical physics and relativity?

In fact, the relativistic statement is that a *signal* cannot be propagated faster than c, and this is a particular example in which the signal velocity is not equal to the group velocity. The derivation of v_g as $\partial \omega / \partial k$ implicitly assumed that v_g was a constant over the frequency-band involved in the signal. In this case, however, v_g is large only for a small range of frequencies, and a signal which has a sufficiently sudden cut-off to have an easily measurable signal velocity must necessarily contain a large range of frequencies,

including substantial amounts outside the anomalous dispersion range. Already our ground has become shaky.

The full problem of propagation of a wave-group in a dispersive medium is complicated because of the integrations involved, although it is introduced in § 12.8. When the integral is carried out

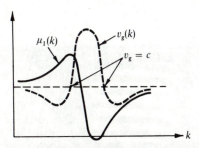

Fig. 10.13. Refractive index μ_1 and group velocity v_g as functions of k in the anomalous region.

for a wave-group in an anomalous-dispersion region, it appears that its form becomes distorted. The signal velocity, which is defined by the time at which the signal has grown to half its maximum value, does in fact turn out to be less than c, and reaches a maximum value of c when the group has frequency equal to that of maximum absorption (Fig. 10.14).

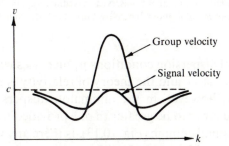

Fig. 10.14. Group and signal velocities in the anomalous region.

Qualitatively, what happens is as follows. Consider a short wave-group travelling in the medium. Initially it will have a Fourier spectrum which will predominantly contain frequencies in the anomalous region (Fig. 10.15), but, because of the absorptive processes taking place, these frequencies will be preferentially absorbed. At a later time, therefore, the spectrum will be as illustrated by Fig. 10.16. The waves which are not absorbed, and dominate

the later spectrum, are waves which undergo normal dispersion and therefore have a group velocity less than c. During a long passage in which the waves in the anomalous region are almost completely absorbed, the signal velocity is therefore less than c. We can, in fact, be a little more specific about the behaviour of the group during the first part of its passage. The absorption process

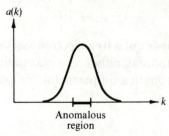

Fig. 10.15. Spectrum of an incident wave-group.

takes place because the re-radiation from atoms excited by a wave of resonant frequency is exactly out of phase with the free-space wave. This free-space wave, however, travels at velocity c, and therefore the absorption process cannot start at position x until a time x/c after the initiation of the wave. However, this sort of microscopic approach is not necessary in order to understand propagation of a wave group in such a dispersive medium, which is discussed a little more completely in § 12.8.

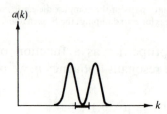

Fig. 10.16. Spectrum of the same wave-group after passage through the medium.

10.3.5   Dispersion remote from an absorption band: X-ray refractive index.
The formulae deduced in § 10.3.2 can be applied when η and ω are far from equality. When $(\eta^2 - \omega^2) \gg \kappa\omega$ absorption is negligible and we can calculate the normal dispersion

$$\mu_1 = 1 + \frac{1}{2}\frac{\Omega^2}{(\eta^2 - \omega^2)}.$$

At very high frequencies, very much greater than the η for the highest-frequency spectral line, we can write

$$\mu_1 = 1 - \frac{1}{2}\frac{\Omega^2}{\omega^2},$$

which shows that the refractive index in the X-ray region is less than unity, but only just so. Substitution of typical values gives

$$1 - \mu_1 \doteq 10^{-7}.$$

10.3.6   Refractive index of a free-electron assembly. If the electrons in a medium are unbound, either as a plasma in the ionosphere or as conduction electrons in a simple metal, for example, we can work

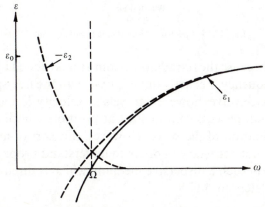

Fig. 10.17. Real and imaginary parts of the complex dielectric constant for a free-electron assembly. The solid line is for zero damping; the broken line for non-zero damping.

out the refraction properties as a function of frequency. Substituting zero for the resonant frequency η, we obtain from (10.10)

$$\epsilon = \mu^2 = 1 + \frac{\Omega^2}{i\kappa\omega - \omega^2}. \tag{10.11}$$

In the zero-damping case, $\kappa = 0$,

$$\epsilon = 1 - \frac{\Omega^2}{\omega^2}, \tag{10.12}$$

which shows that when ω is below the frequency Ω all modes of propagation are evanescent, since ϵ is negative. This can be seen immediately from the diagram (Fig. 10.17); Ω is called the *plasma frequency* because at that frequency collective oscillations of the

whole plasma can occur. When $\epsilon = 0$, we have

$$\frac{\omega}{k} = \frac{c}{\mu} = \infty \; ;$$

therefore, $k = 0$, $\lambda = \infty$. This corresponds to the whole plasma oscillating in phase, a situation which is known as a collective oscillation. At a slightly higher frequency, phase differences will occur between neighbouring parts.

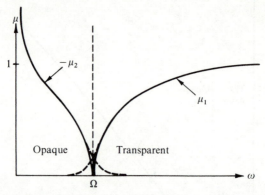

Fig. 10.18. The refractive index arising from Fig. 10.17 $(\mu_1 + i\mu_2)^2 = \varepsilon_1 + i\varepsilon_2$. This figure should be compared with Fig. 10.19, in which experimental results for sodium are shown. Note that the plots in Figs. 10.18 and 10.19 are functions of ω and λ respectively.

Re-introduction of the damping constant κ leads to real and imaginary parts for the dielectric constant

$$\left.\begin{aligned}
\epsilon_1 &= 1 - \frac{\Omega^2}{\omega^2 + \kappa^2}, \\
\epsilon_2 &= \frac{\Omega^2 \kappa}{\kappa^2 \omega + \omega^3}.
\end{aligned}\right\} \tag{10.13}$$

The plasma frequency is thus shifted, zero ϵ_1 occurring at the lower frequency

$$\omega^2 = \Omega^2 - \kappa^2.$$

The plasma oscillations are now damped, however, since at this frequency

$$\epsilon_2 = -\frac{\kappa}{\omega}.$$

The behaviour of the functions in (10.13) is sketched in Fig. 10.18 (and for comparison Fig. 10.19 shows some measurements made in

sodium, which is a fairly good free-electron metal). Since it has a finite electrical conductivity, κ is finite.

10.4 Relaxation effects

It is well known that water and ice have a dielectric constant of about 80 for a static electric field, whereas their refractive index at optical frequencies is about 1·3, corresponding to a dielectric

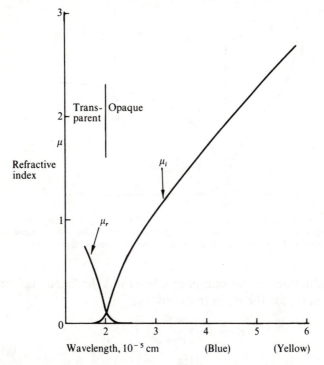

Fig. 10.19. Complex refractive index of sodium measured as a function of wavelength near the plasma wavelength. Calculated from the free–electron density, the plasma wavelength $\lambda_p = \Omega/c = (4\pi n e^2/\varepsilon_0 m c^2)^{\frac{1}{2}}$ should be 2·1 × 10^{-5} cm.

constant of about 1·7. The large change in refractive index occurs in a single frequency range, 10^9–10^{11} c/s for water and 10^3–10^5 c/s for ice (Fig. 10.21); this strong dispersion is accompanied by an absorption band. It is also fairly well known that the H_2O molecule has a permanent dipole moment. When an electric field is applied to water or ice, the permanent dipoles try to align themselves to the field to attain minimum potential energy, and the wholesale rotation of the molecules is naturally resisted by frictional forces.

If the electric field is applied for long enough the dipoles will eventually reach a state of equilibrium in which the considerable net dipole-moment is responsible for the high static dielectric constant. Complete alignment will not be reached for two reasons. Thermal agitation will tend to randomize the directions, as the minimum attained at equilibrium is of free energy, $F = U - TS$, rather than internal energy U, and the free energy is increased in the low-entropy state of complete alignment. If the electric field is applied only for a short time, alignment may not have taken place completely when the field is removed, and so the dielectric constant is time-dependent.

We wish to calculate the dielectric constant as a function of frequency. We shall do this via the susceptibility χ, also a function of frequency, which is related to $\epsilon(\omega)$ by the equation

$$\epsilon(\omega) = \epsilon_0 + 4\pi\chi(\omega).$$

To calculate χ we need to study the variation of $P(t)$, the dipole moment, as a function of time. It is a reasonable hypothesis that the rate of approach of $P(t)$ to the equilibrium state will be proportional to the deviation from that state. When a steady electric field E has been applied to the material for a very long time, P will be related to E by the static susceptibility $\chi(0)$

$$P(\infty) = \chi(0)E. \tag{10.14}$$

$P(\infty)$ is the dipole moment per unit volume achieved after infinite time; $\chi(0)$ is the steady-field susceptibility, that is, for zero frequency. At a finite time t, P will not have reached $P(\infty)$ and, according to the hypothesis above, we have

$$\frac{\partial P(t)}{\partial t} = \frac{P(\infty) - P(t)}{\tau}, \tag{10.15}$$

$1/\tau$ being the constant of proportionality; τ is called the *relaxation time*. Supposing now that E is made to be oscillatory

$$E(t) = E_0 \exp(i\omega t).$$

At any instant, equation (10.15) will be satisfied, the approach being towards the equilibrium state defined by (10.14) at that instant. Equation (10.15) thus becomes

$$\frac{\partial P(t)}{\partial t} + \frac{P(t)}{\tau} = \frac{\chi(0)E_0}{\tau} \exp(i\omega t). \tag{10.16}$$

This equation has a steady-state solution

$$P(t) = \frac{\chi(0)E_0 \exp{(i\omega t)}}{(1 + i\omega\tau)}$$

and this linear relationship between P and E can be simply expressed as a frequency-dependent susceptibility $\chi(\omega)$,

$$P(t) = \chi(\omega)E(t),$$

where
$$\chi(\omega) = \frac{\chi(0)}{(1 + i\omega\tau)}. \tag{10.17}$$

The susceptibility $\chi(\omega)$ leads to dielectric constant with real and imaginary parts

$$\epsilon = \epsilon_0 + 4\pi\chi = \epsilon_1 + i\epsilon_2,$$

$$\left. \begin{aligned}
\epsilon_1 &= \epsilon_0 + \frac{4\pi\chi(0)}{1 + \omega^2\tau^2}, \\[2mm]
\epsilon_2 &= -\frac{4\pi\chi(0)\omega\tau}{1 + \omega^2\tau^2}.
\end{aligned} \right\} \tag{10.18}$$

The expressions satisfy qualitative intuition about their limits. At very low frequency, the static dielectric constant applies:

$$\left. \begin{aligned}
\epsilon_1 &\to \epsilon_0 + 4\pi\chi(0) \\[2mm]
\epsilon_2 &\to 0
\end{aligned} \right\} \quad \text{as} \quad \omega \to 0. \tag{10.19}$$

At very high frequency, the molecule is completely unable to respond to the rapidly-changing field and

$$\left. \begin{aligned}
\epsilon_1 &\to \epsilon_0 \\[2mm]
\epsilon_2 &\to 0
\end{aligned} \right\} \quad \text{as} \quad \omega \to \infty.$$

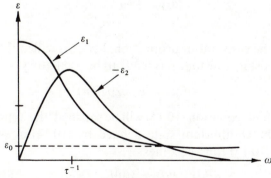

Fig. 10.20. Frequency dependence of the dielectric constant in a medium dominated by relaxation processes.

In between these two limits there is a gradual change in ϵ_1, and an absorption band. The change is not sharp, as it was with the resonant system, but is spread over a considerable frequency range around a frequency

$$\omega = \frac{1}{\tau}.$$

This behaviour is characteristic of relaxation mechanisms which obey an equation like (10.15), and is illustrated by Fig. 10.20. Fig. 10.21 shows experimental measurements made on ice. The

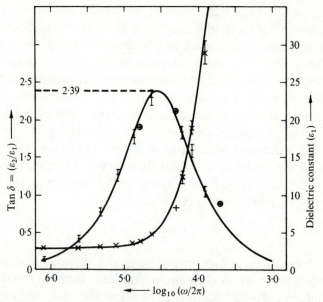

Fig. 10.21. Dielectric constant as a function of frequency in ice at $-5°C$. The two curves show: (a) the real part $\varepsilon_1(\omega)$, and (b) the ratio of real to imaginary parts $\tan \delta = \varepsilon_2(\omega)/\varepsilon_1(\omega)$ which is called the *loss factor*. The points show experimental measurements (J. Lamb, *Trans. Faraday Soc.* **42A**, 242 (1946)) and the curves are the best fit of equations (10.18).

dielectric constants arising from other mechanisms, such as resonances, must be added to the functions (10.18).

10.4.1 The effect of temperature on relaxation dispersion. We have just seen that the assumption of a relaxation time governing any change of polarizability is sufficient to explain, at least qualitatively, the broad-band absorption and dispersion in certain polar materials. In fact the quantitative fit, provided that only a single such

mechanism is involved, is quite good. That the form of the dispersion curve is dependent on interaction between the dipole molecules and their surroundings, and is not a process internal to the molecules, is clear from the change in relaxation time which occurs when water freezes; in water τ is observed to be about 10^{-9} s, while in ice τ is 10^{-4} s, indicating much more resistant surroundings. We shall briefly consider two interesting questions here—first, the origins of τ, and, secondly, the temperature dependence to be expected. Experimental study of the latter is a convenient method of confirming the former.

Debye has proposed a mechanism which is almost unbelievably mechanical in approach. Strictly, the model applies to a dilute solution of polar molecules in a non-polar solvent, so that cooperative effects can be neglected, and it describes the polar molecules as spheres that can rotate hindered by the viscous drag of their surroundings considered as a macroscopic continuum. The dipoles themselves, being microscopic, will have considerable thermal fluctuations about their mean position; in fact, the model describes the effect of the applied electric field as a small perturbation to the otherwise random distribution of dipole moments. The mathematics of the model is described elsewhere (see bibliography), and leads to an expression for τ in terms of the viscosity of the fluid at temperature T and the molecular radius a

$$\tau = \frac{4\pi\eta a^3}{kT}. \tag{10.20}$$

The formula is, in fact, not quite as definitive as it seems; a is essentially an arbitrary constant, the radius of the hard sphere which experiences the same frictional couple as the molecule under the same conditions. Then the microscopic theory of viscosity assumes that relative motion of the molecules involves overcoming a potential barrier of height H, resulting from short-range order in the liquid, and as the dielectric behaviour involves similar motions of the molecules it is not so surprising that the two are connected. The best evidence of this relationship comes from the temperature variation of τ, which is compared with that of η. The potential-hump hypothesis for η is proposed in order to explain its temperature variation,

$$\eta \sim \exp\left(H/kT\right) \tag{10.21}$$

and equation (10.20) leads us to expect that a plot of τ against η/T

should be linear. Experimental results for water in the liquid range show excellent confirmation of this both for normal and heavy water.

Ice has not been studied to such a great extent, but the hypothesis of a potential-hump as a controller of molecular rotation is even more plausible than in water, as the crystal structure will lead to definitely-defined directions for internal electric fields (Problem 33).

10.4.2 The use of electrical analogues for dispersion calculations.

Both oscillatory behaviour and relaxation mechanisms are quite common in electric circuits, and the mathematical analogy between such circuits and dispersion processes is almost complete. The analogy arises because both the medium and the circuit are linear in their response to an applied electric field or voltage. If we can draw a circuit which exhibits the same type of behaviour as our dispersive medium, it is usually a simple matter to write down its complex impedance and hence, by integration with respect to time, its dielectric constant. The integration is necessary because the corresponding quantities are

$$\left.\begin{array}{l}\text{electric field---voltage} \times \text{constant} \\[4pt] \text{dipole moment---charge} \times \text{constant}\end{array}\right\} \tag{10.22}$$

and the impedance of a circuit is the voltage-current ratio. The analogy between the circuit in Fig. 10.22 and the *model atom* of

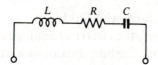

Fig. 10.22. Oscillatory circuit.

§ 10.1.1 is clear; the model atom has a forced equation of motion (10.7)

$$\ddot{x} + \kappa\dot{x} + \eta^2 x = \frac{E_0 e}{m} \exp(i\omega t)$$

and the circuit

$$L\ddot{q} + R\dot{q} + \frac{q}{c} = V_0 \exp(i\omega t).$$

The impedance of the latter is

$$Z = i\omega L + R + \frac{1}{i\omega C}$$

and the charge q is given by $q_0 \exp(i\omega t)$ where

$$\frac{q_0}{V_0} = \left(-\omega^2 L + i\omega R + \frac{1}{C}\right)^{-1}$$

$$= \frac{L^{-1}}{\eta^2 - \omega^2 + i\omega(R/L)} \qquad (\eta^2 = (LC)^{-1}),$$

which is formally similar to (10.9). The two constants in the correspondence relations (10.22) can be chosen at will so long as R/L is made equal to κ. Similarly, the relaxation circuit Fig. 10.23 allows

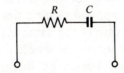

Fig. 10.23. Relaxation circuit.

us to write down the polarizability of a relaxation-dominated medium

$$Z = R + \frac{1}{i\omega C},$$

$$\frac{q_0}{V_0} = \frac{1}{i\omega R + C^{-1}} = \frac{C}{i\omega RC + 1},$$

which is identical in form with (10.17).

An example in which the electrical analogue is very useful occurs in acoustic dispersion. Carbon dioxide is a linear molecule which therefore has rotational degrees of freedom as well as translational.

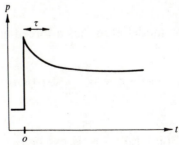

Fig. 10.24. Pressure of carbon dioxide following a sudden compression at time $t = 0$.

If a cylinder containing carbon-dioxide gas were suddenly compressed, the additional energy imparted by the moving piston would entirely be observed as translational kinetic energy during the compression, but by subsequent collisions it would be shared out with rotational modes. The temperature (and hence pressure) of the gas after the compression would drop as in Fig. 10.24, where τ is the relaxation time for the collision process to share out the energy. An equivalent electric circuit is shown in Fig. 10.25; condenser C_1 charges up immediately when a voltage is applied, and

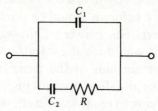

Fig. 10.25. Circuit with a similar transient behaviour to Fig. 10.24.

C_2 follows after a relaxation time

$$\tau = \frac{R}{(1/C_1)+(1/C_2)}$$

and the voltage between the terminals varies in the way shown in Fig. 10.25. It is then a simple matter to work out the impedance of this electric circuit, and hence the acoustic impedance (Problem 37).

CHAPTER 11

QUANTUM OPTICS

11.1 Quantum Optics

The application of optics to quantized systems such as atoms and molecules is so important today that it would be impossible to omit consideration of the subject of quantum optics. Nevertheless, it is difficult to decide where to begin. Were we to treat the subject logically, it would be necessary to discuss a great deal of the foundation of quantum theory before it would be possible to understand the mysteries of interactions between light-waves and quantum systems, and to do this would require a textbook in itself. Even, it seems, to give a short account of the basic quantum theory is almost impossible, since any short account begs so many questions that it is most unsatisfying to read. As a result, we shall start almost in the middle, and assume that the reader has a reasonable physical, if not mathematical, grasp of elementary quantum mechanics. If he does not have this base to work from, he may find the matter in this chapter interesting, but can hardly expect to understand it completely. However, just to serve as a reminder, we shall first discuss very lightly a few basic illustrations of quantum theory, giving an opportunity to derive some simple results which will be of use later on. The illustrations will be chosen with this motive in view.

The subject matter remaining is still, however, too large to be dealt with in a single chapter. It must be heavily restricted, and will be seen to deal mainly with masers and lasers and their influence on optics. This is not an unreasonable choice; masers and lasers have recently prompted a renaissance in optics, and many original experiments have been carried out in homage to the new gods. How long the religion will last it is difficult to say, but it has at least uncovered a number of new effects and it would be unreasonable not to acknowledge their importance.

The plan of this chapter is therefore as follows. We shall quickly skim over some illustrations of elementary quantum mechanics such as the uncertainty principle and the quantum states of a square-well potential. We shall then consider the physical interpretation of time-dependent perturbation theory, which deals with the problems of why atoms absorb and emit electromagnetic

radiation. Then we shall be in a position to understand the workings of masers and lasers, and these are discussed in some detail, followed by accounts of three experiments which have been made possible by the new instruments. The accounts are not exhaustive, but we hope at least that they will be interesting.

The bibliography at the end of the book gives details of one or two books on quantum mechanics. These have been chosen as particularly suitable for the approach used here, and can be used to fill the large gaps which are bound to exist.

11.2 Schroedinger's equation in one dimension

Schroedinger's equation should already be familiar, if only because it was derived as an example of a dispersive wave equation in § 2.2.2. The derivation was not very rigorous, but does illustrate the basic physical thinking behind its formulation. It can be carried through in three dimensions and leads to the equation

$$-i\hbar\frac{\partial\Psi}{\partial t} = -\frac{\hbar^2}{2m}\nabla^2\Psi + V\Psi \tag{11.1}$$

(where V is the potential energy of the particle represented by the wave-amplitude Ψ) of which equation (11.2) is the one-dimensional analogue:

$$-i\hbar\frac{\partial\Psi}{\partial t} = \frac{-\hbar^2}{2m}\frac{\partial^2\Psi}{\partial x^2} + V\Psi. \tag{11.2}$$

This equation can formally be written

$$-i\hbar\frac{\partial\Psi}{\partial t} = H\Psi, \tag{11.3}$$

where H is the *Hamiltonian operator*

$$H \equiv \left(\frac{-\hbar^2}{2m}\frac{\partial^2}{\partial x^2} + V\right). \tag{11.4}$$

The wave amplitude Ψ was introduced as a dummy variable, and has no direct physical meaning. But, since we can assume that if it has zero value there can be no particle present, and that the sort of particles we can understand can only have a positive number density, it is reasonable to assume that this density is given by

$$\rho = \Psi\Psi^* = |\Psi|^2. \tag{11.5}$$

This is doubly reasonable by analogy with the energy density in an electromagnetic wave, for example.

The concept of a *particle density*, ρ, is valid only if there is a large number of particles present. For an isolated particle, or a small number to which the term *density* would be rather misleading, $|\Psi|^2$ is interpreted as the *probability* of finding a particle at the point. Strictly, we say that the probability of finding a particle in a small region of volume dv at $\mathbf{r}$ is $|\Psi(\mathbf{r})|^2 \, dv$. Clearly, for a large number of particles, this definition of the meaning of Ψ leads to equation (11.5). Interpretation of Ψ in this manner means that Ψ must be single-valued; at any one point in space it can only have one particular value. It is impossible for a particle to have two different probabilities of existing at a point.

11.2.1 Waves in a potential-free region. When V is everywhere zero, the equation (11.2) has the simple solution

$$\Psi = \Psi_0 \exp \{i(\omega t \pm kx)\}, \tag{11.6}$$

where
$$\hbar\omega = \frac{\hbar^2 k^2}{2m}. \tag{11.7}$$

This is the dispersion relation for a particle wave. By realizing that energy is given by $\hbar\omega$, we see that

$$E = \frac{\hbar^2 k^2}{2m} = \frac{p^2}{2m} \qquad \text{(as in equation (2.16a)).} \tag{11.8}$$

Often the energy E is a time-independent constant whose possible values we wish to find. Under such conditions the substitution of $-i\hbar(\partial/\partial t)$ for E is unnecessary, and we can write the *time-independent Schroedinger equation* in one dimension,

$$E\Psi = \frac{-\hbar^2}{2m}\frac{\partial^2\Psi}{\partial x^2} + V\Psi. \tag{11.9}$$

Using the Hamiltonian operator H, this equation can be written very simply as

$$E\Psi = H\Psi. \tag{11.10}$$

We shall then find that the equation has solutions $\Psi(x)$ only for certain values of E. These solutions are called *eigenfunctions* of the equation, and correspond to particular values of E which are known as *eigenvalues*. For any particular physical system, such as the square well discussed in § 11.2.4, we can derive a set of possible values of E, which we shall call E_n, and associated with each eigenvalue E_n is an eigenfunction $\Psi_n(x)$. Only for these values does equation (11.9) have a time-independent solution. In a stationary state,

the wave-function of a system must be one of these eigenfunctions, but while the state is changing with time, so that (11.9) must be replaced by the time-dependent equation (11.2), the wave-function will be different from an eigenfunction.

11.2.2 The Heisenberg uncertainty principle. If a particle is restricted to a region of space of dimensions δx its wave-function must similarly be restricted, and must therefore be a wave-group. We know from our studies of Fourier transforms that a wave-group can be expressed as the sum of waves like (11.6) only by using a range δk of k around some central value. This range is derived in § 3.5.6 to be

$$\delta k = \frac{1}{\delta x}. \tag{11.11}$$

The central value of the range is of course given by the energy of the restricted particle and equation (11.8). Using the fact that wave number k and momentum p are related by

$$p = \hbar k$$

we have
$$\delta p \,.\, \delta x = \hbar, \tag{11.12}$$

which is the uncertainty principle in its most useful form. In words, a particle whose position is known to an accuracy δx must have its momentum uncertain to a degree δp given by (11.12).

A statement can be derived likewise between energy and time. If the energy of a particle is measured during a time of duration δt, the measured value is uncertain to an amount δE given by

$$\delta E \,.\, \delta t = \hbar;$$

an illustration of the basic reason for this occurs in the derivation of the line natural width in § 11.4.3. It is important to notice that δt here represents the time during which measurement of E takes place; that is, E is an average value over the time δt.

Diffraction forms an example of equation (11.11) (Fig. 11.1). If a light beam of wave-vector **k** is restricted by an aperture of dimensions δx, the component of wave-vector parallel to δx must be indeterminate to a degree δk which means a spread in the beam over an angle

$$\theta = \frac{\delta k}{k} = \frac{1}{k \, \delta x} = \frac{\lambda}{2\pi \, \delta x}. \tag{11.13}$$

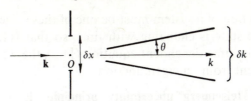

Fig. 11.1. The uncertainty principle and optical diffraction.

This is the same order of magnitude as deduced from the proper theory of diffraction (§ 7.2.1).

11.2.3   Continuity of Ψ and $\partial\Psi/\partial x$. A wave-function which is a solution of (11.2) must satisfy conditions of continuity. We can integrate (11.9) between limits a and b for any eigenfunction ψ:

$$E\int_a^b \psi \, dx - \int_a^b \psi \, V \, dx = \frac{-\hbar^2}{2m}\left[\frac{\partial\psi}{\partial x}\right]_a^b. \qquad (11.14)$$

Let $a \to b$. Then if neither ψ nor V has a singularity, the left-hand side of (11.14) approaches zero, and hence $\partial\psi/\partial x$ is continuous. If V becomes infinite however, this condition does not apply. The function ψ itself must be continuous, otherwise the wave equation (11.2) would be meaningless.

At a delta-function of V, results are not so straightforward. Suppose that the δ-function is defined by allowing $a \to b$ in (11.14), and keeping $V(b-a)$ at a constant value D. Then we can see that, provided ψ remains finite, the equation will become, as $a-b \to 0$,

$$\psi\int_a^b V \, dx = \frac{\hbar^2}{2m}\left[\frac{\partial\psi}{\partial x}\right]_a^b \qquad (11.15)$$

and thus a discontinuity of

$$\Delta\left(\frac{\partial\psi}{\partial x}\right) = \frac{2mD\psi}{\hbar^2}, \qquad (11.16)$$

occurs at the δ-function. This will be zero if the value of ψ at the δ-function is zero (Fig. 11.2).

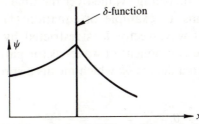

Fig. 11.2. Discontinuity of $\partial\psi/\partial x$ at a δ-function of potential.

11.2.4 Wave-functions in an infinite square well. One of the most illustrative quantum systems is that of an infinitely deep square well, stretching from $x = -a$ to $+a$ (Fig. 11.3). The wave-function

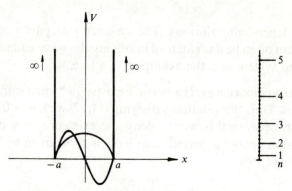

Fig. 11.3. The infinite square well, its first two wave-functions and its spectrum of levels.

ψ must be zero at its boundaries, and within the well must be made up from a linear combination of the two solutions (11.6). Therefore it must be either $\sin kx$ or $\cos kx$;

$$\sin kx = 0 \quad \text{at} \quad x = \pm a, \quad \text{if} \quad k = \frac{n\pi}{2a} \quad (n \text{ even}), \qquad (11.17)$$

and $\cos kx = 0$ at $x = \pm a,$ if $k = \dfrac{n\pi}{2a}$ $(n \text{ odd}),$ (11.18)

where n is an integer. The first of these waves is of odd parity, meaning that

$$\psi(x) = -\psi(-x)$$

and the second is of even parity

$$\psi(x) = \psi(-x).$$

Between them, they give rise to allowed energy states of

$$E_n = \frac{\hbar^2}{2m} \cdot \frac{n^2\pi^2}{4a^2}. \qquad (11.19)$$

Energies other than these, which are illustrated in Fig. 11.3, give rise to waves which cannot satisfy the boundary conditions at the edge of the well.

11.2.5 Symmetry. The symmetry of a potential well determines the symmetry of the particle density in it. In this example the well is

symmetrical

$$V(x) = V(-x)$$

and so

$$|\psi(x)|^2 = |\psi(-x)|^2 \tag{11.20}$$

whence

$$\psi(x) = \pm\psi(-x) \tag{11.21}$$

are two independent solutions. The symmetry or parity of wave-functions can often be a useful tool in solving the wave equation in a complicated system (e.g. the examples in § 11.6.3).

11.2.6 Zero-point energy. If a particle exists, $\psi\psi^*$ must somewhere be non-zero. Thus the solution satisfying (11.17) with $n = 0$ cannot be allowed, because this would deny the existence of a particle. The minimum energy a particle can have is thus given by putting $n = 1$ into (11.19)

$$E_1 = \frac{\hbar^2}{2m}\frac{\pi^2}{4a^2}.$$

This is called its zero-point energy. It can be thought of as a result of the uncertainty principle. A particle is restricted to a region of space by the well:

$$\delta x = a.$$

Hence from the uncertainty principle it must have uncertainty in its momentum

$$\delta p = \frac{\hbar}{a}.$$

This uncertainty in momentum can be associated with a minimum amount of energy

$$E = \frac{(\delta p)^2}{2m} = \frac{\hbar^2}{2m}\frac{1}{a^2}$$

and this is seen to be of the same order of magnitude as the zero-point energy ($\pi^2/4$ is of order unity).

11.2.7 The simple-harmonic oscillator. The simple-harmonic oscillator is a difficult mathematical problem, but it can easily be stated. A particle satisfying

$$\mu x = -F = \frac{dV}{dx}$$

is in a potential well,

$$V = \tfrac{1}{2}\mu x^2,$$

which is illustrated in Fig. 11.4. The Schroedinger equation,

$$E = \frac{-\hbar^2}{2m}\frac{\partial^2\psi}{\partial x^2} + \tfrac{1}{2}\mu x^2\psi,\qquad(11.22)$$

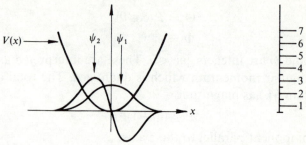

Fig. 11.4. The harmonic oscillator well, its first two wave-functions and its level spectrum.

only leads to solutions which remain infinite as $x \to \pm\infty$ if

$$E = (n+\tfrac{1}{2})\hbar\left(\frac{\mu}{m}\right)^{\frac{1}{2}} = (n+\tfrac{1}{2})\hbar\omega_0 \qquad (n \text{ an integer} \geqslant 0),$$

where ω_0 is the classical oscillation frequency. Once again, we find a zero-point energy, this time $\tfrac{1}{2}\hbar\omega_0$; zero-point energy is a characteristic of any bound system, as a result of the argument using the uncertainty principle.

11.3   Three-dimensional systems

To solve Schroedinger's equation in three dimensions involves expressing $\nabla^2\psi$ in terms of three co-ordinates. The number of problems in which it is convenient to leave $\nabla^2\psi$ in the form

$$\nabla^2\psi = \frac{\partial^2\psi}{\partial x^2} + \frac{\partial^2\psi}{\partial y^2} + \frac{\partial^2\psi}{\partial z^2}$$

is rather small; the number is far larger for which the spherical polar formulation

$$\nabla^2\psi = \frac{1}{r}\frac{\partial^2}{\partial r^2}(r\psi) + \frac{1}{r^2}\left\{\frac{1}{\sin\theta}\frac{\partial}{\partial\theta}\left(\sin\theta\frac{\partial}{\partial\theta}\right) + \frac{1}{\sin^2\theta}\frac{\partial}{\partial\phi}\right\}\psi,$$

is the more appropriate.

11.3.1   Angular momentum.
Spherically symmetric potentials simplify this latter formulation considerably, and lead to two more *quantum numbers* which arise like n out of boundary, continuity or single-valuedness conditions on ψ. We find that the wave-function

is separable into functions of r, θ and ϕ:

$$\psi = R(r)\,\Theta(\theta)\,\Phi(\phi),$$

and that the only allowed functions for Θ and Φ are the Legendre polynomial

$$\Theta = P_l(\cos\theta)$$

and $$\Phi = e^{im\phi},$$

where l and m are integers, $|m| \leqslant l$. These are interpreted as giving rise to angular momentum which is quantized. The total angular momentum **M** has magnitude

$$M = (l(l+1))^{\frac{1}{2}}\hbar \qquad (11.23)$$

and a component parallel to the z axis,

$$M_z = m\hbar. \qquad (11.24)$$

These are clearly satisfied only by certain angles between **M** and the z-axis, which can be illustrated by Fig. 11.5.

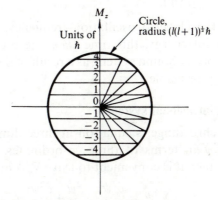

Fig. 11.5. Quantization of angular momentum.

The quantization of angular momentum leads to the quantization of rotational energy in a system. If it has moment of inertia I about a certain axis the energy is given by

$$E = \frac{M^2}{2I} = \frac{\hbar^2}{2I}l(l+1). \qquad (11.25)$$

11.3.2   A magnetic dipole in a field. If a magnetic dipole of strength **d** is placed in a field $\mathbf{H}_0$, its energy is given by

$$E = -\mathbf{d}\cdot\mathbf{H}_0. \qquad (11.26)$$

Because of the restriction of angle between the angular momentum vector and the z-axis, which is the direction of H_0—the only unique axis in the system—E can only take on quantized values. Now it can be shown for orbital angular momentum† that $\mathbf{d}$ and $\mathbf{M}$ are related by the Bohr magneton, μ_B:

$$\mathbf{d} = \mu_B \mathbf{M},$$

and therefore the energy levels of the dipole are

$$E = -m\hbar\mu_B H_0. \qquad (11.27)$$

Thus m is called the magnetic quantum number. The energy levels have a classical interpretation in terms of precession of $\mathbf{d}$ about $\mathbf{H}_0$. Writing down the equation for magnetic couple to equal rate of change of angular momentum, we have

$$\frac{d\mathbf{M}}{dt} = \mathbf{d} \times \mathbf{H}_0 = \mu_B \mathbf{M} \times \mathbf{H}_0,$$

which has the solution that $\mathbf{M}$ precesses around $\mathbf{H}_0$ with a frequency

$$\Omega = \mu_B H_0,$$

This precession corresponds to the difference between two adjacent energy levels of (11.27) and will be further discussed in § 11.4.2.

This much quantum theory will be useful later. We now take a great stride forward and start to consider time-dependent perturbation theory, which is the basis of understanding quantum optics.

11.4   Perturbation theory

11.4.1   Why atoms absorb energy. The basis of perturbation theory is an attempt to discover what happens to a quantum system when its potential system changes slightly. The situation may be as follows. An atom is sitting at time $t < 0$ in the Nth stationary quantum state of the nuclear potential $V(\mathbf{r})$. In this state it has a wave-function $\psi_N(\mathbf{r})$ and a corresponding energy eigenfunction E_N, which is a property of both N and the nuclear potential $V(\mathbf{r})$. At time $t = 0$, we switch on an extra perturbing potential $V'(\mathbf{r}, t)$. Now the atom is no longer in a quantum state, since ψ_N and E_N are not an eigenfunction and an eigenvalue of the new potential $V + V'$. By applying Schroedinger's equation to the atom in the new potential distribution we can find how the wave-function Ψ changes

† For spin angular momentum the ratio between $\mathbf{d}$ and $\mathbf{M}$ is $2\mu_B$.

from its value ψ_N at $t = 0$ to a new function at some later time, and from our knowledge of $\Psi(t)$ so gained we can calculate some macroscopic properties of the atom during the change.

In optical examples, we shall clearly want to use a perturbing potential which is an electromagnetic wave; if it is travelling along the z-direction and has polarization along x,

$$V'(\mathbf{r}, t) = E_0 x \exp\{i(\omega t - kz)\}. \tag{11.28}$$

Moreover, we shall be interested in the changes of energy occurring within the system. If energy can be shown to have been gained by the electromagnetic-wave perturbation, it must have been lost by the atom, since no other source of energy is involved in the problem.

The simplest way of understanding the process of energy transfer is to start by calculating the oscillating multipole moments of the atoms. We shall do this presently. Let us concentrate our attention on its dipole moment $\mathbf{P}$. A dipole $\mathbf{P}$ in an electric field $\mathbf{E}$ has a potential energy

$$W = -\mathbf{P} \cdot \mathbf{E}^*.$$

If $\mathbf{P}$ changes with time, it absorbs energy from the field at a rate

$$\frac{\partial W}{\partial t} = \frac{\partial \mathbf{P}}{\partial t} \cdot \mathbf{E}^*. \tag{11.29}$$

Any positive change $\partial W/\partial t$ represents a transfer of energy from the field to the atom. In general we shall be interested in periodic changes of $\mathbf{P}$ and $\mathbf{E}$, so that we can write

$$\left.\begin{aligned} \mathbf{P} &= \mathbf{P}_0 \exp(i\omega_P t), \\ \mathbf{E} &= \mathbf{E}_0 \exp\{i(\omega_E t + \alpha)\}, \end{aligned}\right\} \tag{11.30}$$

and consequently (11.29) gives us

$$\frac{\partial W}{\partial t} = -i\omega_P \mathbf{E}_0 \cdot \mathbf{P}_0 \exp[i\{(\omega_P - \omega_E)t - \alpha\}]. \tag{11.31}$$

To see whether there is any interaction on a long-time scale, we must average (11.31) over a period of many oscillations; we see immediately that unless both $\mathbf{E}$ and $\mathbf{P}$ have identical frequencies, that is unless

$$\omega_P - \omega_E = 0, \tag{11.32}$$

the average value of $\partial W/\partial t$ over a long period will be zero. When (11.32) is satisfied, the average value of $\partial W/\partial t$ is then

$$\overline{\frac{\partial W}{\partial t}} = -\omega_P \mathbf{P}_0 \cdot \mathbf{E}_0 \exp\{i(\pi/2 - \alpha)\}$$

which involves geometrical factors which we shall study in § 11.4.5.
Notice that the mean value can be either positive or negative.
From the electromagnetic wave point of view it is possible to see
this energy transfer taking place, in terms of concepts already discussed in § 4.5.1. The oscillating dipole moment **P** acts as a dipole
radiator and produces an electromagnetic field around it. In the
absence of any other field **E**, this field represents an outflow of
energy from the atom. But if an oscillating field is already present
we must add the radiated field to it, and the result will depend on the
phase relation between the two. If the two fields are of different
frequency, the phase-relation will change with time and any

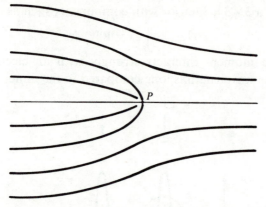

Fig. 11.6. Lines of energy flow around a dipole oscillating with such a phase as to absorb
energy from an electric field oscillating with the same frequency.

interaction will average to zero. But if the fields have exactly the
same frequency any phase-relation will be maintained. Under
certain conditions ($\alpha = -\frac{1}{2}\pi$), the radiated field strengthens the
applied field **E** on the outgoing side, so that the travelling wave **E**
leaves the radiator carrying more energy than it arrived with;
when $\alpha = \frac{1}{2}\pi$, destructive interference between the radiated wave
and **E** occurs on the outgoing side and the wave leaves the dipole
weaker than when it arrived. Fig. 11.6 shows the lines of **Π**, which
is the energy flow vector, schematically for these two cases. Similar
arguments apply to the higher multipoles.

It is quite easy to calculate the dipole and higher multipole
moments of an atom. The dipole moment of a point charge e at
position **r** is

$$\mathbf{P} = e\mathbf{r}$$

and so, for a distributed charge-density

$$\rho = e\Psi\Psi^*(\mathbf{r}),$$

the dipole moment is

$$\mathbf{P} = \int_{\text{all space}} e\mathbf{r}\Psi\Psi^* \, d\mathbf{r}. \tag{11.33}$$

The quadrupole moment of such a distribution is a tensor, whose xz component, for example, is

$$Q_{xz} = \int exz\Psi\Psi^* \, d\mathbf{r}. \tag{11.34}$$

This quadrupole is the one illustrated in Fig. 4.21(a); Fig. 4.21(b) is the zz component of the quadrupole tensor. Similarly, the octopole moment is a $3 \times 3 \times 3$ tensor with components such as

$$O_{xzz} = \int exz^2\Psi\Psi^* \, d\mathbf{r}. \tag{11.35}$$

The dipole moment interacts strongly with an electromagnetic wave whose wavelength is long compared to the dimensions of the

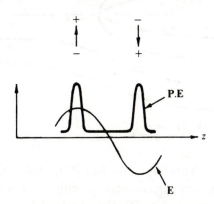

Fig. 11.7. To illustrate strong interaction between a quadrupole and a wave of similar wavelength to the quadrupole dimensions.

atom. The quadrupole and higher moments generally interact very weakly. However, if the wavelength is of the same order as the atomic size, the quadrupole moment can interact strongly as well, as is illustrated in Fig. 11.7, because its two dipole components act in sympathy instead of in opposition. Normally a quadrupole is a bad radiator, and therefore a bad absorber because the radiated waves from its two opposed dipole moments interfere destructively. However, if their separation is of the order of one wavelength the interference becomes constructive over part of the polar diagram

and a quadrupole can become quite a good radiator at such wave-lengths. This type of transition can be important in nuclear studies, because the γ-rays emitted may have wavelengths of the order of nuclear dimensions.

To illustrate the basic behaviour of a perturbed system we shall consider one having only two energy levels, or quantum states. An atom containing a large number of levels can be interpreted as a number of such systems each corresponding to one particular pair of levels. We shall see, however, that the conditions for interaction with a wave are sufficiently stringent for the probability of more than two levels in an atom participating to be very small, and there-fore for the two-level system to form a good approximation to a multi-level atom.

11.4.2 Transition in a two-level system. We consider a system, then, that has two eigenstates, with eigenfunctions Ψ_1 and Ψ_2, and corresponding energies E_1 and E_2. The eigenfunctions Ψ_1 and Ψ_2 can be broken down into space- and time-dependent parts, the latter being the complex exponential $\exp(i\omega t)$, where ω is $E/\hbar$. Thus

$$\Psi_1 = \psi_1(r)\exp(i\omega_1 t), \tag{11.36}$$

$$\Psi_2 = \psi_2(r)\exp(i\omega_2 t). \tag{11.37}$$

Because wave-functions form a complete set, the perturbed wave-function occurring at time $t \doteq 0$ can be written as a linear com-bination of Ψ_1 and Ψ_2, the combination depending on time,

$$\Psi(t) = a(t)\Psi_1 + b(t)\Psi_2. \tag{11.38}$$

We know an initial condition to apply to this equation: if the atom was in state Ψ_1 at $t = 0$,

$$a(0) = 1; \qquad b(0) = 0.$$

At some later time, both a and b will probably be non-zero, and we can easily write down the dipole moment, for example, following equation (11.33):

$$\mathbf{P} = \int_{\text{all space}} e\mathbf{r}(a\psi_1 + b\psi_2)(a^*\psi_1^* + b^*\psi_2^*)\,d\mathbf{r}$$

$$= \int e(aa^*\psi_1\mathbf{r}\psi_1^* + bb^*\psi_2\mathbf{r}\psi_2^* + ab^*\psi_1\mathbf{r}\psi_2^* + a^*b\psi_1^*\mathbf{r}\psi_2^*)\,d\mathbf{r}.$$

Using (11.36) and (11.37) to separate space and time variables, the

dipole moment can be written as

$$\mathbf{P} = aa^*\mathbf{p}_1 + bb^*\mathbf{p}_2 + ab^*\mathbf{p}_{12} \exp\{i(\omega_1 - \omega_2)t\}$$
$$+ a^*b\mathbf{p}_{12}^* \exp\{-i(\omega_1 - \omega_2)t\}, \tag{11.39}$$

where $\mathbf{p}_i$ is the moment in state i (from (11.33)) and $\mathbf{p}_{12}$ is the *matrix element*:

$$\mathbf{p}_{12} = \int_{\text{all space}} \psi_1(r)\mathbf{r}\psi_2^*(\mathbf{r})\,dr. \tag{11.40}$$

The first two terms in (11.39) are the static dipole moments in states 1 and 2. If $\mathbf{p}_{12}$ is non-zero, and neither a nor b is zero, the last two terms can be summed to give a term with a sinusoidal (not complex exponential) time-variation

$$\mathbf{P}(t) = \mathbf{c}\cos\left[(\omega_1 - \omega_2)t + \delta\right] \tag{11.41}$$

where $\mathbf{c} = 2ab\mathbf{p}_{12}$ and $\tan\delta = \arg(ab^*p_{12})$.

Thus the system can have an oscillating moment, with frequency equal to the difference between the two levels:

$$\omega_1 - \omega_2 = \frac{1}{\hbar}(E_1 - E_2). \tag{11.42}$$

The moment may be zero, if p_{12} is zero, however; if so, we can calculate the quadrupole moment in a similar way, and shall find it to have the same time-variation, and magnitude depending (from (11.34)) on

$$q_{12} = \int_{\text{all space}} \psi_1(\mathbf{r})xz\psi_2^*(\mathbf{r})\,dr. \tag{11.43}$$

To illustrate these moments, we have drawn schematically in Fig. 11.8 some of the hydrogen-atom wave-functions, $1s$, $2p$ and $3d$. It is easy to see that the charge density $\psi\psi^*$ in the mixed state $\psi_1 + \psi_2$ oscillates in a characteristic way between $|\psi_1(r) + \psi_2(r)|^2$ and $|\psi_1(r) - \psi_2(r)|^2$ and that these give rise to monopole, dipole and quadrupole moments in the four examples. The question of energy transfer is then easily solved as described in § 11.4.1. Only if the oscillating dipole and the applied wave have the same frequency ω_E, that is

$$\omega_E = \omega_2 - \omega_1, \tag{11.44}$$

will there be a net transfer of energy over a period of time considerably longer than one cycle. The energy transfer may be either positive or negative however, depending on the phase-relation between $\mathbf{E}$ and $\mathbf{P}$; the application of a randomly phased wave $\mathbf{E}$

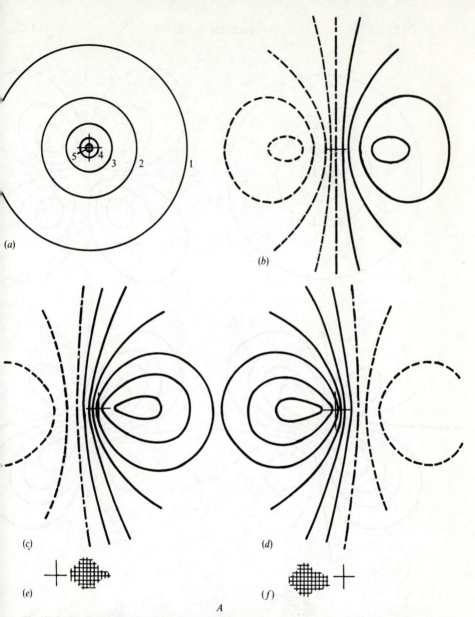

(a)

(b)

(c)

(d)

(e)

(f)

A

Fig. 11.8. To illustrate the origin of matrix elements for transitions in a hydrogen atom. The drawings, with the exception of (C), are schematic contour-maps of the wave-functions in an equatorial plane. They all have the same vertical interval. The line —·—·—· indicates zero; solid lines are positive and broken lines are negative.

A (a) Wave-function $\psi(1s)$ in the 1s state. This function oscillates in sign with frequency $\omega(1s)$. (b) Wave-function $\psi(2p)$ in the 2p state. This function oscillates in sign with frequency $\omega(2p)$. (c) The sum $\psi(1s)+\psi(2p)$. (d) The difference $\psi(1s)-\psi(2p)$. The sum of (a) and (b) oscillates between (c) and (d) with a frequency $\omega(1s)-\omega(2p)$. (e) The regions of maximum charge-density in (c). (f) The regions of maximum charge-density in (d). The charge distribution oscillates between (c) and (d) with frequency $\omega(1s)-\omega(2p)$, and thus the mixed wave-function gives rise to an oscillating dipole moment. Here $\Delta l = 1$.

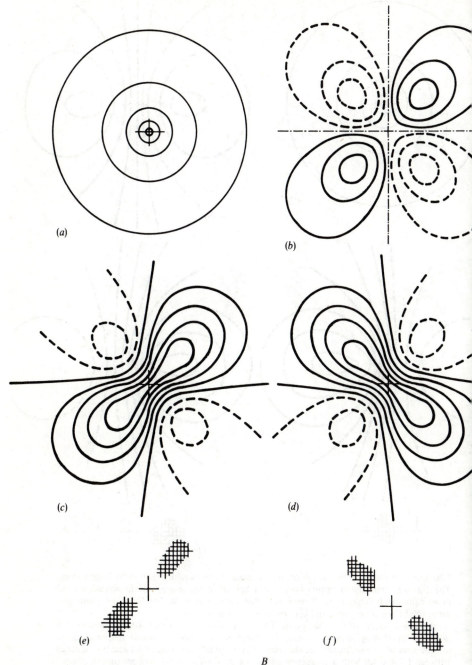

(a)

(b)

(c)

(d)

(e)

(f)

B

B *(a)* Wave-function $\psi(1s)$. *(b)* Wave-function $\psi(3d)$. In this case the oscillating charge distribution represented in *(e)* and *(f)* is a quadrupole $\pm\mp$; here $\Delta l = 2$.

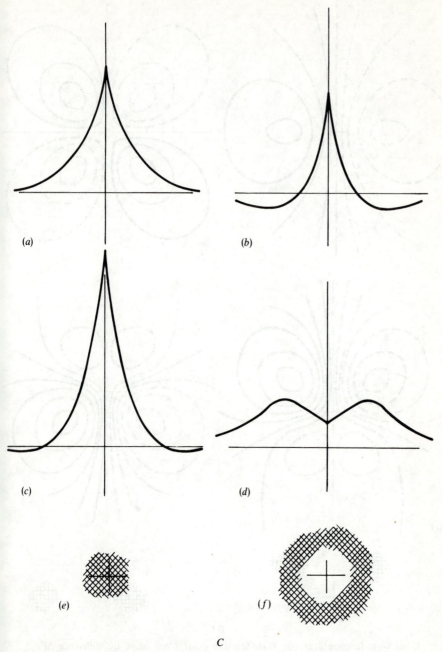

C (a) Graph of $\psi(1s)$ as a function of r. (b) Graph of $\psi(2s)$ as a function of r. Both (a) and (b) represent spherically symmetrical functions. The oscillating charge distribution is a monopole; it always remains spherically symmetrical. $\Delta l = 0$

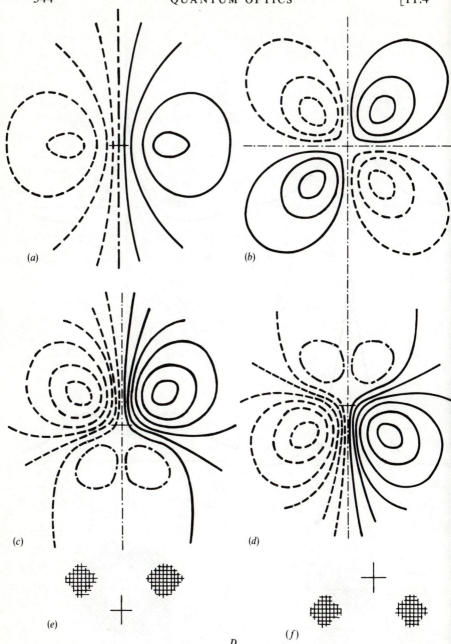

D (a) Wave-function $\psi(2p)$. (b) Wave-function $\psi(3d)$. Once again, the difference $\Delta l = 1$ gives rise to an oscillating dipole moment.

It should be noticed in all these examples that the symmetry alone of the wave-function is responsible for the type of multipole obtained. The radial distribution plays a relatively minor role. Thus the selection rules can be expressed simply in terms of Δl.

is therefore just as likely to induce the atom to emit radiation as it is to cause energy to be absorbed. This discovery leads to the investigation of stimulated emission and the invention of the maser (§ 11.5 et seq.).

11.4.3   The natural line-width. Were we to follow the theory through completely we should now calculate how the coefficients

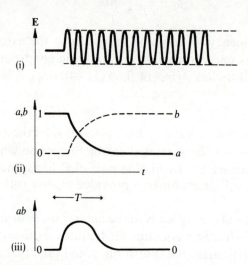

Fig. 11.9. Effect of a perturbing electric field **E** (i) on the *x* coefficients *a* and *b* (ii) in the expansion of Ψ and on the amplitude *ab* (iii) of the dipole moment **P**.

a and *b* in the expansion of Ψ change with time. We should do this by writing down the Schroedinger equation (11.2)

$$-i\hbar\frac{\partial\Psi}{\partial t} = (H_0 + V')\Psi, \tag{11.45}$$

where H_0 is the unperturbed Hamiltonian, which has eigenfunctions ψ_1 and ψ_2 and corresponding eigenvalues E_1 and E_2. Using the substitutions (11.38), (11.37), (11.36) and (11.28) we can easily write down equations that are soluble to find $a(t)$ and $b(t)$. When these are solved, subject to conservation of energy within the uncertainty principle, we indeed find that under the condition (11.44) the coefficients *a* and *b* change from 0 to 1 and from 1 to 0 respectively with a characteristic time *T* (Fig. 11.9). The calculation is not of great importance here, except to notice the implications of the time *T*. According to the interpretation of ψ as a probability distribution (§ 11.2), aa^* gives the probability that the atom has

remained in state 1 until time t, and bb^* the probability that it has changed states by that time. In other words, the existence of a time T during which aa^* has changed from 1 to 0 indicates that the atom can be expected to stay in the state 1 only for a time of the order of T. During this time only can we measure the energy of state 1, and therefore this energy must be uncertain to an extent

$$\delta E = \frac{\hbar}{T}. \tag{11.46}$$

Thus the frequency ω_1 must be uncertain to the extent $1/T$ and, if we take this uncertainty into account, the condition for energy transfer is slightly less stringent than (11.44), since it becomes

$$\omega_2 - \omega_1 + \frac{1}{T} > \omega_E > \omega_2 - \omega_1 - \frac{1}{T}. \tag{11.47}$$

Another way of looking at this result is to consider the average value $(\overline{\partial W/\partial t})$. It can only be evaluated during the period when neither a nor b is zero (since the oscillating part of $\mathbf{P}$ has a multiplier ab^*) and therefore $\overline{\partial W}/\partial t$ is non-zero provided ω_E lies within the limits (11.47).

This uncertainty in ω_E leads to the *natural width* of spectral lines, since the emission line contains all frequencies satisfying (11.47). If $\mathbf{p}_{12}$ were very small, the transition would take place slowly and T would be very large; thus small matrix elements lead to narrow spectral lines. As pointed out in § 8.3, the natural width is not the only contribution to the observed width of a spectral line, and is usually insignificant, but now at least we have seen its origin.

11.4.4 A multi-level system. We can now understand why the two-level system is a good beginning for a multi-level system. If the applied wave has only one frequency, only if there are two levels lying in the range (11.47) will there be a reasonable chance of a transition occurring. The other levels will not be able to conserve energy, and therefore transitions to them will not take place. Only on a very short time-scale can other levels be affected. If there is a level ω_3 not too far from ω_2, so that

$$\omega_1 - \omega_3 - \omega = \Omega$$

is small, a transition can occur provided that it is undone again within a time $1/\Omega$ to conserve energy on a long time-scale, since within that time (11.47) is satisfied for ω_3 replacing ω_2. Such *virtual transitions* can be important when two of them in succession

with non-zero p_{12}'s can satisfy conservation of energy, whereas the direct transition not involving the intermediate level has p_{12} zero. We shall not consider them further.

11.4.5   Matrix elements and selection rules. The interaction component $\mathbf{p}_{12}$ in (11.39) is generally known as a *matrix element*, a terminology which arises out of the matrix formulation of the Schroedinger equation (11.45). Since the probability of a transition depends on the matrix elements, it is clear that they are of great importance and we should at least have some idea of the conditions under which we might expect them to be zero.

We shall therefore calculate the matrix elements for dipole transitions in a one-dimensional infinitely-deep square well, whose wave-functions were introduced in § 11.2.4. There we had:

even solutions $\qquad \psi = \cos \dfrac{\pi x}{2a}(2q-1),$

odd solutions $\qquad \psi = \sin \dfrac{\pi x}{2a} \cdot 2q,$

where q is any integer. The functions are zero at and beyond $x = a$. We therefore carry out the integral

$$p_{mn} = \int_{-a}^{a} \psi_m x \psi_n \, dx, \qquad (11.48)$$

where m and n are any two integers. Without any mathematics we can see that certain integrals are going to be zero for symmetry reasons. If ψ_n and ψ_m are both of even parity, or both odd, the presence of x, which is odd, in the integral (11.48) ensures that contributions from positive and negative x will cancel, and p_{mn} will be zero. When ψ_n and ψ_m have opposite parity we have

$$p_{mn} = \int_{-a}^{a} x \cos \frac{x \pi n}{2a} \sin \frac{x \pi m}{2a} \, dx$$

$$= \frac{4a^2}{\pi^2} \left\{ \frac{1}{(m-n)^2} - \frac{1}{(m+n)^2} \right\}. \qquad (11.49)$$

The largest dipole moments therefore occur when m and n are adjacent ($m-n = \pm 1$). Values of (11.49) are tabulated in the table on page 348.

A *selection rule* is a general statement about matrix elements made in terms of quantum numbers of a particular system. For

example, in the square well we have just deduced that dipole transitions can occur only if $m-n$ is odd. Since dipole transitions are usually the only important ones this would lead to a selection rule:

$$\Delta m \text{ odd.}$$

	n \\ m	1	2	3	4
e	1	0	0·89	0	0·07
o	2	0·89	0	0·96	0
e	3	0	0·96	0	0·98
o	4	0·07	0	0·98	0

Values of the matrix element p_{mn} for a square well: e = even parity, o = odd parity. The units are $4a^2/\pi^2$.

In the hydrogen atom, following from the illustration in Fig. 11.8, we can see that dipole transitions are allowed only for

$$\Delta l = \pm 1,$$

quadrupole transitions for

$$\Delta l = \pm 2.$$

There is also a selection rule for changes in the magnetic quantum number m and so on. Selection rules are the most usual way of giving qualitative information about matrix elements, and arose from empirical observations before the origin of matrix elements was understood.

11.5 Stimulated emission and absorption

The important fact has emerged so far—that the energy transfer stimulated by an applied electromagnetic wave can be either positive or negative. If the atom is in the state of higher energy at time $t = 0$, the application of a wave of the correct frequency will stimulate a transfer to the lower-energy state, the radiated energy increasing the energy of the wave by constructive interference. If the atom starts in the lower state, the radiated radiation interferes destructively with the perturbing wave, and transfer of energy to the atom occurs. At a temperature T, the number of atoms thermally excited to states E_1 and E_2 are related by Boltzmann statistics:

$$\frac{n(E_1)}{n(E_2)} = \exp\left\{-\frac{(E_1 - E_2)}{kT}\right\}, \tag{11.50}$$

and therefore there are always more atoms in the lower energy state than in the upper. Consequently, application of a perturbing wave of the correct frequency will result in absorption rather than emission, since atoms in the lower state are absorbers. If, however, we can invert the populations, thereby achieving what can be described as a *negative temperature state* in which

$$\frac{n(E_1)}{n(E_2)} > 1,$$

the emission process will predominate, and the collection of atoms will amplify the incoming wave. This is the principle of the *maser* (microwave amplification by the stimulated emission of radiation) and *laser* (light amplification) and will be discussed shortly.

The phase of the wave is important here. Only if E and dp/dt are in phase will the interaction take place. The re-radiated energy from the atom has electric field which varies as $d^2[p]/dt^2$, which is therefore in quadrature with E, and would appear neither to interfere constructively nor destructively with it. The situation is, however, the same as that discussed in § 10.1.2, where it is shown that an extra $\pi/2$ phase change is introduced when the contributions from all points in the material are added together; thus the stimulated emission wave-field is able to influence the amplitude of the wave. Because of this strong link between the phase of the perturbing and emitted waves, the amplification occurs with complete phase coherence. Thus very long coherence times can be achieved when a maser or laser is used as a radiation source.

Before proceeding to build a maser there is one further consideration to be dealt with. This is the problem of a spontaneous emission, which is responsible for almost all observed spectral lines.

11.5.1 Spontaneous emission. The electromagnetic field behaves in many ways like a bound oscillator. This arises because its energy is given by

$$\mathscr{E} = \frac{1}{4\pi}(E^2 + H^2), \tag{11.51}$$

which is formally similar to the simple harmonic oscillator energy

$$\mathscr{E} = \frac{1}{2m}(p^2 + \omega^2 x^2), \tag{11.52}$$

and it turns out that, in the same way as quantum theory proves the oscillator to have zero-point energy because of its being bound,

it also proves the electromagnetic field to have zero-point energy. In both cases this energy is

$$\mathscr{E}_0 = \tfrac{1}{2}\hbar\omega.$$

For an electromagnetic field this must be half a quantum of every frequency that it is allowed to have; such frequencies will be determined by the resonances of the cavity in which it is enclosed. The zero-point energy of the electromagnetic field is therefore infinite, since any cavity has an infinite number of resonant frequencies. This infinite energy cannot be extracted, and its magnitude need not be worrying, but the component of frequency within the allowed range (11.47) for stimulated emission can cause downward transitions from E_1 to E_2 independently of any incident radiation. This is called spontaneous emission. Of course, spontaneous absorption cannot occur, because one whole quantum of the stimulating frequency would be absorbed.

Spontaneous emission occurs with random phase, and does not possess much time-coherence, although it is possible that the emitted quantum of energy can stimulate further stimulated (and therefore phase-related) transitions. It is still necessary for the matrix element for the transition to be non-zero, since the zero-point wave must have some way of coupling its oscillations to those of the atom.

11.5.2 The Einstein A and B coefficients; relative probabilities of spontaneous and stimulated transfers. A simple argument due to Einstein allows us to see the relative probabilities of spontaneous and stimulated energy transfers. We consider the detailed balance between two energy levels n and m in the presence of black-body radiation of density $I(\omega)$. The probability of stimulated transitions is proportional to this intensity. In equilibrium the populations of the two states will be $N_n > N_m$ and related by (11.50); the number of transfers from each level will be proportional to the number of atoms available to transfer. It should also be noted that we are dealing with an assembly of many atoms which are distributed statistically between the various energy levels.

The number of upward transitions, which are all stimulated, is

$$A(\omega)I(\omega)N_n,$$

$A(\omega)$ being the probability of a stimulated transition of frequency ω per unit energy density of stimulating radiation, and the number

of downward transitions is

$$A(\omega)I(\omega)N_m + B(\omega)N_m,$$

$B(\omega)$ being the probability of a spontaneous transition. The same probability $A(\omega)$ applies to both upwards and downward stimulated transitions, since both depend on the same matrix-element. These two numbers must be equal, hence

$$\frac{A(\omega)}{B(\omega)} = \frac{N_m}{I(\omega)(N_n - N_m)} = \frac{1}{I(\omega)}\left[\exp\left(\frac{\hbar\omega}{kT}\right) - 1\right]^{-1}.$$

Now for black-body radiation at temperature T

$$I(\omega) = \frac{\hbar\omega^3}{4\pi^2 c^2}\left[\exp\left(\frac{\hbar\omega}{kT}\right) - 1\right]^{-1},$$

so that

$$\frac{A(\omega)}{B(\omega)} = \frac{4\pi^2 c^2}{\hbar\omega^3}.$$

The important fact to notice here is the ω^3 dependence; for a given intensity of applied radiation the ratio of the probabilities of stimulated and spontaneous emission is proportional to ω^{-3}. Spontaneous emission becomes very important at high frequencies. At low frequencies, however, emission stimulated by quite modest $I(\omega)$'s can be considerable compared with the spontaneous noise, and gives rise to the possibility of an amplifier working on this principle, the *maser*.

11.5.3 Masers and lasers. To illustrate the possibility of an amplifying device working on the principle of stimulated emission we shall next put some figures into the preceding analysis. Experimentally we have a cavity containing a material with two energy levels separated by energy $\hbar\omega$ and linked by a non-zero matrix element; the upper level is artificially over-populated compared with the lower one (details of the pump mechanisms used will be discussed later) and a small amount of radiation of frequency ω allowed into the cavity. The question we ask is: what density of radiation is necessary so that the probability of a proportional burst of stimulated radiation is much larger than that of a random burst of spontaneous emission of the same frequency? Mathematically, we want

$$\frac{A(\omega)I(\omega)}{B(\omega)} = \frac{4\pi^2 c^2}{\hbar\omega^3}I(\omega) \gg 1. \tag{11.53}$$

At a frequency $\omega = 10^{10}\ s^{-1}$ this gives

$$I(\omega) \gg 3 \times 10^{-22}\ \text{erg cm}^{-3}. \tag{11.54}$$

A microwatt of radiation per cm^2 corresponds to $10c^{-1}$ erg cm^{-3} = 3×10^{-10} erg cm^{-3}, so that the criterion above is well satisfied even for such low powers. We can also look at the energy density in terms of photons—quanta of electromagnetic radiation—per cc. The photon at $10^{10}\ s^{-1}$ has energy $\hbar\omega = 10^{-18}$ erg, so that even an input of one photon per cc is well above the noise level. A further point in our favour is that by using a resonant cavity tuned to the frequency in question the radiation density can be enhanced many times at the expense of making the frequency selectivity even more stringent. It appears, then, that at microwave frequencies— $10^{10}\ s^{-1}$ corresponds to 18 cm wavelength— an amplifier working on these principles should be quite feasible.

Before discussing details we shall carry out a similar calculation at optical frequencies. A frequency $\omega = 3 \times 10^{15}\ s^{-1}$ corresponds to $\lambda = 5000\ \text{Å}$, and the energy density for reliable stimulated emission then comes out to be:

$$I(\omega) \gg 7 \times 10^{-6}\ \text{erg cm}^{-3}, \tag{11.55}$$

corresponding to 2×10^7 photons/cm^3 or a power of 0.02 W/cm^2. This is a large energy density, about 10^{15} times the threshold sensitivity of the human eye, for example. The laser would therefore appear to be completely useless as an amplifier of light waves, as a photoelectric cell with a very poor quantum efficiency would be better by orders of magnitude. In fact it was this type of argument which convinced the pioneers of masers that there was no future in extending the device to higher frequencies than microwaves. However, the laser, while useless as an amplifier, is an extremely valuable source of radiation, since if it operates within a cavity from which there is only a small leak to the outside world, such enormous energy densities can build up that condition (11.55) is easily satisfied. The same cannot, unfortunately, be said for X-rays. For a frequency of $3 \times 10^{19}\ s^{-1}$ ($0.5\ \text{Å}$ wavelength) the necessary intensity is 2×10^{10} W/cm^{-2}, which cannot be achieved because the construction of an X-ray resonator would require a dimensional accuracy of one atom.

11.5.4   The laser as a highly coherent source. It was pointed out in § 11.5 that when stimulated emission takes place, the light

wave resulting has a definite phase relation to the oscillation of the atomic wave-function, which itself is locked in phase to the initiating wave. As a result, if an avalanche process takes place in which the emitted light causes stimulated emission in a number of other atoms it will be seen that all the radiation produced will have a definite phase coherence. This is a direct contrast to light produced by spontaneous emission, or from a black body, where the emission of each photon is a separate event, completely unrelated to emission of any other photon. A laser beam therefore consists of something which can be described as a giant photon, of energy many $\hbar\omega$. From the electromagnetic wave point of view it is a very long and large sine wave with no phase discontinuities. The period of coherence is, with a continuously pumped maser (§ 11.7.3), essentially infinite, and therefore the wavelength and the direction of travel of the wave are very accurately defined.

Having seen the principle of operation of the maser and laser we shall now go back to discuss the most important practical aspect, that of obtaining the inverted population, corresponding to a negative temperature state.

11.6   Two-level masers

11.6.1   Maser pumps. The problem in the design of a maser is that two separate operations are involved. The first is to obtain the inverted population; the second to allow maser action to occur. There are three practical solutions.

(i) The earliest masers used space-separation. The material was a beam of ammonia molecules, and inversion of the population was achieved in one place, maser action following further along the beam.

(ii) The second mechanism to be used involved time-separation, the inversion occurring first to be followed by maser action. Since the amplification is a function of the degree of inversion, which clearly falls during the maser action, the device is no use as an amplifier, but may be quite satisfactory as a pulsed source.

(iii) The third and most important mechanism is the three-level pump, which is frequency-separated. It uses three energy levels (Fig. 11.23) which are all linked by non-zero matrix elements. Pump radiation is applied from A to C, maser action occurs from C to B, and the levels are chosen so that a fast natural decay from B to A keeps the level B relatively unoccupied.

We shall now discuss these mechanisms in more detail, because of the quantum mechanical principles involved.

11.6.2 The ammonia maser. The ammonia molecule is tetrahedral in structure (Fig. 11.10). The position of the nitrogen atom relative to the centroid of the molecule lies on a sphere, as the molecule can point in any direction in space. Another way of stating the

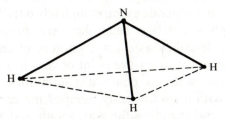

Fig. 11.10. The ammonia molecule.

same fact is that the potential function for the molecule, measured as a function of the **r** of the nitrogen nucleus in centre-of-mass space, has a minimum lying on a sphere of some radius r_0, but is otherwise spherically symmetrical. The function plotted against r is shown in Fig. 11.11. To find the energy levels we must solve the

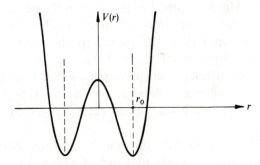

Fig. 11.11. Double potential well in ammonia.

Schroedinger equation subject to this potential distribution. Solution of the angular part of the equation is exactly the same as for any other spherically symmetric system, and leads to quantization of the angular momentum of the molecule. The energy levels for such rotations are very widely spaced, and are not of interest here. The radial wave-equation, with its double potential well, is more interesting. It corresponds classically to two coupled oscillators,

and on solution of the Schroedinger equation we find a spectrum of
energy levels which is the same as for one oscillator, but with each
level split into a doublet, the amount of splitting depending on the
separation or degree of coupling of the oscillators. To illustrate
the solution for the ammonia potential function, we shall consider
the one-dimensional problem of two infinitely deep square wells of
width a, separated by a δ-function of strength D (Fig. 11.12). We
shall see that the level structure is related to that of *one* of the two
wells by the splitting of each level, the splitting becoming sufficient
at high energies to produce a level-scheme approaching that of a

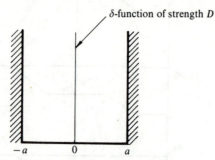

Fig. 11.12. Model of two wells separated by a δ-function.

well of width $2a$ without the δ-function. This scheme is very similar
to that obtained for the ammonia double well, and is illustrated in
Fig. 11.13.

The ammonia molecule, therefore, has a level scheme consisting
of pairs of energy levels with fairly small separation compared to
the separation of one pair from another. To use ammonia as a
maser material we concentrate our attention on one pair of levels,
the lowest-lying pair, and neglect all others in the same way as we
did in § 11.4.2. In normal thermal equilibrium, the lower level has the
greater occupation, and it is only by using some differing physical
property of the atoms in the two levels that we can separate them
and hence produce two non-equilibrium distributions. The one
consisting of atoms entirely in the upper state has an equivalent
temperature

$$T = -\infty,$$

and is ideal for maser action. The property that is used is the dipole
moment induced by an applied electric field. The dipole moment

in the presence of a field E can be written as

$$P = P_0 + \alpha E + ...O(E^2) \qquad (11.56)$$

($O(E^2)$ means that second- and higher-order terms are neglected) and for an ammonia molecule in the lowest pair of energy levels

$$P_0 = 0,$$

as will be seen from the details of the calculation. The polarizability α is, however, of opposite sign in the two states of the doublet, and

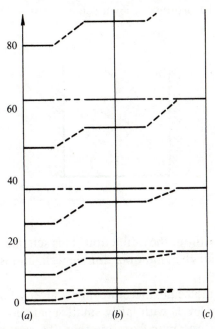

Fig. 11.13. Energy-level scheme for the double well compared with two single wells: (a) is for a single well of width $2a$; (b) is for the double well in Fig. 11; (c) is for a single well of width a. Corresponding levels are indicated by broken lines.

as a result the forces on the molecules are different when it passes through an inhomogeneous electric field. By suitable arrangement of the field (Fig. 11.14), the forces can be arranged to focus the beam of molecules in the upper energy level and to defocus the lower-state molecules. The population at the focal point is thus inverted.

Finally, the inverted population is used to allow stimulated emission of radiation at the frequency corresponding to the difference between the energies of the pair levels. In the ammonia case, this radiation has a wavelength of 1·25 cm. Inversion takes

place within a microwave cavity tuned to the resonant frequency (Fig. 11.15).

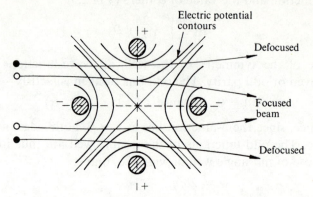

Fig. 11.14. Quadrupole electric field produced by four charged conductors, and trajectories of even-parity (●) and odd-parity (○) ammonia molecules.

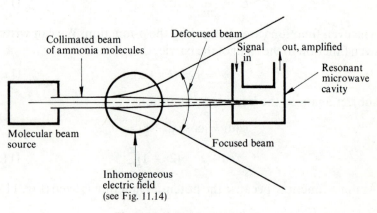

Fig. 11.15. Ammonia maser.

11.6.3   The calculation for a double potential well.
In its zero-potential regions, the double well of Fig. 11.12 leads to a wave ψ of wave-number k related to the eigenstate energy:

$$E = \frac{\hbar^2 k^2}{2m}. \tag{11.57}$$

We must consider the possible values of k that satisfy both boundary and δ-function conditions; that is:

(a) at the boundary, where $V \to \infty$, $\psi = 0$;

(b) at the δ-function, ψ is continuous, but the gradient $\partial\psi/\partial x$ suffers a discontinuity related to the strength D of the δ-function and the value of ψ there (§ 11.2.3),

$$\Delta\left(\frac{\partial\psi}{\partial x}\right) = \frac{2m}{\hbar^2}\psi D. \tag{11.58}$$

Because of the symmetry of the well, all wave-functions are of either even or odd parity. The odd functions must satisfy

$$\psi(0) = 0 \quad \text{because} \quad \psi(x) = -\psi(-x)$$

and hence, since the δ-function lies at $x = 0$, both sides of (11.58) are zero. The odd functions of the double well are thus identical with those of the single well of width $2a$, that is

$$\lambda = 2a/n,$$

$$k = \frac{\pi n}{a} \quad \text{with } n \text{ odd};$$

$$E = \frac{\hbar^2\pi^2}{2ma^2}\cdot n^2. \tag{11.59}$$

The even functions are changed by the δ-function. We can write an even function to the right of the barrier ($x \geqslant 0$) as

$$\psi = \cos(kx + \alpha), \tag{11.60}$$

subject again to the boundary conditions

$$\psi(a) = \cos(ka + \alpha) = 0,$$

$$ka + \alpha = (2n - 1)\frac{\pi}{2}. \tag{11.61}$$

At the δ-function, because the potential function is even (Fig. 11.16),

$$\Delta\left(\frac{\partial\psi}{\partial x}\right) = 2\left(\frac{\partial\psi}{\partial x}\right)_0 = -2k\sin(kx + \alpha) = -2k\sin\alpha,$$

and therefore (11.58) gives

$$-2k\sin\alpha = \frac{2mD}{\hbar^2}\cos\alpha,$$

or
$$\tan\alpha = -\frac{2m}{\hbar^2}\cdot\frac{D}{2k}. \tag{11.62}$$

On expansion, equation (11.61) gives

$$\tan\alpha = \cot ka,$$

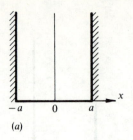

(a)

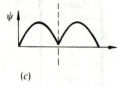

(b)

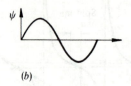

(c)

Fig. 11.16. The lowest-energy wave-functions in the double well: (a) the double potential well; (b) the first odd-parity function; (c) the first even-parity function. The discontinuity of gradient at $x = 0$ is the result of the functions having a non-zero value there.

whence (11.62) leads to the equation

$$\tan ka = -\frac{\hbar^2}{2m} \cdot \frac{2k}{D},\qquad(11.63)$$

which can be solved graphically as is illustrated in Fig. 11.17. Obvious points from the diagram are as follows:

(1) The values of ka satisfying the even equation (11.63) approach $(2n-1)\pi/2$ as $n \to \infty$. They thus asymptotically approach the solution for the well of width $2a$.

(2) For large Da, the even solutions lie very close to the odd solutions, the separation being linearly proportional to n for small n. Large Da corresponds to small coupling between the two wells of width a.

(3) The even function of a pair always has a lower value of k, and hence lower energy by virtue of equation (11.57).

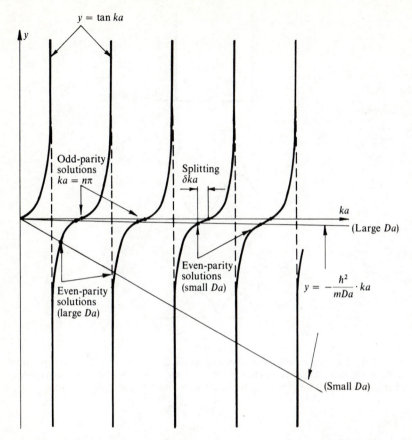

Fig. 11.17. Graphical solution of the equation $\tan ka = -\hbar^2 k/mD$ for small and large values of the parameter Da.

The separation of the levels, which can be considered as the splitting of the levels of the double well of width $2a$, is illustrated in Fig. 11.18 and this leads to the level system in Fig. 11.13.

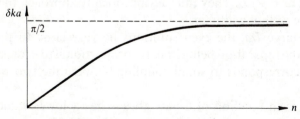

Fig. 11.18. The splitting δk as a function of quantum number n.

11.6.4　Physical interpretation of the result. It is tempting to think that one of each pair of levels corresponds to the nitrogen atom in each well. This is quite wrong. From Fig. 11.16 we can see that each wave-function leads to identical $|\psi|^2$ in each well, the only difference being that the phases are the same in the even state and opposite in the odd state. The problem is identical with the classical problem of the two identical linked pendulums (Fig. 11.19). If they were independent they would have the same period; however, the linking allows transfer of energy from one pendulum to the other.

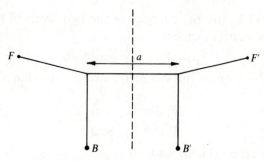

Fig. 11.19. The double-pendulum experiment F, F' are fixed points; B, B' are the pendulum bobs. All the lines in the diagram are string. The degree of coupling can be altered by changing a.

The two time-independent states (normal modes) correspond to both pendulums swinging with identical amplitudes but in phase or out of phase; the frequencies of the two modes are slightly different. Any other state, such as one pendulum swinging alone, must be expressed as a linear combination of these two, and since they have different frequencies the linear combination changes with time. It results in periodic transfer of the oscillation from one pendulum to the other, the transfer frequency being the beat frequency between the two modes. Any reader who has not seen this experiment in action is well advised to set it up for himself. If the nitrogen atom in the ammonia molecule is initially in one of the two wells, it will oscillate backwards and forwards between the two, and it is this oscillation at the beat frequency

$$\omega = \frac{1}{\hbar}(E_1 - E_2),$$

which couples to the electromagnetic wave and produces stimulated emission.

11.6.5   The polarizability in the two states of a doublet. The energy change on application of an electric field can be calculated to give the polarizability. In a field **F**, the energy E becomes

$$E' = E_0 + \tfrac{1}{2}\alpha \mathbf{F}^2 + \dots \qquad (11.64)$$

The problem is a simple piece of second-order perturbation theory,† and for a two-level system the energy is the solution E' of the secular determinant

$$\begin{vmatrix} V_{11} + E_1 - E' & V_{21} \\ V_{12} & V_{22} + E_2 - E' \end{vmatrix} = 0, \qquad (11.65)$$

where E_1 and E_2 are the energies of the two levels of the doublet and V_{ij} is the matrix element

$$V_{ij} = Fp_{ij} = \int \psi_i x \psi_j^* \, dx. \qquad (11.66)$$

Now consideration of the symmetry of the wave-functions shows that

$$V_{11} = V_{22} = 0,$$
$$V_{12} = V_{21} \neq 0.$$

Thus the equation (11.65) leads to

$$2E' = E_1 + E_2 \pm \sqrt{(E_1 - E_2)^2 + 4V_{12}^2}.$$

For small V_{12} this gives approximately

$$E' = E_1 + \frac{V_{12}^2}{(E_1 - E_2)},$$

or

$$E' = E_2 - \frac{V_{12}^2}{(E_1 - E_2)},$$

For these two states, therefore, (11.64) gives

$$\alpha = \pm \frac{2p_{12}^2}{E_1 - E_2}$$

respectively. Thus the defocusing–focusing action of the inhomogeneous field in Fig. 11.14 is possible.

11.6.6   Time-separated masers. The ideas behind a maser in which the population inversion and the maser action are separated in time rather than in space are in some ways easier to grasp than those behind the space-separated maser. We provide a cavity containing the maser material and excite it by the provision of

† For further details of the principle on which this calculation is based the reader must consult a textbook on quantum mechanics. A suggestion is given in the bibliography.

radiation at or near the resonance frequency. The exciting radiation is then switched off, leaving the population in (we hope) an inverted state, and the input radiation is applied. This will stimulate emission, with a consequent return of the system to thermal equilibrium; the amplification factor will drop and the device will clearly be unsuitable for any form of quantitative work, although well adapted to detection of resonance radiation. The one advantage it might have over a maser working by the space-separated mechanism is that it could use a solid material and not only a gas, because no physical movement is required.

So much said, we ought now to enquire into the inversion procedure. How, by applying a resonance radiation, can we be sure of getting population-inversion from the equilibrium state? If we solve the mathematical perturbation theory for perturbation of a two-level system by an electromagnetic wave we find that for a system initially in one of the two states the proportion of the other state (b in equation (11.38)) contained in the perturbed wavefunction oscillates with time over a range with amplitude dependent on the frequency of the applied radiation. The amplitude approaches unity at the resonance frequency. Clearly, then, the application of a pulsed field of resonant frequency of carefully controlled amplitude and duration should ensure a high probability of interchange of the populations of the two states. This seems a rather awkward and difficult procedure, but is in fact used in nuclear magnetic-resonance work for interchanging populations (Fig. 11.20). A rather neater technique used to achieve the same end is that called *adiabatic fast passage*, in which the applied frequency of the pump radiation is swept from a value considerably below the resonance frequency to one considerably above resonance. The effect of this, provided the rate of sweeping lies within fairly generous limits, is to interchange the populations. Physically, the process is rather difficult to understand; the explanation that it is a consequence of the perturbation theory is insufficient until we can see exactly what is happening qualitatively. But if we think in terms of one specific two-level system the process is reasonably clear, and we can then resort to the mathematics to show that all two-level systems can be described in an identical manner to this one system and should therefore behave similarly.

The two-level system we choose is that of an atom with spin $\frac{1}{2}$, and no orbital angular momentum, in a magnetic field $\mathbf{H}_0$. The

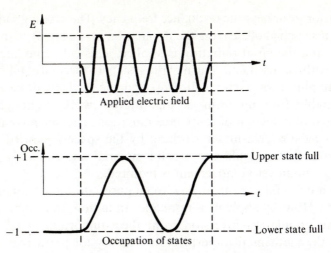

Fig. 11.20. Population inversion by the application of a controlled resonant pulse of radiation.

atom thus has two levels corresponding to moment **d** parallel and anti-parallel to H_0:

$$E = \pm \hbar \mu_B H_0.$$

As described in § 11.3.2, the difference between these energy levels corresponds to precession of the magnetic moment vector **M** around the field H_0 with frequency $2\mu_B H_0$, and this precession gives rise to a rotating magnetic moment which can couple to the magnetic vector in a circularly polarized electromagnetic wave of the same frequency. Suppose that a circularly polarized wave travelling along H_0 is now applied to the atom, which starts with its moment almost parallel (as opposed to anti-parallel) to H_0 and precessing round it at frequency

$$\omega = 2\mu_B H_0.$$

The wave is assumed to have angular frequency δ and amplitude H_p (Fig. 11.21(*a*)). We shall show, by considering the state of affairs when looked at in a frame of reference rotating with H_p at frequency δ, that as δ changes slowly through ω the direction of the moment **M** changes from being parallel to anti-parallel to H_0.

In this frame of reference rotating at δ, the perturbing field H_p appears stationary, and, because electromagnetic waves are transversely polarized, it is normal to H_0. However, the precession

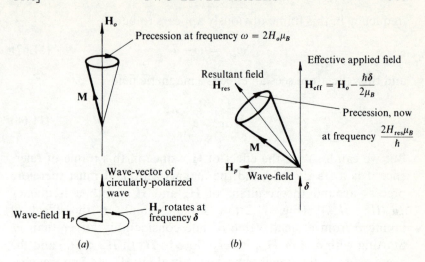

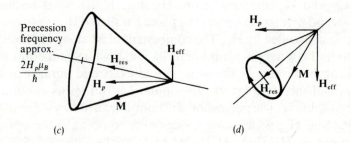

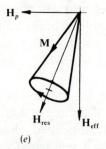

Fig. 11.21. Adiabatic slow passage:
- (a) System in stationary coordinates.
- (b) System in coordinates rotating at angular frequency δ. $\delta \ll \omega$.
- (c) As (b), but δ only just below ω.
- (d) As (b), but $\delta > \omega$.
- (e) As (b), but $\delta \gg \omega$.

frequency in this frame obviously appears to be

$$\omega_{eff} = \omega - \delta \qquad (11.67)$$

and thus the atom sees an effective magnetic field

$$H_{eff} = \frac{\omega - \delta}{2\mu_B} \qquad (11.68)$$

But we can also see the effect of H_p, since in this frame of reference it is a steady field and the magnetization M must therefore precess around the resultant of H_p and H_{eff} with a frequency $2\mu_B(H_p^2 + H_{eff}^2)^{\frac{1}{2}}$ (Fig. 11.21(b)). Finally, think of the effect of taking δ from a small value to one considerably larger than ω. Starting with $\delta \ll \omega$, H_{eff} is very close to H_0 (if $H_p \ll H_0$) and the average magnetization is almost exactly along H_0. As δ approaches ω, H_{eff} approaches zero, and the precession axis along the resultant of H_{eff} and H_p tilts away from H_0 (Fig. 11.21(c)). At resonance $\delta = \omega$, and precession occurs in a plane parallel to H_0 at a frequency entirely controlled by H_p. The component of M along H_0 therefore oscillates between plus and minus its initial value, and application of H_p at the resonance frequency for an exact odd number of half-cycles will therefore invert the population. But let us continue to change δ slowly. The precession will continue to follow the resultant of H_{eff} and H_p, which now is beginning to point in the opposite direction to H_0 (Fig. 11.21(d)). And, finally, when $\delta \gg \omega$, the magnetization M is seen to be almost exactly anti-parallel to H_0, and inversion has been achieved (Fig. 11.21(e)). It merely remains to switch off the perturbing field within a very short time—a cycle or two—to avoid the whole process going into reverse again. During the inversion process the component of M parallel to H_0 has gone through a cycle which is schematically illustrated by Fig. 11.22.

The physical conditions for the process are clearly defined by this illustration. The rate of change of δ must be such that an axis of precession can always be defined, that is, the resultant field $H_{eff} + H_p$ must change slowly compared with the precession rate. This is called a *quasi-static* change. The other limit, of minimum rate of change, is set by the natural relaxation of the system, which will return from the higher to the lower level by various processes, including spontaneous emission, with a time-constant T. The rate

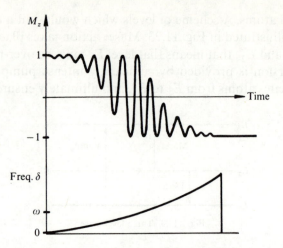

Fig. 11.22. The component M_z of the magnetic moment along H as δ changes. The diagram is only schematic; in practice the precession frequency of M would be much faster relative to the time-scale of the change.

of change is thus limited to a range

$$|\Lambda|^2 \gg \left|\frac{d\delta}{dt}\right| \gg \frac{|\Lambda|}{T},$$

where Λ is the frequency $2H_p\mu_B$. These limits are generous.

It remains to state that for any two-level system the quantum-mechanical equations can be written in a form which reproduces the precession properties of this one; that is, as

$$\frac{\partial \mathbf{R}}{\partial t} = \boldsymbol{\omega} \times \mathbf{R}$$

in which the vector $\mathbf{R}$ has as its components three combinations derived from the wave-functions ψ_1 and ψ_2 and their complex conjugates. Then $\boldsymbol{\omega}$ is a vector derived from the perturbation field, and the solution follows algebraically the same process as that described here pictorially.

11.7   Three-level masers

Having dealt with the two most complicated forms of masers we now turn our attention to three-level masers, conceptually the easiest to understand. A three-level maser, as its title suggests, relies on a triplet of levels, between two of which maser action occurs, and the third of which acts as an inexhaustible supply of

unexcited atoms. A scheme of levels which would suit a three-level maser is illustrated in Fig. 11.23. Maser action takes place between levels E_3 and E_2; that means that level E_3 must be over-populated. The inversion is provided by sufficiently intense pump radiation which excites atoms from E_1 to E_3, and ultimately ensures that the

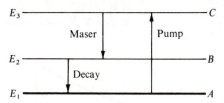

Fig. 11.23. Three-level maser.

populations of E_1 and E_3 are made equal (i.e. spontaneous emission is negligible). The population of E_2, which must be smaller than E_3 to ensure maser action, must therefore be kept down below that of E_1, which is ensured simply by choosing a material in which the transition probability $E_2 \rightarrow E_1$ is very large, so that E_2 and E_1 are kept in thermal equilibrium. If E_1 is in fact a broad level the device is made more efficient for two reasons; first, that the transition probability $E_2 \rightarrow E_1$ is enhanced, and, secondly, that the transition $E_1 \rightarrow E_3$ is not highly tuned, so that the pump frequency does not need to be very precise. This is of further assistance in the design of a practical maser.

11.7.1 Practical problems. To make the maser work efficiently the radiation to be amplified should be kept for a long time in contact with the maser material, which can be either gas or solid —or, presumably, liquid, although liquid energy levels tend not to be sharp because of the lack of long-range order. This is achieved by putting it in a microwave cavity tuned to frequency $(E_3 - E_2)/\hbar$. If the level E_1 is fairly broad it should be possible to design the cavity so that it is also tuned to the pump frequency $(E_3 - E_1)/\hbar$ sufficiently closely to lie within the bounds set by the broad level. The pump-frequency radiation is then applied continuously at sufficient power to saturate the transition $E_1 \rightarrow E_3$ (i.e. to equate the populations of the two levels) and the small signal at the resonance frequency $(E_3 - E_2)/\hbar$ applied. A receiver tuned to this frequency will pick up the amplified signal.

A maser is, of course, a very-narrow-band amplifier; it is because of its narrow band that the noise-level achieved is very low, since there is a theoretical minimum noise-level per unit band-width. If the cavity is highly tuned, the band-width is determined by the cavity, but for microwave amplifiers it is often the width of the energy levels themselves that determines the bandwidth.

11.7.2   Pulsed lasers: ruby laser. As an example of a three-level maser we shall describe a ruby laser, which works in principle in the way described. The level scheme is similar to that of Fig. 11.23 except that the broad level A is at the top, the laser transition occurring between the lower two levels. The important levels of the Cr ion in an Al_2O_3 crystal (ruby) are shown in Fig. 11.24, and pumping at 5500 Å from a xenon discharge tube overpopulates A, resulting in a subsequent fast transition to the level B, the transition occurring with the emission of phonons. Laser output follows from B to C.

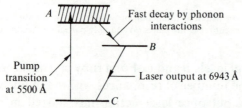

Fig. 11.24. Level scheme for ruby (Cr^{+++} impurity in Al_2O_3).

The requirements of the optical system are two-fold. First of all it must be highly tuned, so that the energy density is concentrated within a very narrow frequency band. Secondly, provision must be made for extracting the radiation. The ruby crystal is therefore cut with accurately parallel and optically flat ends, so as to form a Fabry–Pérot interferometer; one end is completely silvered and the other almost completely. Before laser action begins, the Fabry–Pérot plate has a finite resolving power because of the partial reflectivity (see § 7.5.1). This arises because we consider each of the multiple beams to be a factor R weaker than the previous one due to incomplete reflexion. During the pumping the occupation of level B grows, and the probability of emission with it. Eventually the system becomes unstable and the emitted waves stimulate a greater amount of extra radiation during one transit of the crystal than they lose through the partial reflectivity of one face. The resolving

power of the interferometer therefore increases, because the factor R has now become unity, and the output radiation therefore has a very narrow line-width (Fig. 11.25). The line-width is determined by the pulse length eventually, because the laser action drains level B so quickly that the unstable condition only lasts for a time of the order of 10^{-8} s, although the power delivered during this period may be very great. Powers of the order 10^5 MW in 10^{-8} s pulses have been observed. The actual wavelength of the emitted line is determined by the interference conditions rather than the

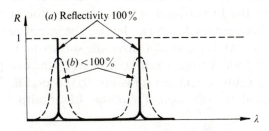

Fig. 11.25. Reflexion coefficient as a function of wavelength for a Fabry–Pérot interferometer with 100 percent reflecting plates (*a*) and only partially-reflecting plates (*b*).

intrinsic widths of levels B and C. For a ruby crystal a centimetre or two in length, the number of resonances within the line width may be considerable, but once laser action has started in one of the resonance modes this particular mode will become more selective as described above and the energy will be concentrated within it (Fig. 11.26).

The complete ruby laser is illustrated in Fig. 11.27. Its xenon discharge tube produces discharges lasting for about 10^{-6} s from a condenser bank at about 5 kV, and the light output pulses a number of times during this period.

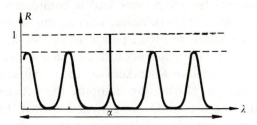

Fig. 11.26. When laser action occurs, in one particular mode the effective reflectivity becomes 100 percent. The line-width of normal emission from the atom may be of the order of α.

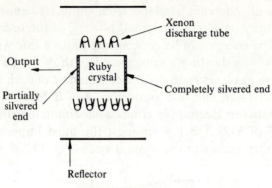

Fig. 11.27. Ruby laser.

The power available in a single pulse can be increased by 'frustrating' the interferometer. We replace the silvering of the completely reflecting face by an external movable mirror, which is set non-parallel to the far face. The pump is allowed to fill level B under these conditions, and, because the interferometer will not resonate, laser action does not occur. When level B is filled well past the degree necessary for catastrophic emission in a resonator, the mirror is moved to become accurately parallel to the far surface, and all the stored energy is released in a burst of much greater power than could otherwise be attained. A mechanical system for achieving this is illustrated in Fig. 11.28; electronic systems involving polaroids and Kerr-cells (§ 5.5.2) are the logical development of the mechanics.

11.7.3 Continuous lasers: helium–neon laser. More important from the point of view of classical optics are lasers which can be operated continuously, and which can therefore make use of the exceptionally

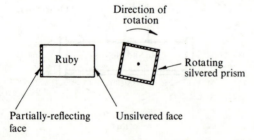

Fig. 11.28. Frustrated ruby laser. The flash tube has been omitted (see Fig. 11.27).

high degree of coherence available from stimulated emission. Such lasers generally develop quite small powers, of the order of milli-watts, but the energy can be concentrated into a line width of the order of $1\,s^{-1}$, indicating a coherence length of 3×10^{10} cm. The helium–neon gas laser is one of the commonest of such lasers. It is a three-level laser, the fast transition $A \to B$ being induced by collisions between He and Ne atoms, and stimulated emission at a wavelength of 6328 Å being amongst the most important of the possible return routes to the ground state (Fig. 11.29). One of the

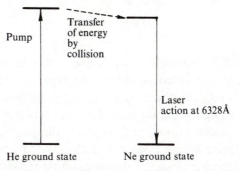

Fig. 11.29. The helium–neon laser: one of the many possible level-schemes leading to laser action.

advantages of a gas is that a very long laser can be made, thus reducing the degree of amplification necessary in the material to offset losses occurring at the reflecting faces. A typical He–Ne laser contains He gas at 1 mm Hg pressure and Ne at 0·1 mm and has a length of up to 100 cm (Fig. 11.30). It is excited by a discharge within the gas itself.

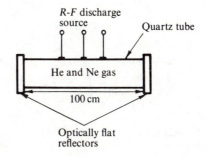

Fig. 11.30. Construction of a helium–neon laser.

11.7.4　Semi-conductor lasers. A further type of laser has been developed using semi-conductors. Gallium arsenide is the most satisfactory material, and laser action occurs in the transition between the conduction and valence bands, the pumping occurring as the result of an applied voltage.

11.8　Laser optics

Under the title of *laser optics* we shall discuss a few interesting experiments which have become possible as a result of either the long coherence times or the high instantaneous powers available from lasers. Some of these experiments could in fact be repeated under more difficult circumstances with ordinary light now that the conditions for operation have been elucidated, and we should point out that there are also many experiments for which lasers offer no advantages whatsoever over ordinary light, but were still left undone until someone wanted an excuse to buy and play with one of the new toys! The experiments we shall discuss are

(a) non-linear optical experiments, in which the refractive index is a function of the light intensity,

(b) the observation of Raman spectra, including Stokes and anti-Stokes lines,

(c) Brillouin scattering, or Raman scattering by phonons.

11.8.1　Non-linear optics. We have become used to regarding the polarization of an atom by an external field as a linear process, i.e. that the dipole moment produced is proportional to the applied field. This must, of course, be true for small fields, as we can always expand the dipole moment P per unit volume as a Taylor expansion

$$P(E) = P(0) + E\left(\frac{\partial P}{\partial E}\right)_0 + \tfrac{1}{2}E^2\left(\frac{\partial^2 P}{\partial E^2}\right)_0 + \dots \qquad (11.69)$$

and provided E is small the third and higher terms above can be neglected. For a molecule with no static dipole moment $P(0) = 0$ and the second term, the linear induced moment, is all that is left

$$P(E) \doteqdot E\left(\frac{\partial P}{\partial E}\right)_0. \qquad (11.70)$$

Now, in the equivalent magnetic case of a ferromagnetic material we know that the magnetic moment $M(H)$ becomes saturated at quite a small field, and that values of H large enough for the linear

approximation

$$M(H) \doteq M(0) + H\left(\frac{\partial M}{\partial H}\right)_0,$$

to be seriously inaccurate can easily be achieved. But it is not such serious deviations from the linear rule that concern us here. We do not need ferroelectric materials to show non-linear effects in optics, but anything in which the linear approximation (11.70) goes wrong. In fact, ferroelectric and ferromagnetic behaviour do not persist at very high frequencies. If we take a material which needs an expansion like (11.69) to do it justice and apply a wave $E = E_0 \exp(i\omega t)$ to it we get

$$\begin{aligned} P(E) &= \chi E + \tfrac{1}{2}\chi' E^2 + \dots \\ &= \chi E_0 \exp(i\omega t) + \tfrac{1}{2}\chi' E_0^2 \exp(2i\omega t) + \dots \end{aligned}$$

$P(E)$ has a harmonic content; a frequency 2ω has been generated and will be reradiated by the oscillating dipole. Of course, all the higher terms in the expansion will also occur, giving frequencies $n\omega$ in general, but we shall assume for the moment that these effects are negligible. What governs the intensity of the observed harmonic waves? First of all the intensity of the 2ω component in P is proportional to E_0^2 so that the high intensity from a laser will be a great help in producing observable effects. But there is one further point of importance, and that is that matching of the propagation velocities of the ω and 2ω waves is necessary. The 2ω wave is produced coherently with the ω wave at its point of origin. It then propagates at the phase velocity $v(2\omega)$. If the 2ω waves are being produced at all points within the material they can add constructively only if the phase velocities of the 2ω and ω waves are equal. Once this condition is satisfied, it becomes quite easy to observe harmonic generation, and in fact the use of a laser is hardly necessary any longer. But the laser was necessary to create the harmonics before the matching condition on the velocities was realized, and it was only when harmonics had been observed that the problem of conditions was seriously considered.

A second, associated, question is that of mixing light frequencies. If two light beams are shone on a non-linear material we have

$E = E_1 \exp(i\omega_1 t) + E_2 \exp(i\omega_2 t)$

$P = \chi E_1 \exp(i\omega_1 t) + \chi E_2 \exp(i\omega_2 t):$ fundamental frequencies

$\qquad + \tfrac{1}{2}\chi' E_1^2 \exp(2i\omega_1 t) + \tfrac{1}{2}\chi' E_2^2 \exp(2i\omega_2 t):$ first harmonic frequencies

$\qquad + \chi' E_1 E_2 \exp\{i(\omega_1 + \omega_2)t\}:$ sum frequency.

If we make the electric fields real by writing $E_1 \cos \omega_1 t$, etc. we find both sum and difference frequencies $(\omega_1 + \omega_2)$ and $(\omega_1 - \omega_2)$ occurring. Again, phase-velocity matching must be achieved to allow the waves to build up to an appreciable magnitude.

The crystal symmetry of the dielectric material may often put conditions on the derivative polarizabilities χ', χ'', etc. If the crystal has a centre of symmetry for example, χ' and all odd derivatives must be zero, for there can be no difference in the effect produced by electric fields $+E$ and $-E$ if r and $-r$ are identical. Consistent with the requirement that χ' should not be zero are some biaxial crystals, and the anisotropy of propagation velocities can then be used to find a direction in which the velocities of ω and 2ω waves are equal (Fig. 11.31). One of the most well-known examples is potassium di-hydrogen phosphate.

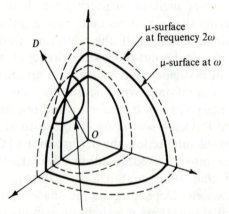

μ-surface at frequency 2ω

μ-surface at ω

D

O

Intersection between inner surface at 2ω and outer surface at ω.

Fig. 11.31. To illustrate the matching of refractive indices, or phase velocities, at frequencies ω and 2ω in a biaxial crystal. In all directions such as OD lying on a cone around the optic axis, $\mu_i(2\omega) = \mu_o(\omega)$, the suffices i and o referring to the inner and outer branches of the surface.

Another closely-related type of experiment is the *double photon absorption* experiment in which a transition which corresponds to frequency Ω is achieved by the simultaneous application of two frequencies ω_1 and ω_2 such that either

$$\Omega = \omega_1 \pm \omega_2.$$

This might be described in two ways. We can consider the non-linear behaviour of the system as generating the sum and difference

frequencies $\omega_1 \pm \omega_2$, one of which, corresponding to the transition, is then absorbed. Alternatively, we can think of the system absorbing ω_1 and going into a non-existent *virtual* state which differs from the nearest bound state by energy ε. It can stay in this state for a time $t = h/\varepsilon$ as, by the uncertainty principle, the bound-state is not defined in energy to better than this accuracy in a time t. If the second photon is present within this period, the second transition to a truly bound state $(\omega_1 \pm \omega_2)$ will occur by either absorption or stimulated emission. Clearly, large fluxes of photons are necessary to satisfy the conditions; the velocity-matching condition is also needed to ensure that the phase relation necessary for right combination of absorption-absorption or absorption-emission is maintained at all points in the sample.

11.8.2 Observations on Raman spectra. Raman scattering of photons is a type of inelastic scattering which is most simply explained by saying that a photon exchanges a quantum of rotational or vibrational energy with the scattering atom. Looked at from a wave mechanical point of view the process is as follows.

A light wave of frequency Ω is incident on an atom which has, say, angular momentum states with energies $\hbar\omega_1, \hbar\omega_2$, etc. (§ 11.3.1). The atom becomes polarized by the wave and re-emits most of its energy by elastic Rayleigh scattering (§ 10.2) also at frequency Ω. However, during the interaction, the perturbation of the light wave has put the atom into a mixed quantum state, like that discussed in § 11.4.1 and that state contains real charge oscillations at frequencies ω_1, ω_2 etc. Depending on the phase relations between Ω and these oscillations, there is a slight probability of re-emission at combination frequencies

$$\Omega \pm \omega_1, \qquad \Omega \pm \omega_2, \text{ etc.}$$

However, because they do not conserve energy and momentum, such processes are rather unlikely. If the atom can lose the spare energy, emission at the lower frequencies $\Omega - \omega_1, \Omega - \omega_2$ can occur; emission at the higher frequencies requires an extra source of energy, such as thermal energy, and is less likely. The emission lines at $\Omega - \omega_1$, etc., are called *Stokes lines*; those at $\Omega + \omega_1$, etc., are *anti-Stokes* lines, and are generally very weak.

If the incident light is very intense, however, there becomes possible an alternative method of conserving energy and momentum. This is by the simultaneous (or nearly-simultaneous) incidence

of two photons Ω. Energy can thus be conserved if re-emission takes place simultaneously at

$$\Omega + \omega_1 \quad \text{and} \quad \Omega - \omega_1.$$

Moreover, for certain angles of scattering the momentum $\hbar\mathbf{k}$ can also be conserved, and thus the intensity of emission can be large. We can draw a vector diagram (Fig. 11.32) for conservation of $\mathbf{k}$ in which we represent the wave-vector for the Ω waves by the vector $\mathbf{k}$, and those of $\Omega \pm \omega_1$ by $\mathbf{k}_\pm$ respectively.

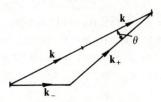

Fig. 11.32. Conservation of $\mathbf{k}$-vector for Raman-assisted double-photon transition.

We write $|\mathbf{k}_+|$ and $|\mathbf{k}_-|$ by Taylor expansions:[†]

$$k_+ = K \pm \omega_1 \frac{\partial K}{\partial \omega} + \tfrac{1}{2}\omega_1^2 \frac{\partial^2 K}{\partial \omega^2} + \ldots$$

and using the cosine rule for the triangle we find that

$$\cos\theta = 1 - \frac{\omega_1^2 (\partial^2 K/\partial\omega^2)K}{2[K^2 + \omega_1\{(\partial K/\partial\omega)K\}]}.$$

For small angles θ this gives:

$$\theta = \omega_1 \left| \frac{1}{K} \frac{\partial^2 K}{\partial \omega^2} \right|^{\frac{1}{2}}$$

$$= \omega_1 \left[\frac{1}{\mu}\left(\frac{\partial^2\mu}{\partial\omega^2} + \frac{2}{\omega}\frac{\partial\mu}{\partial\omega}\right)\right]^{\frac{1}{2}}, \qquad (11.71)$$

since $k = \mu\omega/c$. The strong Raman scattering in the directions satisfying these equations is evident as rings around the direct beam $\theta = 0$ (Fig. 11.33); it has been observed particularly well when a collimated laser beam from a ruby laser induces Raman scattering in nitrobenzene.

Unfortunately, the refractive index and dispersion $\mu(\omega)$ have not been measured well enough in nitrobenzene to check whether the

[†] The abbreviation $\partial K/\partial\omega$ means $\partial k/\partial\omega$ evaluated at Ω where $\mathbf{k} = \mathbf{K}$.

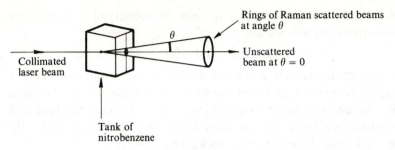

Fig. 11.33. Observation of Raman rings in nitrobenzene.

expression (11.71) for θ is quantitatively correct, but it certainly has the right order of magnitude (a few degrees). We should point out that there are, of course, a number of such rings, corresponding to the various frequencies ω_1, ω_2, etc. The rings are not caused by diffraction!

11.8.3 Brillouin scattering, or Raman scattering by phonons. If a longitudinal sound wave $(\omega_p, \mathbf{k}_p)$ travels through a solid, periodic variation in the density occurs as a result of local compression and rarefaction. If the atomic polarizability α is constant, the dielectric constant will have corresponding periodic variations:

$$\epsilon = \epsilon_0 + 4\pi\alpha\rho$$
$$= \epsilon_0 + 4\pi\alpha\rho_0[1 + a\exp\{i(\omega_p t - \mathbf{k}_p \cdot \mathbf{r})\}].$$

When an electromagnetic wave $(\omega, \mathbf{k})$ is incident on the material it gives rise to an electric displacement D which contains the mixed frequencies ω':

$$\omega' = \omega \pm \omega_p \qquad (11.72)$$

corresponding to $$\mathbf{k}' = \mathbf{k} \pm \mathbf{k}_p. \qquad (11.73)$$

Thus the incident wave suffers inelastic scattering by the sound waves, and the angle of scattering (which arises from the solution of (11.73)) gives the distribution of scattered frequency as a function of angle. The problem is similar to that in § 12.4.5 concerning the diffraction of neutron waves by sound waves in a crystal; except that here the velocities of sound and light are so different that the angles involved are very small, and the intensities very weak unless a powerful incident beam is used. Since ω_p can take a continuous range of values, no rings are observed.

The above is certainly not a complete account of laser optics, but should serve to illustrate some of the results of the use of very high

intensities and very long coherence lengths in optical experiments. The reader might, for instance, amuse himself by working out the light pressure that can be achieved with a laser, and remembering that this is oscillating at twice the light frequency, invent some effect that would result. It has probably been observed!

CHAPTER 12

SOME APPLICATIONS OF OPTICAL IDEAS

12.1 Introduction

Optics has played such a large part in the development of physics that it might almost be said that the history of optics is the history of physics. The point is not so much that optical instruments have always been important in experimental research, but that optical ideas and optical results have often influenced physics and physicists in unexpected ways which have turned out to be of fundamental significance.

This is all the more remarkable because optics by itself might seem to be far removed from what some people consider to be the main stream of physics—down the scale of dimensions and up the scale of energies. If we liken physics to a great river, of which the estuary—classical physics—is clear and unequivocal, we may consider the development of physics to be the attempt to discover the source. As we explore deeper, so we find more tributaries, and at each junction recognition of the main stream becomes difficult. Is nuclear physics, for example, really the main stream?

The question becomes less meaningful if we liken physics to a system of canals, with many cross-connexions, rather than to a river. Each physicist feels a strong affection for his own particular section, but he knows that it is affected by happenings in all parts of the system. If he is to understand his own part properly he must know something of the rest of the system as well. Optics is one of the strong connecting links in physics, and in this chapter we shall give some examples of how it has influenced other branches of the subject—from simple practical applications to basic fundamentals.

12.2 Some general uses of optics

12.2.1 Basic units. Of the three basic units of measurements—the gram, the metre and the second—only the first is not fixed by optical means. The time interval, the second, has always been defined in terms of the rotation of the Earth, and the telescope is therefore involved; the metre—once defined in terms of a length of material in Paris—is now a number of wavelengths of light.

There are three main properties that a basic unit should possess; it should be absolute, it should be precisely defined, and it should

be reproducible. None of our present units satisfies the first condition; they depend upon the properties of this particular planet and upon one of its constituents—water. Perhaps if we were starting again we would choose a different basis, but any change now would be too drastic to accept.

Let us consider the unit of length—the metre. Its accuracy is reasonably good—about one part in 10^7, but its reproducibility to this accuracy is not. It was realized by Michelson that his interferometer (§ 7.8.2) provided a method of re-defining the metre much more accurately and with a reproducibility that would enable anyone with the appropriate source of light to have access to it. The practical details of the measurement are described in many books; we shall deal here only with general principles.

The basic idea is simple; we move the mirror in the interferometer through a known distance and measure the number of fringes that pass the cross-wire in the telescope. In practice this is impossible; for any reasonable distance, the number of fringes would be much too large. The method therefore was to count the number of fringes corresponding to a given short distance and then use this to obtain the number for approximately double the distance. If we count the number corresponding to say 0·01 cm (say 200), to $\frac{1}{10}$ of a fringe, we need not count the number in 0·02 cm, since we can identify the 400th fringe to $\frac{1}{5}$ of a fringe; this can be measured to $\frac{1}{10}$ and so used to identify the 800th fringe. We can thus see that in ten steps we can count, to $\frac{1}{10}$ of a fringe, the number of fringes in 10 cm.

The method therefore involved having, first, a number of pieces of glass (Michelson called them etalons) whose lengths were accurately known in terms of the metre, secondly a strictly monochromatic source of light, and thirdly considerable patience and indefatigability. New sources of light, more precisely monochromatic, are now available; the metre is now defined as 1,650,763·73 wavelengths of a line in the spectrum of krypton 86.

12.2.2   Testing of surfaces. In contrast to this fundamental application interferometry is also of great value in applied physics—to the testing of surfaces. Here the use of optics in maintaining accuracy is of outstanding importance, and the mass production of machinery is dependent upon it.

To test the flatness of a surface we can use fringes of equal thickness (§ 7.1.6). We must have a standard flat and this can be

tested with two others; if all of the three possible pairs give straight fringes when they form small-angle wedges they must all be flat. These flats can then be used to test the flatness of other surfaces to about $\lambda/10$—about 10^{-5} cm. This is better than can be obtained by mechanical means.

The accuracy can be still further improved by multiple-reflexion methods; surfaces can then be examined down to molecular dimensions. For example, steps in mica of the order of 2×10^{-7} cm have been measured (Fig. 12.1).

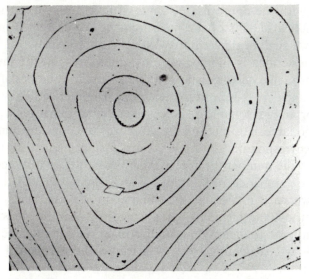

Fig. 12.1. Cleavage surface of mica as revealed by multiple-beam interference. (By courtesy of Professor S. Tolansky.)

There is also a feed-back to optics itself. Lens surfaces can be tested to a high degree of accuracy by forming Newton's rings with a known surface; small departures from circular symmetry can easily be detected. Such tests will not, however, give any information about aberrations, for which more appropriate methods, such as the knife-edge test (§ 9.6.2), should be used.

Fringe methods also enable other properties to be measured. For example, if Newton's rings are formed between a lens and a flat plate, the curvature of the plate when a uniform bending moment is applied can be measured by the change in the diameters of the rings. The rings will be no longer circular and the diameters

measured across the bending give the transverse curvature; thus Poisson's ratio can also be derived.

Coefficients of thermal expansion of quite small crystals can be measured by counting the fringes that pass through the centre of a Newton's ring system as the crystal is heated; a crystal face provides the flat surface. Moreover, the expansion can be measured in different directions, and the method therefore enables the three principal coefficients of an anisotropic crystal to be measured—one of the few methods available for this type of measurement.

12.3   Examination of matter

12.3.1   The electron microscope.
We have seen in §§ 1.7.2 and 1.7.3 that the limit of resolution of a microscope can be extended by the use of radiation of shorter wavelengths than those of visible light. By far the most successful of such radiations is the electron beam; the principle of the electron microscope is exactly that of the light microscope, but it uses electrostatic or electromagnetic fields to produce focused images.

The basic fact that allows electrons to be focused is that their trajectories can be varied so as to simulate refraction. In fact, the theory of refraction is exactly that which was put forward by the supporters of the corpuscular theory of light (§ 1.2.3); if an electron is accelerated through a potential difference V_1 it will acquire a velocity $(2eV_1/m)^{\frac{1}{2}}$ and this will be constant in the region of constant potential; if it now enters another region at potential V_2 the velocity will be $(2eV_2/m)^{\frac{1}{2}}$. Thus the refractive index of the second region with respect to the first is $(V_2/V_1)^{\frac{1}{2}}$.

The exploitation of this result is in some ways more difficult and in other ways more easy than designing glass lenses. Curved equipotential surfaces arise naturally and so some focusing is bound to occur. But the surfaces do not have the right configuration for *accurate* focusing and so aberrations (Appendix II) are always present. Only very small apertures can therefore be used, and the limit of resolution of electron microscopes still falls two or three orders of magnitude short of that theoretically possible.

An electron lens must have cylindrical symmetry. The simplest type is that shown in Fig. 12.2. The theory of even this simple type of lens cannot be worked out exactly, and it may be said that, while theory is necessary to see what possibilities exist, ultimately the precise design of electron lenses is based upon empiricism.

To assist in the design of such lenses, two experimental methods are helpful. The first is the electrolytic tank, which consists of a non-conducting vessel containing a weak electrolyte; in the electrolyte conductors of various shapes can be inserted to represent electrodes and the equipotential lines can be found by means of a probe. Having found these lines, the second device can be used; this is a gravitational analogue which allows electron paths to be derived. A surface is constructed—a plaster model or a rubber sheet—in which the height is proportional to the potential at every point; a spherical ball allowed to run along this surface will then trace out the path of an electron.

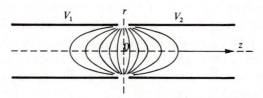

Fig. 12.2. Electron lens formed between two coaxial cylinders. (From Cosslett, *Electron Optics*, Oxford, 1950.)

Electrostatic fields are now not much used in electron microscopes because the higher fields necessary for short focal lengths may cause ionization in the residual gas; magnetic fields produced by electromagnets are almost always used. The theory is much more complicated because the motion of an electron in a magnetic field can be described only in three dimensions; in a uniform magnetic field electrons move in helical paths.

The type of electromagnetic field necessary for high magnification is that produced by a short solenoid enclosed in a soft-iron sheath, the best dimensions being chosen empirically.

How do we set about making an electron microscope? The first requirement is a source which must produce a beam of *monochromatic* electrons; it is called an *electron gun*. A typical form is shown in Fig. 12.3; it can use an accelerating voltage V of 100 kV, giving $\lambda = 0.04$ Å, since

$$\lambda = \frac{h}{\sqrt{2meV}}. \tag{12.1}$$

This beam is focused on the specimen by a lens that corresponds to the microscope condenser. After traversing the specimen—which

must be thin enough not to cause a spread of velocities of the electrons—the beam passes through a stronger lens, which corresponds to the objective (Fig. 12.4); an image with a magnification of perhaps 100 is produced. This is further magnified by a factor of

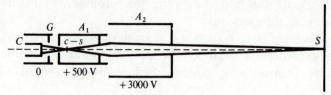

Fig. 12.3. Electron gun. (From Cosslett, *Electron Optics*, Oxford, 1950.)

up to about 200 by a third lens—the projection lens. The final image, as shown in Fig. 12.4, then falls on a fluorescent screen or on to a photographic plate.

The whole apparatus must be highly evacuated, and thus only specimens that are not distorted by being placed in a vacuum can

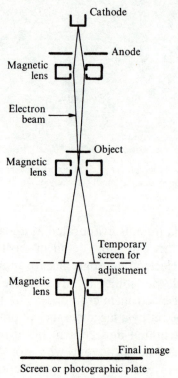

Fig. 12.4. Electron microscope. (From D. H. Thomas, *Applied Electronics*, Blackie, 1948.)

be examined. Moreover, they must be very thin, in order to have negligible absorption of electrons. Metals, for example, can normally be examined only by producing a plastic replica of the surface, and methods of producing such replica have received a great deal of attention. Very fine microtomes can be used to produce very thin sections.

If a specimen is so thin that it does not absorb electrons, there will be no contrast in the image. Some sort of staining must be used. The most successful procedure is called *shadowing*; a beam of heavy

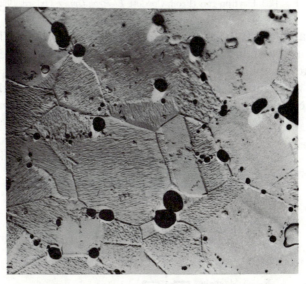

Fig. 12.5. Electron electromicrograph of nickel surface with particles of thoria on it, showing shadows cast by shadowing. (By courtesy of Dr. D. W. Ashall.)

atoms, such as palladium, is evaporated at a glancing angle on to the specimen and this can show detail in most convincing relief. Some examples of electron micrographs are shown in Fig. 12.5.

There seems little possibility of any extreme break through in resolving power of electron microscopes. The limit of 7 Å so far claimed seems to be set by a large number of practical factors such as accuracy of machining and control of currents and voltages. Much credit will accrue to anyone who can design a corrected electron lens and so lead the way to production of micrographs with detail of atomic dimensions.

12.3.2 X-ray diffraction. X-rays have wavelengths comparable with interatomic distances and are much more manageable than electron beams; they are little absorbed in air and can be diffracted by specimens of reasonable size. The theoretical basis of such diffraction (§ 7.6) is well understood. X-rays lack only one property: they cannot be refracted in any appreciable sense and thus image formation by means of lenses is impossible. If we wish to find out what the object is, we have to recognize it solely from its Fraunhofer diffraction pattern.

We know, however, that an image is the Fourier transform of the vector-amplitude distribution in the diffraction pattern of the object (§ 9.3.3), and if such a transformation could be effected we could produce a representation of the object. We have seen in § 9.3.9 that the procedure required for a crystal is the summation of a three-dimensional Fourier series, each coefficient being an order of diffraction. We cannot, however, carry out this procedure because we know only the scalar amplitudes of the orders of diffraction and not the phases. This difficulty is known as the phase problem (§§ 1.7.4 and 9.3.8).

There is no general solution to the phase problem. For crystals that are centrosymmetric—that is, for any atom at position (x, y, z) there is another similar atom at $(-x, -y, -z)$—the relative phases are either 0 or π; this statement corresponds to the result that an even function is expressible in terms of cosine curves only, positive and negative at the origin corresponding to phase angles of 0 and π respectively. But even with this limitation the phase problem is not generally solvable.

Over the years, however, since the original discovery of X-ray diffraction (§ 1.7.4), experience has accumulated and methods of approach have been devised that enable quite complicated crystal structures to be solved, culminating in the structure of the proteins, haemoglobin and myoglobin, determined by Perutz and Kendrew. An outline of the physical basis of this type of work is given below.

Suppose that the crystal structure that we are concerned with has a number of atoms in the unit cell, of which a few (one to four) are of predominant weight. These few atoms may be found easily because their effect on the diffraction pattern will also be predominant. We can calculate the phases given by atoms in these positions; a Fourier summation with these phases should show the other atoms. The most well-known example of successful work of

this sort is the determination of the structure of phthalocyanine (Fig. 12.6), the phases being all fixed as 0 by a heavy platinum atom at the centre of the molecule. In effect, this method is equivalent to having a clear point on which to focus, and when this focus is found, the rest of the detail also becomes visible. The similarity to the hologram method of image reconstruction (§ 9.7) is very great.

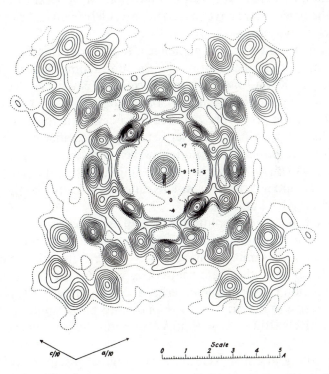

Fig. 12.6. Electron density in projection of a platinum phthalocyanine molecule. Contours are at intervals of 1 electron per Å² except near the centre where some values of electron densities are indicated. (From Lipson & Cochran, *The Determination of Crystal Structures*, First Edition, p. 209.)

If it is not possible to find an atom heavy enough to enable this procedure to be carried out successfully, a more powerful method may be used; the heavy atoms may be replaced by others of different weight, and the amplitude of the various orders compared. An early investigation involved the compounds $CuSO_4 5H_2O$ and $CuSeO_4 5H_2O$. The *changes* of intensity gives clearer evidence than the effect of one heavy atom alone. This method is called the

isomorphous replacement method. If the crystal is not centro-symmetric, so that general phase angles are involved, two different atoms have to be replaced.

One can sometimes arrange for a single atom to exhibit a change in scattering by using radiations of different wavelengths. If the wavelength is just short enough to excite the K electrons in an atom, the phase of the scattered wave is affected, and the scattering factor has to be represented by a complex quantity. Comparison of the intensities of the same order of diffraction with two different

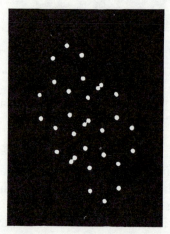

Fig. 12.7. Mask of holes representing two molecules of pyrene, the contents of the unit cell of the crystal.

X-radiations can give some information about the phase angle. This is called the *anomalous-scattering* method.

A completely different approach that may be of particular interest to readers of this book involves the use of optical transforms (§ 9.3.7). Suppose that we have some idea of the positions of the atoms in the unit cell and wish to see if the calculated intensities of the orders of diffraction agree with those observed. We can make a mask (Fig. 12.7) with holes representing atoms, and prepare its optical transform by means of the optical diffractometer (Appendix IV). We may superimpose upon this a representation of the diffraction pattern of the crystal as a reciprocal-lattice section (§ 7.6.2) in which each point has a black spot whose size is roughly related to the observed intensity (Fig. 12.8). One can see immediately whether

the sampling (§ 7.4.4) of the transform by the reciprocal lattice produces intensities which have some relation to those observed.

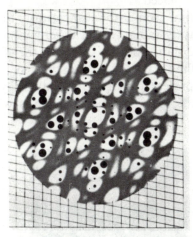

Fig. 12.8. Transform of Fig. 12.7 superimposed on the representation of the X-ray diffraction pattern. Note how each strong order of X-ray diffraction lies upon a strong part of the transform.

12.3.3 Electron diffraction.

Electron-diffraction patterns (Fig. 12.9) are observed over much larger angles than are possible for image formation in the electron microscope, and therefore the resolving-power limitation is absent. But all the problems associated with X-ray diffraction occur, and in addition there are the difficulties introduced by having to put the specimen and recording

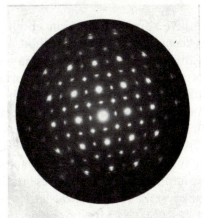

Fig. 12.9. Electron-diffraction pattern of mica crystal.

film in a vacuum, and by requiring the specimen to be very thin. Why then is electron diffraction worth while?

First, it gives information that is complementary to X-ray information; X-rays are scattered by electrons whereas electrons are scattered by electric fields, and a light atom such as hydrogen, which hardly scatters X-rays, can produce appreciable effects on electrons. Secondly, the structure of matter in the form of the thin film may be different from that in bulk. Thirdly, some materials are obtainable only in the form of fine powder, but an electron beam may be able to pick out single crystals. Finally, for imperfect structures, electrons may be able to provide information by selecting a much smaller volume of specimen than X-rays can.

Although the first electron-diffraction experiments were rather crude, considerable improvement occurred when electron-beam focusing (§ 12.3.1) became possible. A typical instrument for electron-diffraction experiments is shown in Fig. 12.10; it can be seen that it has much in common with the electron microscope (Fig. 12.4) and usually the same instrument is used for both purposes.

12.3.4 Neutron diffraction.
Neutrons (§ 1.6.4) are scattered mainly by nuclei and so provide still further information that is complementary to that provided by X-rays and electrons. For neutrons there is no simple relation between scattering and atomic number (Fig. 12.11) and light atoms such as hydrogen scatter as strongly as most other elements.

It will be noted from Fig. 12.11 that some scattering amplitudes are negative; in other words, such nuclei scatter exactly out of phase with most others. Scattering amplitudes may also be quite different for isotopes of the same element. Moreover, the magnetic moment of neutrons may interact with the moments associated with the incomplete electronic shells of the transition elements. All these facts enable information of a completely new type to be obtained; the last, in particular, has cast new light upon the subject of magnetism and this will be discussed in greater detail later in this section.

Provided that one has a nuclear reactor, the production of a beam of neutrons is relatively simple; one uses the fact that neutrons are in thermal equilibrium with the rest of the reactor core, and are therefore moving with considerable velocities. The energy $\frac{1}{2}mv^2$ is

equal to $\frac{1}{2}kT$, where k is Boltzmann's constant; thus at temperature T

$$\lambda = \frac{h}{mv}$$

$$= \frac{h}{\sqrt{mkT}}.$$
(12.2)

If T is of the order of $300°K$, λ is of the order of 10^{-8} cm—about the same as the wavelength of X-rays.

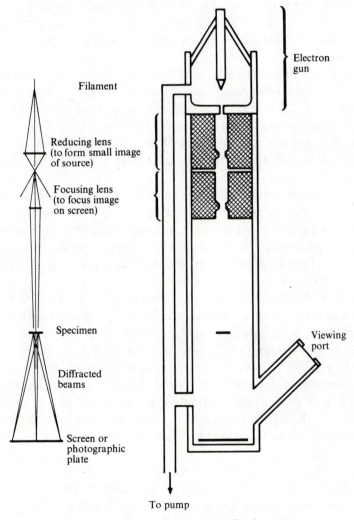

Fig. 12.10. Instrument for recording electron-diffraction patterns.

The neutrons are allowed to leave the reactor through a channel in absorbing material, as shown in Fig. 12.12, thus producing a well-defined beam. It still has a non-uniform distribution of velocities, and to produce a 'monochromatic' beam it is reflected

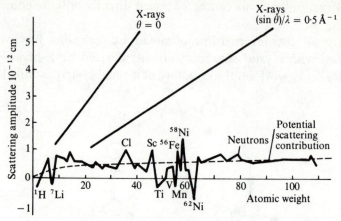

Fig. 12.11. Scattering cross-sections of atoms. (From G. E. Bacon, *Neutron Diffraction*, Oxford, 1962.)

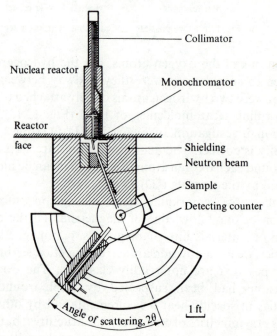

Fig. 12.12. Neutron diffractometer (DIDO at Harwell). (From *Research*, London, **7**, 257, 1954.)

from a crystal (Fig. 12.12) so that Bragg reflexion (§ 7.6.1) occurs for wavelengths near to the maximum of the distribution. This reflected beam can then be used in the same way as an X-ray beam, with one exception: neutrons do not affect photographic film and thus diffraction patterns can be obtained directly only by counter methods.

Nearly all the information obtained by neutrons has been concerned with crystal structures already derived by X-rays. For example, X-ray work on the structure of ice had clearly established

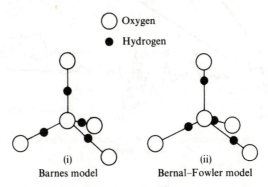

Fig. 12.13. Two possible configurations of atoms in ice.

the positions of the oxygen atoms, but the hydrogen atoms were left open to speculation; were they midway between the oxygen atoms or were two hydrogen atoms closely attached to each oxygen atom forming clear molecules of H_2O (Fig. 12.13)? A neutron-diffraction investigation of heavy ice, D_2O, shows that neither possibility is correct. The deuterium atoms are statistically distributed round each oxygen atom in a way that can be most effectively described by the formula $(\frac{1}{2}D)_4O$.

But the most remarkable result of neutron diffraction is the extension of our knowledge of magnetism. To the classical subdivision of materials into diamagnetics, paramagnetics and ferromagnetics, we must now add antiferromagnetics, ferrimagnetics and other types that are not readily classified. The existence of the subdivisions had been suspected by Néel around 1932 from anomalies in specific-heat measurement, and by others from odd changes in symmetries of certain crystal structures; but the complete elucidation of the subject had to wait for the advent of neutron diffraction.

The reason for this is that the spin of the neutron interacts with the resultant spin of the electrons in an atom. If the resultant spin is zero, there is no interaction, but if it is finite there is an interaction which results in the atom's having a scattering factor that varies with angle; this scattering factor is the Fourier transform of the density of unpaired electrons (compare § 7.6). Neutron diffraction is therefore the ideal method for studying these electrons.

In an ideal paramagnetic the moments of the individual atoms are randomly oriented and the scattering is incoherent; the intensity

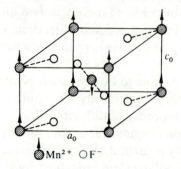

Fig. 12.14. The unit cell of MnF_2, showing the antiferromagnetic arrangement of the magnetic moments of the Mn^{2+} ions. (Erickson, 1953.)

of scattering is therefore a continuous function and is not confined to reciprocal-lattice points (§ 7.6.2). In a ferromagnetic however the spins are aligned and thus coherent crystal-type scattering occurs.

The existence of the new types of magnetic materials appeared when the X-ray diffraction patterns and the neutron-diffraction patterns of certain compounds were compared; it was found that the latter contained orders of diffraction that should not occur. A simple example is given by MnF_2 (Fig. 12.14). It will be seen that the manganese atoms lie at the corners of the unit cell and at the centre; accordingly they give no contribution to the order of diffraction for which $h + k + l$ is odd. The neutron-diffraction results, however, indicated that the atoms at the corners were different from those at the centres; the obvious difference is that their moments are oppositely aligned (Fig. 12.14). This is the anti-ferromagnetism predicted by Néel in 1932.

Since the spins cancel, the compounds would appear by ordinary magnetic measurements to be paramagnetic. Nevertheless, the ordering of the spins is as perfect as in a ferromagnetic and the

variation of the degree of order follows the same law as ferro-magnetism. In the same way that ferromagnetism disappears at a particular temperature (the Curie temperature), antiferromagnetism also disappears at a particular temperature (the Néel temperature) and it was the specific-heat and latent-heat anomalies associated with this temperature that first led Néel to the conclusion that the materials that he was examining were antiferromagnetic.

A ferromagnetic material is one in which the spins of two different atoms are opposite but unequal; such a material would therefore appear to be weakly ferromagnetic. Other types of magnetism exist because spins are not confined merely to two different directions; differently related, but still ordered, directions may occur, and it would take too long to discuss here the structures that have been found.

Another device remains to be discussed. Neutrons are scattered from magnetic materials selectively according to their spins. It is usual therefore for an order of diffraction from a magnetic crystal to have a distribution of spins that is not random, and such a beam is said to be partially polarized. (It is rather remarkable that this is exactly the type of polarization envisaged by the corpuscularists, such as Newton, in the seventeenth century.) The polarization may be complete, and the beam is then said to be plane-polarized. The 220 order of diffraction from magnetite (Fe_3O_4) is an example.

This discovery opens up a new field. Plane-polarized neutrons can be obtained by replacing the crystal in Fig. 12.12 by a magnetic crystal, and with such beams experiments can be carried out more precisely. A great deal has been discovered about the magnetic properties of crystals in this way. It is a pity that nuclear reactors are so rare and that strong beams of neutrons cannot be obtained by any other means. (The suggestion that they could be obtained holding the two halves of an atomic bomb at a judicious distance apart is inadmissible!) There is obviously a great deal of work that can be done by these methods. Another example is discussed in § 12.4.4.

12.4   Some more complicated applications of Fraunhofer diffraction theory

We shall next discuss some extensions of the simple Fraunhofer diffraction theory in Chapter 7 which will enable us to deal with two particular types of problem—an object whose properties are statistical, and a moving obstacle.

12.4.1   The self-convolution function and its relation to the diffraction pattern. If we could observe the amplitude and phase at each point on a diffraction pattern it would merely be a matter of computation for us to work out to an accuracy of about one wavelength, which corresponds to the finest detail that diffracts at a real angle, a complete description of the object. Unfortunately, all observing and measuring instruments are sensitive only to intensity, which contains no information about the phase, and, unless we compare the pattern with a coherent wave that has not been diffracted (§ 9.7), it is impossible to deduce this information. The question of what is the maximum amount of information that can be derived unambiguously from the observed intensity pattern is therefore important; we cannot, of course, make any estimate of what can be achieved as a result of intelligent guesswork and preconceived ideas of the answer!

We shall consider diffraction in two dimensions again, to avoid the necessity of repeated statements about which part of the Fourier transform can be observed. The intensity I of the diffracted beam ψ in the direction (u, v) is the product of the amplitude with its complex conjugate, and the transform of this is therefore the convolution (§ 3.5) of the object with its complex conjugate;

$$I(u, v) = \psi\psi^*(u, v),\tag{12.3}$$

is the transform of

$$F(x, y) = \iint f(x - x', y - y')f^*(x'y')\, dx'\, dy'\tag{12.4}$$

where $f(x, y)$ is the transmission function of the object. This function is the *self-convolution* of the object, or its *self-correlation function* (§§ 8.4.1 and 3.5.7) and must necessarily have a real positive Fourier transform (12.3). The concept is particularly useful when applied to objects for which the self-correlation is an important parameter; for example, we shall discuss the effect of thermal disorder of a lattice in § 12.4.3.

12.4.2   Simple self-convolutions. Let us first consider a very simple example. The idealized Young's interference experiment, with pinholes separated by a distance a, has

$$f(x, y) = \delta(y)\tfrac{1}{2}\{\delta(x - a/2) + \delta(x + a/2)\}\tag{12.5}$$

and gives

$$\psi(u, v) = \cos\frac{au}{2}.\tag{12.6}$$

As $f(x, y)$ is a product we can consider correlation in the x and y directions independently. In the y direction, the function is concentrated entirely at $y = 0$, and therefore the integrand of (12.4) is zero unless $y = 0$. $F(x, y)$ thus has y-dependence $\delta(y)$. In the x direction, f consists of two δ-functions A and B (Fig. 12.15(a)). The integrand of (12.4) is thus zero unless (i) $x = a$, when it is the

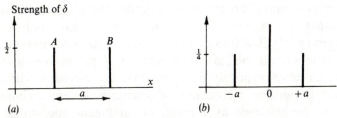

Fig. 12.15. (a) Two δ-functions separated by distance a; (b) the self-correlation function of (a).

product of A and B, which is a δ-function of strength $\frac{1}{4}$; (ii) $x = -a$, when it is the same product; or (iii) $x = 0$, when it has two contributions, one from $A \times A$ and the other from $B \times B$. The self-correlation function is therefore as illustrated in Fig. 12.15(b), the centre

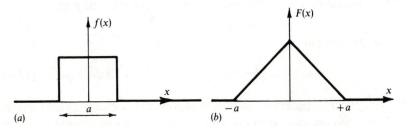

Fig. 12.16. (a) A square pulse; (b) the self-correlation function of (a).

δ-function having twice the strength of the outer ones. The transform of this function is

$$I(u, v) = \tfrac{1}{4}\{e^{-iua} + 2 + e^{iva}\}$$
$$= \tfrac{1}{2}(1 + \cos au)$$
$$= \cos^2 \frac{au}{2}$$
$$= \psi^2(u, v). \tag{12.7}$$

A second example we can consider is that of a slit of width a. It is a simple matter to show that the self-correlation function is as

shown in Fig. 12.16 and, as was shown in the examples in §§ 7.2.1 and 7.2.2, the transforms of $f(x, y)$ and its self-correlation function are respectively,

$$\frac{\sin ua/2}{u} \quad \text{and} \quad \frac{\sin^2 ua/2}{u^2}. \tag{12.8}$$

Such examples are of academic interest only, but we shall now consider an example which is of real importance.

12.4.3 Thermal disorder in a lattice.
A crystal is never exactly perfect. At any temperature the atoms are vibrating about their true lattice positions, and as the frequency of vibration is very much less than that of the X-rays which are used to investigate them the diffraction pattern observed is that of a stationary crystal whose atoms are displaced by random small distances from their true lattice positions. We shall consider a two-dimensional model of this.

The self-convolution of such a model is as shown in Fig. 12.17(a); it forms a two-dimensional lattice of which all the 'points' are broadened except that at the origin, which is sharp because all the atoms are at exactly zero distance from themselves. The intensity distribution in the required diffraction pattern is the Fourier transform of this self-convolution. We can derive this transform by taking the transform of a lattice with *all* the 'points' broadened, subtract the transform of the broadened central 'point' and add the transform of a true point at the origin.

The transform of a lattice of broadened 'points' is a perfect lattice in which the heights of the peaks fall off in some sort of quasi-Gaussian way (Fig. 12.17(b)), the central peak having a height N^2 where N is the number of atoms in the crystal. The transform of the broadened central 'point' is a continuous curve (Fig. 12.17(c)) with the same form, the height at the centre being N. This curve must be subtracted from the transform of the central point, which, being a true point, is now a uniform distribution of height N. The difference (Fig. 12.17(d)) gives a continuous distribution that is zero in the centre and increases with distance outward.

We have thus reached the conclusion that the diffraction pattern of a lattice with thermal disorder is a lattice of sharp points with a background that is zero in the centre and increases in intensity with angle of diffraction.

This is an idealized treatment. In practice, thermal displacements are not independent of each other, and so the peaks in the self-convolution function are not all equal. Moreover, the dependence of the displacements on each other is a function of direction and so the peaks may have odd cross sections. Although these facts do not alter the conclusion that all the diffraction peaks remain sharp,

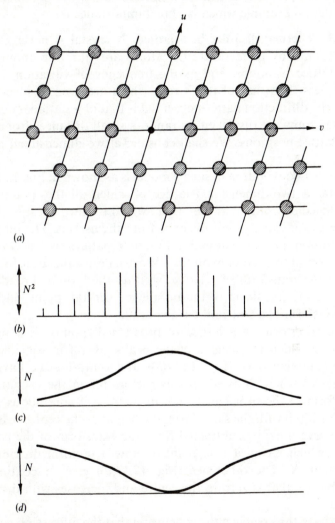

Fig. 12.17. (a) The self-correlation function of a structure with randomly displaced atoms. All peaks have a strength N. (b) One-dimensional representation of the transform of (a) assuming that the origin peak were as broad as the rest. (c) Transform of the origin peak alone. (d) The difference between the transform of a δ-function at the origin and the transform of a broadened peak.

they do lead to structural features in the background (Fig. 7.53). Consideration of this subject would take us far out of the realm of this book.

12.4.4   A moving system: neutron diffraction by lattice vibration. In the previous section we assumed that the X-rays used in a crystal-diffraction experiment saw an instantaneous snapshot of the vibrating crystal because the X-ray frequency is very much greater than that of the atomic vibrations. The same is true of an experiment in which, for example, the wavelength of ultrasonic travelling waves in a liquid is measured by using the periodic density changes in the liquid to form a phase-grating (§ 7.2.5), as the light-frequency is orders of magnitude greater than the ultra-sonic frequency. However, light and X-rays are not the only waves which can be diffracted, and many useful experiments have been performed using the wave-nature of particles such as electrons and neutrons. For neutrons, quite-low-energy particles can be used, and it is possible to do experiments in which a crystal which is vibrating thermally is used to diffract neutrons which have a similar frequency. The neutron beam can no longer be assumed to see a stationary lattice. We shall consider the elements of the problem in one dimension.

The thermal vibrations of a crystal can be Fourier analysed into a set of waves with various frequencies and wave-vectors, and as one particular term of such an analysis represents a sinusoidal displacement of atoms moving through the crystal—in other words a sound wave—the frequency Ω and wave-number $\mathbf{K}$ of the term will be related by the sound velocity $V(\mathbf{K})$:

$$\frac{\Omega}{K} = V(\mathbf{K}), \tag{12.9}$$

which is in general a function of the wave-number and direction of travel of the wave. Only in isotropic material at very low frequencies is the sound velocity a constant. The waves can also be longitudinal or transverse; only in fluids are sound waves restricted to be longitudinal. Such a Fourier component of the atomic vibra-tions of our one-dimensional crystal can be written

$$\zeta(x) = \zeta_0 \exp \{i(\Omega t - Kx)\}, \tag{12.10}$$

where $\zeta(x)$ is the displacement—either longitudinal or transverse—of the atom originally at position x. These original positions lie on

a lattice of spacing a, the stationary lattice of the crystal. Fig. 12.18 shows the situation for transverse displacements. Consider now a wave incident on this linear crystal in the z direction

$$\phi = \phi_0 \exp \{i(\omega_0 t - k_0 z)\}. \tag{12.11}$$

We follow the same procedure as in § 7.1.8, where we dealt with stationary gratings, but here we must assume that the diffracted

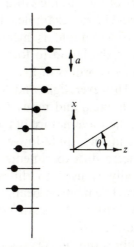

Fig. 12.18. Transverse displacements of the atoms in a crystal transmitting a sound wave.

wave at angle θ has frequency ω and wave-number k. Then the diffraction integral becomes

$$\psi(\omega, k, \theta) = \iint_{-\infty}^{\infty} \phi_0 f(x) \exp [i(\omega_0 t - k_0 \zeta)]$$

$$\times \exp [-i(\omega t - kx \sin \theta)] \, dx \, dt$$

$$= \sum_{n=-\infty}^{\infty} \int_{-\infty}^{\infty} \phi_0 \exp [i\{\omega_0 t - k_0 \zeta(na)\}]$$

$$\times \exp [-i(\omega t - kna \sin \theta)] \, dt, \tag{12.12}$$

since $f(x)$ is non-zero only at atomic positions. We now assume that the displacements ζ are small compared with the wavelength; this is reasonable since in applications the wavelength is of the order of a and the condition $\zeta \ll a$ is necessary if the crystal is to

be solid. If this condition holds we can expand the exponential of ζ:

$$\psi(\omega, k, \theta) = \sum_{n=-\infty}^{\infty} \int_{-\infty}^{\infty} \phi_0 \exp\{i\omega t\} \cdot [1 - k_0\zeta_0 \exp\{i(\Omega t - Kna)\}]$$
$$\times \exp\{-i(\omega t - kna\sin\theta)\}\, dt$$
$$= \phi_0\delta(\omega_0 - \omega)\delta(ka\sin\theta - 2m\pi)$$
$$- ik_0\zeta_0\phi_0 \cdot \delta(\omega_0 + \Omega - \omega)\delta\{(k\sin\theta - K)a - 2m\pi\},$$

$$(12.13)$$

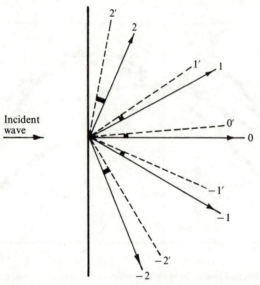

Fig. 12.19. Extra orders of diffraction produced by a sinusoidally disturbed crystal.

where m is any integer. The diffraction pattern therefore consists of
(a) the usual orders of diffraction at angles satisfying

$$u = k\sin\theta = \frac{2m\pi}{a},$$

which have frequency equal to that of the incident wave, ω_0, and
(b) a series of weaker beams displaced from the usual orders by
  $\delta u = K$ having frequency $\omega = \omega_0 + \Omega$, and intensity $(k_0\zeta_0)^2$
  times the intensity of the usual orders.
Since $\zeta \ll a \sim k_0^{-1}$, it follows that $k_0\zeta_0$ is much less than unity and
the beams are weak. Fig. 12.19 shows the positions schematically.
This describes what happens when the crystal is disturbed by a

single sinusoidal sound wave. Clearly by measuring the displacement δu and the frequency change Ω in the secondary diffracted beams, the values of K and Ω can be compared experimentally and the velocity $V(K)$ deduced. In a practical case a crystal, which will diffract neutrons as a three-dimensional obstacle subject to the same conditions as discussed in § 7.6, will be disturbed by the whole spectrum of sound waves, which are necessary to describe uncorrelated motion of the atoms. Each of the orders of diffraction from the undisturbed crystal will therefore be surrounded by weaker beams scattered by the sound waves, and by careful experimentation

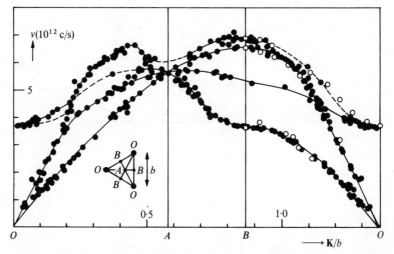

Fig. 12.20. Experimental results for the phonon dispersion relation in magnesium, obtained by slow-neutron diffraction. The frequency v is $\Omega/2\pi$, and the vector **K** lies along symmetry directions in the basal plane of the hexagonal unit cell. The inset diagram shows the basal plane of the reciprocal-lattice unit cell, and the **K** values investigated follow the lines $OABO$. Notice that both acoustic modes ($\Omega \to 0$ as $K \to 0$) and optic modes ($\Omega \nrightarrow 0$ as $K \to 0$) of various independent polarizations are present. (By courtesy of Dr G. L. Squires.)

the frequency shift as a function of displacement from the normal beam can be evaluated, and as a result the whole $\Omega(\mathbf{K})$ spectrum for sound waves in the crystal can be deduced. This information is valuable in understanding interatomic forces. Fig. 12.20 shows some typical results.

12.4.5   Interpretation as neutron-phonon collisions: momentum and energy considerations. In the same way as a neutron, which is generally considered as a particle, has been treated here as a wave,

it is possible to consider the sound wave as a particle which is called a *phonon*. The relationship between the wave and particle properties are (§ 2.2.2)

$$E = \hbar\omega \qquad (E \text{ is energy}), \qquad (12.14)$$

$$\mathbf{p} = \hbar\mathbf{k} \qquad (\mathbf{p} \text{ is momentum}). \qquad (12.15)$$

When a neutron is scattered by a cold crystal, its wavenumber changes by a reciprocal-lattice vector $\mathbf{g}$ (§ 7.6.2), and its energy remains unaltered:

conservation of momentum $\mathbf{k}' = \mathbf{k} + \mathbf{g}$ for diffraction

conservation of energy $\omega' = \omega$ by a cold crystal.   (12.16)

This is called *elastic scattering* because the energy of the particle is unchanged in the process. For scattering by a hot crystal, containing a phonon $(\Omega, \mathbf{K})$ we have

$$\left.\begin{array}{l} \mathbf{k}' = \mathbf{k} + \mathbf{K} + \mathbf{g} \\ \omega' = \omega + \Omega \end{array}\right\}, \qquad (12.17)$$

which is called *inelastic scattering*. Ω may be either positive or negative. One further condition must be met, and that is that the velocity of the diffracted wave is right, that is:

$$\omega'/k' = v, \qquad (12.18)$$

where v may be a function of $\mathbf{k}'$. If we apply this condition to (12.17) we can solve the equations by means of a vector diagram, of which a two-dimensional section is shown in Fig. 12.21(*a*). The various allowed vectors $\mathbf{k}$ lie on the reciprocal lattice, and it is obvious from the diagram that we have constructed the sphere of observation (§ 7.6.1). For a particular value of Ω equation (12.17) can be solved simultaneously with (12.18) using an extension of the same vector diagram; Fig. 12.21(*b*) should make the construction clear, but it follows that interpretation of the observations when there is a range of values of Ω is not trivial.

12.5 Astrophysics

12.5.1 Stellar constitutions.
Until recently, our knowledge of the Universe has been obtained solely from optical measurements; visible light provided the only means of communication with the rest of the universe, and thus all that we know about it depends upon an ability to interpret this light.

The spectrometer has played an invaluable part in this work; the spectra of the stars has enabled the emitting elements to be identified, and so far no elements other than those present on the Earth have been found. This fact is highly important; it indicates that the same elementary particles exist everywhere and that the laws of their combination are universal. However far the science-fiction

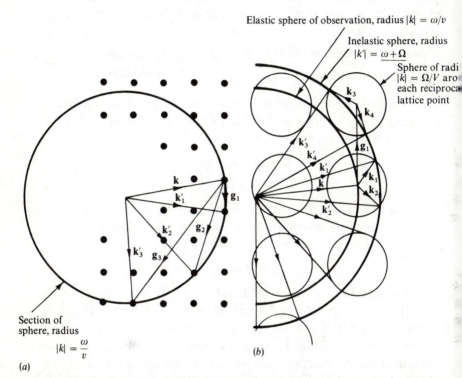

Elastic sphere of observation, radius $|k| = \omega/v$

Inelastic sphere, radius $|k'| = \dfrac{\omega + \Omega}{}$

Sphere of radi
$|k| = \Omega/V$ aro
each reciproca
lattice point

Section of sphere, radius
$$|k| = \frac{\omega}{v}$$

(a)

(b)

Fig. 12.21. (a) Solution of equations (12.17) representing elastic collisions. Reciprocal-lattice vectors $\mathbf{g}_1$, $\mathbf{g}_2$ and $\mathbf{g}_3$ can be added to $\mathbf{K}$, to give $\mathbf{K}'_1$, $\mathbf{K}'_2$ and $\mathbf{K}'_3$ all with the same frequency ω as the incident wave. (b) Solutions of Fig. 12.17 and Fig. 12.18, for inelastic collisions with phonons of frequency Ω. For example, the wave $\mathbf{K}'_3$ is observed after scattering by $\mathbf{g}_1$ and $\mathbf{K}_3$.

writers are prepared to stretch their minds to admit forms of life different from those on Earth, at least they must accept the confines of the known periodic table!

12.5.2 Stellar temperatures. Several methods are available for measuring stellar temperatures, but we shall mention only one of them here. It is based upon the distribution of energy in the spectrum, a property that is dependent upon the absolute temperature.

It was this observation that was responsible for the introduction of the quantum theory by Planck in 1900 (§ 1.6).

We can use either the complete spectrum, fitting an ideal curve as closely as possible to the observed one, or we can take merely the wavelength at which maximum intensity is observed. Since both these observations are dependent upon absorption in the Earth's atmosphere, the results do not agree precisely, but they generally give the same order of magnitude.

12.5.3   Stellar distances. The simplest way of finding a stellar distance is to measure the parallax of the star—the angular displacement that occurs as the star is observed at the opposite ends of the diameter of the Earth's orbit. The method uses this diameter —about 3×10^{13} cm—as a gigantic base line. Since parallaxes can be measured to a fraction of a second of arc, this method can be used for distances up to about 10^{20} cm which is about 30 light years, or with the best possible instruments up to about 100 light years.

At larger distances an empirical discovery has extended the limit considerably. In a galaxy known as the Lesser Magellanic Cloud, it was discovered that there were certain variable stars whose periods were proportional to their magnitude (luminosities). Since these stars are all effectively at the same distance from the Earth, these periods must also be proportional to their absolute magnitudes. To find the constant of proportionality, observation of other variables at known distances—unfortunately not measurable by parallax methods—could be used. From the ratio of absolute and apparent magnitude, the distance of the variable stars—known as Cepheids—could be determined.

12.5.4   Stellar velocities. There would seem to be no method of determining the transverse components of the velocities of stars that are at very large distances from the Earth. The radial components, however, can be measured by finding the Doppler shifts of the spectral lines. This method can also be used for finding the velocities of the edges of a rotating star, for the spectral lines will be broadened; likewise the motions of double stars will lead to a periodic shift of the lines.

The method is simple to apply if the Doppler shift is small. But if it is large, the lines may not be easily recognized, and several lines must be used to establish the emitting elements. Some shifts

observed are so great that when the lines were first observed they were thought to belong to unknown elements. These results bring us to one of the most extraordinary and puzzling observations in the whole of astrophysics—the red shift.

12.5.5   The galactic red shift. If the stars are moving at random throughout the Universe, the Doppler shifts would also be expected to be random—some to the red and some to the violet. In fact, however, they are predominantly to the red, and, in general, the fainter the stars, the greater the displacement to the red (Fig. 12.22);

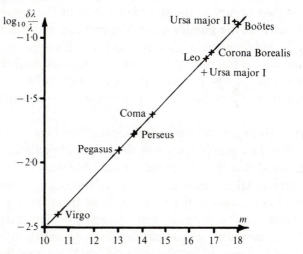

Fig. 12.22. Linear relationship between the magnitude m of a star and log of the red shift, $\delta\lambda/\lambda$. (After Hubble.)

this observation is known as the galactic red shift. Since the fainter stars are probably, on the whole, at greater distances, Hubble in 1929 put forward the suggestion that the red shift—and hence the radial velocity—was proportional to its distance from the Earth. At that time only 24 observations could be advanced to support this suggestion and some of these were not at all definite. Now there are about 500 measurements that are grouped roughly about a straight line. But it must be emphasized that Hubble's hypothesis is not accurately established; the constant of proportionality has changed from $50 \text{ cm s}^{-1} \text{ parsec}^{-1}$ to $7.5 \text{ cm s}^{-1} \text{ parsec}^{-1}$ from 1929 to 1958. (The parsec is the distance that would give a parallax of 1 second of arc and is equal to 3.2 light years.)

Up to about 1965 the greatest observed red shift, measured as the proportional change in wavelength, was about 0·2, corresponding to a speed of $6 \times 10^4 \, \text{km/s}^{-1}$. More recently more extreme speeds have been found, and these will be discussed later in connexion with radio astronomy.

The implications of Hubble's hypothesis are so far-reaching that there has been some reluctance to accept it. It means that the Universe is expanding at a tremendous rate, and this idea is naturally repugnant to those who feel that the universe should be basically stable. They have tried to think of other possibilities of producing the red shift: for example, do photons become less energetic after traversing large distances? But explanations such as this are unacceptable. Alternatively, are we merely in the expanding stage of a cycle of expansion and contraction? This we can never know.

If we accept the red-shift as a true indication of an expanding Universe, we can extrapolate backwards to the instant in time when all the matter in the Universe was at the same point; the fastest-moving matter is then furthest away from the centre. (It can easily be seen that this idea does not put the Earth in any privileged position.) The origin of the Universe is then considered as the explosion of this concentration of matter—the Big-Bang theory. There is still much room for speculation about this suggestion.

12.5.6 Other radiations. All electromagnetic waves can travel through empty space. Why then is visible light so important? Why are not other types of electromagnetic radiation, such as radio waves and X-rays, also reaching us?

The answer is that we are shielded from such radiation by our atmosphere. They do exist and travel for immense distances, only to be stopped in the last few miles before they can reach us. It would be possible to observe these radiations if we could place instruments in the upper levels of the atmosphere and modern techniques make such experiments possible. Platforms can be supported by balloons 20–30 miles above the Earth's surface, and can be stabilized to assume specific orientations to about 1 second of arc. Telescopes and spectrometers can be used to make observations in unusual radiations.

For example, by means of filters it is possible to take photographs of the heavens in infra-red radiation, and some outstandingly

bright objects are found that emit no visible light at all. It is clear that there are many bodies in the Universe that are not hot enough to be observed normally. At the other extreme photographs can be taken by means of X-ray spectrographs. Fig. 12.23 shows the Sun's disc taken in X-rays of about 20 Å wavelength. It is obvious that it shows much more variation in X-ray emission than in visible light.

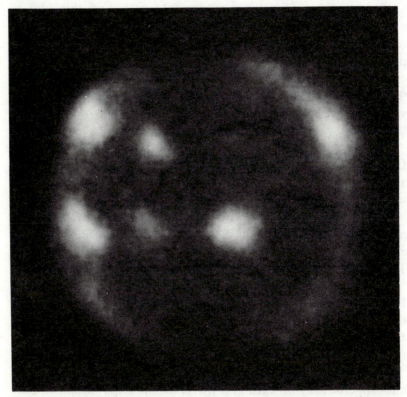

Fig. 12.23. X-ray photograph of the sun taken on 17 December 1964 from a stabilized Skylark rocket (SL 302). Wavelength band $\lambda < 40$Å. (By courtesy of Prof. E. A. Stewardson.)

It is unlikely that instruments on guided platforms will be able to match the size and complexity of those mounted on the Earth's surface and therefore that results obtained with them could be as accurate and detailed. It was therefore an important event in astronomy when it was discovered by Jansky in 1932 that another band of radiation, of a few centimetres in wavelength, would also penetrate the atmosphere. This has produced a new and rapidly

growing subject—radio astronomy—which is so important that it deserves a section to itself.

12.6 Radio astronomy

The first requirement, after the initial discovery that such radiation was reaching the Earth from space, was a form of telescope. Metals, because of their free-electron content, reflect the radiation and therefore a reflecting telescope can easily be built. Accuracy is not difficult to attain; a tenth of a wave is a few millimetres. The real problem is simply that of size. As we shall see in § 12.6.3 even the largest aperture that has been constructed is optically very small, and therefore one tries to see whether optical principles suggest any devices that can improve resolution. These will be discussed in the following sections.

12.6.1 The radio receiver as an optical instrument.
A radio receiver and a telescope have much in common. Each of them receives electromagnetic waves, albeit of very different frequencies, and converts them by some means into electric currents in a circuit; the aerial may be connected to a radio receiver in which the electric currents are converted into audible sounds, whereas the telescope is connected to an eye, which turns visible light into wave-impulses which are eventually interpreted by the observer's brain. As well as this functional similarity, the designers of both telescopes and radio aerials are often faced with similar problems of sensitivity and resolution. Since the solutions illustrate optical principles which should by now be familiar to the reader, it seems appropriate to discuss them briefly.

12.6.2 The resolving power and directional properties of telescopes and aerials.
The resolving power of a telescope is a measure of its directional properties. To cast the problem in the same mould as would a radio-receiver designer, we should ask the following question: if we fix the position of the observer's eye (assumed to be a point), how does the signal received by it depend on the angular position of a point object which is being viewed? For a telescope of finite aperture the answer is quite simple. The point object produces an Airy-disc image in the focal plane of the eyepiece, and so, as the subject changes its angular position, the image will sweep past the observer's eye point, being visible over the angular diameter of the Airy disc. The Airy disc is, of course, the diffraction

pattern of the objective lens of the telescope (§ 7.3.2) and depends on its dimensions. We can illustrate the directional properties of a telescope by a curve showing signal S received as a function of the angular position θ of the source, as in Fig. 12.24(a).

Now consider the same problem as applied to a dipole aerial. We have discussed the properties of an oscillating dipole as a radiator in § 4.5.1, and as a receiver it behaves in an identical manner because the relationship between aerial-current and electric field is independent of which one causes the other. Following Fig. 4.20 we can plot the relationship between S and θ the same way as in Fig. 12.24(a), except that in this case there is a difference between the directional properties in the plane perpendicular to

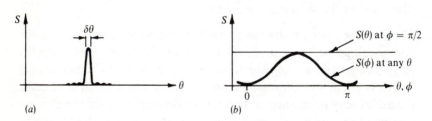

Fig. 12.24. (a) Directional properties of a telescope, the relationship between received-signal, S, and angular position of the source, θ. (b) Directional properties of a dipole aerial.

the dipole (ϕ varies) and in a plane containing the dipole (θ varies) (Fig. 12.24(b)). Clearly the dipole is behaving as if it had an aperture which is infinitely thin and of length $\lambda/2$, which is a fairly accurate description of the average radio aerial! In order to increase the selectivity we need to increase the dimensions of the aperture, or effective aperture.

12.6.3   Large-aperture dish aerials. The simplest way of increasing the effective aperture of a radio aerial is to back it by a parabolic reflector, which collects waves over a large area and presents them at a central dipole aerial with phase changes independent of position in the aperture. A point-source object now produces a signal spread over an Airy disc at the aerial position, and the directional properties are exactly the same as those illustrated in Fig. 12.24(a), since we are now restricting our use of the dipole aerial to a small angular range around $\phi = \pi/2$ (normal incidence).

The orders of magnitude are worrying, however. A telescope of

aperture diameter D gives rise to an angular resolution (§ 9.4.1)

$$\delta\theta = \frac{1\cdot2\lambda}{D}. \qquad (12.19)$$

If the telescope is optical, with a 10 cm diameter lens and wavelength 5×10^{-5} cm (12.19) gives

$$\delta\theta = \frac{1\cdot2 \times 5 \times 10^{-5}}{10} = 6 \times 10^{-6} \text{ radians}$$

$$= 4 \times 10^{-4} \text{ degrees.} \qquad (12.20)$$

A radio telescope, however, with dimensions 250 ft or $7\cdot5 \times 10^3$ cm, working at a wavelength of 20 cm, has a limit of resolution

$$\delta\theta = \frac{1\cdot2 \times 20}{7\cdot5 \times 10^3} = 3 \times 10^{-3} \text{ radians}$$

$$= 2 \times 10^{-1} \text{ degrees.} \qquad (12.21)$$

This is one order worse than the resolution achieved by the human eye, unaided by any optical instrument! And the Jodrell Bank telescope, whose diameter is used in the above calculation, represents a maximum order of magnitude for the practical construction of adjustable parabolic dish aerials.

Of course, the difference between the 2×10^{-1} degrees of the dish aerial and the 90° of the unaided dipole is considerable, but we have overlooked one important factor in the favour of the former —the intensity of the signal, which is collected over an area some 10^5 times larger. But intensity considerations are outside the limits of this discussion. However, with the growing interest in more and more distant, and therefore smaller, objects, it has become of prime importance to increase the resolving power of radio telescopes as much as possible.

12.6.4 The interferometer approach. It will be remembered from § 8.4.2 that Michelson succeeded in increasing the resolving power of a telescope by using it as part of an interferometer. This he did at the expense of simplicity of the image, by producing an interference pattern out of the simple image of a star and observing the properties of the interference pattern. The same approach can be used with a radio telescope. Suppose we consider two dipole aerials separated by a distance L. They can be connected to an electronic device which measures the sum of their signals at a point midway between them, so that the phase lags between the

aerials and the electronics are the same. This system has an aperture corresponding to a pair of infinitely thin Young's slits, and is illustrated in Fig. 12.25. It has a resolution angle

$$\delta\theta = \frac{\lambda}{2L}. \tag{12.22}$$

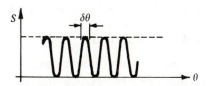

Fig. 12.25. Directional properties of two dipole aerials.

By using a large value of L, the resolving angle can be reduced as much as required; for example, a base-line

$$L = 1 \, \text{km} = 10^5 \, \text{cm},$$

gives, for a 20 cm wavelength

$$\delta\theta = 10^{-4} \, \text{radian} = 6 \times 10^{-3} \, \text{degrees}, \tag{12.23}$$

which is as good as a 1 cm optical telescope. However, the observations of anything but a monochromatic point star are likely to be quite difficult to interpret by this method. The situation may not be quite as bad as the above discussion would indicate, because of the finite coherence-time (§ 8.2.4) of the radio-emission from stars. If the path difference between the waves arriving at the two aerials is greater than the coherence-length of the radiation (§ 8.4.1), no interference pattern will be seen. By using receivers tuned only to a certain bandwidth, the coherence length of radiation from *white* radio stars (ones emitting at all wavelengths) can be artificially lengthened to, say, a few λ, and as a result the $S(\theta)$ curve for the interferometer would appear as in Fig. 12.26. Thus the signals

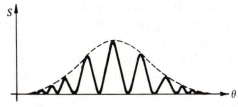

Fig. 12.26. $S(\theta)$ for two-aerial interferometer observing a star emitting waves with a coherence-length of about 5λ.

received from well-separated stars can easily be resolved, and the position of each one determined to the accuracy of the interferometer. An example of the signals received from two sources, Cygnus A and Cassiopeia A, is shown in Fig. 12.27; the angle θ is swept by the rotation of the earth. The process of adjusting the number of visible fringes by altering the receiver bandwidth is exactly equivalent to introducing a coloured glass filter into a

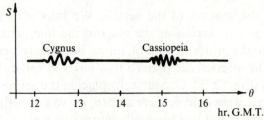

Fig. 12.27. Signals from two sources with finite coherence lengths—or observed within a finite band-width. (From F. G. Smith, *Radio Astronomy*, Penguin, 1962.)

white-light fringe system. With white light, only one or two fringes can be seen; the average piece of coloured glass increases this to seven or eight. A much more selective interference filter would increase the number even more.

Just as in the Michelson stellar interferometer, the angular diameter of a source will also modify the interference pattern. This leads to a reduction of the amplitude of the oscillations in $S(\theta)$ as the base-line L is lengthened, as a result of the finite coherence area of an extended source (Fig. 12.28), and it is easy to see that the interference vanishes just when L becomes large enough for the interferometer to be able to resolve the star as other than a point source.

12.6.5   Diffraction gratings and aerial arrays. To return, however, to the achievement of the highest possible resolving power, we can

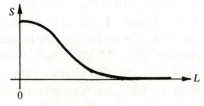

Fig. 12.28. Reduction in signal amplitude as the base-line is increased, when illumination is by an extended source: the analogue of the Michelson stellar interferometer.

follow the progress of interferometry from Young's slits to the diffraction grating (§ 7.4.2). By arranging a line of n regularly spaced aerials, all connected to a summation device by transmission lines introducing equal delays, we can increase the angular resolution to

$$\delta\theta = \frac{\lambda}{2l(n-1)}, \qquad (12.24)$$

where l is the spacing of the aerials. We thus achieve the same resolution as two aerials at the ends of the line, with separation $(n-1)l$, but the introduction of the extra aerials between them simplifies the interference pattern to a series of spikes at a spacing of $\sin^{-1} \lambda/l$ (Fig. 12.29). Of course, by placing the aerials at intervals of less than λ we would achieve an $S(\theta)$ curve consisting only of a zero-order peak, but this is usually impracticable.

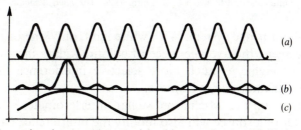

(a)

(b)
(c)

Fig. 12.29. Comparison between (a) two aerials with separation $(n-1)l$; (b) an array of n aerials at separation l; and (c) two aerials with separation l.

A further improvement uses the principle of the blazed grating (§ 7.7.5) by employing two or more dish aerials beamed in a certain direction.

12.6.6   The Mills cross. The one-dimensional array of aerials has only a limited use. It can sweep the sky as the Earth rotates, and has a high angular resolution along its length, say east–west, but no resolution at right angles. The *Mills cross* is an extension of the same idea to two dimensions. By using two aerial arrays at right-angles, a high resolution in both north–south and east–west directions can be achieved (Fig. 12.30). Once again the east–west sweeping is achieved by using the Earth's rotation, but to sweep north–south requires variable interconnexion between the individual aerials, so that a progressive phase difference can be achieved. Then phase differences progressing by ψ radians from aerial to

aerial are equivalent to tipping the aerial through an angle ϕ given by

$$\sin \phi = \frac{\psi}{2\pi} \times \frac{\lambda}{l}. \tag{12.25}$$

This is a difficult procedure, and is therefore inconvenient; it can be replaced by a process called *aperture synthesis* which uses the Fourier transform relation between coherence area, or more strictly correlation function, and source-intensity function, which was proved in §8.4.1.

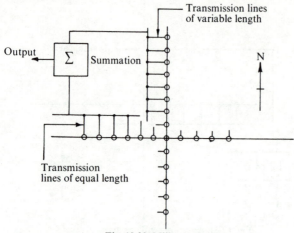

Fig. 12.30. Mills cross aerial.

12.6.7 Aperture synthesis; the use of the correlation function.

If the Earth were stationary, we could build up a picture of the radio universe by studying the correlation between signals V at pairs of points on the Earth's surface. By averaging over a long time the product signal from two aerials separated by vector $\mathbf{r}$, we could calculate the correlation function:

$$\gamma(\mathbf{r}) = \frac{\langle V_1(0)V_2(\mathbf{r})\rangle}{\sqrt{\langle V_1^2\rangle\langle V_2^2\rangle}} \tag{12.26}$$

and by Fourier transforming this function we could then derive the brightness of the radio sky as a function of position. Of course, each evaluation of $\gamma(\mathbf{r})$ would involve observations of V_1 and V_2 over a long period in order to make an accurate assessment of the mean value. The computation involved would be enormous, and would need an electronic computer. The fineness of structure observed in the sky depends only on the range of $\mathbf{r}$ employed. The

larger the maximum values that can be achieved, the finer the detail observable.

In practice this process can be made simpler by employing the rotation of the Earth to sweep in an east–west direction, so that correlation measurements are only necessary with **r** in a north–south direction. The aerial array used is therefore as illustrated in Fig. 12.31; the east–west array is used as an ordinary interferometer, and the north–south pair as a correlation interferometer.

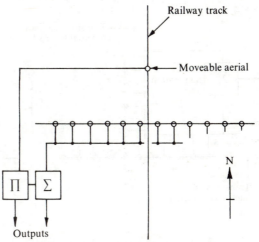

Fig. 12.31. Aperture synthesis aerial array.

12.6.8   Some results of radio astronomy. It would be out of place here to devote much space to a discussion of the results of radioastronomical research. It is sufficient to say that the sky observed in centimetre waves appears quite different from that observed in visible light; although the former picture is crude by optical standards, it is clear that there are few stars that are both visible and radio emitters.

It is not possible to find the distance of radio emitters directly; even the red-shift cannot act as a guide since the only characteristic emission is a faint hydrogen line at 21 cm (§ 8.3.2). The only evidence is that a few radio emitters can be identified with visible objects and thus their distances are known by means of the methods mentioned in § 12.5.3. Quite remarkably, it is found that the radio emission from these is very strong and it can be detected by means of fairly crude instruments. Some of the bodies are at extreme distances, and detectable only with several hours' exposure on the

largest telescope. Since there are many much fainter radio emitters it must be concluded that radio telescopes can probe much deeper into space than optical telescopes can.

There are some strange objects, discovered in 1963, that must be near the extremities of the observable universe. Because of their remarkable properties they cannot be stars of ordinary types and therefore called quasars (quasi-stellar objects). Their red-shifts are remarkably high, indicating velocities up to 0·8 of the velocity of light. To be detected at the distance that this velocity corresponds to according to Hubble's hypothesis, they must be emitting an enormous amount of light, yet they are much more compact than would be expected.

The originally identified quasars were strong radio emitters; this was the reason why attention was focused upon them. But now a large number of non-radiating quasars has been found, also with very large red-shifts, which move ultra-violet hydrogen lines into the visible region. These stars do not fit into the ordinary system of classification, and their presence is giving a great deal of scope for discussion amongst astrophysicists.

It must be remembered, however, that all these results depend upon the interpretation of the red-shift as a Doppler effect. If some other explanation of the observation were to be found the major problem would disappear; the Universe would stop expanding, and the quasars might be ordinary stars relatively near to our galaxy!

12.7 An introduction to magnetoionic theory

Slightly nearer home than the far reaches of the Universe, radio waves can be used to investigate the ionized outer layers of the atmosphere, where their propagation is affected by the Earth's magnetic field. Crystals represent one type of anisotropic medium in which all the components of the dielectric tensor ϵ are real, and because there is no applied magnetic field the relationship (5.33) holds. However, if the anisotropy is a result of the application of a magnetic field, the equivalent relationship to (5.33) is

$$\epsilon_{ij}(H) = \epsilon_{ji}(-H) \tag{12.27}$$

and because the propagation of electromagnetic waves in such a medium is so very different from that in a crystal, it is worth saying something about it, particularly as it illustrates the generality of the approach introduced in Chapter 5.

The medium we shall consider is a model of the ionosphere, and for convenience we shall define it as having n free electrons per unit volume and an equivalent number of much heavier ions of opposite charge to maintain charge neutrality. We shall completely neglect any effects of the heavy ions (which will have at least 10^3 times the electronic mass, m) and also of collisions between the electrons and either ions or other bodies. Such aspects of the theory are outside the scope of this account.

12.7.1   The dielectric tensor.

When an electron of mass m and charge e is acted on by fields $\mathbf{E}$ and $\mathbf{H}_0$ ($\mathbf{H}_0$ is the applied steady field) it experiences a force

$$\mathbf{F} = m\ddot{\mathbf{r}} = \mathbf{E}e + e\dot{\mathbf{r}} \times \mathbf{H}_0. \tag{12.28}$$

Using the operator $\partial/\partial t \equiv i\omega$ we then get

$$-m\omega^2\mathbf{r} = \mathbf{E}e + i\omega e\mathbf{r} \times \mathbf{H}_0. \tag{12.29}$$

Let us define the z-axis to be that of $\mathbf{H}_0$. Written out in components, (12.29) then gives us

$$-m\omega^2(x, y, z) = e(E_x, E_y, E_z) + i\omega e(yH_0, -xH_0, 0). \tag{12.30}$$

Since moving a charge e by distance $\mathbf{r}$ is equivalent to adding a dipole $e\mathbf{r}$, we can write (12.30) as a tensor relationship between the dipole moment per unit volume, $\mathbf{P}$, and the electric field $\mathbf{E}$:

$$ne\mathbf{r} = \mathbf{P}$$

$$\mathbf{E} = \frac{1}{ne^2} \begin{bmatrix} -\omega^2 m & -i\omega eH_0 & 0 \\ +i\omega eH_0 & -\omega^2 m & 0 \\ 0 & 0 & -\omega^2 m \end{bmatrix} \mathbf{P} = \boldsymbol{\chi}^{-1} \cdot \mathbf{P}. \tag{12.31}$$

Using the relationship between dielectric constant ϵ and polarizability $\boldsymbol{\chi}$, which is obtained by straightforward inversion of $\boldsymbol{\chi}^{-1}$ above, we can work out the dielectric tensors:

$$\boldsymbol{\epsilon} = \epsilon_0 \boldsymbol{I} + 4\pi\boldsymbol{\chi} \quad (\boldsymbol{I} \text{ is the unit tensor}),$$

$$\frac{1}{\epsilon_0}\boldsymbol{\epsilon} = \boldsymbol{I} - \frac{\Omega^2}{\omega^2 - \omega_0^2} \begin{bmatrix} 1 & \dfrac{i\omega_0}{\omega} & 0 \\ \dfrac{-i\omega_0}{\omega} & 1 & 0 \\ 0 & 0 & 1 - \dfrac{\omega_0^2}{\omega^2} \end{bmatrix}, \tag{12.32}$$

where $\Omega^2 = 4\pi ne^2/\epsilon_0 m$ (Ω is called the plasma frequency—see

§ 10.3.6) and $\omega_0 = eH_0/m$ (ω_0 is the electron cyclotron frequency). To give an idea of the orders of magnitude involved, the ionosphere at 60 km height contains of the order of 10^4 ions cm^{-3}. This gives a value of the plasma frequency:

$$\Omega \sim 10^6 \, s^{-1}.$$

In a magnetic field of 10^{-1} gauss, the order of the Earth's field, the electron cyclotron frequency

$$\omega_0 \sim 2 \times 10^6 \, s^{-1}.$$

Plasma propagation effects therefore take place at frequencies of the order of megacycles.

Our immediate impulse should be to refer the tensor (12.32) to principal axes. On doing this, we find to our satisfaction that the tensor has three real principal values, but unfortunately that they correspond to complex principal directions:

$$\frac{1}{\epsilon_0}\epsilon = I - \frac{\Omega^2}{\omega^2} \begin{bmatrix} (1+\omega_0/\omega)^{-1} & 0 & 0 \\ 0 & (1-\omega_0/\omega)^{-1} & 0 \\ 0 & 0 & 1 \end{bmatrix}, \quad (12.33)$$

with principal directions $(1, i, 0)(1, -i, 0)$ and $(0, 0, 1)$. The meaning of the complex directions is not difficult to see. They have R-values (§ 5.2.3) of i and $-i$, and correspond to two circularly polarized waves travelling along $(0, 0, 1)$, the z-axis. One of them, the one corresponding to the second value above, represents a wave in which the angular frequency of rotation of the electric vector is in the same sense as the rotation of the free electrons in the magnetic field, which is clockwise about the field. ($R = -i$ corresponds to clockwise rotation.) It is therefore not surprising that there is a singularity in the principal value at $\omega = \omega_0$.

12.7.2 Frequency dependence. One fact which is immediately obvious is that the components of ϵ are highly frequency-dependent; all waves in the ionosphere are very dispersive. Since it is necessary that ϵ should be positive for real propagation (the wave is evanescent if $\mu = \epsilon^{\frac{1}{2}}$ is imaginary) we can place lower limits on ω for each of the three waves to be propagated. This is done in Fig. 12.32 in which ω is plotted vertically and H_0 horizontally. The boundary lines between regions are simply the solution of the equations:

$$\frac{\Omega^2}{\omega^2(1 \pm \omega_0/\omega)} = 1; \qquad \Omega = \omega; \qquad \omega = \omega_0(H). \quad (12.34)$$

12.7.3   The dielectric surfaces. Strictly the surface represented by (12.33) should be drawn in six dimensions, so that any direction, real or complex, plane- or elliptically polarized, can be represented. Fortunately, however, it is possible to manage with a judicious choice of three dimensions; we can make a useful three-dimensional projection of the six-dimensional surface. This is not as abstract as it sounds. We shall simply define $(1, i, 0)$, $(1, -i, 0)$ and $(0, 0, 1)$ as

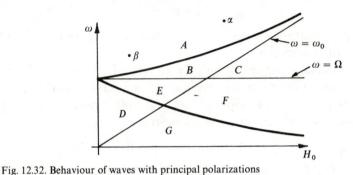

Fig. 12.32. Behaviour of waves with principal polarizations

Polarization:	$(1, i, 0)$	$(1, -i, 0)$	$(0, 0, 1)$
Mode	Clockwise	Anticlockwise	Plane polarized
	$\mathbf{k} \parallel z$	$\mathbf{k} \parallel z$	$\mathbf{E} \parallel z$
Region A	Propagated	Propagated	Propagated
B	Propagated	Evanescent	Propagated
C	Propagated	Propagated	Propagated
D	Evanescent	Evanescent	Evanescent
E	Propagated	Evanescent	Evanescent
F	Propagated	Propagated	Evanescent
G	Evanescent	Propagated	Evanescent

the three orthogonal directions in the projection, and then the tensor ϵ can be drawn as a surface in terms of them in exactly the same way as we drew the optical indicatrix in terms of its principal axes. The actual form of the tensor is dependent on the frequency and field. At very high frequencies, for example, α on Fig. 12.32, all three components of ϵ are positive, and the surface is an ellipsoid with semi-axes equal to the square-roots of the three principal values (Fig. 12.33). At infinite frequency it becomes a sphere. Suppose that we now change the frequency ω at constant field. As ω falls the length of the axis of the ellipse representing anti-clockwise polarization drops, reaching zero on the dividing line between A and B. In B the ellipsoid has become a hyperboloid of one sheet (Fig. 12.34). As we reduce the field still further the hyper-boloid rapidly lengthens along $(1, -i, 0)$, to become a cylinder at

$\omega = \omega_0$ and an ellipsoid once more in region C. Meanwhile, the ellipsoid-axis representing the plane-polarized mode has been gradually shortening, and when the frequency reaches Ω the ellipsoid once again turns into a hyperboloid of one sheet, this time with its open ends along H_0. At the boundary between the regions

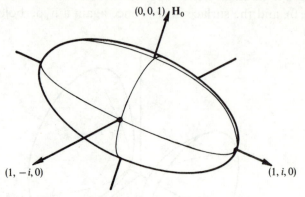

Fig. 12.33. The dielectric surface in region A of Fig. 12.32.

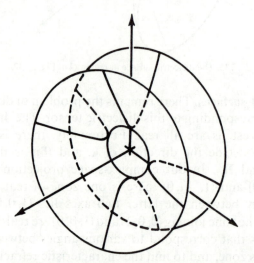

Fig. 12.34. The dielectric surface in region B of Fig. 12.32.

F and G the hyperboloid-axis representing the clockwise mode also vanishes, and in region G the surface is a hyperboloid of two sheets, the only real axis of which corresponds to anti-clockwise propagation (Fig. 12.35).

A similar process of frequency reduction from β on Fig. 12.32 shows that the hyperboloid of one sheet in B becomes a hyperboloid of two sheets in E, the real axis now corresponding to clockwise propagation. On reaching the D–E boundary this remaining axis also shrinks to zero, and the surface is non-existent in region D. At the DG boundary it re-appears with infinite semi-axis along $(1, -i, 0)$, and the surface in G is once again a hyperboloid of two sheets.

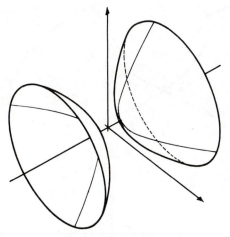

Fig. 12.35. The dielectric surface in region G of Fig. 12.32.

12.7.4   The μ-surfaces. There remains the problem of deducing the μ-surfaces corresponding to this dielectric tensor. The directions of **k** which interest us are all real. Fortunately, there is only one parameter to decide the direction of **k**, and this is the angle θ between **k** and $\mathbf{H}_0$. In our complex-space projection with axes $(0, 0, 1)$ $(1, i, 0)$ and $(1, -i, 0)$ there is one zone of real directions, since half-way between the latter two axes lies $(1, 0, 0)$, and all directions in the zone joining $(0, 0, 1)$ and $(1, 0, 0)$ are real (Fig. 12.36). The **k**-vectors that correspond to various angles between $\mathbf{H}_0$ and **k** all lie in this zone, and to find the characteristic refractive indices we must draw the normal diametric plane for each **k** in the zone and investigate the conic section in which it intersects the dielectric surface (Fig. 12.37).

As with the crystal problem in § 5.4.4, where the characteristic waves were polarized along the symmetry axes of the section-ellipses, in this case the characteristic waves are similarly polarized.

The two symmetry axes of the sections, which can now be either ellipses or hyperbolae, are at right angles, and the meaning of their perpendicularity is simply that the elliptical polarizations of the two waves are orthogonal. In the sense of § 5.2.3 $R_1 R_2^* = -1$. However, of the two axes of a hyperbola, only one is real length; if the section of the dielectric surface cut by the plane normal to **k** is a hyperbola, one of the characteristic waves is evanescent. We therefore expect that there will not always be two characteristic waves.

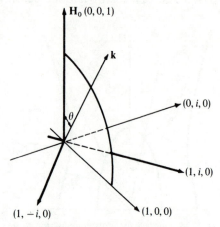

Fig. 12.36. Real and complex directions.

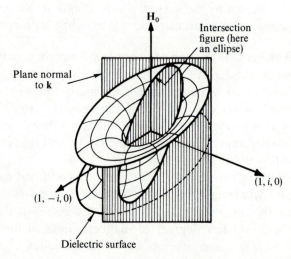

Fig. 12.37. Intersection of a hyperbolic dielectric surface with the plane.

It would take too much space to enumerate all the possible forms that a μ-surface can take, since some of the regions *A* to *G* can give rise to two different types of section. However, the interested reader has all the material available at least to see the form qualitatively under any given conditions, and we shall content ourselves here with two examples.

Propagation with frequency in region *B* gives rise to a μ-surface with section as in Fig. 12.38. Since the propagation depends only on the angle θ between **k** and the field H_0, the μ-surface is axially symmetric about H_0. The ray vector is once again normal to the

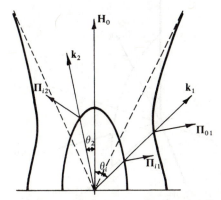

Fig. 12.38. μ-surface for propagation in region *B*.

surface, as is shown by the vectors on the diagram. Notice that k_1 has two propagating characteristic waves, while k_2 has only one.

12.7.5 Whistlers. Whistlers are very-low-frequency radio waves propagated in the Earth's magnetic field. They lie in region *G* of Fig. 12.32 whose dielectric surface is a hyperboloid of two sheets, the asympotic surface approaching the axes $(1, 0, 0)$ $(0, i, 0)$ and $(0, 0, 1)$ as $\omega \to 0$ (Fig. 12.39). The μ-surface follows very simply from this construction; it has one branch only, and that disappears just below $\theta = 90°$ (Fig. 12.40).

The important property of the wave-surface illustrated in Fig. 12.40 is that whatever **k** is chosen, the propagation ray vector is almost exactly along the magnetic field; the energy is thus channelled to within a few degrees of magnetic lines of force. These waves are highly dispersive, as the refractive index $\epsilon^{\frac{1}{2}}$ varies as $\omega^{-\frac{1}{2}}$ in the limit $\omega \to 0$.

The phenomenon of *whistlers* is connected with thunderstorms at the opposite end of a line of force of the Earth's magnetic field from the observer (Fig. 12.41). A lightning flash produces a substantial pulse of audio-frequency radio waves, which are channelled along the line of force and arrive, high-frequency components first, to interfere with the observer's radio-set. The result is a whistle,

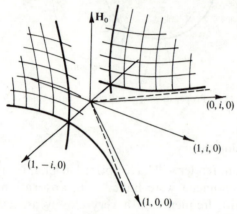

Fig. 12.39. Dielectric surface at very low frequency (region *G*).

which drops from high- to low-pitch in about a second or two. The signal can be reflected and returned after a further reflexion and three trans-world flights; the drop in pitch then takes three times the period of the first, and further reflected signals of even longer duration are occasionally heard.

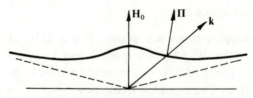

Fig. 12.40. μ-surface for whistler mode (region *G*).

12.7.6   Optic axes. Since the circular section-plane which is the requirement for the optic axis must contain the intermediate axis of the surface (§ 5.4.5), and since this axis is always [001] in the above examples, it follows that the ionosphere (excluding collisions) has no optic axes.

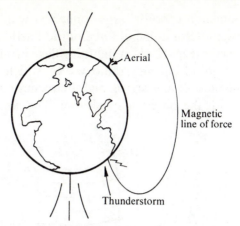

Fig. 12.41. Propagation of whistler along Earth's line of force.

12.8   Dispersion theory

The observant reader will have noticed in Chapter 10 that certain dispersion phenomena were linked with absorption mechanisms that varied with frequency in a very closely associated manner. For example, in anomalous dispersion, the smaller the frequency range of the transition from $\mu > 1$ to $\mu < 1$, the larger the absorption coefficient. It was also evident that the real and imaginary refractive indices were just the real and imaginary parts of a single analytical complex refractive index. Dispersion theory is concerned with studying the basic properties of complex response-functions. It has implications particularly in elementary-particle theory, and is introduced here mainly because optical phenomena provide good illustration of its application.

12.8.1   The complex-frequency plane. The notion of a complex frequency was introduced in Chapter 2 and has been used sufficiently often for the reader to be assumed by now to be thoroughly conversant with it. The complex frequency

$$\omega = \omega_1 + i\omega_2$$

represents a wave whose amplitude is changing exponentially with time; if ω_2 is positive, the amplitude is decaying with a time-constant ω_2^{-1}; if ω_2 is negative, the amplitude is exponentially increasing. We can represent the complex ω as a point on the Argand diagram in which ω_1 is plotted as the x-coordinate and ω_2

as the y-coordinate. Having done this, any function, such as a susceptibility $\chi(\omega)$, can be represented as a function of the complex variable by drawing it as a contour map on the complex-ω plane. There will be two sets of contours, because $\chi(\omega)$ is in general complex; for example, one set of contours represents the amplitude $|\chi|$ and the other the phase, arg χ. Fig. 12.42 illustrates this for the susceptibility $\chi(\omega)$ arising from anomalous dispersion. The two sets of contours are orthogonal; that is, they always intersect at right angles.

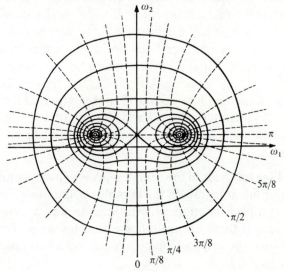

Fig. 12.42. The function $\chi(\omega) = 1/(p^2 - \omega^2 + i\omega k)$ plotted on the complex-frequency plane as a contour map. Solid lines represent contours of equal amplitude; broken lines contours of equal phase (angles as shown). The two poles represent the resonances at frequencies $\omega = ik \pm \sqrt{p^2 - k^2}$. The observed resonance–response curve is the intersection with the real axis ($\omega_2 = 0$).

12.8.2 Resonances, poles and causality.

There is one important type of singularity that a complex function can have, and that is a *pole*—a point at which the function becomes asymptotically infinite. Fig. 12.42 shows that two of these occur for the anomalous dispersion $\chi(\omega)$. A pole in a physical function represents a resonance, which is a frequency at which the amplitude of oscillation of the system or medium becomes infinite for a driving-force of finite amplitude.

Any physical system has a 'memory' which lasts a certain while; it is impossible that a physical system should have precognizance

of events to come. This is known as the *principle of causality*. The only way that a physical system can achieve infinite amplitude, therefore, is as a result of its memory of an infinite driving force at some earlier time; it cannot achieve infinite amplitude in anticipation of an infinite force to come. Now we have seen that a pole represents infinite amplitude of oscillation for a finite driving force; hence it must arise from a force that has exponentially decreased from infinite amplitude at $t = -\infty$ which means that the driving force has a complex frequency with positive ω_2. If ω_2 were negative, the amplitude of the force would be increasing from zero at $t = -\infty$ and the system could never achieve infinite amplitude of oscillation by means of a memory extending only to earlier times. Thus the poles of a real system must all lie in the upper† half-plane of complex-frequency space, corresponding to decaying amplitudes. An alternative way of seeing this result is to consider the resonance frequency as the frequency of natural oscillation. Since the oscillations of all real physical systems decay naturally with time, the resonance frequencies all have positive ω_2 and lie in the upper† half-plane.

12.8.3   Line integrals in the complex-plane. There is one important property of line integrals in the complex plane. If an integral of an analytic complex function is performed around a closed loop, its value is zero if there are no poles within the loop. This property arises because the real and imaginary parts of all complex functions satisfy separately

$$\frac{\partial^2 f}{\partial \omega_1^2} + \frac{\partial^2 f}{\partial \omega_2^2} = 0,$$

(f being either the real or the imaginary part of the function) and therefore behave like single-valued potential functions. A contour integral will therefore not change its value when the contour is distorted provided that the distortion involves crossing no poles.

When a pole is included within a contour, the integral is no longer zero, but has a value related to the properties of the function around the pole. We shall eventually be using contours which come close to poles, and we shall therefore carry out a calculation of this relationship. The function $u(\omega)$ has a pole at ω_0 (Fig. 12.43). Let us draw a circular contour C around it, at a radius ρ, so that its equation

---

† Many works state *lower* half-plane here. This is a result of using the wave-form $\exp\{i(kx-\omega t)\}$ in place of our $\exp\{i(\omega t - kx)\}$. There is no difference in principle.

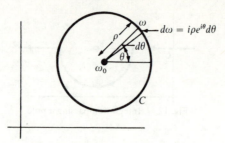

Fig. 12.43. Integration round a pole.

is given by

$$\omega = \omega_0 + \rho \, e^{i\theta}. \tag{12.35}$$

The integral

$$\oint u(\omega) \, d\omega \tag{12.36}$$

is thus

$$\int_0^{2\pi} u(\omega_0 + \rho \, e^{i\theta}) i\rho \, e^{i\theta} \, d\theta. \tag{12.37}$$

Because the point ω_0 is a pole, we cannot expand $u(\omega_0 + \rho \, e^{i\theta})$ by a Taylor expansion. However, since $1/u$ approaches zero, we can expand this:

$$\frac{1}{u(\omega_0 + \rho \, e^{i\theta})} = \frac{1}{u}(\omega_0) + \rho \, e^{i\theta} \left[\frac{\partial u^{-1}}{\partial \omega} \right]_{\omega_0} + \dots O(\rho^2). \tag{12.38}$$

Denoting

$$\left[\frac{\partial u^{-1}}{\partial \omega} \right]_{\omega_0} \quad \text{by} \quad \frac{1}{v(\omega_0)}, \tag{12.39}$$

we have the integral (12.37) becoming, as $\rho \to 0$,

$$\int_0^{2\pi} \frac{v(\omega_0)}{\rho \, e^{i\theta}} i\rho \, e^{i\theta} \, d\theta = 2\pi i v(\omega_0). \tag{12.40}$$

The function $v(\omega_0)$ is known as *the residue at the pole*. Thus the integral round a complete loop enclosing a pole is equal to $2\pi i$ multiplied by the residue at the pole. If the contour involves only half the circle (Fig. 12.44) the contribution to the integral from the region near the pole is just $\pi i v(\omega_0)$, proved in an identical manner. This result will be used in § 12.8.4.

12.8.4   The Kramers–Krönig relations. There is a pair of extremely useful relationships in dispersion theory called the Kramers–Krönig relations, and they relate the frequency variation of the real

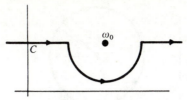

Fig. 12.44. Integration passing a pole.

and imaginary parts of response functions such as the susceptibility, $\chi(\omega)$. The proof of these involves complex-plane integrations.

We consider the functions

$$u(\omega) = \frac{\chi(\omega) - \chi(\infty)}{\omega - \omega_0}, \tag{12.41}$$

where ω_0 is some chosen arbitrary real frequency. This function has poles

(a) at ω_0, where the residue is easily seen from (12.39) to be

$$v(\omega_0) = \chi(\omega_0) - \chi(\infty)$$

since $\chi(\omega)$ can have no singularity at a real ω_0;

(b) at the poles of $\chi(\omega)$ which are in the upper half-plane.

We can now carry out a contour integration of $u(\omega)$ around the closed loop in the lower half-plane of Fig. 12.45. The contour contains no poles, and therefore the integral is zero. It can be written as the sum of three parts:

(i) $\displaystyle\int_{-R}^{\omega_0-\rho} u(\omega)\,d\omega + \int_{\omega_0+\rho}^{R} u(\omega)\,d\omega$ along the real axis,   (12.42)

(ii) $\displaystyle\int_{\omega_0-\rho}^{\omega_0+\rho} u(\omega)\,d\omega$ along semi-circle C,   (12.43)

(iii) $\displaystyle\int_{R}^{-R} u(\omega)\,d\omega$ along semi-circle S.   (12.44)

Let us dispose of these in reverse order.

The integral (iii) can be written, when R is large, as

$$\int_0^{\pi} \frac{\chi(\omega) - \chi(\infty)}{R\,e^{i\theta}}(-iR\,e^{i\theta}\,d\theta), \tag{12.45}$$

which approaches zero as $R \to \infty$ if $\chi(\omega) \to \chi(\infty)$ continuously. Thus we can dispose of (iii) by letting $R \to \infty$.

The integral (ii) approaches $\pi i v(\omega_0)$ as $\rho \to 0$ (from § 12.8.3). Therefore let $\rho \to 0$.

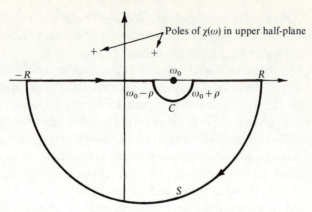

Fig. 12.45. Contour integral.

The integral (i) can now be evaluated. It is written as

$$\mathscr{P} \int_{-\infty}^{\infty} u(\omega)\, d\omega \equiv \lim_{\rho \to 0} \int_{-\infty}^{\omega_0 - \rho} + \int_{\omega_0 + \rho}^{\infty} u(\omega)\, d\omega \qquad (12.46)$$

and called the *principal part* of the integral; it is the integral from $-\infty$ to ∞ missing out a vanishingly small region around ω_0. The fact that the sum of the integrals (i), (ii) and (iii) is zero means that

$$\mathscr{P} \int_{-\infty}^{\infty} \frac{\chi(\omega) - \chi(\infty)}{\omega - \omega_0}\, d\omega = -\pi i [\chi(\omega_0) - \chi(\infty)]. \qquad (12.47)$$

We can separate real and imaginary parts of this equation and use the known facts that

(a) $\qquad\qquad \chi_1(\infty) = 0; \qquad \chi_2(\infty) = 0,$

(b) $\qquad \chi_1(\omega) = \chi_1(-\omega); \qquad \chi_2(\omega) = -\chi_2(-\omega),$

for all physical systems. As a result, (12.47) gives the Kramers–Krönig relations in their most convenient form:

$$\mathscr{P} \int_0^{\infty} \frac{2\omega_0 \chi_1(\omega)}{\omega^2 - \omega_0^2}\, d\omega = \pi \chi_2(\omega_0), \qquad (12.48)$$

$$\mathscr{P} \int_0^{\infty} \frac{2\omega \chi_2(\omega)}{\omega_0^2 - \omega^2}\, d\omega = \pi \chi_1(\omega_0). \qquad (12.49)$$

The dielectric constant and refractive index can easily be written down from $\chi(\omega)$ using the relationship that

$$\mu^2 = \epsilon = \epsilon_0 + 4\pi\chi. \qquad (12.50)$$

12.8.5 Qualitative implications. We shall consider two examples to show qualitatively how the relations (12.48) and (12.49) can be used to deduce one χ from the other.

Suppose that a material is known to have the same real susceptibility in two separated frequency regions around ω_1 and ω_2. We can immediately deduce that χ_2 must be zero between these two frequencies, so that there is no absorption band between them. For, if χ_2 were not zero in this range, (12.49) shows that the contribution it would make would oppositely affect $\chi_1(\omega_1)$ and $\chi_1(\omega_2)$ because the signs of $\omega_1^2 - \omega^2$ and $\omega_2^2 - \omega^2$ are opposite when ω is in this region. Thus no absorption can occur between ω_1 and ω_2. It is important to notice that there must be *regions* of equal χ_1 around ω_1 and ω_2 because it is always possible that isolated frequencies in regions of rapidly changing χ_1 will have the same value. This occurs in the anomalous regions.

Similarly, at very high frequencies, we can see that χ_1 approaches zero from below, when all absorption has taken place at lower frequencies. The imaginary susceptibility χ_2 is always negative, representing absorption, and (12.49) shows that $\chi_1(\omega_0)$ will also be negative when ω_0 is well above the absorption frequencies.

Around an absorption band, such as occurs in anomalous dispersion (§ 10.3.2), it is clear that χ_1 will rise at a frequency just below the absorption and fall to a negative value just above the absorption.

12.8.6 A wave-group in a dispersive medium. The same type of integration is involved in studying the propagation of wave-groups in dispersive media. One of the most important general results than can be proved easily is that for any real dispersive medium the signal velocity must be less than c, irrespective of whether the group velocity is greater than or less than c. We can then resolve in general the problem posed in § 10.3.4.

If we have a wave-group which passes $x = 0$ as a function of time $f(t)$ whose Fourier analysis is given by

$$f(0, t) = \int_{-\infty}^{\infty} a(\omega) \exp(i\omega t)\, d\omega, \qquad (12.51)$$

its function at x is found by re-integrating after each component has travelled a distance x at its own characteristic velocity, ω/k. Thus

$$f(x, t) = \int_{-\infty}^{\infty} a(\omega) \exp\{i(\omega t - k(\omega)x)\}\, d\omega. \qquad (12.52)$$

We shall study the properties of this integral at a fixed point $x \neq 0$, and show that if $f(0, t)$ is zero for all negative times (the pulse starts at time $t = 0$), $f(x, t)$ will be zero for all times $t < x/c$ showing that propagation is slower than velocity c.

The proof hangs on one important fact, and that is that the limit of velocity at high frequency is c

$$\lim_{\omega \to \infty} \frac{\omega}{k} = c. \tag{12.53}$$

In all practical media this is so, and has been assumed by putting $\chi_1(\infty) = \chi_2(\infty) = 0$ in § 12.8.4. We could consider a simple wave-group having the above property of zero value at $x = 0$ until $t = 0$. It is a decaying pulse of frequency Ω and decay time T (Fig. 12.46) and its Fourier spectrum is

$$a(\omega) = \int_0^\infty A \exp\left(i\Omega - \frac{1}{T}\right) t \exp\left(-i\omega t\right) dt$$

$$= -i\left(\Omega + \frac{i}{T} - \omega\right)^{-1}. \tag{12.54}$$

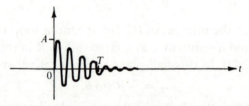

Fig. 12.46. The decaying wave-group, starting at $t = 0$.

This has a pole at $\omega = \Omega + i/T$, which is in the upper half plane, in common with the poles of all functions whose transforms are zero until $t = 0$. The pole is indicated in Fig. 12.47.

We write (12.52) in terms of the *retarded time*

$$s = t - \frac{x}{c} \tag{12.55}$$

and the refractive index $\mu = kc/\omega$, whence

$$f(x, t) = \int_{-\infty}^{\infty} a(\omega) \exp\left\{i\omega\left(s - \frac{\mu - 1}{c} x\right)\right\} d\omega. \tag{12.56}$$

This is a line integral along the real axis of the complex frequency plane. Two points about μ must be noticed. Firstly, in accordance

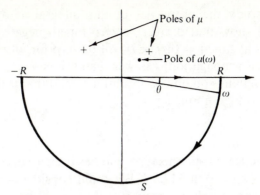

Fig. 12.47. Integration for a wave-group in a dispersive medium.

with our remarks about equation (12.53)

$$\mu - 1 \to 0 \quad \text{as} \quad \omega \to \infty, \tag{12.57}$$

and secondly, it has poles corresponding to those of $\chi(\omega)$ and therefore in the upper half-plane, because

$$\mu^2 = 1 + \frac{4\pi}{\epsilon_0}\chi. \tag{12.58}$$

Now carry out the integral of (12.56) around a loop consisting of the real axis and a semi-circle at a large radius R in the lower half-plane (Fig. 12.47). In this half-plane ω_2 is negative, and has value

$$\omega_2 = -R \sin \theta.$$

The loop integral, which must have zero value because it encloses no poles, gives, since $\mu - 1$ becomes zero as $R \to \infty$,

$$0 = \int_s a(\omega) \, e^{i\omega_1 s} . \, e^{sR \sin \theta} \, d\omega$$
$$+ \int_{-R}^{R} a(\omega) \exp \left\{ i\omega \left(s - \frac{\mu-1}{c}x \right) \right\} d\omega. \tag{12.59}$$

Allow R to approach ∞. When $s < 0$, that is, at times $t < x/c$, the first integral vanishes because of the negative exponential $\exp(sR \sin \theta)$, and hence the second integral, which is (12.56), must also vanish. There is no signal at time $t < x/c$; that is, the signal velocity must be less than c. Of course, at time $t > x/c$ we should have to complete the loop with a semi-circle in the upper half-plane for the s-integral to vanish, and poles would now be included within it. The signal therefore begins at time $t = x/c$, although we can make no more deductions about its form without considerably more

mathematics. However, we have proved, without reference to any particular system or wave-group, that the signal velocity must necessarily be less than c, the important hinge being that waves of infinite frequency travel with velocity c. The exact form of the group is discussed fully by Brillouin (*Wave Propagation and Group Velocity*).

APPENDIX I

GEOMETRICAL OPTICS

1 Fermat's principle

The elementary principles of optical instruments can best be considered in terms of rays rather than waves, a ray representing the direction in which a wave travels. That rays can be used is the consequence of Fermat's principle (§ 4.4.4), that the path of a ray from one point to another is either of maximum or minimum optical length (actual length multiplied by refractive index).

The law of rectilinear propagation in a uniform medium follows directly from Fermat's principle, and so do the laws of reflexion. The second law of refraction can be seen to follow by the following reasoning. Let PQ (Fig. I.1) be a plane separating media of refractive indices μ_1 and μ_2,

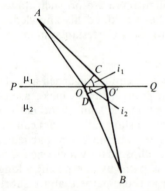

Fig. I.1. Explanation of refraction in terms of Fermat's principle.

and let AOB and $AO'B$ be two possible close paths between two points A and B. The optical length of the path through O is $\mu_1 AO + \mu_2 OB$, and that through O' is $\mu_1 AO' + \mu_2 O'B$. We require to find the condition that these two lengths are equal. They are obviously equal if $\mu_1 CO' = \mu_2 OD$, where OC and $O'D$ are perpendicular to AO' and OB respectively. But $CO' = OO' \sin i_1$ and $OD = OO' \sin i_2$. Therefore the condition

$$\mu_1 CO' = \mu_2 OD$$

is re-stated as

$$\mu_1 \sin i_1 = \mu_2 \sin i_2,$$

which is the second law of refraction.

2 Sign conventions

It is helpful to have a consistent convention for the use of positive and negative quantities in optics. In this book, we use a simple Cartesian

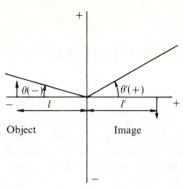

Fig. I.2. Sign convention for distances and angles.

convention, as shown in Fig. I.2. Other conventions—based upon whether real or virtual images or objects are involved—cannot be extended to two dimensions. Although there are no such direct applications in this book, anyone who wishes to extend his knowledge of lens aberrations, for example, will have to use a Cartesian system.

3 Thin lenses and mirrors

An image-forming system can be regarded as a device for equalizing a *limited* group of optical paths. Mirrors make use of the property of an ellipsoid of revolution—that the sum of the paths from a point on the surface to the two foci is constant; all mirrors can be regarded as parts of such an ellipsoid. The parabolic mirror in particular (Appendix III) can be regarded as part of an ellipsoid for which one focus is at infinity.

A lens equalizes optical paths by interposing a longer length of medium of high refractive index in those paths that are shorter. The lens formula

$$\frac{1}{l'} - \frac{1}{l} = (\mu - 1)\left(\frac{1}{r_1} - \frac{1}{r_2}\right)$$

can be proved from this approach. In this equation l and l' are object and image distances, and r_1 and r_2 are the radii of curvature of the two surfaces of the lens.

4 Thick-lens systems

A coaxial lens system is one for which the centres of curvature of all the refracting surfaces lie on a straight line—the axis. When such a system, which may be a single thick lens, has a thickness comparable with the focal length, we can no longer talk of measuring 'from the lens' (Fig. I.3(a)). It can be shown, however, that the thin-lens formula can still be used if object distances are measured from one point on the axis, and image distances from another. These two points (H and H' in Fig. I.3(b)) are called *principal points* and the planes through them perpendicular to the axis are called *principal planes*. Principal points are formally defined as

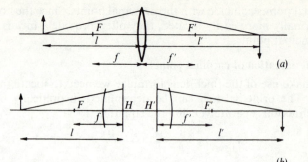

(a)

(b)

Fig. I.3. Comparison of thin-lens and thick-lens systems, showing significance of principal points H and H'.

the conjugate points for which the magnification is unity. The two focal lengths of the system f and f' are the distances from the principal points to the principal foci F, F'.

The two focal lengths are equal only if the image is formed in the same medium as that containing the object. In general,

$$f/\mu = f'/\mu',$$

where μ and μ' are the refractive indices of the initial and final media.

In thin-lens theory it is often convenient to make use of the concept of the optical centre of a lens; for a thick-lens system this point is replaced by two points, called the nodal points N and N'. These have the property that the ray along any line containing N will emerge along a parallel line containing N' (Fig. I.4), so that the nodal points can be defined as conjugate points for which the angular magnification is unity.

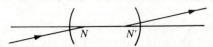

Fig. I.4. Nodal points of a thick-lens system. The incident and emergent rays are parallel.

The points H, H', F, F', N, N' (Fig. I.5), are called the cardinal points of the lens system and suffice for solving any problem concerned with paraxial rays. There are certain relationships between them: e.g. $FN = f'$, and $F'N' = f$. Thus the distance between the nodal points equals the distance between the principal points. If the initial and final media are the same,

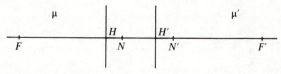

Fig. I.5. Cardinal points of a thick-lens system. $F, F' =$ focal points; $N, N' =$ nodal points; $H, H' =$ principal points. $NH = N'H'; FN = H'F; FH = N'F'; FH/H'F' = \mu/\mu'$.

the nodal points coincide with the principal points. Since the nodal points are normally more easily located, they often provide a means of finding the principal points.

5   Determination of cardinal points

To make use of the thick-lens formulae we need to locate the cardinal points. The principal foci can be determined theoretically by treating each refraction separately, using the equation

$$\frac{\mu'}{l'} - \frac{\mu}{l} = \frac{\mu' - \mu}{r},$$

the sign convention described in Appendix I, § 2, being used for the signs of l, l' and r. After each refraction the position of the image is used as object position for the next refraction. By taking the initial object and the final image at infinity, the two foci can be found. The principal points and nodal points cannot be located so directly.

It is usually best, however, to locate the cardinal points experimentally. The principal foci F and F' can be found by locating the image of a distant object, or by finding the position of an object that produces an image in the same place when a plane mirror is placed behind the lens system. We can then find a set of pairs of conjugate positions, each pair being an object position and its corresponding image position. If the distances of these points from F and F' are p and p', we can then use Newton's equation

$$pp' = -f^2$$

to find the focal length. If the initial and final media are not the same, the equation is

$$pp' = ff'$$

and we need to know the two values of μ in order to find the two focal lengths.

Having found the principal foci and the focal lengths, we can find the principal points and the nodal points from the relationships given in Appendix I, § 4.

APPENDIX II

ABERRATIONS

No image-forming system can form a perfect image of a finite object. Every image has defects, called aberrations, and the best that can be done in practice is to see that the aberrations that would be most noticed in a particular experimental arrangement are made as small as possible— sometimes at the expense of making other aberrations larger.

The classification of aberrations now usually accepted was first introduced by von Seidel about 1860. It is as follows.

1 Spherical aberration

Lenses and mirrors with spherical surfaces cannot form an accurate image of a point object on the axis; usually the more extreme rays are too greatly deviated (Fig. II.1) resulting in a defect known as spherical aberration. This defect can be removed in several ways.

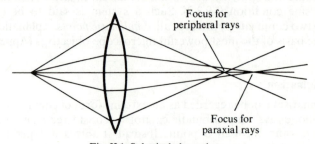

Focus for
peripheral rays

Focus for
paraxial rays

Fig. II.1. Spherical aberration.

(a) The refracting or reflecting surface can be made aspheric and the aberration removed empirically, the Foucault knife-edge test (§ 9.6.2) being used to assess the accuracy of the results. This is usually worth while only for large lenses.

(b) The aberration produced by a converging lens can be corrected by that produced by a diverging lens made from a different glass; the combination is usually in the form of a cemented doublet, and chromatic aberration (Appendix II, § 6) can be eliminated at the same time.

(c) For simple systems use can be made of the rough rule that spherical aberration is reduced if the deviations are spread over several surfaces and is a minimum if the deviations of a particular ray are the same at each surface. Separated combinations—particularly eyepieces (Appendix III, § 3)—make use of this principle.

2 Coma

Even if spherical aberration is eliminated, we may still find that the image of a point slightly off the axis is not perfect. This defect is particularly

important in astronomy, since the image of a star may look like a comet—hence the name *coma*. It can be reduced or eliminated in several ways.

(a) Coma can be eliminated by choosing radii of curvature appropriate to a given object position—the so-called 'bending' of the lens (Fig. II.2). This usually also leads to minimum spherical aberration.

Fig. II.2. A 'bent' lens for eliminating coma.

(b) Coma and spherical aberration are absent in any system that obeys Abbe's sine condition (§ 9.3.2). Such a system is said to be *aplanatic*, and the two conjugate points are called *aplanatic points*. Aplanatic systems form the basis of the most powerful microscope objectives (Appendix III, § 2).

3   Astigmatism

Astigmatism can be regarded as an extreme form of coma; it occurs for very oblique rays when a bundle cannot be considered as even approximately passing through a point. Instead it forms a tapering wedge-shaped pencil, the edge of the wedge (Fig. II.3) forming what is known as a *focal line*: all the rays pass through this line and then diverge; but the taper continues, to cause the rays to pass through another focal line, perpendicular to the first.

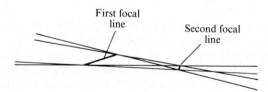

Fig. II.3. Astigmatic pencil, showing formation of two focal lines.

The consequence of this defect is that it is impossible to produce a focused image of the outer parts of a plane object perpendicular to the axis. Radial detail—for example, the spokes of a wheel—may appear to be in focus in one focal line and tangential detail in the other (Fig. II.4). Moreover, the surfaces in which these apparent foci occur may not be

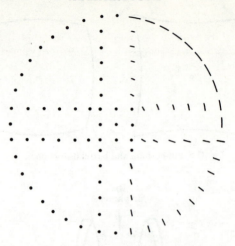

Fig. II.4. Astigmatism. The left-hand side shows the perfect image; the upper right-hand quadrant shows the image in the tangential focal line; the lower right-hand quadrant shows the image in the radial focal line.

even approximately plane, thus leading to the fourth aberration; this can best be considered together with astigmation.

4   Curvature of field

The removal of astigmatism can be regarded as causing the two focal-line surfaces to coincide, and the removal of curvature of field as making these surfaces plane. The defects are particularly important in cameras in which the image has to be focused on a flat plate. Their removal, however, is rather difficult, and the principles cannot be simply explained.

A lens which is corrected for astigmatism and curvature of field is called an *anastigmat*.

5   Distortion

An image in which the previous aberrations have been corrected is still not necessarily a perfect representation of the object; if the magnification varies with the obliquity of the rays then the shape of the object may not be reproduced and the image is said to be distorted; if the magnification increases with obliquity the image of a square will have the shape of a pin-cushion and if it decreases with obliquity the image will be barrel-shaped (Fig. II.5).

It can be seen quite easily that the effect cannot exist for a symmetrical system forming a real image of the same size as the object $(l = -l')$. For since paths of rays are reversible, object and image can be interchanged and thus one cannot be larger than the other. Although this reasoning does not apply to other object distances, symmetrical lens systems have the property of producing little distortion for *any* object position. Most good camera lenses are therefore symmetrical, with the iris diaphragm in the

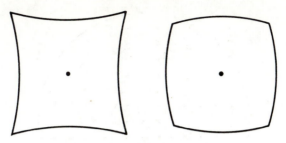

Fig. II.5. Pin-cushion and barrel distortion.

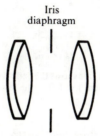

Fig. II.6. A symmetrical camera lens for the elimination of distortion.

plane of symmetry (Fig. II.6). Such a lens is said to be *orthoscopic* or *rectilinear*.

6   Chromatic aberration

Because the refractive index of glass is a function of wavelength, an image produced in white light usually has coloured edges. This defect is known as chromatic aberration.

A rough correction can be made by using two displaced lenses (Fig. II.7). The violet ray is more deviated than the red and so reaches the second lens nearer to the axis than the red ray; it is therefore less deviated by the second lens. The deviations can be arranged to combine in such a way that the red and violet rays emerge parallel to each other.

A more precise correction can be achieved by cemented doublets of two different glasses; such a lens is known as an achromatic doublet. The two

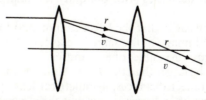

Fig. II.7. Corrections for lateral chromatic aberration by separated doublet. The red ray, *r*, is deviated less than the violet ray, *v*, at the first lens, but is deviated more at the second.

glasses must have different *dispersive powers*, ω, which is defined as

$$\omega = \frac{\mu_1 - \mu_2}{\mu - 1};$$

μ_1 and μ_2 are refractive indices for two different wavelengths λ_1 and λ_2, and μ is their mean. If the two glasses are characterized by primed and imprimed symbols respectively, it is shown in elementary textbooks that the combination of two lenses is achromatic if

$$\frac{\omega}{f} + \frac{\omega'}{f'} = 0.$$

Such combinations work well in practice, but there is always some residual error resulting from the fact that ω is not strictly a constant for a given material; it depends upon the particular wavelength λ_1 and λ_2 chosen to define it. For a better correction a combination of three glasses can be made; this is called an *apochromat*. Such lenses are found to be perfectly satisfactory for even the most exacting work.

A thorough treatise on aberrations would have to deal with the chromatic variation of all the other errors. We shall merely state here that, for thick-lens systems, there are two kinds of chromatic aberration—axial (or longitudinal) and lateral. For the former the images formed by the different colours are the same size, but are not in the same plane; for the latter they are in the same plane, but are not of the same size. The system shown in Fig. II.7 obviously suffers from axial chromatic aberration, but not from lateral. It is not possible to correct for both these aberrations simultaneously except by making the lens system entirely of cemented doublets.

7 Summary

A lens system cannot be produced for which all aberrations are corrected. For any particular use, one must decide which errors are important and to concentrate on eliminating these at the expense of possibly making the others worse. For example, the diffractometer described in Appendix IV has to form a point image of a pin-hole on the axis; therefore spherical aberration is the only error that is important and is eliminated by using corrected doublets. Microscopes for measuring cosmic-ray tracks, however, must produce an image free from distortion and astigmatism, which might make the tracks difficult to measure accurately. It can be seen, therefore, that although the design of lens systems is largely a technical matter, physicists must be aware of the problems involved in order that they can specify their requirements for particular researches.

SOME IMPORTANT OPTICAL COMPONENTS

1 Telescope objectives

The simplest telescope objective consists of an achromatic combination (Appendix II, § 6), which can also be corrected for spherical aberration (Appendix II, § 1). For bigger telescopes, it becomes easier to use mirrors, and all large telescopes now have such objectives, usually of paraboloidal shape (Appendix II, § 1).

It is a property of a paraboloid that all rays parallel to the axis pass, after reflexion, precisely through the focus; that is, spherical aberration is absent. But rays not parallel to the axis do not pass through a single point after reflexion; that is, coma (Appendix II, § 2) is present. If, however, the mirror were spherical all directions would be equivalent, since they are all parallel to radii. A system that takes advantage of both these properties was devised by Schmidt in 1932 and is thus free from both spherical aberration and coma.

The Schmidt system is based upon a spherical mirror, combined with a transmitting plate that has the form of the difference between the paraboloid and the sphere (Fig. III.1). If the plate were in contact with the spherical mirror the two would be equivalent merely to a paraboloidal mirror. If the plate is placed at any other position it maintains this property of correcting the spherical mirror; if it is placed with its centre at the centre of curvature of the mirror it also has the property of treating alike (apart

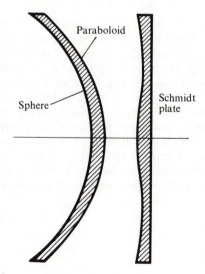

Fig. III.1. The Schmidt correcting plate as the difference between a paraboloid and a sphere.

from an obliquity factor) beams of all directions (Fig. III.2). The system is therefore free from coma.

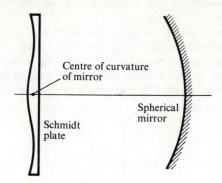

Fig. III.2. Schmidt objective system.

2 Microscope objectives

Low-power microscope objectives pose no great problem. For high powers, producing a limit of resolution near to the theoretical maximum (§ 9.4.1), a special system based upon the aplanatic points (Appendix II, § 2) of a sphere is universally used.

It can easily be shown (Fig. III.3) that rays diverging from a point distant R/μ from the centre of a glass sphere of radius R will, after refraction, appear to be diverging from a point distant μR from the centre;

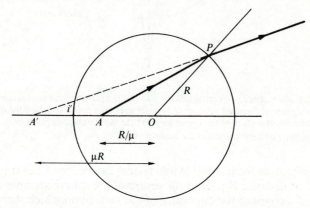

Fig. III.3. Aplanatic points of a sphere. Triangles AOP and POA' are similar.

since no approximations are involved, the result is correct for all angles. A beam with a semi-angle of, say, 64° (sin 64° = 0·90) will thus emerge as a beam with a semi-angle of 37° (sin 37° = 0·60), if $\mu = 1·50$.

This property of a sphere can be used in two ways. First, the sphere can be cut by a section passing through its internal aplanatic point; the

specimen is placed near this point and immersed in a liquid (cedar-wood oil is used) of the same refractive index as the glass (Fig. III.4). The system is known as *oil-immersion* and is used universally for microscopes of the highest resolution.

The second way in which the principle can be used involves putting the object at the centre of curvature of the first face of a lens, making this point the inner aplanatic point of the second surface (Fig. III.4); all the deviation then occurs at the second surface and the image is formed at the outer aplanatic point (Fig. III.4). The semi-angle of the emergent beam is then reduced from 37° to 24°.

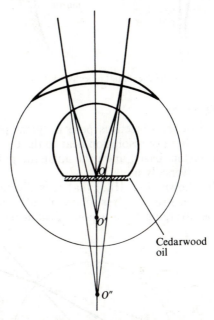

Cedarwood
oil

Fig. III.4. Microscopic objective making use of the aplanatic points of a sphere. O is inner aplanatic point of the small sphere; O' is outer aplanatic point. O' is also the centre of curvature of the lower surface of the upper lens and the inner aplanatic point of its upper surface. O'' is the outer aplanatic point of the upper surface.

The freedom from coma of this system can be seen from the fact that *all* points at distance R/μ from the centre of the sphere are aplanatic points. Thus, if we ignore the curvature of the surface on which these points lie, we can say that all points on a plane object will form a plane image that is free from spherical aberration and coma.

3 Eyepieces

Although there is little noteworthy about eyepieces, they are used so frequently in scientific work that their principles should be well understood. It is quite remarkable that these principles should have been worked

out so soon after the invention of the microscope; Huygens—who has given his name to a prototype eyepiece—lived at the time when the microscope was still quite new. Eyepieces consisting of pairs of lenses are used rather than single lenses because they can be better corrected for both spherical aberration and chromatic aberration. In addition, they can also carry other devices such as cross-wires and scales that can be put in focus with the final image. The lens nearer the eye is called the eye lens and the other is called the field lens.

There are two useful and easily proved rules to remember in dealing with simple lens systems: first, the deviation of a ray incident in a lens at a distance y from the axis is y/f; and, secondly, the chromatic aberration (Appendix II, § 6) of a single lens—the distance between the foci for two different wavelengths—is ωf, where ω is the dispersive power with respect to the same two wavelengths.

The equation for the focal length f of a combination of two lenses separated by a distance a is

$$\frac{1}{f} = \frac{1}{f_1} + \frac{1}{f_2} - \frac{a}{f_1 f_2}.$$

If f_1 and f_2 have a chromatic variation, then

$$\delta\left(\frac{1}{f}\right) = \left(1 - \frac{a}{f_2}\right)\delta\left(\frac{1}{f_1}\right) + \left(1 - \frac{a}{f_1}\right)\delta\left(\frac{1}{f_2}\right)$$

$$= \left(1 - \frac{a}{f_2}\right)\frac{\omega f_1}{f_1^2} + \left(1 - \frac{a}{f_1}\right)\frac{\omega f_2}{f_2^2}$$

$$= \left(1 - \frac{a}{f_2}\right)\frac{\omega}{f_1} + \left(1 - \frac{a}{f_1}\right)\frac{\omega}{f_2}.$$

This is zero if $f_1 + f_2 = 2a$, whatever the value of ω. A combination with this property will be free from axial but not lateral (Appendix II, § 6) chromatic aberration.

To correct for spherical aberration, we try to equalize the deviations produced by the two lenses. The equality can be only approximate, since rays are passing through at all angles, but we take as typical a ray emerging parallel to, and at a distance y from, the axis (Fig. III.5). This must be

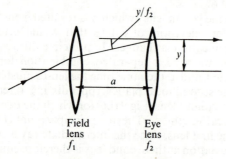

Fig. III.5. Principle of an eyepiece.

inclined at an angle y/f_2 between the lenses and must therefore be incident at the first lens at a distance from the axis $y - a(y/f_2)$; the deviation is therefore

$$\frac{\{y - a(y/f_2)\}}{f_1}.$$

Equating the two deviations, we have

$$\frac{y - (ay/f_2)}{f_1} = \frac{y}{f_2},$$

or

$$f_2 - f_1 = a.$$

If we combine this condition with the previous one, $f_1 + f_2 = 2a$, we arrive at the result

$$f_1 = a/2, \qquad f_2 = 3a/2.$$

This specifies the Huygens eyepiece.

Although it is theoretically the best combination, it has the disadvantage that the focus is between the lenses and so images of cross-wires or scales are not corrected. A more usual combination is the Ramsden eyepiece, for which

$$f_1 = f_2 = 3a/2,$$

which does not have this disadvantage, and which still gives a reasonable performance.

4 Camera lenses

Camera lenses can vary from simple 'bent' lenses (Appendix II, § 2) with displaced stop in cheap cameras, to very complicated symmetric combinations (Appendix II, § 5) in expensive cameras. Only two special types will be discussed here, since they introduce some simple physical principles.

The first type is the telephoto lens, used for taking photographs of distant objects; a large focal length is needed if the image is to be of reasonable size, but it would be inconvenient for the camera to be correspondingly long. Therefore a separated combination of a converging lens and diverging lens is used, with principal planes (Appendix I, § 4) well outside the combination (Fig. III.6).

The second type is the 'zoom lens', which has resulted from the requirements, particularly for television, of a lens that would give a focused image while the magnification is changed. In principle this requirement is not difficult to meet; we need a separated combination for which the separation can be varied, and at the same time the lenses must be displaced in such a way that the second focal plane (Appendix I, § 4) remains fixed.

Let us consider a telephoto lens (Fig. III.6) for which the two lenses have equal and opposite focal lengths, f_1. The first principal point H must be at a distance of f_1 from the first lens, since the intermediate ray is then parallel to the axis, and the deviation at the second lens is therefore equal to that at the first; H and H' are thus nodal points and, since there is no change in

medium, they are also principal points. The focal length f of the combination is, from the first equation in Appendix III, § 3, f_1^2/a. We can thus draw a diagram (Fig. III.7) showing the positions of the two lenses for various separations, in order to give a fixed second focal plane. All we now require

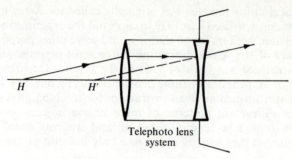

H H'

Telephoto lens
system

Fig. III.6. Positions of principal points for a telephoto lens.

is a mechanical system that, by means of one adjustment, can move the two lenses as required.

Zoom lenses are, of course, much more complicated than this, as the various aberrations require to be corrected, and allowance must be made for the fact that the object is not always at infinity.

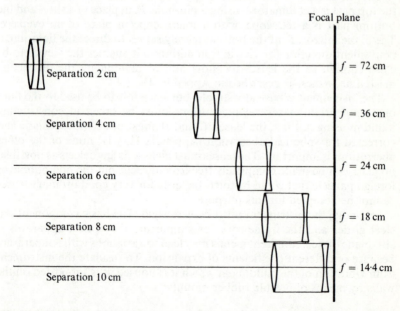

Focal plane

Separation 2 cm $f = 72$ cm

Separation 4 cm $f = 36$ cm

Separation 6 cm $f = 24$ cm

Separation 8 cm $f = 18$ cm

Separation 10 cm $f = 14·4$ cm

Fig. III.7. Simple zoom lens made from two components of equal and opposite focal length
(12 cm).

APPENDIX IV

THE OPTICAL DIFFRACTOMETER

The optical diffractometer was originally called the X-ray microscope by W. L. Bragg, who used it in 1939 to carry out the experiments described in § 9.7.2. Later workers found that it would serve other purposes as well in the study of the X-ray diffraction patterns of crystals, and a more precise instrument was built in 1949 in the Physics Department of the University of Manchester Institute of Science and Technology. It was then realized that it formed an ideal instrument for teaching physical optics; Fraunhofer diffraction patterns of quite coarse objects—even several centimetres—could be readily observed, and students could carry out experiments that they usually experience only in terms of illustrations in textbooks.

The instrument is in constant use in Manchester, and its existence is the main reason why we were prompted to write this textbook. We strongly recommend it as a teaching instrument† and are therefore including details of it here; a more complete description will be found in Taylor and Lipson (*Optical Transforms*).

1 Construction

The instrument is essentially a spectrometer; as shown in Fig. IV.1, the top part is a collimator—using a pin-hole, *B*, in place of a slit—and the bottom part is a telescope, with a microscope in place of an eyepiece. The plane mirror, *E*, at the bottom merely serves to direct the light into a convenient direction for viewing; in addition, it enables the viewer to be close enough to the lenses to allow him to manipulate the diffracting mask if he wishes, as described in Appendix IV, § 4.

The instrument is basically simple, but since it is to be used to the limit of its potentialities several precautions must be taken in constructing it and in using it. First, the lenses, *C* and *D*, must be accurately made and corrected for spherical aberration (Appendix II, § 1); none of the other aberrations is important. The lenses must include as few defects as possible; no glass can be made completely free from defects, but the odd bubble or foreign particle that could be tolerated even for very good ordinary lenses cannot be accepted for this purpose.

Secondly, the instrument must be very rigid. The basic component is a steel girder and the framework for supporting the optical apparatus is also made of steel; different metals may lead to variations with temperature because of different coefficients of expansion. To insulate the instrument from vibration of the building in which it is housed, it is supported on the walls by means of flexible rubber mounts.

---

† It is now made commercially by R. B. Pullin & Co., Ltd., Phoenix Works, Great West Road, Brentford, Middlesex, U.K.

Thirdly, the instrument must be accurately adjusted. One cannot depend upon the precise setting of a lens in its mount, and methods—to be described briefly in Appendix IV, § 2—have been devised to be independent of any initial assumptions.

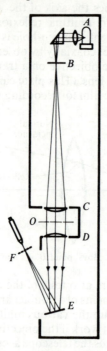

Fig. IV.1. Optical diffractometer. A is the light source; B is the pin-hole; C and D are the lenses; and E is an optically flat mirror. The diffraction pattern of an object at O is seen in the plane F.

2 Adjustment

The requirements of the diffractometer are few: the lenses must be accurately coaxial, and the pin-hole must lie accurately upon this axis; the viewing telescope must also be coaxial and the axis must also pass approximately through the centre of the plane mirror, E, at the bottom. The complete adjustment of a diffractometer is an excellent example of the application of geometrical optics; it is described in full by Taylor and Lipson (*Optical Transforms*) and only a basic outline will be given here.

First, how does one find experimentally the axis of a lens? One of the simplest ways is to locate the *Boys points*—the points that are self-conjugate for reflexion from the back surface of the lens (Fig. IV.2), and which can be used, as shown in elementary textbooks, to determine the radius of curvature of the surface. The line joining the two Boys points—one on each side of the lens—is the axis of the lens. The method of adjusting the diffractometer does not make use of the Boys points themselves, but it

uses the principle of these reflexions, which can be quite numerous if the lens is compound and if the source is bright enough for multiple reflexions to be seen.

The lower lens, D, is set first and its axis—which must be set roughly in the right position—then defines the axis of the whole system. When the second lens, C, is inserted more multiple reflexions are possible and help in setting the two axes coincident. The pin-hole is then placed on this axis. Finally, the telescope can be set coaxially by observing the reflexions from the various components of the objective on a translucent plate, F, placed in the focal plane of the lower lens. (This plate can be replaced by a maximum-resolution photographic film for recording the diffraction patterns.)

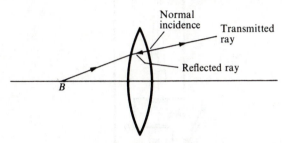

Fig. IV.2. Boys' point B of a lens.

Some of these operations are also tests of the components themselves; for example, if the two components of a doublet are not mounted coaxially, it will not be possible to line up the various multiple reflexions. Also, the test for the microscope will not work if the objective is not an accurate one.

Finally, it is necessary to focus the telescope accurately. For many simple purposes it is merely necessary to form as small an image as possible of the illuminated pin-hole, but for precise purposes, particularly for photographing patterns with fine detail, a less subjective procedure is needed. One method is to form the diffraction pattern of the largest circular aperture that will give a clear diffraction pattern (§ 7.3.2); if the telescope is then raised or lowered, a succession of maxima and minima at the centre of the diffraction pattern will be observed, and the correct plane of focus is that which lies half-way between the two minima on either side of the approximate focus. In this way, the focal plane can be fixed to a fraction of a millimetre. (Anyone who has used an ordinary optical bench may find it difficult to believe that the focus of a lens of 150 cm focal length can be found so accurately; but such sceptics should verify for themselves that an error of 0.01 cm produces a difference of about $\frac{1}{5}\lambda$ between the central and marginal rays for a lens of 10 cm diameter, and this difference should begin to produce observable effects.)

3 Illumination

One of the best sources of monochromatic light is a compact-source high-pressure mercury-vapour lamp. It has a high intrinsic brilliance

(lumens/cm^2) and the lines are not broadened enough by the high pressure to affect the diffraction patterns appreciably. A gelatine or an interference filter (§ 7.9.2) can be used to select the line required; the yellow line ($\lambda = 5790$ Å) is recommended, particularly if the patterns are to be photographed.

The size of pin-hole is important. It is true that the smaller the pin-hole the higher the degree of spatial coherence (§ 8.4.1), but it is unwise to have a pin-hole so small that the patterns can be seen only with difficulty. It is best to use a pin-hole that gives about 90 % coherence over the mask; thus the larger the mask the smaller the pin-hole needs to be. The following table gives a rough guide of pin-hole sizes for masks of given dimensions, for lenses of focal length 150 cm.

Diameter of mask	Size of pin-hole
6 cm	5×10^{-4} cm
3 cm	10
1 cm	30
0·3 cm	100

4   Some possible experiments

It is easily possible to make standard masks out of thin cardboard; old unused X-ray films are particularly suitable because they cut cleanly. For real permanency masks should be made out of sheet brass.

Static demonstrations, however, are never as inspiring as dynamic ones, and the following paragraphs give some suggestions for masks that can be varied as they are viewed by the observer (Appendix IV, § 1).

(a) The diffraction patterns of two holes. Two holes about 5 mm in diameter and 2 cm apart give clear fringes, which disappear when one of the holes is covered.

(b) Variable fringes. The variation of the fringe separation with the separation of two similar apertures can be illustrated by the device shown in Fig. IV.3.

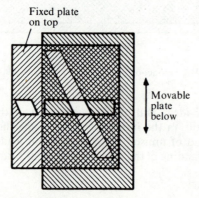

Fixed plate on top

Movable plate below

Fig. IV.3. Device for showing fringes from two similar apertures of variable separation.

(c) Principal and subsidiary maxima for a diffracting grating. An accurate grating with, say, six lines about 0·2 mm wide and 1 mm apart can be produced by means of a fine slitting saw on a milling machine; a raised piece of metal (Fig. IV.4) is very suitable for this purpose. A sliding shutter can be caused to cover up the slits one by one and the changes in the secondary maxima (§ 7.4.2) noted.

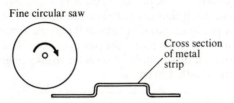

Fig. IV.4. Method of cutting slits for diffraction gratings.

(d) Effect of slit width of a diffraction grating. The effect of changing the width of the slit of a grating, keeping the spacing constant, can be shown by the type of device shown in Fig. IV.5.

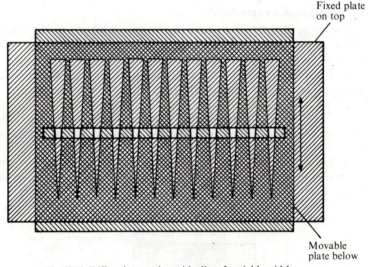

Fig. IV.5. Diffraction grating with slits of variable width.

No doubt other ideas will arise in the mind of the keen teacher of optics or, better still, in the minds of the students themselves. A liberal supply of cards and of unused razor blades can lead to a considerable increase of understanding of the basic principles of Fraunhofer diffraction.

APPENDIX V

PRACTICAL FOURIER COMPUTATIONS

We have emphasized the importance of Fourier theory in optics by devoting a complete chapter (3) to it. Nevertheless, although it is necessary to be able to cope with the basic mathematics, the number of problems that can be solved purely by mathematical methods is severely limited; if one wishes to deal with general problems one must be able to use numerical methods. This appendix is therefore concerned with practical methods of Fourier analysis and synthesis.

1 Fourier synthesis

When the Fourier coefficients of a function have been found, it is advisable to check that the sum of the terms reproduces the function. Of course, with a finite number of terms, the reproduction is not exact, but it is instructive to see how the approximation improves as higher-order terms are added. Fig. V.1(a) shows the first few terms of the Fourier series for the square-wave function, and Fig. V.1(b) shows the summations for successively increasing numbers of terms.

The most direct way of producing these results is to plot the curves as in Fig. V.1 and add the ordinates at chosen points. This operation is, however, rather slow and liable to mistakes. A better method is to use a device known as a set of Fourier strips,† which reduce the operation to the additions of columns of recorded numbers.

The strips record the values of $A \cos nx$ and $A \sin nx$, where n is an integer from 0 to 30, and x ranges from 0° to 90° in intervals of 3°; there are separate strips for values of A in units between $+100$ and -100, and for separate hundreds up to ± 900. Two typical strips are shown in Fig. V.2.

To sum a given series, one merely has to extract the appropriate strips and add the columns together. The result gives only a quarter of the complete period, since x ranges only from 0° to 90°, but the extension to the half-period can be made by adding the strips for n even separately from those with n odd; the strips for n even are symmetrical about $x = 90°$ and those for n odd are antisymmetrical. The use of the strips for summing the series for the square wave is illustrated in Table V.1.

For an even function (§ 3.3.1), only half a period need be computed. For a general function both cosine and sine strips are needed, and again the sine strips can be extended by using the appropriate symmetries of the sine function; the combination of cosine and sine then gives the complete period.

† Available from Dr C. A. Beevers, Chemistry Department, The University, Edinburgh 9.

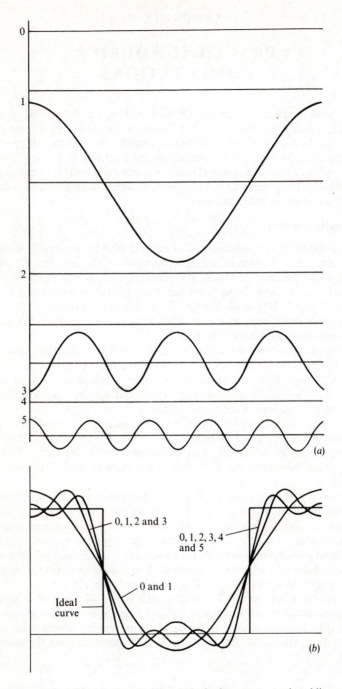

Fig. V.1. Summation of first few terms of Fourier series for square wave by adding ordinates.

Table V.1. *Summation of terms up to the eleventh for the Fourier series representing a square wave; half a period is shown, as the rest is related to it by symmetry. If only the final total (lines 18 and 19) is required, the strips are placed together in sequence and the totals of the columns recorded; there is no need to write down the separate strips as we have done here. The reader might like to plot the various results and see how they fit in with the principles stated in § 3.*

50 C0	50	50	50	50	50	50	50	50	50	50	50	50	50	50	50	50	strip	1
65 C1	65	65	64	62	59	56	53	48	43	38	32	26	20	14	7	0	strip	2
	115	115	114	112	109	106	103	98	93	88	82	76	70	64	57	50	sum	3
	$\overline{15}$	$\overline{15}$	$\overline{14}$	$\overline{12}$	$\overline{9}$	$\overline{6}$	$\overline{3}$	2	7	12	18	24	30	36	43 ↙		differ-ence	4
-22 C3	$\overline{22}$	$\overline{21}$	$\overline{18}$	$\overline{13}$	$\overline{7}$	0	7	13	18	21	22	21	18	13	7	0	strip	5
	93	94	96	99	102	106	110	111	111	109	104	97	88	77	64	50	3+5	6
	7	6	4	1	$\overline{2}$	$\overline{6}$	$\overline{10}$	$\overline{11}$	$\overline{11}$	$\overline{9}$	$\overline{4}$	3	12	23	36 ↙		4−5	7
13 C5	13	11	6	0	$\overline{6}$	$\overline{11}$	$\overline{13}$	$\overline{11}$	$\overline{6}$	0	6	11	13	11	6	0	strip	8
	106	105	102	99	96	95	97	100	105	109	110	108	101	88	70	50	6+8	9
	$\overline{6}$	$\overline{5}$	$\overline{2}$	1	4	5	3	0	$\overline{5}$	$\overline{9}$	$\overline{10}$	$\overline{8}$	$\overline{1}$	12	30 ↙		7−8	10
-9 C7	$\overline{9}$	$\overline{7}$	$\overline{1}$	5	9	8	3	$\overline{4}$	$\overline{8}$	$\overline{9}$	$\overline{4}$	2	7	9	6	0	strip	11
	97	98	101	104	105	103	100	96	97	100	106	110	108	97	76	50	9+11	12
	3	2	$\overline{1}$	$\overline{4}$	$\overline{5}$	$\overline{3}$	0	4	3	0	$\overline{6}$	$\overline{10}$	$\overline{8}$	3	24 ↙		10−11	13
7 C9	7	4	$\overline{2}$	$\overline{7}$	$\overline{6}$	0	6	7	2	$\overline{4}$	$\overline{7}$	$\overline{4}$	2	7	6	0	strip	14
	104	102	99	97	99	103	106	103	99	96	99	106	110	104	82	50	12+14	15
	$\overline{4}$	$\overline{2}$	1	3	1	$\overline{3}$	$\overline{6}$	$\overline{3}$	1	4	1	$\overline{6}$	$\overline{10}$	$\overline{4}$	18 ↙		13−14	16
-6 C11	$\overline{6}$	$\overline{2}$	4	6	1	$\overline{5}$	$\overline{5}$	1	6	4	$\overline{3}$	$\overline{6}$	$\overline{2}$	4	5	0	strip	17
	98	100	103	103	100	98	101	104	105	100	96	100	108	108	87	50	15+17	18
	2	0	$\overline{3}$	$\overline{3}$	0	2	$\overline{1}$	$\overline{4}$	$\overline{5}$	0	4	0	$\overline{8}$	$\overline{8}$	13 ↙		16−17	19

76 C7	76	56	8	$\overline{45}$	$\overline{74}$	$\overline{66}$	$\overline{23}$	31	69	72	38	$\overline{16}$	$\overline{61}$	$\overline{76}$	$\overline{51}$	0
19 S6	0	11	18	18	11	0	$\overline{11}$	$\overline{18}$	$\overline{18}$	$\overline{11}$	0	11	18	18	11	0

Fig. V.2. Two Fourier strips. The first figure is the amplitude; C and S represent cos and sin. The next figure indicates the harmonic and the entries give the values of the ordinates for the first quarter of a period at intervals of $2\pi/60$. (From Lipson and Cochran, *The Determination of Crystal Structures*, first edition, fig. 90(i). Bell, London.)

2 Fourier analysis

The Fourier strips also enable Fourier analysis—the derivation of the Fourier coefficients (§ 3.2.2)—to be carried out very easily. The coefficients can be derived much more quickly than by mathematical integration, but also functions that do not yield to mathematical methods, and arbitrary curves not expressible as analytical functions, can be dealt with.

The method relies upon the fact that Fourier synthesis and Fourier analysis are essentially the same process (§ 3.3.4). To analyse a function we take strips representing successive ordinates at regular intervals—close enough to specify the function reasonably well—and add the numbers in successive columns; these are the Fourier coefficients. They are also the ordinates for the Fourier transform (§ 3.4.1) of a single period of the function.

This method is appropriate only for an even function, which can be represented by cosine terms only. For a general function we need to derive the cosine terms and the sine terms separately. The former are obtained from the even function whose ordinates are $\frac{1}{2}[f(x)+f(-x)]$ and the latter from the odd function whose ordinates are $\frac{1}{2}[f(x)-f(-x)]$.

The example shown in Table V.2 gives the analysis of the square wave carried out by the strip method. Here all the ordinates between $x = -90°$ and $x = +90°$ are equal and are taken as 100: instead, however, of adding

Table V.2. *Fourier analysis of square wave. Each strip represents an ordinate and the totals give the relative values of the Fourier coefficients. The absolute values are obtained by dividing by* 1500—*the product of the ordinate chosen and the number of divisions. The results for the orders up to* 9 *are as follows, the correct results being shown in brackets:*
1, 0·636 (0·636); 3, −0·211 (−0·212); 5, 0·125 (0·127); 7, −0·088 (−0·091);
9, 0·065 (0·071)

50	C0	50	50	50	50	50	50	50	50	50	50	50	50	50	50	50	50
100	C2	100	98	91	81	67	50	31	10	$\overline{10}$	$\overline{31}$	$\overline{50}$	$\overline{67}$	$\overline{81}$	$\overline{91}$	$\overline{98}$	$\overline{100}$
100	C4	100	91	67	31	$\overline{10}$	$\overline{50}$	$\overline{81}$	$\overline{98}$	$\overline{98}$	$\overline{81}$	$\overline{50}$	$\overline{10}$	31	67	91	100
100	C6	100	81	31	$\overline{31}$	$\overline{81}$	$\overline{100}$	$\overline{81}$	$\overline{31}$	31	81	100	81	31	$\overline{31}$	$\overline{81}$	$\overline{100}$
100	C8	100	67	$\overline{10}$	$\overline{81}$	$\overline{98}$	$\overline{50}$	31	91	91	31	$\overline{50}$	$\overline{98}$	$\overline{81}$	$\overline{10}$	67	100
100	C10	100	50	$\overline{50}$	$\overline{100}$	$\overline{50}$	50	100	50	$\overline{50}$	$\overline{100}$	$\overline{50}$	50	100	50	$\overline{50}$	$\overline{100}$
100	C12	100	31	$\overline{81}$	$\overline{81}$	31	100	31	$\overline{81}$	$\overline{81}$	31	100	31	$\overline{81}$	$\overline{81}$	31	100
100	C14	100	10	$\overline{98}$	$\overline{31}$	91	50	$\overline{81}$	$\overline{67}$	67	81	$\overline{50}$	$\overline{91}$	31	98	$\overline{10}$	100
		750 478		0	$\overline{162}$	0	100	0	$\overline{76}$	0	62	0	$\overline{54}$	0	52	0	$\overline{50}$
100	C1	100	99	98	95	91	87	81	74	67	59	50	41	31	21	10	0
100	C3	100	95	81	59	31	0	$\overline{31}$	$\overline{59}$	$\overline{81}$	$\overline{95}$	$\overline{100}$	$\overline{95}$	$\overline{81}$	$\overline{59}$	$\overline{31}$	0
100	C5	100	87	50	0	$\overline{50}$	$\overline{87}$	$\overline{100}$	$\overline{87}$	$\overline{50}$	0	50	87	100	87	50	0
100	C7	100	74	10	$\overline{59}$	$\overline{98}$	$\overline{87}$	$\overline{31}$	41	91	95	50	$\overline{21}$	$\overline{81}$	$\overline{99}$	$\overline{67}$	0
100	C9	100	59	$\overline{31}$	$\overline{95}$	$\overline{81}$	0	81	95	31	$\overline{59}$	$\overline{100}$	$\overline{59}$	31	95	81	0
100	C11	100	41	$\overline{67}$	$\overline{95}$	10	87	81	$\overline{21}$	$\overline{98}$	59	59	$\overline{99}$	31	$\overline{74}$	91	0
100	C13	100	21	$\overline{91}$	$\overline{59}$	67	87	$\overline{31}$	$\overline{99}$	10	95	50	$\overline{74}$	$\overline{81}$	41	98	0
50	C15	50	0	$\overline{50}$	0	50	0	$\overline{50}$	0	50	0	$\overline{50}$	0	50	0	$\overline{50}$	0
		750 476		0	$\overline{154}$	0	87	0	$\overline{56}$	0	36	0	$\overline{22}$	0	12	0	0
		1500 954		0	$\overline{316}$	0	187	0	$\overline{132}$	0	98	0	$\overline{76}$	0	64	0	$\overline{50}$
		0 2		0	$\overline{8}$	0	13	0	$\overline{20}$	0	26	0	$\overline{32}$	0	40	0	↵

them all in, we need take only those for positive values of x, since the negative ones are the same; but the ordinate for $x = 0$ is not repeated and therefore only half the value—50—is taken.

3 Intervals of division

For Fourier analysis, the representation of a function by a set of ordinates is not completely satisfactory, since it introduces a spurious regularity. It is obvious from the preceding section that, if the function is specified at intervals of 3° $(2\pi/120)$ the 120th order will be the same as the zero order; in general, the nth coefficient and the $(120-n)$th will be identical.

To avoid inaccuracies from this cause, the number of intervals of division must be chosen to be much greater than the number of orders required; for example, 3° (120 intervals) will be ample if the orders are negligible after $n = 10$. In fact, an interval of 12° would suffice. A useful generalization is that the number of ordinates should be about three times the number of orders required.

Similar considerations apply to the number of ordinates at which it is advisable to sum a Fourier series; this should be about three times the highest order. Finer division will not reveal any greater detail, although the highest orders will be represented only crudely.

4 Two-dimensional summations

The processes described in the section can be carried over into two dimensions. For example, if we wish to calculate the diffraction pattern of an irregular aperture, we may represent it as a succession of ordinates (Fig. V.3(a)) and then carry out the Fourier analysis taking the ordinates as

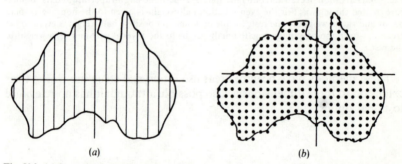

(a) (b)

Fig. V.3. (a) Irregular aperture represented as a set of equidistant ordinates. (b) Irregular aperture represented as a set of lattice points.

the amplitudes of successive terms; one then obtains the transform as a one-dimensional function perpendicular to the ordinates. To obtain the two-dimensional transform one can then take ordinates in different directions, so that the complete result is represented as a set of radial functions.

More satisfactorily, one can represent the aperture by a set of points arranged on a lattice (Fig. V.3(*b*)). The conditions for specifying the dimensions of the lattice are the same as those described in the last section. The transform for an even (centrosymmetric) function is then represented by

$$\sum A \cos{(hx + ky)},$$

where *h* and *k* are integers corresponding to *n* in earlier equations. This may be expanded into

$$\sum A(\cos hx \cos ky - \sin hx \sin ky),$$

and each summation may then be carried out in two stages, as described by Lipson and Beevers (*Proceedings of the Physical Society*, **48**). For a general function, the even and odd parts must be first produced, as indicated in Fig. V.4 (cf. § 3.3.1, where the equivalent procedure in two dimensions is described).

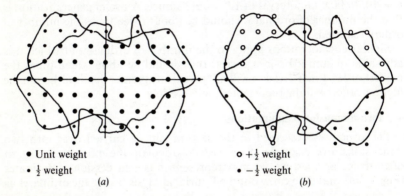

• Unit weight   o + ½ weight

• ½ weight   • − ½ weight

(*a*)   (*b*)

Fig. V.4. Derivation of even and odd functions by superimposing an aperture and its counterpart rotated through π. For the even function half-weight is given to the non-overlapping points and single weight to the rest; for the odd function positive half-weight is given to the erect non-overlapping points, negative half-weight to the inverse part and zero weight to the rest.

These methods have been of great use for crystal-structure work; their extension to three dimensions is also possible although it has no relevance to visual optics.

APPENDIX VI

THE MICHELSON-MORLEY EXPERIMENT

No textbook on optics would be complete without an account of the Michelson–Morley experiment which was carried out around 1887. Since the theme of Chapter 7 would have been interrupted if the account had followed the section (7.8.2) on the Michelson interferometer, we have decided to devote an appendix to it.

The idea of the experiment arose because Michelson realized that his interferometer was sensitive enough to make some measurements that had never before been made. He was concerned by the fact that to explain the aberration of light—the apparent change of the direction of light from a star that occurs because the Earth is in motion around the sun— Fresnel had had to assume that the aether must be at rest as an opaque body moves through it. He therefore set himself the task of measuring the velocity of the Earth with respect to the aether.

The problem had been considered earlier and it had been concluded that it was not possible to construct a piece of apparatus sensitive enough to make the necessary measurement. Michelson showed that, if the velocity of the Earth could be considered as the velocity in its orbit (he had to start with some assumption), his interferometer could make the measurement with reasonable certainty.

The difficulty is that the effect to be measured is a second-order one: the velocity of light can be found only by measuring the time taken for a light signal to return to its starting point; the difference between the time for a journey *up and down* the path of the Earth and that *across* the paths— to take the two extremes—is a second-order quantity derived as follows.

The time t_1 for the up and down journey of a path L is

$$t_1 = \frac{L}{c+v} + \frac{L}{c-v}$$

$$= \frac{L}{c}\left[\left(1 - \frac{v}{c} + \frac{v^2}{c^2} \cdots\right) + \left(1 + \frac{v}{c} + \frac{v^2}{c^2} + \cdots\right)\right],$$

where v is the velocity of the Earth. Thus

$$t_1 = \frac{2L}{c}\left(1 + \frac{v^2}{c^2}\right),$$

if higher-order quantities are neglected.

For the transverse passage, since the light would have effectively to cover a longer path $2L[1 + (v^2/c^2)]^{\frac{1}{2}}$, the time taken would be

$$t_2 = \frac{2L}{c}\left(1 + \frac{1}{2}\frac{v^2}{c^2}\right).$$

The time difference is thus $(L/c)(v^2/c^2)$ which corresponds to a path

difference of Lv^2/c^2. If v is small compared with c, it would appear that the measurement of this quantity would not be possible.

But *is* it too small? The orbital velocity of the Earth is about 10^{-4} of the velocity of light. If L is about 100 cm—a value that Michelson regarded as normal for his experiments—the path difference is 10^{-6} cm, or about $\lambda/50$; this is certainly too small for measurement, but is large enough to suggest that with some modification measurable distance might be possible.

The chief factor in producing a measurable path difference was an increase in the path L; the interferometer was mounted on a stone slab of diagonal about $2m$ (Fig. VI.1) and the light reflected so that it traversed this diagonal several times, giving a total distance L of 1100 cm. Since there

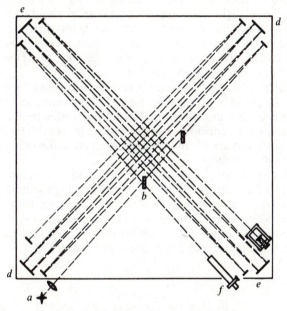

Fig. VI.1. Interferometer used in the Michelson–Morley experiment. (From A. A. Michelson, *Studies in Optics*, Chicago, 1962.)

was no *a priori* knowledge of what might be the direction of the path of the Earth, the whole apparatus was caused to rotate and the maximum difference in path should be twenty-two times that previously calculated—just under half a fringe. Michelson and Morley were confident that they could measure this to accuracy of about 5 %.

This experiment is described in some detail because it is one of the most important experiments in optics. It illustrates the importance of not accepting the impossibility of measuring second-order quantities; and the complete account of the care taken in avoiding spurious effects is well worth reading in the original.

The result was most surprising and disappointing; no certain shift greater than 0·01λ was found (Fig. VI.2). The broken line in Fig. VI.2 shows ⅛ of the displacement expected from the orbital velocity of the Earth. It appeared the velocity of the Earth was zero!

There is just the possibility that the orbital velocity of the Earth happened at the time of the experiment, to cancel out the drift velocity of the solar system. This could not happen at all seasons of the year and therefore more measurements were made at intervals of several months. The result was always zero.

This result was one of the mysteries of nineteenth-century physics. It was perplexing and disappointing to Michelson and Morley, whose skill and patience seemed to have been completely wasted. But now we know that it was not so; it excited Einstein in 1905 to come forward with a new

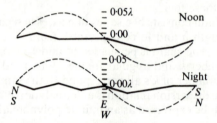

Fig. VI.2. Typical diurnal variation of the fringe shift (From A. A. Michelson, *Studies in Optics*, Chicago, 1962.)

physical principle—relativity—the main assumption of which is that the velocity of light is invariant whatever the velocity of the observer. Thus out of an apparently abortive experiment, a new physical principle arose and a new branch of physics had its beginning.

PROBLEMS

The following problems are intended to give a deeper insight into some of the sections of the book. They are not arranged in a particularly logical order since part of the exercise is to deduce which principles are involved, and, moreover, some of the problems involve more than one section. Notes on a few of them (denoted by asterisks) are given at the end of the section, but it is hoped that these notes will not be referred to prematurely.

*1. Show that the magnifying power of a telescope depends upon the ratio of the focal lengths of the objective and eyepiece.

Why is it not possible to use an objective of infinite focal length and so dispense with the objective altogether?

*2. The foci of a mirror in the form of an ellipsoid of revolution are conjugate points. What is the magnification produced if an object is placed at one of these foci?

3. (a) A long chain consists of a series of masses m separated by springs of equilibrium length a and force constant q (i.e. $F = q(a-x)$ when the spring length is x). The chain is persuaded to undergo longitudinal vibrations of wave-number k and angular frequency ω. Find the relationship $\omega(k)$. Why can a number of k's all correspond to the same ω? Notice that in this example the dispersion relation is non-analytic (i.e. it contains a sine) but that it can still be expressed as an infinite polynomial series (equation (2.9)).

(b) A similar one-dimensional chain of atoms has interatomic forces operating between all atoms, atoms separated by na at equilibrium having force-constants q_n. Show that the $\omega(k)$ relationship can be written as a Fourier series, and illustrate the result in a few simple examples.

(c) If alternate atoms have masses M and m, show that the curve representing $\omega(k)$ splits into two distinct branches. Interpret physically the result that the upper branch has non-zero ω for zero k. Investigate the limiting process $m \to M$.

4. Derive the Fourier coefficients for a zigzag line as an odd function and an even function. Why is the first coefficient predominant?

5. What constituent frequencies are present, and with what amplitudes, in an amplitude-modulated wave:

$$f(t) = (B + a \cos \omega t) \cos pt,$$

where p is the carrier-wave frequency and ω is the modulation frequency? By expanding the wave-form as a power series in $a \cos \omega t$, calculate the constituent frequencies and their amplitudes in a frequency-modulated wave:

$$f(t) = B \cos (pt + a \cos \omega t).$$

When a is much less than unity, so that terms in a^2 and higher powers can be neglected, what properties of the spectrum would distinguish between amplitude and frequency modulation? Use the same ideas to deduce the ghosts occurring in the spectrum from a diffraction grating with periodic errors of (a) density and (b) spacing.

6. An anisotropic medium allows the propagation of two orthogonal plane-polarized characteristic waves with slightly different velocities. An incident wave is plane-polarized with its plane of polarization lying between the two characteristic waves. How does the R-value of the wave (§ 5.2.3) change as it progresses? If the two characteristic waves were circularly polarized, right- and left-handedly, how would the wave progress? And if the characteristic waves were elliptically polarized, as in § 12.7.4, how would it progress?

*7. In Figs. P1 and P2 are given two sets of apertures and their diffraction patterns in arbitrary order and orientation. All the diffraction patterns in each set are produced under approximately the same experimental conditions. Match the apertures and the diffraction patterns, as far as it is possible to do so.

8. Derive the Fraunhofer diffraction pattern of a set of three equally spaced similar slits, by adding the transform of the centre slit to that of the two outer slits.

9. Derive the Fraunhofer diffraction pattern of a set of four equally spaced slits by considering them as

   (a) a pair of identical double slits,
   (b) a double slit in the centre, flanked by a double slit of three times the spacing.

10. Derive the Fraunhofer diffraction pattern of a double slit by considering it as a rectangular aperture with the centre blocked out.

*11. In Fig. P3 are given the Fraunhofer diffraction patterns of two different objects. Deduce what you can about the nature of these objects. You should find that the following properties of the patterns are useful:

   (i) the overall shapes of the patterns,
  (ii) their symmetry,
 (iii) the presence of isolated peaks,
 (iv) the general shapes of these peaks,
  (v) the presence of straight fringes,
 (vi) any pseudo-symmetry.

12. Young's fringes are formed by two coherent point sources side by side. What would the interference pattern be if the one source were directly *in front of* the other?

Thence derive an expression for Newton's rings assuming them to be the interference pattern produced by the images of a point source reflected in the plane surface and the curved surface.

*13. Two similar waves exactly in phase combine to form a wave, which has double amplitude; the intensity is therefore quadrupled. Where does this extra energy come from?

14. By using the concept of a complex refractive index for an absorbing medium, show that

   (a) the angle of refraction depends on the real part of the refractive index only, and
   (b) a medium reflects best those wavelengths which it absorbs best.

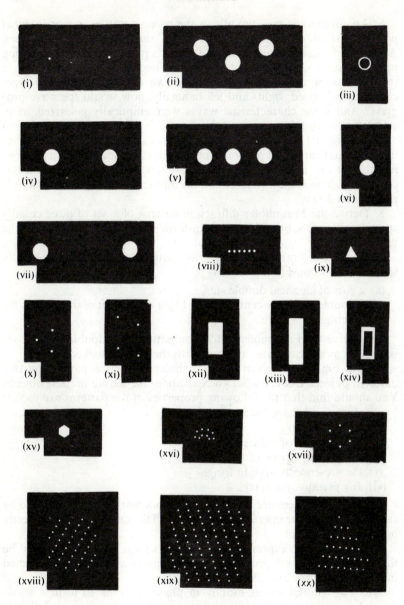

Fig. P.1 (a). A set of apertures.

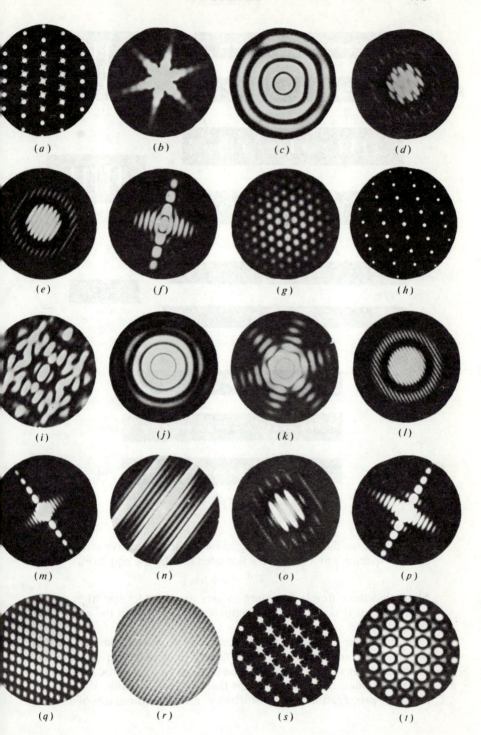

Fig. P.1 (b). The diffraction patterns formed from the apertures in Fig. P.1 (a).

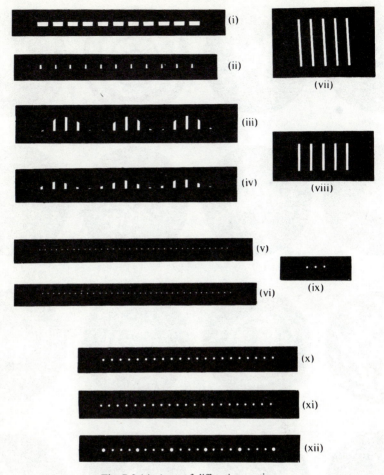

Fig. P.2 (*a*). A set of diffraction gratings.

15. A coarse diffraction grating has a small progressive error, so that the line-spacing s at a distance x is related to x by the equation

$$s^{-1} = a + bx.$$

Show that the diffraction-grating focuses its nth order spectrum on to a plane distant $(bn\lambda)^{-1}$ from it. Compare this result with the principle of the zone-plate.

16. Consider a rectangular waveguide as two pairs of parallel mirrors, of separation respectively a and b (a less than b), which give multiple reflexions of any disturbance between them so that they produce a regular array of similar disturbances. Show that such a waveguide will therefore allow the propagation of the disturbance inside it without loss of intensity

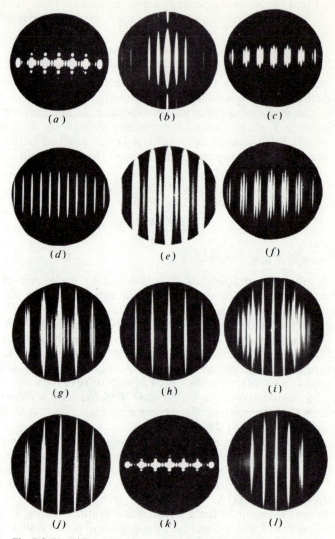

Fig. P.2 (*b*). Diffraction patterns formed by the gratings in Fig. P.2 (*a*).

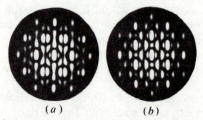

Fig. P.3 (*a*) and (*b*). Diffraction patterns to be investigated.

provided that the walls are perfectly reflecting and that the guide wavelength λ_g in the (m, n) mode is related to the free-space wavelength λ by the formula:

$$4\lambda^{-2} = 4\lambda_g^{-2} + m^2 a^{-2} + n^2 b^{-2}.$$

What is the physical reason for the cut-off wavelength $2b$ above which no propagation is possible? Calculate the effect of partial reflexion by the walls, deducing an attenuation rate in terms of the reflectivity.

17. A Gaussian wave-group of wave-number k_0 and half-width $\sigma(0)$ propagates in a slightly dispersive medium defined by its dispersion relation $\omega(k)$. By expanding $\omega(k - k_0)$ as a Taylor series up to the second order, show that after propagation for a time t the wave-group is centred on position

$$x = v_g t$$

and its half-width has increased to $\sigma(t)$ where

$$\sigma^2(t) = \frac{\sigma^4(0) + u^2 t^2}{\sigma^2(0)};$$

$v_g = \partial\omega/\partial k$ and $u = \partial^2\omega/\partial k^2$.

18. A diffraction grating has lines (denoted by the integer p) whose lengths vary periodically according to the expression $a + b \sin 2\pi p/q$, where b is small compared with a. Find the diffraction pattern of this grating. Derive the result also by using the convolution theorem.

19. The most common observation system for sensitive galvanometers consists of a small concave mirror, about 2 mm diameter and 1 m radius of curvature, mounted on the movement. An illuminated disc containing a fine cross-wire is placed at the centre of curvature of the mirror and its image allowed to fall on a graduated scale. To what accuracy should it be possible to read the position of the cross-wire, assuming that all blurring of the image is caused by diffraction?

20. A reflexion grating is accurately blazed for $\lambda = 7000$ Å in the first order, and the ratio of the intensities of the zero and first orders is found to be 0·09. Treating the grating as composed of flat mirrors of uniform width, find the relative intensities of the other orders. Find also the relative intensities for $\lambda = 4000$ Å.

21. Repeat problem 20 for a transmission grating treating it as composed of prisms of uniform width. If the dispersive power is 0·01, find the ratios of the intensities of the various orders for $\lambda = 4000$ Å.

*22. A strange star consists of a laser with a very long coherence-time, of the order of seconds. Why would it be impossible to measure its diameter with a Brown–Twiss stellar interferometer, but perfectly possible using a Michelson stellar interferometer?

23. Discuss the interference patterns that could be obtained if the mirrors in the Michelson interferometer were replaced by Fresnel double mirrors.

24. A simple microscope views an object illuminated by parallel light obtained from an extended source S. Two variable apertures are fitted.

One is immediately in front of S and therefore controls the coherence of the illumination; the other is in the focal plane of the objective lens of the microscope. How do the degree of resolution and the quantity of spurious detail in the final image depend on the dimensions of the two apertures?

25. A doubly-refracting plate is placed between crossed polarizers, and two perpendicular lines of extinction therefore occur. Show that the transmitted light has a phase difference of π in alternate quadrants defined by these two lines.

26. Assuming that the difference between the principal refractive indices in a photoelastic material is proportional to the strain induced, work out the pattern that would be observed in a model of a simple square-section cantilever beam fixed horizontally at one end with a vertically applied load at the other. Initially, carry out your calculation for a single wavelength, but then consider the effect of white light. If the constant of proportionality is of the order of unity, work out some suitable dimensions and loadings for such a photoelastic experiment. In which direction should the incident light be polarized to give the clearest result?

27. A sandwich consists of three transparent materials with refractive indices μ_1, μ_2 and μ_3, having plane parallel interfaces. The central layer has thickness l.

If a wave of free-space wavelength λ enters normally through the μ_1 layer, show that the reflexion coefficient is

(a) $$\frac{\mu_3 - \mu_1}{\mu_3 + \mu_1} \quad \text{when} \quad \mu_2 l = \frac{\lambda}{2};$$

(b) $$\frac{\mu_2^2 - \mu_3\mu_1}{\mu_2^2 + \mu_3\mu_1} \quad \text{when} \quad \mu_2 l = \frac{\lambda}{4}.$$

In (a) the reflexion is clearly unaffected by the centre layer. Is this also true when μ_2 is complex? In (b) the reflexion can clearly be made zero by choosing μ_2 to be the geometric mean of μ_1 and μ_3. Such is the principle of lens-blooming (§ 7.9.1).

*28. A left-handedly circularly polarized beam of light passes through a half-wave plate so that it emerges right-handedly polarized. By considering the directions and relative magnitudes of the forces

$$\mathbf{B} \times \frac{\partial}{\partial t}(\mathbf{D} - \epsilon_0 \mathbf{E})$$

exerted on the plate (as in § 4.5.4), show that the reversal of the sense of polarization of the wave leads to a torque being experienced by the plate.

29. The problem of the 'gamma-ray microscope' is one of the most famous hypothetical experiments in physics. The idea is to locate the instantaneous position of a moving particle as accurately as possible. The position x in one dimension is observed through a powerful microscope using as short a wavelength λ as possible; the uncertainty in position δx is then given by the resolving power of the instrument and is related to its numerical aperture and λ. During the process of observation at least

one photon must have been scattered by the particle in such a direction as to enter the microscope objective. Conservation of momentum during this scattering process leads to an uncertainty δp in the momentum p of the particle after the observation, since it is impossible to determine exactly in which direction the photon was scattered. Show that δx and δp satisfy the uncertainty relation (equation (11.12))

$$\delta x . \delta p \doteqdot h.$$

30. Show that Snell's law of refraction always applies to wave-vectors in an anisotropic medium, and hence applies to the ray-vectors of ordinary rays only.

31. Investigate the aberrations inherent in a zone-plate with ring diameters as in § 6.3.4. Spherical aberration can be cured for any one focus by correction of the ring diameters in the outer part of the plate; calculate the corrected diameters for the principal focus ($n = 1$). Why cannot an achromatic doublet of zone-plates be constructed?

32. A Michelson interferometer forms fringes from white light which has been passed as a parallel beam through a pair of unsilvered plane-parallel glass plates. How does the visibility of the fringes change with the position of the movable mirror of the interferometer, and what fringe pattern would actually be observed? How would the pattern be modified if the plates were silvered, and how could you use observations of the pattern to deduce the selectivity of such an interference filter?

33. Calculate the relaxation time τ for rotation of permanent dipole in ice in the following manner.

For mathematical simplicity we shall consider a two-dimensional model of a material consisting of an assembly of molecules possessing fixed dipole moments and lying on a crystal lattice. Since the molecules are oriented with respect to the lattice we can assume that the potential energy of a single one is a function of the angle θ between a crystal axis and an axis fixed in the molecule, and can be represented by a function with a number of minima at angles corresponding to preferred directions of orientation. We shall neglect interactions between neighbouring dipole moments (see § (e) below).

(a) Suppose the molecules have two equally preferable orientations, at angles $\theta = 0$ and π. The potential hump between the two preferred directions has height H and the wells can be considered as approximately parabolic in shape (Fig. P4). What is the probability at temperature T that the dipole moment of a molecule will spontaneously reverse during a given period of time?

(b) A steady electric field is now applied parallel to the dipole moment of the molecules in one of the preferred directions. Calculate the dielectric constant of the material as a function of temperature and field.

(c) Show that, for part (b), equilibrium is approached exponentially with a time constant τ. Calculate τ as a function of temperature and field.

(d) Indicate how the calculation in (b) would be modified
  (i) if the field were applied perpendicular to the moment in the preferred directions,
  (ii) if there were more than two symmetrically disposed preferred directions,
  (iii) if one of the two preferred directions were more preferred than the other.
(e) In fact the interaction between the dipoles is very strong. How would this affect the result?

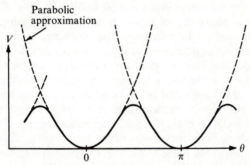

Fig. P.4. Potential function for hindered rotation of a dipolar molecule.

34. By considering atoms on a simple two-dimensional lattice compare the X-ray diffraction patterns (Fraunhofer diffraction) of:
(a) a solid at $0°K$,
(b) a solid at a non-zero temperature,
(c) a liquid,
(d) a gas.

35. This problem is concerned with the detection of underground nuclear explosions by seismic methods.
    A number of detectors at accurately known positions received signals from:
(a) a number of extended random sources within a distance R,
(b) a few definite point sources at a distance much larger than R.
Assuming some simple arrangement for the detectors (e.g. N detectors spaced at uniform intervals along a line), show that studies of the coherence of signals received (by computer if necessary) could distinguish between sources of types (a) and (b), which represent small earthquakes and large underground nuclear explosions. It can be assumed that independent evidence of large earthquakes will be available!

36. Confirm the Kramers–Kronig relations for the relaxation dispersion mechanism. The real part of the dielectric constant is

$$\epsilon_1(\omega) = \epsilon_1(\infty) + \frac{\epsilon_R}{1+\omega^2\tau^2}.$$

From this, deduce the imaginary part by calculating the integral (12.48). (Notice that the fact that the two parts are derived from a complex function which has poles above the real axis is sufficient to ensure that the relation will be obeyed.)

37. Calculate the dispersion curve for acoustic waves in CO_2 by the method suggested in § 10.4.2. How would you expect it to vary with temperature?

38. A Young's slit experiment is carried out with very feeble light so that only one photon is in the system at a given time. In order to observe through which of the two slits the photon passes, a light glass plate of mass M, thickness d, and refractive index μ is placed behind one of them. It will clearly produce a phase-lag of $k(\mu - 1)d$ in a wave passing through it, but this will not destroy interference. The momentum of the photon is reduced while it is in the plate, and so the plate acquires the excess photon momentum. Calculate this momentum transfer, and hence how far the plate moves while the photon is passing through it. Whether or not the photon has passed through can be deduced by measuring the movement. Calculate, however, how much momentum uncertainty must be introduced into the plate in order to make a positional measurement of the required accuracy, and show that this momentum uncertainty affects the time spent by the photon in the plate to such an extent that its phase on leaving is uncertain to the extent of 2π, and hence that the fringes have zero visibility. Consider the significance of this result.

*39. Derive as much information as you can about the cardinal points of the following systems:

(a) a glass sphere in air,

(b) a glass sphere separating two media of different refractive index,

(c) a thick plano-convex lens in air,

(d) a spherical surface separating two media of different refractive index.

Consider the significance of the result for (d) if the surface is plane.

NOTES ON SOME OF THE PROBLEMS

1. Consider an objective of finite focal length and let it approach infinity. Unless the aperture also increases, the resolving power and the intensity will tend to zero.

2. If we consider the system as a symmetrical one the magnification is obviously unity. If we consider the part of the ellipsoid nearest to the object as a small spherical mirror (Fig. N1) the magnification is obviously q/p, and if we consider the farthest part it is equally obviously p/q. In fact, a finite image is *not* formed; the system has zero spherical aberration but infinite coma.

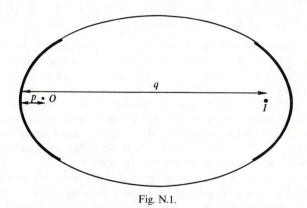

Fig. N.1.

7. The following patterns (P1) should be obvious:

$$e, h, j, l, m, n, o, p, q, r, \text{ and } t.$$

Patterns b and k both have hexagonal symmetry; but (k) is obviously real and (b) is complex and therefore are associated with the hexagon (xv) and the triangle (ix) respectively (§ 3.3.2).

Both (c) and (j) have approximately circular symmetry (the apertures are not precisely circular); but (c) has the smaller 'Airy disc' and is therefore associated with the annular ring (iii) (§ 9.6.4). Similarly, (p) and (f) are associated with the complete and annular rectangular apertures respectively.

The pattern (d) is clearly that of more than two large holes; its aperture is therefore (ii). The intensity distribution along one diameter is the same as that in (o).

The three small holes (x) have diffraction pattern (g). That this looks real, although (x) is non-centrosymmetric, is understandable if we note that with another hole the pattern of holes could be made centrosymmetric.

The patterns (a) and (s) are produced by limiting the lattice (xix) by a triangular (xx) or rectangular (xviii) aperture; thus the diffraction patterns are the convolutions of these two apertures by the reciprocal lattice (h)

(§ 3.5.6). The reciprocal lattice is the interference function, and the diffraction pattern of the aperture (e.g. (b)) is the diffraction function.

The pattern (i) can be recognized as the diffraction pattern of (xvi) only by elimination. There are two ways of finding the correct relative orientations. First, the central peak in (i) is reciprocally related in shape to the overall shape of the pattern; secondly, although (i) has two planes of symmetry, only one is real (approximately NW–SE) and is perpendicular to the plane of symmetry in (xvi).

There is an ambiguity in the orientation of all the non-centrosymmetric apertures; diffraction patterns all have a centre of symmetry.

The correct solution for P2 is as follows.

a	b	c	d	e	f	g	h	i	j	k	l
viii	i	iii	ii	ix	iv	xii	x	v	xi	vii	vi

a, e and k should be obvious, b and d are recognizable by the fall-off in intensities of the orders. c and f show no variation of ghost structure with order and therefore are produced by gratings with regular errors in some property other than the positions of the diffracting elements (§ 7.7.3). g shows a fourfold repetition; also the spacing is not regular. j shows slight regular displacements of the diffracting elements (examine xi carefully!); l shows slight irregular displacements; i shows considerable irregular displacements (§ 7.7.4); h is perfect. All these diffraction patterns have backgrounds that are negligible around the centre.

11. The fact that the patterns cover a circular area suggests that the diffracting objects are sets of circular holes. The patterns are both obviously real and therefore have a centre of symmetry; the symmetry of the diffraction pattern therefore shows that they have two perpendicular planes of symmetry. The elongated shapes of the peaks shows that the overall shapes of the diffracting objects are elongated perpendicularly. The presence of vertical straight fringes shows that they consist of two similar parts. If we allow for these fringes we can see that the separate parts have hexagonal symmetry.

In fact, the diffracting patterns are pairs of hexagonal arrangements of holes, differently orientated in (a) and (b) in the only two ways consistent with the observed symmetry.

13. It is always necessary, in this sort of problem, to find an experimental arrangement for producing two such waves, e.g. Michelson's interferometer. It is always found that there is a loss of energy elsewhere in the system.

22. As is discussed in § 8.4.5, the Brown–Twiss interferometer measures correlation between fluctuations in the beams received by the two photocells, whereas the Michelson stellar interferometer measures correlation between the individual waves. Consequently, since a light beam fluctuates with a period of the order of the coherence time τ_c there would be no fluctuation to correlate in the laser beam unless it were observed for a very long time, much greater than τ_c. In the present example this would involve observation over many hours, and the observation

would then have to be repeated for a variety of photocell separation distances.

39. (a) and (b). The nodal points must coincide at the centre. For (a) the principal points coincide with the nodal points.

(c) One nodal point and hence one principal point must lie in the curved surface.

(d) The principal points must lie in the curved surface; the nodal points must coincide with the centre of curvature.

BIBLIOGRAPHY

The following list gives a short selection of books and articles that contain more complete discussions of some of the topics contained in the book.

BORN, M. & WOLF, E. (1964). *Principles of Optics*. Pergamon, Oxford.

BLEANEY, B. I. & BLEANEY, B. (1957). *Electricity and Magnetism*. Oxford University Press.

BRILLOUIN, L. (1960). *Wave Propagation and Group Velocity*. Academic Press, New York.

BUNN, C. W. (1961). *Chemical Crystallography*. Oxford University Press.

FEYNMAN, R. P. & HIBBS, A. R. (1965). *Quantum Mechanics and Path Integrals*. McGraw-Hill, New York.

FRÖHLICH, H. (1949). *Theory of Dielectrics*. Oxford University Press.

GEAKE, J. E. (1967). 'Surfaces of Constant Order for Parallel-Plane Interferometers.' *Optica Acta*, **14**, 71.

LANDAU, L. D. & LIFSHITZ, E. M. (1960). *Electrodynamics of Continuous Media*. Oxford University Press.

LIPSON, H. & BEEVERS, C. A. (1936). 'An Improved Numerical Method of Two-dimensional Fourier Synthesis for Crystals.' *Proceedings of the Physical Society*, **48**, 772.

MARGENAU, H. & MURPHY, G. M. (1964). *The Mathematics of Physics and Chemistry*. Van Nostrand, New York.

MERTZBACHER, E. (1961). *Quantum Mechanics*. Wiley, New York.

MICHELSON, A. A. (1927). *Studies in Optics*. Reprinted by University of Chicago Press, 1962.

SMITH, F. G. (1962). *Radioastronomy*. Penguin Books, Harmondsworth.

TAYLOR, C. A. & LIPSON, H. (1964). *Optical Transforms*. Bell, London.

INDEX

Abbe, 15
  theory of image formation, 15, 18, 270ff
  sine condition, 272
aberrations in lenses, 269, 287, 382, 443–7, 453
  astigmatism, 444
  chromatic, 443, 446, 451
  coma, 443–4, 448, 450
  curvature of field, 445
  electron lens, 295, 383
  spherical, 287, 443, 451, 454
aberration of light, 465
absorption, band, in relaxation dispersion, 320–1
  coefficient, 309
  in crystal optics, 132, 136
  by double-photon transition, 375
  of electrons, 386
  related to change in refractive index, 428–34
  of spectral line, 245, 310–11, 349–50
acoustic, beats, 255
  boundary conditions, 34
  dispersion in CO_2, 324
  impedance, 325
  waves, 26, 34
    scattering by, 378
    spectrum in crystal, 404
adiabatic fast passage, 363ff
aerial, radio, 412
  array, 415–18
  effective aperture of, 412–13
Airy disc, 185–6, 199, 252, 411–12
alkali metals, 244
alloys, X-ray diffraction by, 216
ammonia maser, 354–62
Ampère, 8
  circuit theorem, 64, 99
amplitude, 23
  of Fourier component, 39
  fluctuations in, 240, 254, 262
  relation to intensity, 60
  vector, 36
amplitude-phase diagram, 147, 152
  for coherent scattering, 307–8
  in Fresnel diffraction, 152–9
  integration by, 160
analogue, gravitational, 384
  electrical, 323, 384
anastigmat, 445
angular diameter, 235, 249, 252–5
angular frequency, 24–5

angular magnification, 441
angular momentum,
  of photon, 260, 376
  in quantum mechanics, 333–5, 354
anisotropic materials, 103ff, 375, 383, 419–28
anomalous dispersion, 33, 308–15, 428–9, 434
  experimental investigation, 311–12
  group velocity in, 313–15
anomalous scattering method, 389
antiferromagnetism, 395–6
aperture, 268
  of diplole, effective, 412–13
  effect on instruments, 277ff
  of electron lens, 383
  of microscope, 268, 277
  numerical, 268, 278
  stop, 267–8, 278
  synthesis, 417–18
aplanatic, points, 444, 449
  systems, 444
apochromat, 447
apodization, 280, 284–5
Arago, 4
Archimedes, 2
Argand diagram, 152, 288–9, 428
argument of complex quantity, 301, 340, 429
Aristophanes, 9
array, of delta-functions, 51–2, 55, 205, 238, 256
  of radio aerials, 415–18
astigmatism, 444
atomic, electric dipole moment, 301, 336, 338–49, 355, 373
  magnetic dipole moment, 334
  'photograph', 296
  polarizability, 303, 306, 356, 362, 373
attenuation, 29–31

Babinet, compensator, 134
  theorem 198–200
    conditions for validity 200
Bartholinus, 7
beats, acoustic, 255
  between laser beams, 256
  between light waves, 255
bending of lenses, 444, 452
Bertrand lens, 136
Bessel functions, 184–5
Betelgeuse, 254
biaxial crystal, 126, 131, 135, 375

483

Kitty Tatsh and friend doing the high kick on over-hanging rock,
1890's-early 1900's.

Courtesy of Yosemite National Park Collections

Women and Western American Literature

Women and Western American Literature

by

Helen Winter Stauffer
and
Susan J. Rosowski

The Whitston Publishing Company
Troy, New York
1982

INDEXED IN MLA

Copyright 1982
Helen Winter Stauffer & Susan J. Rosowski

Library of Congress Catalog Card Number 81-52812

ISBN 0-87875-229-3

Printed in the United States of America

For

Virginia Faulkner and Bernice Slote
whose work reminds us of the excellence we strive toward

TABLE OF CONTENTS

I
SHAPING THE WESTERN FRONTIER:
WOMEN IN HISTORY

II
FROM FACT TO FICTION: MYTH AS FILTER

PREFACE

The idea for this collection of essays grew naturally from our awareness that women have been—and still are—largely excluded from discussions of literature of the American West. This is a serious concern in itself, but it becomes especially so in view of the West's enormous influence in shaping American thought. Frederick Jackson Turner's essay on the American frontier remains the starting point for discussions of the American character. Affirming Turner's premise, if not his conclusions, scholars agree "as America's most formative myth-subject the West has altered the presumptions of Americans about their place in both the political world and the moral universe."[1] In literature, this myth of the West has taken various forms. It is seen in the traditional western formula which glorifies violence and conquest as "the imposition of a Lockean scheme of property, labor and law on a wilderness originally controlled by a people with an opposing scheme" (pp. 127-8); and it is seen in the concept of a heroic that indiscriminately glorifies male endeavor: "A male character in American literature may be a hero in almost any circumstance; all he has to do is struggle, see things as they really are, and benefit from his knowledge."[2]

Assumptions such as these provoke reappraisals. Following World War II, a broadened global perspective led to the counterculture of the Fifties and the anti-politics of the Sixties, with their "widespread refusal to believe in our foreign policies, domestic programs, traditional leadership, customs—past" (p. 129). Changes in western literature followed, for "inevitably, the debunking of the past led to the central myth of the Western Hero and Western Settlement. The Old West had to go. How could we believe in the right of anti-social gunslingers to shoot down opponents in the townstreets once we began to believe that America was an international gunman whose victims were crying out against her" (p. 129). And inevitably, Western heroes assumed new forms: *Butch Cassidy and the Sundance Kid, The*

Wild Bunch, and *Easy Rider,* for example, present the antihero and the outmoded hero. Unable to conquor the wilderness and no longer confident of even a personal code, the hero turns inward, gains a new self-consciousness and an awareness of "life's insoluble complexities" (p. 148). Yet these new western heroes remain as sadly—and dangerously—limited as their predecessors. They remain isolated from full adult human experience, for in them, "disconnection. . .continues between the new western hero and the western woman" (p. 145), and they continue patterns of oppression and exploitation, for to them "women are strictly sexual and work objects" (p. 148).

A second reappraisal is asking more basic questions of the western American tradition, both past and present. Where are the women in this tradition? What were the historical circumstances of these women, and in what ways are (and aren't) these circumstances reflected in literature? What are these women's criteria for value, and what perceptual patterns do they use to order their world? In asking such questions of those for whom the male westering myth is impossible or unacceptable, we may come to understand more fully what it is to be an American—to struggle to survive in the face of this myth and to find more realistic, human, and satisfying ones to counter it.

Authors of essays in this volume have contributed to ongoing efforts to answer these questions. *Women and Western American Literature* is in some respects a sequel to *Women, Women Writers, and the West,* edited by L. L. Lee and Merrill Lewis in 1979. Like that volume, *Women and Western American Literature* includes many essays written by members of the Western Literature Association and presented at one of the Association's annual meetings. And as did the earlier contributors, authors here have written on a wide range of subjects and have employed a broad variety of critical approaches. Some critics return to first-hand accounts, listening to voices previously ignored and, after doing so, reexamining historical and literary versions of women in the West. Susan Armitage goes to letters, diaries, oral histories, and autobiographical novels to explore the image of women as reluctant pioneers, noting "the female subculture did not exist in the first stage of the pioneer process" and discussing implications of forced frontier individualism. June Underwood looks at the historical facts of the second stage

of the westward movement, concluding that there was an "immediate transplanting of women's concerns and women's subculture" into village settlements, discussing the historical significance of women's clubs and their absence or distortion in literature, then considering reasons that "literary visions [are] so antithetical to historical truth." Two accounts by individual women further illustrate these generalizations: Darlene Ritter finds in one woman's diary an eloquent description of emigrating to Nebraska from Switzerland; Margaret Solomon reveals the feminist dimensions of Julia Archibald Holmes's account of traveling West and (the first woman to do so) climbing Pikes Peak.

Other critics concentrate upon the ways in which myth filters reality. Barbara Meldum looks at western literature that does—and doesn't—present "women who go beyond the image stage to become vital, active human beings." David Remley compares the historical Sacajawea of the Lewis and Clark Expedition with the mythical Sacajawea in various fictional accounts, and Caren J. Deming explores broad implications of this distortion in "Miscegenation in Popular Western History and Fiction." Two critics interpret the shaping of fact into fiction in individual works: in "The Emergence of Helen Chalmers," Frances Malpezzi discusses Frank Waters' use of a historical prototype to develop his fictional protagonist in *The Woman at Otowi Crossing;* in "The Western Roots of Feminism in Agnes Smedley's *Daughter of Earth,*" Kathleen L. Nichols interprets Smedley's use of autobiographical details to present the effect of the westering myth of women and children. And two authors—Dorothy M. Johnson and A. B. Guthrie, Jr., in interviews with Sue Mathews, discuss their own fictional treatments of women in the West.

Other essays concentrate upon differences between myth and reality. Frances Kaye points out that Hamlin Garland's writing about women was inconsistent: Garland spoke against historical inequities; at the same time, he perpetuated the myth of women as morally different from and superior to men. John J. Murphy interprets contrasting versions of the American West by recognizing that *The Virginian* and *My Ántonia* are "different sides of the western coin." The contrast helps explain Beret's madness in *Giants in the Earth,* Catherine Farmer argues.

Rölvaag uses Norse mythology to suggest that Beret's natural sexuality, which aligns her with the fertility goddess Freya, is misdirected and absorbed by the land as it awakens, then takes its revenge upon its human interlopers. Patricia Lee Yongue reveals economic dimensions of Cather's treatment of Marian Forrester in *A Lost Lady,* comparing it with Defoe's *Moll Flanders.* The contrast extends to more recent writing about women. Joseph J. Wydeven explores Wright Morris's changing treaments of women whose natures reflect or conflict with American myths. And Mary Ellen Williams Walsh, in her discussion of Jean Stafford's somber short stories of young women struggling to survive, reveals modern forms of the Western myth of women as adjuncts to male heroes.

Finally, alternatives sought by individual writers are the subjects of several essays. Barbary Rippey argues that in *Cheyenne Autumn* Mari Sandoz renders the white myth of conquest from an Indian perspective and attempts to move the reader to a new mythic paradigm. Samuel Bellman discusses Constance Rourke's "mental language" of the West—themes and images that inform her work and express her ideals. Melody Graulich writes of Eudora Welty's *The Robber Bridegroom* as a "woman's tall tale because power comes through emotional rather than physical strength" and suggests that "Welty's interpretation of western values presents an implicit criticism of the dominating male tradition." Two critics discuss writers who stress relationships of interaction and continuity with nature. James C. Work argues that Mary Austin's *The Land of Little Rain* "will be recognized as one of the touchstone works of American nature writing" and that it is incomparable in two respects: "one is the set of abstract impressions left. . .in the reader's mind, and the other is the set of moral statements concerning the proper relationship of the human animal to the land in its natural state." Elaine Jahner sees in the writing of the Indian poet, Paula Gunn Allen, explorations of ways in which "a traditional tribal heritage can be a source of insight to the meaning of contemporary America."

These essays, while certainly valuable for the answers they provide, are perhaps even more so for the questions they provoke. Graulich, writing of Eudora Welty's *The Robber Bridegroom* as a woman's tall tale, suggests possibilities for reinterpreting the male-oriented mode. Walsh, Nichols, Work, Malpezzi,

and others, in discussing ways in which women identify with the land, lead to broader questions of this relationship: do common images, metaphors, and perceptual patterns run through women's writing of the land, and, if so, do these images, metaphors, and patterns differ significantly from those employed by male writers? Certainly, as all the authors suggest, we need to continue to search for literature that deals with aspects of women's lives previously ignored or misrepresented, and to continue to speculate on their significance to larger interpretations of western American literature.

* * * * * * * * * *

In conclusion, we wish to express our appreciation to some of the people and organizations who made this volume possible. First, we wish to thank the contributors for the essays we are proud to present here and for cooperation and support throughout the project. Second, we are indebted to the English Department, Kearney State College, and to the English Department, University of Nebraska at Omaha, for financial aid and staff support. We are especially grateful to Diane Peterson, Pat South, and Jane Moshier for their secretarial help. Finally, we owe much to the Western Literature Association, for it is providing a forum by which we may explore such subjects as women and western American literature.

Susan J. Rosowski
Helen Winter Stauffer

NOTES

[1]Jay Gurian, *Western American Writing: Tradition and Promise* (Deland, Florida: Everett/Edwards, 1975), p. 127. Subsequent references to this source will be provided in the text.

[2]William H. Gilman, "The Hero and the Heroic in American Literature: An Essay in Definition," in *Patterns of Commitment in American Literature,* ed. Marston LaFrance (Toronto: University of Toronto Press, 1967), p. 17.

ACKNOWLEDGEMENTS

We wish to thank the Nebraska State Historical Society (Solomon Butcher collection) and Yosemite National Park Collections for permission to use photos in this volume and Adrienne Rich and the W. W. Norton & Company for permission to use lines from "An Old House in America."

Russian-Germans arriving at Lincoln, Nebraska

I

SHAPING THE WESTERN FRONTIER:

WOMEN IN HISTORY

The Civilizers:
Women's Organizations and Western American Literature

June O. Underwood

Western American literature, almost from the moment of its inception, has had to deal with uncomfortable confrontations of myth and reality. Because we are continually seduced by those magnificent images of the Yeoman Farmer and the Conquering Cowboy, writers have had to grapple with ways to embody the deepest hopes and fears of a people (represented by the grand archetypes) and still maintain historical actuality.[1]

This struggle to incorporate authenticity into the reverberating formulas of the unconscious is even more difficult when writers deal with women. Literary tradition has been a particularly strong force in the making of Western and Plains literature. And, literary traditions about women in the West and on the Plains, like those elsewhere, view women as "the other"—not creatures who grow, learn, and expand to heroism—but as vehicles for enlarging the male hero's sense of the challenge and terror of the land. Cather is, of course, an exception to this generalization, as is Mari Sandoz. Both these writers depict women who, as heroes themselves, must carve out a space for themselves in a society which would wish to keep them "merely female." But most women characters in western literature exist as the female archetypes—the mother, the victim, the seducer, the seduced.[2]

These images are not absolutely wrong: they are, however, distortions and narrowings of the reality of women's lives. In particular, the study of women's relationships to one another has opened up new understandings of how ordinary women lived and thought. In the last ten years, feminist scholars have examined closely nineteenth-century women's bonds to other women. However, much of this research on the women's subculture is

related to English and east coast American communities. My task, then, is to show the applicability of these historical studies to western women settlers, and to show how, in areas like Kansas, the eastern patterns were reinforced by frontier conditions. Then I will examine Western literature for its use and abuse of the historical actualities.

One limitation of this study is that it deals with white middle-class women and is perhaps more applicable to town women than to farm and ranch women. Studies of the sub-cultures of chicano, native American, and black women remain to be done. White agricultural women would have participated in the ideology of women's sphere, but been less able to fulfill the roles I will speak of because of the conditions of their lives. Thus the "civilizing" spoken of in the title was, insofar as I am able to determine, predominately a white middle-class concept.

Women's history in America begins to differ significantly from male mainstream history during the period of American industrialization (1800-1830). With the movement of manufacturing out of the home came a separation of male and female spheres—woman's becoming exclusively private and domestic, man's public and economic. "Work" became differentiated from "home." Women were closed out of the public economic into the private domestic sphere, and, in response to that separation and increasing isolation, they closed ranks into what Nancy Cott calls "The Bonds of Womanhood." During the nineteenth century, women's most intimate emotional relationships were likely to be with other women. Sexually and economically a woman's ties were with the male, but emotionally and spiritually, she reserved for herself and her female friends a powerful separate sphere. In addition, she was given almost total responsibility for the moral and spiritual well-being, first of her family, then of the nation. Both male and female, in the nineteenth century, generally agreed that while the female was physically, intellectually, and economically the inferior of men, spiritually and emotionally and for purposes of nurturing, she was clearly the superior.[3]

The important aspect of this history for my purposes is that women bonded together and came to believe in that bonding as natural. This bonding can be seen in the rapid rise of formalized

female organizations in the period from 1800 to 1840. Female moral reform societies, sewing circles, missionary support groups, and benevolent societies were ubiquitous and indicate that women formed separate social groupings and welfare functions. These groups were sometimes mixed and sometimes they had a male clergyman as their public figure, but they were predominantly female.[4]

By 1840 women were becoming prominent in abolition societies; by 1850 in the women's rights movement. Women gained political and practical experience in the Sanitary Commissions of the Civil War and learned politics the hard way when the black suffrage movement jettisoned the feminist cause after the Civil War. By 1880 the women had taken over the temperance movement. Through organizing into groups, learning parliamentary procedure, and fighting their way to self-confidence through politicized structures like the Woman's Christian Temperance Union, women became accustomed to public and political roles. They extended their private concerns to the community, crusading with a call for "Home Protection" and "Municiple Housekeeping." By 1900, the General Federation of Women's Clubs, which arose from study clubs originally functioning as support and self-help groups, was advocating such measures as tough child labor laws, minimum wage and maximum hour laws, woman's suffrage, clean water and pure food, and decent public charities and correctional institutions.[5]

What has this phenomenon to do with women on the frontier? The women who moved west brought with them all the concerns and ideologies which were part of their eastern existences. The period of the ideological and emotional bonding of women preceded the movement across the Mississippi to the western frontiers. In "Women and Their Families on the Overland Trail to California and Oregon, 1842-1867," Faragher and Stansell document the ways women tried to reinforce the domestic ideology on their trek across the continent. Beyond carrying with them the domestic ties and nurturing roles of which Faragher and Stansell speak, they also carried knowledge and community approval of female organizations. C. I. H. Nichols, activist in eastern suffrage groups, sat in on the state constitutional convention in Kansas and gained property rights and child custody for women, reforms impossible in states further east.

Mother Bickerdyke, a Civil War nurse and reformer, goaded the Kansas Woman's Relief Corps into fighting for the rights of Civil War veterans and their families. The WCTU had its greatest impact in Kansas during the heyday of the cattle frontier there. Between 1900 and 1905, throughout the West, rest rooms (lounges) were built for the relief of wives and children of farmers in town for market days.[6]

In other words, the women who went west were civilizers in that they felt a moral imperative, a god-given duty, to transmit religious, social, and humane values to a lawless land. They brought with them and worked hard to cultivate the seeds of public welfare and reform organizations. Men were the economic explorers; consequently, sheriffs protected horses, not children. Women were concerned with human welfare; hence they became the strongest advocates of reforms like temperance.

Historians have tended to see women's reform work as primarily urban, growing out of the horrors of industrialization. But in the village settlements of the West, there was an immediate transplanting of women's concerns and women's sub-culture. The first state referendum for women's suffrage was held in Kansas in 1867. Lawrence, Kansas, had raids on saloons in that town before the Civil War. The PEO, an educational study club, was established in Meade, Kansas, in 1888, three years after Meade County and the town came into existence. Wherever there was a group of women, women's clubs and organizations sprang up. Because of their isolation, rural women would have remained outside the strongest club movements. But few women were exclusively rural. We tend to forget the extreme mobility and transient nature of frontier settling. In any given span of ten years, historians have shown that a large proportion of a given population will have moved on.[7] Thus farm and ranch women often had been or became town women. And it was in the towns and villages of the Western frontier, far more numerous then than now, that women fought to civilize.

These reforms, temperance for example, are often seen as foolish. Yet Mary Austin reminds us that for women in the nineteenth century, liquor had ugly manifestations:

> One observes, on the part of the younger generation who know

nothing about it, a disposition to sentimentalize about the saloon of the last quarter of a century. . . . But to the women who prayed against it, who went on from that to organize against it, who achieved an unbelievable legislation against the saloon, it was nothing of the sort. . . . It [the saloon] was a place of sour, stale smells, of loud foolish laughter. . .raucous, quarreling voices. It was a place from which might issue at any moment people you knew, other girls' fathers, forcible ejections of sodden and bleary men who proceeded to be violently sick on the sidewalk. . . . There was always a stench coming out of saloons in the eighties, stale beer, hot whiskey breaths, the smell of vomit, the faint un-mistakable odor of maleness on the loose. . . . For Mary there grew up an implication of disgust about the half-screened doors of saloons in the Middlewest, the odors and suggestiveness, that had no counterpart in her experience until years after she en-countered, in the half-screened latrines of the French capitol, the same odors and implications of offense. . . .[8]

Women who were members of Ladies Benevolent Societies had to do battle for the victims of male greed and economics. In Dodge City and Wichita, the Ladies Benevolent Societies had to fight the towns' businessmen to be allowed to aid the starving settlers living through the drought and grasshopper years of 1872-1874. The businessmen, speculating that bad news about conditions would hinder immigration to the area, sabotaged the women's efforts. After the drought passed, the women pub-lished open letters to the town fathers, exposing their calloused disregard for human life.[9]

However, even granting that western women, in their own sub-culture, were powerful forces for important social welfare and reform, we have yet to show the relevance of this historical data to the literature of the West. In Western fiction, women's organizations are used in one of two ways: they are either trivial, used primarily to establish character, or they are more important and used to establish the malevolence of woman's desire to control. However, in autobiography, particularly in the work of Mary Austin and Wallace Stegner, the organizations and their work are seen as crucial to women's experiences and to the civilizing of the West.

References to women's clubs are quite sparse. While his-

torically these groups were pervasive, they scarcely exist in literature. When they are present, it is most often in scarcely notice-
able asides. In *Giants in the Earth,* for example, those women
who can't keep their minds on the sermon think about forming a
congregation and a ladies aid society: "and that would be great
fun, with meetings and cakes and coffee and sewing. . . ."[10] In
Bess Streeter Aldrich's *Spring Came on Forever,* Ida, wife of the
Lincoln, Nebraska, banker, helps organize, and becomes a leader
in, the City Women's Club. Her activities are part of her hard-
working, common-sense benevolence.[11]   Passing references,
then, to female organizations appear but have little significance
other than establishing a general sense of personality. When women's clubs are given a larger role, however, the literary uses
form a significant pattern.

In the novels where such organizations have a strong importance, they are used to trivialize or reveal the malevolence
of the women involved. In Sinclair Lewis's *Main Street,* Carol
hopes to find culture and wisdom in the Thanatopsis Club, but
instead discovers twittering, bubble-headed pretentiousness.
In *Cimmaron,* Sabra forms the Philomathean Club as "part of a
defense against these wilds." The first member she plans to
invite turns out to be the mistress of a local gambler. Sabra is
suitably chastened by her *faux pas.* The work of the club can be
summed up by the women's reactions when Sabra reads a paper
entitled "Whither Oklahoma?" "It had been received with much
pleasure on the part of Osage's twenty most exclusive ladies, who
had heard scarcely a word of it, their mind being intent on
Sabra's new dress."[12]

Even more often, women's organizations and activities are
used in Western literature to show the pernicious nature of pub-
lic-minded women. Myrtle, in *Spring Came on Forever,* is a generation later than Ida, and is also a joiner. However, Myrtle's joining is part of her unpleasant, insensitive character. She is a social
climber and neglects her home and husband for her clubs. Aldrich is sarcastic about Myrtle's activities: Myrtle "had many
interests outside her home by that time, belonging as she did to
so many organizations in town for the betterment of her mind,
and one or two for her soul."[13]   Neither Myrtle's mind nor her
soul seems to have derived much from her club work. In Cather's
One of Ours Claude Wheeler's wife, Enid, works for prohibition

in Nebraska. Enid's tight-lipped temperance work is clearly at odds with the open-hearted nature of her Bohemian neighbors who abhor prohibition. Worse, her temperance activity is a piece with her religiosity, her meticulously uncomfortable housekeeping, and her sexual and emotional frigidity. Leonard Dawson, a neighbor of the Wheelers, says about Enid: " 'That woman is a fanatic. She ain't content with practicising prohibition on humankind; she's begun now on the hens.' " Claude is a sensitive, warm human being whose existence is doomed by the frigid insensitive persons who surround him. Enid is by far the worst of the group. Her club work seems to have as its only identifiable end making men miserable.[14]

To generalize, women's activities within organizations when they appear have either little importance in Western fiction or are shown as trivial or pernicious. The most frequently occurring image seems to be kin to that of the women in the movie *Stagecoach,* the old biddies and harridans who run the whore-with-the-heart-of-gold out of town.

Why are these literary visions so antithetical to historical truth? One simple reason is that popularizers like Edna Ferber have accepted the traditional ideas about the West, ideas which, even when dealing sympathetically with women, tend to view their communal activities with suspicion. Moreover, Ferber wrote *Cimmaron* after the reform impetus for the clubs had declined. Her personal experience of women's clubs may well have been of their status-seeking rather than their reforming.

Moreover, American literature has always idealized the loner, the individual who acts in isolation, and who, when his space gets too crowded, "lights out for the territory." This impulse is naturally magnified in literature about the West, where space and isolation become basic themes. The romantic individualistic streak in the literature is especially damaging to writing about ordinary women's lives, since community rather than individualism was basic to them.

Finally, when the bonding is not ignored or trivialized, it is seen from the perspective of an outsider. Cather is a genius, but a lonely one. Women's clubs must have seemed antithetical to her memories of the freedom of the space and the land which

she celebrates so well. The cramped parlors in which women met would have seemed symbolic to her of their cramped lives and ideals.

Men writing about women's bonding have almost always feared it and thus turned it into something used against themselves. Some of the fear is undoubtedly Freudian; most is probably cultural. In a society in which groups separate themselves from one another, a mutual distrust will inevitably grow. Nineteenth-century America fostered that kind of mistrust, and it shows in the literature.

It would probably be unnecessary to say any more or even to have written this paper if this were just a sad demonstration of another failure. But I did find more. At a conference on Women's Studies a few years ago, when I was first thinking about women's organizations, I heard Meridel LaSoeur, a Plains poet, describe the WCTU women as "guerilla warriors." Her mother, a staunch member of that organization, had had to kidnap her children and take them from Texas to Kansas to get them away from her alcoholic husband.[15] Kansas gave women the right to custody of children because of the work of suffragists at the first state constitutional convention.

Thinking of LaSoeur's testimony, I stopped investigating novels and turned to non-fiction.

In Mary Austin's autobiography, *Earth Horizon*, Austin speaks at length about the activities and meanings of women's groups. In the 1880's women believed that children were genetically deformed because of the father's alcoholism:

> I realized there is doubt in high quarters as to the harm a habitual drunkard can do to his unborn offspring; there was less doubt when Mary was young. It was in view of the possibilities that a drunken father was believed to visit on his unborn offspring that the question of divorce and the right of women to choose when and under what conditions they will bear children was first admitted to the Protestant consciousness in the U.S. .... I remember the first woman who was allowed to speak in our church on the right of women to refuse to bear children to habitual drunkards, and my mother putting her arm across my knees and taking

my hand in one of the few natural gestures of a community of woman interest she ever made me.[16]

One of the lost items of women's history is what was said during the closed, women-only meetings of the suffrage and temperance workers. These closed meetings, held every few months from 1880 to 1916 in just about every town and hamlet, evidently were revolutionary, advocating a woman's right to control her own body and to refuse to visit the sins of the father on the children.

Austin not only examines the question of alcoholism as it affected economically and sexually powerless women of her mother's generation but also describes the impetus for women's bonding:

> I remember a pretty German woman who used to bring her three children to our house to be left until their father recovered from "one of his spells." I recall how she came one night with a great bloody bruise on her face, and my mother insisting on treating it. . .and the unwiped tears on my mother's face while the two women kept up between them the pretense of a blameless accident.[17]

Besides this testimony to the extent of feeling and community bonding among late nineteenth-century women on the frontier, another prominent western writer testifies to the impact of their organizing. In *Wolf Willow*, Wallace Stegner looks at the various civilizations which inhabited and then deserted his childhood home on the northern prairies. These include the Indians, the Metís (half French, half Indian nomads), the French traders, the Mounted Police, ranchers, and finally, his kind, the sodbusters. Stegner's final concern is not so much with his boyhood as noble savage and part of the last mythic frontier, but with the question of indigenous civilization. What groups would take root and grow in his country? Most of those he describes left no trace of their presences. However, at the end of the book, he takes a walk through the village of Whitemud:

> My walk has brought me back around by the elevators and a vacant lot full of rod weeders and tractors. . . . I come up toward Main Street. . .and just short of the side street leading to the post

office. . .I find myself looking in a half-curtained window of an applegreen ceiling and part of a bare applegreen wall. It is a tiny shack. . .the sign above the doorway reads "Farm Wives' Rest Home."

Weather-beaten, warped, the paint flaking off its shiplap, its windows flyspecked and with alluvial fans of dust in the corners of the frames. . .it hardly suggests rest. Behind it a path leads to a privy. . .the wind has cornered candy-bar wrappers and gum wrappers in the doorway. . . . I stand bemused. . .thinking here is a quintessential Whitemud. Here is a human institution, born of a compassionate and humane impulse, and tailored to a felt need, falling so short of its intention that it would draw a snicker from anyone who didn't stop to think first. If he thought first, he might elect to honor the impulse, rather than scorn the result, however shoddy.

Stegner's sensitivity to the history of the peoples of his region makes him instantly move beyond the apparently trivial nature of the ugly building. He sees it for what it is and what it represents:

For the snickerer should remember that in all of Whitemud, . . .there is not a service station with a toilet to which a woman from the country can take a desperate child. There is not a park where a tired woman can sit down, not a public library where she can wait out the hours of heat and tedium while her husband buys feed or seed or gopher poison. . .or sprawls around the Grain Growers elevator gassing with friends, or visits the licensed premises of the hotel. . . . Hamlin Garland did that rural unfortunate tenderly in the story called "A Day's Pleasure," and Sinclair Lewis's stepmother spent a lot of her time promoting just such a place as this Farm Wives' Rest Home in the town that would become Gopher Prairie.[18]

Stegner recognizes the need for these particular amenities (part of a thorough campaign by the Federation of Women's Clubs to alleviate the discomforts of rural women's lives). He also sees the rest rooms as one of the few, but important, signs of the vitality of the community spirit. It is a sign of civilization, growing out of local conditions, answering local needs. "It is little enough. . .but it is the most humane institutuion in

all that village, and it is purely native, the answer to a local need. If it is given up as soon as the town gets plumbing and a well-equipped service station, well and good. What matters is that it exists now to acknowledge a community responsiblity. . . ."[19]

Stegner, if you remember the last paragraph of *Wolf Willow*, decided not to fault Whitemud for not being great, for having only "marginal or sub-marginal community and cultural life. . . ." because "with its occasional impulse to the humane. . .[exemplified by the Farm Wives' Rest Home] not unhopeful. Give it a thousand years."[20]

Thus, while fiction has tended to deny the validity or dignity of women bonding together in a separate sphere, autobiography has recorded it vividly. The women who civilized the West brought more than teacups and lace doilies with them. They brought the moral imperatives of humane nurturing and valuing, valuing not property—horses and lands and cattle—but other human beings. Out of their organized concern, the West became a different place.

The chronicling of that change has been, at least in fiction, somewhat inadequate. I would like to be presumptuous enough to suggest that fiction writers might make use of this rich vein of heroic virtue, a vein which encompasses the communal rather than the individual. Our historical knowledge of the women's sub-culture and their struggles for public welfare could supplement the older ideals, making them part of a larger whole. That this would have to be done without condescension, without preconceptions, with loving craftsmanship and creative imagination, I do not deny. But I would like to suggest, and suggest strongly, that it does need doing.

NOTES

[1]Jackson K. Putnam, "Historical Fact and Literary Truth: The Problem of Authenticity in Western American Literature," *Western American Literature*, 15 (May, 1980), 18-23, has common-sense directives on this subject. He does not, however, discuss re-discovered history.

[2]See Barbara Meldrum, "Images of Women in Western American Literature," *The Midwest Quarterly*, 17 (Spring, 1976), 252-267.

[3]Nancy Cott, *The Bonds of Womanhood: Woman's Sphere in New England, 1780-1835* (New Haven: Yale University Press, 1979). Another important study of women's bonding is Carroll Smith-Rosenberg, "The Female World of Love and Ritual: Relations between Women in Nineteenth Century America," *Signs*, 2 (Autumn, 1975), 1-30. Similar work with westering women is found in Johnny Faragher and Christine Stansell, "Women and Their Families on the Overland Trail to California and Oregon, 1842-1867," *Feminist Studies*, 2 (1975), 150-160; Johnny Faragher, *Women and Men on the Overland Trail* (New York: Yale University Press, 1979); and Julie Roy Jeffrey, *Frontier Women: The Transmississippi West, 1840-1880* (New York: Hill and Wang, 1979).

[4]See Barbara Berg, *The Remembered Gate: Origins of American Feminism* (New York: Oxford University Press, 1978); Mary P. Ryan, *Womanhood in America: From Colonial Times to the Present* (New York: Harper and Row, 1975); and Ryan, "The Power of Women's Networks: A Case Study of Female Moral Reform in Antebellum America," *Feminist Studies*, 5 (1979), 66-85.

[5]The only published study of this phenomenon is Karen J. Blair, *The Clubwoman as Feminist: True Womanhood Redefined, 1868-1914* (New York: Holmes and Meier Publishing Inc., 1980).

[6]See June O. Underwood, "Civilizing Kansas: Women's Organizations, 1880-1920," unpublished typescript, under the auspices of the Research Institute on Women's Public Lives (Ford Foundation), Lawrence,

Kansas, June, 1980.

[7]See, for example, James C. Malin, "Kansas: Some Reflections on Cultural Inheritance and Originality," *Midcontinental American Studies Journal,* 2 (Fall, 1961), 3-19. Malin shows that from 1860-1880, of every 9 persons present in Kansas, 8 were new. Losses of 60% in eastern Kansas were not unusual.

[8]Mary Austin, *Earth Horizon: An Autobiography* (New York: Houghton-Mifflin Company, 1932), pp. 139-140.

[9]Robert Dykstra, *The Cattle Towns* (New York: Alfred A. Knopf, 1968), pp. 190-206.

[10]Ole Rölvaag, *Giants in the Earth* (New York: Harper and Bros., 1927), p. 365.

[11]Bess Streeter Aldrich, *Spring Came on Forever* (New York: D. Appleton-Century Company, 1935), pp. 205, 222.

[12]Sinclair Lewis, *Main Street* (New York: Harcourt, Brace, and World, 1920); Edna Ferber, *Cimmaron* (Garden City, New York: Doubleday and Company, 1929), pp. 171, 217.

[13]Aldrich, p. 210.

[14]*One of Ours* (Toronto: Macmillan Company, 1922), pp. 203-204. While Enid's prohibition work is not necessarily all female, it was probably primarily so. Her escape to nurse her missionary sister is part of the same pattern of women's bonding and organizational activities.

[15]Address, National Women's Studies Association Conference, June, 1978, Lawrence, Kansas.

[16]Austin, pp. 141-142.

[17]Austin, p. 142.

[18]Wallace Stegner, *Wolf Willow: A History, a Story, and a Memory of the Last Prairie Frontier* (Toronto: Macmillan, 1955), pp. 304-305.

[19]Stegner, p. 305.

[20]Stegner, p. 306.

Marie Louise Ritter:
The Pioneer Woman in Fact and Fiction

Darlene Ritter

The addition to the population of the United States between 1815 and 1914 of thirty-five million Europeans is as significant a chapter in American history as the preceding two centuries of colonization.[1] The arrival of these millions altered
America, but it must be remembered that immigration also altered the immigrants. Immigration resulted in one's becoming a
foreigner, ceasing to belong. The disruption of a familiar life
and surroundings often caused broken homes, and the effect of
the movement was harder upon the people than upon the society they entered.[2]

The role women played in the settlement of the West has
been of special interest to many authors. Cather presented her
great heroines, Ántonia and Alexandra, who seemed to belong
to and with the land, but still paid a price for their roles in developing the land. The prototypes of these characters came from
Cather's Red Cloud years. O. E. Rölvaag wrote of Beret and her
problems in adjusting to the many moves and final settlement in
the open plains of South Dakota. He drew upon information
from his wife's family and upon memories of his own mother to
create the fictional character Beret. Sophus Winther, similarly,
in *Take All to Nebraska* used his mother as the prototype for the
character Meta Grimsen. Although Mari Sandoz used her father
as the subject of *Old Jules,* she also wrote of the problems of his
wives and other women as they tried to adjust to life in the Sand-
hills. In other works she wrote of the problems of fictional
women. Suicides and insanity provided escape for many who
could not deal with the adjustments. These heightened, intensified fictional characters speak for the women from whom they
were drawn.

Later generations often forget that immigration uprooted

these people from their traditional environment and replanted them in a strange setting among strangers. Old behavior patterns were no longer adequate because the problems of life were new and different. Once old ties are snapped, where and how does one define her significance as an individual? Alienation was an inevitable result. Dorothy Skårdal deals with this dilemma in her book *The Divided Heart,* in which she records experiences of Scandinavians whose problems in belonging to two worlds reflect the divided loyalties of many immigrants. The importance of kinship naturally continued in the New World since it was one constant element where all else was different. Skårdal records the homesickness which continued regardless of prosperity. Some cured their homesickness by a return to the home country, but for many that was impossible.

The letters that people have written home describing a new situation or location have always been invaluable sources for individual attitudes. Blegen in his book *Land of Their Choice* presents a collection of letters written by Norwegian immigrants to their homeland. He speaks of these letters as "a little-known human story that is a part of the larger saga of America."[3] One of the "little known human stories" is told through the collected letters of a Swiss immigrant woman, Marie Louise Ritter, who wrote from Nebraska to her relatives in Switzerland during the years 1893 to 1925, from her arrival in Nebraska to her death.[4] Similarities between the fictional women and Marie Louise Ritter reveal that characters such as Beret, Meta, and Ántonia speak for real women.

Marie Louise began her journey when she left Iffwyl, a small village in Switzerland, in March of 1893. She was accompanied by her husband, Fritz, and three small sons, ages six years, four years, and two months. They traveled by train to Le Havre, took the *City of Paris* to New York, and then again traveled by train to Nebraska. Her first letter was written in August of 1893, about five months after their arrival in Tilden, Nebraska. She described some of their travel experiences for her sister. "In the hotel in New York all ate with such good appetites that one would not believe that they had felt so miserable on the ship."[5] The train trip to Nebraska was long, but she felt they were fortunate because they "were always favored by co-travelers, train personnel and hosts, and no one objected to the warming of

the milk with the ethyl lamp." She knew of another family who were not allowed to warm the milk for their baby (27 August 1893). Her husband's older brother had come over earlier to find a house and farm for the family, so they moved into a comfortable frame house containing much of the furniture of the previous inhabitants.

Although they lived in a comfortable house, they had to struggle for economic survival. Skårdal used the term "dog years" to describe the period of painful adjustment which continued as long as an immigrant suffered considerable physical hardship.

> You will understand we don't have it as the ones who have been here for a long time. The meat is all gone, and it is too hot to be able to slaughter. We could buy so much; we ought to spend money ten different places. Instead of buying, we kill chickens and make chicken soup or we shoot rabbits which are here in abundance. . . . There are also many pheasants and big and small prairie hens whose melancholy calls one can hear every day. Everybody has here the right to shoot on his land what there is, also there are snakes which horrify us. (27 August 1893)

She wrote of the abundance of wild grapes and plums: "We also preserved a barrel of plums. We have to wait to see what they taste like" (29 August 1893). This preserving reminds one of Cather's description of Mrs. Bergson in *O Pioneers!* for whom preserving was almost a mania: "She could still take some comfort in the world if she had bacon in the cave, glass jars on the shelves, ..."[6] Scrubbing, cooking, and preserving did help pioneer women to order their lives in the new environment.

Rölvaag and Winther wrote of crop losses and the effect of these losses on Beret and Meta. Marie Louise felt obliged to apologize to her parents for not writing sooner: "I was always so busy and the main reason is that I was very worried about our corn harvest. When I wrote you last, the cornfields were exceptionally beautiful but then because of the scorching south wind and lack of rain the leaves hung down limp and withered" (22 October 1893). The following year she wrote: "I don't want to bother you with our grievances. It is just like this, no crop, have to buy the feed and always the same. Thank God we

are all well. All of us have to struggle through like thousands of others who may be even worse off than we" (29 November 1894). Beret, Meta, and Marie Louise soon discovered their crops could be destroyed by drought, grasshoppers, or early frost.

The violence of the weather in the plains has always been a shock to newcomers. Marie Louise described an electrical storm: "About midnight a storm stood directly over us. A terrible noise made us almost faint and believing that our living room was on fire, we seized in our deadly fear our dearest ones, our children." The house did not burn down, "but how close it had been, we saw the next morning! In the kitchen in the wall just below the loft behind the stove there was an enormous hole. The lightning must have gone down the pipe from the outside" (27 August 1893). Storms were not like this in the homeland. The bitter cold of the winter was another problem: "It is so cold that it almost bites away the skin. Just to feed the chickens, I put on a coat and wrapped my head with a shawl and still almost died from the cold." She was critical of the English, her name for those who were not European immigrants. "You should know that here in this barbaric land the cattle have no warm refuge in stables. There are people who try to make you believe that the animals are used to the cold weather and to ice on their backs" (28 January 1894). Marie Louise clung to those who were Swiss and wrote with scorn not only of those English who did not built stables to protect their livestock but also of the "English too lazy to plant potatoes."

The English were not the only new people she encountered. She wrote of her fear when Indians stopped at their house, but her curiosity overcame her fear: "I watched them secretly, these copper-brown fellows with their wives. . . . One I saw naked. My fear was quite unnecessary; no one came to our house. They pitched three tents and camped here overnight, hardly 200 to 250 steps from our house. No one can claim to have slept particularly well that night. The next morning they departed early" (27 August 1893). In her next letter she reassured her sisters, telling them that the Indians were not dangerous, but "better than many a white man and they don't bother us" (October 1893).

Holidays that had been joyous family occasions for pioneer women became reminders of how far they were from their families and homelands. Marie Louise wrote to her family:

> Now we are standing at the threshold of the year 1894. We have experienced a lot in the time which soon will be passed, turned our backs to our dear and beautiful homeland with all you beloved ones in order to found a new home here in the strange foreign land. But I can never really be happy although we are getting along all right, but it is the homesickness that will plague me here in America. I wish and hope that you all over there can celebrate today a Merry Christmas and enter in the best of health in a week's time a happy and peaceful New Year. (Christmas 1893)

Later in the letter she grieves that the pine Christmas tree they had in Switzerland must be replaced with a cedar tree, not nearly so beautiful. The pine tree was symbolic of the many familiar things she missed. Seven years later she wrote again of the tree decorated for the boys—not a pine tree but a cedar tree.

Marie Louise's desire for familiar things reminds one that the struggle was not only for economic survival, but also for peace of mind. Rölvaag and Winther wrote of women who lived with homesickness and feelings of guilt for having left loved ones behind who needed them. Some of these same fictional characters had to deal with personal tragedies without the support of parents or brothers and sisters.

Marie Louise left Switzerland with her husband and three sons and gave birth to two more sons in Nebraska. Her parents, two sisters, and one brother remained in Switzerland. She grieved she could not share her joy in her new sons with the family and that she could not see her sisters' children. After the birth of her fourth son, she wrote: "Oh, if only I could come to you with my sweet Willie and darling Rudolf—how you would enjoy them. Do come and all brothers and sisters. There is much room here, and my children would enjoy so much visiting people whom they love" (25 October 1896). With pride she wrote of their improved economic situation: "We are thinking of building a nice brick cellar and a large kitchen this summer. They are both much needed" (26 February 1899). The January 1902 letter included the announcement of the birth of her last child,

Ernest. "A dear little fellow is our little Ernest, so gay and round, just as one would wish him to be. It was a difficult birth, and I thought that I would never get back my strength." In this letter she repeats what she was to write again and again to her family: "If we could only speak together once again in our lives. One gets old and has so little of each other."

This refrain was a foreshadowing of the letter from home which told of the sudden death of her younger sister. She longed to be able to help the four motherless children and her parents. Marie Louise wrote to her mother and father: "The news of the death has shaken me no end. How it hurts to know a beloved sister is in the grave whom I hoped so much to see one day again and who hoped it, too, and wrote about it in every letter." She continued by asking if her sister had received the last letter from her. "How sad I would be if the beloved one had not heard from me and thought I had long forgotten her." Marie Louise would have liked to have the smallest child come to her home, but had to content herself with wishes that the grandparents would live long to help the "poor motherless orphans." She asked for details. "Was Emma always conscious? Did she think of me sometimes? Did she know she had to die? The departure from her beloved ones must have been heart-breaking" (20 June 1902). It was difficult for her to accept the finality of this separation.

In her next letter to Switzerland, Marie Louise had her own tragedy to report. The child who had been a baby in arms when they immigrated had been killed by a runaway team of horses when he was ten years old. "You have to forgive me when I say that the fate that has happened to me so suddenly is too hard—I believe I shall never overcome it." Her grief was still so immediate the letter is almost incoherent:

> Even now I can hardly put a short letter together; it is turning and twisting in my head—oh, I have often been afraid to lose my senses. . . . He was my best child. And then death breaks this darling flower so mercilessly, unasked for out of the circle of seven happy people—and that forever.   (8 September 1903)

She reached an acceptance, but the next letter reveals the pain and struggle she had experienced:

> A long and anxious time has passed since I wrote you last. You will understand that I lived since through many terrible hours. On Christmas Eve I went with the four children to the Tilden church. I was frightfully shaken, thinking of my deceased darling, who a year ago recited his little Christmas verse. . .and so soon afterwards was torn from us, oh hard, bitter fate!
>
> (27 December 1903)

She described "the quiet grave that holds a piece of my life that was richly decorated with flowers during the summer." In this same letter she shared another concern: her husband had blood poisoning and had been unable to work for three months. "What would become of us if he would have to pass away?" He recovered, but she again received sad news from the homeland. Her father was dead. Now, she wondered about her mother.

> Oh, were we closer, I would love to have you with us. But dear sister Emma's children would not like to miss their dear Grandma. Oh, yes, three years ago all was still different with us, and the sorrow came; the dear sister, the dear Rudolf, and now our beloved father. One after the other had to depart.   (March 1905)

She was torn two ways. She would have gone back to see those still living, but asked how could she leave her children who cried when she spoke of the journey. "Oh, dear Mother, in all your letters I most enjoyed hearing that you were well, and now this had to happen. Never again can I look into the eyes of my dear father; maybe not into yours either. I shed hot tears for both of you." Since she cannot bear to leave her children, all she can do is ask her mother to understand and plead: "Please write me soon all about my dear father. Did he think of me in his last days?" (5 March 1905).

Marie Louise found strength in her Nebraska family and her religion, and she had to accept as did the fictional Meta and Beret that they were a part of the new world. She continued to grieve over the death of her son, but wrote "it is a great comfort to me to know him to be with our beloved Savior although the longing for him almost kills me" (19 July 1905). She continued in the same letter, "but there will be a reunion again, there in the beautiful land. That is the comfort and hope for those hearts who are united in a holy faith."

She found peace in hard work. She cooked for threshers, put up food for the family, and made cheese as she had in the homeland. Her homesickness was always with her. "Maybe in the spring we will have our house and cattle photographed. Better still you all come here to stay. I am often very lonesome. We are doing well here, but who is happy in Switzerland should remain there" (January 1902).

In June of 1908, she wrote: "Had I known fifteen years ago that you, dear ones, would not come here or we return, I believe I would never have come to America. Life is good here but one ought to see each other once in a while."

No one else of her family came to the United States. Her family here continued to prosper, and as her sons married they established homes on farms nearby. When their youngest son married, she and her husband moved to a new house opposite their church. In her last letter, she conceded that the old way was gone.

> All our grandchildren do not know any German and won't ever learn it. In the beginning when we found that out, there was many a harsh word said. If the mother and father were both of Swiss origin, they would have spoken in Bern dialect, but so they speak English. You know our boys didn't want to speak high German and their wives don't know Swiss German.   (13 January 1925)

In the same letter, she told her sister that she was not well, but "everything happens according to God's will. We will trust in Him. The golden youth belongs to our children."

Marie Louise Ritter died December 26, 1925, one day before her beloved Rudolf's birthday. She was sixty-two years old. According to her obituary, services were given in both German and English. The obituary included this summary of her life: "Mrs. Ritter was a woman of ideal character who made and held friends—to know her was to love her. No matter whether in her home or outside she was always the same. The greatest heritage to her loved ones will be the memory of life well lived."[7]

Marie Louise was one of the thousands whose individual stories tell the story of the settlement of the Great Plains. Her

letters reveal the experiences of one individual woman, and these experiences parallel many of the fictional accounts of pioneer women. These pioneer women, real or fictional, came with varied hopes and dreams. Many of these dreams were lost or postponed; some were achieved. Mistakes were made; trage-dies were commonplace. Marie Louise's obituary puts it well—their heritage to their loved ones is the memory of life well lived. Many sustained Marie Louise's faith: "Everything happens according to God's will. We will trust in Him, He will do it well."

NOTES

[1] Marcus Lee Hansen, *The Immigrant in American History* (Cambridge, Massachusetts: Harvard University Press, 1948), p. 191.

[2] Oscar Handlin, *The Uprooted* (Boston: Little, Brown and Company, 1951), p. 5.

[3] Theodore C. Blegen, *Land of Their Choice* (St. Paul, Minnesota: University of Minnesota, 1955), p. v.

[4] Fritz Ritter, my grandfather, was a widower for thirty-four years. He said little about Marie Louise, but in his room he had a large picture of her, and when he spoke of her it was with emotion. Six years after his death, I traveled to Europe and visited Iffwyl to see where my grandparents lived before they immigrated. During my visit, I met many relatives and learned for the first time that after my grandmother's death there had been no communication between the families until the letter telling them I would arrive for a visit. I also learned that Marie Louise, their aunt and my grandmother, had maintained this correspondence from 1893 to 1925. These letters were kept by her sister Anna until her death in 1951. Then the letters were kept by Anna's youngest daughter, Klara. It was in her home that I was shown the letters and learned of their importance to the Swiss branch of the family. In 1972, Klara gave me most of the letters. She said that they now meant more to me than they would to anyone of the next generation in Switzerland. These letters provide me with knowledge of the grandmother I never knew.

[5] Marie Louise Ritter, Series of Unpublished Letters, 1893-1925, translated by Marie Rosenblatt, edited by Darlene Ritter, 27 August 1893. Subsequent quotations will be in the text with the date indicated within parentheses.

[6] Willa Cather, *O Pioneers!* (Boston: Houghton Mifflin Company, 1962), pp. 29-30.

[7] *Tilden Citizen,* Tilden, Nebraska, 31 December 1925, p. 1.

A Study of Feminism as a Motif in
"A Journey to Pike's Peak and New Mexico,"*
by Julia Archibald Holmes

Margaret Solomon

The recent interest in women's experience of historical phenomena has led scholars to re-examine well-known events, even epochs, with a view to determining what the feminine experience of that moment might have been.[1] In the case of Julia Archibald Holmes (1838-1887), one of the members of the historic Lawrence (Kansas) gold-seeking party, whose movements precipitated the Gold Rush to Pikes Peak, the prospects are especially rich. Holmes was not only one of just two women on the trip, but she was a feminist and a writer. Her account of the experience, published in 1859 in *The Sibyl*[sic]: *A Reform Magazine of the Tastes, Errors, and Fashions of Society*, yields the nineteenth-century feminist perspective of the journey west and is a fascinating tale besides, rich in conflict and marked by a singular climax, for Holmes finally climbed Pikes Peak itself, and so became the first woman to do so.

We know little of Holmes's early life, except the saliant facts—that she was born in Nova Scotia, the daughter of John and Jane O'Brien Archibald, who later came with the first wave of Free-State settlers to Kansas and helped found Lawrence.[2] In 1857, when she was nineteen, Julia married James Holmes, a notorious Free-Stater, an emigrant from New York who had ridden with John Brown and fought with him at Osswatomi. According to family tradition, in fact, the two were introduced by Brown at the Archibald family home, a site on the Underground Railroad in Kansas. The next spring, James, Julia, and Julia's eighteen-year-old brother, Albert, set off with the rag-tag group from Lawrence, one of the first three in the country to set their sights on the Rocky Mountain gold. On her trip, Julia wore the bloomer, the feminist costume, and clashed repeatedly with

the other members of the train before finally managing to climb the famous mountain. Directly afterward, the Holmeses travelled to New Mexico, where in 1861 James won an appointment from Lincoln as Secretary of the Territory.[3] During this time, Julia occupied herself with teaching, writing the article, based on her journal, which has not survived, and caring for the couple's first child, Ernest Julio. In 1862, however, James Holmes was court martialled for speaking out against the New Mexican administration's martial law and so lost his post. The couple left New Mexico under a cloud, but settled finally in Washington, D.C., where in 1867 they founded an organization to agitate for the vote for women and blacks.[4] Sometime in the 1870s the two parted, for reasons that are not clear; Wheeler notes, "James increasingly harassed Aunt Julia" (p. 10), and then falls silent. In any event, Julia Holmes went to work for the Bureau of Education and remained there until her death in 1887.

All her life, Holmes maintained an interest in feminism. In 1868 her tract "Women as Clerks and Postmasters" was published by The Universal Franchise Association, and the next year, she, her sister, and mother were arrested for attempting to register at the polls in Washington, D.C.[5] It may be, too, that she is "Julia N. Holmes, the poet, and one of the most admired ladies present" at a suffragist meeting in Washington, D.C., as reported in *The History of Woman Suffrage* (p. 99). Unfortunately, few of her letters survive, but she remains a colorful, intriguing figure, an emblem of the reform-minded woman with her roots planted in Romanticism.

Holmes's feminism clearly helped shape her two-part article, "A Journey To Pike's Peak and New Mexico." With the first lines of the piece, she announces that her theme is the woman's experience of the overland journey, and particularly the feminist vs. the male-dominated culture: "I think an account of my recent trip will be received with some interest by my sisters in reform, the readers of The Sibyl—if not by the rest of mankind— since I am, perhaps, the first woman who has worn the 'American costume' across the prairie sea which divides the great frontier of the states from the Rocky Mountains."[6]

Holmes was not the first woman to have worn bloomers across the plains, as she might very well have known—they were

quite popular in the early fifties and continued to be worn sporadically after that. It is possible, however, that Holmes meant she was the first to wear them for political reasons as well as for comfort, a fact that would be hard to dispute. In any event, her assertion serves the narrative well, for with it she strengthens the theme of feminism, her "angle" in journalism terms. In effect, she says, her article will be read, not because of what she has seen, as might be the case in the ordinary travel account, but because of *who* she is—the feminist on the journey, the feisty fighter, isolated, in some sense like the prairie itself, strange and unappreciated.

Besides this, the first lines, with their biting reference to the "rest of mankind," introduce an antagonism toward nonfeminists, particularly men, that will make itself felt through the article itself. She seldom seems to miss an occasion for pointing a finger at the men—it is they who cannot tell a buffalo from a hillock in the distance, for instance, or who waste time "vigorously discussing" the merits of various camp sites. Gradually this sniping at men and the hostility that seems to underlie it become a strong subtext to the narrative itself.

Finally, the opening lines reveal a pull between description of the passing scene and the personal response to it, a tension between persuasion and exposition, to put it in writerly terms, that keeps the piece taut, the reader wondering just when and how Holmes's values shall next surface to disturb the tranquility of the journey west.

The first of these disturbances centered on her costume, the bloomer dress. Hers was a comfortable traveling outfit, "a calico dress reaching a little below the knee, pants of the same, Indian mocassins. . .and. . .a hat" (p. 16). Like the feminists who adopted it briefly from 1852-1854, Holmes wore the dress because, she said, "I found it to be beyond value in comfort and convenience, as it gave me freedom to roam at pleasure in search of flowers and other curiosities while the cattle continued their slow and measured pace" (p. 16). But this very freedom Holmes felt, this independence, brought her into confrontation with the other members of the party. The men actually talked among themselves of asking her to change clothes, but finally gave up that plan, assuming that dressed in "breeches" she would be less

likely to attract attention from natives than if she had worn a dress.[7] Interestingly, it is not the men's arguments that Holmes describes. Instead, she focuses on the fact that another woman in the group, Mrs. Middleton, disagreed with her. What seems to bother Holmes most is that she had expected to be friends with the woman and found that was impossible: "I was much pleased to learn on my arrival that the company contained a lady, and rejoiced at the prospect of having a female companion on such a long journey. But my hopes were disappointed. I soon found there could be no congeniality between us" (p. 16).

She goes on to note the root of those differences: "She proved to be a woman unable to appreciate freedom or reform, affected that her sphere denied her the liberty to rove at pleasure, and confined herself the long days to feminine impotence in the hot covered wagon" (p. 16). When Mrs. Middleton suggested to Holmes that she change to a skirt, Holmes demurred: " 'I could not positively enjoy a moment's happiness with long skirts on to confine me to the wagon' " (p. 17), and then tried to convince Mrs. Middleton of the virtues of the reform dress. There was no further discussion between them, she notes; the friendship was short-lived.

The implication is that feminist ideas will disrupt the codes of society, not only the code as it applies to the relationships between men and women—that is a foregone conclusion, a minor matter—but the code even as it applies to the relationship among women themselves, a vitally important element of the nineteenth century women's world. Where one expects to find friendship, one may no longer find it. Again, the theme of the feminist as lonely outcast, friendless, is brought into play.

Yet Holmes has, as it were, traded in friendship for something else—and that is power, with the undercurrent here of sexual potency as well. She acts purposefully, with self direction; she can roam where she wants, do as she pleases. And this sense of her own power buoys her up: "I rejoiced I was independent of such little views of propriety as wearing skirts, and felt I possessed an ownership in all that was good or beautiful in nature, and an interest in any curiosities we might find on the journey as much as if I had been one of the favored lords of creation" (p. 17).

Having shed female trappings, Holmes is not simply equal to men, she is above them, a "lord of creation." But how telling in this context is masculinity of the figure! Its very usage suggests the constraints the nineteenth-century feminist felt. For all her independence, she could not assert a sense of power (an "ownership" in nature, and "an interest in any curiosities") and still retain her womanliness—not in society's eyes, not even in her own.

Alone, roaming the fields, Holmes may have taken a measure of power to herself, but she was kept from assuming the responsibilities it implied in the community. Toward the end of the first installment of her two-part article, she recounts a second clash with the company, this time directly with the men themselves. A few days after joining the company, she asked to take a turn with James at guarding the camp, a disagreeable duty the men shared, "Believing as I do," she explained, ". . .that when it is in our power, we should, in order to promote our own independence at least, be willing to share the hardships which commonly fall to the lot of men" (p. 20).

The guardmaster, a Virginian of the old school ("and who, to use his own expression, was 'conservative up to the eyes' "), refused her on the grounds that "gentlemen of the company could not permit a woman to stand on guard" (p. 21). Holmes seethes at the refusal, recalling that although the guardmaster witnessed the "heroic exertions" of Kansas women on behalf of freedom, he persisted in his belief that women were fragile. Like men who deny women the vote, "He believes woman is an angel (without any sense), needing the legislation of her brothers to keep her in place; that restraint removed, she would immediately usurp his position, and then not only be no longer an angel, but unwomanly" (p. 21). Man, she suggests, is a willful, somewhat dimwitted but cunning enemy, determined to keep women voiceless and literally out of this world.

The issue of gaining the vote, of determining appropriate womanly and manly behavior—these were crucial to the nineteenth-century feminist. Holmes may have left Kansas hoping to leave problems of such political dimension behind, but she believed she found herself face to face with them in a new, particularly pointed way out on the plains. If the earlier confronta-

tion suggests that the feminist will forfeit the comfort of the wagon, this one suggests that she will find no place in the community at large either. There seems no place for her in the world of the overland journey: not in the wagon, nor in the community. Where can she turn now?

Holmes's own narrative supplies the answer. Immediately after describing the encounter with the guardmaster, she turns to the passing scene where, she notes, she found "many new varieties of flowers, some of them of exceeding beauty." She particularly admires the "sensitive rose, a delicate appearing flower, one of the most beautiful I ever saw, having a fine delicious aroma. It grows on the running vine. In an eastern observatory, it would be the fairy queen among roses—the queen of flowers" (p. 21). Nature itself will crown the feminine alternative and validate the feminine experience, she seems to say. Women must keep their vision of themselves constant in their own minds; the rose would be queen of flowers in the East, although here it seems of no account. Holmes does not sound here either oppressed or defeated, for all her problems, and in singling her rose out for such prominent notice, she even suggests she may emerge triumphant. Such a triumph was yet to come, however. Before Holmes reached Pikes Peak, she clashed at least once more with the others in the train, as she sought to be "counted" in the little group.

In the opening paragraphs of Part Two of her account, she notes that the company had been scheduled to pass a camp of Cheyenne and Arapahoe Indians. Recounting the incident, her sarcasm bubbles up: "Fifty men armed with Sharps rifles and revolvers were afraid to allow the Indians to know the company contained any women. . . . I was, therefore, confiined to the wagon, while we passed many places of interest which I wished very much to visit" (p. 22).

This, of course, was the contemptible wagon, which she wished so to avoid. The results of the attempt to confine her are not surprising: "Notwithstanding this care to be unobserved, my presence became known. At one time, by opening the front of the wagon for ventilation, at another by leaping from it to see something curious which two or three Indians had brought, not knowing, as afterward proved true, that we were very near a

village" (p. 22). Holmes was caught then: "It was of no use to hide now, for every Indian within a mile knew of my whereabouts. . .and red men have an unaccountable fancy for white women. My husband received serveral flattering offers for me. One Indian wanted to trade two squaws. . . . Others. . .approaching the wagon made signs for me to jump behind them on their ponies, but I declined the honor in the most respectful language I knew of their dialect—a decided shake of the head" (pp. 22-23).

Although Holmes sounds embarrassed by her behavior ("I was sorry I had been seen on account of the feeling existing in the train" [p. 22], she adds), the suggestion is that one is justified in using any means to escape confinement, and, further, that any threats, especially sexual ones, will come to nothing, if one only remains in control, with that "decided shake of the head." Again, she implies that while men think they know best—even native men who want her—they actually do not.

Interestingly, although Holmes here seems willing to acknowledge the fact of men's attraction to her—and by extension, her own attractiveness—she is not so willing to acknowledge openly her anger at being confined to the wagon. She resorts to sarcasm in reporting the event, just as at the time, she resorted to trickery to get her own way, even to tricking herself into believing she opened the flap and leapt from the wagon, all without meaning to at all. The entire substance of the incident underscores the point that, while it was permissible for any feminist to be angry about not being given the vote, it was less easy for her to challenge the cultural biases against women that were more deeply ingrained—here, for instance, that men are the better judges of a dangerous situation, and it is they who should dictate behavior.

The careful reader sees too that Holmes herself cannot shed nineteenth century values. She too believed natives were savages who "fancied" white women in particular. More to the point, in this story the native men's attentions to her become her reward for acting as she did; their attention, in effect, exonerates her for having broken her confinement. Nowhere, we notice, does she suggest that the men's attentions held no meaning for her. On the contrary, their offers are "flattering." For all she might protest to the contrary, Holmes was ready to set store by

the men's opinion of her worth to them.

The company moved on; tempers eased. Eventually, on July 8, the Lawrence Party reached Pikes Peak and their camp-site, an area now known as the Garden of the Gods. Before setting out on the trail, Holmes had decided she would "learn to walk," as she put it, by traipsing alongside the cattle for a number of measured miles each day. Encamped, she hated the inactivity, and on August 1, set out with her husband and two guides to make the two-day climb to the top of the mountain, just as a few men of the party had done three weeks earlier.[8]

In her article, Holmes does not comment on their climb, but moves directly to recounting her own adventure. Like Edwin James, the botanist who had taken Pikes Peak first in 1820, she found the roughest going on the lower portion of the mountain, where the angle was steep and surface crumbly.[9] Past that point, the climbing was easier, and with many stops for resting, the party found themselves ready to take the summit.

Holmes is reserved in her description of the actual experience: "It was cold and rather cloudy, with squalls of snow," she says,"consequently our view was not so extensive as we had anticipated. . .a cloud capped bleak region" (pp. 35-36). She left quickly, although before leaving, she notes, she read aloud the lines that precede Emerson's essay "On Friendship":

> A ruddy drop of manly blood
> the surging sea outweighs;
> The world uncertain comes and goes,
> the lover rooted stays.[10]

Shortly thereafter her "letter," as she calls it, closes, recounting how she, James, and Albert drove to New Mexico and there left the Kansans.

Julia Holmes is somewhat reserved in print about her triumph—she does not comment at all on its meaning for her. But then again, she doesn't have to. The event itself says it all. She has literally done what she has wanted to do all along—raised herself above all others, proved herself man's equal. A letter to her mother written from the top of the mountain fills the gap and

tells us all her feat meant to her:

Pikes Peak, August 5, 1858

> I have accomplished the task which I marked out for myself and
> now feel amply repaid for all my toil and fatigue. Nearly every-
> one tried to discourage me from attempting it, but I believed that
> I should succeed; and now, here I am, and I feel that I would not
> have missed this glorious sight for anything at all. In all proba-
> bility I am the first woman who has ever stood upon the summit of
> this mountain and gazed upon this wondrous scene, which my eyes
> now behold. How I sigh for the poet's power of description, so
> that I might give you some faint idea of the grandeur and beauty
> of this scene. Extending as far as the eye can reach, lie the great
> level plains, stretched out in all their verdure and beauty, while the
> winding of the great Arkansas is visible for many miles. We can
> also see distinctly where many of the smaller tributaries unite with
> it.—Then the rugged rocks all around, and the almost endless suc-
> cession of mountains and rocks below, the broad blue sky over
> our heads, and seemingly so very near; all, and everything, on
> which the eye can rest, fills the mind with infinitude, and sends the
> soul to God.[11]

The letter suggests her triumph was an ecstatic experience;
that she feels especially blessed by God for her efforts, is even in
Beatitude. There is an exultant tone here that is replaced in her
article, it would seem, by the Emerson quote. Even the scene
described in the two pieces of writing is different. In the letter,
written at the moment, the sky is blue, and the plains extend as
far as the eye can see. Not so in the article, written later from
her journal account that was based on memory. By that time,
perhaps, her warmth had cooled and she felt the view was "not
so extensive" as she wished after all.

However, the most compelling lines of the letter, it seems
to me, arise as she describes her perseverance in the face of the
men's opposition: "Nearly everyone tried to discourage me from
attempting it, but I believed I would succeed, and now here I am,
and I feel that I would not have missed this sight for anything at
all." There is a strength, a directness here that attests to the passion with which she fought to maintain her individuality and to
rise above the strictures of her culture. Opposing others, assert-

ing her independence as she did so often on the journey may well have given her the singular will to take her mountain and to appreciate fully all she had done. Perhaps she herself realized that had it not been for the testing of her mettle on the plain, the triumph of taking the mountain might have been far less sweet.

NOTES

*The nineteenth-century spelling of "Pike's Peak" is retained where it is appropriate.

[1]Scholarly interest in women in the nineteenth century has been particularly intense. Studies that I have found especially helpful are now classics and include Barbara Welter's "The Cult of True Womanood: 1820-1860," *American Quarterly*, 18 (1966), 151-174; Gerda Lerner's "The Lady and The Mill Girl: Changes in the Status of Women in the Age of Jackson, 1800-1840," *Mid-Continent American Studies Journal*, 10 (1969), 5-14; Carroll Smith-Rosenberg's "The Female World of Love and Ritual: Relations Between Women in Nineteenth Century America," *Signs*, 1 (Autumn, 1975), 1-29; Johnny Faragher and Christine Stansell's "Women and Their Families on the Overland Trail To California and Oregon, 1842-1867," *Feminist Studies*, 2 (1975), 150-166, and Eleanor Flexner's *A Century of Struggle: The Women's Rights Movement in the U. S.* (Cambridge: Harvard University Press, 1969). There is less research available on the woman's experience of the westward movement, but *Frontier Women: The Trans-Mississippi West, 1840-1880*, by Julie Roy Jeffrey (New York: Hill and Wang, 1979) is valuable and comprehensive as, from another perspective, is *Women and Men on the Overland Trail*, by John Mack Faragher (New Haven: Yale University Press, 1979).

[2]There is no full-length biography of Julia Archibald Holmes, although a brief life history, not complete, is added to her article reprinted in *A Bloomer Girl On Pike's Peak—1858*, edited by Agnes Wright Spring (Denver: Denver Public Library, 1949). The Holmes's years after Pikes Peak are only lightly treated by Spring, however. For the Archibalds, see Louis Barry, "The Emigrant Aid Company Parties of 1854," *Kansas Historical Quarterly*, 12 (1943), 117. The family history is Joseph Wheeler, *Some of the Archibald Tribe: Especially the Family of John Christie* (Benson, Vermont: n.p., 1969).

[3]For James Holmes's career as Secretary, see Loomis Morton Ganaway, "New Mexico and The Sectional Controversy, 1846-1861," *New Mexico Historical Review*, 18 (October, 1943), 325-348; and James B. Rhoades, "The Taming of the West: Military Archives as a Source of Social History of the Trans-Mississippi Region," in *People of the Plains and Moun-*

tains, ed. Roy Allen Billington (Westport, Connecticut: Greenwood Press, 1973), pp. 197-198.

[4] Elizabeth Cady Stanton, Susan Anthony, and Matilda Joslyn Gage, *The History of Woman Suffrage* (Rochester: Charles Mann Printing, 1881) III, 809. See also James H. Holmes, "A Report on the Condition of the Cause of Woman Suffrage Made to The Universal Franchise Association" (Washington, D.C., 1868). This pamphlet also contains a report by Julia Archibald Holmes, corresponding secretary of the organization.

[5] The tract is listed for sale in the Holmes pamphlet, 1868. For the attempt to register, see Stanton, III, 813.

[6] This and further quotes from Holmes's article are taken from her piece, reprinted in Spring, pp. 13-37.

[7] W. J. Boyer, Letter in *The Lawrence Republican,* 15 July 1858. Cited in Spring, p. 21n.

[8] For the Party's activities, see LeRoy R. Hafen, "Historical Introduction," in *Pike's Peak Gold Rush Guidebooks of 1859 by Luke Tierney, William Parsons and Summaries of the Other Fifteen,* ed. LeRoy R. Hafen (Glendale, California: The Arthur H. Clark Company, 1941). Holmes's own account does not mention guides, but in the *Georgetown (Colo.) Courier,* 9 March 1901, J. C. Miller of the Lawrence party asserts that he and another prospector accompanied the couple, according to Spring, p. 44. Albert Archibald refers to four guides for the trip, Spring notes.

[9] Edwin James, "The Ascent of Pike's Peak," in *Colorado, A Literary Chronicle,* ed. A. Storrs Lee (New York: Funk & Wagnalls, 1970), pp. 52-58.

[10] In a statement made to the Kansas Historical Society in 1894, James claimed it was he who read the lines aloud (see his letters in the Hyatt Papers, Kansas State Historical Society, Topeka, Kansas). In any event, the lines are taken from the poem, not from Julia's article. In that piece, and subsequent reprints, the last line has been incorrectly set to read, "the looser rooted stays."

[11] Letter in *Lawrence Republican,* 7 October 1858. Reprinted in Hafen, pp. 65-66, and Spring, p. 39.

Reluctant Pioneers

Susan H. Armitage

I am not the wheatfield
nor the virgin forest

I never chose this place
yet I am of it now
                    Adrienne Rich, "I Am An American Woman"[1]

The American frontier myth is male-dominated. Women, when mentioned at all in western literature, are frequently portrayed as uncomfortable and out of place on the frontier. They are reluctant pioneers: afraid of the wilderness, afraid of the Indians, homesick, and often physically or mentally sick as well.

We know that this cannot be the whole story, for the diaries, journals and letters of actual frontier women paint a much more varied portrait, representing an entire range of human experiences and emotions. On the other hand, the same women's sources tell us that the image of women as reluctant pioneers is not completely false. There were reasons—female reasons—why many women were fearful, homesick, and unhappy on the frontier. In this paper the letters, diaries, oral histories, and autobiographical novels by pioneer women in Rocky Mountain mining towns and agricultural regions of Colorado are used to explore the sources of female reluctance.

Mollie Dorsey Sanford, newly married, was not at first a reluctant pioneer. In fact, she took the initiative, persuading her husband to join the Colorado gold rush of 1859. Work was unexpectedly hard to find in Denver. They went to the mountain town of Gold Hill, where he prospected and she, virtually the only woman in the camp, cooked for the men. Lonely and overworked, Mollie's youthful optimism finally broke. She confessed

to her diary:

> I found a large rock that hung over the side of the hill, which made
> a secure shelter. Into this I crept, and thought, and thought, and
> *wept* for what? I suppose because I was alone, and homesick.[2]

Amelia Buss, who moved to Fort Collins in 1866, was a
different sort. She moved West leaving friends and family behind, because it was a wife's duty to follow her husband. She
could have said, "I never chose this place." Amelia filled her
diary with details of daily housekeeping in a primitive cabin,
and with complaints about hard work, isolation, and loneliness.
She used her diary, which was given to her by her sisters as a
parting gift, as a place to acknowledge her private fears:

> I have not had a letter in over two weeks till today I got one
> from A. and one from L. there was good news from home but
> some how I have felt very low spirited every since and that old
> homesick feeling comes back to me an other week is gon and O
> how cold the wind sounds tonight. G. and V. are a sleep and I am
> a lone.[3]

Amelia had other fears. She had four visits from curious
local Indians who did no harm but nevertheless alarmed her by
their strangeness. Mollie Sanford recorded a similar reaction in
her diary. She wrote, "I keep my doors locked or they would
come in without ceremony. My windows are high up from the
ground, but they manage to darken them with their dirty
visages."[4] This aversion to the dirtiness and persistent curiosity
of Indians is a common sentiment in the writings of pioneer
women.

Amelia's diary ends with a retrospective entry, dated
exactly one year from her arrival in Colorado. She has become
resigned: "Now I have settled down with the belief that here I
shall end my days and the sooner I make it home the better"
("Yet I am of it now.") She goes on to acknowledge what her
diary, her link to her sisters, has meant to her:

> This little book may seem full of trifling troubles to you, but at
> the same time they wer great to me, more than I knew how to
> bear. . .and now farewell little book you shall not carry more

complaint to my friends at home.

Fifteen years later, another woman, in quite different circumstances, used her diary in a similar way. Amelia Buss was poor; Elizabeth Sayre was not. Once a schoolteacher in Central City, she married a miner who struck it rich. Hal Sayre was so wealthy that he could send his wife and children to Paris for a year, but so busy that he could not accompany them. Elizabeth Sayre's diary, dated 1870, begins as she returns to America. The contrast between Paris and Aspen, "this half savage mining camp," was almost too much for Elizabeth to stand. Above all, she hated the rootlessness of her life. Her husband went from one business deal to another, and she followed him. "How I wish I had a home," Elizabeth wrote. She longed for a place where she could settle in, a place that would be *hers*.[5]

The difficulty of dependence is a recurring theme in mining camp diaries and stories. The uncertainty of work for miners affected their wives. "Waiting, always waiting" says Mabel Barbee of her mother in *Cripple Creek Days*.[6] And in the meantime, she endured

> the bare, ugly camp, so alien to her nature; the wide gap between her dream of a home and the drab reality of the house on Golden Avenue, her never-ending loneliness.[7]

The men acknowledged regretfully what mining meant for women: "It's a man's life and his wife often shares it only on sufferance."[8]

Many travellers pitied pioneer women for the harshness that filled their lives. But initial shock over primitive living conditions often gave way to statements of blame. For example, Isabella Bird, the celebrated English gentlewoman who visited Colorado in 1873, noted:

> "But oh! what a hard, narrow life it is with which I am now in contact! Mrs. C. . . .is never idle for one minute, is severe and hard, and despises everything but work. . . . This hard greed, and the exclusive pursuit of gain, with the indifference to all that does not aid in its acquisition, are eating up family love and life throughout the West."[9]

Admiration for the "true woman," who was defined as pious, pure, domestic, and submissive, apparently pervaded nine-teenth-century culture. Most travellers reacted as negatively as Isabella Bird when they noted a falling off in the genteel standards of domesticity on the frontier. Even as sympathetic an observer as Elizabeth Cady Stanton was shocked by the unconcern one Kansas woman showed about the mouse with whom Elizabeth uncomfortably shared her guest bed.[10]

Here, then, is one reason for female unhappiness on the frontier. The eastern, genteel standards of domesticity were impossible to meet. Frontier conditions prompted an apparently endless round of hard work just to maintain minimum standards of cleanliness. One laconic reminiscence from a pioneer woman in western Colorado summed up the struggle: "The hardest thing was gettin' rid of the varmints and the critters."[11]

Nannie Alderson of Montana, in her charming reminiscence *A Bride Goes West*, jokes about her inappropriate clothing: dresses with trains were out of place in cabins with dirt floors![12] Her humor hides the contradiction inherent in female adaptation to the frontier. Mrs. C., of whom Isabella Bird so strongly disapproved, had indeed adapted successfully to primitive conditions only to be judged wanting because she was uninterested in cultured values.

Women like Elizabeth Sayre and Kitty Barbee who did care about genteel values were, in effect, taking on an additional and solitary burden. The physical environment was inimical to their efforts. Isolation compounded the problem. Amelia Buss complained:

> George went to the mountains yesterday morning to be gon all the week. . .after he had gon gave vent to my feeling in a flood of tears. it may seem foolish to those that have neighbors and friends around them. I get a long very well through the day but the long evenings and nights are *horrible*.[13]

This isolation is echoed in Sanora Babb's autobiographical account of the dryland farming area of eastern Colorado in *An Owl on Every Post*. Babb shows the desperate loneliness of her mother cut off from the companionship of other women.

Coffee meant something more to her than a hot drink. Now and then in the afternoon she sat for awhile in a fresh apron, slowly drinking warmed-over breakfast coffee, her face passive, her gaze rapt in faraway memories or in dreams of escape. She did not mind the hard work, only the terrible loneliness. In that solitary rite she reached backward or forward to friends, perhaps, or simply retired within herself to renew her forces.[14]

Recent work by Carroll Smith-Rosenberg and Nancy Cott has shown the existence of a strong female support network among middle class Eastern women in nineteenth-century America.[15] This female subculture had its basis in the sex-role division of labor and in the ideology of "separate spheres" for men and women—men's was the public sphere, women's was the home. The accounts of Sanford, Buss, Sayre and Barbee underline the importance of that female subculture by demonstrating how sorely women felt its absence in frontier Colorado.

The female subculture did not exist in the pioneer West. On the plains women were too far apart, and in the mining camps the diversity of the population and mobility seems to have created something like modern suburban privatization. Women were no longer embedded in a tight community with all the customary attendant female supports. Frontier individualism was forced upon these women: they had to be more self-reliant and less communal than they had been before.

Pity for the lonely woman cut off from female companionship is built into the traditional stereotype of the reluctant pioneer. Perhaps this pity stemmed in part from guilt feelings, for it was indeed true that in the early settlement period men had more mobility than women. Mollie Dorsey Sanford's father and Amelia Buss's husband both left wives and families on homesteads while they took jobs elsewhere. Men often made trips to town by themselves, because there were too many chores and too many children for everyone to go.

Most women keenly felt their isolation from other women and from a shared female value system. As soon as they could, once the hard early years of settlement were past, they joined together with other women to help to build community institutions such as churches and schools. This role is celebrated in

frontier literature in the image of woman as "gentle tamer," as the culture-bearer who brings civilization to the West. What has not been so noticed is the criticism of male values which this female "civilizing" activity represents. The first stage of pioneering required that both men and women adopt the individualism and self-reliance which we have been taught to view as the result of the frontier process. However, what becomes clear from a close look at female sources is how much most women disliked that very process. They did not accept individualism willingly; they missed the shared support of the female subculture; and they re-created that network when they could. In the meantime, they worked side by side with their men.

Rosie Ise, a woman pioneer, homesteaded with her husband in western Kansas in the 1870s. She was widowed while in her fifties, and her children insisted that she deserved the leisure of town life after all her years of hard work on the farm. They tempted her with the suggestion that she would have time to grow flowers. She resisted them with a classic statement of the pioneer ideal of partnership and success:

> I used to think it would be so fine to have lots of time for flowers, but when it comes right down to it, flowers don't seem so important. Caring for the children, planting the trees, and building up our home here, so it would be a good home for us—that always seemed to be something substantial and worth-while.[16]

Some other female accounts echo this agrarian entrepreneurial dream of independence and success. One of the best is *Letters of a Woman Homesteader* by Elinor Stewart, an especially appealing and articulate spokeswoman of an almost forgotten group, single woman homesteaders.[17] Stewart, who homesteaded in Wyoming in the early 1900s, wrote enthusiastically to a former employer in Denver, for whom she had worked as a laundress:

> To me, homesteading is the solution of all poverty's problems, but I realize that. . .persons afraid of coyotes and work and loneliness had better let ranching alone. At the same time, any woman who can stand her own company, can see the beauty of the sunset, loves growing things, and is willing to put in as much time at careful labor as she does over the washtub, will certainly succeed; will

have independence, plenty to eat all the time, and a home of her own in the end.[18]

Stewart was hard-working, but she was also lucky. It was not always so easy. Many people—farmers, ranchers, miners—failed and returned to the East. In the 1860s, Amelia Buss met returning wagon trains as she traveled West, and envied their occupants because they were going home.[19] In the 1880s, the Ise family grimly hung on in western Kansas during drought years, while watching their neighbors give up.[20] In 1915 Sanora Babb's family, returning to town themselves, found a deserted cabin with a sign: "Starved Out."[21]

Some people failed—and stayed. Agnes Smedley's *Daughter of Earth*[22] is shaped by rage at her father and at an economic system which condemned the family to grinding poverty in the Colorado mining town of Trinidad. While her father periodically deserted the family (his only way to cope with failure), Smedley watched her mother try—and fail—to support the family alone.

Her mother's final attempt at independence by taking in washing ended this way:

> There came a morning when she wanted to "lay jist a little longer in bed" and I stayed home from school and started the washing. She lay sick for days. Doctors are only for the rich and it never occurred to any of us to call a doctor. I heated hot bricks all day long and kept them against her back and the side of her head. And each day I cooked potatoes and made a flour-and-water gravy for us all.
>
> Then my father drove up before the kitchen door for the last time. He didn't go away. When the right of women to vote [her previous assertion of autonomy] was even mentioned in the presence of my mother after that, her eyes sought a crack in the floor and followed it back and forth in silence. And her silence was heavy with bitterness.[23]

Rarely has the connection between the oppression of women and the injustice of the economic system been made so clearly. The economic exploitation which characterized the mining industry practically from its beginnings is a staple of labor history, but that perspective has not yet been integrated with our

emerging sense of women's lives on the frontier. Economic insecurity, rootlessness and dependence bore heavily on miners'
wives and families. An uncertain economic future faced most
other groups as well, and especially that large group of homesteaders, like the Babbs and the Ises, who hoped that hard work
would make up for lack of capital. Surely one major reason for
reluctant pioneering was realism: the knowledge that constant
hard work simply wasn't enough to break through the drab
greyness of poverty.

Political and literary recognition of these economic realities
emerged in the 1890s in the Populist movement and in novels
such as Garland's *Son of the Middle Border* and Baum's *Wizard
of Oz.* Some women, however, had seen the reality earlier. Study
of their diaries and reminiscences may well contribute to a wider
understanding of the early years' western economic development.

So too can other reminiscences from the great middle range
of people who neither succeeded nor failed but simply hung on.
Oral histories are a particularly good source for this group of
people, who rarely left written records. An Italian woman in
Sterling, Colorado, remembered her family's survival strategy:

> As the beet industry came into our neighborhood, Dad expected
> the labor would be done by the children as was customary [with]
> the pioneers. . . . So each of us were expected to, as soon as we
> were able to follow a row, to help thin the beets. . . . That also
> became sort of a family chore. Mother would also be out and help
> the rest of us. Whoever was not able to thin beets stayed home
> and took care of the baby.[24]

Dr. Ruth Flowers, a black woman, described the survival
skills necessary for the poor in Boulder, Colorado, in the early
years of this century. Flowers lived with her grandmother, who
was a short-order cook in a restaurant. Ruth, when age fourteen,
was hired as her grandmother's dishwasher. She opened the
restaurant at 6:30 every morning, went to school at 8:30 a.m.,
returned at noon to wash dishes, went back to school, came to
the restaurant again after school, and stayed until 8:30 p.m.,
when she closed up. She studied every night from nine until
one or two a.m., often with her feet in the oven to keep them
warm. This was the routine that Flowers kept from her teens

until she became the first black woman to graduate from the University of Colorado in 1924, overcoming both poverty and persistent racism along the way.[25]

Perhaps the best statement, however, was the matter-of-fact comment of a homesteading woman in eastern Colorado: "We lived an average life. I mean, we worked hard. But that was no different from anybody else."[26]

The traditional frontier myth has been success-biased; we do not know very much about the "failures," or about the pressures and anxieties that everyone, male and female, encountered. Stereotypically, it has been more permissable for women to confide their hopes and fears to their diaries than it has been for men. For this reason, women's sources will be essential to serious efforts to describe the pioneer experience as it really was.

Women were reluctant pioneers for several reasons. Physically draining and monotonous work, inability to maintain domestic and genteel standards, dependence, rootlessness, cultural fears, isolation, enforced self-reliance, the lack of female companionship, and economic injustice—or at least, insecurity—are all among the reasons why women were reluctant pioneers. What is surprising about this list is not its length, but how valid many of the reasons seem when the distorting prism of the sentimental stereotype is removed.

A common theme in the accounts by pioneer women surveyed in this paper is loneliness. Loneliness has many forms—psychological, physical, social—and can foster strength as well as weakness, as these excerpts have shown. Now that we know this, we can move beyond the pitying and limiting stereotype of women as reluctant pioneers. We can use women's sources to answer a whole range of serious and significant questions: from psychological survival on the frontier to a new perspective on economic development. Apparently Adrienne Rich knew this already, for her poem ends where I have proposed that we begin:

> I have lived in isolation
> from other women, so much
> . . . .
> Most of the time, in my sex, I was alone[27]

NOTES

I would like to express my gratitude to the students at the University of Colorado 1976-1977 with whom I developed the thoughts in this paper: Jim Balogh, Libby Comeaux, Rebecca Hensley, Riley Kyle, Roseanna Sneed, Carolyn Stefanco-Schill, Lana Waldron and Faith Williams; to the FIPSE-MLA Project "Teaching Women's Literature From a Regional Perspective" for financial support; and to Sheryll Patterson-Black and Sarah Jacobus for their sharing friendship out of which this paper grew.

[1] Lines from "An Old House in America," from *Poems, Selected and New, 1950-1974* by Adrienne Rich. © 1975, 1973, 1971, 1969, 1966, by W. W. Norton & Company, Inc.

[2] *Mollie: The Journal of Mollie Dorsey Sanford* (Lincoln: University of Nebraska Press, 1976), pp. 144-145.

[3] "Diary of Amelia Buss," Special Collections, Colorado State University Library, Fort Collins, Colorado. A version of the diary, edited by Susan Armitage, is forthcoming by Cottonwood Press, Crawford, Nebraska.

[4] *Mollie*, p. 166.

[5] Elizabeth Sayre Diary 1879, in Hal Sayre Papers, Western History Archives, Norlin Library, University of Colorado, Boulder.

[6] Mabel Barbee, *Cripple Creek Days* (New York: Doubleday, 1958).

[7] Barbee, p. 169.

[8] Barbee, p. 231.

[9] Isabella Bird, *A Lady's Life in the Rocky Mountains* (Norman: University of Oklahoma Press, 1960), p. 47.

[10]Elizabeth Cady Stanton, *Eighty Years and More* (New York: Schocken Books, 1971), pp. 249-250.

[11]Pioneer reminiscence quoted by Anne Saunders, Historical Museum and Institute of Western Colorado, Grand Junction, Colorado, June, 1977.

[12]Nannie Alderson, *A Bride Goes West* (Lincoln: University of Nebraska Press, 1969), p. 42.

[13]Buss diary.

[14]Sanora Babb, *An Owl on Every Post* (New York: New American Library, 1970), pp. 117-118.

[15]Carroll Smith-Rosenberg, "The Female World of Love and Ritual," *Signs,* 1 (Autumn, 1975), 1-29; Nancy Cott, *The Bonds of Womanhood* (New Haven: Yale University Press, 1977).

[16]John Ise, *Sod and Stubble* (Lincoln: University of Nebraska Press, 1967), p. 316.

[17]Elinor Stewart, *Letters of a Woman Homesteader* (Lincoln: University of Nebraska Press, 1961). Sheryll Patterson-Black has shown that in some places the percentage of single women filing homestead claims was at least 15%. See her article, "Women Homesteaders on the Great Plains Frontier," *Frontiers: A Journal of Women's Studies,* 1 (Spring, 1976), 67-88.

[18]Stewart, p. 212.

[19]Buss diary.

[20]Ise, p. 60.

[21]Babb, p. 171.

[22]Agnes Smedley, *Daughter of Earth* (New York: Feminist Press, 1973).

[23]Smedley, pp. 94-95.

[24]Interview with Katherine Pedroni Harley, 1977, by Riley Kyle, Whistlewind Project, Sterling High School, Sterling, Colorado.

[25]Interview with Dr. Ruth Flowers, 1976, by Theresa Banfield, Boulder Women's Oral History Project, Boulder Public Library, Boulder, Colorado.

[26]Interviews with Four Colorado Women, 1977, by Libby Comeaux, in the author's collection.

[27]Rich, "I Am An American Woman."

Sadie Austin

Courtesy of the Nebraska State Historical Society

II

FROM FACT TO FICTION:

MYTH AS FILTER

Women in Western American Fiction:
Images, or Real Women?*

Barbara Howard Meldrum

Joanna Russ, a contemporary writer of science fiction, as-
serted in her essay, "What Can a Heroine Do?, or, Why Women
Can't Write" (1972) that very few central actions can be imagined as being performed by female protagonists. For the most
part, protagonists are male; though there may be many women
in fiction, what we are given are "not women but images of women: modest maidens, wicked temptresses, pretty schoolmarms,
beautiful bitches, faithful wives, and so on. They exist only
in relation to the protagonist (who is male)." These women
characters "do not really exist at all—at their best they are de-
pictions of the social roles women are supposed to play and often
do play, but they are the public roles and not the private women."[1] Is this true of western American fiction? Certainly the
history of the settlement of the West provides many instances
of courageous women doing "men's work" or coping with great
physical or emotional stress. It would seem that fiction writers
would have plenty of opportunities to portray exemplary women. Have they responded with women who go beyond the
image stage to become vital, active human beings?

Let us look first at some of Vardis Fisher's women. This
Idaho author wrote many excellent novels during his long career,
and he is rightly esteemed one of the finest writers of the West.
His last novel, *Mountain Man* (1965), is subtitled "A Novel of
Male and Female in the Early American West." Surely here is
where to look for Fisher's mature reflections on man's and

---

*This essay is a revised and expanded version of one published in
Idaho Humanities Forum, Spring, 1981, pp. 9-10.

woman's nature and potential. The story, which is loosely based on the known facts and legends of "Liver-eating Johnson" and of Crazy Jane Morgan, tells of Sam Minard's love for his Indian wife, Lotus, her death at the hands of Crow warriors, Sam's revenge against the whole Crow nation, and his eventual resolution of that blood quest. Interwoven into Sam's story is that of Kate Bowden, who witnesses the murder of her children and torture of her husband by Blackfeet Indians, retaliates immediately by savagely killing several of the raiders, then retreats from reality into a mostly silent world of faithful, patient tending of her children's graves. Without doubt, this novel is one of the most eloquent tributes to woman that can be found in fiction. Sam senses his need for a woman to fill that empty sense of loneliness in his life, and with open eyes accepts the responsibilities of marriage for the sake of the added dimensions of living that come through that relationship. He is tender and considerate toward his young wife, treating her with respect and deep affection. He respects Kate, too—is, in fact, in awe of her boundless devotion to the memory of her children. As the years pass, he and the other mountain men see Kate more and more as the embodiment of "what mother love should be."[2] Moreover, Sam learns important lessons from Kate's example. When he first vows vengeance against the Crows, his vow is contrasted to the prayer Kate utters for her children. Later, he recognizes that he, the male, is hunted by countless warriors while she, the female, is befriended and left untouched. Woman's influence has a softening effect on his male aggressiveness as he becomes aware of fundamental differences between the sexes. Kate's image of selfless devotion is one important factor leading to Sam's eventual peace with the Crow nation.

Yes—I did say Kate's *image*. She doesn't exist as an individual—only as a type, an extreme instance of motherhood (as Sam sees her), or of psychosis (as many student readers regard her). I have taught this novel to a number of classes and each time have found myself having to explicate and defend (from the text's perspective) Sam's concept of Kate. Most students do not find Kate as convincing an embodiment of motherhood as Sam does. If the problems were simply that she is an extreme instance, then Fisher would be in good company: since Richard Chase's landmark study, *The American Novel and Its Tradition* (1957), it has been a commonplace that American

fiction generally follows the Romance tradition, with its predilection for melodramatic extremes and type characters. But
the problem is not simply that Kate is exaggerated; rather, readers find her unconvincing either because they do not see her actions as motivated by her "motherhood" (she is simply psy-
chotic), or because "motherhood" for them is not conceived in
the terms which she demonstrates: a totally selfless devotion to
one's children. I can't begin to unravel the nature of Kate's
craziness, but I would like to point out a definite pattern in
Fisher's portrayal of women in this book: a tendency to make
the woman other-directed (by spouse or children) and essentially
passive and dependent. Sam believes that Kate ultimately owes
her survival not to her gentleness, but to the mountain men who
have sworn to protect her against hostile Indians. In Fisher's
novel, Sam gives fair warning to the Blackfeet by ramming onto
stakes the heads of four warriors killed by Kate during the massacre; but according to legends, it was Jane Morgan herself who
staked those heads.[3] Fisher's Kate never lights a fire, never kills
a living creature after that one act of fury, and dies during a
severe winter several years after the massacre. The legendary
Jane Morgan, however, endured for twenty years and did kill
game until the winter in which she died, when "she went blind
from a blow she had received from the Blackfeet" twenty years
before.[4]

As for Lotus, Sam's Flathead wife, Sam expects that she
will be his trailmate and warrior at his side and teaches her to
shoot a gun so she can work with him and protect herself. But
he is clearly the one who directs her. He teaches her English,
whereas the legendary Johnson learned his wife's tongue;[5] this
is one small example of the alterations Fisher makes which cast
his fictional woman in a dependent, other-directed role. Moreover, when Sam returns from his trapping to find his wife brutally murdered, he imagines that she was caught off-guard because
she was watching and waiting for his return—again, a passive, dependent, other-directed role—whereas she might have been doing
any number of things when the Crows arrived. Fisher's exemplary women in this novel are images, not real women. Nor do
they demonstrate internal conflicts such as those Sam struggles
with: he is the protagonist, and they are defined in relation to
him.

To find a "real woman" in Fisher's fiction, one must turn
back to his earlier work. Perhaps his most convincing portrait of
a woman is Lela in *Dark Bridwell* (1931), a novel regarded by
many readers as Fisher's best. In this darkly tragic tale, Charley
Bridwell takes his young wife Lela deep into the Antelope Hill
country of southern Idaho, a natural paradise where he hopes to
raise a family close to nature and away from the corrupting ambitions of civilization. But he has not reckoned with the darker
side of his own character nor with the restless spirit of his wife,
who cannot wholly conform to the life vision of her husband.
He cares for her, protects and cherishes her; but his "greatest
mistake" lies in his efforts to make her into "a kind of idle
princess" who is not allowed to work.[6] Though her true nature
is smothered for many years, Lela eventually revolts. The in-
centive for her revolt brings us again to Fisher's notion of a
primitive mothering instinct in woman: it is Lela's desire to
rescue her younger daughter from Charley's influence that
prompts her to throw aside her passive, dependent role and to
become a very active, enterprising woman who labors for seven
years to save enough money to ensure her freedom. The final
break comes during a bitter argument over their sons. Lela
leaves, taking her daughter with her; but her newfound freedom
is undercut by the narrator who asserts that "she forgot that
deeper than ambition, *as deep almost as motherhood itself*, was
her love for Charley Bridwell" (p. 335; italics added). She is a
woman defined primarily by her relationship to the protagonist
Charley and to her children, but she does become something of
a protagonist herself—a thwarted artist, an individual who finally
asserts herself and makes her own way in the world. Moreover,
if her loss of love undercuts her freedom, so too does Charley's
loss of love and family: love is essential to self-fulfillment for
both man and woman. In this novel, if woman is defined in relation to spouse and child, so too is man. The fate is human,
not sexist.

Such a reading of the novel gives Fisher the benefit of the
doubt in his portrayal of a "real woman." I could add that the
obviously male narrative voice simply asserts that Lela forgot
how deep was her love for Charley. We never see or hear of her
life after she leaves her husband. Is it not possible to imagine
that she continued to grow and develop as an individual and that
she found fulfillment in love, though not necessarily marriage?

(There are many kinds of love.) Judging from the strength of character she develops and the loving nature she manifests toward her children, I for one am not convinced that her future is but gloom apart from Charley. Perhaps Fisher created more than he realized in Lela.

Fisher seems to be more successful in portraying a "real woman" in his early fiction. The same may also be true for the most widely recognized woman writer of the West (or Midwest), Willa Cather.[7] Perhaps her best known female character is Ántonia, the title character of *My Ántonia* (1918). Here is the story of a young immigrant girl's struggles in a new land, her growing up and ultimate fulfillment as wife and mother, at one with the abundant earth. Ántonia is surely a vividly realized female protagonist. But she is also defined by her relationship to her children and to men: her husband and the narrator, Jim Burden. Indeed, Jim is a major character; the novel can be read primarily as his story, not Ántonia's. (The same can be said of Mrs. Forrester and the male observer of her story, *A Lost Lady*, 1923). To find in Cather's novels a female character who is indisputably the principal protagonist and is not defined by her role as wife or mother, one must go to the earlier novels, *O Pioneers!* (1913) and *The Song of the Lark* (1915). Alexandra Bergson of *O Pioneers!* takes over her father's farm after his death because she is far more capable as a farm manager than are her brothers. She loves the land and has a vision for its future which is both mystical and practical. She is indeed an achieving woman who is not defined by her relationship to a man. Marriage does come for her at the end of the tale—But when she is middle-aged, and to her lifelong friend. Carl could have become her husband years earlier, but he felt it necessary to become established on his own before marrying the landowner Alexandra. To her, such considerations were superfluous. When she marries, she does so to enjoy the company of a longtime friend and relieve the loneliness of her life. One senses that without Carl she could certainly have managed, though less happily so. She becomes a wife, but is not defined by that role. She is a "real woman," not an image.

In *The Song of a Lark* Cather's female protagonist is even more a career woman than is Alexandra. Thea Kronborg is an aspiring artist, a young girl with musical talent who grows up in a

small Colorado town, encouraged in her musical studies by her devoted friend (a young man), her piano teacher, and the local doctor. Later another male is added: Fred, who also encourages her and falls in love with her, but cannot marry because he is already married (though unhappily so and he does not live with his wife). These men not only encourage Thea, but provide material assistance so she can pursue her studies and become an opera singer. Though their help is important, even more decisive is Thea's own determination, talent, and hard work, which ensure her success. At the height of her career we see her absorption in that work which must take preeminence with her no matter the cost to family obligations or longstanding friendship. The choices to be made are hard ones, and the effects are a part of the aging Thea experiences. Yet in spite of these difficulties, her art is clearly her life: when singing on stage, she is young and vibrant, fully alive and fulfilled. Perhaps we don't normally expect such single-minded devotion to one's career in a woman. Cather here portrays a woman who has chosen work before love, and yet gains some measure of love too through her relationship with Fred. This novel is an early instance in American literature of a predominantly positive portrayal of a woman in search of fulfillment through a profession outside the traditional female role of wife and mother.

Western male authors have not usually been as positive as Cather in their portrayal of career women. Wallace Stegner's *Angle of Repose* (1971) tells the story of Susan Ward, who marries a mining engineer and gives up her hopes for an artistic career in the East to follow her husband to the West of the 1870s. Stegner's tale is doubly complicated. The narrator, Lyman Ward, is Susan's grandson, who is researching and writing the biography of his grandmother as a means of investigating his own roots and understanding his own fate. He is not totally reliable, for he is biased by the subjective factors of his own plight (as well as by his male perspective?). Stegner has complicated his story further by using the life of Mary Hallock Foote as the basis for his narrative, but departing from known facts freely when his fictional urges suggest another direction. Knowledge of those facts which contradict Stegner's narrative generates questions regarding his fictional purposes. Both of these complications are relevant to his portrayal of Susan Ward. The result, it seems to me, is an unnecessarily negative projection of his female protagonist.

Stegner's narrator relies primarily on his grandmother's voluminous correspondence for his sources and professes to stick close to them. He does, however, fictionalize freely by dramatizing scenes he imagines to have taken place. In some instances Susan is sympathetically portrayed, but an undercutting element is present even amidst the otherwise positive portrait. For instance, Susan's husband Oliver seems to be mulishly proud when he refuses to use his wife's money earned through her work as an illustrator to support the family, even though such a refusal works hardship on them all. Like a good wife, she accepts his decision; but we tend to condemn Oliver for his excessive pride.[8] Later in the story, when family finances are more desperate, Susan's earnings become the mainstay; but Oliver clearly resents this necessity (p. 433). Stegner's narrator here imagines a conflict between the husband's self-image and the threat to that image posed by his wife's financial success. No clear source for such a conflict can be gleaned from a reading of Mary Foote's *Reminiscences.*[9] This conflict seems to be part of Stegner's fictionalizing (through his narrator): an imagined resentment of the wife's professional success. Here is a woman who relinquished the career she had dreamed of in the East, but subsequently made a workable adjustment to her Western locale and developed a career in absentia through correspondence. Yet that success is more a threat than an achievement in the context of a family headed by a proud man who resents her financial security while his own ambitions are frustrated and seldom monetarily rewarded. Although we may condemn Oliver's stubborn pride, the legitimacy of the wife's career does become problematic.

Stegner's narrator also insinuates that Susan lacks the moral integrity of her husband. He imagines that she urges Oliver to compromise his honesty for the sake of family security (pp. 342-346); we are duly shocked and disappointed in Susan. Such an incident leads logically to the climax of the novel, wherein Stegner departs most radically from the actual life of Mrs. Foote. In Stegner's tale the narrator pieces together clues from Boise newspaper accounts and Susan's letters to ascertain that she is emotionally unfaithful to her husband at the time of his greatest need, the lowest ebb of his fortunes. As a consequence of her unfaithfulness as wife and negligence as mother, their daughter drowns and her erstwhile lover commits suicide. These incidents

have no basis in Foote's biography; yet Stegner chooses to imagine a woman whose own ambitions leave her so at odds with her husband's Western destiny that she fails as wife and mother. The moral seems clear: if you're a woman with professional aspirations, you had better get your priorities straight, which means you had better not fail as wife and mother, no matter what the cost to your own deepest needs.

Stegner's Susan Ward experiences great difficulty in juggling her various roles as wife, mother, and professional woman (artist and author). It is fascinating to speculate about a reversal of plot roles: what if it had been Susan's career that was in jeopardy? Would her husband have taken the situation so seriously as to get emotionally off-balance and be unfaithful to her? Not very likely. Nor did the real-life counterpart, Mrs. Foote, lose her head during this crisis. True, there was marital tension throughout this stressful period (even a trial separation); but it was weathered, and Mrs. Foote continued writing and drawing, wifing and mothering. What I am suggesting is that Stegner resorts to stereotyped notions of the woman who tries to combine career with marriage. The result is that Susan is revealed as a bit of a bitch—an image that we've seen too many times before.

There is, however, another way of viewing Stegner's novel, and that is as pure novel rather than historical fiction. Assume, then, that the Footes' lives had nothing to do with the story, that Stegner's real-life sources were so various that no clear resemblance to persons living or dead can be traced. All I have said above about the career-woman still stands, it seems to me. But there *are* other considerations: why, for instance, is Susan unfaithful to Oliver—and why does Lyman's wife Ellen run away with his surgeon? Lyman himself stumbles onto the reason, though he responds with contempt rather than sympathetic understanding. He notes her "anxiety" during his illness: "She soaked her pillow the night after they told me I'd have to have the leg off." Yet she left him "only a few months after that. . . when I was helpless." He concludes "that what finally led her to break away from me was my misfortunes." He thereby answers his earlier question: "Does a woman ever leave a man out of intolerable pity? Or because she fears what pity may do to her and him?" (pp. 441-444). Ellen and Susan don't share many traits, but they are alike in that both are "unfaithful" to their

husbands when they are most needed, when the women may feel most keenly their inability to meet those needs—may indeed feel their own identities in danger of being overwhelmed. Their acts of desertion (emotional or physical) may be prompted by a survival instinct; but in both instances, the fact that they choose another man as the haven of rescue may foreshadow their failure (though their impulse affirms their humanness). Perhaps we can say that Stegner has here subtly revealed the tragedy of woman who cannot successfully define herself apart from her role in relation to a man: the tragedy of being an image rather than a "real woman."[10]

Frederick Manfred has also approached the subject of the woman pursuing a "man's career" in his *The Manly-Hearted Woman* (1975). His version is radically different, for his story is about Indians. Nonetheless, we have Manfred's own word, in a published interview, that one subject he was working with in this novel was the women's liberation movement.[11] Manly-Heart is a young Sioux woman who joins the men in hunting game. She is skillful and is accepted by them as a warrior. Moreover, she has a vision—something only the young men of the tribe ordinarily have. That a woman can have a vision says, in the context of this novel, that women are (or can be) equal with men. Surely this is a move away from the old stereotypes. Manfred then carries the development a step further: Manly-Heart obeys the voice of her helper (her spiritual guide, a legacy of her vision) and takes a wife. To my knowledge, this is the solitary instance of portrayal of a lesbian relationship in an Indian story. Manfred handles the subject with some delicacy, much sympathy, and gentle humor. The members of the tribe are perplexed by the arrangement, but accept Manly-Heart as a full-fledged "male" with the right to take a wife. The social tolerance is commendable. What I find disturbing, however, is the latent suggestion that a woman who does things a man normally does thereby ceases to be truly a woman. (Biologically, Manly-Heart demonstrates her new role by ceasing to menstruate.) Surely this is extreme? Must it be either-or?

The dénouement of the tale raises other questions. Manfred's novel features two protagonists: Manly-Heart and a young warrior, Flat Warclub. They are male and female counterparts: both are socially on the fringes of their tribes, both have had

visions, and their secret names are complementary. Comparisons and contrasts are carefully balanced throughout the story. We find that both tend to talk too much when they should be listening to their helper. But Flat Warclub learns to listen well and to obey the spirit voice. As a consequence, he becomes a noble warrior and leader of his people. He dies in battle, but heroically so. Manly-Heart, however, does not learn to listen or obey. Instead, she seems to demonstrate the old stereotype: a talking, inquisitive woman. This is especially so when she spies on Flat Warclub in direct disobedience to her helper. The reason seems to be that she is a woman and therefore can't help doing what she does. Not long after, her helper leaves her and she returns to being a woman in the tribe—alone, without wife or husband, mourning Flat Warclub, whom she has grown to love. For a tale which started out by exploding the old myths about woman's place, this is a disappointing ending. Moreover, Manly-Heart's fate seems not to be hers alone but all women's; the reason she fails lies in her nature as woman.

Mick McAllister has taken a somewhat different position in an excellent essay which focuses on the possibilities for a new sexual covenant. We agree that the novel is more mythic than realistic; but Manly-Heart's archetypal fate seems more individual than gender-determined to McAllister. He sees the source of her failure in her unwillingness to pay the price demanded by the gods: in order to play her part in bringing about a "new sexual covenant," she alone "must renounce sensual pleasure; she is not equal to that renunciation. She cannot be the only person who can never have the lightning; through her a world is lost for love."[12] Stated in these terms, her failure is human rather than sexist; her tragedy is poignant in its very affirmation of human need through disobedience of the gods. If this is so, then those passages which suggest a stereotypical talkative, inquisitive woman should not be confused with a stereotypical conception of woman. (Talking or not talking also fits a major symbolic motif in the novel.) In his response to McAllister's paper, Manfred described how he wrote the novel during a few weeks of intense, inspired composition. He seems to feel that he got hold of something very deep in the unconscious—perhaps archetypal truth (though he did not use these terms). Possibly so. Certainly the tale is provocative and profound, not easily unraveled in spite of its seeming simplicity. Manfred's instincts, however, are very

male.[13]   One can't always be sure that what he portrays is myth-
equals-archetypal-truth, or myth-equals-male-perceived-reality.
There is a difference.   Even the Greek myths are under attack
these days by feminists who see them as the products of a
patriarchy which conquered the earlier matriarchy.   (Manfred
himself is one who frequently "rewrites" earlier myths to suit
his own perceptions—for example, in the poem I quote below.)

Where Manfred is at his best is in his grasp of what it is to
be male.   His achievements in exploring this theme may eventually be seen as his greatest contribution to American literature (no
mean feat).   Here is where his male instincts, tempered by a
"feminine" sensitivity, serve him well.   A poem he wrote in the
early 1950s expresses his concern and his perspective.   Through
a series of images that reverse our usual ordering of events, he
builds to a reversed description of the Biblical creation of man:
God formed woman of the dust of the ground, then took one of
her ribs and formed man.   The poem concludes:

> the truth is true
>   mankind is
>   womankind
> the truth is rue
>   man tries to be man
>   while woman is woman[14]

For Manfred, it is more difficult for man to be (or become) man
than it is for woman to be woman.[15]   Moreover, many of the
problems women struggle with are male-generated.   We see this
time and again in his fiction, especially in the women (or girls)
who are sexually abused by men or boys (often relatives):
Katherine in *King of Spades,* Karen in *Eden Prairie,* Jael and
Jen in *Sons of Adam* are just a few examples.   Taking the last
novel as a paradigm, I think we can see the direction Manfred
points.   Both girls are seduced by their uncles.   Jael is thereby
sidetracked from a possible future as a writer and as wife of the
protagonist Alan to become a cock-crazy young woman who gets
pregnant and elopes with one of her lovers.   Jen is repressed because of her girlhood affair with her uncle, then is brutally
stabbed by her husband when he goes berserk.   But she is long-
suffering and loving; her husband finds himself and learns how to
love her; eventually, they both experience physical and emo-

tional fulfillment in their mutual love. When he decides he would like to live permanently in the Amish community where he had found himself, she accepts his decision: " 'I go where my husband goes. I want him to be happy.' "[16] Alan marries Jerre, a steady young woman who will make a good wife. At story's end, both Jen and Jerre give birth to sons. Manfred portrays a redeemed patriarchy, not a "liberated" world.

Perhaps Manfred is simply being realistic; his novel is set in the 1930s, not exactly the decade for portraying "real women" who are active individuals in their own right. Let us take a look at one more writer, this time one who projects a future New World on another planet with a wilderness that lures dreamers of a new society to a Promised Land. Ursula LeGuin is not usually regarded as a western writer, though she lives in Oregon and some of her works employ setting in a way that suggests concerns of much western fiction. In *The Eye of the Heron* (1978) LeGuin portrays the odyssey of a young female protagonist, Luz, who moves away from the repressive patriarchy of her father's City to the relative freedom of Shantih town (called Shanty-town by her father's people). Her move is influenced by the example of love and freedom she sees in two persons: Vera, an older woman, and Lev, a young man. Lev and Luz are obviously drawn to each other, but their incipient love never blossoms before the idealistic Lev is killed in a pacifist demonstration quelled by the patriarchal City aggressors. Luz eventually helps spur a group of Shantih-towners to emigrate, seeking a new beginning in the eastern wilderness. (On this futuristic planet the direction of hope is East, not West; perhaps this time the mistakes of the past will not be repeated.) In the wilderness Luz begins to discover her inner potential to transcend fear and loneliness. She finds her center, which is not invulnerable; she learns to cope with fear. Through the compassionate wisdom of Lev's father and the influence of nature itself, she begins to learn what the wilderness "where no voice spoke" can teach through its silence: "they must walk in it in silence, until they had learned a language fitting to be spoken here."[17] This new community hopes to build a new world out of mud; it will be a place of freedom and of love, where men and women retain their separate identities and differences, yet share a common destiny united in love.

Are, then, the women in western fiction images or real women? The images which derive from stereotyped notions of female behavior are certainly evident. Some readers (and authors) may believe the images persist because they are true—they are mythic truths. I prefer to think they are false myths: convenient vehicles to express persistent concepts that may not be universally or everlasting true (although they may realistically embody the behavior of many women). Although there is no talisman to differentiate between false myths and mythic truth, the writer who doggedly refuses to resort to stereotypes is most apt to achieve a fresh perspective. Western writers have shown that they are able to move beyond stereotypes and images. Let us only hope that they will continue to explore new frontiers, and not hide in the seeming security of outworn traditions.

NOTES

[1]In *Images of Women in Fiction: Feminist Perspectives*, ed. Susan Koppelman Cornillon, rev. ed. (Bowling Green: Bowling Green University Press, 1973), p. 5.

[2]Vardis Fisher, *Mountain Man: A Novel of Male and Female in the Early American West* (New York: William Morrow & Company, 1965), p. 309.

[3]Raymond W. Thorp and Robert Bunker, *Crow Killer: The Saga of Liver-Eating Johnson* (Bloomington: Indiana University Press, 1958), p. 39.

[4]Thorp and Bunker, p. 105.

[5]Thorp and Bunker, p. 43.

[6]Vardis Fisher, *Dark Bridwell* (Boston: Houghton Mifflin Company, 1931), p. 270. All further references to this work appear in the text.

[7]Carolyn Heilbrun notes the shift in Cather's fiction from strong female protagonists in the early novels to patriarchal milieu in her later works. "It is extraordinarily puzzling that the identity crisis through which an accomplished woman author passes with evident success should so strongly resist imaginative recreation." *Reinventing Womanhood* (New York: W. W. Norton & Company, 1979), p. 81.

[8]Wallace Stegner, *Angle of Repose* (New York: Doubleday & Company, 1971), p. 158. All further references to this work appear in the text.

[9]I am also drawing upon Mary Ellen Williams Walsh's discussion of M. H. Foote's correspondence in her unpublished paper, "Succubi and Other Monsters: the Women in *Angle of Repose*," presented to the convention of the Western Literature Association, October 1979. The correspondence reveals marital conflict which led to a temporary separation, but Mary Foote's financial success does not appear to have been a factor.

[10]For a provocative discussion of Stegner's portrayal of marriage, with emphasis on the male role, see Kerry Ahearn, "Heroes vs. Women: Conflict and Duplicity in Stegner," in *Women, Women Writers, and the West*, ed. L. L. Lee and Merrill Lewis (Troy, New York: Whitston Publishing Company, 1979), pp. 143-159.

[11]"An Interview in Minnesota with Frederick Manfred," James W. Lee, interviewer, *Studies in the Novel*, 5 (1973), 364-365.

[12]Mick McAllister, "The Sundered Egg: The Sexual Issues in *The Manly-Hearted Woman*," paper presented to the convention of the Western Literature Association, October 1980, p. 9.

[13]Delbert Wylder, for instance, says that "Manfred is unashamedly male, and he sees the male principle as the major creative force. He does not espouse the macho image for its own sake, however." "Frederick Manfred: The Quest of the Independent Writer," *Books at Iowa*, No. 31 (November 1979), p. 21.

[14]"Colin," in *Winter Count* (Minneapolis: James D. Thueson, 1966), p. 42.

[15]Similarly, Manfred stated in a 1964 interview: "I think it is more of a problem to be a father, more difficult to be a good father, than to be a good mother. . . . It is very difficult to learn to become a father. Natural instinct and nature are against it." *Conversations with Frederick Manfred,* moderated by John R. Milton (Salt Lake City: University of Utah Press, 1974), p. 62.

[16]Frederick Manfred, *Sons of Adam* (New York: Crown Publishers, 1980), p. 332.

[17]Ursula K. LeGuin, "The Eye of the Heron," in *Millennial Women,* ed. Virginia Kidd (New York: Dell Publishing Company, 1979), pp. 172, 294.

Sacajawea of Myth and History

David Remley

One of the most persistently puzzling important women in western American history is Sacajawea, who travelled to the Pacific with Lewis and Clark. Since about the turn of the century, she has been represented variously in many fictional works. She is also the subject of numerous historical articles and of at least three biographies. These writings represent her as, on the one hand, the "guide" of the famous Expedition and, on the other, as useful in various ways, but hardly as a guide. These writings also tell two widely different stories of what happened to the Indian woman in later life. One story has her travelling throughout the West and settling finally with her people, the Shoshone, on a reservation in Wyoming. There she is supposed to have died late in the nineteenth century; to this day a marker indicates her grave in an Indian cemetery. The other story of Sacajawea's later life has her dying of a "putrid fever" on the upper Missouri River at Fort Manuel in 1812. Grace Raymond Hebard gives the first of these two versions in her biography, *Sacajawea: A Guide and Interpreter of the Lewis and Clark Expedition* (1933). Hebard based her work primarily upon extensive interviews with friends and descendants of an Indian woman who died in Wyoming and who claimed to be the woman with Lewis and Clark. Harold P. Howard gives the other version of Sacajawea's later life in his biography, *Sacajawea* (1971). The virtue of Howard's study is that he uses written documents from the period to reach what he calls "a reasonable conclusion." These documents strongly suggest—though by no means to the satisfaction of two more recent biographers, Ella E. Clark and Margot Edmonds—that the real Indian woman is buried along the Missouri River near the site of old Fort Manuel although no one has located her grave there.[1] Unless someone should discover more hard evidence, it is likely that historians will never be absolutely sure which woman is the real Sacajawea of the

Lewis and Clark Expedition.

It is not nearly so difficult, however, to know certain specific things about the part Sacajawea actually played during her months with the Expedition. Little speculation is required. For anyone interested in reading the *Original Journals of the Lewis and Clark Expedition* (1904-1905), the important elements of the Indian woman's usefulness and of her character become apparent.[2] Both the captains liked the Indian woman; Clark may have been downright affectionate. Most of their references to her state or suggest that she was nearly always uncomplaining and helpful. She was often up and about gathering roots and berries for food. She was both cool and courageous on the day the white pirogue upset in the Missouri River. Sacajawea, seated in the stern, reached out and managed to grab various important small articles while the boat was righted and hauled ashore. She was generous, giving Clark a piece of bread when food was short. Perhaps her most useful quality was that, according to the journal entries, she was nearly always cheerful. This way of accepting optimistically whatever came was undoubtedly a morale strengthener for the overworked, poorly clothed and sheltered, and often underfed men. In short, Sacajawea seems to have been, not a burden, but a completely responsible, contributing member of the Expedition.

Much of the biographical and fictional writing about the Indian woman has, however, carried the legendary or mythical stamp. For nearly a century now some writers and a good many readers have shown a continuing interest in seeing in Sacajawea qualities different from—or at least more exaggerated than—those qualities documened in the journal entries of the captains themselves. Characteristic of this mythical Sacajawea is the notion that she actually piloted or guided the Lewis and Clark Expedition across the West. Nearly as common as this "guide myth" is the notion that Sacajawea and Clark were passionately in love with one another. Many are the stories that have the two secretly embracing, kissing and panting hotly at each other's necks. The "love myth" writers hardly consider the facts that Sacajawea was married by the tribal rules of the day and that she carried her new baby all the way to the Pacific and back. The same writers ignore also the important facts that Sacajawea's husband Charbonneau was ever present as the interpreter of the Expedi-

tion and that, as responsible captains, Lewis and Clark would have had to maintain a dignified distance, sexually at least, from the other members of their group so as to keep discipline and order and a high level of morale.

For years an examination of the literature of the mythical Sacajawea has been in order. No less a historian of the West than Bernard De Voto suggested long ago the need for a study of the legendary or mythical Indian woman. "The tropical emotion that has created a legendary Sacajawea awaits study by some connoisseur of American sentiments," De Voto wrote in the notes to *The Course of Empire* (1952).[3] Because the mythical stories of Sacajawea have continued to appear in print, it seems sensible to accept De Voto's invitation. One cannot help wondering, among other things, why the writers of the guide and lover stories seem more stimulated by their tales than by the actual historical record itself. As anyone knows who has read the *Original Journals,* the captains' own descriptions of this great adventure provide very lively and often very exciting reading.

One wonders not only why this Sacajawea mythmaking has been so persistent, but also why it has been largely a development of the twentieth century. A probable reason is that 1904-1905 honored both the centennial of the Expedition and the publication for the first time of the Lewis and Clark journals in their entirety. These events dramatized the Expedition. Another reason, argued by Ronald W. Taber in "Sacajawea and the Suffragettes" (1967), is that the guide myth was created by feminists interested in promoting women's rights, chiefly by Eva Emory Dye in *The Conquest: The True Story of Lewis and Clark* (1903) and by Grace Raymond Hebard, Sacajawea's early biographer. Taber observes that Mrs. Dye herself believed that she was the creator of the new Sacajawea: "I created Sacajawea and made her a real living entity," she wrote.[4] In fact, however, the myth was already alive by 1902. Elliott Coues, whom Taber calls "the father of the myth," had written earlier that Clark took "the advice of the remarkable little woman, who never failed to rise to the occasion. . . ."[5] As early as 1866, Thomas Bulfinch had prefaced his *Oregon and Eldorado; or, Romance of the Rivers* with a strong suggestion of the urge to make myths out of the Expedition's history: "I indulge the hope," he writes, "that young readers who have so favorably received my former

attempts to amuse and instruct them, in my several works reviving the fabulous legends of remote ages, will find equally attractive these true narratives of bold adventure."[6] One notes in Bulfinch the excitement over "legends" which are both "fabulous" and belonging to "remote ages"—the sense of remoteness in time, distance from everyday living, which mythmaking needs in order to seem persuasive to readers. One also notes the writer's insistence that this particular narrative is "true," that its events actually happened.

Two books before Mrs. Dye's also indicate that the myth was alive earlier than her writing. William R. Lighton's *Lewis and Clark* (1901) states that on the return trip to the Yellowstone, "Captain Clark had an efficient guide in Sacajawea."[7] Noah Brooks' *First Across the Continent* (1901) is more expansive. "With her helpless infant clinging to her," Brooks writes, "she rode with the men, guiding them with unerring skill through the mountain fastnesses and lonely passes which the white men saw for the first time when their salient features were pointed out to them by the intelligent and faithful Sacajawea."[8] It is important to note that upon one occasion Clark had actually called Sacajawea a "pilot." Of the return trip overland to the Yellowstone, he wrote: "The indian woman who has been of great service to me as a pilot through this country recommends a gap in the mountain more south which I shall cross."[9] Hence, the myth makers do have this bit of evidence although it is hardly enough to justify the full-blown romantic conceptions of the Indian woman guide one finds in later writers.

Still another reason for the growth of the myth in the twentieth century may have been the need for faith on the part of readers in the essential goodness of the American system. Mrs. Dye and other Sacajawea writers reveal a strong Jeffersonian urge in an age which was becoming increasingly critical of capitalistic industrialism and of the notion that, let alone to do as he pleased, the American citizen would be morally responsible in his struggle for success. Around the turn of the century, American experience was proving otherwise, or so the critics said. Thinkers like Henry George and writers like Edward Bellamy were widely read. Muckraking magazines like *McClure's*, *Everybody's, Collier's, The Independent,* and *Cosmopolitan* provided committed journalists with outlets for their disaffection

with American abuses. Novelists like Garland, Crane, Norris, London, Upton Sinclair, and David Graham Phillips, in their different ways, expressed their disillusion with aggressive individualism and capitalism in a society that liked to think of itself as Christian. Everywhere in their works one finds characterizations of the unbridled powerful at their worst—the venal politician, the wealthy adventurer, the social climber, the heartless rich—and, posed against these depraved—the urban poor, the prostitute, the overworked factory man, the child laborer, and the farmer thrown off the land by a man from the bank. Herbert Croly, one of the representative critics of the period, argued in *The Promise of American Life* (1911) that the old faith in individual goodness and the common man had been all wrong. That very faith, he believed, had allowed the development, ironically, of a vicious and rampant capitalism. Croly posed against that "wrong" faith the need for firm intellectual commitment and a thoroughly intelligent planning to prevent runaway capital development and the destruction of America's human and natural resources.[10]

In the light of Croly's thinking and the criticism of the muckrakers, Mrs. Dye seems a backward looking romantic, a writer who avoided the ugly realities of the present and gloried in the past out of the hope that the process of benevolent individualism might still work. Appropriately, she idealized the common man. For her, he came to power about 1800 during Jefferson's Presidency. This was the period when, she writes, "the old social systems of Europe were tottering" and "the experiment of self-government had triumphed."[11] It was a time when the American President "in the simplicity of his past" led an essentially simple, forthright, benevolent people.[12] Even before 1800 Americans had been fundamentally good-hearted. "Do you take us for savages?" Clark in Mrs. Dye's book asked the French at Kaskaskia: "My countrymen never make war on the innocent."[13] The Clarks themselves had always been ideal Americans: "A strain of heroic benevolence runs through the red-headed Clarks," Mrs. Dye writes. "They win the world and give it away."[14]

If the muckrakers and the crusading novelists had gone after the banker and the landlord, Mrs. Dye extended her thought to the American Indian. Instead of attacking the

white oppressor, however, she defended him. The major problem for Mrs. Dye and for writers like her appears to have been how to interpret the brutality of land hungry Americans pushing west so as to regain the faith in the ideal of American decency. How does one see the exploration and development of the West in such a way as to excuse or forgive the methods used? It is toward solving this problem, whether consciously or not, that many of the Sacajawea guide myth writers seem to direct their efforts. For all their other possible motives—woman suffrage and the like—these writers are fundamentally apologists for American history, moralists of the westward movement. Brian Dippie has suggested that the poetic celebrations of the Custer disaster attempt "to convert defeat into a kind of moral victory, a glorious if vague triumph of Americanism."[15] He finds a parallel between Custer-worship and Tennyson's transformation of the Balaclava military blunder into a triumph of British manhood in "The Charge of the Light Brigade." Likewise, the twentieth century's Sacajawea literature seems largely an attempt to transform our destructive treatment of the Indian as well as of our once vast wilderness into a victory of some sort—for sheer American effort, for progress, civilization and morality, and for reconciliation between Indian and White American.

Several of the Sacajawea writers work toward these ends in a number of identifiable ways. Mrs. Dye, for example, makes anyone who stands in the way of the westward movement seem like a fiend. In the eighteenth century, in her writing, the French are good because they are helpful, but the English are bad. The Spanish, if possible, are worse. The West, Mrs. Dye writes, "despised and defied the Spaniard as she despised and defied the Indian. They blocked the way, they must depart."[16] Worse still are Mrs. Dye's angry Indians. Those who fought the whites at Detroit, at Niagara, and Michilimackinac are "the red bloodhounds of war."[17] The Blackfeet are "vicious and profligate rovers."[18] On the other hand, helpful Indians are good ones. The Yankton Sioux who were friendly to Lewis and Clark are the "best of their nation."[19] Sacajawea is, of course, the best of all the good Indians.

The same writers create a Sacajawea who understands that not only will the white man's way ultimately prevail but that it is

the best way. Further, peaceful intention is on the side of the whites in much of the Sacajawea guide myth literature, and this fact places accountability upon the Indians for warlike acts. The white man's motives are pure; it is, therefore, the intelligent Indian's responsibility to help the whites. The Indian who chooses to obstruct must be eliminated. Let him realize that the responsibility for his elimination is his. On the other hand, Indians who help the whites will be rewarded with all the benefits of civilization. Finally, these Sacajawea writers attempt to close their case by giving divine backing to the Lewis and Clark Expedition and, in general, to the whole white push westward. Mrs. Dye's book is full of suggestions that an impersonal but exalted being sponsors white Americans. The motive seems to be to reassure the readers that our American guilt is assuaged by high cause and divine backing. Intelligent, sensible Indians like Sacajawea will understand. Those who do not understand will go on hating white Americans, but whites can bear that burden because they know that the cause of the westward movement was right.

Although none but children or the most simple minded and credulous adults in our time could be persuaded, Sacajawea guide myth books continue to appear. At the center of their case is deception in some form or other. Their writers do not or cannot face truths. On the most primary level, they ignore the facts about which the Lewis and Clark *Original Journals* are very explicit. A good example is Jerry Seibert's *Sacajawea: Guide to Lewis and Clark* (1960). Seibert announces fairly accurately that "all we know of Sacajawea is what was written in the journals."[20] With that statement, all accuracy ceases. Seibert claims that his story is taken from the "thousands of facts" given in the *Journals,* but adds, apologetically, that "only a few of the important facts. . .could be crammed into one small book."[21] Certainly Seibert uses few of the facts; his account is mostly imagined. His description of the swamping of the white pirogue on the Missouri above the Mandan villages is an illustration. Here, if anywhere, one would think the *Journals* should be read with care; for this swamping of the pirogue was a point at which the Expedition came very near to failure. Lewis describes the incident in detail, and, in the *Journals,* credits Sacajawea with saving many small items which would, without her nimbleness, have been lost in the muddy river. This "occurence," says Lewis,

"I cannot recollect but with the utmost trepidation and horror." In the pirogue, he continues, "were embarked, our papers, Instruments, books medicine, a great part of our merchandize and in short almost every article indispensibly necessary to further the views, or insure the success of the enterprize in which we are now launched to the distance of 2200 miles."[22]

And it was the Indian woman, Lewis writes, who "caught and preserved most of the light articles which were washed overboard." She was, he adds, of "equal fortitude and resolution, with any person on board."[23] But in Seibert's version, "Sacajawea, with Pompey on her back, was calmly swimming about rescuing the things that had been washed overboard. As. . . [Lewis and Clark] watched, she swam back to the boat and gathered up the articles floating there."[24] Seibert's account is absurd. The *Journals* clearly state that the current was so swift even Lewis refused to go into the river: "I for a moment forgot my own situation," Lewis writes, "and involluntarily droped my gun, threw aside my shot pouch and was in the act of unbuttoning my coat, before I recollected the folly of the attempt I was about to make; which was to throw myself into the river and indevour to swim to the perogue." The waves were running high, "the water excessively could, and the stream rappid" so that "had I undertaken this project. . .there was a hundred to one but what I should have paid the forfit of my life for the madness of my project."[25]

Seibert's book also develops the Sacajawea guide myth. The Indian woman points the way up the Missouri, makes the decisions about which stream to follow at river junctions, and gets spiritual sponsorship for her trouble. In one instance she and Clark watch eagles flying above the river. The captain takes out a ten dollar gold piece to compare the eagle on the coin with the real bird. Seeing the eagle on the gold piece, Sacajawea realizes intuitively that her destiny is to guide the white men to her people. " 'Eagles are Shoshoni,' she thought. 'If eagles are the guardian spirits of the Americans, the Captains speak the truth. We are of the same tribe. It is right for me to lead the Americans to the Shoshoni.' "[26]

Several other titles also illustrate this need for reconciliation which Seibert's eagle-watching Sacajawea exemplifies.

Frances Joyce Farnsworth's *Winged Moccasins* (1954) describes
the Indian woman's remarkable Missouri River swim (Had Seibert read Farnsworth instead of the *Original Journals?*) and
imagines that she leads the Expedition. Indeed Farnsworth's
Sacajawea is ideally equipped to be the leader both because of
her wide experience and her intuitive knowledge. At the junction of the Missouri and the Marias Rivers, she knows "instinctively" which is the Missouri. With her own people, the Shoshone, she barters for horses the Expedition needs to cross the
Rockies because the captains know she has much more experience in such matters than they. While she horsetrades, Lewis and
Clark take care of less important matters: Lewis caches supplies
for the return journey while Clark explores the nearby mountains. The Indian woman's leadership is completely successful;
she makes no mistakes and, therefore, "the men respected her
judgment and had no fear of following her directions."[27] She
succeeds in getting the horses, in prevailing upon her red brothers
to show mercy to these white strangers. The Expedition is saved
by the efforts of a good red woman.

Two other titles, Della Gould Emmons' *Sacajawea of the
Shoshones* (1943) and Anna Lee Waldo's *Sacajawea* (1979)
illustrate more specifically what De Voto called that "tropical
emotion" in the literature of the Indian woman. Although the
Journals, especially Clark's entries, clearly indicate that Clark
valued Sacajawea's services highly and probably felt affection
for her, there is no evidence in the entries that the two were
romantically in love. To imagine that they were and to paint in
the colorful details is to enjoy love fantasies more than to care
about the recorded historical facts and what they may reasonably
suggest. This fictional Sacajawea the lover seems to imply a
many layered wish for romance as well as reconciliation on the
part of writers who indulge themselves and also on the part of
their readers. Emmons' words suggest the matter. "Sacajawea
looked up at Clark and his eyes met hers. . . . He put his arm
tenderly around her waist and drew her close to him and then to
Sacajawea's amazed delight, kissed her lightly on the forehead.
When she thought of it a million times later in life, she remembered it as the one time in her life when she had been supremely
happy."[28]

Anna Lee Waldo's novel, *Sacajawea*, carefully avoids making

the Indian woman out to be the guide of the Expedition, but it offers the reader a more highly developed romance than any of the other books. While the love between Clark and Sacajawea is never consummated because of various inconveniences—such as Sacajawea's belonging to Charbonneau—there is a strong and growing passion between the two. Clark resents Charbonneau; Sacajawea is jealous of Clark's girl who lives in the East. The two embrace passionately, and kiss. Sacajawea keeps noticing how much better, gentler and more sensitive Clark is to her than is her man Charbonneau, she recognizes that white husbands are better to their women than Indian men are to theirs. She wishes she could have white-skinned William Clark for her husband.

One cannot help noticing the evidence that, in preparing to write her own romance, Waldo may have read the romantic books about Sacajawea and the Lewis and Clark Expedition with considerable attention. In one place she appears to have borrowed both the action and the phrasing of one of Emmons' passages describing Clark and Sacajawea embracing and kissing.[29] Elsewhere she imagines actions of which there is no record and little if any suggestion in the *Original Journals.* Like Seibert and Farnsworth, Waldo portrays her Sacajawea going into the river when the white pirogue upsets. The Indian woman swims about in the great Missouri catching articles, stuffing them under her arms, and pushing ashore to unload. She even manages to pack Cruzatte's fiddle under one arm—along with many smaller articles. All this time, of course, she has her baby, Pomp, strapped to her back.[30]

While reading this scene in Waldo's novel, one ought to remember Lewis' entry in the *Journals* for this day. He notes explicitly that he himself was afraid to throw off his clothes and jump into the Missouri because he believed he would drown in the overwhelming current. Consequently he refused to attempt the rescue of the pirogue, its crew and the valuable items aboard. Waldo's novel is imitative, then, not of the historical records and of what they may reasonably suggest, but of the unreliable romances. Apparently the Sacajawea myths, based on urges for romance and reconciliation, continue to delight and seduce both writers and readers.

Anna Wolfrom's play, *Sacajawea, The Indian Princess*
(1918) dramatizes most of the tendencies suggested here. While
seeming to promote, by way of suggestion, feminism, white
racism, Manifest Destiny, and the cultural superiority of Anglo-
Americans, Wolfrom also asserts that the wild freedom of Sacajawea and the Indians is in itself a good and noble quality
(though it nevertheless must give way to the improving influence
of white civilization). In short, the playwright is ambivalent
toward her subject. This ambivalence suggests, on the one hand,
feelings of guilt and, on the other hand, a need to justify American history by lending it high motives. Throughout the play runs
a strong feeling of an urge for reconciliation. Part of the emotional force behind the play may also be the patriotic urgency
produced by the U. S. entry into World War I.

Act I of *The Indian Princess* is set in the Mandan Village.
The captains are wondering how to find their way across all
that unknown space. Sacajawea enters as a naive little girl,
loving Charbonneau and responding to York, a happy, big-
shouldered black, with the line, "I'se so afraid of black."[31] But
when Mme. Jaussaume says of her that she is a mere slave and
Clark responds, "You are no slave, Sacajawea; all daughters of
America's forest were ever born free," her character undergoes
an immediate change.[32] The reason is that her native nobility,
her freedom, and her talent for leading are catalyzed by Clark's
civilized wisdom and his faith in her ability, given the opportunity, to carry responsibility. Clark continues: "Will you, Sacajawea, go to pilot us through your country. . .?" Then: "We
have no money to give. Everyone must give a part of himself to
the land of which he enjoys the freedom. Sacajawea, are you
willing to give your services to this new country. . .that men may
follow in all the years to come?"[33] Unable to resist the inspiration, Sacajawea says she will lead, and the act closes with Clark
taking her hand and announcing: "The key to the Northwest
has been found."[34]

Act II occurs at the Three Forks. Clark tells Sacajawea she
has guided well so far but that she must now help find the Shoshone because his men need horses. Then follows the recognition of her brother, the chief Cameahwait. Between sessions
with her brother, Sacajawea talks with her sister, Natamka. "But
you have no white husband like mine," Sacajawea says.[35]

Natamka remains suspicious, and Sacajawea, trying to convince her of the white man's honesty and superiority, argues: "Be brave and strong for these men come from afar off to make a path that others may come to bring us their life." Then she adds: "Know you not that I love my tribe as much as you do? I go [west with the Expedition] to do. . .[our people] a great service. The Great Spirit has willed it!"[36]

The play closes with Act III, set in a Chinook village near the Pacific. Lewis tells the Indian woman that she has "rendered American civilization" great "services." Her reply indicates that she, the good, the farsighted, the noble, understands, even if her people do not. Through her sympathy whites and Indians are reconciled: "I am glad if I give just a little; it is so little when you think of how you bring peace to the Indian tribes, that have long been weakened from war, and then you find a path for people to come after you to find homes, to make cities, and to cultivate the good earth that the Indian has let lie in waste for so many centuries."[37]

Artistically, Wolfrom's play is the poorest job of all the guide myth fictions. *The Gates of the Mountains* (1963)—by Will Henry, a pseudonym for Henry Wilson Allen who also appears as Clay Fisher—is a much more interesting work. His is a fictional attempt to explore the feelings that may have existed between the captain and the Indian woman, although he too partly succumbs to the appealing Sacajawea-as-lover myth. The narrator is one François Rivet of La Charrette, a "shadowy" member of the Expedition's crew of French boatmen.[38] La Charrette deserts at Fort Mandan on the return trip in order to remain near Sacajawea, with whom he has fallen in love. Clark is also in love with the Indian woman, and La Charrette feels the tension between him and the captain aroused by their competition for Sacajawea's affections. For herself, Sacajawea calls La Charrette "Brother" and never feels for him anything other than friendship.

La Charrette's feelings—and presumably Clark's—are double. The Frenchman first sees Sacajawea as a great beauty, a "dream of beauty." Later, instructed by Clark (who openly admits to La Charrette that he is terribly attracted to Sacajawea) to look more closely at the Indian woman, he sees her at the cookfire

doing all the tasks of the squaw woman—killing and boiling a puppy, eating her fill, belching in satisfaction. La Charrette is at first revolted but then realizes that his first view of her had not been a clear seeing of the "squaw," the "Shoshone slave." Clark had seen her in this other light earlier and had wanted La Charrette to see her that way too. Late in the story the Frenchman comes to an understanding of Sacajawea which includes both his earlier views of her. "She was never the dream of beauty which I had seen step ashore from Charbonneau's canoe at the beach below Fort Mandan," he realizes. "No more was she in actuality the brute female shown by the campfire at Goatpen Creek." What is more important for him, La Charrette realizes that, as he puts it:

> It was not in her mind to love me, or Clark, or old Toussaint, or any white man, apart; it was in her heart to love us all, together. We were the strangers in her land. Unto us she was bidden by her inner light to show the way, to lead us through the wilderness, to guide us and go with us.[39]

The Gates of the Mountains certainly portrays the complex feelings of men in love, the dichotomy of seeing the beloved both as an ideal and as a real woman. The book is also full of the opposites of moral vision built into the Judeo-Christian heritage —the beautiful, the ugly; the saved, the damned; the free, the slave; the good, the bad. Will Henry's is a split vision which tells us much about ourselves but probably has little, if anything, to do with who the American Indian—and Sacajawea—really is, or was. Probably too the love La Charrette thinks Sacajawea feels for him and Clark "or any white man"—not passion for one but brotherly love for all—is, in part, Will Henry's own need for reconciliation projected upon her. It is a need for forgiveness— for release from old guilt—sensitive whites seem driven to ask of the American Indian and of the whole vast brooding continent itself.

Undoubtedly the best novel of the Lewis and Clark Expedition is Vardis Fisher's *Tale of Valor* (1958).[40]   Although it is not a perfect book—Fisher has Sacajawea dashing from one end of the overturned white pirogue to the other busily saving items— *Tale of Valor* seems in most scenes to follow rather closely Fisher's theory about historical fiction, that is that the writer

ought only to imagine characters consistent with what the known facts suggest. Fictional characters must be more than credible; if they were also historical persons, the imagined things they say and do and feel must be carefully limited to what the primary historical sources imply. Is what happens in the book—what is felt and thought and planned and accomplished or failed—in keeping with what is known of the historical personages and their actions? Are the characters' beliefs and values consistent with what historical record suggests about the beliefs and values of their societies, their professions, their time? These are the questions Fisher believed writers must deal with before they could write responsible historical fiction. Otherwise, their work would be irresponsible; they and their readers could never come near to knowing the past as it really was and judge it, if at all, by its own standards rather than by ours.

Tale of Valor comes close to exemplifying the things Fisher insisted upon. Sacajawea often recognizes landmarks—as the *Journals* say she did—but she is not characterized as "the guide" of the Expedition. In two instances Fisher mentions her leading, but probably these were suggested to him by Clark's statement in the *Journals* that she had been "of great service. . .as a pilot through this country." In Fisher's version, Sacajawea and Clark are attached to one another by a bond of affection suggested by the primary sources. Clark appreciated the woman's services, and it is known from his own writing that he proposed to care for her and her husband Charbonneau and to educate her son, whom he often called "Pomp" or "my boy Pomp." Fisher does not falsify these circumstances. He also presents a Sacajawea who is uncomfortable with any prospect that she might be able to advise the captains upon matters involving major decisions for the Expedition. What she does are such things as pointing out landmarks she remembers from her childhood and commenting on the food value and medicinal uses of native plants she recognizes along the way. Fisher's Sacajawea is very much like the Indian girl Lewis and Clark themselves described. One leaves a reading of *Tale of Valor* with the sense that he knows the historical Sacajawea a little better than he knew her after reading the *Original Journals.*

One can hardly help noticing the parallel between the Sacajawea guide and lover myths and the myth which surrounded

the stories of Pocahontas and Captain John Smith. The latter myth appeared again and again in nineteenth century sentimental novels, half fictional biographies, popular poetry, patriotic songs and stage plays. At the center of the Pocahontas myth is the idea that the Indian girl "saved" Captain Smith after she fell in love with him. Leslie Fiedler has called the Pocahontas-Captain John Smith stories a manifestation of the myth of "love in the woods." Fiedler argues that the myth implies a dream of love and reconciliation between alien races—white and Indian—whose actual history has been one of warfare and hatred. To achieve the desired reconciliation, the sentimental myth-makers have, according to Fiedler, tended to make Pocahontas whiter of skin than the typical Indian. They have imagined her as a "princess" and made much of her "noble" connections. They have, in short, removed her "savage" features and tended to convert her into an approving, farsighted, palefaced woodland goddess, not unlike, Fiedler suggests, the American Liberty and the Lady Columbia.[41]

The idea of the Indian woman as benefactor of the white man also appears elsewhere in popular literature. One example is Singing Bird, the Sioux woman in "Buffalo Bill's Fair, Square Deal; or, the Duke of the Dagger's Deadlock," printed in *The Buffalo Bill Stories,* a turn of the century serial interestingly subtitled *A Weekly Publication Devoted to Border History* (1904). Singing Bird saves the bad guy, the Duke of the Dagger, by pulling him out of the flood water which Buffalo Bill, Wild Bill Hickok, and Nick Wharton have let loose into his hiding place in the Dakota Badlands. She nurses him back to health, and, after exacting a promise that he will do anything she wishes, sends him on his way, refusing to tell the illustrious two and Nick Wharton which way he has gone. In a complex chase both sides briefly outwit each other, but at the end, the Duke is caught in his cave, and Singing Bird appears again, this time to demand that he release Nick and Wild Bill, whom he has locked in an underground vault. Her reason: "Your promise, Duke!. . . Those Men are my friends. Save them!"[42] Appropriately, Singing Bird is the general benefactor, the friend to all whites (both "good" and "bad"), or, as Fiedler suggests, the dreamed of Indian mother and lover of white mankind.

There can be little doubt that the Sacajawea guide and lover

fictions—mainly a product of the twentieth century—belong to the same category of writing as the Pocahontas-Captain Smith tales and the story of Singing Bird, the savior of both good guys and bad. That the historical Sacajawea was nearly always approving, uncritical and cheerful—according to the captains—has made her a prime candidate for the kind of figure popular fiction writers have made of her. The "real" Sacajawea lends herself perfectly to writers who would imagine that she guided the Expedition and loved its leaders. As Vardis Fisher understood, most of us at one time or another tend to view the past through those noble sounding myths which flatter us or seem to release us from our guilt. It is this very appeal to the deep seated need for release and reconciliation which seems to keep the Sacajawea guide and lover myths perpetually alive.

NOTES

[1]Harold P. Howard, *Sacajawea* (Norman: University of Oklahoma Press, 1971). Grace Raymond Hebard, *Sacajawea: A Guide and Interpreter of the Lewis and Clark Expedition* (Glendale: Arthur H. Clark, 1933), has been discredited in recent years because there is no known surviving hard evidence—either objects or documents—to prove that the Wyoming woman was the real Sacajawea and also because Hebard seems to have been interested in promoting the guide myth and women's rights through her writing about the Shoshone woman. Also arguing that the Wyoming woman was the real Sacajawea is the recent book by Ella E. Clark and Margot Edmonds, *Sacagawea of the Lewis and Clark Expedition* (Berkeley: University of California Press, 1979). Clark and Edmonds review the oral sources used by Hebard, including the work of Dr. Charles Eastman and others. They conclude that the Indian woman did not guide the Expedition. However, they do agree with Hebard that the historical Sacajawea is the one buried in Wyoming. Clark and Edmonds present little or no new evidence, they all but ignore Harold P. Howard's biographical labors, and they briefly pass over the evidence he used to arrive at his position that Sacajawea died on the upper Missouri in 1812.

[2]Meriwether Lewis and William Clark, *Original Journals of the Lewis and Clark Expedition, 1804-1806*, 8 vols., ed., Reuben Gold Thwaites (New York: Dodd, Mead, 1904-1905).

[3]Bernard De Voto, *The Course of Empire* (Boston: Houghton-Mifflin, 1952), p. 618.

[4]Ronald W. Taber, "Sacajawea and the Suffragettes: An Interpretation of a Myth," *Pacific Northwest Quarterly*, 58 (1967), 8.

[5]Taber, "Sacajawea," p. 7.

[6]Thomas Bulfinch, *Oregon and Eldorado; or, Romance of the Rivers* (Boston: J. E. Tilton, 1866), x.

[7]William R. Lighton, *Lewis and Clark: Meriwether Lewis and William Clark* (Boston: Houghton-Mifflin, 1901), pp. 137-138.

[8]Noah Brooks, *First Across the Continent: The Story of the Exploring Expedition of Lewis and Clark* (New York: Charles Scribner's Sons, 1901), pp. 332-333.

[9]Lewis and Clark, *Original Journals*, Vol. 5, p. 260. Promoters and debunkers of the guide myth tend either to overlook or to interpret Clark's statement. Perhaps the most powerful attempt to debunk the myth is C. S. Kingston, "Sacajawea as Guide: the Evaluation of a Legend," *PNQ*, 35 (1944), 3-18. Kingston cites Clark's statement, but argues that it "is to be understood more as an expression of good natured and generous congratulation than a sober assertion of unadorned fact" (p. 13). A straightforward account of Sacajawea's very real services as they may be read directly from the *Original Journals* is Helen Crawford, "Sakakawea," *North Dakota Historical Quarterly*, 1 (1926-1927), 5-15.

[10]Herbert David Croly, *The Promise of American Life* (New York: Macmillan, 1911).

[11]Eva Emory Dye, *The Conquest: The True Story of Lewis and Clark* (Chicago: A. C. McClurg, 1903), p. 122.

[12]Dye, p. 122.

[13]Dye, p. 25.

[14]Dye, p. 9.

[15]Brian W. Dippie, "Bards of the Little Big Horn," *Western American Literature*, 1 (Fall, 1966), 175.

[16]Dye, p. 110.

[17]Dye, p. 69.

[18]Dye, p. 280.

[19]Dye, p. 179.

[20]Jerry Seibert, *Sacajawea: Guide to Lewis and Clark* (Boston:

Houghton-Mifflin, 1960), p. 192.

[21]Seibert, p. 192.

[22]Lewis and Clark, *Original Journals,* Vol. 2, pp. 34-35.

[23]Lewis and Clark, *Original Journals,* Vol. 2, p. 39.

[24]Seibert, pp. 107-108.

[25]Lewis and Clark, *Original Journals,* Vol. 2, pp. 35-36.

[26]Seibert, p. 102.

[27]Frances Joyce Farnsworth, *Winged Moccasins: The Story of Saca-jawea* (New York: J. Messner, 1954), p. 126.

[28]Della Florence Gould Emmons, *Sacajawea of the Shoshones* (Portland: Binfords and Mort, 1943), p. 188.

[29]Anna Lee Waldo, *Sacajawea* (New York: Avon, 1979), p. 350. In this scene Waldo's phrasing is very much like Emmons' phrasing. For other love passages in Waldo's book, see pp. 531-532, 543-544, and 557-558.

[30]Waldo, pp. 311-312.

[31]Anna Wolfrom, *Sacajawea, the Indian Princess: The Indian Girl Who Piloted the Lewis and Clark Expedition Across the Rocky Mountains* (Kansas City, Missouri: Burton, 1918), p. 5.

[32]Wolfrom, p. 14.

[33]Wolfrom, p. 14.

[34]Wolfrom, p. 14.

[35]Wolfrom, p. 21. Natamka is a fictional character created by Wolfrom. Minnetare Indians captured Sacajawea at the Three Forks of the Missouri River when she was a very young woman. Later, Indians sold her to Charbonneau. The two of them were living near the Mandan village when Lewis and Clark wintered there in 1804-1805. The *Original Journals* state that "all the females and four boys" were captured at the Three Forks (Vol.

2, p. 283) and that at the Mandan village Charbonneau had "two Squars of the Rock Mountains, purchased from the Indians" (Vol. 1, p. 219). On August 17, 1805, Sacajawea rejoined her people, and Lewis describes the scene: "the meeting of those people was really affecting, particularly between Sah-cah-gar-we-ah and an Indian woman, who had been taken prisoner at the same time with her and who, had afterwards escaped from the Minetares and rejoined her nation" (Vol. 2, p. 361). Probably Natamka was suggested to Wolfrom by the "Indian woman" of this incident.

[36]Wolfrom, p. 23.

[37]Wolfrom, pp. 30-31.

[38]Will Henry, *The Gates of the Mountains* (New York: Random House, 1963), xi.

[39]Henry, pp. 301-302.

[40]Vardis Fisher, *Tale of Valor: A Novel of the Lewis and Clark Expedition* (New York: Doubleday, 1958). See also Ronald W. Taber, " 'Vardis Fisher': New Directions for the Historical Novel," *WAL,* 1 (1967), 285-296.

[41]Leslie A. Fiedler, "The Basic Myths, II: Love in the Woods," *The Return of the Vanishing American* (New York: Stein and Day, 1968), pp. 63-83.

[42]"Buffalo Bill's Fair, Square Deal; or, the Duke of the Dagger's Deadlock," *The Buffalo Bill Stories: A Weekly Publication Devoted to Border History,* 170 (August 13, 1904). See reprint under same title by Gold Star Books (Derby, Connecticut: New International Library, 1965), p. 63.

Miscegenation in Popular Western History and Fiction

Caren J. Deming

Miscegenation themes in popular western literature spring from a complex of traditional American assumptions. These assumptions have to do with differences among the races and between the sexes. Fitted neatly together, these racial and sexual assumptions provide a tidy—if somewhat elaborate—defense for a double standard concerning miscegenation. This paper examines some of the assumptions behind that double standard and shows how they manifest themselves in works by several western writers.

The first assumption has anatomical roots. Women, and particularly white women in America, have assumed a "receptacle" function where the culture is concerned. Bearing the white civilization to the frontier, their main function was to preserve it. Willa Cather understood this idea well, giving it extensive development in *O Pioneers!* The narrator describes Mrs. Bergson:

> Alexandra often said that if her mother were cast upon a desert island, she would thank God for her deliverance, make a garden, and find something to preserve. Preserving was almost a mania with Mrs. Bergson. . . .When there was nothing more to preserve, she began to pickle. . . .She had never quite forgiven John Bergson for bringing her to the end of the earth; but, now that she was there, she wanted to be let alone to construct her old life in so far as that was possible. She could still take some comfort in the world if she had bacon in the cave, glass jars on the shelves, and sheets in the press.[1]

England's Lord Bryce observed American women as preservers—if not picklers—of the culture too: "In a country where men are incessantly occupied at their business or profession, the function

of keeping up the level of culture devolves upon women. It is safe in their hands."[2]   The implication in Bryce's remark is that though they safely maintain the culture, there is little danger that women may advance it in a direction of their own choosing.

The passivity of the preserver's role is implicit also in what Mary Ellmann has called "the sexual analogy." In that mode of criticism, women's minds are regarded as "another domestic container of some sort, a recipe file or Thermos jug or umbrella stand (cf. Jung's 'ovens and cooking vessels'), always as an empty object in which others put things."[3]   Put one corrupt notion there, and the whole mind soon is contaminated. The Reverend Silas Pendrake of Thomas Berger's *Little Big Man* makes the point graphically: "Woman is a vessel, and it is within man's power to make that vessel a golden chalice or a slop bucket."[4]

Woman's tendency toward depravity of mind stems from her inherent frailty of body. The heavy physical work that is a traditional builder of American manhood is the undoing of womanhood. Our frontier literature is full of unlovely (though often heroic in their way) women who are made coarse, thick, rigid, and bitter by the rugged work of pioneering. Hamlin Garland's Mrs. Council, "a large, jolly, rather coarse-looking woman," and Mrs. Haskins, "a small, timid, and discouraged-looking woman," are but two examples.[5] Their degraded physical condition makes them particularly susceptible to moral degradation. The belief that hard work can lead women to moral dissipation thus links physical frailty to moral frailty.

Official sanction for this belief extends into the twentieth century. The reasoning behind the belief is summarized in a Supreme Court case that is notorious among feminists, the case of Muller v. Oregon: "In upholding an Oregon statute limiting the hours of women's work, the court sustained the argument of Louis D. Brandeis, counsel for the state. The Brandeis brief declared, with abundant citations from European and American authorities, that the prevailing ten-hour workday was likely to leave a woman exhausted, her higher instincts dulled, craving only excitement and sensual pleasure."[6] In the decision to uphold the Oregon statute, Justice Brewer concluded that the protection of the American woman from depravity induced by

employment would not be "solely for her benefit, but also largely for the benefit of all."[7]

Keeping women at home was not only convenient, but it could also protect a man from the nymphomaniacal female, whose destructive power is archetypal. Quaint as the good Justices' words seem now, the sentiment expressed is not far from that uttered by Judge Archie Simonson in 1977. In the trial of a Wisconsin rapist, Simonson reasoned that women bring rape upon themselves by having legs, breasts, and the temerity to walk down a city street.

Females' "weakness" gives males the obligation to protect them. On the frontier, that generally means against Indians. The tale of the capture of Jemima Boone and the Callaway sisters because they wandered from the settlement is a classic example of females' unwittingly getting into trouble and needing rescue. This motif is recurrent in children's westerns, in which a wise brother saves his foolish sister (who often is older than he) from drowning, from being bitten by a snake, or from some other natural danger. However, the task of rescuing white females from red males is one for grown men only.

The weakness of females is contrasted starkly to the heroism of males in Zane Grey's account of the attack on Fort Henry. Women are supportive, lacking in courage, and—worst of all—susceptible to capture. The image of female vulnerability culminates in the white man's defending white women against rape by savages:

> A man can die. He is glorious when he calmly accepts death; but when he fights like a tiger, when he stands at bay, his back to the wall, a broken weapon in his hand, bloody, defiant, game to the end, then he is sublime. Then he wrings respect from the souls of even his bitterest foes. Then he is avenged even in his death.
>
> But what can women do in times of war? They help, they cheer, they inspire, and if their cause is lost they must accept death and worse. Few women have the courage for self-destruction. "To the victor belongs the spoils," and women have ever been the spoils of war.[8]

As Everett Dick explains, this fear on the part of the white male is not understandable in terms of historical fact: "Many women were taken prisoner by the Indians. Although they were subjected to cruel treatment, privation, and the hardships of travel back to the Indian country, their chastity was never violated by the Indians. When they decided to save a woman's life, they also saved her virtue and honor. They believed that to take a dishonorable advantage of a female would be unworthy of a warrior and would disgrace him in the eyes of his companions."[9] If Indians on later frontiers did, in fact, rape their captives, historians acknowledge the probability that they did so only after the example was set by white soldiers, who were not always reluctant to rape the "spoils" of the Indian wars.

The perceived need to defend women against rape by Indians *is* understandable, however, in terms of two mythic concepts. The first of these is the long-standing suspicion that the savage dark man (whether black or bronze) is more virile and, ultimately, more capable of satisfying the hungry sexuality of the degraded female than the white male is. Dee Brown, relying upon diaries of captive women, suggests a Freudian interpretation of what he calls "the shivering ache of vulnerability" evident in the captives' "curiously unconcealed" admiration for the strong, barely-clad, copper-colored bodies of their captors.[10] (Brown attributes the fact that early captivity narratives do not include accounts of sexual abuse to the influence of "that age of reticence concerning sexual matters.")[11]

The second concept that supports a fear of the Indian's rape of his captive is the susceptibility of females to corruption, which we have known about since the first savage seduced Eve in the first Eden. When captives refused to be rescued, as they sometimes did, their preference for remaining with the Indians could be interpreted as accession to their moral vulnerability: "Some survivors became, in their [own] minds, so degraded by the time they were rescued, that they had little desire to leave the Indians."[12] Brown's comment seems a long way from Fanny Kelly's account of her treatment by the Ogalalla Sioux, who "showed [her] nothing but civility and respect."[13] Kelly's narrative includes an account of Elizabeth Blackwell's decision to remain with her Indian captors because they had treated her more respectfully and tenderly than her own family had.[14]

Brown's judgment also is far different from the standard reasons for the white male captive's preference for the Indian way of life. Leslie Fiedler has labeled the male's preference for remaining with Indians the "Higher Masculine Sentimentality." Fiedler describes the process by which the western hero—Natty Bumppo, Daniel Boone, Davy Crockett, the Lone Ranger—is tempted to give up white civilization out of a "passionate commitment to inverting Christian-Humanist values, out of a conviction that the Indian's way of life is preferable."[15] The white savage, the iconoclast, expresses Higher Masculine Sentimentality through emulation of the red savage's culture (including his mode of dress) and through rituals of adoption into the tribe. What debases the female elevates the male.

Naturally, the double standard operates for miscegenation too. From Little Big Man's point of view, his association with Sunshine does not corrupt him; but the impregnation of the white woman by the Indian results in permanent moral degradation: "As I lay on my buffalo robe and looked at the swell of Sunshine's pregnant belly, all I could think of was how Olga might at this very moment be carrying the seed of that savage in her. She was forever soiled. I could leave my lodge at any time, go back to civilization, take a bath, and be white again. Not her. The *Cheyenne* was inside her."[16] The frontiersman's association with Indian women is viewed as a natural occurrence that bolsters his masculinity without weakening his morality.

This attitude parallels that of the legendary southern gentleman toward the black woman. In Edna Ferber's *Cimarron*, Sabra Cravat's father is critical of intermarriage between Creek Indians and blacks. When his son-in-law jabs, "I understand while you Southerners didn't exactly marry—," the indignant reply is, "Marriage, sir, is one thing. Nature, sir, is another."[17] It is natural to be seduced by the charming Ethiope, though marriage is out of the question.

Although marriages between frontiersmen and Indian women were not uncommon, such marriages often were regarded as temporary arrangements. Squaws, as Brown puts it, "were no problem."[18] In the days of the mountain man, an Indian woman traded security for the husband's highly-prized possessions when she married a white man. The marriage generally

did not require the woman to leave her tribe or to suffer cultural alienation.[19] Rather, her husband would join in the life of the tribe for a time.

When he rode out of camp a few days or a few weeks after his arrival there, she stayed with her tribe to await his next visit (which often never came) and, frequently, to bear his next child. Occasionally, he would wonder about the children he may have fathered, but remorse was not among his feelings. The thoughts of Dick Summers, the hero of A. B. Guthrie's *The Way West,* reveal his perception of himself as outside of the white moral structure when he is with Indians: "He didn't believe in the sin the preacher did. Men and women were made different for a purpose, like hes and shes of any breed, and mostly he had done what he wanted and got up and forgotten, except now and then for a thought of the half-breeds he might have left behind. But they would fare as well as Indians and better than a heap of whites."[20]

Little Big Man is more realistic about the futures of his half-breed offspring, but his realism is hindsight: "I had consumed the night in delivering my masculine services. . . .I might have planted a new human being or two by that night's work, and I never thought about how they would be little breeds, growing up into a world fast turning uncongenial even to full-bloods. No, all seemed right to me at that moment."[21] The mountain man is portrayed as a man whose inconstancy where women are concerned is as natural as his freedom. Those women, in turn, are portrayed as ever-willing, but making no demands that might restrict his freedom.

Alongside white female stereotypes, then, stands the woman of color. She is (to use Fiedler's terminology) the Dark Lady, who may be Catholic or Jew, Latin or Oriental or Negro.[22] On the frontier, she most often is an Indian, but frequently enough a black or Mexican. She is the "sinister embodiment of the sexuality denied the snow maiden."[23] Like the most manly man, the most womanly woman is part of the wilderness. The natural woman in *Little Big Man* is Buffalo Wallow Woman: "She was 100 per cent woman, like Old Lodge Skins was all man, and I don't know that you could get near her quality had you boiled down a score of white females for their essence.

But now what'd you think when you saw that sweet person ripping open some helpless Crow with her knife and unwinding his
guts?"[24]

However dangerous the earth mother's voluptuousness is,
though, it becomes evil only in the context of the white moral
structure, that is, when the Fair Maiden is present. Thus, historians note that no social reproach was attached to unions of
white men and Indian women until white women brought
white civilization to the frontier: "Almost as soon as the first
wagonloads of females arrived from the States—hardly before
they could unpack their household goods—it was considered a
disgrace for a white man to live with a squaw."[25] As if it is not
enough that the white woman is susceptible to decay from within
brought on by intercourse with the Indian man, she also is responsible for the white man's guilt over his mating with the
Indian woman. The domestication of the wilderness—the task of
white women—destroys the milieu in which white men enjoy
guilt-free liaisons with Indian women.

Frederick Manfred's handling of this theme in *Lord Grizzly*
is powerful. Hugh Glass ponders the impending loss: "It made
Hugh sad to think on it, all the she-rips and their cubs coming in
and destroying a hunter's paradise. The white queen bees would
come in with their tame worker bees and build honeycomb
towns and cities just as the real queen bees already were taking
over the wilds just ahead of the oncoming settlements. Ae, the
enslavement of both land and man was coming here too. Ae."[26]
Hugh's white wife, whom he has left in the East, and the grizzly
are the only two things Hugh fears.

In the delirium that results from injuries collected in his
fight with the grizzly, Hugh fuses the grizzly and the woman:
"But Mabel was raking him from behind. Down his back.
. . .She was ripping him up and ripping him down. . . .She roared
him; she ripped him; she gnawed him. She clawed him until
he was finally cowed proper. Laid low."[27] Though both she-
rips (as Hugh calls them both) have the power to bring him
down, he can subdue the grizzly but not the wife.

In contrast, Hugh's Indian wife, Bending Reed, has no such
effect on him. The mountain man glories in his sexual exploita-

tion of the Indian woman as one of the many ways by which he demonstrates his physical prowess. He takes her for granted when she is cooperative and beats her when she is not. While Sunshine (Little Big Man's Cheyenne wife) is off in the woods giving birth to his son one frigid night, he makes the rounds of her sisters, "discharging brother-in-lawly duty" by each one. While such behavior would be unacceptable among white women, Little Big Man makes it clear that by Cheyenne standards (as he perceives them) his actions are "the opposite of loose morals."[28] In the wilderness, where the Indian male is reduced to one element of a dangerous setting, the Indian female represents the beneficent aspect of the bountiful garden. As such, she is merely one of the natural resources to be exploited.

If the Indian woman makes frontier life tolerable for the hero, the white woman takes the fun out of it. This reasoning renders the white woman a force to be reckoned with and the Indian woman simply dispensable. The logic, if it may be called that, flatters neither. Yet the pattern occurs so often in American literature—both fiction and nonfiction—that its power is undeniable. The complex of assumptions behind the double standard of miscegenation denigrates all women and, ultimately, plays white women and women of color off against one another. This familiar theme is a burden carried by the American culture in general, and by the feminist movement in particular, into the present time.

NOTES

[1]*O Pioneers!*, Sentry ed. (Boston: Houghton Mifflin, 1941), pp. 29-30.

[2]James Bryce, *The American Commonwealth*, abridged ed., 2 vols., ed. Louis Hacker (New York: Putnam's Sons, 1959), 2: 511.

[3]*Thinking About Women* (New York: Harcourt, 1968), pp. 14-15.

[4]*Little Big Man* (Greenwich, Connecticut: Fawcett, 1964), p. 137.

[5]"Under the Lion's Paw," in *Main-Travelled Roads* (Greenwich, Connecticut: Fawcett, 1961), p. 163.

[6]Robert W. Smuts, *Women and Work in America* (New York: Schocken, 1971), p. 118, citing Muller v. Oregon, 208 U.S. 412, 28 S. Ct. 324, 52 L. Ed. 551 (1908).

[7]Leo Kanowitz, *Sex Roles in Law and Society* (Albuquerque: University of New Mexico Press, 1973), pp. 46-48, quoting Muller v. Oregon (1908).

[8]*Betty Zane* (New York: Grosset & Dunlap, 1933), p. 268.

[9]*The Dixie Frontier: A Social History of the Southern Frontier from the First Transmontane Beginnings to the Civil War* (New York: Capricorn Books, 1964), p. 259.

[10]*The Gentle Tamers: Women of the Old Wild West* (Lincoln: University of Nebraska Press, 1968), p. 18.

[11]Brown, p. 19.

[12]Brown, p. 35.

[13]*My Captivity Among the Sioux Indians* (Secaucus, New Jersey:

The Citadel Press, 1973), p. 191.

[14]Kelly, pp. 238-240.

[15]*The Return of the Vanishing American* (New York: Stein and Day, 1969), p. 169.

[16]Berger, p. 246.

[17]*Cimarron* (Garden City, New York: Doubleday, Doran, 1930), p. 41.

[18]Brown, p. 293.

[19]Dorothy Gray, *Women of the West* (Millbrae, California: Les Femmes, 1976), p. 9.

[20]*The Way West* (New York: Bantam, 1972), p. 225.

[21]Berger, p. 253.

[22]*Love and Death in the American Novel*, Laurel ed. (rev.), (New York: Dell, 1969), p. 299; Fiedler traces these two images through works by Hawthorne, Melville, Cooper, and other American authors.

[23]*Love and Death in the American Novel*, p. 293.

[24]Berger, p. 99.

[25]Brown, p. 215.

[26]*Lord Grizzly* (New York: New American Library, 1964), p. 160.

[27]Manfred, p. 109.

[28]Berger, p. 252.

The Emergence of Helen Chalmers

Frances M. Malpezzi

In 1922 Edith Warner, the daughter of a Baptist minister, left her family home in Pennsylvania for New Mexico. She soon settled at Otowi, where she spent the remainder of her life. Here she was to come in contact with the inhabitants of San Ildefonso Pueblo and eventually with the atomic scientists of Los Alamos. Her tearoom at Otowi was thus at the crossroads of two very different cultures in American society at a crucial time in our history. The story of this woman who was equally at home with the pueblo *cacique* as with Neils Bohr or Robert Oppenheimer is the basis of Frank Waters' novel, *The Woman at Otowi Crossing.*[1] From the factual Edith Warner emerged the fictional Helen Chalmers, the protagonist of the novel.

As we examine the transformation from fact to fiction, we see the comparisons between the two constantly underscore Waters' thematic concerns in the novel. For Waters, *The Woman at Otowi Crossing* is a tropological application of the Pueblo and Navaho Emergence myth. Waters views that myth not only as the story of human creation and evolutionary development, but as symbolic of the psychic development, the inner journey of every individual. Waters makes clear the significance of the Emergence myth in an earlier work, *Masked Gods: Navaho and Pueblo Ceremonialism.* As critics have noted, what Waters postulates in *Masked Gods* he gives concrete form to in *The Woman at Otowi Crossing.* Jack L. Davis and June L. Davis, for example, draw a relationship between the two works: "Though the novel brings together a multiplicity of now familiar dualities in an unusual display of technical artifice, it is the psychic evolution of Helen Chalmers, cast in the form hypothesized in *Masked Gods,* which provides the primary integrative pattern."[2] The periodic and geographic setting of the novel—the beginning of the atomic age, near the Los Alamos project—further emphasizes Waters'

theme as the world's emergence into the atomic age parallels
Chalmers' psychic evolution. Moreover, Waters believes there is a
strong parallel between an atomic reaction and such a psychic experience. In *Masked Gods,* he points to the relationship between
the physical energy locked inside the atom and the energy contained within the psyche and concludes that "both the transformation of matter into energy, and the transformation of instinctual forces into creative energy, depend upon the reconciliation of the primal dual forces of all life. With the fusion a tre-
mendus conflict takes place, and from it is released a new birth
of energy."[3] Waters' belief in the possibility of a tropological
application of the Navaho and Pueblo Emergence myth, his belief
in the similarity between an atomic and a psychic reaction, his
interpretation of many incidents in the historical Edith Warner's
story as indicative of life lived on a higher plane of consciousness,
his recognition of the setting of that life as one of primal dualities necessary to bring about psychic fusion—all these make possible his fictional transformation of Edith Warner into the mythically amplified Helen Chalmers. In *The Woman at Otowi Crossing* we witness Helen Chalmers' spiritual journey, her awakening
to a new level of consciousness, and finally her Emergence—
through death—in union with the eternal source and, thus, her
transfiguration to the realm of the mythic.

Although no objective, full-length biography of Warner
exists, her story has been partially captured in a memoir by
Peggy Pond Church, *The House at Otowi Bridge: The Story of
Edith Warner and Los Alamos.*[4] Church also appends Warner's
recipe for her famous chocolate cake (with altitude corrections)
and a series of Christmas letters Warner wrote her friends.
Waters, of course, as a resident of this region, must have had
numerous sources to draw on for his information about Edith
Warner—including first-hand knowledge.[5] Yet he was also probably aware of Church's memoir as the preliminary note to his
novel suggests: "Much has been published about the actual woman who lived at Otowi Crossing, including her recipe for chocolate cake corrected for every change in altitude." For readers
who have no other sources for information about Warner,
Church's *House at Otowi Bridge* provides useful biographic
background which enables us to note the many similarities between Warner and Helen Chalmers. Such comparisons also enable us to see how Waters moves beyond mere recapitulation of

Warner's life as he develops the fictional Chalmers and invests her with mythic dimensions.

A transplanted Easterner, Warner moved to the Southwest late in life to recover from a breakdown. As Church illustrates, she soon found strength in her recognition of a sense of place. She found comfort in "the great age and deep-rootedness of the mesas"; and in her small house at Otowi "she felt that the word-less land had accepted her and that if she too had endurance, life in the little house could be deeply satisfying" (pp. 34-35). In this identification with the enduring land, she discovered the source of power within herself.

Almost like Thoreau, Edith Warner came to have an intui-tive response to the simplicity and sacredness of the nature around her. Throughout her journal and letters, she communi-cated the keen sense of unity she felt with nature. She ex-perienced mystic, unaccountable inflowings of the sacred during her daily round of affairs (p. 70). She attributed these sacred impulses not only to her growing awareness of nature and her spiritual maturation, but to a shedding of worldly things as well. In divesting herself of a world that had been too much with her, she found an everpresent world of the spirit in nature. Though she led life often on the verge of poverty, this life was a spiritual-ly rich one. Her contact with nature brought her spiritual peace, harmony, and fulfillment.

Through her identification with the unchanging essence of the land, she was one with the past as well. This is particularly seen in two events. Warner found near an old ruin a sherd of pottery with a woman's thumb print still visible: " 'There alone in the sunlight,' she said, 'I began to understand that nothing men may do, not even the atomic bomb, can in any way touch or change the essence of this country' " (p. 108). In her Christ-mas letter of 1946, she recounted another moving experience:

> This fall as I rested on the ruined wall of Navawii I heard a familiar sound. Looking up, my vision finally caught a thin silver V far above the ruin—wild geese southward bound. I had always thought of geese as following the river. Now I knew that some used the Plateau for their high road and that Navawii women must have listened, too, and watched that undulating silver line against the

blue fall sky, then hastened their preparation for winter.   (p. 133)

Through both experiences she transcended the present, intuitively reaching back to the past and forming a bond of sisterhood with women who lived long before her time, women who had also experienced what she had seen, heard, and felt.

World War II brought many changes to Otowi, changes that touched the life of Edith Warner and her Indian companion Tilano. The Los Alamos School was closed and taken over by the federal government. An atomic energy project surrounded by secrecy replaced the school on "the Hill." As more and more scientists and workers came, the Hill grew into a tightly restricted community. Robert Oppenheimer, who had met Warner when he was a tourist in New Mexico in pre-war years, arranged for the scientists to visit her tearoom for occasional evening suppers. These visits provided the Los Alamos workers with brief respites from the tension of their job and provided Warner with the intellectual companionship of world renowned scientists. But through all the changes that took place at Otowi, Warner represented a point of stability. With Tilano she guarded the "changeless essence" against the forces of upheaval. Warner was cognizant of this role. As she found assurance in the "rhythmic order of nature," she knew others found it in the stability of her tearoom. A piece of remembered chocolate cake symbolized to many the "essence unchanged" in a changing world (p. 130).

So Edith Warner lived out her life at Otowi, providing so much for so many. Nourishing the hungry and comforting the lonely, she was rooted steadfast to a sacred soil in a turbulent time. In Warner's series of Christmas letters and the excerpts from her journal which Church includes we see a single woman of strength, courage, and independence. Ever conscious of nature, in tune with its spiritual harmony, she devoted herself to others but also to the development of her inner well-being.

Helen Chalmers, Waters' protagonist, replicates Warner in many ways. Like Warner she left her family in the East (a wealthy, but drunken husband and an infant daughter) for a new life in the Southwest. Assisted by the aging Facundo, she runs a tearoom at Otowi Crossing, which becomes the haunt of the atomic scientists from Los Alamos who relish her chocolate

cake. Like Warner she is poor in material possessions but rich in spiritual wealth. She is close to the land, in harmony with nature. Like Warner she even discovers a piece of pottery with a thumb print on it. But unlike the picture of Edith Warner presented in *House at Otowi Bridge,* Helen Chalmers begins to garner a reputation for her unusual powers. These spiritual powers are recognized by Facundo, who helps to foster them by initiating her into the secrets of the kiva, and by the *curanderas* and *brujas* of the region who perceive her as " 'An earth woman. A sky woman. *Una Señora que no ha pecado* ' " (p. 63). After her precognitive, apocalyptic visions, her reputation spreads still further. The rumors of her power begin the myth of the Woman at Otowi Crossing. In fiction the story of Edith Warner assumes a new dimension as it is subsumed into Waters' mythic design, his allegorization of Emergence.

It is clear how this story of Edith Warner and Los Alamos could so affect and inspire Waters. A writer always concerned with duality, Waters was, of course, aware of the duality inherent in the Southwest at this time. For instance, in *Masked Gods* he delineates the nature of this duality which is such a fundamental backdrop to the novel as he enumerates the many contradictions and polarities of life in the region: "The oldest forms of life discovered in this hemisphere, and the newest agent of mass death. The oldest cities in America and the newest. The Sun Temple of Mesa Verde and the nuclear fission laboratories of the Pajarito Plateau. The Indian drum and the atom smasher" (p. 425). These same sentiments are echoed in the novel. In one of the many interviews which interweave the narrative, a specialist on mysticism and the occult remarks that Chalmers was in the right place to receive her glimpse of the universal whole:

> At the birthplace of the oldest civilization in America and the newest. Probably in no other area in the world were juxtaposed so closely the Indian drum and the atom-smasher, all the values of the prehistoric past and the atomic future. A lonely woman in a remote spot with few friends, she felt herself at the hub of time.
>
> (p. 159)

Not only is this duality important for the medium of the psychic implosion-explosion which takes place, but also for Chalmers' sense that she is at "the hub of time." Her transcendence of

past/present/future signals her rise to a new level of consciousness.

The process of individual emergence which Chalmers exemplifies is articulated by Waters in *Masked Gods*. In an amalgam of Native American mythology, Jungian psychology, and Eastern mysticism, Waters explains an individual's inner development as an evolutionary journey through worlds or stages which correspond with the growing perception of dimensions. In the first stage of consciousness, things appeared one-dimensional, while a recognition of a second dimension accompanied the next stage. In the third stage "man becomes able to disassociate himself from his environment. He sails over the horizon of the flat world with the new assurance it is a sphere" (*Masked Gods*, pp. 435-436). One also becomes aware of the past and future: "But this first perception of time, the fourth dimension, he still sees as three-dimensional: past, present, future; birth, life, death. He cannot conceive it as an actual dimension at right angles to the three he knows" (*Masked Gods*, p. 436). It is in the next stage that one perceives this fourth dimensional reality: "The faculty of the unconscious develops to correspond with his previous development of the conscious and self-conscious. Through imagination and dreams he enters this unconscious realm of the fourth dimensional past and future" (*Masked Gods*, p. 436). Waters postulates an emergence through as many as six stages until the individual is perfected and ready to emerge to the final stage, "returning to and merging with the eternal source, undifferentiated from the complete cosmos" (*Masked Gods*, pp. 436-437). This progression is not completed in one lifetime. Waters sees the circle as the symbol of the human psyche and the individual's evolutionary Road of Life. Death is only the supposed end of the journey: "But from the after-death state he is reborn to the life-state. So over and over again within the circle he continues his rounds of existence. Until finally, through an inner development, he breaks free and escapes from time into eternity" (*Masked Gods*, p. 434). In this metempsychosis or reincarnation, Waters asserts, the continuity of consciousness remains: "all the memories of his past lives are stored in the unconscious which one day will realease them to his conscious mind" (*Masked Gods*, p. 435). Thus, at death one sheds the three-dimensional physical body and moves to an after-death plane until reentering the conscious plane and once more as-

suming another three-dimensional body. The "essential inner identity," however, never vanishes. And it is this which continually refines itself through the emergence process until the individual makes an eventual escape "from the synonymous circle of the cosmos and the psyche" in a return to the ultimate source (*Masked Gods*, p. 435).

The Woman at Otowi Crossing dramatizes this evolution to a higher level of consciousness, the perfection of the unchanging essence, and the final emergence with the ultimate source as Helen Chalmers tropologically experiences the Navaho and Pueblo creation myth, which depicts the prototypical individual emerging through levels into full, conscious humanity. When Helen Chalmers discovers a lump between her left breast and shoulder blade, her awakening begins and is accompanied by a move to a new level of awareness: "It was as if, in one instant, she had been moved to a plane upon which all the activities and values of life had no substance nor meaning at all" (p. 27). As with all her psychic experiences, Waters' depiction here is replete with language explosively resonant of an atomic reaction as he portrays the psychic fusion that makes Helen aware of the cosmic pattern:

> A cataclysmic explosion that burst asunder the shell of the world around her, revealing its inner reality with its brilliant flash. In its blinding brightness all mortal appearances dissolved into eternal meanings, great shimmering waves of pure feeling which had no other expression than this, and these were so closely entwined and harmonized they formed one indivisible unity. A selfhood that embraced her, the totality of the universe, and all space and all time in one immortal existence that had never had a beginning nor would ever have an end.   (p. 30)

The atomic resonances here and in other passages are underscored even more dramatically later in the novel when Dr. Gaylord, one of the scientists from Los Alamos and the lover of Helen's daughter Emily, explains the process that occurred within Helen:

> The similarity of this implosive-explosive process objectively in the A-bomb and subjectively as it happened to Helen Chalmers is at once casually apparent. Fear, worry, guilt, dread, shame, financial

failure—all this psychological dynamite accumulated within her, re-
called with pain and anguish, and brooded upon, seemed suddenly
on a quiet day to be detonated from all directions; to be driven in
upon her, implosively, with immense psychological force.   (p. 240)

For Helen this implosion resulted in a new sense of oneness with
the world, not unlike that Warner so often knew. Helen felt "the
slow pulse in a stone, the song of the river, the wisdom of the
mountains," and she was able to perceive a universal pattern
that made her recognize the significance of all life (p. 31).

The experience also causes her to feel a strange sense of
dissociation, to see a distinction between the "worldly roles she
played" and her "essential selfhood" (p. 56). Like birth, the
evolutionary process can be laborious and painful; Helen is left
with the uncomfortable sense that "she was caught between two
worlds, belonging to neither" (p. 59). As a result, even more
conflict builds in Helen as she is torn between this new inner
life and her old world. The immensity of what is happening to
her is so great she does not completely understand it. At times,
she even feels resentful because the process is so painful: "She
didn't want to be different! She wasn't ready for an Emergence
to a new world nebulous and unknown" (p. 111).

Yet in spite of the fear, the uncertainty, the pain, Helen
knows she cannot turn her back on the process: "having set her
foot on the ladder, she could not resign herself to going back
into a cramped material existence" (p. 111). And in accordance
with the stages Waters outlines in *Masked Gods,* Helen enters the
unconscious realm of the fourth dimension through dreams and
imagination. After her psychic cataclysm, dreams play a significant new role in her life:

> For now to her who had seldom dreamed, there came dream after
> dream in quick succession. Whatever they meant, if they had a
> meaning, they revealed her increasing receptivity to influences be-
> yond her mental ken. Something was untying the hard knot inside
> her; trying to break through the shell of the rational, materialistic
> world about her.   (p. 64)

Through a synthesis of two episodes from Warner's life—the discovery of the pottery sherd and the sighting of the wild geese—

Waters shows Chalmers actually breaking through that shell and delving within herself and through time as she unearths not merely a piece of pottery but memories of past lives stored in the unconscious. When Helen finds a piece of pottery with the thumb print of a Navawi'i woman on it at the same time wild geese in V formation fly overhead, she has another cataclysmic experience. Time is no longer three-dimensional as she moves through past, present, and future:

> At that instant it happened again: the strange sensation as of a cataclysmic faulting of her body, a fissioning of her spirit, and with it the instantaneous fusion of everything about her into one undivided, living whole. In unbroken continuity the microscopic life-patterns in the seeds of fallen cones unfolded into great pines. Her fingers closed over the splotch of clay on the bowl in her arms just as the Navawi'i woman released her own, without their separation of centuries. She could feel the enduring mist cooling and moistening a thousand dry summers. The mountain peaks stood firm against time. Eternity flowed in the river below. . . . And all this jelling of life and time into a composite *now* took place in that single instant when the wedge of wild geese hurtled past her—hurtled so swiftly that centuries of southward migrations, generations of flocks, were condensed into a single plumed serpent with its flat reptilian head outstretched, feet drawn back up, and a solitary body feather displaced by the wind, which seemed to be hanging immobile above her against the gray palimpsest of the sky.
> (pp. 116-117)

The centuries of migrating geese imaginatively transformed to the mythic plumed serpent become symbolic of Helen's new perception of time—the past of the Navawi'i woman, the future of the trees growing from fallen seeds, and her present are all an instantaneous composite. One of the most powerful passages in the novel, this captures the flow and rapidity of Helen's vision and awareness of her essential self.

The view of the great pines unfolding from the seeds of fallen cones is the first of many precognitive visions Helen has. The most significant of these occurs when she and Jack Turner, a lover renounced after the first of her psychic experiences, come upon a grotesque, huge mushroom so repulsive it gives Helen a feeling of "overwhelming malignancy" (p. 164). When Jack

kicks the fungus, Helen has another psychic experience. Helen is horrified as she watches in slow motion and preternatural silence the "cancerous gray cap" rise in the air and expand "like a mushroom-shaped cloud"; she screams in terror as billions of spores rain down on her:

> They whitened the blades of grass, shrivelled the pine needles, contaminated the clear stream, sank into the earth. Nor was this the end of the destruction and death they spread. For this malignant downport [sic] of spores was also a rain of venemous [sic] sperm which rooted itself in still living seed cells to distort and pervert their natural, inherent life forms. (p. 165)

In these and Helen's later vision of everything "enveloped in one brilliant apocalyptic burst of fire" (p. 194) comes the novelist's dire warning of the potentially destructive consequences of the work at Los Alamos. When Waters in *Masked Gods* compares the atomic and the psychic, he is quick to note that the birth of energy that takes place as a result of the fusion "may be a Monster Slayer or a Monster Bomb, a new faith or a new fear. Only the guiding philosophy determines whether it be constructive or destructive" (*Masked Gods,* p. 422). In the case of Helen Chalmers, the fusion is constructive since it brings about a spiritual refinement that leads to the consummate goal in the individual's Road of Life. The guiding philosophy will determine whether the bomb is constructive or destructive in the fulfillment of our civilization's Road of Life. As the lump of cancer in Helen's breast led to a spiritual awakening, the malignant threat of atomic warfare can awaken mankind or precipitate a reign of horror in the fallout of destruction.

The process Helen undergoes from the time she first feels the lump in her breast readies her for the final Emergence, the bursting forth from the circularity of the Road of Life to join with cosmic oneness. Helen reverts more and more to her inner world. When Emily takes her and Facundo on a trip, stopping at the Grand Canyon, Helen and Facundo stare into its depths. Through Facundo's perspective its meaning is articulated for us; to him and Helen it is the reality which the kiva symbolism— sipapu, the place of Emergence:

> Now before him was the reality, the monstrous chasm, the abysmal

> mile-deep hole which extended down through the nebulous past to
> the rock bottom core of a world that had existed unchanged mil-
> lions of years before his forefathers had made their Emergence here
> in human form to begin their life upon its surface. At sunrise and
> at sunset Facundo stood on the rim to cast pinches of prayer meal
> into the great *sipapu,* the womb of Our Mother Earth, the revered
> Place of Beginning whence came man.   (p. 270)

This womb symbolism appropriately comes as Helen prepares for
death, a death that will bring her final re-birth, the last stage of
her Road of Life, her Emergence with the cosmic.

Helen's moment of release, her transfiguration, significantly
occurs at the same time as an atomic test in the Pacific. Dr. Gaylord, working on this project in the Pacific, far from Helen and
Otowi Crossing, intuits her death and recognizes it as a transfiguration. He describes her Emergence in terms of the blinding
brilliance of the atomic flash. Recognizing in his vision what
Helen saw in her precognitions—"a vision of that apocalypse in
which each planetary body in time bursts into dissolution and
vanishes into eternity" (p. 297), Gaylord at once identifies the
connection between Helen Chalmers and the shot:

> I felt instead an overpowering surge of relief and gladness as if I
> were witnessing, far off in the Pacific, the death and transfiguration
> of that strange and lonely woman at Otowi Crossing whom I had
> never understood till then. The supernatural brilliance of that light,
> blinding as the radiance of a thousand suns; that tremendous re-
> lease of the universal energy confined so long within her mortal
> frame; the final assertion of spirit over matter;—they seemed to me
> then, and they have in some measure presisted ever since, the tri-
> umphant affirmation of her conviction of that enduring mystery
> which having no beginning could have no end, being the light and
> life eternal, and not only the destroyer but the maker of worlds
> without end.   (p. 297)

So Gaylord pronounces his *benedicite* for Helen. Chalmers is
released from the circular journey of the psyche as she bursts
forth in a radiant apotheosis to eternity. And Gaylord, in this
intuitive vision, has just begun his journey to awakening.

The novel concludes with an epilogue, an interview with

M. Meru, an investigator of psychic phenomena. Meru comments generally on the nature of myth and specifically on the myth of the Woman at Otowi Crossing. According to Meru, myth "wells up spontaneously within us in the same involuntary processes which shape the mind, the foetus within the womb, the atomic structure of the elements" (pp. 299-300). So it is with this particular myth:

> We ourselves created it—we of a new age, desperately crying for a new faith or merely a new form that will model old truths to useful purpose. Helen Chalmers affirms our mistrust of the neuter and negative materialism of our time. In the image of a warm and pulsing human being, she embodies the everlasting Beauty combatting the Beast, the spirit versus the flesh, the conscience of man opposed to the will of man. Helen Chalmers is dead and will be forgotten, but the myth of the Woman at Otowi Crossing is woven of a texture impervious to time. We ourselves, each one of us in turn, simply tailor it anew for successive generations.　(p. 300)

Like the Doctor at the end of a morality play, Meru clearly draws the moral for the reader.

In this way Waters has tailored the story of Edith Warner. While working from the basic structure of her biography, he alters some facts—giving her a drunken husband, giving her an abandoned daughter, Emily, who comes to the Southwest as an adult to meet the mother she had never known—to increase the conflicts, the dualities in her life which provide such a fundamental medium for the psychic fusion. He builds on Warner's religious experiences in nature, her intuitive sense of harmony, her transcendence of the present in a preternatural bond with the past—on all of those aspects which he would interpret as a sign of a highly refined spiritual awareness, an existence on a higher plane of consciousness. He dramatizes, too, the backdrop of her life, the world at the birth of the atomic age; Los Alamos, the womb of that age. And, thus, transforming Edith Warner, he creates a new faith in the form of the myth of the Woman at Otowi Crossing, a faith modeled on older truths, modeled on the Navaho and Pueblo creation myth, on Jungian psychology, on Eastern mysticism. Edith Warner fictionally transformed becomes Helen Chalmers transfigured, Helen Chalmers on the onset of *"our greatest experience, our mysterious voyage of discovery*

into the last unknown, man's only true adventure" (p. 300). Helen Chalmers in her awakening and emergence mythically manifests a prototypic pattern for every psyche.[6]

NOTES

[1](Chicago: Swallow Press, 1966). All further references to the novel will be from this edition.

[2]"Frank Waters and the Native American Consciousness," *Western American Literature,* 9 (Spring, 1974), 42. For a similar perspective, see Thomas J. Lyon's *Frank Waters* (New York: Twayne Publishers, 1973), p. 124.

[3](Chicago: Swallow Press, 1950), pp. 421-422. All further references to *Masked Gods* will be from this edition.

[4](Albuquerque: University of New Mexico Press, 1960). All further references to Church's memoir will be from this edition.

[5]Cf., for example, *Masked Gods,* p. 413.

[6]I would like to thank William M. Clements for his extensive help in the revision of this paper.

The Western Roots of Feminism
in Agne Smedley's *Daughter of Earth*

Kathleen L. Nichols

Although many writers have advanced the idea that the American consciousness was shaped, in part, by the frontier experience, western literature too often focuses on only half of the story—namely, the male side of the western experience. However, Agnes Smedley's autobiographical novel, *Daughter of Earth* (1929), can provide us with part of the other half of the story—the effect of the western experience on women's lives, as viewed by a woman who attributed her feminist attitudes to the corrosive effects of growing up female on the disappearing frontier at the turn-of-the-century.

The West that Smedley introduces is a Hamlin Garland world of struggle, poverty, and oppression. In particular, Smedley looks at the oppression experienced by poor women in the West, delineating in her fictional counterpart, Marie Rogers, the damaging effects these negative role models had upon the developing consciousness of a young frontier girl. Yet in the lives of these doubly oppressed western women struggling to survive economic hardship along with their men, as well as sexist exploitation by the western male, Smedley also locates the values of loyalty, courage, and dedication which would later form the basis of her political beliefs and, during the 1930s, take her to revolutionary China, where she became a world-famous political activist.

Smedley's novel begins with the adult Marie Rogers "at the end of one life and on the threshold of another." Having recently sacrificed her marriage to the exigencies of her husband's political career, and planning to leave America forever, Marie faces an uncertain future numbly wondering whether her new political work "that is limitless in its scope and significance" will

be "enough to weigh against love"[1] —lost love, that is. To answer this question, Marie feels the need to sort through the "fragments of [her] life" which she organizes into two phases: the painful western childhood which she had tried to forget, and the young adult years spent primarily in New York ignoring too many of the lessons learned in the West. As the pattern of Marie's memories will reveal, only by recovering and accepting that lost past and her roots in the western soil can she make sense out of her life and justify the future she has chosen as a defender of the oppressed in Asia.

The major theme of the novel is established by the first memories Marie recalls from her early life in northern Missouri in the 1890s—namely, her own oppression as a child by her angry mother. Because the young Marie had a predilection for building "beautiful" red fires and telling stories—"lies," her mother called them—her mother would get a "tough little switch that cut like a knife into the flesh," and "without taking hold of me, she forced me to stand in one spot of my own will, while she whipped me on all sides. Afterwards, when I continued to sob. . . , she would order me to stop or she would 'stomp me into the ground' " (p. 7). The immediate lesson young Marie learned from such beatings was the unjustified basis of oppression—"only by virtue of her size [my mother] had the power to do what she would with me." However, looking back years later, the older Marie understands better her mother's anger, noting that "as the years of [my mother's] unhappy married life increased, as more children arrived, she whipped me more and more" (p. 7). What the rest of the novel will show is that through these beatings, young Marie was receiving her first indirect lessons in what it means to be a woman victimized by her own biology, by her economic dependence on a husband, and by the conditions they both must suffer in the West: "I see now," the older narrator observes, "that she and my father, and the conditions about us, perverted my love and my life" (p. 8).

What were those "conditions" that help explain the mother's cold rages and the way young Marie's life was "perverted"? As Marie retraces her childhood in vivid, painful detail, the answers to her mother's anger are seen to be partly geographical, partly socio-economic, and partly her husband's character, particularly as it was manifested in his responses to the first two

problems. Although Marie can muster up some early memories of joyous harvest festivals at which her flamboyant father sang and led the dances, she also remembers even more vividly how her childhood was "blackened" by the "terrible quarrels" her parents had over their hard way of life. As she summarizes it, her father was a dreamer frustrated by the conditions in Missouri and always convinced that "success and happiness and riches . . .lay just beyond—where we were not" (p. 30), while her more pragmatic mother was "satisfied to work ceaselessly and to save a few pennies a year." To her father, "such an existence was death." As he viewed it,

> there were but three or four festivals a year. The rest of the time he had to follow the lone plow over badly yielding, stony soil, stumbling over the clods with his bare feet. He wanted to wear shoes all the year. . . . (p. 29)

Driven on by the American Dream which promised that "out West" lay the good life, adventure, happiness—whatever it was a person felt was lacking in his life—Marie's father is a familiar figure often idealized in the standard western male myth. However, in Smedley's version, the father serves primarily as a backdrop for her focus on the effects of the conventional western male myth on those usually not treated in it—the women and children. Marie reveals, for instance, how the family was frequently forced to pull up roots so that her discontented father could continue his western search for that easier way of life. On the first "escape" from the Missouri farm that Marie remembers, the family had traveled for days in a covered wagon in which they lived for the summer, while the father earned money by cutting trees on other men's property, only to have the family forced back with the first heavy snowfall to the "little farm where the soil was so gray and hard" (p. 31), at which point the father deserted his pregnant wife, striking off for months on his own in search of opportunity. This was the hopeless, repetitive pattern that was to mark all of Marie's childhood. Marie's father, an impractical dreamer, could neither accept nor break out of their impoverished living conditions; her overworked mother, periodically deserted by her westward-bound husband, would grimly assume all the responsibility for supporting the growing family, then, upon her husband's return, would be moved by him to a new and equally hopeless situation, where the same cycle

would be repeated.

Yet Marie also sees that environment and other circumstances in the West contributed to the problem and to her father's demoralization. For instance, when the father moved the family to Trinidad, a small Colorado mining town near the Sante Fe trail, they lived well for a while in a tent by the Purgatory River, until they lost all their worldly goods in a flash flood. Then followed a series of jobs in a number of extremely isolated mining camps hidden in the canyons far back in the mountains where the discouraged father drank up most of his paycheck. These struggles occur in the context of gas-reeking mines and strike-ridden camps which were "smoldering [with] discontent and hatred. . .and complaints about the weigh boss, the hours, wages, insufficient props and other precautions against falls, the high prices and dishonesty of the Company store [and] the payment of script instead of American money" (p. 110). As the older Marie realizes, this series of impossible situations, along with her father's ignorance of written contracts, repeatedly forced her family back to Trinidad—a pattern which was not broken until her mother died and the teenage Marie left home, striking out on her own first for the far West and then to New York to find a better kind of life.

Despite the mutual suffering of both her parents, the oppression experienced by women in the West is the most difficult memory Marie, as a woman, has to contend with. Young Marie, cruelly whipped by her oppressed mother, understandably enough wanted to identify with her father, who laughed, told wonderful stories, and too often saw glorious adventures somewhere just beyond the horizon; yet one of her early lessons in being female was that females were not highly valued. As she discovered early on the Missouri farm, male animals cost more than females and were "chosen with more care" (p. 11). Even worse, her own father valued more the new male baby than he did the daughter who was so like him in spirit, a resemblance for which her mother had too often whipped the child. However, Marie was more disturbed by her father's devaluation of her female existence, an attitude which made her feel that there was "something wrong with me. . .something too deep to even cry about" (p. 12). No matter how much she wanted to identify with her father, biology, as well as circumstances often created

by her father, forced young Marie to side increasingly with her mother against her father.

As a role model, however, Marie's mother could not offer her daughter much, for the one reality of woman's existence that scarred Marie the most deeply was the miserable lot of married women in the West. Marie remembers, for instance, the way her father used the threat of leaving his wife penniless as a means of getting his own way, often even carrying out the threat and leaving her mother in tears and despair, only to return months later to see if she had learned her lesson. The first time he tried to force his wife into agreeing with him about giving up the hard but secure life in Missouri, he even threatened to take the children with him, a prospect that had at first delighted the young Marie—until she saw the effect of her father's strategy on her mother: "But there was something about my mother that made me disobey my father that night. I ran to my mother and placed my hand on her knee and her tears fell on it" (p. 30). At that moment, Marie instinctively made the first choice which would set the pattern for her life: because she already identified with the oppressed, she sided with her mother, her own oppressor, against her father, her mother's oppressor—a choice which meant that in the future Marie would have to define her feminine identity in terms of oppression or reject her sexual identity so that she could view herself as free. This was, in fact, the central conflict which developed out of young Marie's experiences in the West and which it took her many anguished years to resolve.

The second most important role model for young Marie was her beautiful Aunt Helen, her mother's younger sister about ten years Marie's senior, who left home at age fifteen to work as a hired girl. Through her working aunt, Marie learned an important lesson about the economic basis of sexual politics. As Marie notes, "to be a hired girl drawing your own money gave you a position of authority and influence in the community. . . . You could tell it by her proud bearing and her independent attitude. . ." (p. 23). When the "flaming and vital" Helen was lured further West by the initially enthusiastic letters Marie's parents wrote her from Colorado, Marie was again impressed with her aunt's attitude, noting that before her aunt decided on a job, "she considered what work was worthy of her—for she knew her value" (p. 43), something which Marie's mother had no sense of.

For only six dollars (plus board) a month as a hired girl or, later, as a laundry girl working the mangle for seven dollars a week and then the stiff shirt machine for eleven dollars a week, Marie's Aunt Helen could afford pride and self-respect.

Throughout Marie's important developmental years, her beautiful, independent Aunt Helen functioned as a standard by which Marie could measure and understand the degree of oppression experienced by married women in the West. Not only was Helen self-supporting, she frequently was the sole supporter of the household. Thus, her position in the home was truly powerful for a woman, and when she would defend her sister, Marie's mother, against the abuse of Marie's father, there was little he could do, because he also recognized and accepted her first-class status as worker. As Marie observes, Aunt Helen "paid for her room and board and no man had the right to 'boss her around.' My mother did not; she could never toss her head proudly and freely and say 'I'm payin' for my keep here!' " (p. 44).

The independent, unmarried Helen was an inspiring example for young Marie and her oppressed mother, providing both of them with an affirmative image of woman. Thus, following in Helen's footsteps, even Marie's timid mother would one day find the courage to defy her husband when women were granted the right to vote and he demanded, as a husband's right, to know how she had voted; and after the father began to speak admiringly of men who beat their women, Marie's defiant response which cowed her father on two occasions when he actually tried to carry out the threat was an exact duplication of her aunt's earlier attitudes and actions. Through her aunt, Marie learned, among other things, female self-respect and courage, group loyalty, and resistance to an oppressor.

Yet, in the end, her Aunt Helen failed Marie as an ideal role model. It was discovered that even the proud Helen had one limitation which she, as a woman, could not overcome: her own sexual nature, a culpable condition for women in western society's eyes, which viewed virginity as woman's only marketable commodity, even though, as Marie remembers, "women were scarce in the West even in those days, and it wasn't an easy thing [for a western male] to get a wife" (p. 101). Since early child-

hood, Marie had been developing increasingly negative attitudes toward women's sexuality and fertility, partly because she had too often been the scapegoat of her mother's displaced anger over her own biology which had trapped her in an unhappy marriage, but also because sex was treated as a shameful secret. Marie remembers how, as a farm child in Missouri, she had quickly learned not to mention the birth of a calf which she had witnessed, and how, when her baby brother was born, "we children were hurried off to another farmhouse, and secrecy and shame settled like a clammy rag over everything" (p. 11). The shame of sex had turned to actual revulsion when the young Marie had awakened in the night in the one bedroom house and overheard her parent's love-making in the dark. As Marie puts it, "on my mind was engraved a picture of terror and revulsion that poisoned the best years of my life" (p. 12).

As a teenager, however, Marie had one last lesson to learn about female sexuality—that it is a weapon which men use against women. Despite her aunt's status as worker, when it was revealed that Helen had had lovers and that part of her income, which so often had been the family's only resource, came from her lovers, Helen was immediately demoted, in the eyes of Marie's father, to the subordinate status of a mere woman, and a "bad" woman at that, even though Helen could justifiably point out that women like herself were created by men like Marie's father who abused, overworked, and almost literally starved their wives and children. But since female sexuality had no defense, Helen could still be ordered out of the house by Marie's outraged father who seized on this "flaw" as a justifiable excuse for regaining his lost status in the household. Since Helen was no longer his equal, the father even felt free to use threats of physical violence against his wife and children as a legitimate weapon for putting Helen, a mere woman, in her place. Thus Helen ended with no choice but to submit to male authority and leave. Although conflict about sexual identity and male domination ruined some of the best years of Marie's later life, dominating her relationships with others and destroying her marriage to a man she loved, Marie could still find value in the life of her Aunt Helen, whose bid for freedom got her no further than the emotionally barren life of an aging prostitute: "Greater love hath no woman than she who will sell her body for the sister she loves" (p. 132).

The confused, sixteen year old Marie, however, could accept neither her mother's nor her aunt's ways; after her mother died, what she did to escape the trap which the West represented to her as a woman was to accept her father's way. As the thirty year old narrator puts it,

> Had it not been for the wanderlust in my blood—my father's gift to me—and had I not inherited his refusal to accept my lot as ordained by a God, I might have remained in the mining towns all my life, married some working man, borne him a dozen children to wander the face of the earth, and died in my early thirties. Such was the fate of all women around me. (p. 117)

However, her father's way of ignoring the past and its obligations, while looking only at the future and its opportunities, turned out to be another trap which would also help poison her young adult years because it involved denying her own womanhood, her family, and her western roots. As she recalls, at that time in her life, she "resented everything, hating myself most of all for having been born a woman, hated my brothers and sisters because they existed and loaded me with a responsibility I refused to carry; hated my father and mother for bringing me into [the] world. . ." (p. 137). Her solution for the next decade or so as she struggled to get an education, to survive political imprisonment and betrayal, and to find an enduring purpose to her life was to draw "a dark curtain before my conscious memory and. . .forget I had a family at all" (p. 137).

This dark curtain on her past, however, almost destroyed her emotionally because she could find no continuity to her fragmented life; for the older narrator, at a major crossroads in her life, removing that curtain so that she can find the "unity in [the] diversity" of her past is essential if she is ever to establish a meaningful basis for her future. Thus, through the reawakened memories of the cowboys and rough working men and women she lived among in the West, she achieves a kind of catharsis which allows her finally to reclaim her ties with the past. As she explains,

> I now recall with joy those hearty, rough, hairy-chested, unshaven men. I recall the rougher, unhappy men in the mining camps, and their silent, unhappy wives. . . . But there were years when, in

> search of what I thought were better, nobler things, I denied these,
> my people, and my family. I forgot the songs they sung. . .I erased
> their dialect from my tongue; I was ashamed of them and their
> ways of life. But now—yes, I love them; they are a part of my
> blood; they, with all their virtues and their faults, played a great
> part in forming my way of looking at life.   (p. 119)

The major triumph of her mental journey back to her western roots, however, is the recovery of the "bond of misery" she and her mother, as two oppressed women, forged in the face of unbearable conditions, a bond and an identity which Marie, when she left the West, had rejected in anger: "Love, tenderness, and duty belonged to women and weaklings in general; I would have none of them!" (p. 136). Yet the sense of "nothingness [that] throbbed in beats, like the waves of a sea against a cliff" (p. 129) that so often overcame her in her young adult years and that dominates the narrator's consciousness at the beginning of the novel, began the day her mother, not yet forty, died; and the narrator knows that for her future commitment to her new "family"—to all of suffering humanity that engages in the "struggle of earth"—to mean anything, the story of childhood oppression must be tempered by recovered memories of the positive qualities of her relationship with her mother, qualities which the misery of her western childhood had made her repress for so many years: memories of the mother and daughter, when Marie's father was gone, working happily together as comrades and supporting each other through the grueling workloads and despair of their impoverished conditions; memories of her mother overworking herself so that her daughter could receive an education, something Marie's father scorned, but which her mother knew was the only way Marie could escape duplicating her mother's life; memories of her mother's silent sympathy for the miners striking against oppression when her husband was not sure which side to take, and of her mother's grand moment of pride and defiance when she risked her husband's dangerous wrath to defend her "fallen" sister Helen who had loved her so well; and finally memories of her mother's pride in her daughter's accomplishments, as the mother transferred all her frustrated hopes for her own life to her daughter's future, and on her deathbed announced "as if the words were wrung from her"—"I don't know how I could of lived till now if it hadn't been fer you" (p. 128).

As Smedley shows through the memories of her auto-biographical heroine, the western experience for many women was the antithesis of the standard western male myth which too often ignored the lives of women and children or, in some cases, actually victimized them. Yet in the daily loyalty and endurance of these oppressed western women forming bonds of misery and hope, Smedley also finds the courage, the commitment, and the cause to which she can devote her life. Thus when her fictional counterpart finally proclaims, "I belong to those who do not die for the sake of beauty. I belong to those who die from other causes—exhausted by poverty, victims of wealth and power, fighters in a great cause" (p. 4), she is affirming her legacy from the West, and from her mother who died in the West.

NOTES

[1] Agnes Smedley, *Daughter of Earth* (Old Westbury, New York: Feminist Press, 1973), p. 4. All future quotations from the novel will be cited by page number in the text.

Pioneer Women in the Works of Two Montana Authors:
Interviews with
Dorothy M. Johnson and A. B. Guthrie, Jr.[1]

Sue Mathews

Pulitzer Prize winner A. B. Guthrie, Jr., has a favorite question he poses when the topic of the western movement comes
up in conversation. "I wonder," he asks, "how many men would
have gone West had they been women?" His main female character in *The Way West*, Rebecca Evans, ponders the same question:
"It was like men to be excited and not to feel with their excitement such a sadness as a woman did at saying goodbye to her
home. . . ."[2] But even in her sadness, Becky goes West, pulled
by her husband's dream, if not her own. "A woman ain't cut
like a man," she thinks. "Not so adventuresome or rangin' and
likin' more to stay put—but still we foller 'em round, and glad to
do it, too" (p. 171).

It is for sentiments such as these that Guthrie says he has
been accused of not being sympathetic toward his women characters. "I think I am [sympathetic]," he says. "When I wrote *The
Way West*, for example, I began to think about Rebecca Evans, a
rather hefty woman, jouncing over the plains, and I thought
'that must have been hell on her breasts'—and I put that in the
book to express in a physical way the hardships those pioneer
women endured."

"Of course" he goes on, "the [pioneer] women, largely un-
acknowledged, were real heroines. They made the westward trek,
often with babies, always with more concern for their children or
menfolk than for themselves. By and large," Guthrie suggests,
"maybe the westering experience was easier for men. I'm not
sure, though, that the men had more fun," he adds. "They
weren't burdened with such drudgery, but still, if they were
good men and concerned about their wives and their families,

they had a big burden on them, too. . . ."

Dorothy M. Johnson, whose contributions to Western literature won in 1976 a Levi Strauss Golden Saddlemen award "for
bringing dignity and honor to the history and legends of the
West,"[3] and in 1981 Western Literature Association's Distinguished Service Award, agrees with her fellow Montanan:

> The Western experience was different for a woman than it was
> for a man. It would have to be. She would not go alone for one
> thing. I never heard of a woman who went adventuring by her-
> self—except for Isabella Bird who wasn't planning to settle in the
> West, and possibly the "soiled doves." I think maybe they went in
> pairs and probably it was all arranged ahead of time by somebody
> else.

> Surely, it was different. Most of them had entirely different
> responsibilities than men, and it wasn't perfectly terrible, either;
> some of them had a lovely time going West.

As an example, Johnson points to "Mrs. Wilbur Fisk
Sanders,[4] one of Montana's earliest pioneers," who, she says,
"was a very sunny tempered creature. Nothing was ever as bad
as she thought it might be, and she never thought it was going to
be very bad anyway. Everything came out better than she expected—she loved it."

Johnson admits, however, that Mrs. Sanders' attitude was
the exception rather than the rule for pioneer women:

> She was highly educated and she had a perfectly beautiful dis-
> position, but she's not the only one. Fanny Kelly,[5] who was cap-
> tured by Indians at the age of 19 and had a perfectly horrible time
> getting away from them, had a lovely time, too, until the Indians
> attacked the group that she was with and killed some of them and
> captured her and another woman and Fanny Kelly's little niece
> and another woman's little boy. Then they had a terrible time,
> but up to then they'd enjoyed it. The women did their housework,
> but under different conditions. They didn't have to do any dust-
> ing; they didn't have to do any mopping. Washing clothes was
> harder and cooking would be difficult, especially if it was raining.
> But everything was different and it was a great adventure.

Johnson uses the Fanny Kelly story as a "jumping-off place" for her short story "Journey to the Fort." This technique—basing fiction on an historical event—is one of Johnson's favorites, although she cautions against reading her fiction as history.

"My stories often start with an emotion," she says. "Then I create characters to fit that emotion, and those characters make the plot." Given her wide reading in Western history, it is not surprising that she finds characters who project the emotions and qualities she believes in—"I believe in love and I like strong people," she says; "and the virtues I admire are what people would probably label 'old fashioned': honesty, integrity, stick-to-itiveness."

"Lost Sister," for which Johnson won the Spur Award given by the Western Writers of America for the Best Short Story of 1956, is another example of her use of this technique:

> "Lost Sister" is based on a real event, the story of Cynthia Ann Parker, a little girl who was captured by Indians and raised by them. Her son was the famous Quanah Parker, the Comanche chief. The Comanches are home folk to Ben Capps, and he wrote an excellent book called *A Woman of the People* that was based on the life of Cynthia Ann Parker, too; but if you read those two stories you'd never know they were about the same person because fiction writers just don't work that way. All you need is a jumping off place.

Many of Johnson's jumping-off places have resulted in stories portraying pioneer women. In addition to "Journey to the Fort" and "Lost Sister," these include "Flame on the Frontier," "The Story of Charlie," "A Time of Greatness," and several others. And in "Beyond the Frontier," Johnson uses another of her plotting techniques—the "what if?" approach.

"According to legend," she says, "pioneer wives were always noble. I asked myself, what if one wasn't? Couldn't there be one who was spoiled, demanding, complaining—and who wanted to go back where she came from?" From such "iffing," the character of Blossom was born—Blossom, whom the reader meets for the first time "Standing in the yard in front of the

still-smoking log house, her long skirts blowing, her hands up to her mouth in a theatrical gesture that said Rancher's wife waiting for husband's return after Indian raid."[6]

Guthrie, too, turns to historical record for character proto-types and episodes in his novels. "Everything is based on re-cord," he says. "Not my characters, necessarily; but I try to be totally honest to history. I make up my own characters. I don't like to put words in the mouths of people who have actually lived and are now dead. That seems to be a little like disfiguring headstones. So I won't do that. But still, I try to be true to the time, the events, the techniques, the experiences of people of that time."

Guthrie's truth as it touches the women characters in *The Way West* reflects attitudes current in the mid-1800's. At one point on the trail, a serious shortage of wood for cooking fires is encountered. The men of the wagon train meet to ponder a seri-ous question: Was it right and proper for women to cook over buffalo chips? The men will worry this question through and let the women know their decision. When Mr. Byrd advances the belief that "it's not a lady-like thing" (p. 92), Higgins, one of the men in the party, reflects on this attitude:

> It struck him that Byrd and some of the others, for all that they knew better, stuck to queer ideas of women, not liking to think of them as flesh and blood and stomach and guts but as something different, something a cut above earthly things, so that no one should let on to them that critters had hind ends. . . .   (p. 92)

Higgins thinks the women in their party would find this discus-sion funny—because, he believes, "women had harder heads than men liked to believe" (p. 93).

It is left to Rebecca's husband to put into words Guthrie's admiration for the women who endured the dangers and hard-ships of the Oregon Trail:

> Raw or not, the women did their part and more. They traveled head to head with men, showing no more fear and asking no favor. . . . They had a kind of toughness in them that you might not think, seeing them in a parlor. . . . It was lucky for the pride of

men that few traveled with their wives to Oregon. They'd never
quite believe again a woman was to look at but not to listen
to.   (p. 297)

Not that this realistic view of women's capabilities brought
about any immediate changes in the way women were treated in
the newly settled communities—or on the scattered ranches—of
the Western frontier. "The early Westerner was very courteous
to the womenfolk," Guthrie says. "I think that was half out of
convention, though." Johnson agrees with Guthrie's view on
chivalry on the frontier, and takes the idea of "convention"
one step further. The women in her stories were civilizing forces
in their frontier towns, she says, "and this is not just in my
stories. They really were. They wanted everything to be the way
it was back in Iowa. The women had their responsibility, and the
married men, the fathers of families, did, too."

The conflict that "settling" this wild untamed portion of
the country produced—a product of "the woman's touch"—is
addressed by both Johnson and Guthrie. "The wide open West
was great while it lasted as a resort for the fiddle-footed, those
who didn't want responsibility, and it was better that way because the scum of the earth went West. There isn't anyplace for
them to go now," Johnson says.

In *The Way West,* Guthrie points up the different views of
"civilization" when he brings his wagon train to Fort Laramie:
Dick Summers—who soon will leave the train to return to the
freedom of the mountains—ruminates on a sight that catches his
eye. "A cornfield, even like the sorry patch by the fort, didn't
belong with war whoops and scalping knives. It belonged with
cabins and women and children playing safe in the sun. It belonged with the dull pleasure, with the fat belly and the dim eye
of safety" (p. 138).

To Rebecca, though, the fort represents comforts and concerns that had been left behind when the wagons began to roll
away from "home" toward the far distant Oregon Territory:

> She sighed inside, thinking it would be good to stay at the fort
> the rest of her life and so be done with dirt and hard travel and
> eyes teary with camp smoke and the back sore from stooping over

a fire and the legs cramped from sitting on the ground. . . . Her face, she knew, was a sight, reddened by the sun and coarsened by the wind until it was more man's face than woman's. For all that God had made her big and stout and not dainty, she wanted to feel womanlike, to be clean and smooth skinned and sometimes nice dressed, not for [her husband] alone, but for herself, for herself as a woman, so's to feel she was a rightful being and had a rightful place. . . . (pp. 140-141)

Guthrie is able to speak through Dick and Rebecca with the ring of truth in both voices because, he says, he builds his characters, "really, by thinking, by transposing [myself], if that is possible, by trying to think as they might think. You will note in my books that I always, in every chapter, or if not in the chapter, then divided by space breaks, I try to be totally with the character whose viewpoint I am expressing, whose sensibilities, understandings or lack of understandings are right there. I have the feeling that if the author extrapolates his imagination enough, he can really almost understand everybody, even the other sex."

Johnson, also, needs to live in the skin of her characters. "I can't write about people I don't understand because I have to *be* at least all the main characters," she says. Using this technique has caused her some anguish. "I remember rewriting one story ten times," she says:

The main reason was that the man had to go through such a terrible time out in the woods with a broken leg, lost. He thinks he's going to die, but he has to get ready to pull through if it's possible. I didn't want to be that man, so I approached that story from all kinds of other angles, using flashbacks and trying to avoid going through that misery myself. And finally—on the tenth revision—I thought I might as well face it and just do it. So I sat there with duck bumps on my arms and did it.

Johnson has not only had to adopt the guise of the opposite sex, but to "be" Indian characters as well. Her novel *Buffalo Woman* tells of the life of a Plains Indian woman, Whirlwind, from birth until her death on the flight to Canada following the Custer Battle. At one point in the book, Whirlwind, old and wounded by a grizzly bear, sorrows over what she has come to.

"This is not the way I have lived, being in the way, being waited on! I am the one who looks after others."[7]

Her lament would be perfectly understandable to Rebecca Evans and any number of her real life counterparts who made the journey West. Rebecca sees that "Her man and her boy are happy, and that was enough. A happy family was all a person could ask for. It wasn't in the right nature of things for her to allow herself the miseries when she had that much" (p. 77).

Perhaps this view, and others expressed by Guthrie and by Johnson, who explains the actions of one of her female characters by saying of her simply, "She loved her husband, and I believe in love," will not find favor with contemporary readers. But they present—as truthfully as they know how—the world as it existed a century ago, a world that intrigues the modern reader, perhaps because, as Johnson says in explaining her preference for the nineteenth century over the twentieth, "we know how it came out." Or, perhaps, some of our interest can be attributed to having the leisure time that our pioneer forebears did not, to look to our past and learn from it. Perhaps, too, it signifies a maturation on the part of the country. "As a civilization ages, its interest in antecedents increases," Guthrie says.

For whatever reason we turn to the lives of frontier women —fictional or real—we are sure to find lessons in them that transcend century marks or state lines. In 1954, Guthrie addressed a Montana State Historical Society conference on the subject of the historical novel. The world—especially the world of women —has changed considerably from the decade of the fifties, but Guthrie's remarks ring true—perhaps even truer—today: "I believe all of us become better citizens, better and richer human beings, through a familiarity with the dreams and deeds of the men and women who went before us in this adventure that we call the United States of America." "The men and women"— side by side, equal partners not by law, but in pride in their achievements and in each other. This is part of the western—the Montana—heritage captured and preserved for all of us to enjoy and learn from by Dorothy Johnson and A. B. Guthrie, Jr.

NOTES

[1] Quoted material in this article not taken from the works of Guthrie and Johnson was obtained through interviews with Mr. Guthrie in his Choteau, Mt., home (August, 1979), and with Miss Johnson at her home in Missoula (June, 1977 and October, 1979).

[2] A. B. Guthrie, Jr., *The Way West* (New York: Bantam, 1971), p. 36. Subsequent references to this source will be included in the text.

[3] Golden Saddleman citation, one of the many awards for her writing in Dorothy M. Johnson's personal collection. For further information on Miss Johnson's works, see Sue Mathews and James W. Healey, "The Winning of the Western Fiction Market: An Interview with Dorothy M. Johnson," *Prairie Schooner*, 52 (Summer, 1978), 158-167.

[4] Mrs. W. F. Sanders (Harriett) was the wife of one of Montana's first U. S. Senators. W. F. Sanders served in that capacity from 1890-1893. Harriet Sanders is the subject of a chapter in Virginia Towle's *Vigilante Woman* (New York: A. S. Barnes, 1966).

[5] Fanny Kelly's own account of her capture is told in *My Captivity Among the Sioux Indians* (Hartford, Connecticut: Mutual Publishing Company, 1871), a signed copy of which Dorothy Johnson calls "the pride of my library."

[6] Dorothy M. Johnson, "Beyond the Frontier," *A Man Called Horse* (New York: Ballantine, 1953), p. 116.

[7] Dorothy M. Johnson, *Buffalo Woman* (New York: Dodd, Mead, 1977), p. 199.

(Portion of)

Mrs. Powers House, Kearney

Courtesy of the Nebraska State Historical Society

III

IMAGES IN TRANSITION AND CONFLICT

Hamlin Garland's Feminism

Frances W. Kaye

Hamlin Garland is probably the most interesting of the American male feminist writers of the late nineteenth century. Garland's partial identification with women and his approving though ultimately unflattering reflection of the philosophy of the main stream feminist movement, including its contradictions, lend considerable poignancy to his writing. Garland explicitly announced his intention to speak for women, and he was the only male author of literary significance who specifically endorsed in his writing woman's rights, woman suffrage, and woman's equality in marriage.[1] In this paper, I discuss Garland's specific treatment of feminist issues.

Garland's feminism must be understood in terms of the intellectual currents of his time. The nineteenth century feminist movement demanded woman's rights on two mutually exclusive grounds. On one hand, the feminists claimed for women equal rights as human beings, as individuals, and as citizens on the simple ground of equity. Human rights, they argued, were inalienable, and could not be divided into men's rights and women's rights. On the other hand, the feminists claimed for women political and social equality because, as the moral superiors of men, women were needed in the public sphere to reform it. According to this line of reasoning, women and men were equal in rights but different in powers. This argument agreed in analysis but differed in conclusion from the conservative argument that because women were better and purer than men, they needed to be protected from the harsh political world by remaining confined in the "sphere" of home and family. The nineteenth century suffrage associations accepted the traditional definition of woman's *nature* but challenged the definition of her *role*.[2] That nineteenth century feminists considered the question of woman's moral, sexual nature as fundamental to

woman's political and social role can be seen in the agitation over "age of consent" (statutory rape) laws, an issue that occupied many pages in the *Arena* magazine, which published much of Garland's radical writing.[3]

Garland's feminism was affected not only by the movement itself but by the general currents of thought. He was comfortably in the center of the middle class melioristic reform movement of the nineteenth century, with its three-fold belief in the inevitability of Progress, in a Lockean respect for the individual, and in Spencerian environmental determinism. Herbert Spencer's writings were of particular importance to Garland, who based his system of self-education upon the concepts of the British philosopher and consistently invoked Spencer in the lectures he prepared for Brown's School of Oratory, where he taught off and on during the beginning of his career. He accepted as axiomatic Spencer's lines on equality from *Social Statics,* "The rights of women must stand or fall with those of men, derived as they are from the same authority, involved in the same axiom, demonstrated by the same argument."[4]   On the other hand, Garland had imbibed the Victorian dualism of good woman/fallen woman, and although he would explicitly deny the duality in his novel *Rose of Dutcher's Coolly,* he, like the suffragists, was unable to come to terms with the question of woman's sexuality. His fear of female sexuality as subversive to the order of society coupled with a belief in the "good" woman's innate purity sometimes compromised his dedication to simple equality. Garland's expressions of feminism were also affected by his theories about literature. As a Realist, he felt that the literary portrayal of women as strong individuals had to be tempered by the fact that only a small percentage of women in real life were able to escape from their socially determined weakness to become strong.

During the reformist part of his career, Garland believed in the Single Tax as the panacea to cure all ills. Garland believed that his most effective contribution to the movement was his fiction, in which he showed farm people, especially the farm women, beaten down by the land monopoly, their lives made inhuman. The problem is not that the farmer wants to tyrannize over his wife, or even so much that law and society have given him the right to tyrannize over his wife, but that the economic

system has brutalized him to the extent that he *does* tyrannize over his wife, not out of volition, but out of despair. The wife's lot cannot be changed by equalizing her status in marriage or politics, because only when the land monopoly has been defeated can working men and women be equal in anything but drudgery. Garland was a meliorist who believed in the essential goodness of human nature and, like Henry George, believed that once economic necessity was gone, no person would seek power for the sake of power, and man would not choose to exercise power over woman. Garland's theoretical writings on woman's rights derive directly from his Single Tax beliefs.

In these theoretical writings, Garland thunders rather platitudinously for the absolute equality of women and men. His fullest statement of these beliefs is in his Single Tax "New Declaration of Rights," which is similar to John Stuart Mill's argument in "On Liberty" and "The Subjection of Women." The Single Tax would bring about economic freedom for women, which would "do more for woman than place her equal before the law with man. It will release her from her dependence upon him as a breadwinner, and never till that is done can woman stand a free soul, individual and self-responsible. . . ."

> Woman will at last come to have the right to herself, and be the free agent of her own destiny. Then marriage will be a mutual co-partnership between equals. Prostitution will disappear, and marrying for a home, that first cousin of prostitution, will also disappear.

Political equality would also become woman's right:

> It is not a question whether woman will use the ballot, it is a question of liberty. She must have the liberty to do as she pleases so long as she does not interfere with the equal rights of others. It is not a question of her desires as a woman, it is a question of her rights as a human being.[5]

Garland wrote in the same vein in an essay for the *Standard*, proclaiming, "In my far-off ideal world the liberty of man and woman is bounded only by the equal rights of others. Woman stands there as independent of man as man is independent of woman."[6]

Most of Garland's thinking on feminism, however, must be derived from his fiction, and in examining his theories, I will start with his beliefs about the personal nature of woman and work outward to his conclusions about her role in public life. *Rose of Dutcher's Coolly* is Garland's longest and most complex investigation of what he believed to be woman's nature, particularly her sexual nature. Rose is raised by her widowed father on a farm in southwestern Wisconsin. More intelligent and intellectually ambitious than her school mates, she goes to Madison and, after some preparatory work, enters the University. When she graduates, her father hopes she will come back to the farm and settle down, but she moves on to Chicago to become, she hopes, a poet. Her beauty attracts many suitors, but finally she accepts the slightly cynical, middle-aged newspaper man, Warren Mason. The book ends with their marriage. Garland distrusted male sexuality, but in *Rose* he shows woman's sexuality as healthy, as long as it is controlled by a strong mind in a strong body. As a child, Rose is keenly and sensually aware of her body:

> Sometimes when alone she slipped off her clothes and ran amid the tall cornstalks like a wild thing. Her slim little brown body slipped among the leaves like a weasel in the grass. Some secret, strange delight, drawn from ancestral sources, bubbled over from her pounding heart.[7]

She is reluctant to confine herself in clothes again, and she envies the bodily freedom of the skinny dipping boys. However, female sensuality in a weak woman easily leads to disaster. When Rose is fourteen, her teacher is a kittenish young woman whose flirtatious ways set off a mysterious epidemic of undefined sexual experimentation. Even Rose and her friend Carl are tainted by whatever unspecified things happen, but they are corrected by Mr. Dutcher and their innocent comradeship returns.

Rose's real sexual awakening is intellectual and it occurs when she confronts the double standard. She reads *The Scarlet Letter* and feels Hester unfairly treated. She goes to a play which dramatizes the idea that men outgrow their youthful sexual experimentations, but women are ruined by them. She sets herself to figure out the problem of sex. Her contempla-

tions, we are to believe, are tempestuous and frightening. Like most children, her introduction to the subject has been crude. As a young woman on her way to the University she has been harrassed by a "sex-maniac" of a brakeman.[8] Later, as a student,

> God only knows the temptations which came to her. She had days when all the (so-called) unclean things she had ever seen, all the over-heard words of men's coarse jests, came back like vultures to trouble her. Sometimes when she walked forth of a morning. . .every lithe youth moved like a god before her, and it was then that something deep in her, something drawn from generations of virtuous wives and mothers, saved her from the whirlpool of passion. (p. 120)

> There was nothing she did not think of during these character-forming days. The beauty and peace of love, the physical joy of it; the problem of marriage, the terror of birth—all the things girls are supposed not to think of. . .this thought was wholesome and natural, not morbid in any degree.

> . . .in the most trying moments of her life (and no man can realize these moments) some hidden force rose up to dominate the merely animal forces within. Some organic magnificent inheritance of moral purity.

> She was saved by forces within, not by laws without. (p. 127)

Garland was undoubtedly courageous in choosing to talk about woman's sexuality, but his discussions ultimately do not make much sense. At the end of the book, Garland solves Rose's problems by finding her an appropriate marriage. The marriage is not an evasion, but evasion is an integral part of the whole consideration. Although Garland was in most things an environmental determinist, a Naturalist, he seems to have viewed woman's moral nature as some non-Mendelian, sex-linked genetic trait. Rose's reaction to her sexual awakening is determined by her "organic magnificent inheritance of moral purity" (p. 127), and not by either external laws and customs nor what Garland portrays as the sordid aspects of sex around her. Garland seems to have believed that this was the inheritance of all women, but that most were too weak to put it into play. Like the kittenish teacher, the putative whore in the uncharacteristic story

"The Passing Stranger," and the young divorcee in "A Fair
Exile," most women are too weak to claim this inheritance and
instead reflect and even inflame the impure lust that, in Garland's curious double standard, seems to be the inheritance of
men.

As a Realist, Garland was careful not to include too many
strong women in his writing, but his portrayal of strong women
is significant. Rose is able to think about sex—and the incon-
clusiveness of her musings seems more Garland's fault than her
own—because she is mentally strong enough to defy convention
and physically strong enough to think without becoming "morbid." She also has the advantage of having grown up on a farm
and learned enough about generation to think concretely about
sex. Garland sensibly associated strong-mindedness with good
health and physical fitness. As espoused by the heroine of his
story "Upon Impulse," physical fitness "adds so much to life!
It gives what Browning calls the wild joy of living. Do you
know, few women know what that means? It's been denied us.
Only the men have known. . . ."[9]

The strong woman, Garland believed, had an obligation to
use her inherent purity to influence society for the good through
her domestic relations. A wife had a responsibility to keep her
husband from being a lobbyist or monopolist; she should not live
comfortably on his ill-gotten gains. She was also supposed to
regulate her husband's personal life. Garland's view on this is
most clearly expressed in the play *Margaret Fleming*, by Garland's friend James A. Herne. Garland was Herne's sounding
board during the writing of the play, and it expressed his ideas as
well as its author's, as Garland made clear in his article about
Herne in *The Arena*. Philip Fleming deserts his family when his
wife, Margaret, discovers his infidelity. Four years later they
meet accidentally, and he finds out that she will neither divorce
him nor allow him to return to her. He asks if it is degrading
to forgive. "No," she replies, "but it is to condone." According
to Garland, "She seemed to be speaking for all womankind,
whose sorrowful history we are only just beginning to read truthfully."[10] Since Philip is not an honorable man, Margaret will
not let him resume an honorable position in the eyes of the
world. Clearly, this is an inversion of the usual double standard,
and Margaret's purity seems quite completely to have vanquished

her sexuality.

Most women, however, Garland believed, were weak, and that was man's fault and society's loss. Women were either drudges who had no time or will to think, or they were "protected" from assuming their proper moral duties. Men were strong but filled with lust and "morbid" sexuality. Garland himself was "shocked and horrified" by the sexual attitudes of the hired hands he knew as a boy.[11] There are good men in Garland's books, but they seem to have learned their goodness somehow from mother or beloved. It was to the advantage of the common men whom Garland saw as controlling most of business and government to keep women weak and ignorant so that their inherent morality would not interfere with the men's greed. The argument that men consciously oppressed women for their selfish purposes was more radical than Garland's usual theory that men and women were both oppressed by the system, but it is largely submerged in Garland's horror at the Naturalistic efflorescence of men's sexuality.

Garland seems to have been possessed by the particular sexual fantasy in which the rapist is both ravisher and comforter of his victim. On somewhat the same level, he could identify with his father's pioneering feats, while also identifying with his mother's victimization by the frontier and his father. The same pattern is visible in the otherwise uninteresting "Ol' Pap's Flaxen." The orphaned Flaxen is raised by two bachelors. Still very young she marries a no-good man. He conveniently drowns, and she marries the younger of her two foster fathers, who has been roused to an understanding of his own sexual desire for her by the actions of the first husband. The husband/father shares none of the guilt but all of the fruits of Flaxen's original "rape." The voyeurism of Garland's observer figures, particularly in the story "A Fair Exile," is of the same ilk.[12] Perhaps the strongest occurrence of this pattern is in the unpublished manuscript, "The Stranger Woman." A mysterious woman gets off a train at a country station one Sunday morning, and walks into the wood. Immediately the men of the town are galvanized into lustful pursuit, while their wives and daughters pray in church. In the willows by the river, the woman meets a blond giant of a man. They fall in love, contemplate suicide and, after he accidentally kills one of the pursuers, flee together.

If male sexuality could so easily become brutal even in a civilized village, Garland feared that in the wilderness the beast in man, unchecked by civilized restraints, would develop even more rapidly and dangerously. Of the villain in another unpublished story, a miner and would-be rapist, Garland wrote that he had become sex-mad by living alone and brooding over erotic novels.[13]

Even in civilized society, Garland feared that men were in constant danger of becoming sex-mad and could only be restrained by circumspect behavior on the part of women. This sparked his frequent snarls against "pornography" in literature, and in 1930 it led to his opposition to electing the first women to the National Institute of the American Academy of Arts and Letters. "It is not a question of the ability of these candidates but the probability that their election will lead to others less able and tactful," he wrote in his diary. "It is impossible at present to keep the sex element subordinate the moment a woman comes into a room."[14] Garland's persistent meliorism and his refusal to admit that power may be sought for its own sake led him to see exploitive sexuality as a particular human aberration caused by mysterious, irrational forces that could be conquered only by unceasing and restrictive controls.

Garland rarely attempted to see deeply into his characters, and so he rarely created direct confrontations between his ideas on equality and his fears of sexuality. His ideas on marriage are generally consistent with his ideas on equality. *Rose* is again the major text. After avoiding all the saccharine young men who are in love with her, Rose finally finds a worthy suitor in Warren Mason, a middle-aged Chicago newspaper man. He loves Rose, or at least finds her extremely physically attractive, and admires her talent as a poet. He hesitates to declare himself because he fears marriage will handicap her career and because he is not wealthy enough to be sure he can support her—a sign that he has no faith in at least the economic success of her career. Finally, however, Mason writes Rose a proposal in the form of a tract in which Garland can state his views on marriage:

> I cannot promise to be faithful to you until death, but I shall be faithful so long as I fill the relation of husband to you. . . . I *think* I shall find you all-sufficient, but I do not know. . . .

On the other hand, let me say I exact nothing from you. I do not require you to cook for me, nor keep house for me. You are mistress of yourself; to come and go as you please, without question and without accounting to me. You are at liberty to cease your association with me at any time, and consider yourself perfectly free to leave me whenever any other man comes with power to make you happier than I.

I want you as comrade and lover, not as subject or servant, or unwilling wife. I do not claim any rights over you at all. You can bear me children or not, just as you please. You are a human soul like myself, and I shall expect you to be as free and as sovereign as I, to follow any profession or to do any work which pleases you. . . . (pp. 379-380)

Rose, deeply moved by this "apparently cold and legal," yet actually "manly and passionate" (pp. 381-382) letter, accepts at once, by telegraph.

The proposal is certainly an interesting and creditable one, though neither quite as "cold and legal" nor as "manly and passionate" as Rose, or Garland, thought. This marriage seems to rest on the old economic dependence. Both of the lovers assume that marriage will transfer the responsibility for supporting Rose from her father, where it has rested thus far, to her husband. Mason's role in the marriage is clearly defined. He is responsible for making their living, and to do this he will follow his career as a journalist. Rose's role is open: she *may* do whatever she wants to, but there is nothing she *must* do. In her, Garland has created the truly free individual with no duty except to be herself, neither the traditional "feminine" responsibilities of bearing and raising children nor the "masculine" ones of succeeding in a career in order to support the household. Anything Rose does must be done entirely of her own volition, a prospect that is terrifying and paralyzing as well as liberating. Garland's typical belief in a naive individualism renders him unable to see that he has deprived his character of the usual social pressures available to back up an individual's decision. The marriage proposed is new and improved, but like the new and improved marriages advocated by nineteenth century suffragists, it is traditional in its outline, and leaves unsettled how Rose is to manage a family and a career, both of which Garland seems to assume she will choose.

Another new and improved marriage takes place between a pair of Rose's friends, whose ceremony specifically leaves out the "obey" (p. 255), a useful symbolic gesture but not, unfortunately, legally binding. Nonetheless, Garland's ideas on marriage are liberal and decent, and cognizant of the reality of marriage as a legitimate part of the life of a woman interested in a serious career.

A somewhat more unorthodox and potentially liberating marriage occurs in *A Spoil of Office.* Ida Wilbur is a Grange lecturer in Iowa. Bradley Talcott is a hired hand who is inspired by her to go to school and to make something of himself. He attracts the attention of influential men who launch his political career. He is quickly elected state legislator and then congressman. He also rises from admiring Ida from afar to writing to her and asking to marry her. As they ride back together from a rally, Bradley proclaims, "Henceforward I shall work for these people and all who suffer. My life shall be given to this work." Ida takes his hand and promises, "We'll work *together,* Bradley." After a ten week honeymoon in Washington, Ida leaves Bradley to Congress and goes back to the West. "We mustn't be selfish, dear," Ida tells her husband; "you've got your work to do here, and I've got my work to do there."[15]

Despite the fact that the laws in most states legally limited a wife's freedom to come and go to the wishes of her husband, the pattern of most middle class marriages was actually closer to the freedom Garland advocated. As Garland knew from his life in Boston, when summer came, the families of prosperous businessmen fled the cities for resorts to which the husbands came merely on weekends. Toward the other end of the financial scale, it was not unusual for poor, young congressmen like Bradley to leave their families in the home district and board in Washington, rather than maintaining two residences. Nor was it unusual for the women at home to occupy important independent positions. In an *Arena* article Annie Diggs described one such woman, the wife of Representative Ben Clover, who stayed at home to manage the family farm. "She is much counselled with in the Alliance, and was the first woman ever sent as delegate to the Supreme Council of the National Farmers' Alliance."[16] Like Ida, many nineteenth century feminists left their families for lecture tours and for special campaigns in states where suffrage

laws or amendments were pending.

While Garland, who married at 39, believed marriage was good and fine and strengthened characters who were old enough and strong enough, he believed it could be disastrous for characters who were too young. Bradley and Rose are both threatened by early and unsuitable marriages, and Bradley sees his best friend fall by the wayside as a result of marriage. The disaster of early marriage is the subject of the short story, "A Stopover at Tyre." Albert, a poor young farm boy, is working his way through college as a book agent. Maud, a delicate girl, has had to drop out of school to help her mother, who runs a boarding house where Albert comes to stay. The two fall in love, and when it is time for Albert to leave, he lacks that remorselessness that would enable him to desert the girl. He realizes he will have to quit school to help Maud and her mother. His decency is his ruin. As his friend remarks, "That ends him. . . . A man can't marry a family like that at his age, and pull out of it."[17] Presumably, the Single Tax is the solution. When the general economic system is reformed, the problems of individuals will be solved. In the meantime, Maud is not to blame for ruining Albert's life, although it is clear that, quite unknowingly and most innocently, that is what she has done. Maud's failure seems inherent in her situation in life and in her sex, while his failure will grow out of his marriage.

In the play *Under the Wheel* Garland shows marriage as economic failure for the woman. Alice Edwards, a music student, promises to marry the importunate journalist Walter Reeves, but will not set a date until she has the chance to master her art and "show people that I can earn my own living."[18] However, Alice is the daughter of a working man who decides to leave Boston for "free land" in South Dakota. Alice goes along with her family instead of marrying Walter or trying to support herself in Boston. For a while Alice's meager salary as a school teacher keeps the family farming enterprise solvent, but then a hailstorm flattens the crop that was their last hope, and Mr. Edwards has a stroke.

At this moment Walter shows up, eager to marry Alice and take the whole family back to Boston. Unlike Albert, he can afford to "marry a family," because his career is secure.

Alice accepts him, but she also accepts her defeat. When he burbles about protecting her, rescuing her from the press of the world, she replies, "I am out of the press, *but not by my own merit.* . . . The world's injustice remains, my failure remains."[19] Alice and her father are reconciled to accepting Walter's help only by his infectious belief that they have fought and fallen in a cause that will eventually bring justice and liberty. The play ends, however, with the emphasis on their failure. Edwards discovers that his stroke has left him paralyzed, and Alice, too, has been crippled in her attempt to enter marriage as an independent equal. Garland is unflinching in his portrayal of this failure, avoiding platitudes about sweet dependency or woman's place.

Garland was specific in his ideas of what constituted a true "marriage." Validation came from within the partners themselves, and not from the ceremonies and legalisms of society. The final scene of *The Mocassin Ranch* is an example of Garland's belief both in the internal validity of marriage and the partners' need to have their relationship acknowledged in the eyes of society. The runaway lovers are "married," despite the fact that the woman is legally the wife of another man, by pledging to be true and responsible in front of a third person who, by being a normal decent human being, acquires the power to speak for so much of society as need be respected. In the original edition, *Rose* ended when the lovers pledged themselves to each other and to the responsibilities and sacrifices that marriage entailed. Because this ending left some readers confused, Garland added a final scene in which the two enter Mason's apartment as husband and wife. Garland was not changing his ideas on marriage, but making them clearer to his audience. Like Rose and Mason and his other fictional couples, Garland and his wife were married in a civil ceremony. This partly reflected Garland's agnosticism, but it was also evidence of the distinction he made between the trivial external sanctification of marriage and the real need for the partners to commit themselves and to see that commitment ratified by a representative of society.

Since Garland believed that the real marriage was a private contract that existed outside of or in spite of convention and legality, he believed that the dissolution of marriage was equally private, an individual decision. The right thing to do with a bad marriage, Garland believed, was simply to leave it. Given his

ideas about the sexual nature of women and men, it was for him a foregone conclusion that the offending party would be the man, and that it was the woman's duty, as an individual and as a moral arbiter, to leave an unsatisfactory marriage. However, he saw the formal, legal process of divorce as an evil, calling forth the "divorce colonies" of the Dakotas. As he described them in "A Fair Exile," these were invitations to evil, agglomerations of weak women sending out sexual signals and inflaming lust in rapacious men.[20] Although he paid lip service to the importance of laws and customs that granted custody of minor children to fathers rather than to mothers, he still believed that the honorable solution for a strong individual was to take the children and leave, and to let divorce worry about itself. In both "A Branch Road" and "The Owner of the Mill Farm," Garland advocates that a farm wife should leave or expel her husband, and seems to see personal weakness as the only obstacle to such a course. Garland was optimistic, and probably naive, in his assumption that because the "real," the praiseworthy, element of marriage was personal commitment, personal action was enough to cancel a bad marriage. Philosophically, Garland often seems more of a Romantic than a Realist, with his blithe disregard for social pressures. His emphasis on individualism, his belief that individuals could by their own actions break out of societal bonds, led to an accompanying emphasis in his fiction.

Society impinged on the individual most insistently in the realm of economics. Defining marriage as a partnership that can be dissolved rather than as a legally immutable state of being requires economic independence for women, something that concerned Garland in theory, but which he did not always work out satisfactorily in his stories. The bulk of his important fiction deals with farm folk, where the economic unit is the family, and both wife and husband trudge through their chores, always dependent upon each other and the crops and the livestock. Men, however, controlled the sales of the cash crops and hence the purse strings were in the hands of the husbands, with wives having to beg cash to buy necessities. Garland was sensitive enough to the problem to protect his own wife—"Her signature shall be as good as mine at the bank,"[21] he assured his future father-in-law—but whoever took money out of the bank, it was Garland himself who put it in.

As Garland often noted in his nonfiction, it was economic weaknesses that kept women in bad marriages, but this is not reflected in his fiction. Of Garland's heroines, only Alice Edwards is deeply concerned with economic independence, and she fails. Ida Wilbur's economic standing is apparently not important enough to Garland for him to make it clear. Even though the pay was low and married women were barred, teaching, the most common profession for young women of British stock, did provide a woman with an independence she would not know if she became a farm wife. "I was a fool for ever marrying," the young wife in "Up the Coolly" tells her city brother-in-law. "I made a decent living teaching, I was free to come and go, my money was my own. Now I'm tied right down to a churn or a dish-pan, I never have a cent of my own."[22]   Garland has little to say about other economic fields for women. Garland glossed over working women even in his city writings. A few clerks are somewhat woebegone background figures. In *A Spoil of Office* there are girls fluttering around the lecherous legislators of the Iowa State House, trading, or at least jeopardizing, their virtue for a job. Rose's university acquaintance, Mary, is "a typewriter on trial." Her beau tells Rose, "I don't claim any right to say what women shall do or not do, but I imagine they wouldn't go into shops if they were not, in a way, forced into it. . . . A woman should be free and independent, but is she free when pressure forces her into typewriting or working in a sweat-shop?"[23]   Garland does not seem to be making the point that a woman with a university education is qualified to be more than a typist. It is hard to understand what freedom and independence can mean if they do not include the freedom to find a job. Garland, who took pride in being able to go back to "shingling" if his intellectual pursuits failed to support him, was not able to understand that sexual equality meant that for women, too, economic independence was important in itself, regardless of the merits of the occupation.

Part of the problem is with "woman's work." Garland realized that typing or factory work—or traditional housekeeping chores—would be frustrating and unsatisfying for him, and thus for intelligent, ambitious women. Instead of analyzing the nature of work or the nature of the legal and social barriers to

careers for women, he settled for platitudes, except in one short story which proposes an "individualistic" answer to the question of woman's need for economic independence. In "A Good Fellow's Wife," the town banker is about to flee town to escape prosecution for embezzlement, but his wife makes him stay. She opens a notion store to support the family and pay off the debt. Her store succeeds, and she grows both intellectually and emotionally. After awhile, the speculation for which he had embezzled the money pays off, and he is able to retire the debt. The woman, however, does not retire her store. "I like being my own boss," she tells her husband. "I can't go back where I was." Instead, she asks him to become a partner in her store. "I looked up to you too much," she explains. "Let's begin again, as equal partners."[24] This is a skillfully plotted story showing how the wife's economic independence is necessary for a healthy marriage, but the point is blunted at the end, when the economic factor is submerged in what Garland considered a larger emotional factor.

Garland presented few professional women, and their careers are largely symbolic. Rose's career ambitions are hazy. She considers being an astronomer because she likes looking at the stars, but seems to wind up a "poet" because that job does not have any prerequisites. We do not know what she reads or what she writes, and we never hear her talk shop, unlike Garland's male characters who talk incessantly of their writing, their political strategies, and the other matters of their various trades. Rose meets a woman who is a "famous" lawyer, but we know nothing more of her career than the tag. Rose's doctor friend, Isabel, is the most clearly developed professional woman, but we see her only in her social role. Garland tells us she was the leader of the three young women who integrated her medical school, but once she is within, we get no glimpse of her studies. As far as his writing goes, Garland's interest in economic independence and fulfilling careers for women was more theoretical then practical, while in his own marriage, his ready assumption of economic responsibility helped defuse his wife's need for a career. After their marriage, Garland writes, his wife Zulime Taft left her career as a painter, over her husband's protests, to become a full-time wife and mother. Like Rose, she had lost all external pressure to be anything else, because her husband fully expected to support her.

Like his theories on woman's economic position, Garland's theories on women in politics are more complex than he realized because he did not recognize the social and historical background of the conditions he observed. The woman suffrage movement of the 1880s and 1890s was split, and was strangely convoluted by long disappointment. After the Civil War, the suffragists found to their anger and dismay that many men who had supported woman suffrage out of principle were willing to abandon it in order not to jeopardize the passage of black manhood suffrage. Some feminists, mostly easterners, broke with the Republicans, who had reneged on their promises to the women, and turned their energies to fighting for suffrage and woman's rights alone, not tied to any party or program. Other leaders, mostly westerners, stayed within the Republican party and worked for the whole gamut of Republican reforms. The two groups never disagreed upon their ends, however, and were reunited in one organization in 1890. The question remained for individuals, whether to work in sex integrated groups or alone, and whether to press for all reforms or to press for suffrage first.

Garland was involved in a vehement discussion of this question at and after the Single Tax Convention of 1890. Garland's special concern at the meeting seems to have been for the representation of women. "This conference thus far has just one weak point, it has not women enough in it," he told the group, to applause. "I want to stand, in a way, for the women in our movement."[25] Later in the conference, a male delegate from New York proposed that a national committee should look into the possibility of forming a "ladies single tax union," like the Women's Christian Temperance Union. After some discussion, Garland replied at length:

> I want to state right here that a necessity for this thing exists, for this reason, that the women of the United States have not come into the single tax league. They cannot play billiards or smoke. . . . You can theorize on this matter all you please, but the women won't come in as long as you conduct matters on the present plan. These women, in order to do special work which they are fitted to do, must have organization. Let this conference encourage the women to do this. You say they can go on and do it now. That is very well, but we have so long excluded women and so long said, "You shall not participate in these things," that they

need special encouragement.[26]

Garland was making two separate arguments. On one hand, he held that women were too pure and delicate for the rough and tumble of male defined political life; they could not play billiards and smoke, or travel to the dark meeting houses where the Single Taxers met. On the other hand, he pointed out, more usefully, that since women had habitually been barred from politics, they needed an explicit invitation to enter.

The matter of a separate woman's single tax league attracted a good deal of comment from women in the "Letters" columns of the *Standard,* and the variety of opinion Garland's suggestions evoked shows how little he was in tune with the women in the movement for whom he presumed to speak. Some women applauded the suggestion of a separate organization wholeheartedly, saying that it would give them a chance to study in private, to discuss aspects of the movement of particular interest to women, and to use their natural gifts, such as intuition, to the fullest, without having to suffer the grossness of the men. Others felt that existing conditions made a separate organization desirable. "In our disjointed present," wrote Frances Milne, "we cannot attempt too strictly to conform to codes of procedure which make no allowance for today's disabilities."[27] Other women were less enthusiastic. "I detest 'negro pews'," wrote Frances Russell. While she did not oppose the plan, she thought it unnecessary.[28] Sarah Mifflin Gay violently opposed the idea. Like Mrs. Russell, she pointed out that women did smoke and play billiards and that Single Tax men probably did not play billiards during meetings:

> If the women of the United States choose to form themselves into a ladies national single tax league, nobody can say them nay, but the late national conference could not suggest it without intimating that the room of some of its members would be better than their company and without reflecting upon the choice of delegates by certain clubs.

Any special moves to congratulate or encourage women as women, rather than as comrades in a cause, Miss Gay saw as an insult.[29] Elizabeth Meriwether wrote in to admonish the *Standard* for what she saw as its usual insensitivity to woman's rights.

"Are men utterly unable to see subjection when only women are the sufferers?" she asked.[30]

In the midst of all this controversy, Garland answered. His apology for the smoking and billiards remark shows to what extent his self-proclaimed championship of women resulted from his identifying his goals with his belief in woman's purity:

> Possibly my hatred of smoke and drink led me to be too emphatic, but I hope the single tax men of this country will understand me when I say that not only does smoking and the attendant atmosphere keep away the women from your league meetings, but many men to whom (as to myself) tobacco is an active poison.[31]

Garland believed that encouragement and special invitation to various groups was not patronizing, and he pointed to an actor's single tax league as analogous to a woman's organization. Actors could discuss applications of the doctrine specially pertinent to them, and women could do the same. The analogy is attractive and, as pointed out in some of the women's letters, acceptable to many women. However, it founders on the difficulty that being a woman is not a profession.

Garland was undoubtedly completely sincere in advocating a separate organization for women as a way of strengthening their participation in the movement. He emphasized that in his travels as a Single Tax speaker, he had visited many clubs, and that, with few exceptions, women were badly under-represented, at least in part because of the smoke-filled rooms and the seedy condition of the meeting halls. He cared less about the means of attracting women to the cause than about the necessity of their being attracted. In part, he believed that the movement needed the talents of the women. "Some of the finest minds in the single tax movement, as I know from personal experience and personal acquaintance, are women," he told the conference. In addition, there was the "special work," which women "are fitted to do."[32] Garland clearly did not see that the interdependence of men and women advocated by Miss Gay was part of the total interdependence of all humankind, because he envisioned an interdependence not of individuals but of two separate male and female geniuses. His insistence in seeing men and women as different and separate tended to blind him to the

actual presence of women who had somehow survived the smoking and billiards. It is difficult to tell what proportion of delegates to the convention was women, as many were listed only by initials and surname, but slightly under five per cent seems a reasonable estimate, based on my count of the delegates who were identifiable by sex. Garland does not seem to have realized that the proposal to separate rendered their position somewhat anomalous. Agnes Martin, the most enthusiastic of the women who wrote in to praise a separate organization, certainly seems to have believed that women would not go to and would not be wanted at the regular—the men's—meetings.[33] Frances Russell feared and deprecated that possibility. "I wish to go to the regular single tax league, where the best of men and women consult together concerning the best of measures," she wrote.[34] Garland did not consider the question, because he did not believe women liked rough things.

In his fiction, Garland created no women with the political savvy of Miss Gay nor the steadfastness of the earlier suffragists. He was a moderate; he took the same line as the Alliance writer Annie Diggs and the women who wrote to the *Standard* favoring a separate organization, but by portraying them as the only brand of feminists, the most radical available, and ignoring the women who feared "negro pews," Garland considerably blunted his picture of political feminism. Ida Wilbur is the only one of his characters who is a suffragist. Rose, Isabel, the various teachers and farm wives, all seem to lack a political dimension. When the men gather to talk politics, the women are never shown as resenting their exclusion.

Ida's political speeches are of the rather vague moral uplift sort. She talks of equal rights, but not of specific campaigns to extend suffrage, rights of married women, education, equal employment opportunity, or the other campaigns that occupied suffragists. Ida accepts, moreover, the idea that there is a "woman's sphere" and that women will naturally fill it if left alone. The political implications of this sphere are stated most clearly by Annie Diggs, a woman who very likely did not smoke and certainly did not play billiards:

> . . .women should watch and work in all things which shape and mould the home, whether "money," "land" or "transportation."

So now Alliance women look at politics and trace the swift relation to the home—their special sphere. They say, "Our homes are
threatened by the dirty pool. The pool must go."

Before this question of the salvation of the imperilled homes
of the nation, all other questions, whether of "prohibition" or
"suffrage" pale into relative inconsequence.[35]

A comment on Ida that Garland made many years later in
his autobiography shows how little he understood her in relationship to the suffrage movement.

Ida Wilbur was in advance of her time. As I look back on her, I
see that she was a lovely forerunner of the well-dressed and wholly
competent leaders who followed Susan Anthony's austere generation. I find her not altogether despicable. I knew her type as well
as I did that of Bradley Talcott, but I failed to make her lovable.[36]

Susan B. Anthony, who was "austere" because she was from a
Quaker background, not because she was a feminist, would have
been nearly seventy when Ida's career began, so Ida can hardly
have been a forerunner of the next generation. Ida was plea-
santly liberal, but by no means "in advance of her time," and
would have been completely at home with the WCTU or most
woman's clubs. "Despicable" is an odd word to choose, even
to negate, and seems to show that Garland was himself somewhat
uneasy about woman suffrage.

Throughout *A Spoil of Office*, Garland implicitly negates
the strength and the determination of the suffrage movement
and also inaccurately locates sources of resistance to it. Bradley
speaks sincerely for woman suffrage in the Iowa legislature, but
it is a somewhat *pro forma* exercise. "Defeat came as usual. . . .
They all cheered the speech, but a majority tabled the matter
as usual."[37] Garland was unfair to the highly efficient suffragist
lobbyists in Iowa. Several legislatures, starting in 1870, had
passed woman suffrage amendments to the state constitution,
but amendments needed passage by two successive legislatures,
and it was at this that the suffragists failed.[38] Garland makes
Bradley seem far more daring than he would have been in the
actual situation. Both Bradley and Garland harbor some doubts
about the need or efficacy of woman suffrage, for the same sort

of reasons that Garland found divorce unnecessary. A cynical fellow reformer tells Bradley, "What the women want is not votes; it's brains, and less morbid emotions." Bradley replies,

"I don't know about that, conditions might still—"

"They'd make their own conditions."

"That's true. It all comes back to a question of human thinking, doesn't it?"[39]

Nor was the Alliance and its successor, the Populist party, always the consistent champion of women against the lecherous back room pols of the old parties, as Garland portrayed it in his fiction. Although some state Populist organizations included a woman suffrage plank in the 1892 platforms, the national organization did not. Garland attended their convention in Omaha, but did not seem to notice the lack not only of a suffrage plank but even of the usual courtesy appearance of feminists before the Committee on Resolutions, which had become routine for the major parties.[40] Progressivism and conservatism intermingled in strange ways within both the populist and the suffrage movements. Garland's delineation of political blacks and whites showed a misunderstanding of the reform politics of his day that was as severe as his lack of appreciation for the radicals within the woman suffrage movement.

Garland's feminism has two strains. One is based upon his emotional identification with the farm women of the middle border. He passionately admired art and culture, but he grew up in a society in which these tastes were the province of women, to be mocked in a man. After he had escaped from the farm to the city, he knew he had been right and felt that to be deprived of contacts with other artists, writers, actors, painters, sculptors, would have been unbearable exile. He knew that the women who had shared and encouraged his tastes, and others like them, were pining away in that terrible exile in board shacks on the plain. His intense and troubled empathy led him to identify with the cause of women. Without the empathy, the identification vanished, as in his stories and articles about Indians, which, though sensitive and well-observed, have very little to say about Indian women. Garland's other feminist strain con-

sisted of the rather pious moral equality preached by the conservative wing of the feminist movement and the reformers he met through the *Arena,* the Alliance, and the Populists. Garland was not at all clear about what constituted this "equality," and he does not seem to have believed that women, even extraordinary women, wanted, understood, or were asking for complete political and economic equality.

The psychological rewards of his feminism, including its contradictions, seem to have been immense for Garland. He believed he was helping women into a world far greater than they could imagine, in which they could blossom, but still be less than he was. At the same time, Garland was proving his moral superiority to the men, like his father, who imprisoned the women, like his mother, away from their cultural treasures. Garland's guilt at having left the women on the farm comes through clearly in his autobiographical writings and in the short stories "A Branch Road" and "Up the Coolly." The guilt could be gloriously expunged by coming home relatively rich and famous, distinctly handsome and well-dressed, and displacing the father figure in the eyes of the mother. The Thanksgiving Day dinner in *A Son of the Middle Border* is the culmination of that triumph. Having purchased for his mother the house in Wisconsin he called "The Homestead," and having claimed her from his father in Dakota, he placed her at the foot of the family table and himself at the head. This marvelously Oedipal scene represents the triumph of the man of culture, the woman's man, over the farmer, the man's man, but it reduces the woman to a mere object of desire, not an actor in her own right. The need for this particular triumph helps explain Garland's failure to convince us that Rose is a poet or Ida a suffragist. He can empathize with the struggling woman, but the finally triumphant figure must be a man, himself, superior to men and women alike.

Garland's fear of sexuality and his general prudery also helped blunt his feminism. It was necessary for women to be other, to guard the founts of purity which, if sullied, would, Garland believed, rise up to pollute the earth. Since he believed men were untrustworthy, he had to be sure women were at the ready. Although he stood foursquare for motherhood and saw it as the highest calling of all true women, this was less deleterious than it might seem to his notions of equality for women. He

was equally foursquare for fatherhood and took an equal part in the raising of his daughters, whom he encouraged in careers.

Garland's own psychological needs probably made inevitable the contradiction in his beliefs about woman's role and woman's nature. However, the dichotomy at the heart of the late nineteenth century woman's movement allowed his pronouncements to slip virtually unchallenged into what he saw as the vanguard of the social reform movements. Unfortunately, he never felt himself pressed, either by his own disquiet or by the intellectual milieu within which he worked, to follow up the frightening ramifications of sexuality and power he sometimes glimpsed, or to question their effect upon his simple ideas of equality. There is a certain smugness in Garland's outlook, in his presuming to speak for women, despite his honesty and the essentially honorable beliefs he held. That many women held to the same smug beliefs only illustrates the difficulties of serving as spokesman for a group of which one is not a part. The women at least spoke for themselves. It is difficult to see for whom Garland spoke. Garland was a sincere feminist. His shortcomings illustrate the fallibilities of a meliorist system that ignores the ways in which humans struggle for power over other human beings, men over women and women over men.

NOTES

[1]Most general critics of Garland have to some extent discussed his attitudes toward feminism and woman's equality, particularly in terms of his novel *Rose of Dutcher's Coolly,* which is treated in most detail by Donald Pizer in his introduction to the Bison edition of the novel (Lincoln: University of Nebraska Press, 1969, pp. vii-xxiv). In addition, the 1977 Western Literature Association conference produced four papers dealing entirely with Garland and women. George Day's "Can Rose Dutcher Find Happiness in Liberation" expands on Pizer's analysis, but does not substantially differ with it. Roger E. Carp's "Hamlin Garland and the Cult of True Womanhood," recently republished in L. L. Lee and Merrill Lewis, eds., *Women, Women Writers, and the West* (Troy, New York: Whitston Publishing Company, 1979), is the most ambitious of these in trying to put Garland in context, but Carp's emphasis on the "Cult of True Womanhood" leads him to overlook complexity in both the feminist movement and in Garland's responses. Gary Culbert's "Hamlin Garland and the Twentieth Century Woman" is an excellent account of Garland's betrayals of the later feminist movement, but avoids many of the personal complexities involved in Garland's stand. Robert Gish's "Desertion and Rescue on the Dakota Plains: Hamlin Garland in the Land of the Straddle-Bug" is a Freudian discussion of Garland's "family romance," which finally disappoints because of Gish's attempt to judge Garland's feminism by "today's" standards.

[2]Background information on the nineteenth century feminist movement comes from Elizabeth Cady Stanton, Susan B. Anthony, and Matilda Joslyn Gage, eds., *The History of Woman Suffrage* (1882; rpt. New York: New York Times/Arno Press, 1969) I-III, and ed. Susan B. Anthony and Ida Husted Harper, *The History of Woman Suffrage* (1902; rpt. New York: New York Times/Arno Press, 1969), IV.

[3]*Arena,* 3 (1891), xxi.

[4]Herbert Spencer, *Social Statics* (1850; rpt. New York: R. Schalkenbach Foundation, 1954), pp. 152-153.

[5]"A New Declaration of Rights," *Arena* 3 (1891), 182-183.

[6]"Women and Their Organization," *Standard*, 8 October, 1890.

[7]*Rose of Dutcher's Coolly* (1895; rpt. Lincoln: University of Nebraska Press, 1969), p. 90. Hereafter cited within parentheses in the text.

[8]In the second edition of the novel, Garland toned down some of these references. The unpleasant brakeman no longer "eyed her with the glare of a sex maniac" (p. 90), but was merely "insolent" (New York: Harper, 1899, p. 77). The fence drawings of the other children are no longer "hideous signs" (p. 23), but mere "signs" (p. 19).

[9]"Upon Impulse," *Wayside Courtships* (New York: Appleton, 1897), p. 270.

[10]"Mr. and Mrs. James A. Herne," *Arena* 4 (1891), 557, 559.

[11]*A Son of the Middle Border* (New York: Macmillan, 1917), p. 175.

[12]See Gish, "Desertion and Rescue on the Dakota Plains," for a slightly different and more Freudian view of "Ol' Pap's Flaxen."

[13]"The Stranger Woman," document 184, and "And a Brave Lady Beside," document 69, Hamlin Garland papers, Doheny Library, University of Southern California.

[14]*Hamlin Garland's Diaries*, ed. Donald Pizer (San Marino, California: Huntington Library, 1968), p. 232.

[15]*A Spoil of Office* (Boston: Arena Press, 1892), pp. 377, 385.

[16]"The Women in the Alliance Movement," *Arena* 6 (1892), 177.

[17]"A Stop-over at Tyre," *Wayside Courtships* (New York: Appleton, 1897), p. 169.

[18]"Under the Wheel," *Arena* 2 (1890), 185.

[19]"Under the Wheel," pp. 223-224.

[20]"A Fair Exile," *Wayside Courtships*, pp. 241, 244-246.

[21]*A Daughter of the Middle Border* (New York: Macmillan, 1921), p. 137.

[22]"Up the Coolly," *Main-Traveled Roads,* p. 119.

[23]*Rose,* pp. 194, 217.

[24]"A Good Fellow's Wife," *Main-Traveled Roads,* p. 376.

[25]*Standard,* 10 September 1890, p. 13.

[26]*Standard,* p. 25.

[27]"Women and the Single Tax," *Standard,* 15 October 1890, p. 3.

[28]"No Separate Women's Organization," *Standard,* 24 September 1890, p. 4.

[29]"Why Not Thank the Men?" *Standard,* 24 September 1890, pp. 4-5.

[30]"To Enlist the Women," *Standard,* 15 October 1890, p. 17.

[31]"Women and Their Organization," *Standard,* 8 October 1890, p. 5.

[32]*Standard,* 10 September 1890, pp. 13, 25.

[33]"Favors Separate Clubs," *Standard,* 15 October 1890, p. 17.

[34]"No Separate Women's Organization," p. 4.

[35]"The Women in the Alliance Movement," *Arena* 6 (1892), 165.

[36]Hamlin Garland, *Roadside Meetings* (New York: Macmillan, 1930), p. 186.

[37]*A Spoil of Office,* p. 260.

[38]*History of Woman Suffrage,* III, 626.

[39]*A Spoil of Office,* p. 251.

[40]*History of Woman Suffrage,* IV, 437.

The author would like to thank the Research Council of the University of Nebraska-Lincoln for a Maude Hammond Fling Junior Fellowship during the summer of 1979, which made possible the research for this paper.

The Virginian and Ántonia Shimerda: Different Sides of the Western Coin

John J. Murphy

Owen Wister in *The Virginian* and Willa Cather in *My Ántonia* portray contrasting versions of the American West through characters of epic, almost archetypal, dimensions. The representative purposes of both novelists are inherent in their adoption of the first-person point of view, enabling their heroes to be evaluated and associated with certain ideals and meanings by other participants in the action. Elizabeth Sergeant explains that when *My Ántonia* was being planned, Cather compared her new heroine to an apothecary jar filled with orange-brown flowers in the middle of a table. She was to be a rare object examined from all sides and to stand out "because she *is* the story."[1] The male narrator functioning as examiner involves a difficulty, however; he is placed in the awkward position of being able to appreciate Ántonia from a man's perspective without being romantically involved with her, thus eliminating romantic love from the core of the novel. In presenting his Western hero, Wister avoids this limitation at the expense of violating technique, by having a male narrator focus on certain qualities in the development of the hero and then switching to an omniscient authority to highlight others. In both novels, these technical peculiarities merely reflect similar efforts to embody Western experiences and attitudes in heroic lives. That one hero is of the cattle frontier and the other of the agricultural frontier is an occasional distinction; more importantly, one is a man and one a woman, and the situations and heroic qualities of each underscore distinct concepts of Western potentials, of what constitutes success in individual lives and in the history of the country. After summarizing the development of Wister's hero, I will suggest Cather's conscious dismissal of this type in order to develop her own, summarize that development, and then indicate the clearly divergent views of the West implied in the characterizations.

I

The Virginian[2] begins as a first person narrative distinguishing the hero among the thousand young drifters who comprise
the cowboy brotherhood. He is physically outstanding, characterized by tigerlike movements and healthy bloom that is attractive to men and women. His wholesome facade conceals a
gentlemanly reserve and a suspicion of familiarity. Pride is evident in his confrontation with villainous cowboy Trampas, who
is publicly put down in an attempt to make small of him, and
evident in his outsmarting the American drummer whose friendly presumptions are insulting. Trampas and this drummer are
foils to the hero; the former is his evil counterpart among the
cowboys, and the latter merely an inferior specimen who is rude
to women when the Virginian is polite and who is physically
untidy, not hesitating to use a dirty towel when the Virginian
requests a fresh one. Quick wit and an inventive sense of humor
are among the qualities that make the hero popular among the
young cowboys. Other qualities include kindness to animals and
response to Nature, the "quiet, open, splendid wilderness," and
meticulous responsibility in carrying out Judge Henry's orders
to escort the Eastern narrator, initially a nuisance. His world is
definitely a young man's world, adolescent in its gaiety and care-
free spirit. He is typical in his defense of this world, feels he
"ain't near reached the marriageable age" and that he best
move on "if this hyeh territory is goin' to get full o' fam'ly men
and empty o' game" (p. 42).

Wister switches to the omniscient point of view in the
eighth and following four chapters. These develop the Virginian
as a romantic lover, the very aspect Cather avoids by maintaining
a consistent point of view in her novel. The hero matures, begins
to withdraw from the boys, and becomes Molly Wood's suitor.
Significantly, Steve, who was his companion in the boyish pranks
in the first section, lapses from respectability. When his adolescent world is threatened by the coming of the schoolhouse, the
Virginian must adapt: "with women and children and wire
fences, this country would not long be a country for men" (p.
69). The change begins after he rescues Molly at the river. He
cherishes the handkerchief the frightened girl loses in the scuffle
and no longer sings the bawdy eightieth stanza of his trail song.
He reveals later in the letter to Molly's mother that he stopped

seeing other girls when he met Molly. Also, he becomes clothes-conscious, buys new trousers and an "unnecessarily excellent" scarf. He defends Molly and betrays his feelings for her when he forces Trampas to retract insinuations he has made about her and Lin McLean. A typical courting game develops, Molly coyly insisting that she has not been formally introduced and the Virginian switching babies in retaliation for her slight. Significant changes in the hero include his determination to study. Admitting that he had "hated books and truck when [he] was a kid" (p. 102), he asks Molly to begin the process of preparing him for a place in the Wyoming she is helping to civilize. His confidence in being equal to this world and to Molly, his insistence that he is the kind that moves up, leads him to express his intentions toward her and his intention to be her best scholar.

The second first person narrative section (chapters 13 through 21) develops the natural leadership abilities the Virginian needs to command authority in a civilized Wyoming. He has been appointed Judge Henry's acting foreman and realizes that his boyhood is over. Trampas is again the challenger, encouraging the Judge's cowboys to abandon the acting foreman at Rawhide rather than return to the ranch. Leadership ability is equated here with skill at cards, the ability to outmaneuver opposition demonstrated by England's Queen Elizabeth when her position was challenged. Western democracy, according to Wister, offers opportunities for the exercise and recognition of natural leadership ability, now evident in tall-tale-telling rather than cards, with successful moves by Trampas and the Virginian. The latter conveniently wins the game with his tale of the frogs of Tulare and proves that he "could have played poker with Queen Elizabeth" (p. 145). By this time he has arranged for the feeding of the hungry crowds at Rawhide and passes among them as a natural aristocrat: "Even the Indian chiefs. . .magnetically knew that the Virginian was the great man" (p. 141). Before the end of this section the obvious Christ parallels include the Virginian's preaching his own gospel of "the sunset and the mountains" (p. 157), his rejection of the dark prohibitive religion of Dr. MacBride, and his defeat of Trampas through the fair play gesture of allowing him to keep his job and refusing to use his position against him. Symbolically and literally he kills the serpent, shooting the head off a rattlesnake threatening the narrator. In the end he is made permanent foreman by Judge Henry, after

melting the hearts of the narrator and Molly, and emerges a true aristocrat: "his frame and his features showed out of the mass . . ." (p. 171).

In the fourth section (chapters 22 through 29) Wister returns to the omniscient point of view and combines the hero's leadership role with that of the romantic suitor. The Virginian tells Molly that he left Virginia to get away from "the same old things. . . . [T]his whole world was hawgs and turkeys. . .with a little gunnin' afteh small game throwed in. . ." (p. 188). The opportunities he wants, which his Virginia brothers seemed unaware of, include fulfilling his potential as a leader of men and suitor of a cultivated girl like Molly. He asks Mrs. Henry's help in basic schoolroom skills which will serve him as foreman and enable him to write his first letter to Molly, to warn her that he is coming to ask for her hand. His studies also provide him with self-reliance in evaluating the failures of Shorty, a good-natured weakling fallen under Trampas' influence. He offers Shorty a job, a chance to save himself, and advises him to invest his earnings (the Virginian himself had invested in land that is proving valuable), but Shorty is poisoned by discontent.

Wister now inserts the Balaam and Pedro story, which brings about the wounding of the hero and Molly's acceptance of his offer; more importantly, it establishes his dimension as a champion of justice and provides an opportunity for depth of character. When he thrashes Balaam for gouging the pony's eyes, the "sledge hammer blows of justice" (p. 221) clarify Wister's perspective on the subsequent lynching of Steve and final shootout with Trampas. Not only does the hero's languishing near death from Indian wounds soften Molly's resistance, but the physical suffering and soul-searching involved prepare him for the disturbing experiences of the Steve and Trampas affairs. At one point he feels incapable of achieving Molly's level of civilization: "I ought to have seen from the start I was not the sort to keep you happy" (p. 255). Of course he *is* the sort and proceeds to write a very revealing self-explanation which Mrs. Wood fails to acknowledge and which contains, I think, the key to his heroic qualifications: "I am of old stock in Virginia English and one Scotch Irish grandmother my father's father brought from Kentucky. . . . We have fought when we got the chance, under Old Hickory and in Mexico and my father and two brothers were

killed in the Valley sixty-four" (p. 268).

The last first person narrative section (chapters 30 through 32) contains the final test of the Virginian's leadership ability, in which he is forced to administer justice in spite of corrupt Wyoming law and his affection for cowboy friend Steve. Steve's shunning of him before the hanging causes the hero to experience guilt without being guilty, to be haunted by the dead man's face and the cluster of cottonwoods where the hanging took place. He feels he must justify his actions to the narrator by contrasting Steve's life with his own and explaining how Steve made the choice to join Trampas and the other rustlers for easy money and suffered the consequences of that choice. This is the Virginian's most difficult moment: "he [loses] his bearings in a fog of sentiment" (p. 287). He sobs and is comforted by the narrator but then, because such heroes are "always very shy of demonstration" (p. 287), quickly resumes his manly facade. The seriousness of this period is evident in his complaints of lonesomeness (p. 287), previously the necessary context of his life (p. 54), and in his unusual alienation from Nature. The Tetons become depressing: "I'll be pretty near glad when I get out of these mountains. . . . They're most too big" (p. 296). Underworld experience is suggested in his feeling pursued by the dead, which he characterizes as the little kid in the grown man afraid of the dark, who "keeps a-crying and holding on to me" (p. 301). The message from Steve found on Shorty's body clears up the mystery and provides the assurance of Steve's respect and affection for the Virginian even as the instrument of death.

In the last section (chapters 33 through 36) Wister returns to the omniscient point of view and tests his hero's integrity as a man, a test he must undergo on the eve of his wedding in order to feel worthy of his bride. The difficulty here is that it involves the alienation of the bride, who insists that if he stands up to Trampas's ordering him out of town "there can be no tomorrow for you and me." He responds that he would be "a poor sort of a jay" if he didn't "value [his] nature enough to shield it from. . .slander. . ." (p. 343). Because his trouble with Trampas involves his defense of Molly's good name, this test has significance, and coupled with his shooting a snake after Trampas rides by, becomes the final showdown with evil complicated by conventional female opposition. The hero is equal to the test;

Trampas is killed, and Molly's New England conscience capitulates to love.

The apotheosis of the hero following the shootout occurs within the setting of the honeymoon island in the Bow Leg Mountains. Here the Virginian expresses his desire to mix with Nature, to shed all the responsibility of his hard-earned manhood and "become the ground, become the water, become the trees, mix with the whole thing. Not know myself from it. Never unmix again" (p. 356). Molly regards her man/boy and recognizes the transformation "their hours upon the island had wrought, filling his face with innocence" (p. 357). Of course, Wister refuses to leave his hero in such an otherworldly condition. This is a mere interlude in which Molly can focus on her husband's heroic stature while he relaxes. She had recognized on the eve of their wedding that he was her master, her superior, that the tables had turned; and now, in the mountains, she watches him with "eyes that were fuller of love than of understanding" and realizes that he is unfathomable and that "it was she who renounced, and he who had his way" (pp. 358-359). In the last picture we have of Wister's hero, he is in New England, in a finely cut Scotch homespun suit and straw hat, discussing his investments with Molly's great-aunt. An epilogue passage reveals that he became Judge Henry's partner, a very wealthy and important businessman in the West, and the father of many children.

II

In *My Ántonia,*[3] Cather's Virginian, Jim Burden, expresses an affinity with Nature similar to Wister's. When he sits in his grandmother's sheltered garden, the earth feels warm under him, and as he crumbles it through his fingers, "I was something that lay under the sun and felt it, like the pumpkins, and I did not want to be anything more. . . . [T]hat is happiness; to be dissolved into something complete and great" (p. 18). This Nature philosophy, Virginia origins, and the fact that he moves to the West are about all he shares with Wister's hero. Jim is too passive and too inexperienced for a heroic role, which is not Cather's intention for him. Assuming instead a role similar to that of the tenderfoot narrator, he will focus on a heroic character very

different from Wister's. The circumstances of the opening of *My Ántonia* are curious variations on the opening of *The Virginian*. Each begins on a train, and the narrator first meets at a railway station the special character who will symbolize his West. Cather's intentional altering of typical Western formulae is obvious. Jim is reading a life of Jesse James when informed by the conductor of the Bohemian family in the car ahead but is too shy to visit them and returns to his Wild West biography. At the Black Hawk station he sees Ántonia huddled with her family but is quickly diverted by his grandfather's hired man, Otto Fuchs, a typical citizen of the Wild West, who "might have stepped out of the pages of 'Jesse James.' He wore a sombrero hat, with a wide leather band and a bright buckle, and the ends of his mustache were twisted up stiffly, like little horns. He looked lively and ferocious, I thought, and as if he had a history" (p. 6). It is not Fuchs, however, but the humble immigrant girl who will become the "central figure" that will "mean. . .the country, the conditions" of Jim's Western experience (p. ii).

In the penultimate chapter Jim recalls Ántonia in "a succession of. . .pictures, fixed [in his memory] like the old woodcuts of one's first primer: Ántonia kicking her bare legs against the sides of my pony when he came home. . .with our snake; Ántonia in her black shawl and fur cap, as she stood by her father's grave; Ántonia coming in with her work-team along the evening skyline" (p. 353). To these might be added: Ántonia in the cheerful Harling kitchen; Ántonia in a copied velveteen dress dancing at Firemen's Hall; Ántonia in a man's overcoat, pregnant, driving her steers homeward in the snow; finally, Ántonia, battered and brown, surrounded by the children tumbled from the dark fruit cave into the sunlight. Such pictures trace her development as a symbol of the West. We meet her earlier than we do Wister's hero and take our last look when she is about forty-four.

During her childhood phase Ántonia is distinguished among the Shimerdas as the favorite of her father, who provides the family with aristocratic quality. However, the Shimerdas are generally degraded. Swindled by their countryman Krajiek, who lives off them like a rattlesnake among prairie dogs, they inhabit a cave (Ántonia and her little sister Yulka are forced to sleep in a hole in the earth wall), depend on handouts and even come to expect them. Mrs. Shimerda's crude resentfulness and her son

Ambrosch's sullenness are aggravated by hard times and cold and give the family a poor reputation. Mr. Shimerda remains sadly refined, however, taking whatever solace he can in daughter Ántonia's potential, appealing to Jim to teach her English. Like her father, who tries to explain that they were not beggars in the old country, Ántonia is embarrassed by her mother's alternating moods of scorn and subservience.

During the few months her father survives in Nebraska, she is free to discover with Jim the country she will one day symbolize. They share the golden foliage of autumn and spectacular sunsets, and sled through snow-covered fields. Ántonia makes distinctions between the Old World and America, and provides cultural dimension through European references. This happy sharing of the land by the two children, despite the recurring reminders of Shimerda disasters, contributes the novel's most delightful pages. The highlight of these days is the snake episode, in which Ántonia, the heroic character, instigates the situation, must be rescued by Jim, the narrator, and then through her enthusiasm romanticizes the event. Childhood ends abruptly for Ántonia when her father takes his life. We see her in the icy snow, dressed in handouts and hugging her sister Yulka, while the neighbors nail down the coffin lid.

The second phase of the hero is largely one of brutalization, but it is also the beginning of her involvement with the soil. Her brother Ambrosch, ambitious to improve the farm and make money, replaces her father as the force in her life, and Ántonia soon grows boastful like her mother, refuses Jim's reading lessons, and decides against school: "I ain't got time to learn," she tells Jim. "I can work like mans now. . . . I help make this land one good farm" (p. 123). She also dismisses housekeeping and domestic niceties: "Oh, better I like to work out-of-doors than in a house! . . . I not care that your grandmother say it make me like a man" (p. 138). Shimerda arrogance during this phase leads to a falling out with the Burdens. Previously embarrassed by her mother's crude behavior, Ántonia now follows the old lady's example, taunting "in a spiteful, crowing voice" (p. 131) when she meets Jim and Jake on the road after the horse collar incident. Boastful of her muscles, careless in her habits, sloppy at table, she disgusts Jim because she has become coarsely masculine: "Whenever I saw her come up the furrow, shouting at her

beasts, sunburned, sweaty, her dress open at the neck and her throat and neck dust-plastered, I used to think of the tone in which poor Mr. Shimerda, who could say so little, yet managed to say so much when he exclaimed, 'My Ántonia' " (p. 126).

Much of her bravado and fidelity to Ambrosch amounts to a survival effort, and Jim initially fails to detect the sacrifice involved in her neglect of the finer things she still associates with her father.   At times she reveals a desire for what she gives up: "Sometime you will tell me all those nice things you learn at the school," she asks at one point, "won't you, Jimmy?" (p. 124).   That the girl must be brutalized by the conditions of the country her family has come to for opportunities is, of course, an irony; it becomes poignant as well when, after all her boasting, she reveals to Jim her attraction to the refined life at the Burdens': " 'I like your grandmother, and all things here,' she sighed."   But she immediately defends cooperating with Ambrosch: "If I live here, like you, that is different. Things will be easy for you. But they will be hard for us" (p. 140).

Cather's hero needs rescue, not in a mock adventure from a rattlesnake but from brutalizing labor in the fields. Grandmother Burden and Mrs. Harling convince Ambrosch to allow her to take a job with the Harlings in Black Hawk, and thus begins her domestic refinement.   Although the Black Hawk experience will lead to disgrace, Ántonia can appreciate its benefits in retrospect: "I'd never have known anything about cooking or housekeeping if I hadn't [come to town]. I learned nice ways at the Harlings', and I've been able to bring my children up so much better. . . . If it hadn't been for what Mrs. Harling taught me, I expect I'd have brought them up like wild rabbits" (pp. 343-344). She achieves some self-sufficiency at this point, due to Mrs. Harling's insistence that an allowance be kept from the wages sent home to Ambrosch, and she rewards the efforts made in her behalf, excelling in housekeeping and baking and demonstrating the unusual maternal instincts that will eventually define her mission. She is in every way a perfect partner for Mrs. Harling. Strong, independent, and original, they share fondness for children, animals, and gardening. "They liked to prepare rich, hearty foods and to see people eat it; to make up soft white beds and to see youngsters asleep in them" (p. 180).   In the picture we have of her at this point she is surrounded by children in the Harling

kitchen baking cookies and telling stories.

As a foil to Ántonia and this picture of domestic happiness, Cather introduces Lena Lingard, a hired girl companion who has rejected marriage and motherhood for a career in dressmaking. Lena is disruptively sexual and causes Ántonia to grow dissatisfied with the restrictions of life at the Harlings'. From the start, Lena makes an issue of independence and freedom. When Ántonia hesitates to accept an invitation to her room because, she says, Mrs. Harling "don't like to have me run much," Lena's response shows pluck: "You can do what you please when you go out, can't you?" (pp. 163-164). After Ántonia is "discovered" by the young bloods of Black Hawk and noisy backyard rendezvous ensue, she informs the disapproving Harlings that "A girl like me has got to take her good times when she can. . . . I guess I want to have my fling, like the other girls" (p. 208). She leaves the Harlings to work for the Cutters, who pay more and have no children.

Ántonia now becomes one of several hired girls considered dangerous to the social order maintained by Pennsylvanians, Virginians, and other established settlers. The immigrant girls are ambitious to improve themselves but forced into menial positions because they are too deficient in English to teach school and are presumed inferior: "All foreigners were ignorant people who couldn't speak English," and all hired girls are simply servants whose "beauty shone out too boldly against a conventional background" (pp. 200-201). With Lena's help Ántonia acquires a cheap, stylish wardrobe and becomes the outstanding member of this "free and easy" set, parading in feathered bonnets and high heels before the local high school boys. Jim reflects that these girls "were growing prettier every day, but. . .I used to think with pride that Ántonia, like Snow-White. . .was still 'fairest of them all' " (pp. 214-215). Ántonia is pursued, first by the iceman, the delivery boys and young farmers, then by the sons of established Americans, including Jim, whose efforts are awkward and ridiculous, evoking from her responses which reveal her own conservatism. She is careful to protect him from the hired girls and expects him to do better: "You are going away to school and make something of yourself," she insists. "I'm just awful proud of you. You won't go and get mixed up with the Swedes, will you?" (p. 224).

Ántonia's lifestyle during this phase is no more genuine than the mannish one assumed after her father's death. Her natural innocence and refined femininity become clear when she congratulates Jim on his commencement oration and, at the picnic, when she tells him the circumstances of her parents' marriage. Her friend Anna Hansen suggests the compromise she and many of these girls have made in America: "It must make you very happy, Jim, to have fine thoughts. . .and words to put them in. I always wanted to go to school, you know" (p. 230). Despite her worldly-wise facade, Ántonia is vulnerable to the dangers of Black Hawk. The evil money-lender Wick Cutter tries to rape her, and she is exploited by Larry Donovan, a railroad conductor and notorious womanizer. We see her at this time in her inexpensive velveteen dress copied from Mrs. Gardener's original velvet, dancing and obviously infatuated with Donovan at Firemen's Hall.

Ántonia's darkest period, her most difficult test of character, is subsequent to her abandonment by Donovan. She later reveals to Jim that her tendency to doglike infatuation and her inability to believe harm of anybody she loves contributed to her trouble. Her trusting, open temperament becomes her weakness; as Lena comments during the Donovan affair, "She's so sort of innocent" (p. 268). Jim's and the reader's distance from the events of Ántonia's disgrace enables Cather to transform it into a heroic test. When Jim returns to Nebraska after two years of study at Harvard, he hears the story from Widow Steavens, who got the details from Ántonia herself. Donovan had promised marriage, arranged for Ántonia to come to Denver, got her pregnant, and jilted her. She returned to the farm, worked in the fields as she had after her father's death, and seemed "so crushed and quiet that nobody seemed to want to humble her" (p. 314). She confided her thoughts of death to Mrs. Steavens, and her feeling that she was "not going to live very long. . ." (p. 316).

The climax of this dark period is the birth of the baby one cold night after a day full of chores. The simplicity of the telling is evocative, almost biblical, transforming disgrace into a heroic event: "She got her cattle home, turned them into the corral, and went into the house, into her room behind the kitchen, and shut the door. There, without calling to anybody, without a

groan, she lay down on the bed and bore her child" (p. 316). Ántonia now revealed her independent spirit in her dedication to her baby, and publicized her pride in it by having a crayon enlargement displayed in a gaudy frame at the Black Hawk photographer's. A new sense of purpose replaced her thoughts of death: "[E]verybody's put into this world for something," she later tells Jim, "and I know what I've got to do. I'm going to see that my little girl has a better chance than ever I had. I'm going to take care of that girl, Jim" (pp. 320-321). There is little indication at this time of the magnitude of her maternal destiny. Although Mrs. Steavens recognizes that Ántonia "is a natural-born mother," she laments, " 'I wish she could marry and raise a family, but I don't know as there's much chance now' " (p. 318).

Twenty years later when he visits Ántonia, Jim explains the unique quality of her mission. Although flat-chested and without teeth, she possesses "something which fires the imagination, could still stop one's breath for a moment by a look or gesture that somehow revealed the meaning in common things. She had only to stand in the orchard, to put her hand on a little crab tree and look up at the apples to make you feel the goodness of planting and tending and harvesting at last" (p. 353). Although she resembles the Queen of Italy in her sensitivity toward all of life, her apotheosis does not depend upon accomplishments associated with worldly prestige. References to Tiny Soderball's fortunes and Lena's glamor are foils to scenes of Ántonia on her farm: at the dinner table, with "two long rows of restless heads in the lamplight, and so many eyes fastened excitedly upon her as she sat at the head of the table, filling the plates and starting the dishes on their way" (p. 347); at the fruit cave, when her children "came running up the steps together, big and little, tow heads and gold heads and brown, and flashing little naked legs; a veritable explosion of life out of the dark cave into the sunlight" (pp. 338-339).

Nor does her apotheosis derive from the dominant culture. Her rescue has not been by an established American but by a fellow Bohemian immigrant, Anton Cuzak, a cousin of the Black Hawk saloonkeeper. This "crumpled little man, with. . .one shoulder higher than the other" (p. 356), works the soil beside her as a yoke mate more than romantic partner. Ántonia has

reverted from the Americanization of her Black Hawk years and
has difficulty speaking English because her family speaks Bohemian at home: "The little ones could not speak English at
all—didn't learn it until they went to school" (p. 335). Pictures
of Prague once sent by Jim are the prized decoration in the
parlor. Old World identification and the obvious struggle to provide for so many children ("You wouldn't believe, Jim, what it
takes to feed them all!") become conditions of her enthrone-
ment in the orchard like a maternal goddess, "a rich mine of life,
like the founders of early races" (p. 353).

III

As a consequence of being symbols of the West, the Virginian and Ántonia Shimerda share certain characteristics and experiences. Both are remarkably attractive and naturally distinguished. From the beginning the tenderfoot senses unique
qualities in the Virginian: "in his eyes, in his face, in his step, in
the whole man, there dominated something potent to be felt
. . ." (p. 6). Jim finds Ántonia's presence exciting, singles out
"that something which fires the imagination, could. . .stop one's
breath. . .by a look or gesture that somehow revealed the meaning in common things" (p. 353). Both heroes respond to Nature,
to the landscape, animals, and growing things. Both progress
from adolescence to adulthood, experience periods of trial, and
risk ostracism by lesser men. Both experience reversals of fortune which contribute to their development and independence.
The Virginian must violate the law to follow his conscience, must
respect himself more than the opinions of others. Ántonia returns in shame to her family but is as proud of her baby "as if
she'd had a ring on her finger, and were never ashamed of it" (p.
318). Also, both are pursued by evil: snakelike Trampus threatens the Virginian's leadership opportunities, and snakelike Wick
Cutter preys on Ántonia's sexual and social vulnerability. Finally, the natural distinction of each is confirmed by reference to
European royalty. As a leader the Virginian is comparable to
England's Elizabeth; as a mother Ántonia is as sensitive to life as
the young Queen of Italy.

The Virginian and Ántonia possess unique powers of vision,

although what they envision is complementary rather than similar. Molly compares the "cold lustre" of the Virginian's eyes to "looking. . .down into clear water" (p. 102). Capable of detecting details on the distant range, his eyes suggest far-reaching prospects and leadership ability involving awareness of future conditions and the ability to take advantage of them. With Molly's great-aunt he discusses "Western questions: irrigation, the Indians, the forests. . ., revealing to her his wide observation and his shrewd intelligence" (p. 363). Ántonia's eyes are her memorable feature: "They were big and warm and full of light, like the sun shining on brown pools in the wood" (p. 23). They suggest inward and backward more than outward and forward vision. She merely had to "look up at the apples, to make you feel the goodness of planting and tending and harvesting at last" (p. 353). Much is made of these sympathetic eyes, which Jim recognizes after twenty years as "simply Ántonia's eyes. I had seen no others like them since I looked into them last, though I had looked at so many thousands of human faces" (p. 331). Taken together these visions fuse the future enterprises and cultural pasts, and the physical and metaphysical dimensions of the West. Taken separately they make the West of Willa Cather distinct from Owen Wister's.

Social distinctions between the Virginian and Ántonia Shimerda are important for what they reveal about opportunities of life in the West. Although in a moment of self-pity the Virginian laments being a giant in a narrow gauge world, he does move up socially. He sets his sights on Molly, the only high-class young woman around, and much of his story involves his acquiring enough finish to enhance his natural intelligence and quality, feel comfortable in her world, and demolish her resistance to him as a specimen of the Wild West. He gets his refined woman and a responsible job and becomes an influential leader in the West. His task is easy; he is of established American stock, like all the Westerners who count in Wister's novel: Judge and Mrs. Henry, Mr. and Mrs. Taylor, the Westfalls, the Thomases, etc. Being a good man and a responsible worker, he needs only school skills and new clothes to overcome superficial barriers and pass for a New Englander—and a distinguished one to boot.

Wister's West is a place where natural superiority will be recognized and rewarded, but Cather's West is not the same kind of

opportunity land—at least not for many of the non-English speaking Westerners she celebrated. The late Ellen Moers noted that while Cather herself "came from 'old' people, that is, good, solid, Eastern-seaboard Virginian stock," she dealt as much with "the 'new' people she encountered [who] were crude, poor, not well spoken, servant people who had illegitimate children, and were dirty people. . . . She was doing something very bold in using immigrants, using what today we call ethnic people to stand for old and deep and superior kinds of civilization."[4]   A shiftless Yankee or barely literate Virginian will have it easier than an enterprising or cultivated Norwegian or Czech immigrant in Cather's West. The immigrants are forced to compromise themselves, have difficulty taking advantage of public education, and are relegated to menial positions. Ántonia, like Anna Hansen, preferred school but decided that such opportunities were beyond reach and went to work in the fields. Lena Lingard decided against marriage simply because the well-fixed, traditional American men who could improve her lot married their own kind. Ántonia is so conditioned by her limited options that she accepts the social inferiority of girls like herself and warns Jim against Lena because she expects better things for him. This sense of inferiority explains her seduction by Larry Donovan, who represents a step up for her. Hurt by an American and rescued by one of her own, Anton Cuzak, her cultural reversion is understandable. She inhabits an immigrant West opposed in many ways to the dominant culture, and identifies with the differences which have limited her.

Cather's making her Western hero a woman increases the scope of Western fiction; the kind of woman she chose adds a touch of boldness to a conservative tradition. Ántonia and her friends, who are idealized by Jim Burden and related to the poetry of Virgil, are the kind of girls the Virginian stopped seeing when he met Molly. The last of these was the golden-haired landlady of Medicine Bow, whose look said: "I am one of your possessions," and who left a "long gold thread of hair" on the Virginian's flannel shirt (pp. 35-36). The Virginian admits he is "the kind that moves up" (p. 103), and such girls would hardly help. What would have happened to Ántonia if Cuzak had been this ambitious "kind"? Readers are not to ask such questions, I suppose, but the fact remains, as Moers comments, "that this marvelous, golden hazy figure of Ántonia is a girl who, as we say,

is 'knocked up' and has an illegitimate baby. This is not a matter of accident. Cather chose to celebrate a figure who is sexually not respectable, and she is very much aware of what she is about."[5]

To have such a girl "stand for old and deep and superior kinds of civilization" is an alternative to the usual Western formula of a prim and proper woman representing the dominant American culture. Molly's is the conventional woman's role, Antonia's is not. Molly civilizes her cowboy sweetheart according to New England standards, and he develops what she contributes, reducing her in the end to a support in his enterprise. In *My Antonia*, Jim Burden is associated with aspects of the dominant culture Molly represents, teaching Antonia reading and the country's history, but Antonia fails to be accepted by the dominant culture and thus fails to embrace it. She becomes curiously independent, the source in Nebraska of an "old and deep and superior" civilization; it is in this sense that she is "like the founders of early races" and her husband a support in her enterprise. He is the "instrument of Antonia's special mission" (p. 367), not living the life of his choice, but serving her, functioning as the "corrective" to her "impulse" (p. 358). She represents a counterculture in the West, a backward life rather than progress, poverty rather than riches, family rather than town society, and spiritual rather than material prosperity. The values Cather loved she allowed to be represented in a "knocked up" girl, and that was very bold indeed.

Beret as the
Norse Mythological Goddess Freya/Gerthr

Catherine D. Farmer

In his masterpiece, *Giants in the Earth*, Ole E. Rölvaag pitted Norse mythology against Christian belief, both of which prove finally inadequate against the "Great Prairie. . .giantlike and full of cunning"[1] who, in the last chapter, "Drinks the Blood of Christian Men and Is Satisfied." The Great Plain achieves its own animate existence through contact with its human inhabitants: it takes from Beret a sexual identity and absorbs from her the powers traditionally associated with the Norse Freya/Gerthr; then the Plain turns on the men who have presumptuously come to "break prairie" and brings about Ragnarok deaths for the transplanted Norsemen, Per Hansa and Hans Olsa.

Initially in *Giants in the Earth*, the relationship between Per Hansa and Beret suggests a fruitful mating of male and female forces reminiscent of Norse mythology. Beret incorporates aspects of femininity embodied in the Norse goddess Freya/ Gerthr, the female counterpart of the fertility god Frey. A goddess of fertility, birth, and death, Freya is an amorous and seductive figure; she is also a witch of the disreputable magic called *seithr*. Gerthr, whose name is related to the word *garthr* (field), personifies a winter cornfield. When Frey and Gerthr meet in the grove Barri, fertilization and springtime occur.[2] Per Hansa bears striking similarities to the Norse vegetation god Frey/Freyr, a god of sunshine and fertility, pictured as *skirr* or shining. Frey is a god of peace, a protector of the gods, also a warrior and defender.[3] Like Frey, Per Hansa possesses a seemingly supernatural "creative force" and an unusually vibrant empathy with growing things:

[B]right emanations of creative force seemed to issue out of his

square, stocky figure (p. 127). A divine restlessness ran in his
blood (p. 109). [E]verything that had life he touched with a gentle
hand. . .talk to it he must; his voice sounded low, yet it thrilled
with a vibrant energy. . . . She felt a force that made her tremble,
emanating from him (p. 288). Now he was binding his own wheat,
his hands oily with the sap of the new-cut stems. . .he rubbed his
hands together and felt a sensuous pleasure welling up within him.
His body seemed to grow a little with every bundle he tied.

(p. 328)

The Norse god Frey or Freyr is the keenest of riders and owns a
splendid chariot that symbolizes death, fertility, and rebirth;
Frey is also owner of Skidbladnir, a wondrous ship made for him
by dwarfs.[4] In like manner, Per Hansa is a skilled sailor and
master of an oxen-powered sleigh (pp. 207, 269).

When Beret and Per Hansa arrive in Dakota Territory, the
Great Plain is "lifeless" and "desolate" (p. 9). It is a silent prairie
(p. 37) which has been "slumbering there undisturbed for countless ages" (p. 47). As Per Hansa and Beret sow their first garden,
the prairie shows its "upturned face" to the sun and gives "promise of fertility" (p. 47). Per Hansa and Beret, as Frey and Freya,
are bringing life to the desolation. As Per Hansa and Beret establish their family on their own section of land, the prairie becomes a presence (p. 56) which demonstrates its first consciousness when Per Hansa establishes a mutually beneficial relationship with the Trönder settlement: "The Great Plain watched
them breathlessly" (p. 59). The Plain becomes sexually particu-
larized as it assumes Beret's sexual identity, then becomes a
hostile female giant (pp. 241, 321, 339).[5] The attributes of
Freya/Gerthr were volatile but beneficent in the mistreated
Beret, but once the Great Plain has absorbed these characteristics, *She* wreaks vengeance on the domineering Per Hansa and
on his friend, Hans Olsa, whom Beret sees as having usurped her
husband's devotion and loyalty.

Before their marriage, Beret and Per Hansa have a free,
joyful sexual relationship that results in the conception and birth
of their child, Ole, outside wedlock (pp. 216-217). Their fertility
god-goddess relationship is clear: "Where Per Hansa was, there
dwelt high summer and there it bloomed for her. . . . He was
like. . .the gentle breeze of a summer's night" (pp. 217, 221).

Significantly, it was in the spring that Beret became pregnant with the child who would be named Peder Victorious. At the time of the first spring planting, Beret functions as a fully developed fertility goddess: approximately three months pregnant, she "produced all kinds of seeds" and worked alongside Per Hansa in the planting (p. 49). This is the last time that Beret is directly involved with the planting because each succeeding spring Per Hansa takes this job on himself (pp. 288, 324, 439); thus, Per Hansa (Frey/Freyr) takes from Beret (Freya/Gerthr) her proper duties.

As Per Hansa turns his attention—and his allegiance—toward the awakening land and the development of the settlement, his creative balance with Beret is broken. After reaching Dakota Territory, Per Hansa fails to exhibit his earlier spontaneity and joyfulness in the sexual act. In the scene of the first spring planting, Per Hansa grudgingly gives Beret a sexual reward for her industry and fruitfulness:

> The moment he stirred, she put her arms lovingly around him and told him that he must stay in bed awhile longer. . . .She begged him so gently and soothingly that he gave in at last and stayed in bed with her. But he was ill at ease over the loss of time. . . .This Beret-girl of his meant well enough, but she didn't realize the multitude of things that weighed on his mind—things that couldn't wait. . . . During the last two days she had hurried through her housework, and then. . .had joined in their labour. . . . He thought of other things that she had done. When they had harrowed and hoed sufficient seed ground, Beret had looked over her bundles and produced all kinds of seeds. . .turnips, and carrots, and onions, and tomatoes, and melons, even! . . .What a wife she was! Well, he had better stay in bed and please her this time, when she had been so clever and thoughtful about everything. (pp. 48-49)

Although the Norse Freya was the female counterpart of the god Frey and the two can be thought of as halves of a creative principle, Per Hansa comes to treat Beret as his sexual and mental inferior rather than as his mate in the sense of completion. Per Hansa's first transgression against Beret's gender is his insisting on their making the journey from Minnesota to Dakota Territory during her pregnancy. Wishing to protect the growing life within her, Beret "argued that they must tarry where

they were until she had borne the child" (p. 220). Per Hansa lacks respect for the female's overwhelming labor in the birth process: "Oh, well, she would have to bear the brunt of it herself, as the woman usually did" (p. 44). Instead of feeling excitement and pride at having fathered the first child to be born in his New World settlement, Per Hansa begrudges the time caring for the child will take and views the coming of the baby as "the main hitch in his calculations" (p. 44), certain to interfere with his acquiring farm animals and the gleaming white mansion with green cornices (pp. 44, 45, 108). For a fertility-god figure who has a loving and fruitful counterpart (Beret), Per Hansa has strangely misplaced loyalties: he forces Beret to start the journey to Dakota Territory so that he can keep up with his friend Hans Olsa (pp. 220-221, 372-373, 404-405).

As the relationship between Beret and Per Hansa deteriorates, Beret becomes a "corrupted" Freya, rendered incapable of fulfilling her natural potential for fertility first by Per Hansa's denial of her natural sexuality, then by her subsequent turning to Christian fanaticism. This process is one that begins with Per Hansa's mistreatment of Beret.

Per Hansa does not confide in Beret as a helpmate or even as "an help meet [suitable] for him." He does not tell Beret his worries and plans for their family as he makes his first trip to the Trönder settlement. Instead, he confides in Hans Olsa (p. 54). Beret feels "a twinge of jealousy because he had not confided in her" (p. 57) concerning his settlement plans. He did not confide in Beret during the landstakes affair (p. 116). Beret is jealous of Hans Olsa, for it seems to Beret that Hans Olsa "took something that rightfully belonged to her" (p. 218). Beret's jealousy of Hans Olsa flares again when the deranged Kari and her pitiable family arrive at their home and Per Hansa goes to Hans Olsa to discuss plans for helping Kari and family (p. 313).

Per Hansa pays no attention to Beret's opinions. He overrules Beret's reasonable objections to taking Store-Hans to the Indian camp (pp. 70-71). He overrules her sensible suggestion that Sam or Henry Solum (instead of Per Hansa) go to look for the missing cattle since the Solum boys have no one waiting at home for them (p. 99). Beret and Per Hansa clash in front of their friends concerning his removal of the landstakes, and her

opinion counts for nought (p. 150). Per Hansa, believing that women are intrinsically more fearful and inherently less understanding of business matters than men, warns Hans Olsa not to breathe a word about the landstakes affair to the women (p. 133). Later, Sörrina is the unwitting recipient of Per Hansa's highest (though unspoken) compliment to a woman: "her equal was not to be found! She could be both minister and father confessor, that woman!" (p. 212). In other words, Sörrina is capable of having been a good *man*! And Per Hansa passes on to his sons a belief that women are silly and are mentally inferior to men by joining with the boys to make fun of their mother's objections to their going on an expedition to catch ducks: "The boys only laughed at these objections; their mother sounded just like Sofie; probably all women were alike—they had no sense. . . .The father joined in with them" (p. 194).

Per Hansa's destructive treatment of Beret is three-fold: his thinking of her as less than an intelligent adult; his cursory, condescending physical attentions toward her; his regarding her pregnancy as a sickness and resenting the time he spends with her during her pregnancy. In his thinking of Beret, Per Hansa has to remind himself that she is a grown woman. The first instance of this occurs when Beret sensibly asks Per Hansa, " 'What do you think you're doing here?' " as he forces his sailor remedies on the sick Indian's blood-poisoned hand (pp. 76-77). The second instance occurs when Beret's pregnancy is far advanced and they are snowed in (an understandably depressing situation); Per Hansa gruffly commands her to "sit up and eat like a grown woman" (p. 202). At this time, he is "seized by a sudden, almost irresistible desire to take Beret. . .on his knee like a naughty child— just *make* her sit there. . .talk some sense into her!" (p. 206). Near the conclusion of the novel when Hans Olsa is ill, we are told that a "paternal attitude had become fixed" with Per Hansa and that "Even now that she was well again, it did not change. . . . To him she was still the delicate child that needed a father's watchful eye. To desire her physically would be as far from his mind as the crime of incest" (p. 440). This attitude robs Beret of the most elemental aspect of her identity as a female, her strong sexuality.

Throughout the novel, Beret retains sexual desire toward Per Hansa (pp. 48, 188-189, 220-221), even though she later

stifles this instinct due to her fanatical belief that it is evil (pp. 322, 443). Per Hansa's physical attentions to Beret become cursory and condescending (pp. 160, 187). As Per Hansa becomes more concerned with his personal prestige in the community and the amazing feats he can accomplish, he is able "to forget his wife's condition" when he sees

> . . .how everything was growing on the farm—meadows and fields, cattle and youngsters—then he was filled with an exultant joy. . . . He had a larger field than any of his neighbors, and there wasn't a doubt that his grain was the finest—theirs was just ordinary dumb grain, while his seemed alive! (p. 323)

Per Hansa's physical attentions to Beret, once thrilling to her, are now coarse and domineering. Before leaving on a trip to town which bolsters his already enormous ego, he takes hold of Beret and swings her around "trying to cheer her. . .beyond that he was too busy to pay much attention to her" (p. 160). When he returns from town, he denigrates Beret's ability to handle Store-Hans and Ole by saying to them, " 'Mother couldn't manage you, eh? Well, now you'll soon be dancing to a different tune' "; then he forces on Beret two drinks of whiskey which she does not want:

> "Come here, Beret-girl of mine! You have earned a good drink, and a good drink you shall have!" . . .he poured out a good half cupful of whiskey and offered it to her. She put out her hands as if to push him away. Yes, indeed, she would have to take it, he told her, putting his arm around her waist and lifting the cup to her lips. "There, that's a good little wife! You're going to have just another little drop!. . . Two legs, and one for each! Just drink it down! And now you take care of the bottles!" (p. 187)

Beret hungers for true tenderness from her husband, but Per Hansa dares not respond to Beret's "delicate" tenderness toward himself and the children because he notices that when he does "show her any tenderness. . .the tears were sure to come. And that, certainly, was not good for her" (pp. 203, 205).

The final blow to Beret's womanliness is Per Hansa's resentment of staying home with her during the ninth month of her pregnancy: " 'If *he* didn't have to sit there like a sick women, *he*

would have had enough lumber on hand for the finest farmstead, long ago. . . . Was she in such a condition that he could ever leave the house?' " (pp. 210-211). Beret replies truthfully that " '. . .she was in the condition he had brought her to—no worse and no better. . . . No, indeed, he didn't need to sit home on her account!' " (p. 211). Per Hansa cannot bear the truth and again tries to make her his mental inferior: " 'You talk like a fool! That only shows how much sense you've got!' " (p. 211).

As Per Hansa's neglect contributes to the destruction of Beret's original personality (that of a confident, sexually respon- sive and sexually initiatory woman), she becomes increasingly despairing and obsessed with the belief that she is being punished "for having broken God's Commandment of filial obedience" by leaving "parents, home, fatherland, and people. . .gladly, even rejoicingly" to journey to America with Per Hansa and their children (p. 219). Beret was an intrinsically joyful person, never overly concerned with Judeo-Christian sinfulness or its con- sequences (pp. 216-217); she loses her joy in herself and in her relationship with Per Hansa, and becomes obsessed with sin and its resulting punishment (pp. 149-150, 190, 216, 219, 227, 338, 368). She comes to conceive of herself not as a wife or even as a helpmate but as "a hindrance to him, like chains around his feet"; she believes that her presence has "burdened and imped- ed" her husband (p. 221).

As she retreats from her physical world, Beret becomes in- creasingly absorbed in the supernatural. She has, for example, many witch-like premonitions and visions: at the beginning of the story she foresees that the road west is taking them to a Ragnarok kingdom (p. 8); she senses "strange movements" and "strange things abroad" in the still room immediately before the grief-crazed Kari abducts And-Ongen (pp. 313-314); she hears an inaudible voice that warns her of Kari and And-Ongen's whereabouts (pp. 315-316); she talks with her dead mother re- peatedly, knowing "that her mother was dead half a year before the letter came" (p. 376). These powers fulfill Beret's identity as the vegetation/fertility goddess Freya, a witch of *seithr*, a disreputable magic. Beret's witch-like qualities and her abundant fertility become transferred to the Plain as she loses her identity as Freya/Gerthr. Beret senses that a magic circle is centered about her new home (pp. 36, 123, 124) and that she and her

family "had been bewitched into straying out here!" (p. 123). As her sexual identity was absorbed earlier, now her supernatural powers are absorbed by the Plain.

After Beret comes to see herself as a burden to Per Hansa, she makes her plans to die in childbirth (pp. 221-223). No longer confident in her ability to bring forth children, she incorrectly assumes her attempt to do so will result in her death. But the Plain, having absorbed the supernatural elements of Beret's personality, is now a monstrous female who practices witchcraft (pp. 241, 245) and who is prepared "to guard herself and her own against. . .man" (p. 241).

The Great Prairie's threat that "she would know, when the time came, how to guard herself and her own against him. . .man and his works" (p. 241) is made good when "a penetrating wind blew over the prairie, as if searching for signs of life to wither and blight" (p. 291) and when it seems to Per Hansa, Hans Olsa, and Tönseten as if "the unseen hand of a giant were shaking an immense tablecloth of iridescent colours" (p. 331) upon the first arrival of the glittering, ominous locust clouds. Significantly, the locust plague raged "with unabated fury throughout the years '74, '75, '76, and part of '78" to "pounce upon and destroy. . .all that grew above the ground, with the exception of the wild grass [which]. . .it left untouched because it had grown here ere time was and *without the aid of man's hand*" (pp. 339-340). With the advent of the locust plague, Beret is reduced to an almost mindless terror: she can only hide in the immigrant chest from a Judeo-Christian devil (p. 338). Mentally and spiritually, Beret has departed from the physical world of the Great Plain and from her married life with Per Hansa.

Beret's mystical re-entry into the actual world of the Plain contains both Judeo-Christian and Norse mythological elements. The minister had laid his hands on Beret and released her from the "bonds of Satan," but her mind was still clouded. She continued to expect the arrival of her dead mother every day and had preparatory mental conversations with her (pp. 400-401). Beret's mind clears as a result of overhearing Per Hansa's conversation with Hans Olsa, a conversation in which Per Hansa greatly praised Beret and expressed love for her. Beret was so enraptured that she

did not know where she was going nor what she did. In the southern sky floated transparent little clouds; rainbow ribbons hung
down from them. She saw the rainbow's glow; her face was transfigured. . .as Beret lay there playing with the child she was suddenly overcome with drowsiness. . .in a moment she had dozed off and
was carried away into an infinite, glittering blue space with rainbows hung all around it.   (pp. 405-407)

When she awakens, everything looks strange to her, and she has
difficulty finding certain kitchen utensils and food items: "It
seemed to her that she hadn't been here for a long time. . .but
the feeling of home-coming filled her with such joy, that she
could only laugh at her bewilderment" (p. 408). At the point
when the rainbow motif is first mentioned, Beret's mind is still
unclear and it is not until "she had dozed off and was carried
away into an infinite, glittering blue space with rainbows hung
all around it" that her mind is unclouded. The sequence recalls
Norse mythology, in which Asgard was the home of the gods,
access to which was gained only by crossing the bridge Bifrost
(the rainbow).[6] From a Norse point of view, Beret had spiritually crossed this mystical bridge, which had been apparent earlier
in the book only in the incomplete form of the sun-dogs or
partial rainbows visible in the worst winter weather (pp. 254,
274).

The change in Beret was perceptible and lasting. Per Hansa
had to hold to the door jamb to steady himself when he first saw
her after her mystical journey. Near the conclusion of the book
when Beret is sitting up with the dying Hans Olsa, we get a view
of her by way of Tönseten:

> On entering the room Tönseten greeted them both cheerily; but
> instantly he began to feel ill at ease. . . .Since Beret had recovered,
> he couldn't stand her. She had become so pious that if a fellow
> made the most innocent remark, she was sure to preach at him.
> And never a drop of whiskey would she tolerate, either for rheu-
> matism or for cough. One ought to have some sense, even if one
> was going to be religious.   (p. 426)

Whether we take it to be a Christian experience or a mythological journey via the Norse rainbow-bridge Bifrost, Beret was freed
from her delusions by an epiphany. Beret's becoming extremely

rigid and narrow from this gloriously freeing experience is an ironic comment on the paradoxical nature of man's consciousness: Per Hansa expresses such disregard for Beret's role as a sexual, fertile woman that she loses all sense of herself and those characteristics that identify her as Freya/Gerthr; she convinces herself that she will die as a result of the sin of filial disobedience in leaving her parents and fatherland; her mind is not cleared by the minister's actions but as the result of her mystical transportation experience, yet at recovery she espouses a pseudo-Christian doctrine that forbids her and her husband to live together "as one flesh."

Per Hansa, too, is radically changed from the vital young man who caressed every living thing he came near and who spoke in a voice which "thrilled with a vibrant energy. . .a force. . . emanating from him" (p. 288). In Hans Olsa's thoughts at the Communion Service, Per Hansa "had become an old man before his time: his hair and beard were gray; his face was thin and worn" (p. 398). Instead of a vital Frey/Freyr, he has become aged, a dangerous state, for when the course of nature is dependent on a man-god's life, he must be killed as soon as he shows symptoms that his vigor and virility are failing.[7]   Per Hansa is "ripe" for destruction.

The image of Per Hansa at his death, "a heavy stocking cap pulled well down over his forehead, and large mittens on his hands" (p. 453), extends the mythological reference, for it suggests the Northern European representative of winter: "The representative of Summer was clad in white and bore a sickle; his comrade, who played the part of Winter, had a fur-cap on his head, his arms and legs were swathed in straw and he carried a flail. . . .   Formerly, the part of Winter was played by a straw-man."[8]   The position of Per Hansa's body, "on the west side of the stack. . .with his back to the mouldering hay" (p. 453) is similar, too, to an old Norwegian folk-practice. When the hay-making was over in the Romsdal and in other parts of Norway, people said that "the old Hay-Man has been killed." The corn-spirit was often represented by a man who lay down under the last corn, which was threshed upon his body; the people then said that "the Old Man is being beaten to death."[9]   In like manner, Per Hansa, having fulfilled his seasonal cycle, has become the embodiment of winter rather than that of the "creative force"

of springtime.

With its immense power to bring about change, the Great Plain inspired fear in all the characters of *Giants in the Earth,* but only Beret articulates this fear. Before Peder Victorious is born, her thoughts foreshadow Per Hansa's and Hans Olsa's deaths: "Was it only by ruthless sacrifice of life that this endless desolation could ever be peopled?" (p. 185). As Beret loses her identity as Freya/Gerthr, the Plain seems an increasingly animate and malevolent force, a force that bides her time in waiting to destroy:

> Monsterlike the Plain lay there—sucked in her breath one week, and the next week blew it out again. Man she scorned; his works she would not brook. She would know, when the time came, how to guard herself and her own against him! But there was something she did not know. Had it not been for the tiny newcomer, who by mysterious paths had found his way into the settlement on Christmas morning, the monster might have had her way; but the newcomer made a breach in her plans—a vital breach! (p. 241)

But the newcomer, Peder Victorious, has made only "a breach in her plans"; he has not totally destroyed them. At his christening, Beret had cried out, " 'How can a man be *victorious* out here, where the evil one gets us all!' " (p. 368), the question she returns to later, when she reflects, "Here Earth takes us. What she cannot get easily she wrests by subtle force, and we do not even know it. I see what happens in my own home. It is awful!" (p. 432). Her forebodings suggest her sense of exile in a land of pre-Christian terrors, where even the gods are doomed to eternal destruction. A distinctive feature of Norse mythology is that its followers believed their gods to be of a finite race. Born from a mixture of divine and gigantic elements, they bore within them the germ of death and were doomed to endure a Ragnarok destruction toward which the entire scheme of Northern mythology inevitably leads.[10] Ragnarok, the final "Twilight of the Gods," will have climatic forerunners: a triple winter untempered by a single summer, during which snow will fall from the four corners of the heavens; war and discord will spread over the universe; the earth, seas, and heavens will be torn and dislocated, and men will perish.[11] Near the conclusion of *Giants in the Earth,* Rölvaag seems to suggest an impending Ragnarok:

They say it rained forty days and forty nights once in the old days, and that was terrible, but during the winter of 1880-81 it snowed twice forty days; and that was more terrible. Day and night the snow fell. From the 15th of October, when it began, until after the middle of April, it seldom ceased. From the four corners of the earth it flew. . .and all winter the sun stayed in his house. . . . The suffering was great that winter. Famine came; supplies of all kinds gave out for no one had thought, when the first snowfall began, that winter had come. Who had ever heard of its setting in in the middle of autumn? . . . Some had to leave their potatoes in the ground; others could not thresh the grain; fuel, if not provided beforehand, was scarcely to be had at all; and it was impossible for anyone to get. . .to town to fetch what might be needed.

(pp. 415-416)

The sons of the gods were sheltered from the conflict of Ragnarok; they survived the holocaust to join the god Balder returned from the dead.[12]   Per Hansa's final thoughts are of Peder Victorious/Permand (p. 452), and Per Hansa makes an unusual parting remark to Permand (considering the season of the year) that could be taken as his surrendering to his son his identity as a vegetation god: "And now you must be a good boy, and get a lot of threshing done before I come back" (p. 450). Here, as in Norse mythology, Ragnarok is not the final end: after the destruction, the earth will arise again from the waves—free of all sufferings and evil, to be ruled by the sons of the great gods.[13]

That is the pattern we find in *Giants in the Earth.* Per Hansa, who bears unmistakable similarities to the Norse god Frey/Freyr, and Hans Olsa, who is described as a Norse mountain giant, die as a result of the Prairie's harshness. The final chapter begins with this statement: "Many and incredible are the tales the grandfathers tell from those days when the wilderness was yet untamed and when they, unwittingly, founded the Kingdom" (p. 413).   Per Hansa and Hans Olsa are Norse supermen who found a Ragnarok kingdom; they are also "Christian men" whose blood is drunk by the malevolent Plain.

From a Christian standpoint, the book is pessimistic: an egotistical man undertakes an arduous, postponable journey over the protests of his pregnant wife; over her protests, he settles his family in an area so desolate as to cause madness; he single-

mindedly directs his efforts toward accumulating earthly possessions which "moth" and "rust" will destroy; he considers himself any man's equal—or superior—and dares to challenge Satan; he never understands Hans Olsa's sense of urgency that a minister be present at his deathbed, undertaking the journey to fetch the minister because it is expected of him as a doer of impossible deeds. Although Per Hansa realizes that "Wyrd biđ ful ãrãed!"[14] or "Fate is fully fixed," he struggles heroically to win fame and earthly joys. The Ragnarok of Per Hansa and Hans Olsa proves inescapable,[15] but the two men leave their sons a glorious post-Ragnarok Kingdom, described in the poem *Balder Dead* as the heritage of the sons of the dead gods Odin, Thor, Balder, and Frey:

> . . .an Earth
> More fresh, more verdant than the last, with fruits
> Self-springing, and a seed of man preserved,
> Who then shall live in peace, as now in war.[16]

The final paradox of *Giants in the Earth* is evident in the destruction wrought upon Per Hansa and Hans Olsa. The Great Plain wins; she "Drinks the Blood of Christian Men and Is Satisfied." Thus, the dominant male characters, Hans Olsa and Per Hansa, are destroyed through the actions of a monstrous female. In the Hebrew and Hellenic traditions, destruction was wrought upon the human race through the actions of evil and insatiably curious women—Eve and Pandora. But in *Giants in the Earth*, it is Per Hansa's failure to treat his wife according to the Christian teaching, "so ought men to love their wives as their own bodies . . . . Let every one of you in particular so love his wife even as himself" (Ephesians 5:28, 33), that contributes to the destruction of Beret's intrinsic personality as a volatile but beneficent Freya/Gerthr. The Great Plain absorbs Beret's Freya/Gerthr characteristics but sets herself against those men who have come to "break prairie"; Per Hansa and Hans Olsa are destroyed through the wiles of the monstrous female prairie, but unlike the woman-wrought destruction of the Hebrew and Hellenic myths, a man is the transgressor—Per Hansa. In this novel of male dominance, Beret's mistreated and redirected female nature is the final victor.

NOTES

[1] Ole Edvart Rölvaag, *Giants in the Earth: A Saga of the Prairie* (New York: Harper & Row, 1955), p. 339. (Further references to this book will be cited by page number within the text of the paper.)

[2] Edward Oswald Gabriel Turville-Petre, *Myth and Religion of the North* (Westport, Connecticut: Greenwood Press, 1964), pp. 159, 174, 176-177.

[3] Turville-Petre, pp. 168, 174-175.

[4] Turville-Petre, p. 173.

[5] The world of Norse mythology was made from the body of the frost giant Ymir: his body formed the earth's surface, his blood became the seas, and his skull formed the heavens. A great wall built from Ymir's eyebrows defended Midgard, the place where humans were to live. Edith Hamilton, *Mythology* (New York: New American Library, 1969), p. 312.

[6] Thomas Bulfinch, *Mythology* (New York: Dell Publishing Company, Inc., 1959), p. 242.

[7] Sir James George Frazer, *The Golden Bough: A Study in Magic and Religion* (New York: The Macmillan Company, 1923), p. 265.

[8] Frazer, p. 317.

[9] Frazer, pp. 428-429.

[10] H. A. Guerber, *Myths of Northern Lands* (Detroit: Singing Tree Press, 1970), p. 263.

[11] Bulfinch, pp. 258-259.

[12] Hilda Roderick Ellis Davidson, *Scandinavian Mythology* (New

York: Paul Hamlyn, 1975), p. 122.

[13]Hilda Roderick Ellis Davidson, *Gods and Myths of Northern Europe* (London: Penguin Books, Ltd., 1964), p. 38.

[14]Frederick G. Cassidy and Richard N. Ringler, eds., *Bright's Old English Grammar and Reader* (New York: Holt, Rinehart and Winston, Inc., 1971), p. 324.

[15]A Norse belief expressed in the Old English poems *The Wanderer, The Seafarer,* and *Beowulf* and expressed by Per Hansa on pages 264 and 404 of *Giants in the Earth.*

[16]Guerber, p. 271.

Marian Forrester and Moll Flanders:
Fortunes and Misfortunes

Patricia Lee Yongue

In addition to sharing a set of initials, the heroines of Daniel
Defoe's *Moll Flanders* (1722) and Willa Cather's *A Lost Lady*
(1923) resemble one another in ways that indicate greater correspondence between the two novels than might at first be presumed likely.[1] Specifically, the special emphasis on Marian Forrester and Moll Flanders as fortunate, if desperate, survivors in
worlds described as caring little or nothing about their human
rights unites Cather with Defoe in an inquiry into an aspect of
social history and morality important to them both: the economic situation of women in a man's world and the psychological and moral ramifications of that situation. Indeed, a view of
the charming and aristocratic Marian Forrester in the light of
the oppressed and wicked Moll Flanders introduces a fine ambiguity into Marian's characterization, at the same time that it
contributes to the layering of theme, action, point-of-view, and
irony in *A Lost Lady*, a remarkable novel which is proving to
be one of Willa Cather's most intricate studies.[2]

A Lost Lady is, perhaps, Willa Cather's most explicit,
though characteristically subdued, treatment of society's diffi-
dence with respect to women and their needs.[3] The subtle traces
of *Moll Flanders* in the novel, which seem deliberate, serve to
remind the reader that Marian, like Moll, is "unprotected"—even,
or especially, in the company of the men and mores so eagerly
claiming to be her protectors. Marian's affiliations with heroines
as diverse and psychologically complex as Moll Flanders, Hawthorne's Hester Prynne, and Flaubert's Emma Bovary offset the
more prominent resemblance she bears to women like Queen
Guinevere and Robin Hood's Maid Marion.[4] The tension created
by these myriad images of woman—each representing a different
perception or facet of her character—approximates the tension

Marion herself endures, as she is caught up in a web not of her own weaving, and as she must face alone the consequences of her entrapment.

Insofar as Marian's combined financial, psychological, and moral predicament emerges from the aristocratic but self-serving dreams of males like Niel Herbert and Captain Forrester who treasure her as one might treasure a piece of jewelry, and from the vulgar, more obviously self-serving motives of men like "shyster" Ivy Peters, it is appropriate that the echoes of Guinevere and Maid Marion (the Captain calls his wife "Maidy") precede the echoes of Moll Flanders. By and large, Cather suggests through this strategy, it is the one- or, at best, two-dimensional image of woman that has dominated society's relationship with her, just as it dominates Marian's treatment at the hands of the men in *A Lost Lady*. Cather adroitly counterpoints the more fixed Camelot/Sherwood Forest associations of the novel's action and Marian's behavior with the equivocality intrinsic to most human intercourse. The tangible insinuations of "coarseness" in Marian's character—such as her early engagement to an adulterous, criminally suspect "gaudy millionaire," and her later liaisons with "coarse worldlings" like Frank Ellinger and "coarsegrained" Ivy Peters—do not transform her from goddess to bitch, save, perhaps, in young Niel Herbert's eyes. What these insinuations do accomplish, however, is the interruption of Niel's fantasy and Captain Forrester's dream of a non-human, nonsexual Marian.

Marian's humanity invades Sweet Water not merely as greed, adultery, and vulgarity invade Camelot and Sherwood Forest, and as harsher economic realities invade the Nebraska town "of which great things were expected" (p. 14), but even as *Moll Flanders* invaded established literature's portrait of woman, and as woman's humanity intrudes upon the view of her that has been singularly blind to that humanity. Willa Cather may, in this regard, be infusing additional irony into the Marian/Maid Marion of Sherwood Forest association. The name "Forrester" links Marian not only with the forest of popular romance and with the pastoral, mythic West that is endangered by encroaching industrialization and capitalism ("as the match factory splinters the primeval forest" [p. 106]), but also, in the Hawthornean sense, with the moral and emotional wilderness in which she,

like Hester Prynne, is forced to exist by virtue of her ignored humanity.

It is important to emphasize, however, that Willa Cather does not make of *A Lost Lady* Woman's Story alone. In her own elegant way, at her own superbly measured pace, she integrates this dimension into the novel so that it expands the meaning and the action of the other stories she tells. What happens to Marion Forrester as "unprotected" woman happens to her as the feminine ideal—"the mirage"—of a maturing Niel Herbert and a dying Captain Forrester, and also as Cather's symbol of the West, America, and the American dream. The sympathy and understanding that Cather extends to Marian, even in her "coarseness," she extends to America as well. Both Marian and the country are described as being victimized by idealists and opportunists; both are trapped between two generations and two value systems; and, both must struggle for survival, independence, and respectability and pay dearly in the process. It is in the context of the latter action especially that *Moll Flanders* becomes kin to *A Lost Lady*. Moll, whose struggles are quite similar to Marian's and who herself is finally—if ironically—associated with the American ideal of freedom and respectability for all, becomes a touchstone to our understanding of Mrs. Forrester's essential dilemma.

It is difficult, admittedly, to do more than just suggest a compatibility between *Moll Flanders* and *A Lost Lady*. Although Willa Cather's admiration for *The Scarlet Letter* and *Madame Bovary* is documented, there is no indication in her correspondence or elsewhere of any particular attraction or indebtedness to Defoe. The fact that both *A Lost Lady* and Cather's Introduction to the 1924 Knopf edition of Defoe's *The Fortunate Mistress* (*Roxana*) were written within about eighteen months of one another during the bicentennary period of *Moll Flanders* is suggestive but, of course, not conclusive. So is the fact that the first two decades of the twentieth century produced much feminist activity and important acknowledgment from writers like Virginia Woolf of Defoe's special contributions to the goals of women's rights advocates.

Ironically, Cather herself may have deflected attention away from any specific connection between her fiction and Defoe's

by an extremely unflattering appraisal of his art in her Introduction to *The Fortunate Mistress.*[5] Here she claims, almost angrily, that with the exception of Robinson Crusoe, who admirably "practice[s] his ingenuity upon a desert island and the untamed forces of nature," the typical Defoe hero—like Roxana—blandly and unsympathetically "uses his wits upon the persons and pocket-books of his fellow mortals."[6] Roxana well illustrates what Willa Cather thought to be Defoe's usual "poverty of emotion and lack of imagination," his inability either to invest action with "feeling" or to evoke sympathy from his readers. He, like his heroine, seemed "blind to everything but francs and pounds."

Despite her objections to Defoe and *The Fortunate Mistress,* it still remains somewhat curious that, unlike Virginia Woolf in 1919, Cather makes no attempt at all in her essay to compare/contrast Roxana with her more illustrious counterpart, Moll Flanders. Curious, too, is the fact that so many of Cather's insights into and reservations about *The Fortunate Mistress,* whether acceptable or not as solid literary criticism, reflect her own interests in *A Lost Lady.* As one colleague suggests, perhaps Cather had *A Lost Lady* in mind while she was writing about Roxana; perhaps she thought that she could have written *The Fortunate Mistress* or even *Moll Flanders* better than Defoe, or that she may have, in fact, already done so.

Willa Cather chastises Defoe for caring too much about "francs and pounds" and for being too preoccupied in his fiction with the vulgarities of "making a living"; yet, she herself agitated considerably over these same matters. Frequently, she agitated over her agitation. On the one hand, as I have elsewhere explained, her own deeply aristocratic sensibilities prohibited worrying the issues of money and economics, especially publicly.[7] On the other hand, she realized, like Marian Forrester, that "Money is a very important thing" (p. 114). She was ambitious and fiercely dedicated to the "unladylike" business of making her own money and her own way in a man's world. A character such as Alexandra Bergson in *O Pioneers!* (1913), who does not marry until long after she has achieved financial independence and success through hard work and economic shrewdness (neither of which the reader is allowed to observe in process), expresses Cather's commitment to woman who not only survives in

a man's world, but survives beautifully without sacrificing her femininity or her ladyship.[8] Marian Forrester, however, is more directly affected by the exigencies of her sex and social class with respect to respectability and survival.

At first, the glaring differences between Moll and Marian seem to negate the possibility of any sustained intimacy. Moll's lowly birth (in Newgate prison to a condemned thief) and social status, her blatantly criminal as well as immoral deeds, her lack of Marian's grace—not to mention the episodic structure of her narrative and the abundance of sordid detail she chooses to include—all disparage a view of the lovely Marian as any relative of the infamous Moll. Nevertheless, there are important similarities between the two, not the least of which is a "coarseness" nurtured by their position as women faced with the problem of survival in an unfeeling world. Lacking independent incomes, Moll and Marian are of necessity preoccupied with money and come to represent how woman's need for money, and the few options society has allowed her for its procurement, has confused her emotionally and, often, morally.

Moll Flanders' private history unfolds as a series of attempts to make money merely by securing it from others. Moll early concedes that "Money is the thing" women must consider in establishing their relationships; men, she explains, have *always* considered that factor first (*MF,* p. 54). In Moll's case, whoring, marriage (Defoe terms it Matrimonial Whoredom), and eventually stealing become her means of obtaining money and also the kind of respectability she quickly learns money can purchase. As an orphan child fortunate enough to get a position as a serving girl, Moll determines to become a "Gentlewoman" and is at first willing to work for the title. According to her simple definition, "being a Gentlewoman. . .was no more, than to be able to get my Bread by my own work" (*MF,* p. 12). But she soon discovers that mere mending and cleaning will allow her at best only to "eek" out a living and will certainly never bring her the luxuries she has begun to covet. Discovering this, she alters her definition of "gentlewoman" and her *modus operandi* considerably. Immorality and crime bring her money and respectability and survival more surely than does her "Needle."[9]

Marian Forrester's way of living off the "persons and

pocket-books" of her "fellow mortals" is undoubtedly more gracious and socially acceptable, although her affairs with the "gaudy millionnaire," Frank Ellinger, and Ivy Peters gradually reveal her unbecoming vulgarity. But like Moll's baser crimes, both Marian's travesties and her more charming ways are depicted as consequences of the female's struggle for survival and of the emotional and moral confusion wrought by her socioeconomic bondage. For Marian, as for most women of her generation, marriage is the only acceptable strategy in the quest for survival, a quest she herself remains fairly innocent of as long as there are men available to her who can easily provide her the marriage, money, and material advantages she desires. Like a child, Cather seems to be saying, Marian instinctively "knows" the way to survival. As such, her marriage to Captain Forrester, a kindly man twenty-five years her senior, effectively represents what marriage has in fact become for most women—not a fulfilling sexual/love relationship between two adults, but a necessary extension of the financial dependence that women have learned at the knees of their fathers.

After the Captain's death, when Marian leaves Sweet Water and goes "West,—people supposed to California" (p. 171), she resumes the pattern of marrying for money that is first registered in the single detail of her engagement to the "gaudy millionaire." She ends up in South America married to a "rich, cranky old Englishman" who had "been married twice before, once to a Brazilian woman," and who, though "quarrelsome and stingy" (unlike the Captain), gives her "everything" (p. 173). When Niel Herbert hears, many years later, that Marian "was well cared for, to the very end," he thanks God; but it nevertheless remains that, despite her restoration to a life of French carriages, maids, and valets—to the kind of life in which her aristocratic attributes flourish—she may not have escaped completely, if at all, what Defoe calls Matrimonial Whoredom, what Willa Cather also describes as a form of protracted girlhood, and what both authors agree is a means of survival that exacts a stiff toll.

It is only when Captain Forrester's financial base collapses and he falls gravely ill that Marian becomes acutely aware of just how vulnerable and powerless she is, how desperately she needs money in order to survive, and how much her survival depends upon the men who control the money. She also realizes that her

age—she is no longer fashionably young—is a factor now working against her continued success in the only "trade" she knows. Her desperation reduces her to drunkenness, unattractive *déshabille* (which opposes the charming *déshabille* in which she often coquettishly indulges), and loss of dignity. In Niel's aristocratic eyes, she becomes "common." The frantic, midnight phone call she makes to her lover Frank Ellinger, whose marriage to the young, rich Constance Ogden has just been announced in the newspaper, embodies Marian's plight. The sexually attractive, graying, and somewhat shallow Ellinger, scorned as a "coarse worldling" by a jealous and naive Niel Herbert, has obviously been perceived by Marian as her protection against imminent poverty and widowhood. But Ellinger suddenly marries Constance, leaving the older woman helpless and raging.

> . . .She was watching the telephone as if it were alive. Her eyes were shrunk to hard points. Her brows. . .kept twitching in the frown which held them,—the singular frown of one overcome by alcohol or fatigue, who is holding on to consciousness by the strength of a single purpose. Her blue lips, the black shadows under her eyes, made her look as if some poison were at work in her body. . . .

> The telephone buzzed. Mrs. Forrester darted toward the desk. . . .

> "Is that you Frank? this is Marian. I won't keep you a moment."

> "Play safe! When have you ever played anything else? You know, Frank, the truth is that you're a coward: a great hulking coward. Do you hear me? I want you to hear! . . . Now let me tell you the truth: I don't want you to come here! I never want to see you again while I live, and I forbid you to come and look at me when I'm dead. I don't want your hateful eyes to look at my dead face. Do you hear me? Why don't you answer me? Don't dare to hang up the receiver, you coward! Oh, you big. . .Frank, Frank, say something! Oh, he's shut me off, I can't hear him!"

> She flung the receiver down, dropped her head on the desk, and broke into heavy, groaning sobs. . . .   (pp. 131-134)

Marian's desperation here recalls Moll Flanders' accounts of similar periods of despair, but especially her situation at forty-eight years of age, following the untimely death of her husband, which leads to her first real act of theft.

> . . .I was now left in a dismal and disconsolate Case indeed, and in several things worse than ever: First it was past the flourishing time with me when I might expect to be courted for a Mistress. . . and the Loss my Husband had sustained had reduc'd his Circumstances so low, that tho' indeed I was not in Debt, yet I could easily forsee that what was left would not support me long; that while it wasted daily for Subsistence, I had no way to encrease it one Shilling, so that it would be soon all spent, and then I saw nothing before me but the Utmost Distress. . . .
>
> In this Distress I had no Assistant, no Friend to comfort or advise me, I sat and cried and tormented myself Night and Day; wringing my Hands, and sometimes raving like a distracted Woman. . . .
>
> Let 'em remember that a time of Distress is a time of Dreadful Temptation, and all the Strength to resist is taken away; Poverty presses, the Soul is made Desperate by Distress, and what can be done? I was one Evening, when being brought, as I may say, to the last Gasp, I think I may truly say I was Distracted and Raving, when prompted by I know not what Spirit. . .I dress'd me. . .and went out.　　　(*MF*, pp. 148-149)

Although Willa Cather is not as garrulous as Moll/Defoe, she captures in Marian's raving phone call to Frank Ellinger all of Moll's fright, concern, and hysteria in the face of the threat to her survival.

Moll's continual emphasis on her lack of true friends and an "Assistant" has its parallel in *A Lost Lady*, even though Marian at first seems to have many champions, all of them men. Niel Herbert is even willing to "chuck school for a year" to help the Forresters through their crisis and to protect Marian from the Sweet Water "gossips" who seem to delight in her misfortunes and who are more than ready to pounce upon all her fine things. It is important to remember, however, that Niel, because of his immaturity and his aristocratic bent, is himself quite innocent

about money and economics. And for psychological reasons having to do with the death of his mother and his deep resentment over his own father's financial "failure and defeat" (p. 30), he avoids facing up to the urgency of Marian's dilemma and to her need to abandon him in favor of Frank and Ivy. Added to this is the fact that Niel does not have to provide for himself in the way the others boys, including Ivy Peters, have to; at twenty-one he will inherit several thousand dollars his mother has left for him. Currently, he is in the care of his uncle, Judge Pommeroy. All of this makes for a Niel who is so snobbish, unsympathetic, and insensitive to anything but his own ideals and taste, that he ungallantly deserts the lady he believes he has been chivalrously defending.

Judge Pommeroy, who has handled the Forrester accounts for many years, is as incapable as his nephew of helping Marian reclaim her losses; " 'his methods don't work nowadays' " (p. 123), she claims with probable cause. Frank Ellinger, having married Constance Ogden, will no longer be available to her as either a short- or long-term successor to the Captain. Finally, when the Captain suffers his fatal stroke, Marian is left completely alone and unprotected. Ivy Peters is the only one who can assist her in the way she needs assistance most—financially. Like Moll, who claims loudly and somewhat facetiously that the Devil "laid the Snare" which made her steal in order to survive, Marian succumbs to Ivy Peters, the ugly fellow whose eyes have the "fixed, unblinking hardness of a snake's or a lizard's" (pp. 21-22), and who "cheats the Indians" in order to insure his own and Marian's survival. " 'He's invested a little money for me in Wyoming, in land,' " Marian explains to Niel on one occasion. " 'He gets splendid land from the Indians in some way, for next to nothing. . .I've no doubt it's crooked' " (p. 123).

Although the immediate source of Marian's desperation and aloneness is, like Moll's, her financial powerlessness, Willa Cather's portrait of unprotected woman goes beyond a study of this one aspect and considers a greater source of her woe. More than Defoe, Willa Cather attributes woman's vulnerability and isolation to the unrealistic image of her by which society evaluates her and by which she often evaluates herself and her sister. If, like modern America, Marian Forrester is at "the mercy of men like Ivy Peters, who had never dared anything, never risked

anything" (p. 106), she is every bit as much at the mercy of Niel Herbert's idealized view of her as the ageless madonna—he first sees her in black and white attire leaving her carriage and going into church (p. 42)—and of Captain Forrester's dream of her as well. She is "valued" (p. 143) by these men as an object or flower or projection of their romantic fancies. Niel, in fact, is so absorbed in his fantasy of Marian that he refuses to allow her even the voice of human frailty and hurt. When she makes the phone call to Frank Ellinger and the "quivering passion of hatred and wrong leaped into her voice," Niel takes "the big shears left by the tinner" and cuts "the insulated wire behind the desk." He congratulates himself for this deed: "For once he had been quick enough; he had saved her" (p. 134). What he is trying to save, of course, is not Marian at all, but his own romantic vision of her. He cuts one wire only to secure another.

By contrast, Captain Forrester does seem to understand his young wife's needs and her feelings of confinement in the small, unpolished town of Sweet Water. To Niel's dismay, in fact, the Captain indicates some knowledge of Marian's infidelities and yet chooses to remain silent. The reasons for this behavior, though never stated, are implied. Perhaps the Captain feels that Marian's obvious sexual and social needs are better satisfied by younger men like Ellinger than by him. Or he may simply want to keep his wife and himself from the embarrassment of a "scene" and possible public humiliation; the Captain, after all, observes an aristocratic code of behavior. But his silence can also reflect the same egocentric motives as Niel's act of cutting the telephone wire reflects. The Captain does not want to risk losing Marian and the dream he has been protecting for many, many years. " 'When I came here a young man,' " he tells his dinner guests one evening, " 'I had planned it in my mind, pretty much as it is today; where I would dig my well, and where I would plant my grove and my orchard. I planned to build a house that my friends could come to, with a wife like Mrs. Forrester to make it attractive to them' " (p. 53).

With respect to this dream, the Captain and Marian seem to have struck a bargain: in exchange for wealth and silence, Marian will provide him with her youth, beauty, and charm. Like Niel Herbert, Captain Forrester gets a great deal of pleasure just looking at his young wife dressed in her finery and wearing the

jewels he has brought her and serving as hostess at his table. Marian gets pleasure from these things too; but, she needs and wants more than her aging husband can provide. What their subsequent complicity amounts to is immorality—not merely the conventional "sin" of adultery which Marian commits, but the "sin" of consent which the Captain also commits by refusing to put his dream in jeopardy. Moreover, his silent acceptance of Marian's adultery encourages her, whether either is aware of it or not, to continue her extramarital affairs and thus to sink deeper into moral and psychological confusion. Again, this is not a situation which Willa Cather delineates; it is a possibility she intimates.

Marian Forrester is a prisoner, a prisoner of the male imagination and of the socio-economic, psychological, and moral conditions which issue from that initial imprisonment. Like Moll Flanders, who describes herself as a "meer Newgate-bird" and a "Partridge" caught in a net, Marian is bird in a cage. Perhaps the single, most salient use of the metaphor occurs in the surprisingly violent picnic scene, when Ivy Peters disturbs the pastoral quiet of the other boys by his "ugly" presence and his even uglier action—the sadistic blinding of a female woodpecker whom he "carelessly" addresses as "Miss Female."

> . . .He held the woodpecker's head on a vice made of his thumb and forefinger, enclosing its panting body with his palm. Quick as a flash. . .he slit both the eyes that glared in the bird's stupid little head, and instantly released it.
>
> The woodpecker rose in the air with a whirling corkscrew motion, started to the right, struck a tree trunk,—to the left, and struck another. Up and down, backward and forward among the tangle of branches it flew, raking its feathers, rallying and recovering itself. (pp. 23-24)

Besides representing Ivy's own disturbing attitudes about women and besides prefiguring his draining of the Forrester marsh, his cheating of the Indians, and his eventual capture of Marian herself ("he unconcernedly put both arms around her, his hands meeting over her breast" [p. 169]), the woodpecker episode images the fundamental predicament of a woman who has been mutilated to the point of blindness as to her own real

needs and goals. The desperation of the blinded, "stupid" woodpecker is comparable to Marian's desperation and foreshadows
her behavior, possibly even the behavior of woman in general.

> . . .There was something wild and desperate about the way the
> darkened creature beat its wings in the branches, whirling in the
> sunlight and never seeing it, always thrusting its head up and
> shaking it, as a bird does when it is drinking. Presently it managed
> to get its feet on the same limb where it had been struck, and
> seemed to recognize that perch. As if it had learned something
> by its bruises, it pecked and crept its way along the branch and
> disappeared into its own hole. (p. 25)

Young Niel tries to climb the tree to put the bird out of its
misery, but he cannot. He breaks his arm trying. Likewise the
adolescent Niel, blind himself to certain realities of the human
condition, cannot help Marian in her distress. His own romantic
notions, in fact, have locked Marian into a cage, a prison, and
Niel is actually thrilled by the very idea of her imprisonment.
On one occasion of a visit to Marian, for example, Niel finds her
lounging in a hammock "slung between two cottonwoods, in the
low glade. . .where he had fallen the time he broke his arm."
He approaches Marian, reaches out to catch her, and discovers
the sensation produced by the Marian "caught" in his arms to be
most delightful: "How light and alive she was! Like a bird
caught in a net. If only he could rescue her and carry her off like
this,—off the earth of sad, inevitable periods, away from age,
weariness, adverse fortune!" (pp. 109-110). Although Niel's
romantic illusions are on the surface less abrasive than Ivy's
determination to get back at Mrs. Forrester for always being
"high-and-mighty" with him, they are no less suggestive of a desire to control her. His supposedly gallant cutting of the telephone wires with the shears is prefigured in his worshipful
cutting of the roses with his knife on the fateful morning when
he makes the pilgrimage to Marian's, only to find her not on her
pedestal but in bed with Frank Ellinger (pp. 85-86). And both
acts are, in the end, aligned with Ivy's blinding of the woodpecker. They are efforts to dominate woman, to destroy something natural.[10]

For her part, of course, Marian glories in being the traditional lady of romance, in being the dark heroine as well as the

light.   Cather frequently uses black/white imagery to describe Marian's appearance or to predict Niel's simplistic, romantic perception of her.   She loves to be worshipped as a goddess and a seductress (the scene in which the bull chases a delighted Marion who is "stubbornly clinging to the crimson parasol that had made all the trouble" [p. 13] metaphors this characteristic), and she loves being envied by other women.   She delights in her aristocratic possessions and leisure, her beautiful clothes, and her expensive jewels.   And she is always a determined coquette.   Her preference for entertaining younger men is well known.   Everything she does, in fact, she does in order to attract men.   In good times and bad, Marian seems to be doing little else but courting men.

In addition to representing what Willa Cather accepts in part as Marian's natural enjoyment of male attention, Marian's behavior and delight can also be regarded as a function of her dependency and, hence, a consequence of her entrapment.   As such, it may be something akin to what Moll Flanders claims affected her during her long imprisonment in Newgate.   At first, Moll explains, she was disconsolate and desperate over the wretchedness of her physical and spiritual torment.   As time passed, however, she "became as naturally pleas'd and easie with the Place, as if indeed I had been Born there" (*MF,* p. 217).

Moll, no doubt, is tendering a doubly ironic statement.   She *was* born in Newgate prison, and her feelings of ease and pleasure, besides affording her a kind of *deja vu* experience, were the result of the madness to which she fell victim as a result of her wretched state.   But there is another truth embedded in Moll's irony, a truth which applies to Moll's general state of imprisonment in a society Defoe regarded as unresponsive to woman's rights and needs.   Prolonged exposure to society's neglect and abuse of her has forced her to find her pleasures within the context of that essential neglect.   Thus, as Moll realizes that she actually learned to enjoy stealing, she also realizes that woman has learned to enjoy the perverse behavior which has been necessitated by her low socio-economic status.   In short, she has adapted.

The very same truth may apply to Marian Forrester who, as representative woman, has become "pleas'd and easie" with her

place in society. Her form of adaptation, however, particularly her quenchless thirst for male attention, is as deleterious as Moll's penchant for stealing gold watches. Because of their respective "professions," Moll and Marian live virtually without the friendship of other women, a situation that Moll openly rues time and time again. Although she accepts some responsibility for this situation, admitting that she has used other women for her economic ends much as they have used her, she regrets the loss nevertheless. Unlike Moll, Marian Forrester never expresses any sorrow over her lack of female camaraderie, but her actions reveal a void that Willa Cather, who cherished her own friendships with women, would consider harmful. Marian, in fact, scorns other women, paticularly those like Constance Ogden whom she perceives to be competition. More than once, Niel Herbert witnesses—with approval, no less!—Marian's disdain for her own kind: he "noticed that in describing the charms of other women, Mrs. Forrester always made fun of them a little" (p. 37).

The vulgar townswomen—the "gossips" who come to the Forrester home during the Captain's final illness more to scavenge than to assist are, in one sense, a reflection of the less attractive dimensions, the Moll-like coarseness or dark side of Marian's own behavior—just as Ivy Peters can be viewed as the dark side of Niel's and the Captain's behavior toward Marian. Their own situations, moreover, mirror the essence of Marian's situation when the superficial finery is stripped away. Like Marian, these hapless women "trained to petty economies" must survive off the "persons and pocket-books" of their "fellow mortals." Lacking Mrs. Forrester's advantages and aristocratic bearing, the "Mrs. Beasleys and Molly Tuckers" are true sisters of Marian nonetheless. Described contemptuously in Niel's viewpoint as "ants," these graceless women reveal the "Creature," to use Moll's favorite word, woman has become.

A final important parallel between Marian and Moll Flanders involves their rehabilitation and recovery of fortune. Released from the horrid hole of Newgate, Moll is transported to America, to Virginia, where she is united with her Lancashire husband and, after a period of indenture, becomes respectable not only in terms of material prosperity but also in the more important terms (she claims) of spiritual and emotional regeneration. She avows true repentance for her evil deeds and considers

herself most fortunate that America, land of freedom and opportunity, has made possible her liberty and the chance to become a
good Christian wife and mother at last. Whether she is, in fact,
honest in her assertions of spiritual renewal is the question Defoe
leaves his readers to entertain. Is it the money, the Virginia inheritance, that provides her with the kind of rebirth she really
seeks?

Two hundred years later, Marian Forrester finds herself in
much the same circumstances as Moll Flanders, except that the
place which symbolizes Moll's freedom is Marian's prison. After
years of alliance with Ivy Peters—" 'Mrs. Forrester's name is
everywhere coupled with Ivy Peters. . . . She does not look happy. . .her health is failing. . .she has put herself in such a position
that her husband's friends cannot help her' " (pp. 170-171)—
Marian leaves Sweet Water "pretty well gone to pieces" (p. 174).
She goes West to California, the new frontier, where she meets
and marries "rich, cranky old" Collins. Then suddenly Willa
Cather spirits her away to South America, where she is once
again restored to the material pomp and circumstance that she
loves. Ladyship, in the feudal way Marian has come to enjoy it
(i.e., the material benefits of aristocracy and the devotion of lads
like the Blum brothers who "regarded her. . .as one of the rich
and great of the world"), is anachronistic and even suspect in
modern, industrial America. But it is still very much a reality
in other lands where there is a dramatic gap between rich and
poor, where "such a fortunate and privileged class was an
axiomatic fact in the social order" (p. 19).[11]

Marian's "transportation" to another country, like Moll's
transportation to America, is also a measure of the relief she can
achieve by removal from the locale of her sin and her imprisonment. It becomes a form of psychological as well as sheer physical survival. But it has yet another meaning. Unlike Moll Flanders and Hester Prynne, Marian never returns to the site of her
ignominy "to spend the Remainder of [her] Years in sincere
Penitence"—except, that is, by way of the "cheque" she sends
"to the Grand Army Post every year to have flowers put on
Captain Forrester's grave for Decoration Day" (p. 174). However sincere the gesture, it is in one sense also ironic, for it symbolizes Marian's return to the Captain in the only form he and
Sweet Water had ever known her—as a purchased hot house

flower, a decoration. If there is love and loyalty in this remembrance, there may also be defiance and poetic justice.

The upshot of Marian's expatriation and financial recovery, however, which Willa Cather attributes to her personal need for ladyship and to her representative feminine predicament, is as ambiguous as Moll's claim of true rehabilitation. Although the ambiguity does not issue, as it does in *Moll Flanders,* from the unreliability of the I-narrator, it is conveyed through *A Lost Lady's* complex narrative point-of-view which goes beyond Niel Herbert's perceptions and evaluations. As a survivor Marian is to be congratulated. Her methods of surviving and the price she pays for survival, however, are the problematic issues for which Cather supplies some possibilities. Expatriation may permit Marian survival and also wealth; in the context of *Moll Flanders,* it may also slyly imply punishment and penance. But it seems doubtful that Marian finally escapes the original prison, the larger labyrinthine Newgate that man's world is for woman.

Combined with her marriage to another rich and older man, the act of sending a "cheque" for flowers to decorate Captain Forrester's grave may indicate Marian's fundamental, if unconscious, acquiescence to her position as a decorative and cherished object. Her effort to look younger and beautiful, an effort society demands of woman, results in a Marian who is "a good deal made up. . . . Her hair looked as if she dyed it" (p. 173). Moreover, the fact that Ed Elliott and Niel Herbert are delighted that "she was well cared for, to the end" is not necessarily representative of Willa Cather's point-of-view. For all of the genuine "warm" feeling toward Marian this attitude conveys, it also expresses the masculine paternalism and control that have been the problem all along. Like the mutilated woodpecker that creeps back into its hole, Marian has adapted to this domination—this injury—and her removal to South America may, in the larger sense, be more a necessary repetition of the posture of submission than it is rebellion. Like Moll Flanders, whose spiritual recovery suspiciously coincides with financial recovery, Marian's survival and restoration to aristocratic grace depend upon her financial solvency, which in turn depends—now, as always—upon her acceptance of masculine guardianship.

NOTES

[1] Daniel Defoe, *Moll Flanders,* ed. Edward Kelly (New York: W. W. Norton & Company, Inc., 1973); Willa Cather, *A Lost Lady* (New York: Alfred A. Knopf, 1923). All page references to the texts are from these editions.

[2] See, especially, David Stouck, *Willa Cather's Imagination* (Lincoln: University of Nebraska Press, 1975) and Susan J. Rosowski, "Willa Cather's *A Lost Lady:* The Paradoxes of Change," *Novel,* 11 (Fall 1977), 51-62.

[3] Willa Cather was very much opposed to the use of fiction as blatant social protest.

[4] This is not to say, of course, that Malory's or Tennyson's Guinevere lacks complexity as a character, but only that her situation as woman is less profoundly explored.

[5] Daniel Defoe, *The Fortunate Mistress,* introd. Willa Cather (New York: Alfred A. Knopf, 1924).

[6] Cather, Introduction to *The Fortunate Mistress,* p. vii.

[7] Patricia Lee Yongue, "Willa Cather's Aristocrats," Part I, *Southern Humanities Review,* 14 (Winter 1980), 43-56; Part II, 14 (Spring 1980), 11-25.

[8] Alexandra Bergson is not without her problems, including the effects of postponing a love/sex relationship with Carl Linstrum. But her moral situation is simply not as complicated or as studied as Marian's.

[9] Hawthorne's celebration of sewing as a "woman's special art" (in *The Scarlet Letter*) might be construed as a rejection of Moll Flanders' rejection of sewing as the most ambitious profession for a "gentlewoman." Despite her preference for Hawthorne, Willa Cather would probably take Moll's side in this case!

[10]Susan Rosowski (see n. 2) perceives in Niel's act of taking a knife to the roses a subtle yet stunning similarity to Ivy's maiming of the female woodpecker. She penetrates to the essence Niel's efforts to limit Marian, to isolate her, to deny her her humanity.

[11]Defoe's economic theories (see Maximilian Novak, *Economics and the Fiction of Daniel Defoe* [Berkeley and Los Angeles: University of California Press, 1962], pp. 74ff.) supported the idea of a necessary partnership between rich and poor, an idea interesting in the light of Cather's own representation in *A Lost Lady* of the relationship between social classes.

Wright Morris, Women, and American Culture

Joseph J. Wydeven

With the publication of *Plains Song for Female Voices* (1980), Wright Morris has continued his acute probing into the psychology of American culture, this time by focusing directly on women and their lives within that culture. *Plains Song*, published just in time for the author's seventieth birthday, is Morris' thirtieth book, and it is a remarkable one, dealing with material which is at once both familiar and new. Morris has often insisted, sometimes to the exasperation of critics, that his works must be seen as a whole, the novels related to each other through sheer accumulation and the recasting of old themes through the light of new and fresh concerns. Despite the difficulties which this presents to critical scholarship, there is an important sense in which that demand must be honored, for Morris has frequently been misunderstood as a novelist and his themes distorted by critical unwillingness to view him as a writer whose themes have been in continuous development from the start, with *My Uncle Dudley*, in 1942. To a degree which is unusual in American literature, Morris has always reserved the right to change his mind, so that the novels which have already been written become added experiential grist for his mill. *Plains Song for Female Voices* is another Morris novel which must be put into context for its riches to be examined in a critically satisfying way.

As *Plains Song for Female Voices* is both about American culture, specifically as it developed on the Nebraska plains, and about the lives of women, it may be useful at this time to focus on Morris' fiction in its perspectives on women and on the relations between the sexes as consequences of that culture. Morris' project in dealing with these issues has been, despite diversity of method, fairly consistent from the outset, that being to delineate and examine that fine point where nature and culture merge and provide sometimes ambiguous conclusions. About women Morris

has had much to say, and much of that appears at first view to be shot through with contradictions; nevertheless those apparent contradictions are more the result of Morris' view of the nature/culture bifurcation in lived experience than of deliberate obfuscation on the author's part. "Man's culture [is] a hoax," Alexandra Selkirk says to Sharon Rose Atkins in *Plains Song;* "Perhaps a decade, no more, [is] available to women to save themselves, as well as the planet."[1] But Sharon, from her own perspective, understands that Alexandra speaks out of her *nature;* it is her nature to be so bombastic and dogmatic about her own values. This conflict between nature and culture is found frequently in Morris' work, and it is the purpose of this essay to grapple with this pattern in a few of the novels, in order to show that the strengths of *Plains Song for Female Voices* are the result, not of a change of attitude on Morris' part, but of a new development of his thought on a crucial issue.

Often enough our memories of Morris' female characters include portraits of repression and suppression, vengeful resentment, and stifled consciousness—including bitter snipings against men: the expression, almost always uttered with exasperation, of "You men!" echoes throughout the fiction, especially in those novels set on the plains, in which the men, having tamed the frontier, have failed to make good on the living promise of the American Dream inherent in the myth. We recall, for instance, the dogmatic righteousness of Aunt Clara in *The Home Place* (1948), the pathetic indifference of the various women in *The Works of Love* (1952), the vengeful recriminatory attitude of Lois McKee in both *The Field of Vision* (1956) and *Ceremony in Lone Tree* (1960). In the latter book, Lois McKee is near hysterics in her rejection, not only of the culture controlled by men, but of the male principle itself. She equates violence with the male, and the instrument of violence, the gun, with the penis: she would like to do away with things, as she says, which point, and thus she is portrayed in at least part of that novel as the castrating bitch.[2]

But nowhere has Morris attempted to confront the thorny issue of American sexual relations more squarely, working out from his own apparent obsession with the problem, than in *Man and Boy* (1951) and *The Deep Sleep* (1953), both of which are set in suburban Pennsylvania in the early 1950s. Morris' own

commentary on these books is revealing. In 1957, David Madden posed to Morris a question "raised emphatically by your works: how do you regard women in our society?" In his response, Morris converted "women" into the archetypal American "Woman," and noted that Henry James, in *The American Scene*, had already provided the context: "Betrayed by Man (deprived of him, that is), woman is taking her abiding revenge on him—unconscious in such figures as Mrs. Ormsby [in *Man and Boy*] and Mrs. Porter [in *The Deep Sleep*], where she inherits, by default, the world man should be running. Since only Man will deeply gratify her, the Vote and the Station Wagon leave something to be desired. One either sees this, or one doesn't. As of now both man and woman are tragically duped: the Victor has no way of digesting the spoils."[3]

Mrs. Ormsby and Mrs. Porter are presented as qualified harridans, ruling over the home and its occupants with an iron hand and a curious rigidity of emotion. In *Man and Boy* Mrs. Ormsby is held responsible for failing to provide a viable home for the "boy," Virgil, and both he and his father live their lives in fear of female tyranny. Virgil, unable to find peace in the home, becomes a hunter of the very birds which Mrs. Ormsby claims to love, and ultimately, he seeks a new life in the army— and is killed in action. Most of *Man and Boy* has to do with how Mrs. Ormsby attempts to monumentalize that death for her own purposes, failing to perceive her own crucial role in bringing the death about. The navy—and the implication is that the navy is simply following through on the American Way—has asked *her* (to the exclusion of *Mr.* Ormsby) to dedicate the new ship to be called the *Ormsby* after her son. Mother, as she is called, insists on doing things her own way at the ceremony— including bringing the amazon-like Mrs. Dinardo on board with her and forcing the Commander to hold the women's parasol. The male involvement in the proceedings is stripped away at every turn, presumably in the name of American Motherhood. Readers are left with the understanding that Mother is a revengeful tyrant, with little self-knowledge, but with an uncanny ability to put men in their places and a savage desire to do so. She is a study in the psychology of institutionalized sexual revenge.

Mrs. Ormsby is reconsidered in the character of Mrs. Porter in *The Deep Sleep* two years later, in a novel which is at once

more complex and more artistically satisfying.[4] If *Man and Boy* (and the short story from which it derived, "The Ram in the Thicket") is sometimes too blatant, too grudging against Woman, *The Deep Sleep* is a more subtle and a more penetrating book, certainly one of Morris' most significant despite the fact that critics seldom focus upon it. It is in this book that Morris most confidently works out from Henry James and confronts the issue of sexual relations most candidly. Presented through Morris' use of the multiple point of view, it focuses upon the often bewildered and beleaguered artist Paul Webb—and upon his understandings, grudged as they are, of the role which women play both in his own life and in the culture at large. He returns, with his wife Katherine, for the funeral of his father-in-law Judge Porter, to the house run by Mrs. Porter.

Morris announces early in the novel that the house has much to do with the whole of American life, and that Webb's role of "getting the picture" has more to it than simply coming to understand the Porter "arrangements," but of coming to comprehend the relationship of the Porter household to the wider implications of American life as a whole: the house is a microcosm. "Beginning at the back, beginning with the kitchen, each room seemed to open on a wider vista, a deeper, more ambitious prospect of American life," Webb observes. He had traveled abroad "in order to return to this room and rediscover America. To find in this house the spaciousness of American life. . . . It was the house, the house itself, set in its miniature surburban [sic] forest, that brought the conflicting forces together and gave them shape. It added up to more than the sum of the separate lives."[5]

The house, he discovers, is run by a woman who is self-assured, abrupt in mannerism, principled, and undaunted by anything she fails to understand. (Katherine concludes that her mother is a "hermetically sealed unit," breathing free of "the life that distracted everybody else" [*DS*, p. 152].) Judge Porter's life had been lived largely outside the house, on "Porter's Island," or hidden away in the bushes where he consumed the banana candy forbidden him in the house; or else in private hideaways in the basement (where his private booze and his law books are hidden away: "The law hiding under the basement stairs. . ." [*DS*, p. 141]) or in the attic where he had hidden the

fine Swiss watch which symbolized his marriage to Mrs. Porter, and where he had retired for his secret smokes, leaving the butts to float in the water at the bottom of a lidded nightpot. Mrs. Porter's principles had always proved too much for the Judge. Too much, too, for Katherine, who had once attempted suicide and later run off, with her father's good wishes, to college in England. And too much, too, for the son, Roger, who like Virgil Ormsby, had found his life outside the house and looked upon running off to war as a preferable alternative to emotional deprivation.

The house is run by Mrs. Porter on inflexible principles, causing the family members to lead lives of guarded emotion—to the point of neurosis. The grandmother, in constant revolt, maintains a discreet emotional distance, yet she subtly defies domestic principles at every turn; Webb, despite his caustic critical attitude towards her, sees in her "the last hope of the world for privacy" (*DS,* p. 145), perhaps because of her rebellious independence. In her, Morris suggests, the past lives on as a kind of judgment on the present. Webb's usual antipathy to her stems, one must conclude, from both her indestructibility *and* her ineffectuality: her judgments are tacit ones, self-centered, more in the interests of her own integrity (and hunger: her physical appetite is enormous), than in the interests of an emotional life. She exists, rather, as a principle of life: she eats, sleeps, and endures. But she had not, apparently, been able to provide for the Judge the proper equipment for dealing on an emotional level with women. In short, she seems to represent an appetite for experience and longevity, tradition and privacy which is essentially passive. Haunting the house, she has yet no part to play in its management.

Worse, the Grandmother had trained the Judge to be emotionally passive. In the middle of the novel, Webb observes a woman holding firmly to a boy's hand; the more the boy struggles to free himself, the more determinedly the mother grasps him. The boy is then forced to sit on the woman's lap, straddling her leg:

> They were, it seemed to Webb, not two people at all but one joined
> person, and the child was a mirror in which the mother saw herself,
> . . .she searched him like a map for some key word, some familiar

sign, something that pointed to the past, or the future, some likeness of a lover or some conception of her better self. They were not, for the moment, two people but one, the child straddling the leg was still part of the mother, as if the hydra-headed monster had learned to spawn and admire itself. Nothing, it seemed to Webb, would ever tear them apart. *Through the clasped hands a current seemed to pass, the same force that drew the salmon up the river, leaping, and drove the lemmings on their suicidal movement to the sea.* (*DS*, pp. 182-183; my italics)

Webb sees in this tableau of mother and child something of greater significance: "The woman and the child, the hook-up of nature that was both public and private, seemed to sum up all the problems that he was powerless to resolve" (*DS*, p. 183). Several pages later, Webb sees the Judge's photograph in the newspaper, a photograph which "made him look strangely distracted, as if the Judge, as well as Webb, had just turned his gaze from the mythic, hydra-headed mother and child. The pair of them drawn together by the same force that drew the salmon, leaping, up the river, and men, as well as lemmings, to some fatal rendezvous with the sea" (*DS*, p. 186).

What Morris is suggesting here through reiteration is that there is something more than cultural in the relationships between the sexes, that in fact the bond between the mother and boy is a natural determinism not to be overcome through merely social change—or cultural explanations. In fact, Webb finds the image of the hydra-headed monster appalling because it suggests something "natural" (that is, in congruence with Nature) in the entrapment of the male by the female. As Mrs. Porter operates by principle, so does Nature and by extension, so do the instinctual drives of men towards "some fatal rendezvous with the sea."

Principles, in Webb's understanding, can be comprehended but they are difficult to change once they have atrophied—and in their reification or automatization they contradict autonomous growth: in the American system as it is the boy will always be subject to the mother, the male to the female. If such is the nature of things, then the matriarchate of American life is beyond salvation; it is a "given" opposing rationality or will. When Webb pays final homage to Mrs. Porter by hiding the

Judge's Swiss watch where she will easily be able to find it, he is not surrendering his right to protest; he is merely doing obeisance to a principle which he feels he can't change, but which must be respected for its own logic and integrity. He can't change it because it goes beyond the scope of intellectual synthesis, rooted in the life-force itself (as that life-force has evolved through the American cultural system).

In this manner Morris may be said to wed Henry James to D. H. Lawrence, cultural problematics to "blood consciousness." It is an uneasy alliance. Women, repressing their own inner natures for the sake of a culture run by men, turn *against* Nature and their own best qualities, and they become destructive victims of a debilitating system. *The Deep Sleep,* as a whole, serves as a variation on Freud, from *Civilization and Its Discontents:*

> . . .women soon come into opposition to civilization and display their retarding and restraining influence—those very women who, in the beginning, laid the foundations of civilization by the claims of their love. Women represent the interests of the family and of sexual life. The work of civilization has become increasingly the business of men, it confronts them with ever more difficult tasks and compels them to carry out instinctual sublimations of which women are little capable. Since a man does not have unlimited quantities of psychical energy at his disposal, he has to accomplish his tasks by making an expedient distribution of his libido. What he employs for cultural aims he to a great extent withdraws from women and sexual life. His constant association with men, and his dependence on his relations with them, even estrange him from his duties as a husband and father. Thus the woman finds herself forced into the background by the claims of civilization and she adopts a hostile attitude towards it.[6]

Morris' response to this problem of the female capitulation to male culture is, in novels which followed *The Deep Sleep,* to create female characters with audacity and will to rebel. These audacious females include the *ewige weibliche* figures of Eva Baum, Cynthia Pomeroy, and Etoile in the novels, respectively, *Love Among the Cannibals* (1957), *What a Way to Go* (1962), and *Ceremony in Lone Tree* (1960). In these books Morris, drawing upon the "wisdom of the body" from Sir Charles Sherrington, utilizes something of Lawrence's notions regarding

human vitality, and according to G. B. Crump, of the vitalism of Bergson.[7]

Similar to these figures, but with less of the *ewige wei-bliche* connotation, are Alec in *One Day* (1965)—who protests futilely against the culture lying behind the Kennedy assassination by giving up her newborn child to the dog pound—and the rebellious hippie hitchhiker of *Fire Sermon* (1971). Indeed, this movement towards rebellious females unwilling to bend to male culture is intentional on Morris' part. Speaking to Wayne Booth in 1975, he noted: "In short, I am shifting over to the female some of the audacity that seemed to be wasted on the males. I am becoming more sympathetic with the new than I was with the old. . . . My fiction seems to be changing. Again."[8] In *Plains Song for Female Voices* that new sympathy receives full—and triumphant—treatment.

* * * * *

Plains Song for Female Voices, as has been remarked by reviewers, functions through counterpoint, layers and layers of female voices (worked out through third person and omniscient methods of narration) swelling into a chorus: through these female voices Morris writes of the emotional lives of women in a manner close to social history, so that the reader is left, not only with particular voices, but also with voices singing in unison. What this amounts to is a kind of paean to womanly endurance within the crippling American Dream, as well as a recasting of a crucial segment of American history (the century ending with Vietnam) from the viewpoints of women. Its focus on the Nebraska plains, the book deals with the movement to the frontier and with twentieth century backtrailing to the East, with West and East, in addition to their presence as geographical concepts, serving as the emotional antipodes in the lives of the two central women portrayed.

Plains Song deals with three generations of women in the Atkins family, beginning with Cora, with whom the book opens: it is her emotional presence which haunts the novel as well as the individual lives within it; it is she—for better or for worse—

against whom the other women in the family measure themselves. Like many another woman in nineteenth-century America, Cora had made the move west as a young bride; settling with her husband Emerson in Madison County, Nebraska, she then lives out her life there. Certainly not a cerebral type, she is a woman whose sheer powers of endurance mark her place in social history as courageous and, above all, as faithful to the principles which are part of her heritage. She and Emerson have one child, Madge, but more important to the course of the novel is the daughter of Emerson's brother Orion and his wife Belle Rooney (a woman with the hillbilly "wildness" of the Ozarks in her blood). This daughter is Sharon Rose, and she is reared by Cora after the death of Belle; Madge and Sharon grow up nearly as sisters. If Cora is the best representative of the stifled, but valiant, life on the plains, Sharon Rose is the chief opposing force, for she rejects the plains, and although she rejects the people who inhabit the plains as well, she finds that she is attached emotionally to them. This attachment, indeed, is perhaps the largest issue which the novel attempts to probe and clarify.

If Cora and Sharon Rose embody the principles of two distinct ways of life, there are two central events which receive symbolic and metaphoric meaning through reiteration, and finally, in the case of Cora, through combination in memory. The first of these occurs early in the novel: Cora, having sexual intercourse for the first time (and apparently the last) with Emerson, is so aghast at the brutality of the experience that she bites through the knuckle of her hand, to the bone, in order to keep from screaming out. Emerson's explanation to the doctor the next day is that a horse bit her, and this is an explanation which is acceptable to all, including Cora, who senses the need for a public explanation for something which cannot really be discussed.

The second event takes places years later, and it is used to clarify Sharon Rose's relationships to other people, specifically to Madge, and indirectly to all of the others: the event precipitates her departure for Chicago. Already appalled by the social understanding that girls are reared specifically to become wives, Sharon Rose, on her return from a trip, finds Madge spooning with a boy. " 'Is he looking for a wife or a housemaid?' " Sharon screams out, within hearing of Cora.

Cora had been on the screened-in porch, ironing; she had stood leaning on the iron, speechless. Nothing had prepared her to believe that Sharon Rose had such resentment, such bitterness, in her. Cora had followed her into Fayrene's room, off the kitchen, seized her by the wrist, and whacked her palm with the back of a hairbrush, sharply. How well they knew what Sharon Rose thought of her hands! "That will teach you!" Cora cried, knowing that it wouldn't even as she said it. Not Sharon Rose. She had turned from Cora and run up the stairs.[9]

Cora's anger in striking Sharon Rose with the hairbrush is remembered well by both the women. For Sharon Rose it seems to symbolize both Cora's rigid acceptance of the limited role which women are meant to play in life and her half-stifled understanding of human motivations. Ironically, the physical act itself seems to draw the women closer together in relation to their separate statuses as women; certainly the act forces Cora to re-examine her own situation with Emerson. For Cora the event becomes linked to the horrors of her own experience with intercourse. Two-thirds through the novel, Cora remembers Sharon's words on seeing Madge and Ned Kibbee kissing, and she sees Sharon Rose's similarities to herself: "It might have been last summer, it might have been this morning, Cora standing in the pickle-sharp draft off the kitchen, except that now she knew, as she hadn't before, that Sharon Rose had meant it just as she had said it. It had not been a horse that bit her, she had bitten herself" (*PS,* p. 164). What Cora understands in this juxtaposition of memories is that both she and Sharon Rose have been victimized by a male-oriented system which tends to limit women's potentials. Sharon's rebellion against that system is more open and concrete than Cora's biting of her hand. As for Sharon, she realizes later that her resentment of the system is founded on the fact that it severs close relations between women—as in her own relations with Madge.

When later in the novel Sharon invites Madge's daughter Blanche to Chicago, supposedly to "save" her from the plains environment, she does so out of "suppressed feelings of guilt" (*PS,* p. 146), and she is determined to make amends for her previous neglect of the folks on the home place. The form which this takes is revealing, for Sharon Rose takes Blanche under her wing for interesting, and personal, reasons: "Sharon could no

longer bear the thought, nor avoid it, that this girl child would soon appeal to some loutish youth stimulated by the seasonal fall of pollen, and be thick with child. The thought almost sickened her. In a family of girls one sacrifice (Fayrene's) was enough. Before the cocoon of Blanche's childhood had peeled away she would be locked into the trap that nature and man had set for her" (*PS*, p. 148). Blanche stays with Sharon for an extended time, but finally when the young girl is discovered to have an interest in boys, Sharon appears to give up on her, and Blanche is returned to Nebraska. Sharon tells Madge that Blanche is simply "not a city girl. Madge was relieved to hear her say so, because her father had been wondering why they had her in the first place if she wasn't at home where they could enjoy her, before she got married" (*PS*, p. 161).

There is a third event which serves as an epiphany in the novel, showing us something of the ambivalence and ambiguity in Sharon's motivations for moving away from Nebraska. Returning east after one of her home visits, Sharon sits next to a young man on the train. The young man clears a spot in the window to catch a last glimpse of what is outside—to see, that is, the place he will in the future be *from,* having escaped it.

> [Sharon] saw nothing but his reflection. "Boy, am I glad to see the last of that!" he said, happy in his freedom, in his expectations that whatever life held for him in the future, it would henceforth be his own life, it would not be the life of Battle Creek or Colby, it would not be the trauma of birth or burial, or mindless attachments to persons and places, to kinships, longings, crossing bells, the arc of streetlights, or the featureless faces on station platforms, all of which would recede into the past, into the darkness— wouldn't it?   (*PS*, p. 137)

The question at the end is Sharon Rose's, based on her own discoveries that one does not simply leave the past behind. In seeing the young man Sharon sees herself, for if he is from Colby, it is *she* who is from Battle Creek. The passage reflects upon her own ambivalent misgivings.

The major issue of the novel receives its crucial treatment in yet another of Sharon Rose's returns to Nebraska, this time for the funeral of Cora near the end of the book. Sharon is met this

time by Caroline, another of Madge's daughters, who drives her past the place which was once the home place, but which is now being bulldozed out of existence. In the car, Caroline and Sharon Rose have a conversation which puts their relations with Cora into perspective:

"Poor Cora!" Sharon blurted.

"I'll never forgive her," said Caroline. "Never."

"Caroline!" Sharon cried. She almost barked it, but her eagerness to hear more shamed her.

"She never complained. An animal would have complained. She would still be in all that rubble if they hadn't moved her."

A hand to her eyes, Sharon felt her head was splitting. The air trapped about her face smelled of flint.

"At least I can complain," Caroline said. "She couldn't."

With an effort Sharon said, "She *could* have, Caroline, but she simply *wouldn't.*"

"Could or wouldn't, she didn't," said Caroline, "and now she's dead." *(PS,* p. 201)

Caroline prides herself on being a "modern" woman, free to indulge her emotions; she is clearly one of the interim results of a growth of consciousness in women: she is as least able to articulate her understandings. But Sharon is appalled and stunned at the apparent savagery of Caroline's remarks, the crassness of her rejection of Cora's strength of character. By this time in the novel Sharon has come to realize that Cora's strength is something useful to all women: the "animal" qualities of the plains people in general speak to traditional forms of faith and endurance which the younger generations are apparently rejecting out of hand.

All of this has final relevance when Sharon returns to the motel to keep her appointment with a woman she had met earlier in the Boston airport, Alexandra Selkirk, described as similar in

appearance and character to Cora. Alexandra is a feminist of some reputation, dogmatic in her belief that "Women's previous triumphs had been by default. Men had simply walked away from the scene of the struggle, leaving them with the children, the chores, the culture and a high incidence of madness" (*PS*, pp. 188-189). Together with Alexandra later, Sharon hears a rooster crowing:

> The sound was piercing, but cracked, shrill with young male as-surance, transporting Sharon to the hush of a summer dawn, the faint stain of light between the sill and the blind at her window, the house dark as a cave, in the stairwell the sounds of stove lids being lifted, shifted, the pungent whiff of kerosene spilled on the cobs, the rasp of a match, and in the silence following the whoosh and roar of the flames the first clucking of the hens in the hen-house, all of it gone, vanished from this earth, but restored to the glow of life in a cock's crow.

> "You hear that?" said Alexandra. "The same old tyrant!" Was it a smile she turned to share with Sharon or a grimace? This would be a young tyrant, not an old one, but it seemed unim-portant in the context. His voice gained in assurance. . . .
>
> (*PS*, pp. 227-228)

Like *Ceremony in Lone Tree, Plains Song for Female Voices* ends with dawn providing a hopeful, reinvigorated sense of the fullness of life. Beginning with Cora on her death bed, the novel moves first backward in time and then forward to this conclu-sion, in a fairly typical sense of cyclical movement found fre-quently in Morris. With Cora's death now in the past, and with the home place inexorably plowed under, Sharon makes mani-fest her realization that if she has rejected Man's culture, she has not rejected Man. The burden of her life might have been easier to bear if she had been able to come to terms sooner with the meaning of the rural past into which she had been thrust at birth. Her rejection of the plains psychology carries with it the knowledge—accumulated through time and memory—that wo-men on the plains, as elsewhere, are to be valued for their in-tegrity and for their refusal to submit wholly to male culture. In the end, in accepting Cora as well as Alexandra Selkirk, Sharon is also able to accept the meaning of the past as that meaning is reshaped in the present: Alexandra, that is, has her

own nature which links her—and Sharon—to the past as embodied and identified in Cora Atkins. Sharon's feminism, then, is this complex understanding, not to be simplified in Alexandra's terms.

Thus, over a distance of thirty years, Morris returns closely to the materials of two novels written in the late forties, *The Home Place* and *The Works of Love,* both of which take their resonance from the plains experience in cultural history and the stifled life of the emotions consequent upon that history. If in *The Home Place* we are given an account of the return of a native, so also in *Plains Song:* Sharon Rose returns several times in the course of the book, always freshly shocked at what she sees upon her return, at the same time that she comes to understand the invisible threads which hold her heart to its origins. Moreover, as in *The Home Place,* we are given again those wonderful scenes in which family conversations take place—point, counterpoint, pointcounterpoint—which is certainly one of the things which Morris does most compellingly, with the returned native trying to fit all the pieces of her life together from the welter of voices speaking all about her. And finally, the use by Morris of one of his poignant photographs as chapter divisions adds a haunting and resonant quality to *Plains Song.* This photograph, reminding us of the phototext experimentation in *The Home Place,* is of a mirror which reflects back to us a group of photographs, the only sign of life in the picture. The mirror holds us, reflecting back to us the photographs which recall the past, while the mirror itself speaks to us of our own potential reflections. Thus, the photograph enhances the novel's theme of the necessity for rethinking the past, and of the continuous process which humans must undergo as they re-evaluate their memories in the light of present needs. The photo is itself counterpoint to the prose which carries the novel forward.[10]

But I find that *Plains Song for Female Voices* is closest of all to *The Works of Love,* certainly a strange pairing in light of the passivity and the failure of the protagonist of that book, Will Brady. But in many ways, the problem announced in the opening pages of *The Works of Love* is crucial also to *Plains Song,* particularly as that problem pertains to Sharon Rose. Brady, the inheritor of the plains psychology from his parents, goes east, as does Sharon Rose. In Brady's case, "This desolate

place, this rim of the world, had been God's country to Adam Brady, but to his wife, Caroline Clayton, a godforsaken hole. Perhaps only Will Brady could combine these two points of view. He could leave it, that is, but he would never get over it."[11] Brady never manages to understand the psychology he had been born into; his emotional passivity stifles even his abilities to comprehend the nature of reality. But, like Sharon Rose, he deliberately attempts to escape the Nebraska plains, backtrailing to the East—and both Brady and Sharon Rose come to rest (temporarily in Sharon Rose's case) in Chicago. But whereas Brady wastes away his days still grappling with the American Dream, Sharon Rose—somewhat reminiscent of Willa Cather—pursues a life in art: in music she senses the underpinnings of an emotional life which she had been denied on the plains. Nevertheless, like Brady, she only dimly senses her motives at first, and much of her life remains submerged. Like Brady, that is, Sharon Rose could leave the plains environment, but she would never get over it; and she recognizes that her motives have been more complex than she had known.

Both *The Works of Love* and *Plains Song* deal with the issues of hidden motives, submerged emotions, the problems involved in the articulation of complex feelings—all of which result from plains upbringings and subsequent inabilities to find the city of Chicago a sufficient place to quiet the yearnings for a better life. But having noted these similarities, I must point out that whereas *The Works of Love* dwells in pathos through the character of an *individual, Plains Song,* through its point of view and method of counterpoint, works out its themes through the *family;* and rather than showing failure, *Plains Song* stresses the powers of endurance and the growth of consciousness through interplay with family members and an intelligent use of memory. If *The Works of Love* attempted to grapple with the problem of the inarticulation of love in American culture (at least in the Midwest, using Sherwood Anderson as a guide), *Plains Song* deals primarily with change over time and through generations, showing both the rootedness of female strength and the invisible umbilical cords which stretch from one generation to another, from Chicago to northeastern Nebraska. It is not the least of the similarities between the two books that in so many ways they are the obverse of each other.

Finally, *Plains Song for Female Voices* is a moving and compassionate study of American life and of the women whose lives have been silenced as a result of the peculiarities of American history and of the failures of the male-oriented system to provide emotional meanings which are necessary for the attainment of human fulfillment. That Morris has consistently set as one of his goals as a novelist and critic the understanding of this emotional diminishment in our culture is clear. With *Plains Song* Morris returns to his thematic concern with the plains, but he does so now with a new sense of compassion. There is a wisdom in this book which, as I have tried to demonstrate, is at least an interim summation of the concerns for American culture which Morris has always evinced. If in the fifties Morris dealt with the apparent tyranny of women in the figures of Mrs. Ormsby and Mrs. Porter, his work has evolved now to a fresh focus on the strengths of the will to survive and to achieve human freedom for both men and women.

NOTES

[1]Wright Morris, *Plains Song for Female Voices* (New York: Harper & Row, 1980), p. 188.

[2]See Wright Morris, *Ceremony in Lone Tree* (1960, rpt. Lincoln: University of Nebraska Press, 1973), p. 58, but see entire section, pp. 57-69.

[3]Wright Morris, "Letter to a Young Critic," *The Massachusetts Review*, 6 (1964-1965), 99. The letter is dated 7 December 1957.

[4]See John Aldridge and Wright Morris, "The American Novelist and the Contemporary Scene," in *Conversations with Wright Morris,* ed. Robert Knoll (Lincoln: University of Nebraska Press, 1977), p. 17, where Morris comments on Mrs. Porter as a "reconsideration" of Mrs. Ormsby.

[5]Wright Morris, *The Deep Sleep* (1953, rpt. Lincoln: University of Nebraska Press, 1975), p. 7. Future references to this novel are noted in the text, with the abbreviation *DS*.

[6]Sigmund Freud, *Civilization and Its Discontents,* trans. James Strachey (New York: Norton, 1961), pp. 50-51.

[7]I have discussed Morris' indebtedness to Sir Charles Sherrington's *Man in His Nature* in my dissertation, "Structures of Consciousness in the Works of Wright Morris," Purdue University 1979, pp. 169-248; G. B. Crump discusses Bergson in relation to Morris in *The Novels of Wright Morris: A Critical Interpretation* (Lincoln: University of Nebraska Press, 1978), pp. 11-15.

[8]Wright Morris and Wayne Booth, "The Writing of Organic Fiction," in *Conversations with Wright Morris,* ed. Robert Knoll (Lincoln: University of Nebraska Press, 1977), p. 100.

[9]Wright Morris, *Plains Song for Female Voices,* p. 75. Future references to this novel are noted in the text, with the abbreviation *PS*.

[10]The Penguin paperback edition, disappointingly, utilizes a different illustration, not the photograph found in the original edition of *Plains Song*.

[11]Wright Morris, *The Works of Love* (1952; rpt. Lincoln: University of Nebraska Press, 1972), pp. 12-13.

The Young Girl in the West:
Disenchantment in Jean Stafford's Short Fiction

Mary Ellen Williams Walsh

In the Pulitzer Prize-winning *The Collected Stories of Jean Stafford,* Stafford groups ten stories under the heading, "Cowboys and Indians, and Magic Mountains."[1] The heading, which suggests a romantic, mythic West of the past filled with red men and white men in conflict, ironically comments on the contemporary, restricted lives of the characters in Stafford's stories who grow up overshadowed by that myth. For Stafford's central characters are girls and young women and a small Indian boy. They live in a modern West, most of them in one small town, a vantage point from which they get only occasional glimpses of the glorious West that was. They are, for the most part, separated both by time and by sex from the expansive Western tradition which provides a sharp contrast to their cramped and painful lives.

Seven of the stories are set in Adams, Colorado. In the "Author's Note" to *The Collected Stories,* Stafford writes that her "roots remain" in this semi-fictitious town. Adams, Colorado, is in an important sense Stafford's Yoknapatawpha. The stories she sets there strongly define her perception of the reality of the lives of girls and young women in the West. Adams is a quiet college town in the foothills of the Rockies. For each of Stafford's characters, however, the geography of the town is more narrowly defined than in this generalization. For most, the geography is rather bleak; for some, grotesque. The restrictions on their lives are exemplified in how they see where they live.

Nine-year-old Jessie, "The Healthiest Girl in Town," sees Adams as a place where three different classes of tuberculars live out "their static, cautious lives" (p. 197). The rich live in a re-

sort-like hilltop sanitarium. The very poor live on the edge of town in "a settlement of low, mean cottages" (p. 200). The houses of the middle class, the kind of people for whom her mother works as a practical nurse, are epitomized by the home of the Butlers, which smells constantly of witch hazel and which is always quiet except for the sounds of illness and approaching death. For Kitty Winstanley, in "The Tea Time of Stouthearted Ladies," Adams is a world of near bankrupt boarding houses where her mother and other boarding house keepers rest their swollen feet and their "tumid hands mutilated by work" (p. 220) in kitchens such as the Winstanley's—"a room all skin and bones: a coal-oil range with gaunt Queen Anne legs, a Hoosier cabinet ready to shudder into pieces, a linoleum rug worn down to gummy blackness save in the places that were inaccessible to feet and still showed forth its pattern of glossy bruises. . ." (p. 221). The narrator of "In the Zoo" and her sister Daisy, who also grew up in the geography of the boarding houses, remember Adams as an "ugly town" with a "dreary park," "mongrel. . . churches," a "high school shaped like a loaf of bread" (p. 285). For them, the college campus was "an oasis of which [they] had no experience except to walk through it now and then. . ." (p. 285).

For Cora Savage, in "The Philosophy Lesson," the college is not an oasis, but a place where she poses nude and immobile for a life drawing class, three mornings a week for three hours at a stretch, ignored by the other students except as she is an object which they paint or draw. Although Polly Bay, in "The Liberation," teaches at the college, for her Adams is reduced to a city block, lined by the ancestral homes of the Bays, a place which induces in her a feeling of claustrophobia. The homes are in various stages of dismantling, which suggest the decay of the Bay family. One has become a museum, one has been made into apartments, and one has been torn down. The fourth is the one in which she lives with her widowed aunt and widowed uncle, a house so "gorged with furniture and with garnishments and clumps and hoards of artifacts of Bays, you had no sense of space. . .and felt cornered and nudged and threatened. . ." (p. 308).

Emily Vanderpool, the narrator of "Bad Characters" and "A Reading Problem," inhabits yet another Adams. While her

own home is a "normal" middle-class household, her travels around Adams take her to the "bedlam" of a Woolworth's, where old men "look as if they were walking over their own dead bodies" (p. 278); to the library, where the librarian wears a yellow wig; to the lobby of a hotel whose permanent residents are querulous old men; to the waiting room of the jail where she overhears obscenities shouted by drunken moonshiners; and finally to a roadside campground where the single occupants are a traveling evangelist-bootlegger and his daughter.

The Adams, Colorado, in which these girls and young women live is, then, collectively a place of illness, poverty, stasis, and grotesquerie. In this landscape, they are allowed little freedom of action. For months, Jessie is forced to spend several afternoons a week enduring boredom and harassment as the captive playmate of the children of her widowed mother's employer, so that her mother will not lose her job. Throughout the deadly afternoons the sickly Butler children lovingly caress their illnesses and deride Jessie's healthiness. The sisters in "In the Zoo" are equally trapped. None of their movements goes undetected or untaunted by their foster mother. She does not object to their visits to their one childhood friend, a gentle, drunken Irishman who lives by the railroad tracks with two capuchin monkeys and several other animals, because these visits allow her to heap verbal abuse on Mr. Murphy. Her greatest triumph over the sisters and their friend is turning the gentle dog given to the girls by Mr. Murphy into a killer that destroys one of his beloved capuchins.

Emily Vanderpool, whose family and social class at least allow her the freedom of choosing her own friends and moving with relative ease about the town, is nonetheless not shielded from painful and grotesque human situations, which come to her in the persons of Lottie Jump and Opal Gerlash. Emily bewails her "bad character" which causes her to alienate all her friends. Lottie Jump, whom Emily first encounters as a thief in the Vanderpool home, is a hardened, eleven-year-old criminal, "evilly ugly," dressed in filthy, ill-fitting clothes (p. 268). She is a real "bad character," the extension in all details of Emily's somewhat refined fears. Similarly, Emily's "reading problem" is parodied by the situation of Opal Gerlash. When Emily finally finds a place where she can read and memorize the names of

the books of the Bible, Opal and her father intrude upon Emily's peace. Opal, a twelve-year-old con artist who assists her father in selling hell-fire-and-brimstone religion and an alcohol-based liver medicine, recites by rote some of her religious spiel.

The actions of Emily, Jessie, and the sisters in "In the Zoo" are limited partly because they are children. The actions of the older young women in the other Adams stories are, however, equally limited. Cora Savage and Kitty Winstanley are both students at Nevilles College. That they are educating themselves suggests a possible means for them to achieve greater freedom and eventually to escape their current situations. It is important, however, that neither do they consciously consider this point nor does Stafford imply it, other than by portraying them as college students. In fact, in the most stunning image of restriction in the stories, Cora is literally immobile throughout the episode of "The Philosophy Lesson." She poses nude, only her eyes and her mind active, enduring the psychological pain of becoming an object and servant to her fellow students and the harsh physical pain of her straining muscles. Kitty, like Cora, is restricted to the role of servant to her fellow students each evening in her mother's boarding house. Each summer she escapes to the comparative freedom of a dude ranch, where as a hired servant she is in a less ambiguous position than she is in at home, but where she exists at the whim of the dudes and her employers and where her day is circumscribed by chores from 5 a.m. to 9 p.m.

Polly Bay spends her almost thirty years hemmed in by her family's Western chauvinism and inherited bigotries, symbolized by the city block on which they all lived, which Polly feels as a "zone restricted for the use of her blood kin, for there lingered in it some energy, some air, some admonition that this was the territory of Bays and that Bays and ghosts of Bays were, and forever would be, in residence" (p. 309). She acquiesces to all the family's demands, living to please them, so that she feels her life is "a dream of smothering" (p. 309).

The family situations of the girls and young women in the Adams stories contribute to their powerlessness. Most of the characters are in fact either orphans or the children of invalid fathers. Thus, early in their lives they have experienced the deep

emotional loss caused by the death or lingering illness of a parent and the resulting psychological and physical deprivation. While Emily Vanderpool's parents are both very much alive, the distortions in the lives of her alter egos are at least partially explained by missing or disabled parents. Opal Gerlash's mother had died a year before Emily encounters her. Lottie Jump's father was slowly dying of tuberculosis. Although Cora Savage fondly remembers some childhood experiences with her father, he is absent from her reflections on the present. It is only her "anxious United Presbyterian" mother whom she has had to reassure about her posing nude (p. 361). Kitty Winstanley's father has lost a lung. His inability to find work and the constant fear and bitterness of his wife as they live "hand to mouth, one jump ahead of the sheriff" (p. 222) unman him, in the eyes of Kitty, who hates him for his weakness and hates her mother "for her injustice" and hates "herself for hating in them what they could not help" (p. 222).

The other characters are true orphans. Jessie, in all her health, is "possessed with the facts of dying and of death" (p. 198), especially by the memory of her father's death from gangrene. While she retains the consolation of a "valiant, pretty" mother (p. 200), the two of them are subject because of her father's death to having to please people like the Butlers so that they may live. The deaths of both their parents place the sisters in "In the Zoo" in the hands of the paranoiac Mrs. Placer, herself the widow of a tubercular husband. Griefstricken for their parents and with no responsible relatives to offer them comfort, the girls are left to grow up "like worms," in a house "steeped in. . .mists of accusation and hidden plots and double meanings. . ." (p. 287).

Both Polly Bay's parents are also dead. Her mother died when she was a child. Her father's death, seven years prior to the action of "The Liberation," has placed her at the mercy of her aunt and uncle: "Both widowed and both bereft of their heartless children, [they] had cajoled her and played tricks upon her will until she had consented to go and live with them. It was not so much because she was weak as it was because they were so extremely strong that she had at last capitulated out of fatigue. . ." (p. 307).

Orphaned or near-orphaned, caught like insects in amber in restricted situations, living in a nightmarish landscape, the girls and young women cope with their situations, but they do not resolve them. Jessie is unable to free herself from spending the obligatory afternoons with the Butler children. She does however defy them with her vitality and frees herself from the feeling they had imposed on her that her health was a "disgrace" (p. 206). In a purging of fear and anguish and as a reaction to their torture, she admits she has lied about her father's dying of leprosy. She exultantly exclaims: " 'He got shot out hunting, if you want to know. . . . My father was as tall as this room. The district nurse told Ma that I am the healthiest girl in town. Also I have the best teeth' " (p. 216).

The sisters in "In the Zoo" cope by adapting their behavior to the suspicions of Mrs. Placer, living "in a mesh of lies and evasions, baffled and mean, like rats in a maze" (p. 300). As adults, they wonder why they had not fled their situation as soon as they were old enough to work. They realize, the narrator concludes, that Mrs. Placer had "held us trapped by our sense of guilt. We were vitiated, and we had no choice but to wait, flaccidly, for her to die" (p. 301). The sisters as adults feel themselves at last free of the "succubus" who had preyed on them. Their farewell remarks to each other, however, reveal that they have been permanently damaged by the suspicion and hostility toward other people that Mrs. Placer ingrained in them, even to the point of their unconsciously using her favorite phrase, "I had to laugh," to preface their spiteful remarks about the narrator's fellow passengers.

Polly Bay is awakened to her situation when she falls in love and begins planning to leave her aunt and uncle. She begins to understand how she had coped. She sees, "appalled and miserably ashamed of herself, that she had never once insisted on her own identity in this house. She had dishonestly, supinely (thinking, however, that she was only being polite), allowed her aunt and uncle to believe that she was contented in their house, in sympathy with them, and keenly interested in the minutiae that preoccupied them. . . . She had never disagreed with them. . ." (p. 310). She counts herself lucky that unlike Aunt Lacy, her uncle's wife, she had not had to die to free herself of the Bays. In an outrageous irony, her fiancé does die. Nonetheless, her

love for him and the realization that her love has brought to her about her life continue the impetus for her "liberation." She leaves Adams, not triumphantly as she has expected, but fleeing, taking with her only the clothes she is wearing.

Kitty Winstanley survives by being absolutely realistic about her situation. Her mother and her mother's friends *must* live by illusion, "lest the full confrontation with reality shatter them to smithereens" (p. 220). They cannot admit "to the monotonous terror of debt that kept them wakeful at night despite the weariness that was their incessant condition, or to the aching disappointment to which they daily rose, or to their hopeless, helpless contempt for their unemployed husbands. . ." (p. 200). Kitty does. Despite the rosy picture her mother paints of her as a college student, she knows that she and the children of similar households are "exhausted from classes and study and part-time jobs and perpetually starved for status. . .and clothes . . .and fun" (p. 224). The summers at the dude ranch, which her mother describes as Kitty's "vacation with pay," Kitty knows to be "friendless, silent, long and exasperating" (p. 228). Nonetheless, Kitty lives through the summers "in pride and without woe" (p. 228), because there at least she can escape the hypocrisy of her life at home.

Cora Savage's body remains frozen in a pose, but her active mind seeks release. The avenues she finds remove her farther from, rather than connect her to, humanity. First she glories in the falling snow, because it dematerializes the studio and conceals "the harshness of the world" (p. 364). Then she reflects on Bishop Berkeley's philosophy and concludes that "she would be at peace forever if she could believe that she existed only for herself and possibly for a superior intelligence and that no one existed for her save when he was tangibly present" (p. 365). Finally, she considers the ultimate dematerialization of self, the possibility of suicide.

Emily Vanderpool, who seems to lead a life that Jessie and Mrs. Placer's foster children would long for, cannot control or resolve by herself the bizarre situations into which she falls. Lottie Jump mesmerizes her. She is afraid that Lottie will "get revenge" on her if she does not join Lottie in the shoplifting venture. Finally, it is she, not Lottie, who is punished when they are

caught. She is trapped by the Gerlashes first because she has been taught to answer when adults ask her a question and secondly because Gerlash physically restrains her while they threaten her.

As the powerless often do, many of these characters turn their frustration inward and begin to hate themselves. Jessie begins to loathe her own health. She sees herself as a "pariah" and begins to be ashamed, she says, "not only of myself but of my mother, who was crassly impervious to disease. . . .I felt left out, not only in the Butler's house but in this town of consumptive confederates" (p. 206). In a terrible irony, she longs to be as ill as her tormentors. Under the tutelage of Mrs. Placer, the orphaned sisters develop a suspicion of themselves which makes them "mope and weep and grimace with self-judgment" (p. 288). As Mrs. Placer destroys their friendship with Mr. Murphy, they wish they were dead and wish they were "something besides kids! Besides girls" (p. 299). Kitty Winstanley hates herself for hating her parents. Cora Savage's thoughts of suicide reveal her self-loathing. Polly Bay feels "an ebbing away of self-respect" (p. 310) and under her uncle's harassment doubts "the testimony of her own eyes, the judgments of her own intellect" (p. 313). Even Emily Vanderpool says, "My badness never gave me half the enjoyment Jack and Stella thought it did. A good deal of the time I wanted to eat lye" (p. 274).

The backdrop against which the lives of these characters are played out is the West of "cowboys and Indians, and magic mountains." None of them, however, participates in the heroic West. Polly Bay comes closest. Her family had migrated to Colorado in a covered wagon in the 1840's, and her senile great-grandmother had talked "without pause of red Indians and storms on the plains" (p. 309), chastising her descendants by saying, "Not a one of you knows the sensation of having a red Indian arrow whiz by your sunbonnet with wind enough to make the ribbons wave" (p. 309). The family's pride in its forebears has calcified to a defense of all things Western, and a hatred of all things Eastern. As Polly contemplates her escape to the East, she realizes the Bays have been "too busy defending the West even to look at it. For all their pride in their surroundings, they had never contemplated them at all but had sat with the shades drawn, huddled under the steel engravings" (p. 319). She

looks forward to a time after the deaths of her aunt and uncle when the young Bays may return, free to view the landscape, when "in their mouths there would not be a trace of the dust of the prairies where, as on a treadmill, Great-grandfather Bay's oxen plodded on and on into eternity" (p. 319).

For Emily Vanderpool, the heroic West is reduced to a collection of "seedy" souvenirs in the lobby of the hotel: "a rusted, beat-up placer pan with samples of ore in it, some fossils and some arrowheads, a tomahawk, a powder horn, and the shellacked tail of a beaver that was supposed to have been trapped by a desperado named Mountain Jim Nugent, who had lived in Estes Park in the seventies" (p. 325). This West has no meaning for Emily except that the collection is the source of an argument between the old men at the hotel that ultimately forces Emily from her reading place.

Other characters have made westward treks which parody the pioneering of the Bays and the tarnished glory of the souvenirs in the hotel. The pastor who sends the orphaned sisters west to their foster home talks to them "of Indians and of buffaloes" (p. 285), trying to use the romance of the West to quiet them. Jessie moves west with her mother "because there were enough [sick] people there to need her [mother's] services and therefore to keep a roof over our heads and shoes on our feet" (p. 197). Kitty Winstanley's family has sought a new life in the West because of her father's health. The same is true of Lottie Jump's family. The situation in "A Philosophy Lesson" suggests the same is true for Cora Savage's family. For these families, with absent or invalid fathers, there is no possibility that the West will yield riches from a placer pan or a trap line or glory from a brush with the Indians.

The image of the young female in the West that emerges in the Adams stories is that of a human being who is powerless, who has few defenses, who exhibits some degree of self-hatred, who lives in a confined psychological and physical space, and whose actions are restricted to surviving in that space, rather than redefining it. Stafford herself fled the West. "As soon as I could," she says, "I hotfooted it across the Rocky Mountains and across the Atlantic Ocean."[2] She was pursued no doubt by the smothering image that she presents in the Adams stories. Staf-

ford does give us glimpses of girls and women whose lives do not seem as circumscribed as the lives of her central characters. Cora Savage and Kitty Winstanley go to school with young women who enjoy all the advantages of wealth. The Butler children can control, not be controlled by, Jessie. Mrs. Butler holds a Phi Beta Kappa key, was a student of Professor Kittredge, and writes plays. It is important to recognize, however, that the lives Stafford chooses to reveal fully *are* circumscribed. The stories also make clear that had she examined the lives of these others, she probably would have found that they too have little freedom. Polly Bay, after all, is a member of a wealthy, prominent family. Emily Vanderpool suffers no economic or physical deprivation.

The other three Western stories in the *Collected Stories* further develop the idea of the West as a place from which romance and heroism have vanished and as a place which is antithetical to young women. "A Summer Day" is set in the Indian territory, in the capital of the Cherokee nation. Jim Littlefield, the eight-year-old orphan who follows his own trail of tears to Oklahoma, symbolizes the diminished stature of the red man in the West. He and his fellow Cherokees, adults and children alike, are wards of Uncle Sam. He is placed in an orphanage, where most of the children are sick, and one has died, as a result of drinking bad water, because the bureaucrats in Washington have failed to provide an adequate septic tank for the orphanage. While Jim enters the orphanage with plans to escape as soon as night falls, he is overpowered by his experiences of the day—by the heat, the isolation, the bureaucracy, the sickness—and decides to delay his escape. As he falls asleep, outside in the heat, alone and unprotected, lying on the "sickly grass," he sees himself "growing smaller and smaller and lying in a bureau drawer" (p. 359). Jim's sense of himself as diminished, his inability to carry out his escape, his confinement in an institution which is riddled by disease—all re-enact the fate of the conquered Indian nations. It is perhaps no accident that Stafford portrays the powerlessness of Jim Littlefield, an Indian, in terms very similar to those she uses to describe the lives of young women in the Adams stories.

Judy, the narrator and central character of "The Mountain Day," has all the advantages that the Adams characters lack. She

is a student at Bryn Mawr, engaged to a handsome and intelligent Harvard student. Her family is loving and wealthy. Vacationing in Colorado with her family, Judy, in this summer of her love, finds the West more beautiful than it has ever been: "The aspen leaves were more brilliant. . ., the upland snow was purer, the pinewoods were more redolent, and the gentle winds in them were more mellifluous; the berries I ate for breakfast came from the bushes of Eden" (p. 235). The same landscape holds danger, however. Huge turtles and hellbenders live in the heart-shaped lake which lies between her father's cabin and her grandmother's house. While Judy is protected from these and other dangers, the young Irish maids who work for her grandmother are not. When they capsize a canoe in the lake, they drown and their bodies are mutilated by the turtles and hellbenders. Thus, against Judy's "storybook summertime romance" (p. 235), Stafford juxtaposes the stark image of the corpses of two young women, "their lovely faces and their work-swollen hands" eaten away (p. 247), an image of what can happen to women in the West infinitely more powerful than the happy ending suggested for Judy.

The last of the ten Western stories, "The Darkening Moon," is emblematic of Stafford's portrayal of the young girl in the West. Ella, the central character, is eleven years old. Her father has been dead for one year. She lives in a small, nameless mining town. Her story takes place completely at night. When we first see her, she is "alone beneath the black firmament and between the blacker mountains that [loom] up to the right and to the left of her like the blurred figures of fantastic beasts" (p. 252). She makes a trip she often makes, riding her brother's horse several miles through the dark to babysit at an isolated farm on the other side of town. Sometimes she dreads the trip because the horse tries to throw her if it is frightened by the sight of the high bluffs along the highway. Once it had tossed her in the path of a bus and left her to walk a mile and a half home in the cold. Tonight she has the added danger of carrying through town ten pounds of elk meat her brother has poached. She postpones her arrival at the farm as long as she dares, knowing that this will be like all the other evenings she has spent there: "Afraid to move lest by moving she make a noise that would obscure another noise. . ., she would sit motionless all evening in a big pink wing chair. . . . By midnight, she would be wringing wet with sweat,

although it was cold and she had let the fire go out. And yet, as soon as she had mounted for the ride back, her fear had changed its focus and she was not anxious to get home, but only to get Squaw safely past the bluff" (p. 254). This night is like the others, except that Ella endures the additional horror of an eclipse of the moon.

Stripped of its narrative particulars, this story embodies Stafford's version of the mythic journey possible to young girls in the West. An orphaned child travels through a dark landscape riding a steed which she has difficulty controlling because the landscape itself threatens the beast. Her destination is a place where she sits paralyzed by fear. She is released from her place of paralysis only to travel once again through the threatening landscape and to return to where she began. This is not the triumphant journey of a hero. Her dark night of the soul does not release her finally into the light of new perceptions and new possibilities. Instead, it is a journey which she is doomed to repeat. The repetition and the willingness with which the young girl reenters her state of paralysis distinguish the horror of her situation. She has accepted the journey as normality.

The stories in the *Collected Stories* do not provide us with a means of comparing the lives of the central female characters with those of boys and young men in similar settings and situations. Stafford's western novel, *The Mountain Lion,* does. Stafford places Molly and Ralph Fawcett, a young sister and brother, in exactly the same situations, makes them equally misfit, and has them share an emotional bond which makes them the male and female sides of the same coin. Their destinies, however, are very different. Molly, unlike the characters in the stories, does not cope and is unable to accept the limited life open to her as a female. Consequently, she must die. She is accidentally shot to death by Ralph, who thus frees himself so that he can reach his full masculine possibilities. Interestingly enough, in commenting on *The Mountain Lion,* which, as nearly as any novel can, equally examines the lives of a young boy *and* a young girl, one critic doesn't even mention Molly.[3] Another critic apparently considers Molly's death a lesser tragedy than the fact that Ralph must grow up with his principles compromised.[4] Only Blanche H. Gelfant, in my opinion, has fully explained the uncomfortable truth the novel presents:

Molly dies, I believe, in a sacrificial ceremony disguised as accident. Her death is demanded by the great masculine myth of the
West—a symbolic place: where boys like Ralph become men; and
girls like Molly become not only extraneous and intrusive, but ac-
tively threatening to the ritual of male initiation. For just as the
West held the promise of innocence, so also it promised manhood.
It defined the terms for manhood by its ritual, which, in the
American novel, might be modified in its details, but never in its
exclusion of women. The young hero going West was to leave all
women behind. In the wilderness he was to join a male tribe of
archetypal hunters. They were to designate a sacred spot of wilderness and a legendary animal, usually personified, as the place and
object of the hunt. When the boy and animal met, in a mystically
charged encounter, he achieved courage, skill and pride—and became a man. . . . Ralph has committed himself to a timeless ritual
of initiation, and implicitly to the decision to break with Molly.
For as a female she encumbers him in his obsessive stalking of the
mountain lion, and of the masculinity that is for him the real
trophy of the hunt. Her constant presence reminds him of a part
of himself he can no longer endure as he grows up, and indeed
must kill: the feminine part of his nature.[5]

The female characters in Stafford's stories do not have to
make Molly Fawcett's ultimate sacrifice to the myth of the West.
What is clear from the stories, however, is that the myth equally
excludes them. The reality of their lives denies the ideas in the
myth of boundless individual opportunity, of freedom and open
spaces, of the chance to form one's own destiny. Instead, the
dominant images are repressive ones: girls and young women
trapped inside unpleasant houses, frozen in immobile positions,
surrounded by the trappings of illness and death, often harassed
by grotesque people. The uncomfortable truth suggested by the
stories is that the initiation ritual for these young women is learning to accept their condition—to live with fear and pain and restraint as a normal consequence of their being female.

NOTES

[1] (New York: Farrer, Strauss, and Gireaux, 1969). Page references for the stories will be placed parenthetically in the text and will refer to this edition.

[2] "Author's Note" to *The Collected Stories.*

[3] Sid Jenson, "The Noble Wicked West of Jean Stafford," *Western American Literature,* 7 (Winter, 1973), 267-268.

[4] Stuart L. Burns, "Counterpoint in Jean Stafford's *The Mountain Lion,*" *Critique,* 9 (1967), 31.

[5] "Reconsideration," *New Republic,* May 10, 1975, p. 22.

(Portion of)
Chautauqua tent and people at Kearney, Nebraska

Courtesy of the Nebraska State Historical Society

IV

SHAPING IMAGINATIVE FRONTIERS

Toward a New Paradigm:
Mari Sandoz's Study of Red and White Myth in
Cheyenne Autumn

Barbara Rippey

Recent criticism has demonstrated the mythic dimension in the works of Mari Sandoz. In her broad study of Sandoz, Helen Stauffer writes that, "Sandoz's allusions clearly indicate her affinity for various kinds of myth,"[1] and that Sandoz's "sense of the mythic was the means by which she presented her creative historical vision."[2] Sandra Warman in her work, "The Mythic Vision of Mari Sandoz," argues that "in *Crazy Horse* Sandoz's writing clearly conveys a mythic message," and then extends her interpretation to encompass the way in which Sandoz understands and portrays how "things done" or the "drama" of a people's life becomes "things said" or "myth."[3] These interpretations concentrate either on Sandoz's presentation of Indian myth as an expression of Indian tradition and culture, or on Sandoz's creative vision as a shaping influence in bringing into being a new understanding, an enlarged and altered myth. The new myth is created from the "drama" of her writings in which universal truth and scientific (historical) truth exist in a unique blend.[4] This unique blend becomes a "drive toward a verbal circumference of human experience," which Northrop Frye sees as necessary in the formation of myth.[5] To understand the mythic dimensions of her works, however, we must consider also her incorporation of white myth. For Sandoz vividly demonstrates how the myth, or world view, of white people was instrumental in their action on the frontier, particularly in terms of their conquest of the Plains Indians, and white acquisition and use of the land.

In *Cheyenne Autumn*, Sandoz does much more than tell us of the brutal pursuit of a small group of Indians by the white military in the winter of 1878. She impresses upon our con-

sciousness the way in which whites invaded Indian culture, violating it as they violated Indian land and Indian people. First Sandoz creates for us "something of the rhythm, the idiom and the figures of Cheyenne life" in the narrative.[6] We learn how capable the Indians are of traveling in a diffuse and intuitive manner, guided by an intimate knowledge of and feeling for the land. They travel like the animals with which they are so familiar as "scattered in little parties over the pale, moon-touched prairie, they moved like Little Wolf's name animal, the sly coyote." The idiom and figures of white culture are interposed by Sandoz in passages that are dissonant and jar by their contrast. Diction and tone suggest methodical, military ways: "At Fort Reno Colonel Mizner reported good progress. Rendlebrock, out 30 miles by late afternoon the first day, sent a courier to Camp Supply for more cavalry because the Cheyennes were traveling very fast" (*CA*, pp. 25, 35). We read that "four companies of infantry and some cavalry were headed out along the line of the Platte to take the Cheyennes at the probable crossing," giving us a tactical, unemotional account of pursuit. Sandoz follows this bareness with a picture of the Indian's preparation for the soldiers, beginning with an image which conveys to us the time and quality of day "when the sun was over the head and the panting grouse had nothing except her own shadow to stand in," as well as the action as "Little Wolf signaled two gun seekers in" (*CA*, p. 36).

Ultimately, Sandoz reverses our familiar historical view, and we find ourselves questioning the white way-of-being. At the same time, she enables us to perceive the Indian way-of-being as a viable, ethical community, imperiled by white aggression. We see that basic to the white myth is the view of the white man as righteous heir and proud possessor of all desired land as promised land, promised if not personally to him, then at least eventually and rightfully to the white way-of-being. The white man wanted the Indian land by treaty, guile, or usurpation, and "with millions of men hungry for a new start. . .the romantic Red Hunter [became] a dirty, treacherous, blood-thirsty savage standing in the way of progress, in the path of manifest destiny." Sandoz also points out that it took only twenty-three years for the region to change from "white men. . .only a few little islands in a great sea of Indians and buffaloes," to "only a few little islands of Indians in a great sea of whites." She adds that "this

exploit of modern man is unrivaled in history: the destruction of a whole way of life and the expropriation of a race from a region of 350,000,000 acres in so short a time" (*CA*, pp. v, vi).

Sandoz heightens the impact of white aggression by contrasting it to the initial hospitality of the Indians; the Indians accommodated visitors even from abroad, "to ride in the surrounds, to eat roast hump ribs, to study and become one with this great Red Hunter" (*CA*, p. vi). And when it became obvious that the whites intended to displace the Indians, the Cheyennes made an attempt at co-existence:

> It was then that one spoke of something new, so quietly that his soft Cheyenne was barely to be heard. "We want a thousand white women as wives," he said, "to teach us and our children the new life that must be lived when the buffalo is gone. . . ." The chiefs saw the bearded dignity of the white men break into anger at this. Plainly they did not understand that the children of Cheyennes belong to the mother's people and that this was a desperate measure to assure the food and survival of their descendents, although in a few generations there might be not one left to be called Cheyenne anywhere under the blue kettle of the sky.[7]

Despite anything the Indians can do, the greed of the whites overwhelms them. In *Cheyenne Autumn* Sandoz presents the final defense of the Northern Cheyenne against the conditions of confinement, starvation and disease—a defense by flight from Indian territory (now Oklahoma) back to their lands in the Yellowstone Country, "through settled regions netted with telegraph, across three railroads, and straight through the United States Army" (*CA*, p. vii). She highlights the tension and tragedy of this defense, portraying its vulnerable, desperate nature, by first presenting to us the community of the Cheyennes and then revealing that community assaulted again and again by a myth-driven white action that interferes with increasing frequency and frenzy. For "the general policy was for extermination. The Indian and his treaties stood in the way of progress" (*CA*, p. 83).

The basic narrative of the text concerns the Cheyenne struggle under the leadership of two chiefs, Dull Knife and Little Wolf, to escape their white pursuers and reach their homeland, to survive the onslaught of winter with minimal food and shelter,

and, most importantly, to maintain their community as they travel under extreme duress. Within this narrative, Sandoz establishes the rhythm of Cheyenne life: "sometimes bits of information about the customs and village life are incorporated inconspicuously into conversations or the ruminating of one of the characters."[8]   The Indian man's regard for his wife, her place in the community, his respect for the sacred beliefs of his tribe, and his regard for his sustenance are suggested through the most casual of actions that make up the patterns of everyday life: When Little Wolf says, "as though speaking to no one. . . . 'You know you are not to get near the fighting,' " Feather does not look up but gives food to her husband. "Gravely, with his knife point, he offered a bit if the meat to the sky and the earth and the four directions. Then he ate." Now "Feather sang her little song of happiness, very softly, so not to be an embarrassment":

> I have a good man.
> In the village circle
> The women have called out his name many, many times,
> And the children follow his tracks.   (*CA*, p. 44)

Figurative language reinforces action.   After a fight with the soldiers, the boys hunt for the "mushroomed bullets they needed so much" (*CA*, p. 45).   Sandoz speaks not only of the shape of spent lead, but also gives a sense of the "mushrooming" or increased intensity of gunfire we are soon to encounter in the narrative, yet uses a woodland image to do so.   Often "the idioms are related to the customs and traditions of the Cheyenne."[9]   When "a small girl, six, an orphan," is shot in the foot she is lifted up, "light as a doll made of rushes or willow sticks" (*CA*, pp. 45, 46).

When white action, white words, and white ways intervene, they do so with a harsh brutality.   A context of death envelops birth.   Sandoz shows the Indian community in a fight for life, but taking time in the next few hours for a celebration of birth. As the soldiers draw near the Cheyennes turn to meet them, "the little row of dusty men in plain leggins and old cotton shirts, their braids unadorned, the blankets folded formally over their arms, the hands all empty except Dull Knife's, carrying the pipe."   Rendlebrock sends his shouted message   " 'The whites want you to turn around. . .if you give up now, you will receive

your rations and be treated well. If not, you will be whipped back.' " While the Indians are responding that they want only to go home, to be well and whole again, "the soldier guns roared out" (*CA*, pp. 38, 39).

It is not until after the day's fighting that there is a chance to welcome the new one born on the trail: "The little one was shown for a moment at the red coals of the council fire and named Comes Behind by Old Bear, his great uncle. The Bear made the motions of the pipe to the Great Powers as he said the words" (*CA*, p. 43). There is no birth in the camp of the soldiers. Dull Knife "ruminates" later in the flight:

> Somehow unlimited killing never turned the [white] officers from their path. Was it because the white man's fighter was not from a home, not returning to his house to eat and sleep and to live as the Indian warrior did, but was a pay man who did nothing but kill? Was it because the stink of all the blood could be kept away from the living, off in the distant forts? (*CA*, pp. 67, 68)

Sandoz contrasts this often alienated and fractured attitude of whites toward life, which she represents by white narrative, with Indian narrative, which she has written "to convey something of these deep, complex, and patterned interrelationships which I myself sense only imperfectly" (*CA*, p. vii). Through this contrast of attitude and idiom Sandoz moves us beyond the history of the flight to the emotional and spiritual conflict of the two cultures. And when the journey ends with so few of the 300 who fled still surviving, Sandoz has made certain that we know who has died, the manner of their death, and who killed them. Even those Indians who do survive, lose. Among them are the chiefs: "Dull Knife is a disillusioned man at the end, and we understand why; Little Wolf becomes a drunken killer, and we understand that."[10]

Our understanding begins not only with Sandoz's preface, but also with the two chapters of exposition that appear before the first chapter of narrative, the beginning of the flight. At first glance these chapters—"The People and the Time" and "Gone Before"—appear to be a singularly unemotional account. They include a straightforward presentation of the main characters—the Old Man Chiefs, Little Wolf and Dull Knife—and of the

background of the story. The use of subtitles—"The Indians," "The Indian Agent," "The Military Departments," "The Military Men"—suggest a familiar historical format. But gradually we question our first impressions. Looking more closely at Sandoz's style, we see that this is a matter-of-fact recitation of the extremity of human condition. On the one hand she delineates the desperate situation of the Indians, who wait for an "agency [that] was never established and the goods [that] seldom came," and who try hard "to remain at peace with the encroaching whites," even when they are repeatedly provoked by attack. We see the futility of Little Wolf's trip to Washington to receive "a big peace medal from President Grant." We are angered that the Indians are told "that there would be no more food for their families until they started to the hated Indian Territory," and when we realize that they are also told that "they could return— one more promise that was like the wind on the grass" (*CA*, pp. xiii, xiv, xv).

On the other hand Sandoz reveals that moral desperation of the conqueror, striving to hold on to what he wants with some semblance of humanity and show of integrity, but betrayed by brutality and practicality. She tells us of John A. Miles, who "was one of the Quakers appointed as Indian agents after years of scandal and graft," but underscores the tragedy with the dry comment, "but honesty was not the sole requirement for dealing with the proud, independent element of a nomadic hunting people suddenly pushed upon an agency with nothing to do or to eat." We smile at the comment General Nelson Miles made to an old chief who explained that he had never joined a warrior society: "I'm not a West Point man myself," Miles said, but our smile stops when we discover that his gracious, identifying answer did not stop him from his "relentless pursuit of the Sioux and the Cheyennes. . .[which] had helped reduce them so near to nakedness and starvation that they finally had to surrender." And we are galled at Sandoz's report that civilian agents and army officers were exchanged at will in Indian agencies—the army being sent when there was a hint of trouble and then pulled out because "it was argued that the military was really not equipped to make good citizens of the aborigines" (*CA*, pp. xvi, xvii, xviii).

As we recognize that human reality resides beneath the

account's apparent historical distance, we rebel against this telling of human events as though it were only of historical consequence. By the end of her extended introduction, Sandoz has provoked in her reader a feeling of displacement, of preparation gone on too long, of anxiety to be on with the story, and especially of a desire for resolution to the growing tension between real and wooden emotion, between the human and the historical account. Sandoz has prepared the reader to move to a mythic account, and with that movement to accept "an unequivocal moral obligation to which we respond at the deepest level of our imagination."[11] We move into the atmosphere of Indian culture with the sharp realization that something of value was and is at stake, that something of value was destroyed and is still in danger.

It is with the apparent contradiction of "was" and "is" that Sandoz makes that move from historical, linear time to mythic, cyclical, Indian time:

> Now it was the night, but there were no friendly clouds to run before the face of the climbing moon. Little Wolf sat alone at the deserted council fire, the big silver peace medal given him by the President in Washington shining softly on his breast. But under his shirt hung the Cheyenne Chief's Bundle and across his knee was his rifle, ready. (*CA*, p. 13)

As we accept the "Now it was," we accept the mythic combination of past and present—"It was a stream of many and complex dimensions, one in which man, the tree, the rock, the cloud and all the other things were simultaneously in all the places they had ever been; and all things that had ever been in a place were always in the present there, in the being and occurring" (*CA*, p. vii). Many times in *Cheyenne Autumn* we return to the symbols Sandoz has given us in those opening lines—the moon, the fire, the peace medal, the Chief's Bundle and the rifle—as if each were metaphor, again existing in the present as it had in the past, as though the past could be persistently recreated by the same form in a different time, or the same time in an altered form.

Sandoz recognizes that for the Indians the moon was a significant symbol of the diminution of the Great Power that had for so long protected them. On the first night of flight the moon

shown bright even though Bridge, the medicine man, had fasted for three days working on his cloud ceremony, yet "this night laid naked every living thing" (*CA*, p. 14). And later Sandoz reports, "Always the weather was against them now, with storms to hide the attacking soldiers, moonlight to reveal the fleeing Indians. Truly the Cheyennes had lost the sacred way somewhere, long ago" (*CA*, p. 195). The fire epitomizes the warmth of community, or even of life itself, as Sandoz relates that, "Here and there the diffused glow of a little fire showed through the old skins, or a few coals lay red inside a lifted lodge flap— fires that had been kept alive all through the hot summer against the chills of the shaking sickness and starvation" (*CA*, p. 13). Fire may be another kind of protection, throwing into relief the ignorance of whites in knowing and using the ways of the land, a point Sandoz was always quick to highlight:

> Little Wolf found other work to do. He helped to set a row of little fires to run together in the dry weeds and grass and move down over the rifle pits, the horses plunging and afraid in the little draw of the holders when the wind rolled the smoke that way. . . . Finally the troops took their stock back into a deep rocky ravine to escape the fire and the arrows too, but in another place without water."   (*CA*, p. 41)

The peace medal, Sandoz tells us, was placed on Little Wolf by President Grant, and "Little Wolf smelled the hated whiskey on the general who was the Great Father, and yet they had to beg him to pity their hungry children" (*CA*, p. 4). Once again we have been given a sharp negative picture of whites. It is a particularly poignant picture, for if it is the sign of Little Wolf's accommodation and desire for peace at any necessary price, Sandoz wants us also to know that it is a sign of the white man's bad faith, lies and treachery:

> Out in front of them stood Little Wolf, the President's silver medal of peace shining on his breast. . . . So once more Little Wolf said what he had been saying for a year. They were going back north as they had been promised they could. . . . But the dusty Rendlebrock, his blond face burnt raw by sun and whiskey, seemed to notice the Indians moving away through the ravines as though to escape. . .the trumpet made its call to war.   (*CA*, pp. 38, 39)

Sandoz presents the Chief's Bundle as an effective symbol of the Cheyenne's strong faith in the Powers, even when those Powers fail him. It is also the symbol of Little Wolf's particular responsibility for all the northern Cheyenne tribe. Little Wolf is known for his bravery and his survival power for, "he bore the bundle brought to the Cheyennes by Sweet Medicine very long ago, and so was selected as the dedicated one of all the tribe, the man who must always forget himself, as their culture hero had done, and remember only the people" (*CA*, p. 16). Once again Sandoz deftly brings in the invading influence of the whites, even in the Cheyenne's own sacred symbol, for while the Bundle is the repository of the most sacred memories of the tribe, yet the man, Sweet Medicine, from whom it had come, foretold "a time to happen here in the north country. Many people were to die, perhaps all the Cheyennes" (*CA*, p. 246). The Cheyenne Chief's Bundle, then, carries the message of the invasion of the whites by the Indian's own prophecy, yet Sandoz depicts Little Wolf as charged by possession of the bundle with the protection of his people. The rifle, the remaining symbol from the opening scene, becomes one of his chief means of protection, but it is also the white man's tool, as though what corrupts and what protects had become for the Cheyennes, with the coming of the white man, an inescapable tangle in which they were inextricably captured.

In the figure of Little Wolf, Sandoz graphically illustrates the pollution of Indian culture and mythos by white culture and mythos. As white narrative invades Cheyenne narrative, so is Little Wolf invaded in both exterior and interior attacks. The inner attacks come as he struggles to adapt to the realities of survival. Sandoz details for us the early hours of the flight, giving us a taste of the Indian way, before we must cope with the words and world of white pursuit. Her telling is full of metaphor and simile, suggesting that this is the way the Indian understands his world, himself, and the meaning of his life in every passing instant, the eternal instant. This is Little Wolf's world— a world of community, as the Cheyennes, "humped as buffaloes with their burdens," leave in a "contagion of anxiety," with, as a single organism, a "loud throb of the drumming heart" (*CA*, pp. 14, 15). Human and natural imagery combine as the Dog soldiers, members of a warrior society, will stay behind for "all the people here and all those to be born so long as the sky stood

over the earth were given into the palms of their warrior hands, to be saved or to lie scattered and lost forever on the wind" (*CA*, p. 16).

Little Wolf watched his "wife, Feather on Head, and the women after her, moving like smoke from shadow to shadow toward the little pass in the hills." Sandoz interjects into this action for community survival the realization of a rift that already exists in the community, brought on by a white man's act: "They moved carefully, keeping from the moon's rounding face so no white-man eyes could see the going, nor the Indian policeman the agent had made" (*CA*, p. 14). There is a foreseeing of death. Young Eagle is blowing his love flute softly on the hillside, for "he must go with them, leaving his beloved one here in the south, go even if his blood was to be spilled in a red blanket on the ground" (*CA*, p. 13). Now his flute signals the sentinels who will watch the "husks of the village" when the Indians have stolen away, as Sandoz suggests that the husks of Indian life will be increasingly scattered in front of the white reaping. "So the young man blew his plaintive eagle-wing flute, while on both sides of him lay the dark rifle pits. . ." (*CA*, p. 21).

Little Wolf recognizes "each darkening of the shadows below him, knowing each one as intimately as though of his own lodge." They were following Dull Knife without question because "his wisdom was of the old days—of the wool-blinded buffalo feeding with his nose always into the wind. . .the old wisdom of the time when a man spoke what he believed and his word was his life." Here, juxtaposed with Indian wisdom, Sandoz tells us of the interior attack upon Little Wolf's deepest values, for "something new had come into this. . .and to Little Wolf it seemed that the whites had to be met on their own terms, for now the power of numbers and of guns and the twisted tongue was with them" (*CA*, p. 20).

So Sandoz shows the Cheyennes moving into land once traveled in freedom, when they "left their corn patches near the great sweetwater lake and moved with the sun," now traversed in fear and mortal danger, and when we have become one with the flight of the Cheyennes, Sandoz interposes the pursuit of the whites, in white thought, words and action (*CA*, p. 31). Her

presentation of the military idiom—direct, assertive, factual, and impersonal—conveys to us the sense of the values of those pursuing the Indians:

> A few days later Mizner reported that the Indians were well mounted. The best he hoped now was that they could be overhauled at the Arkansas River, high in flood this wet summer. Although these Cheyennes had complained repeatedly about the meat rations, abandoning their standing lodges and their few goods showed a greater desperation that he had realized. (*CA*, p. 35)

That this was not the kind of realization to bring either understanding of or reparation for the Indians, Sandoz is quick to show us, for she continues in the same style:

> A special train would take mounted infantry to west Kansas, while troops from Lyon were to scout the rail line east and west. Washington ordered that, unless the intercepted Indians surrendered at once for dismounting and disarming, they were to be attacked. (*CA*, p. 36)

Sandoz is careful to indicate how seriously the white mind took this brooking of white orders to stay in Oklahoma by recounting for us the commanders' strategy against the Indians: "From Kansas General Pope wired his plans. Lewis of Fort Dodge would take command when the southern troops neared there, and the two companies of infantry from Hayes, to be joined by over a hundred civilians" (*CA*, pp. 35, 36).

After this dry and chilling account of mobilization, Sandoz returns to the Cheyenne narrative and we find a deepened sense of urgency, a new resolve and heightened tension. Little Wolf is counting the cost of the few guns they have been able to get from a trader "hidden in the jack oaks." Not only did it take "two fine quilled otter skins from the old, old grandmothers," but the seekers had to "give up even the saddle trappings of their wives, and so if there were ever horses again and a peaceful life, they must ride poor as any agency woman in the ceremonials" (*CA*, p. 36). Once again Sandoz has demonstrated how the Indian life was stripped of its meaning, sacrificed here for white weapons for defense against white aggression.

As the narrative lengthens and the path of flight continues, Sandoz lets us see more and more of Indian life. There are brief moments when the Cheyennes can catch a breath of community while the soldiers are hunting for them or regrouping. Humor helps them reconcile themselves to disruption:

> Little Wolf talked for the pleasantness of big fires, so they stopped near wood. . . . There was even a little singing tonight. Girls and older boys. . .went along the scattered fires, a Contrary Society youth with them, making the people laugh in his turned-around way, his from-behind clothes. With the white-man hat over his face he walked backward, showing only the black Indian hair where a nose and eyes should be. . .it seemed very funny in this anxious time.   (*CA*, p. 49)

Returning to their own rhythms provides some solace, though "a settler's light like a star pinned to the ground, or several together, and many of the rough places where a plow had traveled the earth" was a new danger and "the people became more and more fearful, with these unexpected enemies everywhere." This is a new white menace, for it is unknown whether the settlers will be friendly or hostile, and much travel was done at night. When the group halted for good reason "the Indians rested in the darkness or slipped away to their needs—but not far, with none knowing when night-charging soldiers might come. The men smoked their red willow bark, women fed their babies, and some of the young men went for a whispered word with the girls" (*CA*, p. 50).

This context of community is savoured by Sandoz even as she portrays adversity, for adversity is set always in the larger picture of the Cheyennes caring for and sharing with each other. So while Sandoz shows the fear Little Rope's people had for his mind sickness, she also shows their understanding, for they knew he "needed a long time of good village life, the easy cycle of eating, hunting, and sleeping, and then eating and sleeping again, not this running, running, with danger behind every hill, riding through every gully, and never a lodge over his head or even a willow shelter that need not fall before the sun returned" (*CA*, p. 51). When Sitting Man's leg is broken in the fighting, Sandoz tells of many people playing a part in his medical treatment as "fearfully the wife of Sitting Man brought the needed water and

wood" while Bridge, the medicine man, "gave the wounded man a red drink and by rattle and song put him to sleep almost at once." Young Eagle is "blowing his medicine flute" as Bridge is "making his medicine gestures to the flute's song" and covering the leg "with the green hide of a solider horse" which had been quickly skinned by the warriors and would dry to a fine cast (*CA*, p. 53).

Sandoz moves from the thanksgiving song of the wife of Sitting Man to the increased frenzy of the white reports as the Cheyennes continue to evade them. She leads us to question just who is the savage and who the civilized as the whites turn on each other with anger and consternation in their own adversity: "To the query, 'Where is Sherman, our General of the Army?' political enemies answered that he was probably in a sulk somewhere because, not a Catholic himself, his only son had become a priest" (*CA*, p. 55-56). Sandoz also reflects the white's paranoid distortion of proportion in their perceptions in her report of "many hundreds of telegrams and letters from everywhere demanding arms, guns in hundred lots, ammunition by the 20,000 rounds" from the governor and army posts in Kansas where newspapers were flooded with stories of "a great Indian uprising" (*CA*, p. 55). She documents the overkill response of the military as:

> Around the Dodge City saloons it was said that Captain Hemphill's gray-horse troops were too weak against 250 or 300 Indians. He had retreated to get the reinforcements he knew were due. That night a train of stockcars was ready to haul everybody up to the Dull Knife crossing of the Arkansas: five companies of cavalry, two of infantry, about fifty cowboys and ranchers, and wagons to haul the infantry and the supplies. (*CA*, p. 56)

Sandoz presents old facts in a new way. It is the whites' killings that become difficult to understand or excuse. Even when "many men showed up who had been counted as dead, and trail herds that were considered lost," the whites cried for the ruthless squelching of the Cheyennes and demanded that "the raiding Indians must be stopped. Colonel Lewis, it was said, considered the campaign shamefully mismanaged. He was taking up the trail on the first train west, and he would wipe out those murdering redskins or leave his body dead on the ground" (*CA*,

p. 70). Sandoz researched carefully the Cheyennes' reprisal against the settlers for earlier white atrocities against Indians in the Sappa region through which they were traveling. There was "a settler [killed] for every Cheyenne [male] killed in 1875. She was told, 'There is no way to pay for women and children killed.' "[1 2]

Sandoz presents white reprisals and threats of reprisal as grandiose and without entreaty for divine assistance. The whites' sense of power seems to reside in themselves, their arms, and their words, as when one brags, "We'll rake them Cheyennes in at the river like a grizzly rakin' in berries, leaves 'n' all" (*CA*, p. 118). Yet Sandoz tells us that the Indians were aware of and puzzled by:

> the white man's sacred object, the Cross of Wood—not one, as with the Hat, or the sacred number of four, as the Arrows, but many, little and big, and made of many things. The white man's medicine was surely very strong, for he was the biggest tribe of the whole earth, bigger even than the Sioux. But his cross did not seem to work for all the people as the Arrows and the Hat did. . .they were certain that the power of their Hat was not the same thing.
>
> (*CA*, p. 32)

Sandoz suggests that the Powers of the Indians are a most persuasive influence in their life: "The mysticism of the Plains Indians attracted her because of its relationship to nature and to the universal."[1 3] She demonstrates the humility of Little Wolf in his method of preparation for conflict:

> Cross-legged before the handful of coals, the Cheyenne chief made his bundle medicine. He laid a little silver sage to smolder on the coals and took out the Sweet Medicine bundle from under his shirt. Four times he passed it through the fragrant smoke of the sage and then offered it to the Great Directions, the sky, the earth, all around, and put it carefully back. When this was done and his mind quiet and composed for whatever was ahead, he called his horse out of the night.   (*CA*, p. 167)

When Sandoz does emphasize the spirituality of a white man, it is accompanied by the introduction of Indian idiom into white narrative. At the surrender of Little Wolf and his

diminished band to his friend, Lt. "White Hat" Clark, for whom he has scouted earlier, Clark says, "I have prayed to God that I might find my friend Little Wolf, and now I have done so" (*CA*, p. 265). Sandoz continues, "White Hat said he was sad to see his friends so poor. The people standing away, afraid, could not know his words, but the close ones saw the water as of a raining stand in his whiteman eyes" (*CA*, p. 266). In the use of Indian idiom she celebrates the discovery of a white man the Cheyennes can love and trust.

It is in Sandoz's skilled use of white idiom that she accentuates the alienation of the whites from themselves, from the Indians, and even from the very ground on which they stand. For if "[one] way Sandoz's idioms and figures characterize the Cheyenne is through contrast with the whites," with "the Cheyenne as the people of nature and of the land," then she at the same time characterized the whites by that same contrast. They "seem to have lost contact with many of their instincts concerning the land."[14] From the beginning of the narrative Sandoz portrays the whites from the Indians' point of view in terms of their strangeness, encroachment, and senseless attack, as "more and more blue-coated troopers came riding, and the emigrants began to run on the trails like dark strings of ants hurrying before the winter, bringing strange sicknesses, eating up the grass of the pony herds, killing the buffalo until the wind stank and the bleaching bones lay white as morning frost on the valleys of the Platte and the Arkansas" (*CA*, p. 2).

As the conflicting images of white and Indian multiply, Sandoz raises the reader's level of awareness and encourages change in basic perceptions, with the possibility of social action based on that perceptual change. The idea that Sandoz was interested in educating for action is supported by Helen Stauffer in her study of Sandoz as biographer. She relates that when Sandoz was frustrated in her attempt to take direct action in the war (in 1944), "she continued to use her historical writing to draw attention to the mistakes made in the past, mistakes she hoped men would avoid in the future."[15] Sandoz believed that "the United States had destroyed much of its own potential for greatness in its destruction of the Indians. . .she saw her material as magnificent in both heroism and tragedy, but damning to the white man."[16] It is in the selection and presentation of her

material, in her contrast of white and Indian myth that Sandoz cries for a new way. It has been said that:

> History is an ideal which the best of men can only hope to approximate. Wherever there is selection and emphasis by human agency, there will be myth. No man can live a day of his normal life, much less write a book, without selecting narrowly from all that competes for his attention. What governs his selections and the emphasis he places upon them will be his myth.[17]

Stauffer feels "Sandoz's mythic vision was predominantly that of the Indian rather than that of the white man of 'manifest destiny.' "[18] In an expression of her own openness to another culture, the myth of the Indian, Sandoz effectively uses the figure of Little Wolf, whose willingness to try to understand white culture has left him especially vulnerable. Her desire is to impress upon us the need for change in the white myth before such openness to change as Little Wolf's can be of any help in achieving a synthesis of red and white myth and culture. She presses upon us the conflict felt by Little Wolf as he realized change was necessary to insure survival for himself and his people:

> The Indian had always lived by knowing the ways of the things about him. Now, far too late, he must study these whites and their Great Father who could talk soberly of peace while big bunches of their young men did nothing but practice charging up and down, shooting at a target that was like a man, stabbing with the bayonet, crushing with gunstock. Then when what they wanted was already clutched in the palm, they said, "Sell us this for peace. . . ."
>
> (*CA,* p. 107)

Sandoz confronts the agony of integrating conflicting cultural messages as Little Wolf "tore at himself, as though he were both the rabbit and the eagle who fed on the quivering entrail" (*CA,* p. 107). Throughout the flight he has worn both the medal and the Bundle. They "represent the two great goals of his life: to learn to live peacefully with the whites and to guide and counsel his people in finding a relatively safe tribal existence."[19] He is afraid of how much he and his people will have to change to be acceptable. Sandoz realizes change is difficult, especially when one must turn from values long affirmed. Must

the Indian "learn to smile too when his heart was bad, and say 'Hou!' when he meant a roaring against it, say the 'Yes, yes, this will be done,' when it is only for so long as the eye was there to see" (*CA*, p. 107)? Sandoz shows Little Wolf, in his doubt, turning again to his basic mythic faith for strength and resolution as he makes a song:

> Great Powers, hear me,
> The people are broken and scattered,
> Let the winds bring the few seed together
> To grow strong again, in a good new place.

> But as he sang, the sky grayed and he knew that there would be more snow and that he must get his camp to a protected canyon before it came. (*CA*, p. 259)

But Sandoz reveals the "protected canyon" Little Wolf and his people reach as ultimately a snare and a delusion, even though Clark saw that the chief and his group of Cheyennes were taken safely to Yellowstone Country. In the telling Sandoz remains faithful to her presentation of the crushing influence of white myth by the use of white idiom. They are "facts so bleak that Sandoz need do little but report them in white-man words. Her tone is impersonal, without the Indian idiom, or even her characteristic imagery."[20] We are back to the historical distance, the wooden emotion of the introductory chapters. Sandoz shows a man who through great difficulties and with great heroism and skill brings his people home, home to a place where there is no longer anything of worth, of their worth, to do. They only "talked over the glories of the past and played games, gambled, and drank the bit of whiskey they managed to get now and then from the plentiful supply around the post" (*CA*, p. 271). Sandoz deftly develops the picture of Indians following white pastimes, including Little Wolf, who "obtained a little bottle. Hiding it under his blanket, he slipped away and drank it up fast" (*CA*, p. 271). In this condition he shot and killed another Cheyenne— a man who had long provoked him but from whom he had to withhold his anger, for the Medicine Bundle required his anger be only for the good of the tribe. Though he lives for twenty-five years after this tragedy, it is in isolation for the most part. Sandoz has shocked us to awareness of what white cultures had done to an Indian who "survived" and who was even befriended

by a good-hearted faithful white. She charges her reader to ask what there is about the white myth, the white way-of-being, that is so destructive to the red myth and the red way-of-being, and why an integration of the two cultures has not occurred. She encourages us to search for that in the Indian myth that might still be saved and for that in the white myth that is exclusive of others and should be excised that the good of both might be retained in a new blend: "Sandoz made clear in her numerous taped interviews and other writing that her primary interest was not in the past but in the significance of the past to the present and to the future. . .thus she binds two distinct and hostile cultures together in a unity with the land and with the past and the future."[21]

In Little Wolf, Sandoz has stripped the red man and clothes him in white man ways for all to see, and she does so with white words. The white officer said to him, " 'Little Wolf, you are no longer the chief' " (*CA*, p. 271). Sandoz has made clear that the reasons for Little Wolf's disintegration lie in the white culture, and that an integration of red and white myth demands a new paradigm. She has said that there are things "that I cannot watch with detachment, things that anger me to the violence of my father. One is the sight of the earth exploited, and the other is the knowledge of man, red, white or whatever color, deprived of the right to walk in pride and dignity before all the world."[22] In our realization of this need for justice, Sandoz has left us with the framework, the heightened perception that engenders new myth, new meaning. The "circumference of our human experience has changed." She has managed "both to disclose the world and to offer it as a task to the generosity of the reader."[23] The perspective we gain in *Cheyenne Autumn* calls for us all to "grow strong again, in a new place." Sandoz's artistry works to move us firmly toward this, her goal.

NOTES

[1] Helen W. Stauffer, "Mari Sandoz: A Study of the Artist as a Biographer," Diss. University of Nebraska, 1974, p. 76.

[2] Helen W. Stauffer, "Mari Sandoz and Western Biography," in *Women, Women Writers, and the West,* ed. L. L. Lee and Merrill Lewis (Troy, New York: The Whitston Publishing Company, 1979), p. 64.

[3] Sandra E. Warman, "The Mythic Vision of Mari Sandoz," MS, dated January 16, 1980, and submitted to the Nebraska Committee for the Humanities, pp. 7, 22.

[4] Stauffer, in "Mari Sandoz and Western Biography," p. 64, says, "Mari Sandoz, I believe, saw myth as a universal truth or equivalent to truth, not competitive with scientific (historical) truth."

[5] Northrop Frye, "Myth, Fiction, and Displacement," in *Literary Criticism,* ed. Lionel Trilling (New York: Holt, Rinehart and Winston, Inc. 1970), p. 584.

[6] Mari Sandoz, *Cheyenne Autumn* (New York: McGraw Hill, 1953), p. vii. All further references to this work appear in the text, except where special notes apply.

[7] Sandoz, p. 3. Sandoz is quoting from the Commissioner of Indian Affairs, *Annual Report,* 1854.

[8] Stauffer, "Study of the Artist," p. 364.

[9] Pam Doher, "The Idioms and Figures of *Cheyenne Autumn,*" in *Where the West Begins,* ed. Arthur R. Huseboe and William Geyer (Sioux Falls, South Dakota: Center for Western Studies Press, 1978), p. 144. Doher uses this illustration: "Another Cheyenne custom. . .is for the people to draw their robes or blankets to their eyes to hide sorrow or anger which might be seen in their faces. Hence Sandoz speaks of 'blankets of anger' or

'sorrowful blankets.' "

[10]Stauffer, "Study of the Artist," p. 329.

[11]Warman, p. 26.

[12]Stauffer, p. 376. For more information on Sandoz research on the reprisals this is excellent. The quote is from the University of Nebraska Archives (UNA) Sandoz to Neckyoke Jones.

[13]Stauffer, "Mari Sandoz and Western Biography," p. 63.

[14]Doher, p. 150.

[15]Stauffer, "Study of the Artist," p. 315.

[16]Stauffer, "Study of the Artist," p. 348. Stauffer quotes UNA, Sandoz to Louis Lightner, 3 March 1938.

[17]Richard McKenna, *New Eyes for Old* (Winston-Salem: John F. Blair, 1972), pp. 112-113.

[18]Stauffer, "Mari Sandoz and Western Biography," p. 63.

[19]Stauffer, "Study of the Artist," pp. 333-334.

[20]Stauffer, "Study of the Artist," pp. 359-360.

[21]Warman, p. 12.

[22]Sandoz, Brief Biographical Resume, MS 1953-1954, UNA.

[23]Jean-Paul Sartre, "Why Write?" in *Literary Criticism,* ed. Lionel Trilling (New York: Holt, Rinehart and Winston, Inc., 1970), p. 507.

Where the West Begins:
Constance Rourke's Images of Her Own Frontierland

Samuel Irving Bellman

Among the more active terms at work in the mental language of Constance Mayfield Rourke, American cultural historian and specialist in folk criticism, was the principle of the American West. Born in 1885 in Cleveland, Ohio, which was once part of the Western Reserve, she was to spend most of her life in Grand Rapids, Michigan, and allow her fancy a free rein in imaging the rich potentialities of that glorious region invitingly below New England, beyond the Alleghenies, the Mississippi also, possibly as far from main-travelled roads as California itself, and maybe farther away even than that.

There is a telling line in Rourke's chapter on Horace Greeley in *Trumpets of Jubilee* (1927), describing Fourierism, the radical social-reorganization system of the Frenchman Charles Fourier, as it made its way across the country in the mid-nineteenth century. "*Like a great* pavanne, *or a child's dream of a far* country, or a perpetual circus, the Fourieristic scheme spread its sweetly assembled elements."[1] Embedded within the line are certain features prominent in the landscape of Rourke's mind, presented straightforwardly or in veiled fashion. These include: the charm and splendor of a slow, stately dance; the enchanted land of faery; the rich pleasure of continuous theatrical entertainment; children's delights; being on the go; a new life.

This constellation of themes has a bearing, in Rourke's thought, on an important concept which is treated in a chapter in her masterwork, *American Humor: A Study of the National Character* (1931). That chapter takes its title from Walt Whitman's 1860 poem, "Facing West from California's Shores," and Rourke quotes it entire, with its eternal-child's baffled wonderment. "Facing West from California's shores,/Inquiring, tireless,

seeking what is yet unfound,/. . . . ./Now I face home again, very pleas'd and joyous,/(But where is what I started for so long ago?/And why is it yet unfound?)"

Taking into account all that Rourke wrote about the American West, considering particularly her keen delight in describing the California-Nevada region during and after the Gold Rush, one may detect hints about her "westering" impulses in her few tentative ventures into fiction. "Portrait of a Young Woman," printed in the November, 1921, issue of *The Dial,* describes a poor little rich girl living alone with her father, but giving the impression that she just may drive away in her expensive motorcar or fly away with some stunt pilot. Nothing specific is mentioned about this alter ego of Rourke's going West, but the sketch's companion-piece, "The Porch," printed in the preceding month's *Dial,* is far more explicit about such a move by the female protagonist.

In this little quasi-story, Maude Fassett, a high-spirited girl of the lower-middle class, lives in a little house with her colorless, unintelligent mother, in what may be the town of Grand Rapids. Mr. Fassett, a travelling salesman, is practically never home. Maude too is away much of the time, gallivanting around on short trips in motorcars with her riffraff friends. In actuality she is a shameless wanton, to the gossipy delight of the nosey neighbor women and the quiet consternation of her long-suffering mother. Finally Maude takes off on a long motor trip, this time to California, and it is understood by Mrs. Fassett and Maude that there will be no returning home. Her scandalous promiscuity would, this last time, cause too much talk on the street. Covering for her daughter, unsuccessfully as always, Mrs. Fassett says only that Maude has now gone to Alaska and that Maude's husband, a promoter, is doing well.

Again and again in her major writings, Rourke invokes the spirit of the Great West. Four aspects of the "call of the West," four particular visions or images, may be discerned, although there is a certain amount of blurring and blending in this quartet of modes. The four are: (a) the "making all things new" impulse that carried a myriad of utopian and religious reformers and their followers ever farther from New England and the Atlantic Seaboard into the hinterland river valleys and mountain fastnesses,

the plains and deserts and New Zions of the ever-widening West;
(b) the jolting and prodding of "the creative imagination" by
this westward prospect; (c) the great pioneering spirit of the frontier settlers and colonizers, seeking the kind of Lebensraum that
could not be found in the East; and (d) the world of the "stroll-
ers" and mobile entertainers: the people's theater on wheels,
on the water, and on the hoof.

Constance Rourke treats the "making all things new" impulse of social and religious reform most effectively in her first
book, *Trumpets of Jubilee.* This work, confined almost entirely to nineteenth-century American life, is actually a series of
five long biographical sketches of Easterners who were for a
time at least popular leaders, capable by virtue of their strong
personal drive and penetrating vision of making their presence
felt far beyond their original habitat and lifespan. Three were
Beechers: Lyman Beecher and two of his many children, Harriet
Beecher Stowe and Henry Ward Beecher; the remaining two were
Horace Greeley and P. T. Barnum.

Rourke's descriptions of the fervor of nineteenth-century
renewal sects, from Lyman Beecher's controversial but flexible
brand of Calvinism to the secular utopian movements, leave no
doubt in the reader's mind as to her basic feelings on the subject.
She herself, though never a formally religious person or follower
of any cult leader, was sympathetic to something that underlay
these impulsive efforts to usher in a new mode of living. And
what underlay them quite often was the notion of a new land,
beyond the pale of settlement, where a glorious fresh start could
be made. This was in essence the West, extending over much of
the length of what is now the continental United States. Because of her response to the potential of this enormous un-
bounded and alluring region, Rourke could describe it as exerting
a powerful effect on the imagination.

But the religious element, the philosophical-theological core
of hope or belief, which prompted many of the westward migra-
tions should be kept in mind; otherwise Rourke's treatment of
Lyman Beecher and his daughter Harriet will lose much of its
meaning. An idea was current in the 1820s of a religious and
social Millennium, inspired by the dream visions and apocalyptic
prophecies of the book that concludes the New Testament, The

Revelation of St. John the Divine. In accordance with a cyclic pattern of submergence and ascendancy of beneficent Divinity, a glorious era of all-pervasive blessedness symbolizing the renewal of God's protection and love was soon to come about. Yet by no means all of the eager sectarians anticipating a glorious new day were essentially religious or Bible-oriented; secular philosophies with their own historic rationale blended into or coexisted with the religious ones.

"On the fringes of frontiers," according to Rourke's lively account, men and women were laying the foundations of eternal cities or nearly perfect temporal settlements. Joseph Smith's Latter Day Saints, Jemima Wilkinson's New Jerusalem cultists, "the Shakers, the Harmonists, the Separatists of Zoar, the schismatic Rappites,"[2] the Fourier communards, the followers of Robert Owen in his colonies in New Harmony, Yellow Springs, and various other locales: all of these and more were seeking some sort of radical renewal, at the least a drastic improvement in their lot. To provide an image for this broad aggregate of renovating movements Rourke applied the term "trumpets of jubilee." The expression was adapted from one of Lyman Beecher's exaltations on the glorious promise of the great new American experiment in government. It harks back, however, to the Jubilee Year of ancient Israel, which came after every seven Sabbaths of years and was heralded by the blowing of the ram's horn, as described in Leviticus.

Rourke's descriptions of Lyman Beecher's removal with his family to the Middle West in 1832, where he would remain for roughly two decades and Harriet for eighteen years, convey a certain measure of excitement. However, those passages can be appreciated far more if one takes into account Rourke's pride in her pioneer ancestors and her lifelong concern with what she felt was the wholesomely unifying effect of our cultural history and folk traditions. All at once, Rourke explained, Beecher seized "the emotion arising from the half-broken, half-settled" Western expanse. The trailblazers and settlers taming the wilderness felt that an unprecedented new way of life was opening up: "Catching the thrilling intimation, Beecher fitted it to a primary pattern. The supreme issue was that of the new birth—on an epic scale."[3] The problem however for the energetic but restless Beecher, currently occupying a church post in Litchfield, Con-

necticut, was where to start.

Lyman Beecher's first move was hardly into the West, however; his new pulpit was in Boston. Melancholy and seemingly unable to avoid harsh, unpleasant controversies within his church organization, relating to hairsplitting doctrinal details, Beecher was soon ready to move on. Amid his painful embroilments "he saw the finger of destiny pointing unmistakingly [sic] toward the West." Sometime later, in 1832, he was able to move where the finger pointed. The exact spot as it turned out was a thriving but still primitive town on the Ohio River, Cincinnati, which the enthusiastic Beecher had earlier called " 'the London of the West,' " while anticipating that only in the West could his mission to further Calvinism, through Presbyterianism and/or Congregationalism, succeed: " 'If we gain the West, all is safe; if we lose it, all is lost.' "⁴ He was to take over the presidency of a newly founded ministerial institution, Lane Seminary, and to preach at Cincinnati's Second Church.

Ironically, gaining the West, he was nevertheless on the point of losing all more often than once during his stormy administration of the poorly supported school. There were, for example, severe religious and political storms, among them a heresy trial for Beecher, and the loss of most of his students when their rights were curtailed as a result of anti-slavery agitation. Yet, "The West—the West! The exhilarated cry ran through all his talk, his letters, his public utterances." Here would begin the Millennium, "the evangelization of the world" also, beyond a doubt. Beecher made of it almost a sacred myth. It was " 'a young empire of mind, and power, and wealth, and free institutions, rushing up to a giant manhood, with a rapidity and a power' " hitherto unknown. Its destiny, in his view, was to be America's " 'great central power' "; this was a region " 'eight thousand miles in circumference, extending from the Alleghany to the Rocky Mountains, and from the Gulf of Mexico to the lakes of the North; and it is the largest territory, and the most beneficent in climate, and soil, and mineral wealth, and commercial facilities ever prepared for the habitation of man.' "⁵

That Lyman Beecher ultimately failed to find his anticipated Millennium in the Cincinnati region or elsewhere in the West does not accordingly render his geographical fixation un-

important or ludicrous. Rourke's portrait of him is vividly and forcefully drawn. But in her treatment of the author of *Uncle Tom's Cabin,* Rourke showed herself to be particularly sympathetic to the financial and psychological pressures under which that lady labored for so long. Lyman's daughter Harriet had come to Cincinnati with the other Beechers in 1832, and under her father's spell had also nourished soaring hopes of good times coming. She was twenty-one years old when her father "migrated to Cincinnati, singing *Jubilee* along the hard route over the Alleghanies and preaching revivals." The young woman "was lifted to a high buoyancy, now at last in the lush new western country, amid spreading scenes, encircled by far horizons, every moment would be touched with glamor."[6]

Rourke's biographical chapter on Harriet Beecher Stowe, repressed daughter of the severe authoritarian head of the Beecher clan, is particularly interesting in regard to at least one phase of her life. That phase has to do with her marriage to the Calvinist theologian-scholar Calvin Stowe, a man so neurotic, emotionally immature, and improvident that for many years she was on close terms with hardship and misery. For roughly two decades Calvin Stowe was affiliated with Beecher's Lane Seminary in Cincinnati. His wife Harriet's residence in that frontier town in the 1830s and 1840s had far-reaching effects on her thinking about the new American frontier and about the human condition in general. To explain this point, a bit of background information will be helpful.

For one thing, Harriet, living for so many years in the Ohio-Kentucky border region where pro-slavery feeling was strong and even Negro freemen endured a precarious existence, absorbed much of the nightmare of Negro slavery without conscious effort. Her father was outwardly indifferent to the "peculiar institution." Yet shortly after Harriet and her own family removed to Brunswick, Maine, in 1850 she produced the monumental anti-slavery novel *Uncle Tom's Cabin.* She had been affected, according to Rourke, by a Boston relative's letter regarding the Fugitive Slave Law; the writer had wanted Harriet to compose a protest. Likely, she had also been strongly affected by her father's millennial theology and somehow adapted his new-era apocalyptic preachings to the story of an innocent people held in bondage and of one particular Christian slave willing to yield up

his life if it would redeem the soul of his heartless oppressor. As for Harriet's later anti-slavery novel *Dred* (1856), Rourke directly connected the terrifying fantasy of the demon-ridden story and the influence of Lyman Beecher's Calvinistic religion on Harriet. "Those signs and wonders and predicted overturnings which had filled Lyman Beecher's mind in the West as he considered the coming Millennium were turned to account—as if [she] were still under their spell, as if she had gained from them a touch of prophecy, for out of *Dred's* wailing utterances. . .came an un-mistakable foreboding of the black chaos of war."[7]

For another thing, Rourke pointed out, in what may have been her best writing, Harriet identified with Uncle Tom and was in effect rewriting her own life story of enslavement by male oppressors such as her father and that other Calvinist tyrant, her spirit-sapping husband Calvin Stowe. She attributed to Uncle Tom "a pity akin to self-pity, endowing him with a mild faith which she had struggled so long to attain."[8] Third, and this is but a suggestion, Rourke may have felt some subtle personal bond with the author of *Uncle Tom's Cabin*, who had clearly yielded to the scented romanticism of Madame de Staël's *Corinne* but had had to endure decades of painful self-denial before she could recreate herself as an individual in her own right, one of the world's most celebrated authors. Rourke, living alone with her crotchety, unremittingly demanding mother in Grand Rapids, was outwardly calm but aspired to genuine auctorial success; and she projected an unforgettable account of a brave and almost unbelievably resourceful woman who ultimately achieved per-sonal triumph over family and custom.

Rourke's second image of the West is that of the "creative imagination" aroused out of a sluggish acceptance of things as they are, and brought in effect to a high level of artistic energy. This reviving of a dormant imagination involves the West in a dual role: it is to provide not only a forward prospect, but—if not an actual backward one—a local prospect, as well. Rourke was aware of Frederick Jackson Turner's classic paper of 1893, "The Significance of the Frontier in American History." Turn-er's crediting the continuing settlement of our westward-moving frontier region with the promotion of American democratic practices accorded well with her folk-culture philosophy, bor-rowed largely from Gottfried von Herder. According to that

philosophy, art and other cultural expressions develop upward and outward from the common people and their native traditions. The forward-thrusting American West thus held for Rourke two powerful sources of intensely meaningful value. One was based on what was happening right there in the frontier zone; the other was based on the unlimited potential for human fulfillment, of the far-distant extensions of that frontier.

Rourke's excitement at the local prospect, whose concomitant was the consolidating of the gains from the continuous "winning of the West," was shown in her 1935 article, "American Art: A Possible Future." Since the time of the American Revolution, she argued, the American people have harbored immense "expectations as to esthetic fulfillment." Instantly "we were to have the arts, on the epical scale. Small Western newspapers foretold the certain event in the eighteen thirties and forties. We are still strangely afflicted by that obsession."[9]

On the other hand, when Rourke took up the far-Western prospect, an even more intense feeling of exhilaration was communicated to the reader. California, which had become a state in 1850, was the great new Western frontier, for the time being at least, and that might mean any number of things to a still-developing nation: "treasure trove," "a new sense of union," a vision of empire, gateway to the South Seas. Thinking apparently of the aftermath of the Mexican War (1846-1848) and the Gold Rush, Rourke claimed enthusiastically: "The whole outflowering of the American tradition came in those first brief years of acquisition and discovery." Herman Melville was "always facing west"; Walt Whitman and Nathaniel Hawthorne produced their more important writings within little more than five years "after the conquest of California; and national legends took new forms." During this very period "the mythical Crockett went west and to the South Seas," while "the strangest scattered tales of far islands, verging upon the supernatural, crowded the almanacs." Even Horace Greeley is quoted, exulting in 1859 that he has brought himself, as will be the case with how many other Americans, to the Pacific shore. "The new empire haunted the popular imagination, this was the greatest of the nomadic adventures."[10]

But then, such were the vagaries of Rourke's thoughts on

the subject that she veered away from the maritime prospect and concentrated at length on humorists and raconteurs of the West such as Mark Twain and Bret Harte, on regionalists the nation over, on tall tales and a variety of inland expressions of the American temper of the 1860s and thereafter. From that welter of Rourkean impressions and associations there emerged a grand statement of just what the above image ultimately embodied. "Facing west from California's shores meant the spacious view and a fresh sense of unity; it also meant the long breath taken as a last boundary was reached, and a turn toward entrenchment in local life."[11]

Rourke's third image or view of the West, involving the great pioneering frontier spirit, partakes of a newspaper slogan and stereotypical figures of American folklore. Her chapter in *Trumpets of Jubilee* on the journalistic and political rise and fall of Horace Greeley (1811-1872), famous editor and publisher of the New York *Tribune,* accents his famous clarion call to upward mobility: " 'Go West, young men [sic] , and grow up with the country!' is remembered as the cry of an era." While a member of the U. S. House of Representatives, Greeley (a Whig) adopted some of the principles of the Free Soil party and introduced a bill that would give U. S. Government land, without cost, to bona fide settlers. Though a meaningful homestead act would not be passed by Congress until 1862, Greeley was an early advocate of such a measure. The West, where he enjoined young men to go, might effectively be settled by such means as homestead legislation. "Land, free land. . .to the actual settlers; this cry he raised above all others, and remained first and last the" leading supporter "of a dynamic measure. For [many] years his agitation was to continue."

Now, "From the backwoods, from a half-tilled acreage, from tracts exhausted by [careless] farming, the movement westward was. . .streaming far into the Valley of the Mississippi and past it, over the plains, with breaking fringes in" Oregon and California. At the threshold of the 1850s, following the victorious outcome of the Mexican War, and the Gold Rush, that "swing toward empire in its loudest, noisiest phases" was on and there was much talk about "manifest destiny." Speaking of the stringencies brought on by exhausted farmland, Rourke observed that "the country had been harried by reckless farming until

whole sections looked as though they had been devastated by fire, blight, or war." Greeley's family had experienced the effects of such abuse of the soil when he was growing up, and his "passion for the land," Rourke noted, reflected a basically rural view of the United States. Even when warming up to the subject of the Gold Rush, Greeley visualized not monetary treasure, but rather "an intoxicated human movement, and an effect of magnitude in a superabundantly rich, uncharted country."[1] [2]

Two powerful folk stereotypes reflecting life in the West strongly attracted Rourke. The first of these, which had some basis in fact, she called the "gamecock of the wilderness." This rough-and-ready countryman, as described in her *American Humor,* parodied to some extent the fiercely independent wilderness tamer who helped settle the frontier territories from the Atlantic Seaboard throughout the Tidewater region, the Midwest and Great Plains, through to the West Coast. The gamecock was a bombastic boaster, a pugnacious bantam or burly rooster whose chief claim to notice was his "Cock-a-doodle-doo!" battle cry. "He was not only half horse, half alligator, he was also the sea-horse of the mountain, a flying whale, a bear with a sore head." He was also "a steamboat, or an earthquake that shook an enemy to pieces, and he could wade the Mississippi." With a crack of his heels this self-inflating noisemaker jumped "into the air to proclaim his attributes against all comers."

The generic backwoodsman, who in many ways might be identified with the gamecock figure, came to prominence following the War of 1812. But there was actually another exemplification of the gamecock: the boatman, whom Rourke traced to the French *voyageur* of a slightly earlier time. The latter "came by the rivers and kept to the rivers." He "was livelier than the Kentucky scout and had the habit of song." With the coming of the settlers in the early 1800s, the *voyageurs* were largely displaced by the backwoodsmen in their broadhorns and other river craft. Yet the tradition of song was preserved, "as Negro oarsmen joined their number and broke into rowing-melodies." Traversing our inland waterways by canoe, flatboat, keelboat. . . the boatman was a robust and fearless trader, freight handler, and explorer. He "blew his magic horn," Rourke wrote of this figure, following a beautiful lyric passage on the Ohio River in Spring, "and improvised sentimental songs." Pulling on his oar,

he went into "a highly posed melancholy," growing "elegiac over lost loves."[13]

The second folk stereotype within Rourke's vision of westward movement is that of the giant, the earthmover and miracle worker. Enchanted throughout her life by the very thought of human colossi of folklore and legend, she loved retelling the tall tales that had accumulated around such figures; but, as was the case with other interpreters of the Great American West, Rourke in her account blended common experience and dreamy myth. Not only were vast hordes of determined, energetic young men and their families needed to settle the western lands and to keep pushing the frontier back ever further toward the limitless Pacific. A few men bigger than life, heroic giants really, were needed as well—if only as ideal forms.

Two particular early-nineteenth-century exemplars of the folklore figure of the gamecock of the wilderness loomed large in Rourke's imagination: a backwoodsman and a boatman par excellence, Davy Crockett and Mike Fink. Two of her great-aunts had known stories about Crockett, and she in fact wrote a juvenile biography of him, stressing his exploits and achievements as hunter, backwoods sage, Congressman and war hero. He represented "to the popular imagination all that had been known or guessed about life in the western woods or on the western waters." Fantastic tall tales grew up around his remarkable career, but nevertheless they contained a measure of truth and "they belonged to the western country—its great rivers, trees, high winds, storms, earthquakes, wild beasts."[14] Somewhat less famous than Crockett, Mike Fink, also an actual historic figure, was celebrated for his extraordinary skill as a boathandler and his prowess as a hunter and fighter. A revealing hint as to a possible reason for Rourke's profound fascination with such legendary heroes of the expanding West is given in her *American Humor.* Mike Fink "was in fact a Mississippi rivergod, one of those minor deities whom men create in their own image and magnify to magnify themselves." As for Davy Crockett, one might surmise that Rourke, in according him even more homage than she gave Mike Fink, was tapping an even stronger symbolic power source: "In the end [Crockett] became a demigod, or at least a Prometheus."[15]

Lastly, there is Rourke's image of the West as a great outdoor stage or crudely improvised theater-house, where dedicated
performers, show people of every description, followed closely
behind the trailblazers and mining prospectors, singing, dancing
and playacting, sometimes under the crudest conditions, and
loving every minute of it. Describing our American theater with
special reference to the West, Rourke again showed how deeply
moved she could be when one of her favorite subjects was conceived of in these geographic terms. Such theater represented to
her "a composite of native feeling," significant because it was intimately involved "with the American character and the American experience," going onward "with the forces of dispersal."[16]

Rourke's descriptions in *American Humor* of the "strolling
actors" making their way across the largely-undeveloped country
are derived from memoirs and theatrical records. Her accounts
are high-spirited, suggesting vicarious participation in the rolling
and rollicking life of these stage folk. The actor was a madcap,
a free-living blithe spirit. The actor's existence was haphazard
and precarious, but packed with so much fun and excitement as
to make a complacent social conformist envious. The Alleghany
was a route to the West for many of the mobile troupers, who
left in their wake "white flags flying" along the riverbanks to indicate "a friendly reception" awaiting others of their kind coming later. In towns such as Pittsburgh, where the constables were
notoriously unsympathetic to deadbeats from out of town, a
trouper cast in the role of Hamlet's gravedigger "saw the bailiffs
in the wings and popped into the grave, and was never heard of
again." All the troupers in another company, "caught on the
wing for debt as they tried to leave town," hired "themselves out
as waxworks at a museum to raise the necessary money."[17]

A number of these bands of wandering players moved by
raft and broadhorn, down the Mississippi and Ohio rivers. Others
travelled in wagons through the Kentucky hills, where the steep
roads forced them "to unload their properties and carry them,
and where they often left their watches and chains behind as
toll." One particular company, happening to be in Florida during
one of the Seminole wars, performing "at forts and garrisons on
the way," was attacked by the Indians; some of the actors were
put to death, "and their wardrobe seized." Following this the
Seminoles might have been seen galloping "through the sandy

lowlands" in the apparel of "Romans, Highlanders, and Shake-
spearean heroes." The inventors of the showboat, the Chapmans,
made their way "up the Arkansas River to wild country," meeting dangerous rowdies there, on occasion being "besieged, [and]
dealing out grape and canister" by way of self-defense; yet they
became quite hardened to this kind of floating show business
under fire, and were content to keep it going for an extended
period of time.[18]

The stage-world in the *far* West enchanted Rourke most of
all. She devoted most of an entire book to the life of a long-for-
gotten stage entertainer who from her childhood onward performed—as singer, dancer, actress of sorts—in the California and
Nevada mining camps following the period of the Gold Rush.
Unfortunately Rourke's attempts to make Lotta Crabtree (1847-
1924) an exciting and even mysterious figure are unsuccessful,
for all the log-book minutiae of Golden West theater, for all the
speculations about who Lotta's father really was and whether
Lotta ever married. It is interesting that in the above book,
Troupers of the Gold Coast (1928), which also deals briefly with
other femmes fatales of the western stage such as the famed
spider-dancer Lola Montez and the equally famous Adah Men-
ken, auctorial commitment and emotional involvement overrode
literary judgment. This is not to say that the life of a nineteenth-
century "actress" in San Francisco and the mining camps was not
worth writing about—though, incidentally, none of these ladies
restricted her sphere of influence to the Pacific Coast-Nevada
region. It is merely that Rourke failed to bring Lotta and the
others to life. They remain names and data-clumps, thwarting
the biographer's intentions as skillfully as they might have be-
guiled (with impunity) some lonesome prospector or randy bar-
room brawler into hormonal madness.

The value of this strange book probably lies in its suggestive
power. The far West may be seen as one vast congeries of theaters, formal and makeshift, to suit all comers. If San Francisco
not long after the Gold Rush was filled with performers and
stages, numerous small troupes found their way into the interior.
"Theaters were being built at Marysville and Grass Valley, and
as far up into the mountains as Downieville. Sacramento had two
handsome new theaters. Stockton had had a charming small
playhouse." And at a place called "Mokelumne Hill, a riotous

camp near rich gulches which had been successfully worked since the winter of '49," a successful theatrical program had been maintained practically from the time that the inhabitants settled in. Nowhere else in our land "had the theater come into such unchastened, free and abundant life." In other parts "the theater had always suffered from repression," with the possible exception of some "few scattered cities of the South." But here on the "new frontier nothing was repressed, either plays, actors, or the audience [sic] ."[19]

Constance Rourke would always make much of the West, regarding it as more than a mere frontier zone between settlements on the Atlantic Seaboard and the raw wilderness. The West held the promise of transformation and renewal, and the key to the release of the American's "creative imagination." The West was where we had once been bidden to go, not just by some colorful newspaper editor but by an irresistible prompting of the human spirit. The West was a place for giants in the earth to exert their strength. Finally, and this was a matter particularly dear to her, the West was the Great Theater of American Life, with all the magic that the world of the stage represented to her, with a cast of millions cementing American cultural traditions, and with continuous performances daily. Rourke's West, the land of her own romance, began in her secret heart, and she would follow it all of her days.

NOTES

[1]Constance Rourke, *Trumpets of Jubilee*, introd. Kenneth S. Lynn (New York: Harcourt, Brace & World Harbinger Books, 1963), p. 201.

[2]*Trumpets of Jubilee*, p. 41.

[3]*Trumpets of Jubilee*, p. 25.

[4]*Trumpets of Jubilee*, p. 38.

[5]*Trumpets of Jubilee*, p. 40.

[6]*Trumpets of Jubilee*, p. 69.

[7]*Trumpets of Jubilee*, p. 87.

[8]*Trumpets of Jubilee*, p. 82.

[9]"American Art: A Possible Future" appeared originally in *Magazine of Art,* July, 1935; the reference here is to its reprinting in Rourke's posthumously published collection, *"The Roots of American Culture" and Other Essays,* ed. with preface Van Wyck Brooks (New York: Harcourt, Brace & World, Inc. Harvest Books, 1942), p. 279.

[10]Constance Rourke, *American Humor: A Study of the National Character* (1931; rpt. Garden City, New York: Doubleday & Company, Inc. Anchor Books, 1955), pp. 163-164.

[11]*American Humor*, pp. 177-178.

[12]*Trumpets of Jubilee*, pp. 180, 223-226.

[13]*American Humor*, pp. 39-40, 42, 43.

[14]Constance Rourke, *Davy Crockett* (New York: Harcourt, Brace

and Company, 1934), p. ix.

[15]*American Humor,* pp. 52-53, 55.

[16]*American Humor,* p. 93.

[17]*American Humor,* p. 94.

[18]*American Humor,* pp. 94-96.

[19]*Troupers of the Gold Coast or the Rise of Lotta Crabtree* (New York: Harcourt, Brace and Company, 1928), pp. 16, 56-57.

Pioneering the Imagination:
Eudora Welty's *The Robber Bridegroom*

Melody Graulich

". . .in the best sense, of course, the western boundaries are inward
and the West is a territory of imagination, in a recurring drama of
the American character shaped by exigencies of place, then reshaped by subsequent generations who have had to rub the strangeness about the past from their eyes to be sure who they were. . . .
Consequently, an exactly defined region is less important, we
would argue, than the perceptions of the region, than the westering mind itself."[1]

American humor, says Mark Twain, having read earlier
western writers like "Davy Crockett," T. B. Thorpe, and George
Harris, is not in the tale but in the telling; in western soil, humor
is germinated from character and richly fertilized by the western
voice, with its outrageous exaggeration and gaudy imagery.[2]
Like their independent and inventive bull-shooting characters,
western comic writers, seeking ways to recreate the West's
imaginative force, have viewed conventional narrative as a prison.
Eudora Welty joins this gang of westering jailbreakers with her
tall tale of frontier history, *The Robber Bridegroom,* set in a
wilderness whose "savage breath. . .covered the sky with black,
yellow, and green clouds the size of whales."[3] Such exuberant
images characterize Welty's narrator, undramatized but possessing an idiosyncratic voice. Like the characters who have been
unable "to rub the strangeness from their eyes. . .to be sure who
they were," Welty's narrator wonders at the West's liberation of
the imagination. Her western vision moves Welty to search, as
she says, for a "*narrative* truth that. . .the times themselves had
justified," for a voice capable of testifying that "life was so full,
so excessively charged with energy in those days, when nothing
seemed impossible in the Natchez country. . . ."[4]

In her talk in 1975 to the Mississippi Historical Society, Welty decided to discuss her frontier tall tale, she said, because "it set its foot, lightly enough, across the border between my territory and yours and for you, I'm going to call it my historical novel."[5]   And yet she hastened to recognize that her merger of history, legend, and fairy tale is not conventional western history:

> In *The Robber Bridegroom*, the elements of wilderness and pioneer settlement, flatboats and river trade, the Natchez Trace and all its life, including the Indians and the bandits, are all to come together. The story is laid in an actual place, traces of which still exist, and in historical times. . . . And you historians and scholars would be the first to recognize that this is not a *historical* historical novel.[6]

Like other western mythologizers, Welty is interested not in the literal past but in its effect on the modern imagination; her book, she told the historians, "instead of burying itself deep in historical fact. . .flew up like a cuckoo, and alighted in the borrowed nest of fantasy."[7]   Fantasy, as Bruno Bettelheim has argued, enriches the inner life: "The unrealistic nature of these tales makes obvious that the fairy tale's concern is not useful information about the external world, but the inner processes taking place in an individual."[8]   While Welty bases her plot on historical fact to show, as Warren French has persuasively argued, that the time for physical pioneering is past, her "narrative truth" focusses the reader's attention on the inner reality of the narrator who proves that it is possible to recapture the freedom of individual spirit the West once symbolized.[9]   Welty borrows the exaggerated style of the tall tale tellers who rebelled against the restrictions of "reality," but she revises their narrow definitions of human values while at the same time affirming the triumphant power of the human imagination through her narrator's fantasies, her comic and poetic language, and her ability to condense experience into a single image, symbol, or gnomic phrase. Her narrative vision shapes that of the reader who becomes himself a pioneer, his imagination open to the wonders of America's westering past.

While some reviews called the novel a dream, Welty's own metaphor suggests that her technique is one of revelation. "I think," she says, "it is more accurate to call it an awakening to a

dear native land and its own story of early life, made and offered by a novelist's imagination in exuberance and joy."[10]   Welty mingles the sleeping and waking worlds, repeated images throughout the tale, accepting that the exaggerations of the tall tale world and language express a distorted psychic truth, just as dreams do.   Talking decapitated heads are economical guilt symbols—and funny, too.   Welty's narrator affirms those characters who share her vision, a vision shaped by the anti-rational power of the imagination to re-organize and comprehend reality; narrow, restricted characters are symbolically blinded by images of caves, blindfolds, or eye-gouging.   While some of Welty's southern contemporaries like Faulkner or Penn Warren see the past as repressing individual growth, she turns to the history and legends of the Natchez Trace, part of the old southwestern frontier and the setting of much of her later fiction, to liberate, to *awaken*, the inner self.

For Welty, fantasy is pioneering within the imagination, a conscious breaking free from experienced reality, from what one has always known, in an effort to create a new world, to see beyond the accustomed mountains, to explore the unexpected, to live freely and independently, yet in harmony.   Its boundaries, like western ones, are inward, limited only by the author's vision. If Welty's western territory mirrors her narrator's inner landscape, then within her imagination "nothing seemed impossible," or, as one of my students once said of the book, "Anything goes."   Earlier romancers like Hawthorne and Robert Montgomery Bird have used wilderness legend and landscape to convey symbolically their fears about the primitive irrationality of the inner self released from the governing laws of civilization; repression and guilt are major themes in their works.   Welty responds to these writers and to Faulkner (a "big mountain" in her fictional landscape) when her hero, the outlaw Jamie Lockhart, says, " 'Guilt is a burdensome thing to carry about in the heart. . . . I would never bother with it,' " to which the innocent planter Clement replies, " 'Then you are a man of action. . .a man of the times, a pioneer, and a free agent' " (p. 27).   In the West's liberation of the inner self, Welty also finds irrationality, but with different results: instead of a chaotic unconscious filled with dark impulses, she discovers a creative vision, capable of synthesizing fragmentary experience.   There may be danger in accepting freedom and instinct over regulation and restraint:

Salome and Little Harp are both capable of murder and rape, while Big Harp (the decapitated head) is a persistent reminder of violence. But these short-sighted characters eventually die, losing to those who, like Jamie, are free to "look both ways and to see a thing from all sides" (p. 185). These characters triumph because they accept the irrational as one more mystery in human experience and because they, like the narrator, integrate reality and fantasy, responding creatively to the wilderness's savage disorder by accepting the possibility of whale-filled skies. They exert some control over their lives by seeing more than is "really" there—and by living to tell the tale.

Such a character is Rosamond, whose imagination is eager to convert the bizarre things that happen to her into exaggerated stories that cannot forestall disaster but often help protect her from it: from the assaults of the Indians who appear like magicians from out of the wilderness; from the incompetent con man, Goat, who literally butts his way into other people's business; and especially from her stepmother, Salome, so greedy that "the poor contamination of her heart broke out through her words until it showed even on her skin, like the signs of the pox" (pp. 100-101):

> Now Rosamond was a great liar, and nobody could believe a word she said. But it took all the starch out of her stepmother, you can be sure, to send Rosamond out on a dangerous errand, hoping some ill might befall her, and then to have her come safely back with a tale of something even worse than she had wished upon her. As for Rosamond, she did not mean to tell anything but the truth, but when she opened her mouth in answer to a question, the lies would simply fall out like diamonds and pearls. (pp. 38-39)

In more conventional "old world" fairy tales, heroines who lie are rewarded with mouthfuls of snakes and toads and with princes who remain frogs. Rosamond, however, captures the rebellious Jamie, who can out-roar even Mike Fink, his bed-mate in the book's opening scene,[11] and who "knew that he was a hero and had always been one" (p. 185). Both shape-shifters who often mask their true identities with their lies, the two are well mated. As the free children of the wilderness, they declare their independence of any convention: when her father suggests that a tutor might teach her to become a truthful lady, Rosamond

responds, " 'Never! I will learn it all for myself' " (p. 39), a line Jamie echoes when he says, " 'No one tells me and no one needs to tell me. . . . I think of everything for myself' " (p. 47). Self-reliant seekers of their own identities, fast-thinking and faster-talking, the two share the swaggering self-assertion and indomitable mastery of fate of the heroes of western tall tales.

And yet these protagonists, unlike most tall tale heroes, do not tell their own tales, perhaps because there is no conflict between their voices and that of the narrator. Most tall tales have a frame narrator, an educated and urbane easterner whose dull diction and stilted syntax emphasize the natural vitality of the images in the speech of such "ring-tailed roarers" as Thorpe's Big Bar or Harris's Sut Lovingood. While the characters' dense imagery is as anarchic and energetic as their actions and conveys their disgust at society's hypocrisies, the frame narrator establishes distance from the physical comedy, violence, and obscenity, implicitly allowing the author a tone of superiority so dull and inflexible that the reader's sympathies usually lie with the rambunctious roarer. Thus art frames, and often seeks to limit, chaos through convention.

Like the roarers, Welty accepts that experience is fragmentary, mysterious, and irrational, that our efforts to shape and control life are largely acts of defiance against limitation, not impositions of it. Unlike the frame narrators, she refuses to imprison the contradictory vitality of life within conventional boundaries. While the traditional tall tale writers separate art from life by intruding the formal writer between storyteller and audience, Welty creates another character who "looks both ways" by uniting the frame narrator and the storyteller into one voice. Her narrator is not distanced from her materials because the western spirit has enriched her imagination. Her tale reminds critics of a dream because there is no frame to ease the reader out of and back into "reality," because the plot seems to be largely a vision of the dominating voice of the storyteller, and because Welty mingles subjectivity and objectivity by showing how fantasy begins with fact. She awakens to the necessity of fusing an American Dream with American storytelling, which she achieves by assuming the role of the frame narrator, removed from the narrative action, while accepting the fantastic visions and playful language of the roarer as her own. Diamonds and

pearls of American myth fall from her mouth.

The narrator's fantasies amuse the reader, as do those of the tall storyteller. Roarers, however, are often con men, shape shifters like Hooper's Simon Suggs, who manipulate others to their own selfish ends; they con their audiences into giving up something, sometimes money, always disbelief. Telling tales was often an initiation rite, the story's language testing the newcomer's "green-ness." The story becomes a hoax, the listener a victim. The roarer's defiance of limitation, too, often results from violent individualism which ignores human consequences; Sut Lovingood destroys not only Mrs. Yardley's quilts, a symbol of the imposition of feminine order, but also Mrs. Yardley herself, whose "deserved" death provokes laughter. Although Welty's narrator, like Simon Suggs, finds it useful to be shifty in a new country, her motives are quite different. She does not seek to victimize the readers she draws into her "new country." Welty reshapes the convention: her tall tale demands a willing suspension of disbelief, but she demonstrates not her power over others but the power of the imagination. She liberates the reader's imagination from the constrictions of realism to awaken an awareness of more mysterious, inner truths, not to free the individual from responsibility to others. Where the roarer's fantasies tend to suppress human needs, Welty's narrator's fantasies explore the power of emotional freedom.

Southwestern humor and tall tales blunted emotion, exposing the sentimental or the hypocritical, particularly in such social institutions as family, church, and politics. The broad, blind cruelty and grotesquerie is one kind of response to the terrors of wilderness life; so many corpse jokes debunked the dignity—and fear—of death. Usually social criticism, these tales postulate a reduced social world in contrast to a powerful natural world. Characters like Sut Lovingood, a verbal wizard and acute observer of social failings, learned from Emerson, perhaps, that natural facts are symbols of spiritual facts, but Sut's natural similes usually herd the human spirit right into the barnyard or pig sty where it roots with its fellows for food or sex. Expressed emotions, particularly love or affection for another, were one of western humor's major targets; the barrage was strongest against any hint of sentimental language.

While Twain's satire in *Huckleberry Finn* grows from this tradition, he manipulates the conventions to convey genuine emotion, probably influencing Welty's later experiments. The King and the Duke fake emotion in order to hoax their victims, while Emmeline Grangerford demonstrates how fixed conventions paralyze emotion into sentimentality. This dark and satiric view of human nature dominates the novel, but readers tend to remember best the moving passages where Huck and Jim speak both truly and emotionally, revealing their shared humanity. Through Huck and his language, Twain twists the tall tale to express the validity of our emotional needs without resorting to sentimentality. Working in the tall tale tradition, he moves toward realism, Welty toward fantasy.

And yet *Huckleberry Finn* is a clear exception to the tall tale rule, and Twain, as many have noted, seems incapable of dealing with adult love. Welty's interpretation of western values presents an implicit criticism of the dominating male tradition. Hers is a woman's tall tale because power comes through emotional rather than physical strength. Rosamond and Jamie are heroes not only because their spirits and tongues are free, but more importantly because they carry in their hearts not the contamination of selfish greed, but "nothing less than a dream of true love" (p. 74). This tale ends with harmony and reconciliation, with an affirmation of human possibility, for Jamie and Rosamond, as fertile as the land they inhabit, pass the westering spirit on to the twins they produce at the book's close. For Welty, the imagination feeds and is fed by strong feelings. The natural and comic symbols and images, exaggerations, puns, and strange reversals of the narrator express an emotional response to the Natchez wilderness, not so remote a region, as a recent comment of Welty's implies:

> Time is *passing*. Places are *changing*. This is what speed is. There is suspense everywhere, all the time: we are living in its element, racing to keep up with being alive. And in the end there is no rest or help for anything but what lies in the acceptance of love.[12]

Her narrative structure allows Welty to challenge conventional emotional responses to experience without dulling or denying the importance and complexity of emotional needs.

Although the narrator of *The Robber Bridegroom* never uses the first-person "I," her values and responses shape those of the reader, familiarly addressed as "you." The fantasy clearly belongs to someone, and a very eccentric someone indeed. When Goat sings out five questions without waiting for answers, the narrator comments, "Little Harp blinked his eyes and smiled, for nothing pleased him on a fine day like a lack of brains" (p. 92). When Rosamond tries to convince Clement and Salome that a mysterious bandit did indeed steal all of her clothes, the narrator says, "And at first they did not believe her, but by dark she had told it the same way at least seven times, until there was nothing else to do but believe her, unless they jumped down the well" (p. 54). She moves easily from incongruous and unexpected humor to lyrical meditations: "The only thing that could possibly keep [Rosamond] from being totally happy was that she had never seen her lover's face. But then the heart cannot live without something to sorrow and be curious over" (p. 88). This "curious" voice seeks to explain the world in terms of human feelings: Rosamond feels safe from Indians and wildcats "for she was wearing her mother's locket, which kept her from the extravagant harms of the world and only let her in for the little ones" (p. 45). The *locket* knows of Rosamond's sorrows, for it "spoke and said, 'If your mother could see you now, her heart would break' " (p. 43), a persistent refrain that implies the protecting influence of love. The repeated heart image recalls Hawthorne's injunctions: Welty's narrative truth would "sin unpardonably so far as it [might] swerve aside from the truth of the human heart."[13]

This voice, as these examples suggest, is both comic and poetic, extravagant and lyrical. The narrator intrudes upon the already bizarre story, playing with language, speaking through lockets, heads, and tamed ravens, emphasizing emotional needs and inner reality. Her puns are both entertaining and thematically significant: when, after Rosamond disappears, Jamie runs "wild" through the woods, the single word echoes with meanings. Her repeated use of natural imagery suggests that the wilderness provokes fresh associations, and re-asserts the analogizing power of natural facts for spiritual ones. The images are economical, simple, and comic: Salome's ears open "like morning-glories to the sun" (p. 51); later she "danced as naked as a plucked goose" until she fell "blue as a thistle" (p. 163), "stone

dead" because her heart is only a "stone image." And yet the narrator, capable of seeing both sides at once, mocks her own poetic powers through Rosamond, who produces this "pearl": " 'Here I stand all ragged and dirty!/If you don't come kiss me I'll run like a turkey!' " (p. 73).

The narrator's implicit judgment of characters also reinforces Welty's mockery of her own themes as American archetypes. Rosamond and Jamie learn the limits of frontier independence when Salome declares, " 'No one is to have power over me! . . . No man and none of the elements! I am by myself in the world' " (pp. 160-161), and dies, defying the sun. Jamie, a western hero, refuses the guilt that pervades the literature of Welty's region. He prefers his heart to his head (both images are used satirically and seriously), but he knows the importance of maintaining a balance, unlike Little Harp, who chants, " 'Oh, the way to get ahead is to cut a head off!' " (p. 145). And Rosamond becomes a pragmatic western hero by refusing to follow the conventions of her hundred of "feminine" predecessors: when the mysterious bandit asks her if she would die to save her name, she answers, " 'Why, sir, life is sweet. . .and before I would die on the point of your sword, I would go home naked any day' " (p. 50).

Fairy tales and tall tales alike confront experience from an innocent viewpoint; they rely not upon accumulated knowledge to attempt to explain the world but upon imagined possibilities. Rosamond is safe from her evil stepmother so long as she wears her mother's locket because she *feels* secure in the memory of her mother's love. For Welty's narrator, emotions become manifest in fantastic and exaggerated circumstances and symbols. Clement, Welty's version of the innocent American Adam, makes his way through his wilderness life unharmed because he "trusted the evil world" (p. 102); he is incapable of violence until he seeks the bandit who stole his daughter:

> Clement's horse stopped, and all of a sudden there was a rustle of the leaves and a ghost or a shape went by behind him. In the next moment Clement was riding in pursuit, for he thought it was the bandit now for sure, and he rode and rode furiously, though it seemed to him that he had lost the way and that he was only charging in a circle; and this had happened to him before. But

then he heard the same sound, and he brought his horse to a stop and jumped off his back. And although up until that moment he had thought all he defended too sacred for the privilege of violence, he now flung himself forward with such force that the wind left his body for a moment. He ran headlong through the dark, and then it seemed he clasped the very sound in his arms. He could feel the rude powerful grip of a giant or a spirit, and once he was brushed by a feather such as the savages wore, and they threshed about and beat down the earth for a long time. It was as dark as it could possibly be, for the stars seemed to have gone in and left the naked night overhead, and so Clement wrestled with his monster without any aid from the world at all. He tossed it to the ground and it flew up again, he bent it back with all his strength and it would not yield, it fought with the arms of a whirlwind and flung him on the ground, and he was about to give up, but then it clung to him like the Old Man of the Sea and he could not get out from under. At last with a great crash he threw himself upon it and it went down, and he sat there holding it down where it lay with his own body for the rest of the night, not daring to close his eyes for his concern, and for thinking he had won over wickedness. And it was not till the eye of the red sun looked over the ridge that Clement saw he had fought all night with a willow tree .   (pp. 105-106)

Clement "wrestled with his own monster," his protective fear for his daughter. He imagines wickedness where he has not seen it before, but even so, he is incapable of imagining *real* evil, unlike Salome, who "divined these things for herself by means of the very wickedness in her heart" (p. 119). One type of pioneer, "Clement Musgrove was a man who could have. . .had his choice of the fruits of the Garden of Eden without making up his mind" (p. 182); only love and generosity tempt him. His meditations on history, on the "lateness of the age," prove that his time is past:

"But the time of cunning has come. . .and my time is over, for cunning is of a world I will have no part in. Two long ripples are following down the Mississippi behind the approaching somnolent eyes of the alligator. And like the tenderest deer, a band of copying Indians poses along the bluff to draw us near them. Men are following men down the Mississippi, hoarse and arrogant by day, wakeful and dreamless by night at the unknown landings. A trail

leads like a tunnel under the roof of this wilderness. Everywhere the traps are set. Why? And what kind of a time is this, when all is first given, then stolen away?" (pp. 142-143)

The literal time of American innocence is past and Clement must leave Eden, but through the use of fantasy, the narrator recaptures the spontaneity of his wondering vision. Clement's life, expressed through symbol, image, the supernatural events of the tall tale, but most of all through the tone of the all-accepting narrator, becomes a fable for the proper westering spirit, an unconventional treatment of the inner self.

Clement is one example of many. Welty uses her narrator's symbols and images to condense character and theme, while expanding connotations. Like Rosamond's locket, Salome's "eagle claw" serves as both metaphor and symbol, expressing both individual and American character: the ugly, grasping hand the description implies suits her greedy nature, while it is an *eagle* claw because Salome is a wicked satire of the pioneer who believes that the "land is there for the taking" (p. 99).

Tall tales are always more about the teller than about the tale. Through her narrative voice, Welty focusses the reader's attention on how to tell a story, on the imagination at work. She manages to restore the spirit of the West, while questioning some of its assumptions about human behavior, to imply to the reader that a pioneering expedition into America's past, a wonder-filled place, is a natural symbol for an exploration into the powers of the extravagant American imagination. Here is Welty's closing to the Mississippi Historical Society. She describes her characters and her technique, but she might be describing her own response to westering:

So I present them all—the characters of *The Robber Bridegroom*— to you historians in order that you may claim them. They're fanciful, overcharged with high spirits, perhaps, and running out of bounds when advisable or necessary, some of them demented— but they are legitimate. For they're children of their time, and fathered, rather proudly, by its spirit. If I carried out well enough my strongest intentions, fantasy does not take precedence over that spirit, but serves the better to show it forth. It partakes, in a direct way possible to fantasy alone, of the mood and temper

and drive of those challenging times, in the wild and romantic beauty of that place.[14]

NOTES

[1]Arthur R. Huseboe and William Geyer, "Herbert Krause and the Western Experience," in *Where the West Begins,* ed. Huseboe and Geyer (Sioux Falls, South Dakota: Center for Western Studies Press, 1978), p. 9.

[2]Throughout this essay my discussion of the tall tale takes as a foundation Constance Rourke's seminal explorations of the American character in *American Humor* (New York: Harcourt, Brace, and Jovanovich, 1931).

[3]Eudora Welty, *The Robber Bridegroom* (New York: Atheneum Press, 1963), p. 2. All subsequent references are to the same text and follow quotations in text.

A number of critics have noted the influence of tall tale humor on Welty's story. Alfred Kazin first said that the book "captures. . .the lost fabulous innocence of our departed frontier" ("An Enchanted World in America," in *The New York Herald Tribune Book Review* (25 October 1942, p. 19). He is quoted by Ruth Vande Kieft in *Eudora Welty* (New York: Twayne, 1962, p. 166), while Alfred Appel Jr. echoes the same words without quotation in *A Season of Dreams* (Baton Rouge, Louisiana: Louisiana State University Press, 1965, p. 72). No critic, so far as I know, has studied carefully how Welty varies the narrative conventions of the tall tale to convey her historical vision. Most dismiss the connection in one line; for example, John Peale Bishop remarks in the *New Republic,* 16 November 1942, "If Miss Welty meant to establish that our tall tale is the equivalent of the European folk tale she fails to do so." Although I do not deal with Welty's mythic or fairy tale sources, much discussed in general studies of her work, I do not mean to imply that her use of the tall tale style is her exclusive interest in the novel.

Many later Welty stories show the influence of western storytelling, particularly her experiments in first-person narration (*The Ponder Heart* and "Why I Live at the P.O."). *Losing Battles,* like *The Robber Bridegroom,* accepts the incongruous chaos of the frontier or backwoods world, while

suggesting a possible transcendence through what Welty would call "the acceptance of love."

[4]Eudora Welty, "Fairy Tale of the Natchez Trace," in *The Eye of the Story* (New York: Vintage Books, 1979), pp. 310-311, my emphasis.

[5]"Fairy Tale of the Natchez Trace," p. 300.

[6]"Fairy Tale of the Natchez Trace," p. 302.

[7]"Fairy Tale of the Natchez Trace," p. 311.

[8]Bruno Bettelheim, *The Uses of Enchantment: The Meaning and Importance of Fairy Tales* (New York: Knopf, 1977), p. 25.

[9]Warren French, " 'All Things are Double': Eudora Welty as A Civilized Writer," in *Eudora Welty: Critical Essays,* ed. Peggy Whitman Prenshaw (Jackson, Mississippi: University Presss of Mississippi, 1979), pp. 179-188.

[10]"Fairy Tale of the Natchez Trace," p. 314.

[11]Throughout *The Robber Bridegroom,* Welty parodies memorable and important passages in American literature. Much of the humor in the opening bedchamber scene relies upon the reader's acquaintance with the opening chapters of *Moby Dick.*

[12]Eudora Welty, "Seventy-Nine Stories to Read Again," in *The New York Times Book Review,* 8 February 1981, p. 22.

[13]This quotation is from Hawthorne's well known definition of romance in the introduction to *The House of the Seven Gables.*

[14]"Fairy Tale of the Natchez Trace," p. 314.

The Moral in Austin's *The Land of Little Rain*

James C. Work

Mary Hunter Austin was born in 1868, the year Alcott published *Little Women,* and died in 1934, the year Millay published *Wine From These Grapes.* During those sixty-six years she published thirty-four books and plays as well as an extensive assortment of articles in periodicals; became known as a mystic, a philosopher, a naturalist, a feminist, an editor, critic, and compiler (as well as an author); had the acquaintance of Charles F. Lummis, Jack London, John Muir, and Ambrose Bierce (among others) in America, and met Henry James, Joseph Conrad, George Bernard Shaw, Hilaire Belloc, and W. B. Yeats (among others) in Europe; and managed overall to leave behind her enough evidences of her literary significance to occupy quite a respectable number of critics and scholars.

In the final assessment of Mary Austin's contribution to literature—if a final assessment is ever possible—*The Land of Little Rain,* published in 1903, will be recognized as one of the touchstone works of American nature writing. In subject matter it may be said to be similar to Krutch's *The Desert Year* or Eiseley's *The Night Country,* and in its use of the autobiographical approach it reminds one of Thoreau's *Walden* or Muir's *Yosemite.* But there are two respects in which *The Land of Little Rain* is incomparable. One is the set of abstract impressions left by the book in the reader's mind, and the other is the set of moral statements concerning the proper relationship of the human animal to the land in its natural state.

The best initial approach to *The Land of Little Rain* is the impressionistic one; the reader should simply let the book affect the sensibilities and then should analyse the resulting impressions to whatever extent seems natural. No other approach, for the first-time reader, fits the material so well.

To begin such an impressionistic approach, we could hardly do better than to let our impressions be guided by the words Austin wrote in appreciation of her neighbor's field:

> It is a still field, this of my neighbor's, though so busy, and admirably compounded for variety and pleasantness,—a little sand, a little loam, a grassy plot, a stony rise or two, a full brown stream, a little touch of humanness, a footpath trodden out by moccasins.[1]

The Land of Little Rain, being composed of tranquility, does seem to be a "still" little book; but just as patient vigils prove that the apparently still and lifeless desert is in fact full of movement, so does close reading prove this to be a "busy" book indeed. We have a sense of watching the author walking through the country, or riding through it, in constant motion. She is always coming away, it seems, from an encounter with her plants, her terrain, her animals, her people, it is a book busy with life— no passive statistics of "Economy" or bean fields, no tiresome detailing of motionless specimens. Of the dead and inanimate she has as little to say as possible, as if they were to her nothing more than objects of merely momentary curiosity:

> Once below Pastaria Little Pete showed me bones sticking out of the sand where a flock of two hundred had been smothered in a by-gone wind. In many places the four-foot posts of a cattle fence had been buried by the wind-blown dunes.   (p. 159)

She takes far more interest in the "unshepherded, small flocks" of clouds moving in the sky than in the bony remnants of the earthly kind.

Being busy, the book also has the "variety" of the neighbor's field. From the dry desert in the title chapter to the marshy "Water Borders," from lonely "Scavengers" and "The Pocket Hunter" to the less lonely individuals gathered in "Jimville" and "The Little Town of the Grape Vines," from the "Streets of the Mountains" to the starker scenery of "The Mesa Trail" and thence to the "Neighbor's Field," Mary Austin seems the most self-indulgent of authors in responding not just to the richness of things in her arid world nor just to the surprising fullness of life there, but to the sheer unending variety of terrain,

creature, plant, weather, sky, and mood as well.

Like the busy and various field, her book has a rich "pleasantness" to it. Here are no urgings of a philosophic system, no real pressure put upon the reader to perceive deeper meaning; rather, Austin seems to offer an invitation to us to look over her shoulder as she contemplates—very closely—the arid land. A reader gets the pleasant sense of listening to one of those "lyric improvisations" she insists have died out (p. 119). We are tempted to confront her with her own lyric passages in the book—the meal described at Las Uvas, the tribute to the arid land, the picture of the wildfowl in the tulares, the poetry of a stream's course, the smells of sage. "Pleasant" seems, indeed, an inadequate term for a work of such lyric quality.

About that "touch of humanness" I intend to say more later. But one does have a sense, with Austin, that contact with land in the arid regions—where any life that can exist is precious and a marvel—has brought something of one's "humanness" closer to the surface, has caused the memory to be more acute, has somehow given new significance to thinking, to the sense of irony, to sadness, to joy. It is not a tale of Austin struggling to drive life into a corner to know it, but of Austin in deep yet self-forgetting sympathy with the desert life-struggles.

"A footpath trodden by moccasins"—*The Land of Little Rain* is that, certainly. It is a light trail to follow, made as if by one walking in moccasins that are soft to allow the feet that necessary "sense of intimacy" with the land (p. 57).

If the neighbor's field is planned, is the book? I am content to leave the question to the formalists. There is, perhaps, some pairing of chapters—the scavenger and the pocket hunter have at least as much in common with each other as do the streets of the mountains, the water borders, and the nurslings of the sky—some sense of movement from the dry desert and its hard Jimville town to the well-showered mountains and the green softness of Las Uvas. On a philosophic level the reader is first told that "after having lived there one does not wonder so much about those who stay" (p. 11), then is shown the deep satisfactions of it all from barren flats to verdant mountains, and finally is invited to "come away" to enjoy the "even-breathing days" in

the end (p. 171).

Beyond these few abstract impressions, *The Land of Little Rain* presents an almost organic regularity. I began examining it by separating Austin's more philosophic comments into categories, of which there appear to be three of major importance: these include observations about the land, observations about the animal and plant life native to the land, and observations about humans in the land. Later, reviewing the quotations and notes I had gathered under each category heading, I realized that Austin is addressing three questions: What are the essential qualities of the land? What is the relation of life forms to the land and to each other? And what is the proper role of the human animal in relation to the land and the life of it?

The replies Austin gives to these questions are of far more importance than any sort of order she may put them in, for they support what she was later to set down as a central premise of her own humanistic beliefs:

> Man is not himself only, not solely a variation of his racial type in the pattern of his immediate experience. He is all that he sees; all that flows to him from a thousand sources, half noted, or noted not at all except by some sense that lies too deep for naming. He is the land, the life of its mountain processions, the involution and variation of its vegetal patterns. If there is in the country of his abiding, no more than a single refluent color, such as the veiled green of sagebrush or the splendid wine of sunset spilled along the Sangre de Cristo, he takes it in and gives it forth again in directions and occasions least suspected by himself, as a manner, as music, as a prevailing tone of thought, as the line of his rooftree, the pattern of his personal adornment.[2]

The "prevailing tone of thought"—what does Austin tell us is the essential character of the land that can so determine our own character? It is first of all a rewarding land, this desert, and a seductive one:

> If one is inclined to wonder at first how so many dwellers came to be in the loneliest land that ever came out of God's hands, what they do there and why stay, one does not wonder so much after having lived there. None other than this long brown land lays such

a hold on the affections. The rainbow hills, the tender bluish mists, the luminous radiance of the spring, have the lotus charm. They trick the sense of time, so that once inhabiting there you always mean to go away without quite realizing that you have not done it. (p. 11)

The land is, moreover, a place where one can retain some measure of individuality, where one can have the joy of knowing "special places" and private pleasures. "The earth," Austin writes, "is no wanton to give up all her best to every comer, but keeps a sweet, separate intimacy for each" (p. xvi).

But despite the lotus charm and sweet intimacy of the land, relation with it must be entered into with great care. In every chapter, death is never overlooked as a necessary adjunct to life: "Go as far as you dare in the heart of a lonely land, you cannot go so far that life and death are not before you" (p. 8). And, pleasant as it is to know that the experience of the land becomes a part of one's very person, it is necessary to remember what is stamped on the other side of that coin: "The manner of the country makes the usage of life there, and the land will not be lived in except in its own fashion" (p. 59).

Here, then, is a view of a nature that can be sweet, but not beneficient, a nature which, while not taking extreme measures to deprive an inhabitant of life, makes no effort to keep one alive. Neither malicious nor benevolent, Austin's is a nature much like that of Stephen Crane—the leaden sky and apathetic sea in his story, "The Open Boat," have their counterparts in her characterization of Death Valley:

Properly equipped it is possible to go safely across that ghastly sink, yet every year it takes its toll of death, and yet men find there sun-dried mummies, of whom no trace or recollection is preserved. To underestimate one's thirst, to pass a given landmark to the right or left, to find a dry spring where one looked for running water—there is no help for any of these things. (p. 6)

And if we turn to the green and cooler regions also described by Austin, go up into "The Streets of the Mountains," we find in the waters the same impersonal characteristic:

> But the storms of hill countries have other business. They scoop
> watercourses, manure the pines, twist them to a finer fibre, fit the
> firs to the masts and spars, and, if you keep reasonably out of the
> track of their affairs, do you no harm.

> They have habits to be learned, appointed paths, seasons, and
> warnings, and they leave you in no doubt about their perform-
> ances. One who builds this house on a water scar or the rubble of a
> steep slope must take chances.   (p. 151)

Perhaps it is because of the indifferent surroundings that
Mary Austin so keenly feels the fellowship, the close interrelationships of the living things. These she largely personifies, thus
bringing them, in her moral system, into kinship with the human
intruder. Writing as she did within two or three years of the turn
of the century, when each coyote and wolf had a price on its
head and when anything with wings was considered only a challenging target, she extends a humanitarian fairmindedness to even
the most repulsive of them. Even toward the "curmudgeon"
badger she shows some understanding—at least she does not use
her human status as a bench from which to hand down judge-
ment upon him:

> This short-legged meat-eater loves half lights and lowering days, has
> no friends, no enemies, and disowns his offspring. Very likely if
> he knew how hawk and crow dog him for dinners, he would resent
> it. . .he may be met nosing a trail hot-foot to the home of ground
> rat or squirrel, and is with difficulty persuaded to give the right of
> way. The badger is a pot-hunter and no sportsman.   (p. 96)

Similarly, Austin is content to deal rather objectively, yet
in the personifying tone, with those canine inhabitants which
many of her fellow "outdoor" humans go out of their way to
destroy:

> Both the red fox and the coyote are free of the night hours, and
> both killers for the pure love of slaughter. The fox is no great
> talker, but the coyote goes garrulously through the dark in twenty
> keys at once, gossip, warning, and abuse. . . . The coyote is your
> real lord of the mesa, and so he makes sure you are armed with no
> long black instrument to spit your teeth into his vitals at a thou-
> sand yards, is both bold and curious.   (p. 96)

The Land of Little Rain also employs personification—and pathetic fallacy—to lesson us in what appear to Austin to be some human-like qualities of interaction in nature. Her road-runner, for instance, who reminds us of Twain's bluejay, goes "peeking and prying" about the desert; perferring dustbaths himself, he "never had any patience with the water baths of the sparrows," so "after daunting them with shrill abuse and feint of battle," he would go away "in fine disdain, only to return in a day or two to make sure the foolish birds were still at it" (p. 26).

When she describes, with the disinterest of one who truly understands the nature of things, the five coyotes in their hunting down of the stray antelope, she notes that the eagles and buzzards also only watch, and that

> hawks came trooping like small boys to a street fight. Rabbits sat up in the chaparral and cocked their ears, feeling themselves quite safe for the once as the hunt swung near them. Nothing happens in the deep wood that the blue jays are not all agog to tell. The hawk follows the badger, the coyote the carrion crow, and from their aerial stations the buzzards watch each other. What would be worth knowing is how much of their neighbor's affairs the new generations learn for themselves, and how much they are taught of their elders.   (p. 37)

Speaking of the buzzards, Austin says: "All their offensiveness notwithstanding, they have a stately flight. They must also have what pass for good qualities among themselves, for they are social, not to say clannish" (p. 33). After describing how an acquaintance of hers was sickened at the sight of carrion-eaters rising from the bodies at San Juan Hill, Austin still gives the carrion crow his due: "He is nice in his habits and is said to have likable traits. . . . Once at Red Rock, in a year of green pasture, which is a bad time for the scavengers, we saw two buzzards, five ravens, and a coyote feeding on the same carrion, and only the coyote seemed ashamed of the company" (p. 36).

Examples of Austin's empathy toward the living inhabitants of the land—and "empathy" is here the exact word we want—are plentiful in *The Land of Little Rain*. The best one, however, is in the chapter titled "The Streets of the Mountains." In those water-canyons she finds the same oversoul sense that she

did in the desert, what she calls here the "sense of the hills."

> Whether the wild things understand it or not they adapt themselves
> to its processes with the greater ease. The business that goes on in
> the street of the mountain is tremendous, world-formative. Here
> go birds, squirrels, and red deer, children crying small wares and
> playing in the street, but they do not obstruct its affairs. Summer
> is their holiday; "Come now," says the lord of the street, "I have
> need of a great work and no more playing."

> But they are left borders and breathing-space out of pure kind-
> ness. They are not pushed out except by the exigencies of the
> nobler plan which they accept with a dignity the rest of us have
> not yet learned. (p. 123)

The third category in *The Land of Little Rain* is the human
animal. On this topic, Mary Austin's theme is consistently based
upon two watchwords: "awareness" and "simplicity." To promote the first of these two virtues, she often surprises the reader
with observations on human habits, such as "Men have their
season on the mesa as much as plants and four-footed things,
and one is not like to meet them out of their time" (p. 99) and
then challenges one to break out of them:

> Never believe what you are told, that midsummer is the best
> time to go up the streets of the mountain—well—perhaps for the
> merely idle or sportsmanly or scientific; but for seeing and under-
> standing, the best time is when you have the longest leave to
> stay. (p. 116)

Seeing humans and animals as co-equals in the land, and
dealing with animals in human terms, it is natural that Austin discusses human beings as a species. At Jimville, for instance, she
finds she cannot get into "any proper relation" with the town—
meaning to be aware of the people—unless she could "slough off
and swallow acquired prejudices as a lizard does his skin" (p. 73).
Having done that, she finds herself free to agree with the basic
simplicity and rightness of the town's social codes:

> . . .almost every latitude of behavior is allowed a good fellow, one
> no liar, a free spender, and a backer of his friends' quarrels. You
> are respected in as much ground as you can shoot over, in as many

pretensions as you can make good. (p. 74)

It is true, of course, that Austin becomes fascinated with individual specimens, such as the Pocket Hunter and Seyavi the basket maker, but even in her examination of these obviously unusual samples she formulates several generalizations about the race as a whole. She makes the reader see them not just as individuals, but as abstractions as well. Speaking of the pattern changes in Seyavi's baskets, for instance, Austin observes that

> In our kind of society, when a woman ceases to alter the fashion of her hair, you guess that she has passed the crisis of her experience. If she goes on crimping and uncrimping with the changing mode, it is safe to suppose she has never come up against anything too big for her. (p. 105)

Austin can, of course, see the human weaknesses. And she does not let her high moral perspective keep her from pointing out the mean and obvious examples:

> Man is a great blunderer going about in the woods, and there is no other except the bear makes so much noise. Being so well warned beforehand, it is a very stupid animal, or a very bold one, that cannot keep safely hid. The cunningest hunter is hunted in turn, and what he leaves of his kill is meat for some other. That is the economy of nature, but with it all there is not sufficient account taken of the works of man. There is no scavenger that eats tin cans, and no wild thing leaves a like disfigurement on the forest floor. (p. 40)

> The wind, too, is a besom over the treeless spaces, whisking new sand over the litter of the scant-leaved shrubs, and the little doorways of the burrowers are as trim as city fronts. It takes man to leave unsightly scars on the face of the earth. (p. 97)

But more in the humanitarian vein—especially the examination of the human capability and need for improvement as a moral being—is the lesson in nature that humans are not some sort of elect beings. To the land, the human is just barely the equal of the other creatures and the plants. Speaking of the Pocket Hunter, Austin paints him as a creature of simplicity but one lacking in awareness of ". . .a big, mysterious land, a

lonely inhospitable land, beautiful, terrible. But he came to harm in it; the land tolerated him as it might a gopher or a badger. Of all its inhabitants it has the least concern for man" (p. 46).

Even though he developed an unconscious sense for self-preservation, an attunement to nature that saved him from the flood (pp. 47-48), and although he had acquired that "weather shell" that made all seasons the same to him (p. 47), the Pocket Hunter still went about his searching as a man more or less oblivious to the Spirit of Place. He is as morally blind to that Spirit as Browning's Caliban, this prospector who ". . .had seen destruction by the violence of nature and the violence of men, and felt himself in the grip of an All-wisdom that killed men or spared them as seemed for their good" (p. 47). When he does leave the desert country, "the land seemed not to miss him any more than it had minded him" (p. 42).

The Pocket Hunter seems a sort of tragic example of a person with the impulse for the simple life and the ability to live it, but without the awareness of the larger Impulse behind the life of the land. And Austin does not hesitate to apply the lesson to her reader: "You of the house habit," she writes, "can hardly understand the sense of the hills. No doubt the labor of being comfortable gives you an exaggerated opinion of yourself, an exaggerated pain to be set aside" (p. 123).

Besides setting aside that overblown self-esteem, we need to adopt some proper perspectives for observing the land and the life. Those who have read Storm's *Seven Arrows* will remember how he explores the seeing ways of mice and of hawks, how the mice see and feel only what is immediately under their whiskers and how the eagle misses the nearby feel and smell of things but sees an immensely larger view of the world. Compare this with the perspective lesson in "Water Trails of the Ceriso."

> By the end of the dry season the water trails of the Ceriso are worn to a white ribbon in the leaning grass, spread out faint and fanwise toward the homes of gopher and ground rat and squirrel. But however faint to man-sight, they are sufficiently plain to the furred and feathered folk who travel them. Getting down to the eye level of rat and squirrel kind, one perceives what might easily

be wide and winding roads to us if they occurred in thick planta-
tions of trees three times the height of man. . . . It seems that
man-height is the least fortunate of all heights from which to study
trails. (p. 17)

To really see the life beneath our feet, we need to ascend, up to
the "tall hills" if necessary, to that height which is "also the level
of the hawks."

Even with that height, however, comes more need for
awareness. Achieve the level of the hawks and you need to add
inquisitiveness and perhaps some cunning—traits of the fox and
coyote—to your improved viewpoint:

High as the camp may be, so it is not above timberline, it is
not too high for the coyote, the bobcat, or the wolf. It is the
complaint of the ordinary camper that the woods are too still, de-
pleted of wild life. But what dead body of wild thing, or neglected
game untouched by its kind, do you find? And put out offal away
from camp over night, and look next day at the foot tracks where
it lay. (p. 39)

Or, sometimes, we need to look not down at the ground but up
at the heavens to re-acquaint ourselves with our proper place in
the large scheme of things:

For all the toll the desert takes of man it gives compensations,
deep breaths, deep sleep, and the communion of the stars. It
comes upon one with new force in the pauses of the night that the
Chaldeans were a desert-bred people. It is hard to escape the sense
of mastery as the stars move in the wide clear heavens to risings
and settings unobscured. They look large and near and palpitant;
as if they moved on some stately service not needful to declare.
Wheeling to their stations in the sky, they make the poor world-
fret of no account. Of no account you who lie out there watching,
nor the lean coyote that stands off in the scrub from you and
howls and howls. (p. 13)

Our proper awareness of ourself may indeed come from such
apparently simple things as rat-level inspection, offal-watching,
and sky scanning. The last of these, done in the night only, may
finally make Calibans of us all, simple half-human-half-animals

who believe we are free of moral obligation just because we are of "no account" in the universe. But our sky-watching must also be done in the daytime if we are to keep a balanced perspective, for daytime observations will bring us back to knowing ourselves to be subject to—and thereby responsible to—a Spirit of Place.

> The first effect of cloud study is a sense of presence and intention in storm processes. Weather does not happen. It is the visible manifestation of the Spirit moving itself in the void. It gathers itself together under the heavens; rains, snows, yearns mightily in wind, smiles; and the Weather Bureau, situated advantageously for that very business, taps the record on his instruments and going out on the streets denies his God, not having gathered the sense of what he has seen. Hardly anybody takes account of the fact that John Muir, who knows more of mountain storms than any other, is a devout man.   (p. 152)

The Spirit that moves itself in the void. The Sense of Place. The "God" discovered under the walnut tree by Mary Austin at age six—or was it three? Surely we can exist unaware of it, and even with a measure of content, as does the Pocket Hunter. But how much the better for us, and for all of nature, to live in appreciation of it. We are creatures not only of being but of imagination: we create for ourselves, if we will, a constant spirit of wonder and belief, a spirit which science can neither explain away nor prove. A complex soul, indeed, and therefore the more in need of simple wonderment. "I am persuaded," Austin writes, in the final pages of *The Land of Little Rain,* "only a complex soul can get any good of a plain religion. Your earthborn is a poet and a symbolist. We breed in an environment of asphalt pavements a body of people whose creeds are chiefly restrictions against other people's way of life, and have kitchens and latrines under the same roof that houses their God" (p. 170).

Far from being a naturalist who is an advocate of the hermit existence, Mary Austin recognizes the need for a social environment. But people in impersonal crowds which inhabit asphalt pavements are almost as isolated from the essential good of group living—and as isolated from the earth—as if they *were* alone there. People are at their best, in terms of moral behavior, in intimate association both with the land and with other humans, living in such an environment as she describes in the final chapter of *The*

Land of Little Rain. It is significant in understanding her stance with regard to desirable human behavior, I believe, to realize that she does not recommend or even particularly condone the hermit life of the Pocket Hunter, the basket weaver, or the borax mule-skinner, and to further note that she uses the final words of her book to recommend not the empty land, but rather the little town of the grape vines, where "every house is a piece of earth." Would you be better than you are? Then to that town,

> Come away, you who are obsessed with your own importance in the scheme of things, and have got nothing you did not sweat for, come away by the brown valleys and full-bosomed hills to the even-breathing days, to the kindliness, earthiness, ease of El Pueblo de Las Uvas.   (p. 171)

NOTES

[1]Mary Austin, *The Land of Little Rain* (Albuquerque: University of New Mexico Press, 1974), p. 87. All subsequent page references are to this edition.

[2]Mary Austin, *The Land of Journey's Ending* (New York: The Century Company, 1924), p. 437.

A Laddered, Rain-bearing Rug:
Paula Gunn Allen's Poetry

Elaine Jahner

Poetry written by American Indians is beginning to gain the recognition it deserves. Much of it is superbly crafted art, remarkably free from the clever banality that characterizes too much of today's poetry. There is good reason for so much strong writing among American Indians. Within the tribal traditions that helped to shape the aesthetics of these poets, art is closely linked to survival. Vital oral traditions include prayers, songs, chants, tales and oral history that bind the artistic use of language to almost every aspect of daily living. American Indians can not take survival for granted, even today, and continuity is still dependent upon the community's artistic resources. The women seem especially aware of the fragilities in human experience; their writing is often painfully exhilarating in the way it shows life at high intensity.

There are many good American Indian women poets. Paula Gunn Allen, Roberta Hill, Wendy Rose, Linda Hogan, Joy Harjo, Leslie Silko, Marnie Walsh and Elizabeth Cook Lynn are only a few of the better known ones.[1] Studying one poet in depth is a good way to gain some basic understandings about how a traditional tribal heritage can be a source of insight to the meaning of contemporary America; such insight can help one read the other poets with enough awareness to find genuine pleasure in the experience. My choice of Paula Gunn Allen as an exemplary figure among American Indian poets is not entirely arbitrary. She has now been publishing poetry since 1963, so we possess a body of work from a mature artist. She has also published several critical essays which explain how she reads other poets and how she views the meaning of her Indian traditions.

Paula Gunn Allen was born in 1939 in Cubero, New Mexico,

"to a Laguna-Sioux-Scotch mother and Lebanese-American father, both of whom were native New Mexicans."[2] She attended schools in Cubero, San Fidel, and Albuquerque, New Mexico, before beginning work on her B.A. in English at Colorado Women's College. She interrupted her undergraduate career when she married but completed the degree in 1966 at the University of Oregon in Eugene. In 1968 she earned an MFA in creative writing at the same university. After returning to Albuquerque to live, she attended the University of New Mexico, finishing her Ph.D. in American Studies in 1975. Her list of publications is long and varied, including poetry, literary criticism, essays on feminist thought and on American history from a minority perspective. Her poetry first gained national attention through the examples John Milton included in his book *Four American Indian Poets.* Her first complete book of poetry, *The Blind Lion,* was published in 1974. This was followed in 1978 by *Coyote's Daylight Trip,* the book that I intend to concentrate on in this paper. The UCLA Center for American Indian Studies is publishing her most recent book of poems, entitled *Shadow Country.* She is also completing a novel tentatively entitled *Ephanie.*

The way in which Allen balances the diverse elements of her heritage with her own voracious inquiry into all systems of human thought—religious, philosophical, and political—is well illustrated in *Coyote's Daylight Trip.* At a first reading the poems seen unconnected to each other, but a careful study of the book's major themes reveals a process of learning documented by the various poems. At first we find nostalgic idealism and longing for the kind of community the poet intuitively believes once to have been in existence at Laguna Pueblo. Then comes a realization that she must identify with contemporary fragmentation and loss. With identification comes the possibility for transformation of the pain found in urban streets, and finally the poet knows she is creating not only poems but the actual patterns for a new way of life.

The entire process implies a belief in the mythic foundations of metaphor and poetry giving language what N. Scott Momaday has called "its deeper and more vital context" than is usually taken into account.[3] Poetry that so directly relates to myth is written in order to function as myth does in society, establishing structures (or metaphors) that not only make the

world intelligible and help people see it in a new way but also teach people about the creative powers of the universe. Belief in these powers is part of the religious tradition of all tribes. Creating poetry that is a contemporary realization of the powers of mythic processes is a quite different matter from merely using myth as a source of imagery or allusions. While the content of specific poems may reflect specific American Indian myths, a poem does not have to include overt reference to anything Native American to show how the energies dramatized in ancient myths can still shape life in today's city streets. Following through her book Paula Gunn Allen's vision of how myths function today can be for the reader a remarkable experience of seeing previously unimagined facets of American life.

The book begins with a poem entitled "Snowgoose." Based on a traditional American Indian belief that how one experiences any meaning depends on *where* the experience occurs, the poem describes a hope that somewhere there is a place where one can still have the kind of relationship to one's surroundings that brings a sense of order and belonging rather than fragmentation and fear. The belief makes it possible for the poet to mean literally her statement that, "North of here where/water marries ice,/meaning is other than what I understand."[4] While the underlying belief about the function of setting is profoundly traditional, the poem itself is about the poet's own search for a setting that would make a new beginning possible. Allen's personal life has been one of frequent new starts in different locations and careers. Because the personal search is real and easily understood, the reader is led directly into a poetic journey that becomes increasingly more complex with each poem until the very last one returns to the simple directness of the first.

"Snowgoose" is a short, lyrical poem. Everything in it points towards a dream of growth and renewal that is to take place in the frozen north where, the poet hopes, rapacious materialism has not yet destroyed basic relationships among natural phenomena. She describes a glacier as a "frozen pentecostal presence, brilliant in the sun—way I have never been." Even the sky proclaims an "untroubled blue song." It is a compelling dream of rebirth with which she begins her volume. But it is chimeric. In the next poem we learn why, and we find a statement of the purpose behind the entire book of poetry.

The second poem, "Passage," is the book's only other expression of nostalgic hope. It moves from the idyllic northern
setting of the first poem to an intensely understated description
of the realities in America's city streets. As it begins, we discover more about the poet's motivation for going north and for
the poetic journey which is the book itself.

> This was another end in the long trip
> Our private search for meaning,
> for certainty, for a silver peg
> to hang ideals on. No one
> had sent us. We had to come
> to the port in the cool north waters
> to see the mountains thundering in pine,
> green, glacial cold.
> This was as far as we could go
> toward the turning of the earth.

The painful boredom caused by the "turning, turning, turning, turn" of daily life has driven the poet to search toward the
farthest point of the earth's own turning, looking for "a silver
peg/to hang ideals on." By the end of the entire book we, along
with the poet, have found that peg. It is not in the north
though. When the travelers arrive at their destination, they do
not find the untouched, natural setting which had been their
dream. Instead they find a terrifyingly ordinary street quite like
any middle-class street anywhere in the world. It is "a narrow
street/lined with fuschia flowers." The travelers' response is to
take the next ferry home, completing the first phase of the poet's
work. If the book is compared to a traditional American Indian
ceremony, the first part is a kind of purification. By actually
testing her unrealistic dreams and finding out for herself that
they can not be realized, the poet rids herself of them. Then the
real creation of meaning can begin. Poems in the next section of
the book describe intense pain, loss, even boredom. She is living
in the city and has no choice but to "surface in private space."

> Turning, turning, turning, turn.
> Barricades and veils for shrouds
> pay your way covering midnight brawls
> knifings in the silent streets before the bars close down.
> I think of the haze-grown, wine dark afternoons pasted up

on fragmented space, unmediated.
Sentimentality is unwanted where all is want,
driven from without, go within.
                    "Surfacing In Private Space"

This poetic description of living on despair's knife edge speaks of an "image of self glazed mindless by touch" and of "meaning hardly captured before it fades," but the poem remains true to the book's themes of hope. The poet takes stock and tries to "redesign the space in this underplace, so it will take on a new measure, go/riverward, cowering."

The river (and water imagery in general) signals renewal. This ancient and universal signification takes on special meaning in Allen's work, where it is so directly opposed to precisely realized desert imagery. Allen is a desert writer. When she wants to describe pain, she says, "life is dead and dry for the most part." Phrases like this, drawn from common speech patterns, avoid triteness in their context because, as we learn in the nine line "Elegy for My Son," death is not merely figurative. This tender poem is a response to her son's crib death. She dreams of stopping time so that she can prevent it from leading to the moment when she sits holding her son's "small body dead."

As the next poem, "Paradigm," states, there is death everywhere and drought in the land and soul. Even love seems no more than a compensatory dream, lost upon waking to the realization that the house is dusty and needs cleaning. Yet this poem about drought also includes the line that indicates the poet's complete acceptance of and identification with her current place and condition. Such acceptance is a turning point, the beginning of rain for the soul's growth.

Life here is here.
Dead and dry for the most part,
we put in time
wondering when we'll be released from drought
and worry and dusty, seamed faces and eternal
dissatisfaction, the politics of getting along
and our fear.

"Life here is here." The statement takes on its proper force

and significance against the background of some of the poet's prose writings about the relationship between the person and land or setting. In an essay entitled "*Iyani:* It Goes This Way," Allen boldly states, "We are the land." This striking sentence is not just a rhetorical device to gain attention. The rest of her essay describes this "fundamental idea embedded in Native American life and culture in the southwest." After adding that the land is not merely a setting, an "Other" that supplies people with their livelihood, she explains that the land is "truly an integral aspect of our being as we are of its being. And the integral nature of this fact continues beyond mortal dissolution of bodies— human, beast or plant. The old ones come from Sipap to participate in the eternal living being of the land/people as rain. The gods come from the skies and mountain peaks to participate in the welfare of this immutable gestalt. In this return the corn and squash, the deer and game, the men and women are renewed. . . . And so, Indian poets of the Southwest return again and again to this relationship. . . . It is within this larger being that we are given life, and in the acknowledgement of the singleness of that being that we eat, hunt, run, heal, sing, chant and write."[5]

When Paula Gunn Allen writes in her poem "Paradigm" that "life here is here," she is acknowledging the oneness she describes in her prose. As we read the essay, we tend to imagine the rural landscape of the reservation as it once was, forgetting or perhaps not knowing that today Laguna Reservation includes a huge uranium mine. Few readers go beyong the mine-pocked reservation scenes of the southwest to imagine an urban skid row or even a middle-class suburb as one part in the "land/ people" entity described by Allen. Yet in *Coyote's Daylight Trip*, the "here" which the poet must accept is a city in turmoil. How then does this "larger being" find renewal? The answer to that question is given us bit by bit throughout the rest of the book of poems.

The first and perhaps the primary emotion that can come from so complete an identification with the technological setting is fear, capable of closing out everything else. In "Jet Plane/ Dhla-nuwa" we overhear the poet arguing away fear. Trying to deal with a debilitating fear of flying she says,

I tell myself not
to feel the fear that rides my gut, it's
only as far down as death.

She knows that "deep canyons hold no power like flute song butterfly"; nevertheless, "heart clings to breath, alongside the north cliff of the Sandias." Mere argument is not enough; it must lead to some new insight, and it does. As she meditates on the nature of the vast machine taking her to Denver, she realizes that it is part of a cycle that began long ago. No alien monster, it is simply a part of what the ancient discovery of fire means to humankind:

. . .(Who
could say in the dark caves of yesterday
that smokedark choking fire could lead
to 80,000 feet in the air and rising?)

Sensing continuity is important for perceiving the right form of action. Throughout her study of world religious traditions, Allen has remained convinced that life is not absurd; some transcendent intelligence guides the ways of peoples and nations. Healing, whether it be for the social body or the individual human one, involves first discovering continuity with the sources of life and then recognition of how illusions have led us astray from these wellsprings of renewal. In "The Last Fantasy" we experience a confrontation with many kinds of illusion. The setting is San Francisco, but it could be any city.

In the inevitable city
exactly how we came here or why we
do not know
but suspect each illusion led
inexorably to the next, steps westward
to the northern shore, surrounded by water,
the harbour that could house the navies of the world
houses final journeys.

In the city illusions turn to stone, "pave each hill:/we watch the swaying tide, singing." Sometimes even the tide is an illusion: that is, if one is watching a washing machine in a laundromat imagining it is an ocean as the poet does in the second part

of "The Last Fantasy." While she watches, she wonders if a crazy old woman, also washing her clothes, is really a duchess in disguise. Allen turns this scenario bordering on the absurd into a transitional statement about how to get beyond illusions to experiences real enough to give meaning to action. Illusion results from an absence of the identity between person and place that has been part of the thematic content in earlier poems. The biggest illusion of all is the notion that somehow a place can be home simply because one lives there. The old duchess in disguise yells at the poet to go home, and she replies, "*I would go home, crazy old woman,*/if I knew where that might be, or how." Even though she recognizes that "Life here is here," and that her task is to turn the city into a home, she still has to find the way to accomplish her goal in a setting where even the identities of people are not quite fixed: "as I read sisters in levis, bewitched princesses in beards, saunter by, unconcerned that they turn into this, into that/in front of my astounded eyes."

If "The Last Fantasy" were a non-Indian poet's work, it would be a well-written description of modern alienation and rootlessness, a theme that has probably been taken as far as it can go without some truly creative variations. But this poem is the writing of an American Indian woman who has herself said that "to one who knows what it is to feel the life force of the land flowing through one's being, home is as near as that bit of earth which one can touch, allowing energy to flow through one's body."[6] Paula Gunn Allen knows this, but the persona in her poems does not yet have that special relationship to the land which is part of viewing the cosmos in the way that myth teaches, as a unified web of life. A poet or artist who understands this unity can observe illusions, turning them into a special kind of metaphor that shows how to make any place a true home. Inherent in this statement is Allen's theory of metaphor. Within the context of American Indian literature, Allen's sense of what metaphor can do is quite usual; but in the much more secular context of non-Indian American literature, it can seem confusing and vaguely mystical. Allen's prose writings can help explain the basis for her sense of metaphor.

> Native American thought. . .does not draw a hard and fast line between what is material and what is spiritual, for the two are seen to be two expressions of the same reality—as though life has twin

manifestations that are mutually interchangeable and, in many instances, virtually identical aspects of a reality that is, essentially, more spirit than matter. The closest analogy in western thought is the Einsteinian understanding of matter as a special state or condition of energy. . .energy in the Indian view is intelligence manifesting yet another way.[7]

By observing accurately the precise physical details of things, even though their momentary manifestation may be illusory, the poet can, like the scientist, come to understand the special condition of energy which things manifest. The physical details form one term of a metaphor; the spiritual reality (known through mythic images) constitutes the other term. Practically, such a theory of metaphor means that patient and careful observation is the most useful response to a world that seems hopelessly unstable. Once the right metaphors have been found, the artist can channel energies capable of renewing what is dying and of pointing to what is essential amidst illusion.

The poet is a powerful person. She can connect—or disconnect, depending on how she chooses to use metaphor. In "The Kerner Report On Camp Creek Road," Allen speaks directly about how she wants to use metaphors. The poem describes the murder of a black civil rights activist and comments on the white response. The poet's sense of what might bring about a solution to the powerlessness many feel is written as though it were a recipe for some gourmet delicacy:

> Take the full length of a club
> And a street full of people crying
> tie them together to make
> a journey as long as a night of rot
> put them carefully in a warm, dark place.
> . . .
>
> If I had a metaphorical knife
> And a metaphorically thick cutting board
> and a whole pile of translucent metaphors
> I would cut them finely and watch
> them quiver in the light:

Poets can control metaphors and use them to tap cosmic energy resources. Metaphor becomes a solution to social prob-

lems because it is a source of strength for action. Allen means literally what she says in the poem "Locus":

> . . .the image is where the
> action is begotten, and undreamed centuries lurk in every
> darkened alley, around every corner, across every intersection
> behind every pane of glass, waiting to be born.

The echoes of W. B. Yeats in this poem are deliberate. Allen points out that she has carefully studied poets whose metaphysical interests paralleled her own. "Locus," though, is a far more optimistic poem than Yeats' "The Second Coming." Like Yeats, Allen implies that "Surely some revelation is at hand," but in Allen's work the revelation is no second coming presaged by an anti-Christ. It is a more universal awareness of the life force permeating the universe. Even the stars represent possibilities for significant regenerative action.

> . . .I
> think stars on a cold summer night know how to move
> and wait: to wonder when New Jersey will be restored.
> "The Film Library"

From this point onward in the book, there is image after image of possibilities for significant, regenerative action. The title poem of the volume, "Coyote's Daylight Trip," occurs in this section. Coyote is Trickster, ancient master of disguise and illusion. Ordinarily he goes about at night playing tricks that sometimes change the face of reality. But in this book, Trickster changes his habits and travels by day through the city where the real gets lost amidst the images of the mass media: "Senses of accuracy in the machine are light." No matter how much else may be mere "question posed in photograph," death is the inescapable reality. It becomes the poet's touchstone for her capacity to distinguish between the illusory and the real. When the poet says, "I bury my dead. I mourn for four full days," she is affirming her ability to see at last through the illusions that once she had feared and to find appropriate responses even to the pain of death.

She can now pray to Grandmother Spider, the creator figure at Laguna Pueblo. As she prays, she adopts her role as one who

works with the Creator to bring into being the thought forms which give life to the people. The "simultaneous thought of this/and other" that "makes the distance between each point disappear" is poetry which teaches that "small things count after all."

> So grandmother,
> Your gifts still go with me
> Unseen.
> To reach,
> Slowly
> To go
> (as the tree makes its way through the earth)
> the simultaneous thought of this
> and other
> makes the distance between each point disappear.
> . . .
>
> Small things count after all:
> each leaf a tale,
> each journey retracing some ancient myth
> told in shadows and whispers
> under the flickering boughs:
> sacred making. (sacrificing)
> The power of spider thoughts
> so small
> mount, thread by thread.
>   "Affirmation"

Grandmother Spider's gifts are those of prophetic poetry. In a recent article, Thomas Buckley has described well the relationship between myth and prophecy. Certainly his description fits Allen's approach to her poetry: "Prophets tell myths of a future. Both myth maker and prophet disrupt presumed structures in order to see what is, before conditioning it again. Out of that sight, in both cases arises a new structure. Myth accounts for origins, prophecy usually for ends—both, that is, for temporal peripheries. The difference between these is relevant only from a static point of view."[8]

Allen's poetry is a collection of "spider thoughts," powerful because of their invincible continuity with other creation accomplished by a mythic being the Laguna Pueblos call Grand-

mother spider. Like the myth maker, the poet participates in "sacred making." The "presumed structures" mentioned by Buckley correspond to the illusions that Allen seeks to disrupt in order to expose them for what they are. By comparing them to the enduring realities encoded in myths, Allen suggests new ways of looking at contemporary life which become prophetic insofar as they are descriptions of actual evolutionary potential. Allen is not alone in the way she chooses to incorporate tradition into her work. The same could be said of almost all the best American Indian writers. A genuine sense of mythic meaning drives the creative writers to a stance that can be called "prophetic."

The partnership between human beings and the creative forces of the universe is something that Allen believes with absolute conviction, a belief that gives her poetry its positive, hopeful momentum even though she derives most of her actual imagery from the most frightening of contemporary realities. In a poem entitled "The Trick Is Consciousness" she describes a childhood experience of watching the blast of a nuclear experiment in the New Mexican desert. She concludes:

> Control is out of reach
> We knew that then
> As now we know that outside these lighted islands of our lives
> the dark is growing
> hurtling toward us at the speed of light

Poetry might help keep some light alive in a world full of "abandoned dream/fallen into silence, left to brood about its dead" ("Woman's Day, 1975"). Poets create the "image. . . where the action is begotten." By arranging images so that the socially creative action of myth may continue, the poet establishes "mythic space" where people can confront the truth of their own and others' existence. Metaphors in mythic space tell the myths of the future; they are prophetic.

In "Premonition" the disjunction between the title's apprehensive quality and the poem's hopeful message helps shape the meaning of the poem. Premonitions drive people beyond the illusory forms described so well in the book's previous poems to the mythic and prophetic stance that characterizes the last

poems in *Coyote's Daylight Trip.*

> Standing in mythic
> space/we
> meet
> . . .
> The present and the past meet, here.
> . . .
> Another space ancient in visioning,
> carved into bark, into rock, into hide, into spear, waits.
> We stare at this meeting, wonder,
> accept its confusion,
> surprised.

The various strands of meaning at work in *Coyote's Daylight Trip* come together when we realize that it is in mythic space that one can be truly at home. By the end of the book there is an answer to the early cry: "I would go home, crazy old woman, if I knew where that might be, or how." The poet has found her way home by freeing herself of nostalgic dreams about finding a place where life could be lived as it once was. Then she had to identify with her own urban existence even though that meant the pain of loss and disorientation amidst a culture that glorifies the illusory. With identification came recognition of possibilities for turning what is illusory into metaphors that link the present with mythic patterns, thus making artistic expression of contemporary life into the prophetic continuation of myth. Poetry is not just passive description. It points toward appropriate action. In "Hanging Out In America," the second to the last poem, the sense of homecoming is humorously linked with clandestine action to bring about the end of all empty useless dreams. "Like Chinese CIA" those who understand the process described throughout the book of poetry watch for clues that the "money glamour dreams of big times" will self-destruct and all will find their way home. Then rain will fall. Drought will end and new growth will occur.

> Blessings
> that rain might fall
> and that/too
> nourishing
> the singing, so high and sweet, like home

coming, like roads that wind through the trees,
like crumpled bodies fallen into tears that
release. . .
. . .

We watch. Everywhere. Like Chinese CIA
running laundry junks up the Mississippi, from the plazas
of our past, from the kivas of our dreams; it's
not much longer: we see the alien way empty, the footprints,
disappeared. Maybe the worlds they seek are
really empty, this time.
Bendito, Bendito, Bendito, sea Dios
Los angeles cantan.
A laban a Dios
I wonder if they know we're watching.
All the time, everywhere.

The volume ends with a poem that is as much a prayer as a poem. Entitled "Grandmother" after Grandmother Spider, it is a retelling of the Laguna creation myth and of the story of Paula Gunn Allen's own creations. Both were given their tasks "from beyond time," and both must create out of their very life substance. There can be no detached intellectualism in Allen's view of poetic creation. Simple and direct, this poem requires quotation in full because it is the perfect capstone for the volume, showing as it does the continuity with mythic creation that is so large a part of the meaning of all of Allen's poetry.

Our of her own body she pushed
silver thread, light, air
and carried it carefully on the dark, flying
where nothing moved.

Out of her body she extruded
shining wire, life, and wove the light
on the void.

From beyond time,
beyond oak trees and bright clear water flow,
she was given the work of weaving the strands
of her body, her pain, her vision
into creation, and the gift of having created,
to disappear.

After her,
the women and the men weave blankets into tales of life,
memories of light and ladders,
infinity eyes, and rain.
After her I sit on my laddered, rain-bearing rug
and mend the tear with string.

Using the strings of poetry to mend the fragile fabric of life is the work and goal that drives many American Indian women to delicate but strong lines. With their intuitions of a mythic order in which their own forms partake, American Indian women like Paula Gunn Allen are exploring various directions toward a future that is hurtling toward us "with the speed of light." Reading these women can be a richly comforting experience as we sense the truth of Allen's statement, "perhaps when the worst has happened one can accept life sanely."[9]

NOTES

[1] For an excellent collection of American Indian woman's poetry see Dexter Fisher, *The Third Woman* (New York: McGraw Hill, 1979), pp. 5-135.

[2] Taken from a biographical sketch in *Shantih*, 4 (Summer-Fall, 1979). Other biographical data is based on an interview with Paula Gunn Allen, July, 1980.

[3] Duane Niatum, ed., *Carriers of the Dream Wheel* (New York: Harper and Row, 1975), p. xx.

[4] *Coyote's Daylight Trip* (Albuquerque, New Mexico: La Confluencia, 1978). All subsequent quotations of poetry are taken from this book.

[5] Geary Hobson, ed., *The Remembered Earth* (Albuquerque, New Mexico: Red Earth Press, 1979), pp. 191-194.

[6] Stated in an interview with Paula Gunn Allen, July, 1980.

[7] "The Sacred Hoop," in *The Remembered Earth*, p. 212. This essay is reprinted frequently in anthologies of American Indian literature.

[8] "Myth and Prophecy," *Parabola*, 6 (Winter, 1981), 88.

[9] "The Remaining Grace," *Book Forum*, 5 (1980-1981), 377.

CONTRIBUTORS' NOTES

Sue Armitage is Director of Women's Studies and Associate Professor of History at Washington State University in Pullman, Washington. Since 1980 she has been Eastern Washington Project Director for the Washington Women's Heritage Project, an NEH-funded effort to collect and publicize the history and experience of women in Washington State. Her special research interests include frontier women, women's oral history, and the development of methodologies to incorporate women's experience into local history.

Samuel I. Bellman is Professor of English at California State Polytechnic University. He received his Ph.D. in English from The Ohio State University; he has taught at USC and Portsmouth Polytechnic in Hampshire, England. He has published "The 'New Woman' in the Space Age" (published by the California Association of Women Deans and Vice-Principals), biographies of Marjorie Kinnan Rawlings and Constance Rourke in the Twayne United States Authors Series, and articles on American women writers in *Notable American Women, Dictionary of Literary Biography,* and *Fifteen American Women Writers: Bibliographical Essays.*

Caren J. Deming received her Ph.D. in Radio-Television-Film from the University of Michigan. She is Associate Professor and Chairperson for the Broadcast Communication Arts Department at San Francisco State University. Her primary research interest is in broadcast criticism, media and culture, women and media, and intercultural media issues. She has articles and reviews in the *Journal of Popular Culture, Comm/ent, Intellect, Women's Studies Quarterly* (London), *Media Report to Women,* and various regional journals. She has contributed biographies of broadcast writers for Ungar's *Guide to American Women Writers* and is contributing editor of *Public Communication Review,* and an Associate of the Women's Institute for Freedom of the Press.

Catherine Dobson Farmer has been a member of the English faculty at Wallace State Community College in Hanceville, Alabama, since 1975. A native of Birmingham, Alabama, Ms. Farmer received her bachelor's degree

and her M.A. in English from Jacksonville State University. She has recently completed all required course work for a Ph.D. in English from Auburn University.

Melody Graulich is on the faculty at the University of New Hampshire. She received her B.A. Degree at Stanford University, her M.A. and Ph.D. from the University of Virginia. Her interests are in American literature and culture, Western and frontier literature, and women's studies. Her publications include " 'They ain't nothing but words': Flannery O'Connor's *Wise Blood*," in *The Flannery O'Connor Bulletin.*

Elaine Jahner is an Associate Professor of English at the University of Nebraska-Lincoln. Her areas of specialty include American Indian literature and Cross-Cultural Literary Criticism. She has published numerous articles. Her study of James Welch's imagery appeared in *Denver Quarterly,* and her analysis of Leslie Silko's novel *Ceremony* appeared in *American Indian Quarterly.* She co-edited the book *Lakota Belief and Ritual,* and she edited a special issue of *Book Forum* devoted to contemporary American Indian art and literature.

Frances W. Kaye teaches plains literature and American studies at the University of Nebraska-Lincoln. She has published essays and articles in *Mosaic, Prairie Schooner, Agricultural History,* and other journals. Her interest in women and western literature dates from at least 1926, when her grandmother published a novel about the Canadian prairies.

Frances M. Malpezzi, Assistant Professor of English at Arkansas State University, has published articles on the poetry of Spenser, Donne, Herbert, Herrick, and Vaughn as well as papers on women's literature. She and her husband, William Clements, are currently compiling an annotated bibliography of Native American folklore for Swallow Press.

Susan Mathews is an Associate Professor of English and Director of Women's Studies at Eastern Montana College in Billings, where she teaches "Montana Writers" and "Women and the Frontier Experience." She is currently working on studies on regional authors who focus on the frontier experiences of women in Montana and Wyoming.

Barbara Howard Meldrum, Professor of English at the University of Idaho, has published essays on Melville, Rölvaag, Winther, Fisher, Richter, Guthrie, and women in Western American fiction. She has been awarded a National Endowment for the Humanities Fellowship to write a book on Western

American pastoral fiction. She is a member of the Editorial Board of *Western American Literature.*

John J. Murphy, Chairman of English at Merrimack College, Massachusetts, has published extensively on Willa Cather and other American novelists in *American Literature, Western American Literature, Prairie Schooner, Queen's Quarterly, The Platte Valley Review,* and other journals. He is presently editing *Critical Essays on Willa Cather* (G. K. Hall) and will be contributing the annual essay "Fiction 1900-1930" to *American Literary Scholarship.*

Katherine Nichols, Assistant Professor of English and Co-ordinator of the Women's Studies Program at Pittsburg State University (Kansas), teaches courses in American literature and women's literature. She has published articles on Cather, Hemingway, early American women novelists, and other subjects, and is currently working on a book about early American women dramatists.

David Remley is the author of *Erna Fergusson* (Southwest Writers Series), *Crooked Road: the Story of the Alaska Highway* (McGraw-Hill), and various articles and poems. He has a continuing interest in the history and literature of the American West.

Barbara Rippey teaches in the English Department, University of Nebraska at Lincoln, where she is working on her Ph.D. She is a native of Nebraska, has lived in the plains area all her life, and is primarily interested in Mari Sandoz and other Nebraska writers. Her master's thesis was a study of Sandoz's use of allegory in *Slogum House, Capital City,* and *The Tom-Walker;* she is currently continuing work on Sandoz for her dissertation.

Darlene Ritter, Professor of English at Midland College, teaches classes in American literature, plains literature, composition, and mythology. She has a special interest in the role of women in the settling of the West as reflected in their letters and diaries.

Susan Rosowski, Associate Professor of English at the University of Nebraska-Lincoln, is the author of numerous studies on Willa Cather, published in *Studies in American Fiction, Western American Literature, Genre, Prairie Schooner, Journal of Narrative Technique, Novel, Where the West Begins,* and elsewhere. Her other publications include genre studies and articles on Atwood, Joyce, and Congreve. She participated in the MLA project, "Teaching Women's Literature from a Regional Perspective," is a Danforth

Associate, and serves on the Executive Council of the Western Literature Association.

Margaret Solomon, for many years a free-lance writer and editor, is now a program specialist for Cemrel, Inc., an educational research and design laboratory in St. Louis Her special interest is women's studies, which she has taught at Washington University, St. Louis. She is now researching the teaching of women's studies in Missouri high schools.

Helen Stauffer, Professor of English at Kearney State College, has worked extensively with the canon of Mari Sandoz. She received an NEH research grant in 1976 to write on Sandoz's works. She has published in *Platte Valley Review, Kansas Heritage, Prairie Schooner, Great Plains Quarterly* and other journals, and an essay included in *Women, Women Writers and the West; Fifty Western Writers* (forthcoming); and *Literary History of the American West* (forthcoming). Her biography of Mari Sandoz is scheduled for publication by the University of Nebraska Press in 1982. She was a participant in the project, Teaching Women's Literature from a Regional Perspective, and was President of the Western Literature Association in 1980.

June O. Underwood, Association Professor of English at Emporia State, has published articles on Victorian fiction, women in Western literature, and women's organizations in Kansas. She won the National Cabletelevision ACE award for her TV production, "Blessed, Blessed Mama: A Chase County Life," about a mother and daughter in Kansas at the turn of the century. She has a continuing interest in women in Western history and literature, expressed in other television programs she wrote and produced in conjunction with the Center for the Study of the Great Plains as well as in her work toward a book on the reforms of women's groups in Kansas between 1880 and 1920.

Mary Ellen Williams Walsh in an Associate Professor of English at Idaho State University. She is the author of *A Vast Landscape: Time in the Novels of Thornton Wilder* (1979) and articles on the humanities, university administration, and Western writers.

James C. Work, Associate Professor at Colorado State University, teaches Literature of the American West, Heritage of the West, and such special courses as The West in Film, Fact, and Fiction, Victorianism in the American West; and Nature Writing as a Literary Tradition. He has published in *The Indian Historian, The Mark Twain Journal, Western American Litera-*

ture, and other journals. Two articles have appeared as chapters in text books. He has co-authored (with Dr. William Fitzgerald) a column of humorous veterinarian advice appearing in the Fort Collins *Coloradoan* and the Denver *Post.*

Joseph J. Wydeven, Assistant Professor and Chairman of the Department of English at Bellevue College, Nebraska, completed his dissertation on Wright Morris at Purdue University. He has published articles on Morris' photography, and has a continuing interest in the relations between literary texts and the visual arts. He is currently pursuing a project on American Indian art, literature, and culture.

Patricia Lee Yongue, Associate Professor of English at the University of Houston, Central Campus, is widely known as a Cather scholar, having published in a number of distinguished journals. She has also lectured on the author.